Sources of South German/Austrian Anabaptism

Classics of the Radical Reformation

Classics of the Radical Reformation is an English-language series of Anabaptist and Free Church documents translated and annotated under the direction of the Institute of Mennonite Studies, which is the research agency of the Anabaptist Mennonite Biblical Seminaries, and published by Plough Publishing House.

1. *The Legacy of Michael Sattler.* Trans., ed. John Howard Yoder.
2. *The Writings of Pilgram Marpeck.* Trans., ed. William Klassen and Walter Klaassen.
3. *Anabaptism in Outline: Selected Primary Sources.* Trans., ed. Walter Klaassen.
4. *The Sources of Swiss Anabaptism: The Grebel Letters and Related Documents.* Ed. Leland Harder.
5. *Balthasar Hubmaier: Theologian of Anabaptism.* Ed. H. Wayne Pipkin and John Howard Yoder.
6. *The Writings of Dirk Philips.* Ed. Cornelius J. Dyck, William E. Keeney, and Alvin J. Beachy.
7. *The Anabaptist Writings of David Joris: 1535–1543.* Ed. Gary K. Waite.
8. *The Essential Carlstadt: Fifteen Tracts by Andreas Bodenstein.* Trans., ed. E. J. Furcha.
9. *Peter Riedemann's Hutterite Confession of Faith.* Ed. John J. Friesen.
10. *Sources of South German/Austrian Anabaptism.* Ed. C. Arnold Snyder, trans. Walter Klaassen, Frank Friesen, and Werner O. Packull.
11. *Confessions of Faith in the Anabaptist Tradition: 1527–1660.* Ed. Karl Koop.
12. *Jörg Maler's Kunstbuch: Writings of the Pilgram Marpeck Circle.* Ed. John D. Rempel.
13. *Later Writings of the Swiss Anabaptists: 1529–1592.* Ed. C. Arnold Snyder.

Sources of South German/Austrian Anabaptism

Translated by
Walter Klaassen, Frank Friesen
and Werner O. Packull

Edited with an Introduction by
C. Arnold Snyder

Published by Plough Publishing House
Walden, New York
Robertsbridge, England
Elsmore, Australia
www.plough.com

Plough produces books, a quarterly magazine, and Plough.com to encourage people and help them put their faith into action. We believe Jesus can transform the world and that his teachings and example apply to all aspects of life. At the same time, we seek common ground with all people regardless of their creed.

Plough is the publishing house of the Bruderhof, an international community of families and singles seeking to follow Jesus together. Members of the Bruderhof are committed to a way of radical discipleship in the spirit of the Sermon on the Mount. Inspired by the first church in Jerusalem (Acts 2 and 4), they renounce private property and share everything in common in a life of nonviolence, justice, and service to neighbors near and far. To learn more about the Bruderhof's faith, history, and daily life, see Bruderhof.com. (Views expressed by Plough authors are their own and do not necessarily reflect the position of the Bruderhof.)

Copyright © 2019 by Plough Publishing House
All rights reserved.

ISBN: 978-0-874-86274-4

Library of Congress Cataloging-in-Publication Data

Names: Klaassen, Walter, 1926- translator. | Friesen, Frank, translator. | Packull, Werner O., 1941- translator. | Snyder, C. Arnold, 1946- editor.
Title: Sources of South German/Austrian Anabaptism / translated by Walter Klaassen, Frank Friesen and Werner O. Packull ; edited with an introduction by C. Arnold Snyder.
Description: Walden : Plough Publishing House, 2019. | Series: Classics of the radical Reformation ; 10 | Originally published: Kitchener, Ontario : Pandora Press, c2001. | Includes bibliographical references and index.
Identifiers: LCCN 2019044927 (print) | LCCN 2019044928 (ebook) | ISBN 9780874862744 (paperback) | ISBN 9780874862768 (ebook)
Subjects: LCSH: Anabaptists--Germany, Southern--History--16th century--Sources. | Anabaptists--Austria--History--16th century--Sources. | Anabaptists--Doctrines--Early works to 1800. | Germany, Southern--Church history--16th century--Sources. | Austria--Church history--16th century--Sources. | Reformation--Early works to 1800. | Reformation--Sources.
Classification: LCC BX4933.G3 S68 2019 (print) | LCC BX4933.G3 (ebook) | DDC 284/.30943309031--dc23
LC record available at https://lccn.loc.gov/2019044927
LC ebook record available at https://lccn.loc.gov/2019044928

*Dedicated
with affection to
past and present colleagues at
Conrad Grebel University College*

*but especially to
John E. Toews
for hope and direction,
enabling
a community at work*

Contents

1 Jörg Haugk von Jüchsen	A Christian Order of a True Christian: Giving an Account of the Origin of his Faith (1524)	1
2 Hans Hut	Comparing and Interpreting Divine Scripture: A Christian Instruction given in the power of the Holy Spirit together with the three parts of Christian Faith and how they are to be understood (1527)	21
3 Hans Hergot	Concerning the New Transformation of Christian Living (1527)	35
4 Ambrosius Spitelmaier	Questions and Answers of Ambrosius Spitelmaier (1527)	50
5 Leonhard Schiemer	Letter to the Church of God at Rattenberg (1527)	64
6 Hans Schlaffer	A Brief Instruction for the Beginning of a Truly Christian Life & Confession and Defence (1528)	81
7 Eitelhans Langenmantel	An Anonymous Anabaptist Sermon & An Exposition of the Lord's Prayer (ca. 1527)	110
8 Anonymous (Simon Schneeweiss?)	Theological Refutation of Anabaptist Teaching (1528)	121
9 Lamprecht Penntz	Recantation Procedures (1528)	129
10 Ursula Hellrigel	*Ausbund*, the 36th Song	132
11 Hans Nadler	Declaration of the Needle Merchant Hans at Erlangen and the Refutation of the Articles of the Needle Merchant Hans (1529)	136
12 Wolfgang Brandhuber	A Letter from our Dear Brother and Servant of Jesus Christ, Wolfgang Brandhuber to the Church of God at Rattenberg on the Inn (1529)	155

Contents / vii

13 Jörg Zaunring	A Short Interpretation of the Last Supper of Christ Presented as a Conversation between the World and a Christian to the Honour and Glory of God (ca. 1530)	163
14 Andreas Althamer & Johann Rurer	Instruction Concerning Anabaptists (1530)	171
15 Georg Gross Pfersfelder	Georg Gross, called Pfersfelder, to Hans von Seckendorf. Concerning Persecution of Anabaptists (1531)	185
16 Katharina Hutter	Testimony of Katharina Hutter, Given before December 3, 1535, at Klausen	191
17 Endres Keller	Confession of the prisoner, Anabaptist Endres Keller (Kentlein) in Rothenburg (1536)	196
18 Urbanus Rhegius	Justification for the Prosecution of Anabaptists (1536)	213
19 Sebastian Franck	Sebastian Franck on the Anabaptists (1536)	228
20 Anonymous	Anonymous Hutterite Leaders to Mathes Hasenhan (1538)	253
21 Trieste Brethren	Confession of the Brethren, Taken to Trieste as Prisoners (1539)	259
22 Hans Umlauft	A Letter to Stephan Rauchenecker (1539)	277
23 Helena von Freyberg	Helena von Freyberg, Confession on Account of her Sin (1539-45)	287
24 Paul Glock	Letter to his Wife Else (1563)	294
25 Paul Glock	First Defense (1563)	309
26 Paul Glock	Letter to Leonhard Lanzenstiel (1563)	325
27 Paul Glock	Letter to Peter Walpot (1566)	329
28 Paul Glock	Letter to Peter Walpot (1567)	335
29 Paul Glock	Letter to Peter Walpot (1569)	340
30 Paul Glock	Letter to Peter Walpot (1569)	344

viii / *Sources of South German/Austrian Anabaptism*

31 Paul Glock	Letter to Peter Walpot (1571)	348
32 Paul Glock	Letter to the Church in Moravia (1573)	354
33 Walpurga von Pappenheim	*Ausbund*, Song 75 (ca. 1571)	362
34 Hans Schmidt	Experiences of a Hutterite Missionary in Württemberg (1590)	366

Notes 381

Index of Names and Places 408

Scripture Index 412

Abbreviations

Bossert, *Quellen I*: Gustav Bossert, *Quellen zur Geschichte der Wiedertäufer, I. Band. Herzogtum Württemberg* (Leipzig, 1930).

Chronicle I: *The Chronicle of the Hutterian Brethren* vol. I (Rifton, N.Y.: Plough Publishing House, 1987).

Chronicle II: *The Chronicle of the Hutterian Brethren* vol. II (Ste. Agathe, MB: Friesen Printers, 1998).

Franck, *Chronica*: Sebastian Franck, *Chronica, Zeitbuch unnd Geschichtbibell...* (Ulm, 1536; Photo reprint edition, Darmstadt, 1969).

Franz, *Quellen IV*: Günther Franz, *Urkundliche Quellen zur hessischen Reformationsgeschichte, IV. Band, Wiedertäuferakten* (Marburg, 1951).

ME: *Mennonite Encyclopedia*. 5 vols. (Scottdale, PA: Herald Press, 1955-59, 1990).

ML: *Mennonitisches Lexikon*. Vols. 1-3 (Frankfurt a.M. and Weierhof, 1913-42, 1958); Vol. 4 (Karlsruhe: Heinrich Schneider, 1967).

MQR: *Mennonite Quarterly Review*.

Müller, *Glaubenszeugnisse*: Lydia Müller, *Glaubenszeugnisse oberdeutscher Taufgesinnter, I* (Leipzig, 1938).

Schornbaum, *Quellen II*: Karl Schornbaum, ed., *Quellen zur Geschichte der Wiedertäufer, II. Band. Markgraftum Brandenburg (Bayern, I. Abteilung)* (Leipzig, 1934).

Schornbaum, *Quellen V*: Karl Schornbaum, ed., *Quellen zur Geschichte der Wiedertäufer, V. Band.(Bayern, II. Abteilung)* (Gütersloh, 1951).

General Editor's Preface

In the last several decades the Institute of Mennonite Studies has been involved in the publication of primary source materials of Radical Reformation and free church documents through its *Classics of the Radical Reformation* (CRR) series. This tenth volume in the series continues an important tradition of providing translations in the English language, which are intended to be faithful to the original documents, yet readable and accessible to a wide audience.

Sources of South German/Austrian Anabaptism is a significant contribution to Reformation studies. In recent years scholars have emphasized the diverse nature of the origins and development of sixteenth-century radical reform in general and Anabaptism in particular. The present volume underscores this growing awareness. It unveils an important current of Anabaptist thought and piety, and sheds light on a stream of spiritualist writings that have been underrepresented in translation collections.

Gratitude for making these writings available to the English-speaking world goes to the editor, C. Arnold Snyder, and to the primary translators Walter Klaassen, Frank Friesen, and Werner Packull. Appreciation is also due to the sponsoring institution of the Institute of Mennonite Studies, Associated Mennonite Biblical Seminary of Elkhart, Indiana. Finally, special thanks must go to Pandora Press Canada for its commitment to publishing this volume, which we trust will make a contribution to both the church and the academy.

Karl Koop, Editor, CRR
Institute of Mennonite Studies

Editor's Acknowledgments

This collection of translated sources had its own peculiar genesis and development, as do all projects of this kind. A core of documents published here dates back to a publication done twenty years ago by the Institute of Anabaptist and Mennonite Studies, Conrad Grebel University College. The collection, entitled *Sixteenth Century Anabaptism: Defences, Confessions, Refutations* (1981), was translated by Frank Friesen and edited by Walter Klaassen. The book contained some rare and valuable material, but it was published as a bound typescript volume, intended for very limited circulation. The book was soon out of print. One of the first projects undertaken by Pandora Press in the mid-1990s was to make preparations to republish the Friesen/Klaassen collection. Thanks to Sam Steiner and the IAMS, permission was granted to proceed with the project, and IAMS has continued its support throughout.

The tasks of scanning and proofreading followed, with Linda Snyder doing the work of converting the material into a workable digital format. At this early point in the project, the intention was to reprint the original book in the *Anabaptist Texts in Translation* series, published by Pandora Press. As work on *Sixteenth Century Anabaptism* continued, however, the germ of a larger project began to take shape. Most of the documents in the Friesen/Klaassen collection related to the early South German/Austrian Anabaptist stream. Translated documentation from the earliest years of this movement was generally unavailable. Could material be added to make the collection more broadly representative of South German/Austrian Anabaptism?

The edition of Anabaptist documents edited by Lydia Müller, *Glaubenszeugnisse oberdeutscher Taufgesinnter* (Leipzig: Nachfolger, 1938; Johnson Reprint, 1971) offered important South German/

Austrian materials hitherto unavailable in English, and consultation with Walter Klaassen and Werner Packull resulted in a proposal for an enlarged and more comprehensive collection of documents. Walter Klaassen agreed to do a series of new translations for the larger collection; Werner Packull worked with his student, Mary Buck, in preparing a translation of Jörg Haugk von Jüchsen's pamphlet; and John Roth, editor of the Mennonite Quarterly Review, extended permission for the inclusion of two pamphlets translated by J. C. Wenger and published some years ago in that journal. Thanks is due to them all for their hard work and cooperation—but especially to Walter Klaassen, who did the lion's share of the new translation work and from his retirement has graciously donated his linguistic gifts and historical expertise to this and other translation projects.

The expanded collection, under its present title, was proposed to the *Classics of the Radical Reformation* editorial board, and accepted for publication in that series. Thanks to the Institute of Mennonite Studies, Associated Mennonite Biblical Seminary, for its continued support of the task of making available radical reformation texts in English. Thanks go also to Karl Koop, editor of the series, for his logistical and editorial help throughout. This volume is being co-published with Herald Press, Scottdale, Pennsylvannia. Their cooperation and support has enabled the continuation of the historic connection with the original publishers of the CRR series.

The provenance of individual translations in this volume is identified at the foot of each new chapter page. The designation "Friesen/Klaassen" indicates material taken from *Sixteenth Century Anabaptism: Defences, Confessions, Refutations*. The original translations were reviewed, revised and corrected, as needed, by the editor for publication in this volume; the essential work, however, remains that of Friesen and Klaassen. Four items contained in the original Friesen/Klaassen volume are not included in the present collection for editorial reasons, namely a brief letter by Melchior Rinck (#8 in Friesen/Klaassen), a letter by Hans Schmidt and Wolf Kürschner (#9 in Friesen/Klaassen), an apology by Georg Schnabel (#11), and a confession by Peter Tasch (#14). The latter two writings were excluded because they represent writings from the Melchiorite tradition, rather than the South German/Austrian tradition. It is hoped that they can be included in a collection of early Melchiorite writings, still in the planning stages at the present time. The two tracts by Langenmantel, translated by J. C. Wenger and previously published in the *MQR*, were substantially reworked and revised by the editor; they are, in effect, new translations. Further additions to the collection were five relevant items previously published elsewhere. Two items in our collection were translated originally by Linda Huebert Hecht (#9, 23), two by Pamela Klassen (#10, 33), and one by Elfriede Lichdi (#16). They were first published in C. Arnold Snyder and Linda H. Hecht, *Profiles of Anabaptist Women* (Waterloo: Wilfrid Laurier University Press, 1996). They are reprinted here with the kind permission of WLU Press.

A large thank you goes to Galen Peters, graduate student in history, Wilfrid Laurier University. Galen spent the summer of 2001 working at Pandora Press, researching and writing introductory material for this volume, laying out the manuscript, and preparing the scriptural and general indeces. Galen's work was subsidized by a generous grant from the Jubilee Charitable Trust, Halifax, Nova Scotia. Our final thanks is reserved for Dr. Robert L. Kruse, trustee of the Jubilee Charitable Trust, for his enthusiastic support of Anabaptist publishing. The "private" support of a public project such as this is a model that, one hopes, will be emulated by others.

It is fitting that a volume dedicated to writings by and about the South German/Austrian Anabaptists—the most "communal" of the Anabaptist groups—should itself have been the result of such a clearly communal effort.

C. Arnold Snyder, editor
August 26, 2001

Introduction

Dating from studies in the 1960s and 1970s, the sixteenth-century beginnings of three primary baptizing groups—Swiss Anabaptists, South German/Austrian Anabaptists, and North German/Dutch Anabaptists—have been identified and described in some detail.[1] Of the three original Anabaptist groups, the Swiss and the South German/Austrian Anabaptists stand closest in time, geography, and mutual influence, even though there are distinct emphases in the original teachings of each. The baptism of adults began in January 1525 in Zürich; its initial appearance in South German territories is not as well documented, but there is evidence of baptizing activity about one year later. North German/Dutch Anabaptism began only in 1530, with the baptism and missionary activity of Melchior Hoffmann. North German/Dutch Anabaptism developed in northern Europe with little visible influence from the Swiss and South German/Austrian movements. In the second half of the sixteenth century—well after these groups had matured and developed beyond their original peculiarities and particular emphases—more contacts developed between the baptizers in the south and the north, with Mennonite influence from the north predominating in these later exchanges.

Historians have noted significant diversity among the earliest Anabaptists in geography, levels of social involvement, faith emphases, and church practices. At the same time, there is also the recognition that along with diverse points of origin and emphasis, the various baptizers also exhibited fundamental commonalities that allow us to speak of a sixteenth century "baptizing movement" as such.[2] To contemporaries of the Anabaptists, their most obvious common teaching was their uniform opposition to infant baptism and their insistence that baptism was to be reserved for adults, following a sincere confession of faith. Among other common emphases visible to the historian are the celebration of a memorial Lord's Supper (as opposed to maintaining a "real presence of Christ" in the elements), belief in the freedom of the human will as a result of God's grace, the conviction that saving faith is the result of the Holy Spirit's activity in the heart, and must include the "fruits" of discipleship and obedience (as a result of God's grace, not by human effort alone), a practice of fraternal admonition (discipline) among members, and a concern for economic sharing and solidarity with the believing community as visible evidence of one's faith in Christ. As the movement matured over the course of the sixteenth century, more points of consensus emerged among the baptizers, for example, that no oaths were to be sworn (only "yes" and "no" were to be used) and that believers were to live without recourse to weapons (*Wehrlosigkeit*).

The documents collected in this volume are writings that emerged from, or that relate directly to the South German/Austrian Anabaptist grouping, that is, the second geographical and ideological wave of the sixteenth century baptizing movement.[3] The geographical boundaries of the South German/Austrian baptizing movement are imprecise, and shift over time. In spite of important points of genesis in Thuringia and the Tyrol, a significant early presence in South German imperial cities like Nuremberg and Augsburg, and refugee membership extending from Silesia to the Rhineland, the geographical core of the movement came to be located in Moravia. Moravia was the place of refuge for many thousands of Anabaptists in the sixteenth century, and was the particular location for the growth and development of the South German/Austrian branch of the baptizing movement.

There is no one document in this collection that, taken by itself, summarizes the birth and development of this branch of Anabaptism. Taken collectively, however, the documents translated here provide important avenues for understanding this unique group of "baptizing brothers and sisters in the Lord" that was active in the south-central regions of Europe.

Looked at in terms of genre, the collection of sources published here contains an eclectic variety of material, well representing the kind of documentation available to historians of this branch of Anabaptism.

–*Edifying treatises and letters.* Some of the writings collected here were composed primarily for the edification of others (#1, 2, 3, 7, 13,

20, 22). Of these, two (#1, 3) date from the pre-Anabaptist period, and illustrate the continuity that existed between the baptizing movement and some of the currents of reform that preceded it.

–*Prison Documents*. By far the most numerous in our collection are Anabaptist writings originating in various prisons, reflecting the reality of religious persecution. The "prison documents" include judicial records of prisoners' replies to questioning (#4, 11, 16, 17) and epistles and treatises written in prison, intended for the edification of the communities (#5, 6, 12, 24-32). The collection also contains a complete confession of faith written in prison by a group of prisoners (#21).

–*Hymns*. Hymns were an important means of communication for the Anabaptists. They generally borrowed well-known melodies (secular as well as sacred) and composed verses to be sung to these tunes. The hymns functioned as memorials and reminders of historical events —above all, of the martyrdoms of brothers and sisters in the faith. The stories (and the teaching hymns) all served didactic purposes, all the more practical as a medium because of the aid to memorization provided by rhyming couplets set to music. Two hymns are included in our collection (#10, 33). This is a disproportionately small number, relative to the number of hymns actually composed and preserved in the sixteenth century, but will provide readers with a sense of this important genre of Anabaptist documentation.

–*Refutations and defences written by non-Anabaptists*. The collection also contains writings composed by opponents of the South German/ Austrian Anabaptists, intended to refute Anabaptist teachings and practices (#8, 11-B, 14, 18). Also included are two writings composed by non-Anabaptists that portray them in a less polemical light, and plead for toleration (#15, 19).

–Finally, rounding out the collection are sources that defy easy classification, but that shed valuable light on the movement. Included here is a translation of the recantation procedures applied in Hapsburg territories (#9), a letter of inquiry from Hutterite leaders to an Anabaptist outside Moravia (#20), a confession by an Anabaptist woman directed to her fellow church members (#23), and the reminiscences of a Hutterite missionary (#34).

Emphases common to all Anabaptists will be plain to see in these writings, but also visible will be the particular emphases that marked the South German/Austrian movement both in its historical origins and in its subsequent development. Of particular interest is the role played by late medieval mysticism in shaping the spiritualism visible in early South German/Austrian Anabaptism—a connection to an earlier spirituality that is less clearly evident in other branches of Anabaptism. A second particular mark of early South German/Austrian Anabaptism is its emphasis on the nearness of the End Times. Anabaptism in south-central Europe began in the midst of a heightened apocalyptic consciousness, in the shadow of the great Peasants' War. Its baptizing practices were shaped initially by apocalypticism. A third feature that will be evident in our collection of documents is the subsequent movement away from apocalyptically-inspired itinerant ministries, toward settled communities. As the movement matured, and apocalyptic predictions proved false, it became more and more important to establish faithful communities that could survive in the longer run. The growing importance, over time, of a congregational mentality and polity, and the apparent influence of the Swiss Brethren in this regard, will also be visible in the documents collected here. Finally, the importance of communal thinking (concrete expressions of mutual aid) will be visible in the documents gathered here. A few documents in our collection will point to the emergence and continuation of Hutterian communal Anabaptism in south-central Europe, but no attempt has been made to adequately document the early years of the Hutterites, since those documents are available elsewhere.

I. Anabaptist Sources in English Translation

English-speaking readers with an interest in the beginnings and development of Anabaptism have not had equal access to the historical sources documenting the sixteenth-century movement. However, there are some source anthologies that survey the field rather well. One of the best collections available in English remains the third volume in the *Classics of Radical Reformation* (CRR) series, Walter Klaassen's *Anabaptism in Outline* (Scottdale, PA: Herald Press, 1981). Also useful, even though more limited in focus, is C. J. Dyck's, *Spiritual Life in Anabaptism* (Scottdale, PA: Herald Press, 1995). Two collections that include Anabaptist writings within the broader Radical Reformation rubric are George H. Williams, *Spiritual and Anabaptist Writers* (Philadelphia, PA: Westminster, 1957) and, more recently, Michael G. Baylor's *The Radical Reformation* (Cambridge: Cambridge University Press, 1991). The anthologized Anabaptist writings translated and collected in these books give English-speaking readers a good sense of the broad panorama of views present in the sixteenth century baptizing movement.

For readers interested in more detailed sources written by specific Anabaptist writers, or for those who wish to study the Anabaptism of a particular geographical area more intensively, the sources available in English are quickly diminished, and only selectively available. The writings of the very early Swiss Anabaptists (1525 to ca. 1530), for example, are well represented in English translation, with three volumes of writings available in the *Classics of Radical Reformation* series for this narrow slice of historical time and place.[4] Writings of the later Swiss Brethren (1530-1600) are extant, but are not well-known in any language, since they circulated primarily in manuscript form and must be individually sought out and read in European archives.[5] However, a Swiss Brethren biblical concordance from this later period is now available in translation,[6] and a *Classics of Radical Reformation* volume translating some central writings of the Swiss Brethren in the last quarter of the sixteenth century is in preparation and, it is hoped, will be available in a year or two from the time of publication of this present book.

The writings of the North German/Dutch Anabaptists are even more selectively available in English, and in fact present a seriously truncated view of the birth and development of the Anabaptist movement in the lowlands. Of the numerous and influential booklets published by Melchior Hoffman in his lifetime, the only writings translated into English are his "Ordinance" (in Williams' *Spiritual and Anabaptist Writers*) and some important selections in Klaassen's *Anabaptism in Outline*.[7] The general unavailability of Melchior Hoffman's writings represents a serious lacuna for serious students of Anabaptism, since understanding Hoffman's thought is central for understanding all that comes later in North German/Dutch Anabaptism, including of course, Menno Simons himself. The considerable body of writing by Bernhard Rothmann, Anabaptist theologian and apologist for the Münsterite group, is available in a German critical edition,[8] but is unavailable in English, with the exception of an occasional excerpt here and there.

In contrast to the unavailability of so many crucial early Melchiorite writings, the selection of writings dating after the fall of Münster (post-1535) is far richer, although also far from complete. As might be expected, writings valued by Mennonites are well represented, whereas the writings of Anabaptist dissidents have fared less well. The writings of Nicholas van Blesdijk and Adam Pastor, for example, are generally unavailable in translation. By contrast, the collected writings of Menno Simons as well as those of Dirk Philips have been available in

English for many decades now, as has the *Martyrs Mirror* and various confessions of faith.⁹ Thanks to the *Classics of Radical Reformation* series, there is now even a good selection of writings by the eccentric spiritualist Anabaptist, David Joris, available in English.¹⁰

In spite of the relative wealth of material for this later historical period of Anabaptist/Mennonite history, it should be clear that readers who rely exclusively on sources translated into English will receive a truncated and selective view of Anabaptist origins and development in the north, with the preponderance of available writings dating from the post-Münsterite period and representing a particular Mennonite perspective.

Against this backdrop, the writings of South German/Austrian Anabaptists are relatively well represented in English, but there are some notable omissions, particularly from the earliest period of baptizing activity. The Anabaptist writings from south-central Europe that have predominated in the English literature have been those of the Hutterites.¹¹ Historically speaking, however, the Hutterites represent a later Anabaptist development in South German/Austrian Anabaptism (much like the Mennonites in the North in this regard). A Huttero-centric picture of the movement in south-central Europe consequently leaves important gaps in documentation. Renewed interest in North America in Pilgram Marpeck has helped to round out the picture. Almost all of Marpeck's writings have been translated, with some work still to be done in this regard.¹² The translation of Marpeck's writings and those of his circle have considerably widened the sources of South German/Austrian Anabaptism, but they likewise left untouched the sources documenting the beginnings and early evolutionary steps of the movement in this region. The primary aim of this volume of translated sources is thus to fill this gap and to make available a representative selection of the rich and interesting material documenting the earliest years of the South German/Austrian movement. Consequently, readers will find a concentration of documents dating from the 1520s and 1530s. As the collection moves forward in time, documentation becomes more selective than representative.

A review of the birth and development of South German/Austrian Anabaptism will allow us to locate the writings in this present collection within the framework of the South German/Austrian movement as a whole.

II. South German/Austrian Anabaptist Sources in Translation

For the sake of this introduction, we will identify three phases of development of South German/Austrian Anabaptism and note some of the source literature available in English that documents these phases of the movement.

1. Beginnings in radical reform and social upheaval (1517-1526)

The immediate context out of which South German/Austrian Anabaptism grew was Martin Luther's call for church reform on the basis of Scripture alone and an understanding of salvation by faith. What sheds particular light on South German/Austrian Anabaptism, however, are late medieval mystical writings that were considered "reforming" literature in their own right in the first decades of the sixteenth century.

Martin Luther's calls for church reform initially galvanized a wide spectrum of support, but as Luther began to define his program in more politically conservative directions, especially following his return to Wittenberg from the Wartburg in 1522, the reforming movement began to fragment. Andreas Karlstadt's estrangement from Luther and Karlstadt's grass roots reforming efforts in the small town of Orlamünde were an early sign of a more radical reforming direction. Thomas Müntzer's dissatisfaction with Luther and his own reform in the town of Allstedt mirrored Karlstadt's experience. In contrast to the increasing clericalization of Luther's reform, and its conscious integration into the reigning political order, both Karlstadt and Müntzer expected common people to be spiritually informed participants in church life and reform; both retained a greater role for the direct action of the Holy Spirit; both expected "true faith" to result in changed lives and a visible, moral reformation; and both were more interested in changing the social-political order (according to what they understood to be biblical models) than they were integrating into the existing order. Luther increasingly insisted that salvation was a complete gift of divine grace, known to God alone, and so saving faith could never be judged by visible works; furthermore, his reformation was to have everything to do with divine salvation, and nothing directly to do with social change as such.

This rupture within the early Reformation movement is well known, and historians have often pointed (rightly) to the social/political "impatience" of the radicals, who pushed for wholesale changes with little consideration of the practical political results. However, there were also significantly different ideological points of departure informing the "mainline" and "radical" reformations. These become visible in the way mystical literature was interpreted by either side.

The early Luther and his early supporters, Karlstadt and Müntzer, shared a common grounding in late medieval mystical theology. In fact, Luther's earliest publications directly promoted mystical theology. In 1516 and again in 1518, Martin Luther published an anonymous writing he called the "German Theology" or *Theologia Deutsch*.[13] It was a Taulerian mystical text that described the process of yielding self-will so that Christ might be born within, all of which would result in a new life. This message appealed to many in the reforming camp. Karlstadt was an enthusiastic supporter of the book and its ideas, and he acknowledged his debt to it.[14] Müntzer was even more deeply immersed in Tauler's writings than were either Karlstadt or Luther.[15] Hans Denck, the important early South German Anabaptist leader, wrote what some have called an abbreviated commentary on the *Theologia Deutsch* which was often subsequently republished with later editions of the *TD*.[16] The Spiritualist Sebastian Franck, who did not share the adult baptism of Denck and the Anabaptists, nevertheless had in common with the South German/Austrian Anabaptists a similar understanding of the mystical process of regeneration and an appreciation of the *Theologia Deutsch*.[17]

South German/Austrian Anabaptism grew out of the late medieval thought-world represented by the *Theologia Deutsch* and in many ways, continued to champion a "protestantized" late medieval mystical spirituality. Martin Luther never openly disavowed the book he had brought to light and published, but he resolutely moved away from some of its central presuppositions. For their part, orthodox Lutheran theologians in the second half of the sixteenth century came to consider the *Theologia Deutsch* a pernicious and dangerous book, and disavowed it openly.[18] The case of the *Theologia Deutsch* thus provides a good point of departure for understanding the theological grounding of South German/Austrian Anabaptist reforming movement and its differences with Luther's later reform.

A central point on which Luther and the later radicals came to disagree, was in their respective understanding of "faith" and the work of Christ. Luther's radical followers continued to insist, much in the manner of the *Theologia Deutsch*, on the necessity of a spiritual rebirth and the subsequent sanctifying work of "Christ in us." True faith, in the radical (and medieval mystical) understanding, could be attained only by going through a painful process of self-negation, leading up to the birth of Christ within—it was necessary to yield to the work of Christ in the heart. The understanding that this ascetic, spiritual process would give birth to "true faith" was a radical protestant interpretation of the mystical process of achieving *Gelassenheit*. Reading the writings of both Andreas Karlstadt and Thomas Müntzer is instructive in this regard.[19]

Martin Luther, by contrast, came to place the atoning work of "Christ for us" at the centre of his theology. In Luther's understanding, faith was a pure gift of God that could not be "attained." The divine gift of faith changed the sinner's standing before God, not because Christ was working within, to transform sinners into actual saints in this world (something Luther considered an impossibility), but rather sinners were forgiven only because of the atonement that Christ had already wrought for all sinners, on the cross. Sinners are forgiven and saved ("justified"), said Luther, by the grace of God and for Christ's sake. Period. It appears that what most impressed Luther in the mystical literature was the initial "self-emptying" phase leading up to a total dependence on God's grace, and not the "regenerationist" steps that followed.

It might be said that these contrasting emphases on the "work of Christ" were differences in degree, not differences in kind. The radicals also continued to stress Christ's atoning work on the cross (without which no one would be saved), and Luther continued to preach that true faith would bear good fruit in the world. Nevertheless, the differing respective emphases on the nature of faith and the work of Christ did lead to fundamentally different understandings of salvation, how the Christian life was to be lived, and how church reform should be carried out.

South German/Austrian Anabaptism built directly upon the radical protestant appropriation of mystical theology, rather than on Luther's stress on Christ's atonement for sin. Readers who move from the *Theologia Deutsch* and the writings of Andreas Karlstadt and Thomas Müntzer, on to the Anabaptist writings of Hans Denck and Hans Hut will see the connections immediately. Hans Denck's Anabaptist writings reflect his continued grounding in the mystical tradition. None of Denck's writings are included in this collection, since they are all readily available in a new and fine translation,[20] but they are nonetheless central background to the writings contained here. Likewise, although our collection includes an important writing by Hans Hut on the interpretation of Scripture, the intimate connection between his thought and that of Thomas Müntzer is most clearly visible in Hut's tract *On the Mystery of Baptism*, recently translated and published elsewhere.[21] Readers wishing to understand the thought-world of South German/Austrian Anabaptism should be aware of the writings of Andreas Karlstadt and Thomas Müntzer, and not omit a careful reading of Denck's works and Hut's tract on baptism, as well as translated excerpts from Hut's prison testimony translated in Klaassen's *Anabaptism in Outline*.

The earliest documents in our collection demonstrate the close link that existed between "protestant mysticism"and early South German/Austrian Anabaptism. Jörg Haugk von Jüchsen's *A Christian Order of a True Christian* (#1) was written before adult baptism had begun anywhere. It therefore belongs to the pre-Anabaptist category of radical reform writings, along with Müntzer's writings and the early writings of Andreas Karlstadt. Nevertheless, Haugk's booklet also belongs in our collection of South German/Austrian Anabaptist writings, not only because Anabaptists like Denck and Hut echoed Haugk's views (with the added feature of adult baptism), but also because South German/Austrian Anabaptists emphatically made Haugk's *Christian Order* their own: they continued to reprint and copy this work into the seventeenth century. Hans Denck and, to all appearances, Pilgram Marpeck, both were responsible for later printings, and the Hutterites made numerous copies of Haugk's tract in their manuscripts. In fact, a review of themes brought to light by Haugk's writing provides a good introduction to the particular emphases visible in the early South German/Austrian baptizing movement that adopted Haugk's writing as its own.

Suffering, Spiritual Regeneration, and Faith

In a manner reminiscent of Thomas Müntzer, Haugk's *Christian Order* emphasizes the process of spiritual regeneration of believers. It is this painful process that leads to "true faith," says Haugk, as opposed to an "invented faith" that wishes to achieve salvation on the cheap. Haugk uses mystical language, concepts, and imagery, but transforms it all by interpreting the mystical legacy through the Reformation lens of salvation by faith. His language and imagery closely echoes Thomas Müntzer's criticism of Luther's "justification by faith alone." This mystical/radical Protestant emphasis on attaining true faith through a painful process of having Christ come to birth in one's heart—in opposition to a "false faith" attained by mere hearing the Word of God

(Luther)—would remain a central feature of South German/Austrian Anabaptism, and re-appears in various configurations in the Anabaptist writings collected here.

It was a foundational conviction in South German/Austrian Anabaptist thinking that suffering is integral to spiritual regeneration and faith. Hans Hut taught that suffering was integrated into the nature of creation and that it provided the key to understanding Scripture and attaining salvation (see #2). He taught that there was a "gospel *of* all creatures" (a mis-reading of Mark 16:15) embedded in the natural order which taught the need for all creatures (including humankind) to suffer the will of those who stood above them in the hierarchical chain of being. In the case of humankind, it was God's will that needed to be accepted into one's heart and life. This would lead to suffering, first because the pleasures of sin, self-love, self-will, and love of the world all resist the call to "yield" before God's will and work. Doing God's will, rather than one's own, was bound to cause pain to the "old Adam." It could not be otherwise. But in the second place, "yielding" to God was bound to be painful because when God adopted the yielded sinner as God's child, Christ was born within and the believer would begin to reflect Christ's nature. Achieving "Christlikeness" in this way meant nothing less than accepting even more suffering, because the believer would be called (as Christ was) to embrace the suffering of the cross.

The atmosphere of persecution into which South German/Austrian Anabaptism was born seemed amply to confirm the link between the birth of Christ within, and the continuation of suffering in this world. The central biblical texts read: "They persecuted me, they will persecute you also." The world would continue to persecute Christ, wherever Christ appeared in "his members," that is, in his adopted brothers and sisters who had followed him, and yielded to the working of God's will and Spirit in their lives. This was the nature of "the world," the way God had created and ordered things, and it guaranteed continued suffering for "the body of Christ," the true church.

The late medieval, ascetic tone of this understanding of the saving process is undeniable, but so also is the resolute application of the "yielding" process to the burning issues of the Reformation. The point of "yielding" was not to attain merit or salvation through good works of penance (even though true penitence was central to the process), but rather the point was to allow true, saving faith to be born within. True, saving faith is a faith tested in the crucible of suffering. It undergoes the pain of self-denial; it does not shrink from the cross; it honours God above all and is obedient to God above all; its commitment is absolute and complete, and is proven in all that is said and done, even unto death. Hypocritical or feigned faith, by contrast, might repeat all the right words and formulae (such as "salvation by faith alone" and reciting the Lord's Prayer), but a false faith will avoid testing and suffering at all cost.

Readers will note the ongoing emphases on regeneration, "true faith," and suffering in virtually all the selections in this collection, but especially in the early Anabaptist writings of Hans Hut (#2), Ambrosius Spitelmaier (#4), Leonard Schiemer (#5), Hans Schlaffer (#6), Eitelhans Langenmantel (#7), Hans Nadler (#11), Wolfgang Brandhuber (#12), and Jörg Zaunring (#13).

The New Life

"A good tree will bear good fruit" (Matt. 7:17ff). This oft-repeated saying of Jesus was also foundational for the South German/Austrian Anabaptists, and grew directly out of their understanding of spiritual regeneration and true faith. Expressed positively, the call for "good fruit" was a challenge to believers to allow Christ's nature, born within, to express itself in Christ-like action in the world. A long list of virtues and virtuous actions often was the result of this positive expression of what "good fruit" would look like. Expressed negatively, Jesus' saying was often applied to the mainline reformation as a reproach: "They claim to have faith, but one look at their works reveals the truth of the matter." Such reproaches were often followed by an impressive catalogue of the sins and failings of so-called "reformed" preachers and their flocks. In a typical example, at his judicial hearing in 1563, Paul Glock answered the priest who had asked him why the Anabaptists did not attend the state churches. Glock's answer (not calculated to win him friends) was: "Your teaching, preaching, church and assembly is a mob and an assembly of fornicators, adulterers, liars, blasphemers, drunkards, proud, usurers, and all unclean spirits in whom the devil has and does his work... Your teaching and preaching is not done according to the counsel of Christ nor in his Spirit. Therefore, also, it does not bear any good fruit." (#25: "First Defense, 1563").

Whether expressed positively or negatively, the conviction was universal in South German/Austrian Anabaptism that true faith would bear the Christ-like fruits of faith, and that these "fruits" would—of necessity—be plainly visible in life. Protestant opponents derided this view as "salvation by works"; the Anabaptists defended their understanding by insisting that any "good fruit" was purely the result of God's grace alone, working in the human heart (not the result of human striving), and merited nothing. At the heart of the disagreement stood two very different understandings of the nature of faith, visible already in the disagreements between Luther on the one hand, and Karlstadt and Müntzer on the other. The "Sermon on Sin," most likely written by Hans Langenmantel (#7), provides a good example of how the link between regeneration and a new life was explained and elaborated by these Anabaptists.

Scripture and the Holy Spirit

Haugk's *Christian Order* illustrates a further theme that played an important role in early South German/Austrian Anabaptism, namely the emphasis on the activity of the Holy Spirit as the primary mode, not only of regeneration, but also of revelation. "The Scriptures give only an outer witness of a true life, but they cannot create a new being in me," writes Haugk. This sentiment, given expression by Hans Denck, Hans Hut and other Anabaptists, gave the early South German/Austrian movement a strongly spiritualist cast that eventually was resolved only by the later departure of the more avowed spiritualist Anabaptists on the one hand, and the establishment of the more biblicistic and rule-oriented Hutterites on the other.

The spiritualistic approach to Scripture, like the regenerationist understanding of saving faith, was an early and crucial point of separation between the radical reformers and the mainline reformers. The radical evangelical reformers insisted that reformation would not come simply by hearing the biblical Word preached by learned pastors interpreting passages of Scripture (that is, by "Scripture alone") but rather, a true reformation of the church would take place only through the birth of the living Word in the hearts of "yielded" people—by the creation of new beings who would become living members ("limbs") of Christ's body. Thomas Müntzer had already identified Luther as one of the "learned doctors" who, in spite of his knowledge of "the letter," did not know what he was talking about because he lacked the living, regenerating Spirit. Hans Hergot's bitter attack on the "Scripture wizards" (#3) makes plain the profound sense of betrayal felt by those who sided with the commoners in 1525, in the face of Luther's call for their extermination by the princes.

The true interpretation of Scripture, the radical wing insisted, had to be the result of a successful process of yielding to God's Spirit by suffering God's work within, and then being brought to life by that same Spirit of God. The true exegete would be one who gave evidence in life of the activity of God's Spirit within. To many observers, Luther's actions generally—and especially his two printed pamphlets of 1525 which called for the peasantry to be killed like mad dogs—were evidence enough of the lack of the Holy Spirit. Certainly that was Hergot's conclusion.

The relentless critique of "the learned scribes" (Protestant clergy and theologians) continued to be heard in South German/Austrian Anabaptist writings; the fact that Protestant clerics supported and justified the persecution of Anabaptists only confirmed for the Anabaptists what "spirit" was at work in the mainline reformation. A thoroughgoing anticlericalism—hostility towards the Roman Catholic "priests" as well as the Protestant "learned shepherds"—is evident throughout the documents in this collection (see #2, 3, 4, 5, 6, 13, 14, *et passim*).

Hans Hut's booklet on biblical interpretation (#2) is an original and ingenious application of the principles that the true "Word of God" is spiritual, not literal, and that therefore true biblical interpretation is carried out only by the spiritually regenerate. Hut's listing of a series of "literal contradictions" in Scripture is intended to make the point that a mere reading of "the letter" is of no avail, and thus the skill in biblical languages displayed by the "learned doctors" is not only useless, but a positive hindrance. To penetrate the true meaning of Scripture, one needs to be able to transcend the literal through a spiritual understanding.[22] Hut's trinitarian interpretive structure is loosely based on the Apostles' Creed, but it does not make a dogmatic point about the Trinity. Rather it serves to make the point that "true believers" must *experience* the Trinity in themselves, in a three-fold process, in order to grasp the true meaning of Scripture. There are strong echoes of this experiential trinitarianism, along with similar conclusions regarding one's fitness for biblical interpretation, in Spitelmaier's response to questioning (#4) and Leonard Schiemer's essay on the "three-fold grace" (#5).

A Commoner's Reformation

The radical emphasis on regeneration by the Spirit, rather than the interpretation of the written letter, had the practical consequence that the educated lost all advantage in the interpretation and understanding of God's will. In fact, the privileged were at a real disadvantage, given the exalted positions they usually assumed in society, since a true spiritual understanding could only come to those who were able to humble themselves enough to yield their self-will to God's will. The poor and downtrodden had a shorter distance to travel in this regard. A very few members of the lower nobility and patrician classes in the Tyrol were attracted to Pilgram Marpeck's Anabaptism, as was the noblewoman Helena von Freyberg (#23), but Anabaptism in south-central Europe was overwhelmingly a reformation of common people, with particular strength among the artisans.

Several documents in our collection provide graphic evidence of how South German/Austrian Anabaptists established an interpretive and educational model geared to the uneducated and even the illiterate. Hut's essay (#2) certainly is geared to the common person and emphasizes experience (and suffering) rather than learning. Spitelmaier (#4) sounds a note commonly heard in South German/Austrian documents, namely that the Gospel is to be taught to the common people "through the trade of each." There is a "gospel" that is written in creation, that is available to learned and unlearned alike. The "gospel of all creatures," taught by Hut to his followers, is most clearly explained in our collection by Hans Schlaffer (#6) in his description of the "first witness" of created things. The "gospel of suffering" that was to be learned from the "creatures," along with related lessons concerning spiritual regeneration, baptism, and living the new life, were in fact the basic Anabaptist teachings that were communicated to converts in the south-central parts of the Holy Roman Empire. The vast majority of these converts were commoners, artisans, and peasants. These teachings were "sealed" publicly by water baptism.

One of the most remarkable documents in the corpus of Anabaptist court records—because of what it tells us about the communication process in the sixteenth century—is the confession and statement by Hans Nadler (#11). Nadler was an illiterate needle peddler who also functioned as an evangelist for the Anabaptist cause. In his confession, taken down by a court scribe, he described the details of his evangelistic method. His testimony thus provides an extremely rare window into the world of reforming commoners, who carried out their calling to preach and convert others in spite of a lack of education and even (as in Nadler's case) without basic literacy. Anabaptism spread primarily through one-on-one contact and conversation. There were innumerable opportunities for social interaction in the sixteenth century, particularly for itinerant salesmen like Hans Hut, who was a book peddler, and Hans Nadler. But artisans such as weavers, tailors, and seamstresses also were notoriously mobile, setting up "shop" in houses and barns, and working together in informal groups. It was in such settings that Anabaptist instruction took place.

It is clear from court testimonies and other sources that Anabaptist religious instruction revolved around key biblical texts that provided answers to the burning questions of the day. Many Anabaptists demonstrated an amazing capacity to absorb and remember Bible verses relating to a variety of topics, as is amply documented in court records across all of Europe. Endres Keller's rambling testimony (#17), written following torture, under horrible conditions in a dungeon with no access to a Bible, demonstrates an astoundingly detailed recollection of Old and New Testament texts that address a wide variety of religious topics. Keller had a rudimentary literacy, but that did not take the place of a zeal for committing Scripture to memory. This emphasis on memory was foundational in a culture that still depended on oral/aural means of communication—and thus depended on mnemonics for the retrieval of information.

The "common people" took the Reformation call to "prove all things by Scripture" quite to heart. In the Anabaptist movement, one way of appropriating Scripture was to collect and remember topically-organized Scripture passages. These biblical concordances were sometimes written, less frequently printed, and most frequently committed to memory, as fully as the person was able. The printed topical concordances that have survived sound remarkably like the prison testimonies still extant in court records.[23] In the case of memorized and printed "texts," both were composed of selected Scripture passages, addressing topical subjects, woven together by a minimum of commentary. Even in the reasoned testimony of a Paul Glock (#24-32)—who was fluidly literate and wrote his epistles with the aid of a printed Bible—the topical and thematic grouping of Scripture texts, so characteristic of oral/aural mnemonics, is quite evident.

It is also evident from the South German/Austrian sources collected here that the Lord's Prayer and the Apostles' Creed were used repeatedly as instructional tools. They were basic Christian texts, known and memorized by virtually everyone, that could be re-interpreted and invested with new Anabaptist content. A "negative" and critical re-telling of the Lord's Prayer (focusing on the supposed hypocritical recitation of the prayer by those in the mainline churches) seems to have been common currency in the proselytization of this part of the Anabaptist movement (see #5, 6, 7, 11). The teaching of the Lord's Prayer, the Apostles' Creed, and the Ten Commandments continued to be central in Anabaptist education and catechism, and later formed the core of religious instruction for children in the settled Hutterite communities.[24]

The effectiveness of underground, grassroots communication was a source of great consternation to the religious and political authorities. The "texts" of biblical interpretation that were spreading orally at the grassroots represented a remarkably coherent, biblically-based, counter-theology that was not subject to the control of the authorities or their sanctioned preachers. Furthermore, these oral texts contained implicit and explicit criticisms of state-sanctioned church reform and social injustices which, the authorities feared, would undermine the existing religious, social, and political order. All this may help explain why the attempt to silence the Anabaptists through persecution was as fierce as it was.

From Social Reform, through Apocalyptic Hope, to Communalism

As noted above, Haugk associated closely with Thomas Müntzer and Hans Hut and, besides sharing their grounding in late medieval mysticism and their criticism of Luther, also was implicated in the Peasants' War, as they also were. Combining mystical thought with church reform and political revolt is rather an odd blend, and calls for explanation. Thomas Müntzer was the one who best put these pieces together.[25] In Müntzer's understanding of divine and human history, God was acting not only to lead individuals to salvation by a process of purgation and cleansing, God also was redeeming the world by an analogous process. The pain associated with social purgation and cleansing was simply a preparation for the new and just world which would be inaugurated by the coming of Christ himself. When Christ returned in glory, those who had humbled themselves and suffered the process of inner regeneration—the elect—would come into their eternal inheritance. On the other hand, those who had proudly resisted the "sharp ploughshare" because of their pride and love of the world, were resisting the movement of God's Spirit both within themselves and in society at large. The most culpable among these stubborn and prideful people were the clergy and "false biblical scholars" (or "snakes"), who would go to a particularly painful eternal reward because of their role in misleading so many others.[26]

When the Peasants' War erupted, Müntzer became convinced that the final act in history had begun and that the peasants were the "elect," the humble means chosen by God to purge the fallen world before Christ's return. In this spirit he preached to the peasant army at Frankenhausen, just before their disastrous defeat on May 15, 1525. Hans Hut was present at that battle, a supporter of Müntzer who soon re-interpreted Müntzer's apocalyptic scenario in Anabaptist terms. There is no evidence that Jörg Haugk von Jüchsen was at the battle itself; at the time he was functioning as preacher to rebellious peasants in his home territory.

Haugk's *Christian Order* belongs to the period leading up to the Peasants' War.[27] There is nothing in the *Christian Order*—or, for that matter, in Hut's *Comparing and Interpreting Divine Scripture* (#2)—that suggests a militant apocalypticism or incipient support for rebellious peasants. The one tract in our collection that openly encourages the establishment of a new and more just society (in its first part) is Hans Hergot's *New Transformation* (#3), although Hergot's tract also reflects (in its second part) the bitter disappointment of betrayal at the failure of the attempt. Hergot's writing is not an Anabaptist tract as such, but belongs in our collection because of the light it sheds on the social and religious aspirations of the common people from whom the majority of Anabaptists in this region were drawn.[28]

In fact, little will be found in our collection of writings that openly refers to the Peasants' War of 1525 in either its Franconian or Tyrolean phases,[29] even though the uprising in both geographical locations was fundamental to the beginnings of South German/Austrian Anabaptism. The lack of explicit comment on the Peasants' War in our collection accurately mirrors the dearth of Anabaptist sources reflecting on those experiences—and this should not be surprising. The systematic baptism of adults in the south-central Europe emerged only after the Peasants' War had failed. People implicated in the revolt were punished severely by the authorities when caught, and it was dangerous to put evidence in writing. The Austrian authorities in particular were convinced that Anabaptism was simply a continuation of the Peasants' Revolt in another guise—another form of insubordination (see also the Lutheran polemic, #14, e). Anabaptist prisoners (however innocent) were routinely questioned under torture about the supposed insurrectionary plot they were carrying out under the cover of

Anabaptism. This was Hans Schlaffer's experience (#6) and it was shared by many other Anabaptist prisoners (see also Hans Nadler's testimony, #11). South German/Austrian Anabaptist beginnings originating with Hans Hut are bound up with Thomas Müntzer and apocalyptic expectations tied to the Peasants' War. There are also evident connections between Gaismair's revolt in the Tyrol and the Anabaptism that emerged there, but the writings collected here will shed little direct light on those original connections. The ideological links to those beginnings, however, are deep and significant and can still be discerned.

A deep-seated concern with social justice and economic sharing runs through South German/Austrian Anabaptism and provides a crucial thread of continuity with the peasants' call for a new social order based on the "Bible alone." Müntzer's pre-Anabaptist view was transmuted into a wary apocalyptic Anabaptism primarily by Müntzer's disciple, Hans Hut, who was baptized into the movement by Hans Denck in 1526. In the face of peasant defeat and the failure of Thomas Müntzer's prophecies, Hut saw in the Anabaptists a purer movement of renewal, in preparation for Christ's return. He transferred the mantle of "God's elect" from the peasants—now discredited by their military defeat— to those willing to accept a baptism of suffering and waiting, for the meantime. Hut became convinced that God himself would precipitate the final conflict and judgment in a direct way, and that Christ's return could be predicted for Pentecost, 1528. Many early Anabaptist converts South German and Austrian lands were convinced by Hut's message, and accepted his baptism with hopes of an imminent judgment for the godless "Big Jacks" and a quick redemption of the social order. In the meantime, they were to share common cause with each other, both spiritually and materially. In these early stages, the extent of material sharing was left undefined, but was nevertheless one of the primary messages communicated to converts.

The earliest South German/Austrian Anabaptist writings still hold out hope for a new and just society, but in the post-Peasants' War context that hope now rested with external forces that were in God's hands—the marauding Turks would lead up to Christ's coming, for example, rather than peasants-in-arms. Ambrosius Spitelmaier's testimony of October, 1527 (#4) gives the most graphic evidence in our collection for this early apocalyptic Anabaptist view that owes so much to Hans Hut and the expectations of the common people for a new social order. However, apocalyptic hope of this kind faded rather quickly. When it did, the hopes for a new society were transmuted into descriptions of (and prescriptions for) the new community of the regenerate, where the new and just society would be modeled and lived out in microcosm. Although both Leonard Schiemer and Hans Schlaffer (see #5, 6) make passing reference to living in "these last perilous times," and both clearly expect the End to come soon, their apocalypticism is muted in comparison with Spitelmaier's. Their writings call for perseverance on the narrow way and a sharing of all things among true Christians. Their writings begin to trace outlines of what a longer-term community might look like.

The legislated communalism of the Hutterites which emerged a few years later thus stands directly in the lineage of Hergot's utopian vision, transmuted by the painful experience of the defeat of the peasants and the subsequent vicious persecution of Anabaptists by the authorities—a persecution that claimed the lives of Hans Hut and Jacob Hutter, as well as the lives of many hundreds more. The connection between spiritual regeneration (which rested on "yielding" the self, me, and mine for the sake of God and the neighbour) and a new and just social order (a commitment to "ours" and what is "common to all") was central to South German/Austrian Anabaptism from the start, and continued in suitably-modified ways as the movement developed. The communalism that is central to Hergot's utopia (#3) can be seen in Hans Hut's true believers holding "all things in common" (#2) as well as in similar expressions of Hut's followers Ambrosius Spitelmaier (#4), Leonard Schiemer (#5), Hans Schlaffer (#6), Hans Nadler (#11), and Wolfgang Brandhuber (#12). The ideological thread connecting the Anabaptist community, the "pure body of Christ on earth," to peasant utopianism is a shared vision of a just social order, finally established as God intended it to be. If society was not yet purged and ready, at least the "true church" could and should be.

From its very inception, South German/Austrian Anabaptism found itself on the margins of religious and civil society. In the context of religious reform, South German/Austrian Anabaptism was an unwelcome stepchild of the mainstream reforming movement already at the moment of its birth. Inheritors of the existing estrangement between Luther and his radical followers, the baptizers were convinced from the start that the Roman Catholic clerics were serving human custom rather than Scripture, and likewise convinced that Luther and his followers lacked the Spirit and had mis-appropriated Scripture and twisted its true meaning. South German/Austrian Anabaptism was thus born at odds with the religious establishment, gathering its first followers among the discontented and marginalized, creating underground and persecuted groups of baptized believers. In the political context of the time, the close connection between the Peasants' War, Thomas Müntzer's failed mystical apocalypticism, and the subsequent rise of mystical-apocalyptic Anabaptism meant that the baptizers were suspect from the start as potential insurrectionaries—and not always without cause.[30]

The socio-political and religious shape of early South German/Austrian Anabaptism is thus a complex one. We see in the early teachings of South German/Austrian Anabaptism a continuation of a unique "protestantized" mystical path that placed an emphasis on spiritual regeneration and growth (Karlstadt, Müntzer, Haugk). Furthermore, the living Spirit of God was seen as the motive force behind the personal appropriation of saving faith and regeneration, as well as the true light of revelation for believers. The same living Spirit would bear good fruit in the lives of yielded believers. These elements, seen so clearly in the teaching and writing of Hans Denck, exercised a significant formative influence on the South German/Austrian movement and remained decisive in shaping the entire movement. We see these same spiritualist emphases in the followers of Hans Hut, but with the added apocalyptic expectation that Christ's imminent return was going to renew all the earth and establish justice soon, and very soon. The path of inner spiritual regeneration and the active role of the Spirit remained central to Hut, but these elements were placed within an apocalyptic scenario shaped by Thomas Müntzer.

The arrest and death of Hans Hut (December, 1527) certainly was a blow to apocalyptic Anabaptism, as was also the uneventful passing of the predicted time of the Second Coming. Christ did not return; the expected Kingdom of justice failed to materialize; the predictions had proven false.[31] Along with these failures came increased persecution in cities and territories that had earlier been somewhat lenient in tolerating the presence of Anabaptists. With these changes came a rapid shift in emphasis in South German/Austrian Anabaptism from a lively apocalyptic expectation—with itinerant apostles hurriedly baptizing the 144,000 elect of Rev. 7:3—to a concern for the establishment of strong communities that could survive the uncertain time until Christ came for his Bride, the church.

2. Persecution (from 1527)

The Reformation was as much a political event as it was a religious event, as the issue of religious toleration made clear. The fundamental political assumption in the sixteenth century was that order in the social-political sphere could only be maintained by a unified religious confession in any given political territory. A "separation of church and state" was virtually inconceivable in the sixteenth century, particularly when seen against the medieval political and religious backdrop. Civil enforcement of a uniform religious confession and the persecution of religious dissenters had a long, if inglorious, political history reaching back to the christianization of the late Roman Empire. The persecution of Anabaptists in the sixteenth century followed this bloody, time-honoured model. It came as no surprise to anyone in the sixteenth century that religious dissent evoked such a response; this had happened to religious dissenters for more than a millennium. What was surprising was that the coming of the Protestant Reformation changed so little in this regard.

The fundamental Reformation teachings, that human beings are saved by their faith (and not by objective sacraments administered by the priests), and that ultimate authority lies with Scripture alone, were critiqued in Catholic circles as calls to political insurrection. Perhaps one of the reasons for Luther's vitriolic reaction to the peasants' uprising was precisely because the peasants were appealing to Reformation principles (particularly to Scripture) in their struggle to change the social and political order—giving Roman Catholic polemicists a case study which they did not hesitate to apply. The Protestant reformers felt the need to demonstrate—to the political authorities in particular—that the call to faith and the appeal to the authority of Scripture could be harmonized with the maintenance of the social and political order—put crudely, that "reformation" would still leave princes and city councils in control of their territories.

If human beings are saved by their individual faith, on what basis could territorial religious uniformity be maintained? The radical reforming movement slowly drew out the implications of their understanding of the evangelical position, and it led to what appeared to be dangerous conclusions: If saving faith is a gift of regeneration from God alone, no human being or human institution can bring this to pass. The Anabaptists took this one step further and insisted that only those who had come to such a conscious, regenerating faith through the inner work of the Spirit (adults, in other words) could or should be baptized into the church. Only those baptized into the church, and who were willing to amend their lives and submit to fraternal admonition, would be welcome at the Lord's Supper. Furthermore, this body of committed believers would be free to elect their own pastors.

The corollaries of such a model of church reform were frightening and almost unthinkable to many contemporaries. The political and religious authorities in any territory would lose control of the religious structures. The response of the political authorities was to reassert the need for civil enforcement of religious uniformity, which meant attempting to coerce religious dissenters into conformity by judicial means.

Much of what we know about the beliefs of Anabaptists comes from judicial records, prison testimonies of Anabaptist believers often extracted under torture. Many of these prisoners knew that they were soon to be put to death in unimaginably cruel ways. In our collection, the testimonies of Ambrosius Spitelmaier (#4), Hans Schlaffer (#6, B), Hans Nadler (#11) and Katharina Hutter (#16) are examples of surviving judicial records of this kind. Our collection also contains numerous writings written as "testaments" by Anabaptist prisoners themselves, as they awaited judicial sentence. The prison writings of Leonhard Schiemer (#5), Hans Schlaffer (#6, A), Endres Keller (#17), the Trieste prisoners (#21), the letters of Paul Glock (#24-32) and Hans Schmidt (#34), and the hymn of Ursula Hellrigel (#10) are examples of this kind of literature. The expectation of suffering, and preparation for it, were not peripheral to Anabaptist faith and life, and it is not surprising that so much biblical reflection was devoted to understanding the reality of persecution and suffering. It also is not surprising that Anabaptists were exponents of religious toleration.

Radical reformers were among the first to issue calls for religious toleration.[32] More cynical observers may say that calls for toleration are always a tactic of the powerless, but there seem to have been more profound religious motives at work as well. Radical reform was grounded in a transformational experience that began when individuals responded freely to God's call to repentance. A freely-chosen decision to testify to one's faith and readiness to follow Christ by water baptism (the testimony of a good conscience before God) was foundational to the formation of the baptizing church. Freedom to choose, and freedom of conscience concerning one's choice, were at the heart of Anabaptism.

It is an odd fact that the arguments for religious toleration that the Anabaptists developed are best summarized in our collection by the Lutheran pastor Urbanus Rhegius, in a systematic treatise written with the intent of demolishing the possibility of such toleration (#18). The main arguments put forward by the Anabaptists (as noted by Rhegius) are:

–No one can coerce faith. Therefore heretics must be opposed by God's Word alone, and convinced in their hearts; coerced "confessions" simply create hypocrites, not believers.

–Those who err may eventually improve.

–The apostles successfully evangelized the world without using the worldly sword.

–Christ commanded preaching the Gospel, not coercion.

–Faith is of the heart and is known to God alone; therefore the state cannot judge concerning it, and should not involve itself in punishment in matters of faith.

–Judgment is ultimately God's, and is not a human responsibility.

To Rhegius' credit, his list included all of the central points used by Anabaptists. Rhegius did what he could to counter these points with biblical and theological arguments.

Regardless of how we may judge the matter from the twenty-first-century vantage point, to most sixteenth-century Lutheran reformers, an ecclesial model based on the toleration of individual religious convictions simply did not fit with the perceived need for territorial churches and political order. Rulers, they were convinced, needed to control the religious content taught to their subjects and practiced by them in their territories, if they were to have any hope of maintaining social and political order.

Anabaptism in south-central Europe was born into a context of persecution of religious dissent, but the levels of persecution varied with place and time. Consequently, political geography played a large role in the development of the movement. Although a crucial link to the beginnings of South German/Austrian Anabaptism was central Germany, that is eastern Hesse and Thuringia (areas where Thomas Müntzer was active and one of the regions where the Peasants' War raged), the flowering of Anabaptism came further to the south and east, first in the south German cities like Nuremberg and Augsburg, but soon centred in Moravia. Similarly, there were crucial links between the Peasants' Revolt in the Tyrol (under the leadership of Michael Gaismair) and later Anabaptists there, but determined persecution in the Tyrol by the Hapsburg king Ferdinand I soon forced Anabaptists to flee to Moravia. Moravia thus became the primary Anabaptist haven, beginning already in 1527—a time when the political and religious pressure on the Anabaptists intensified in other territories. Later in the century, however, Hapsburg power reached into Moravia as well, and renewed hardship ensued for Anabaptist refugees there.

Werner Packull has identified three primary periods of persecution that impacted the Anabaptist communities in south-central Europe. From 1527 to 1529, there was initial pressure exerted by Ferdinand I, particularly in the territories under his direct control. The result of this first wave of persecution was increased migration from Hapsburg territories to Moravia, since the Moravian lords still managed to maintain a fair degree of independence from Ferdinand and his repressive policies. Increased military threat and pressure on Hapsburg territories meant more freedom for the Moravian lords, and more toleration in Moravian lands for Anabaptists. That pressure came primarily on the eastern frontier, from the Turks, and within the Empire from the Protestant states. Documents 1-15 in our collection date from the pre-1535 period which saw increased persecution in the Holy Roman Empire generally, but relative security and freedom in Moravia.

A wave of severe pesecution finally reached the Moravian territories in 1534-1535. The Turkish threat to Hapsburg lands abated towards the end of 1534, at which point Ferdinand I was free to renew political pressure on the Moravian lords. Adding to this pressure were the unfortunate events in the city of Münster, which tainted all Anabaptists with the whiff of sedition and armed insurrection. The Moravian lords finally were sufficiently pressured by Ferdinand, and responded reluctantly by expelling the most visible Anabaptist communities. The wholesale expulsions of Anabaptists from Moravia in 1535 led to disappearance of the Austerlitz brethren, the Philipites, and the Gabrielites as distinct communities. The Philipites migrated back to their homelands in the Palatinate, the Rhineland, and Württemberg, most eventually joining the Swiss Brethren. The Gabrielites migrated back to Silesia and points east, from whence the majority of that community had come. The expulsions were a severe test also for the Hutterites. They lost all of their communities and most of their early leaders. Between 1535 and 1538 Jacob Hutter (see the testimony of Katharina Hutter, #16), Jeronimous Käls, Onophrius Griesinger, Leonhard Lochmair, and Georg Fasser had all met a martyr's death—but the Hutterites managed to survive and reorganized under the leadership of Hans Amon during the easing of the situation in Moravia from 1537 to 1545.[33]

In 1545, Ferdinand I won a resounding victory over the Turks again, and immediately ordered renewed repression of Anabaptist groups in Moravian territories. This phase of persecution resulted in the publication of Peter Riedemann's *Account of our Faith*, published as an apology and an attempt to win living space for Hutterite Anabaptist communities.[34] In 1547, with the dual victory of Charles V over Protestant forces, and the defeat of the rebellion in Bohemia, the Hapsburgs were even more free to enforce their will in Moravia again. At this point, the remaining Hutterites were again driven from their re-established Moravian homes, left to wander to the East, living a precarious existence in caves near the Slovakian-Hungarian border. These years of trial came to an end in the 1550s, with a renewed military threat from the Turks. The Hutterites re-established their communities again on lands of friendly nobles in Moravia. The "golden years" of the Hutterite communities in Moravia began in the 1550s, and bloomed particularly following the death of their implacable enemy, Ferdinand I in 1564. It is estimated that the Anabaptist population in Moravia may have reached twenty-thousand in the second half of the sixteenth century.[35]

Although persecution came and went in Moravia, in inverse proportion to external pressures on the Hapsburgs, in Austrian territories themselves (Austria, the Tyrol, parts of Württemberg), the reaction to Anabaptism (and to any form of Protestantism) was uncompromisingly hostile. The protocol outlining recantation procedures in the Tyrol (#9) demonstrates the sort of harsh treatment faced even by those willing to recant. Very little in the way of mercy could be expected by recalcitrant Anabaptists captured in Hapsburg territories, the only variable being the amount of independence enjoyed by a local lord vis-a-vis Ferdinand I of Austria. Occasionally, local officials could mitigate Ferdinand's demands for blood.

In the south German cities that were open to Reformation ideas (e.g., Nuremberg, Augsburg, Strasbourg) and in Protestant territories generally, there was a willingness to work a little harder at winning over the Anabaptists. Local Protestant pastors and theologians were given the task of convincing imprisoned Anabaptists to join the state church. Their tools were theological and biblical argument and persuasion. They sometimes succeeded in their attempts, but Anabaptist prisoners proved to be uncommonly stubborn. In some Protestant territories, the local authorities sometimes extended efforts at coerced persuasion over a longer period of time. Hans Schmidt, for example, was in a variety of prisons for some five months (#34). Paul Glock's nineteen-year imprisonment (#24-32) was unusual for its length, the occasional leniency of his prison conditions, and the extended discussions that took place in efforts to dissuade him from Anabaptism.

When attempts to convert Anabaptists failed, the pastors made their best case to the public at large and, more importantly, to the political authorities. Sometimes pastors appealed to the authorities for mercy, as Johann Rurer did for Hans Nadler (#11-B); but later polemics increasingly called on the authorities to suppress Anabaptism altogether, and not to allow such "damnable errors" to continue circulating among the people (#14). Still later, in the face of a movement that refused to disappear and that argued for freedom of conscience, the Lutheran pastors found themselves providing biblical and theological arguments in support of civil prosecution of religious dissenters (#18). Four writings in our collection (#8, 11-B, 14, 18) provide a window into the world of Protestant pastors doing theological battle with Anabaptism, and provide an important outside perspective on the movement.

The anonymous "Theological Refutation" (1528) sounds themes that will be heard in later writings by Lutheran apologists: Anabaptism is an heretical sect because it separates from the one true church. The "true church" in the Lutheran definition was where the Gospel was preached and the sacraments celebrated—and it was understood that only in the state-sanctioned church did this take place (see also #14, B). In the second place, the Anabaptists could not be the "true church" because they did not accept the interpretation of Scripture as defined by the state church, which by definition was the "true church." (The circularity of these arguments seems not to have bothered the Protestant theologians; they used them repeatedly.) This second and crucial point of the "Refutation"—that Anabaptists did not accept the testimony of Scripture—was obviously overstated for polemical effect, as is plain to anyone who reads what the Anabaptists were actually writing and saying, but the accusation had at least some basis in fact. The early Anabaptists did hold that a true exegete had to be spiritually regenerated, as we have seen. In the hands of Lutheran apologists, this Anabaptist teaching was re-stated to say that their teaching was "self-invented," not based on "Scripture alone" but rather on dreams and visions of individuals. The "Refutation" (as would later apologies) was trying to shift the ground of the argument back to the literal text of

Scripture, and a learned exegesis of that text by the pastors authorized by the local political authorities (see also #14, C and Anabaptist responses by Hans Umlauft, #22 and Paul Glock, #25).

The "Refutation" also predictably challenged the practice of adult baptism, the rejection of a real presence in the Lord's Supper, and the Anabaptist practice of community of goods, but more fundamental was the final point: the Anabaptists, says the Lutheran apologist, "do not believe in Christ, nor think that the suffering of the Son of God was sufficient payment for sin." The heart of this early "Refutation" of South German/Austrian Anabaptism thus came back to the two crucial questions that were evident already in the disagreement between Luther and Müntzer. First, who has the authority to interpret Scripture, and how is that authority established—i.e., by a proper education and a "legitimate" appointment to the office by a secular authority, or by a spiritual rebirth? Are the Protestant preachers the "false prophets," as the Anabaptists maintained repeatedly, or are the Anabaptists the "false prophets," as the preachers argued (see also #14, C, D)? Second, what is the nature of salvation? Are we saved by faith alone, simply by believing in Christ's atonement for sin, or does salvation entail faithful obedience ("fruit") as well?

Urbanus Rhegius' "Justification for the Prosecution of Anabaptists" reaches another level of hostility by arguing systematically that the authorities ought to punish Anabaptists—if convincing them by biblical argument does not succeed. Rhegius composed his "Justification" in 1536, following the Anabaptist takeover, defense, and military loss of the city of Münster in Westphalia. Anabaptists everywhere experienced increased persecution as a result of the disaster at Münster, being tarred with the same brush as the Münsterites. Rhegius' "Justification" appealed repeatedly to the writings of Augustine to the effect that heretics should be "compelled" to come into the "true church." Rhegius identified the Donatists as "Anabaptists," and applied Augustine's anti-Donatist arguments directly to the sixteenth century baptizers.

Just as consistently, Rhegius appealed to the example of Münster to argue (on the basis of Deuteronomy and other Old Testament Scriptures) that false prophets and "all evildoers" should be punished and even put to death by Christian governments—as long as such punishment were done "in love." His point that heresy "has brought with it revolt and murder" was underlined by the events in Westphalia: "If at Münster they [the government officials] had not watched Bernhard

Rothmann so long, they might have saved the situation," wrote Rhegius. "Since, however, they let matters go and spared the seducer, the terrible distress followed which Germany will never forget..." The moral of Rhegius' story was not lost on most government officials, especially after Münster: Anabaptism was a dangerous heresy that needed to be strictly prosecuted and stamped out, the sooner the better, while there was still time. Anabaptist prisoners after 1536 routinely had to defend themselves by distancing themselves from the Münsterites (e.g. Endres Keller, #17).

The Anabaptists were not completely bereft of public defenders, although they were few and far between, and primarily were persons drawn to spiritualistic religion. The baron Georg Gross (Pfersfelder), who had spiritualist leanings, was one such defender. Pfersfelder was as critical of the mainline reformers as he was sympathetic to the Anabaptists (#15). Klaus von Grafeneck and his wife, who leaned in Schwenckfeld's direction, were more lenient than was usual with their Anabaptist prisoner Paul Glock (#24-32). The common depiction of Anabaptists as heretical seducers and insurrectionists was also countered in print in the sixteenth century by the spiritualist Sebastian Franck. He wrote a description of the Anabaptists he knew (most of whom were from the South German/Austrian branch) in his monumental *Chronica*, published in Strasbourg in 1531 and again in 1536 (#19). Franck's observations are coloured by his own spiritualist convictions throughout, but they are uniquely free of the rancour that characterizes so much sixteenth century literature documenting Anabaptism. Franck's depiction of the Anabaptists as pious, if misled, people who should be extended religious toleration stands in stark contrast to the usual polemical accounts of theological opponents like Urbanus Rhegius and Zürich's Heinrich Bullinger.[36] Franck's observations provide an apt counterpoint to the mainline Protestant critiques.

Ironically, what Franck found most appealing about the Anabaptists, namely the non-dogmatic spiritualism of some baptizers like Hans Denck and Hans Bünderlin, was—at the time of his writing—in the process of being replaced in South German/Austrian territories by the feature Franck disliked the most, namely the propensity among some Anabaptists to cement the boundaries of their communities by establishing external "rules" to accompany the spiritual rebirth.

3. The emergence and growth of communal Anabaptism

Anabaptism was a grass roots movement that encompassed a rich variety of viewpoints. Even sympathetic contemporaries like Sebastian Franck claimed the Anabaptists were so divided amongst themselves, that he could not identify all the groups. Franck's statement was made with ulterior motives, with the intention of convincing readers to embrace a non-divisive, inner, spiritual Christianity. Nevertheless, his point is well taken: whatever fundamental agreements there might have been, the Anabaptists had trouble agreeing on the details. Nowhere was this diversity more evident than in Moravia, the destination for thousands of Anabaptist refugees—their numbers can only be roughly estimated—fleeing persecution in Switzerland, the Palatinate, Württemberg, the Tyrol, and Silesia.

Balthasar Hubmaier was an early refugee in Moravia, unique among Anabaptist leaders in the fact that he managed to establish a state-sanctioned Anabaptist church first in the Hapsburg city of Waldshut on the Rhine in 1525, and then in the small Moravian city-state of Nicholsburg in 1526. Anabaptist refugees in Nicholsburg coexisted, uneasily no doubt, under Hubmaier's leadership for more than a year, but there were contentious issues bubbling just under the surface. Hubmaier accepted the use of the sword in the hands of a Christian magistrate as a matter of course, and established his Anabaptist church in Nicholsburg under the protection of the local lords. There were, however, Swiss Anabaptist refugees who believed that baptized members of the church should not wield the sword—regardless of their role in government. Likewise, Hubmaier had accepted his role as leading pastor in the Nicholsburg church on the strength of appointment to that position by the local lords; some Anabaptists were of the opinion that church leaders should be chosen from the congregation, not appointed by state authorities. Finally, Hubmaier was not convinced that the "signs of the times" could be interpreted to yield precise information on the Lord's second coming, while Anabaptist refugees in Nicholsburg who had been baptized by Hans Hut or by Hut's followers had accepted baptism precisely in the expectation that they would be welcoming the returning Christ at any moment.

In the Spring of 1527, Hans Hut's visit to Nicholsburg brought many of the underlying tensions to the surface, specifically the question of how to interpret the biblical signs of the second coming and, consequently, how to prepare the church for the future. Hubmaier and Hut debated publicly, after which Hut was arrested—only to escape the city with the aid of friends. Hubmaier not only did not share Hut's passion for the End Times, he also did not share Hut's conviction that "goods should be in common," opting for a lower level of mutual aid. A dissident Anabaptist group formed in Nicholsburg under the leadership of Jacob Wiedemann and separated from the official Anabaptist state-church. Wiedemann's group appropriated ideas characteristic of Hans Hut (apocalyptic expectation; community of goods) and combined them with pacifist ideas seen among some Swiss Anabaptists. In early Spring of 1528, 200 of these Anabaptists were asked to leave Nicholsburg. Eventually they found their way to a place of refuge in Austerlitz. On their way there, they decided to pool all their resources and institute a full community of goods.[37]

The "Austerlitz brethren" were thus the first Anabaptist community to practice full community of goods in Moravia, but they soon had plenty of company. From the first baptisms in Zürich, the baptizers had believed that the truly regenerate would share goods with brothers and sisters in need. There is evidence that in the earliest community in Switzerland, in the village of Zollikon, "holding all things common" was the earliest practice, until local conditions made this impossible.[38] Even where a full community of goods was not physically possible, the Anabaptist ideal was the sharing of possessions between brothers and sisters in the faith, with no member of the body of Christ claiming ultimate ownership over temporal goods. The Moravian territories provided a setting conducive to the establishment of communities in which possessions were shared in common. Furthermore, by 1528 apocalyptic hope for an early return of Christ had begun to fade. Anabaptist refugees began to consider how to establish settled and more permanent communities.

In 1528 a group of Anabaptist refugees—the majority originating from Silesia—gathered at Rossitz, Moravia, under the leadership of Gabriel Ascherham.[39] The "Gabrielites" also practiced community of goods in a settlement that came to number some 1200 adults. The Gabrielite community was a parallel and alternative community to the Austerlitz group. The following year, refugees from the Rhineland, the Palatinate, and Württemberg fled to Moravia and were gathered into a community under the leadership of Philip Plenner.[40] The Philipites first joined the Gabrielites at Rossitz, but after an amicable parting of the ways, settled at Auspitz. All three groups, the Austerlitz brethren, the Gabrielites and the Philipites, practiced community of goods, and for a time, all three recognized Gabriel Ascherham as spiritual leader. The first phase of community-building outside Nicholsburg in Moravia was characterized by communities sharing their goods in common.

One exception might be the Marpeckite communities, about whom we know very little. Pilgram Marpeck, originally from the Tyrol, had been ordained an Anabaptist leader by an unknown community in Moravia in 1528, and retained connections to Moravia and communities there all his life. Marpeck seems to have been open originally to communal living arrangements (in the 1530s), but by the 1540s (probably in a negative response to the Hutterite position) he argued for voluntary, not legislated, sharing of possessions.[41] In any case, Marpeckite communities—although small—formed a part of the Moravian landscape from 1528 to the end of the century, as did Swiss Brethren communities, living alongside the more numerous Hutterian communal settlements.

No document in our collection more clearly illustrates the transition from short-term apocalyptic hope to longer-term community-building than does Wolfgang Brandhuber's "Letter to the Church at Rattenberg," written in 1529 (#10). The shifts in emphasis in this letter are subtle, but fundamental. Brandhuber, who probably had been baptized by Hans Hut himself, was leader of the Anabaptist group in Linz but was in touch with the new community in Austerlitz.[42] In his letter, Brandhuber speaks to a new situation with a new vision and language. Persecution is still interpreted as a test and discipline of the Lord, but in response to it, the church is to separate itself decisively from the world ("leave Sodom and Gomorrah"), and structure itself properly to survive in, and witness to, a fallen world. The true church, Brandhuber teaches, must hold all things in common—to the degree that it is possible in any given situation. Brandhuber resolutely maintained that private property has no biblical basis. Even if one could only manage a "community" consisting of a single extended family, it should be organized communally. There must be proper oversight and admonition by leaders appointed to the tasks of preaching, teaching, and stewardship of earthly goods. With the elevation of the "common purse" to the status of a rule concerning communal property (and the forbidding of private property), Brandhuber's letter presages what would become the decisive point of contention between the legislated communalism of Hutterian Anabaptists and the voluntary mutual aid of non-Hutterite Anabaptists such as the Swiss Brethren and Marpeckites.

Also notable in Brandhuber's letter is what appears to be a common appropriation of Swiss Brethren teaching, that no weapons are to be used nor can war or armed defence be allowed to this community or its members. Brandhuber's contemporary followers of Hans Hut had not been so unequivocal about the sword.[43] Hans Nadler, for example, said at his trial that he knew of *some* who had renounced the sword, and that he himself had, but there was no "rule" concerning it (#11). It was otherwise with Brandhuber: He established a "rule" concerning nonresistance that brings to mind the Schleitheim Articles of the Swiss Brethren.[44] The nonresistance or "living without weapons" (*Wehrlosigkeit*) taught by Brandhuber and others soon became the universally approved teaching among South German/Austrian Anabaptists. A decade later (1539) the Trieste prisoners had a copy of the (Swiss) *Schleitheim Articles* in their possession, which they used freely in composing their own confession—including a verbatim copying of large sections of Schleitheim's Article 6 on the sword (#21). As late as 1590, the Hutterite missionary Hans Schmidt could be found quoting Michael Sattler's words concerning nonresistance (#34). In spite of some wavering on the issue of the sword in the early apocalyptic phase of South German/Austrian Anabaptism, nonresistant living soon became one of the non-negotiable, visible signs of the true church, the body of Christ, for this branch of the Anabaptist movement.[45]

Finally, Brandhuber continues to speak the language of spiritual regeneration, but with a significant shift in emphasis. Where the earliest South German/Austrian Anabaptist literature concentrates on the process of coming from unbelief to faith (through yielding and suffering in the heart), and leaves the particulars of the "new life" rather undefined, Brandhuber's letter focuses the living of the new life, returning repeatedly to the continuing struggle between the spirit and the flesh for those who have committed themselves to walk the narrow way. Brandhuber's letter was written to provide guidance and encouragement for a congregation of believers who had already gone through the personal process of repentance and commitment, and were now gathered together facing an uncertain future in a hostile world. In response to this situation come suggestions (not to say "rules") for the structure and organization of the community. The Spirit called the community into being; the Spirit now required a structure that would reflect God's revealed will, but would also ensure continued obedience and faithful perseverance to the end.

We can see clearly in Brandhuber's short letter the beginnings of an intense focus on the visible, gathered community as the real locus of the Spirit's activity. Jörg Zaunring's little exposition on the Lord's Supper (#13) underlines the same point christologically: the "body of Christ" that is present on earth is not Christ's physical body (which was crucified), or his glorified body (now in heaven), but rather is the church itself, where Christ is present as the head of his living members. Zaunring, like Brandhuber, concludes that there will be suffering for the body of Christ—thus continuing this early theme—but the locus of this suffering is now the community in the world, much more than in individual hearts suffering God's ploughshare.

The shift away from earlier interpretations of Hans Hut is seen clearly in the confession of the Trieste prisoners (#21). The confession quotes the Mark 16:15 passage concerning the preaching of the Gospel to/of all creatures—so central to Hut and his immediate followers—but there is not a hint of Hut's distinctive exegesis that extracted a "Gospel of all creatures" from this passage. The point of the passage, as interpreted by the Trieste prisoners, is that it illustrates the "proper order" of preaching, repentance, baptism and salvation—with not a word given to suffering the ploughshare of God in the soul. In fact, the entire confession of 1539 gives one line to the inner birth of the Holy Spirit (in the section entitled "Concerning the new birth"), investing the balance of the text to an extraction of the "commands of Scripture" by which the true church is to be guided in its actions: "Whatever our Lord Jesus has taught, prescribed and commanded us ... we will do," the prisoners emphasize. The suffering that is discussed has to do with the church as Christ's body, in particular (as per Zaunring), symbolized in the cup of suffering in the Lord's Supper.

An analogous shift may be seen in Endres Keller's confession (#17), with its strong emphasis on obedience to the commands of Scripture— an emphasis one associates more with the Swiss Brethren than with the spiritualism of the early South German/Austrian Anabaptists. At the same time, Keller stands comfortably in the South German/Austrian tradition, occasionally utilizing an allegorical exegesis to extract a "spiritual meaning," and reflecting on the importance of apocalyptic Scripture (Revelation, Esdras, Daniel).

The tensions between a more spiritualistic reading of Scripture and one more attuned to the "letter," and the analogous tension between an emphasis on "inner" change and "outer" signs of the inner change, played themselves out as South German/Austrian Anabaptism matured. The spirit/letter tension appeared to increase as apocalyptic fervour decreased. Said another way, the spirit/letter tension increased in direct proportion to the increased concern for the long-term survival of the visible community, the body of Christ on earth—as contrasted with the earlier concern for inner regeneration, baptism of "the elect," and the imminent return of Christ. In Brandhuber's letter and in other South German/Austrian documents after 1529 we see a regulated shape being given to the "new life."

Appeals to "freedom of the Spirit" functioned well when used against the "learned scribes" of established Protestant churches, but the same appeal didn't provide much guidance in shaping communities. The letter of Scripture, on the other hand, provided tangible guidelines for what the "Spirit-shaped community" ought to look like, but inevitably restricted the "freedom of the Spirit." Out of this shift in emphasis came a regulated community structure that probably was responsible for the ultimate survival of Anabaptist communities in South Germany and Austria, but along with those same structures came also the seeds of disagreement and, eventually, schism.

Schism among communal Anabaptists

The story of the schisms among the communal South German/Austrian Anabaptist groups in Moravia is not an edifying one. Strong personalities played their usual leading roles in precipitating the divisions that began to occur in 1531, and it also appears that regional differences among the various groups of refugees and their leaders added to the tensions.[46] All three communal groups were involved in one way or another in the leadership tensions, with a final rupture occurring in 1533. The dominating figure in the final division was Jacob Hutter. He had been a key Anabaptist leader in the Tyrol beginning around 1528. In 1529, Hutter had traveled to Moravia to visit the Austerlitz community. He returned to the Tyrol, in apparent agreement with the teachings and way of life of the Austerlitzers. He organized the flight of hundreds of Tyrolean refugees to the communities in Moravia, including a growing core of loyal followers from his own Puster valley. By 1533, the systematic repression of Ferdinand I made it was clear that the Tyrol would not be a place where Anabaptists could continue living. Jacob Hutter decided to move permanently to Moravia, a move that corresponded with continued leadership conflict among the communal Anabaptist groups.

The end result of Hutter's return was the formation of a communal group under his direct leadership—the group that came to be known as the Hutterian brethren, or Hutterites. Gabriel Ascherham and Philip Plenner were excommunicated, and all subsequent efforts at reconciliation failed. The purported doctrinal issue had to do with the strictness of discipline relating to community of goods. Jacob Hutter insisted on a strict giving over of all goods to the community by all members of the community. The practice prior to this time seems to have been a voluntary community of goods, with some degrees of private ownership remaining. With the mutual excommunications of 1533, however, the lines hardened. The distinctive teaching of the Hutterites became a legislated and total community of goods, without which none could be considered members—or saved, for that matter. The three remaining communal groups in Moravia (Austerlitz Brethren, Gabrielites, and Philipites) as well as the remaining non-communal Anabaptists, continued to practice varieties of mutual aid, ranging from communities where most members lived communally, to churches where most members owned private property but had a "common purse" to help the needy.

The division among the communal Anabaptist groups in Moravia soon came to an end, with the expulsion of all Anabaptist groups in 1535, as noted above. Faced with the need to disband their communities, the different leaders adopted a variety of strategies. The Gabrielites and the Philipites decided to migrate back to their original homes, in small numbers. They never re-established themselves again as distinct groups. A few survivors of both groups later joined Hutterite communities, but the majority of Gabrielites simply faded from view in Silesia, and the majority of Philipites joined with the Swiss Brethren, contributing their rich hymnody to the Swiss. The Hutterites, many of whom had come from the Tyrol, had no safe place to which they could return. The majority of the Hutterites formed smaller groups and remained in secluded places in Moravia, waiting for the wave of persecution to end, with only a few leaders returning to the Tyrol—with disastrous results. In the end, the Hutterian strategy turned out to be the preferred one for group survival, even though, as noted above, virtually all the original leaders, including Jacob Hutter and his wife Katharina, met their deaths back in the Tyrol.

Introduction / xlix

Our collection of sources does not document the history of divisions among the communal South German/Austrian Anabaptists. However there are some selections that shed light on selected aspects of these events. Through Brandhuber's letter (#12) we have a connection with the Austerlitz community and Gabriel Ascherham, and can see communal Anabaptism taking shape. Katharina Hutter, Jacob Hutter's "wedded sister" as she called herself, was arrested at Klausen, Tyrol, along with Jacob and a few companions on November 30, 1535. Her prison testimony (#16) gives a vivid portrait of life on the run for Hutterite leaders in Ferdinand's Tyrol. Our collection also includes two hymns from the *Ausbund*, the Swiss Brethren hymnal first printed in 1564 (#10, 33). The core of the hymns from the *Ausbund* in fact was composed by some Philipite brethren, imprisoned at Passau as they were attempting to flee Moravia following the expulsions of 1535. Finally, the communities that looked to Pilgram Marpeck for leadership are represented by two documents. One of the hymns included in our collection (#33) is attributed to Walpurga von Pappenheim, a young noblewoman who was part of Pilgram Marpeck's circle. The unusual letter of confession by the noblewoman Helena von Freyberg (#23) also stems from the Marpeck circle and reveals the more "lenient" congregational discipline that was in use in Marpeck's circle.

Finally, the concluding group of documents by Paul Glock (#24-32) and Hans Schmidt (#34) date from the "Golden Age" of the Hutterites. Although Glock's letters were written in prison, and read and preserved in the communities in Moravia, readers will discern the outlines of the fully-developed and structured community that had emerged by the 1560s and 70s, most fully articulated in Peter Riedemann's *Account of our Faith*. The tension between the communal Hutterites, and the non-communal Anabaptists becomes quite visible from time to time in Glock's letters. The schism concerning the nature and form of mutual aid that dated back to Jacob Hutter remained a defining line of separation running between the South German/Austrian Anabaptist groups. The missionary efforts of the Hutterites, documented in Hans Schmidt's recollections (#34), were directed primarily to non-communal Anabaptist groups in the western Empire, in efforts to win them to "full community." As might be expected, tensions in Moravia between the communal Hutterites and their non-communal Swiss Brethren and Marpeckite neighbours sometimes ran high.[47]

1 / *Sources of South German/Austrian Anabaptism*

III. Conclusion

It should be clear from the foregoing that this collection of South German/Austrian Anabaptist sources does not (and could not) give a complete picture of the origins and development of this baptizing movement. Nevertheless, English-speaking readers will now be able to see the original roots of this branch of Anabaptism in late medieval mysticism and apocalypticism. Likewise, readers will be able to trace the evolution of early teachings as the movement matured and developed under difficult conditions in Moravia and the Empire.

This introduction has traced the development of an early emphasis on individual spiritual rebirth into its mature emphasis on the visible communal fruits of discipleship—from an "inner" emphasis of "yielding to God in the heart," to an "outer" emphasis on what must be visible if that inner yielding has taken place. Equally evident is the transmutation of a live apocalyptic hope (with its expectation of a just world) into communities where the "biblical order" is visibly established within an unjust world. We have traced the division that took place in Moravia among the communal Anabaptists—a division based on a reading of the "biblical rules" for the establishment of such communities. This division led to the establishment of the Hutterian Brethren—the only communal Anabaptist group in all of Europe that was able to survive as an identifiable group, and the only identifiable group to survive the sixteenth century from the original South German/Austrian Anabaptist movement.

There remains one further note in this story of South German/Austrian Anabaptism, all the more important because no documents in our collection point to it. The early emphasis on spiritual regeneration as the central event in a Christian's life left its mark on many Anabaptists in this region. The majority of South German/Austrian Anabaptists seemed able and willing to place a stronger emphasis on the outer life of conformity to the "commands of Scripture" in structuring their lives as individuals and in community. But for a significant minority, the establishment of rule-oriented baptizing groups was seen as a devolution of spiritual regeneration to a secondary status, when in fact they felt it should have remained the most important thing of all. Hans Denck's last writing, called by some a "recantation" (1527), backed away from the "outer baptism" of water because of its divisive nature and pointed to an inner, more individual "spiritual" Christianity. Denck's lead was followed by two South German/Austrian Anabaptist leaders, Hans Bünderlin and Christian Entfelder. Both had been important Anabaptist leaders in Austrian territory, but by 1528 both had declared themselves to be spiritualists, who would baptize with water no more. Both Bünderlin and Entfelder migrated to Strasbourg, where their spiritualist (and anti-baptizing) writings were opposed in print by Pilgram Marpeck. His replies have been published in English translation, but theirs remain available only in German.[48]

In much the same vein as Bünderlin and Entfelder, but with less radically spiritualistic conclusions, Gabriel Ascherham composed *On the Distinction between Divine and Human Wisdom* (ca. 1540) from his Silesian exile, critiquing the Hutterian "externalization" and division of Anabaptism through the imposition of outer rules. Apart from translated excerpts in Packull, Ascherham's Anabaptist treatise is not available in English.[49] Readers should be aware of the fact that there was a spiritualist challenge to the way in which South German/Austrian Anabaptism had changed and developed, namely in the structured, rule-oriented communal direction.

The earliest documents from the South German/Austrian Anabaptist movement provide clear examples of the spiritualistic and regenerationist principles that underlay all adult baptism in the sixteenth century. Consequently, the documentation from this branch of the baptizing movement also provides clear examples of the tensions that developed as the "spiritual rebirth" attempted to take shape in a concrete and imperfect material world. The inner change will be manifested in external behaviour—but how can that behaviour be measured? The body of Christ on earth will be guided by Christ's Spirit—but what will be the concrete evidences of that Spirit? The regenerated will be enabled to interpret Scripture—but what happens once an authoritative interpretation has been established? Is a "spiritual" challenge to a previous biblical interpretation still possible? The body of Christ will be a community of justice—but how are injustices adjudicated within that body, when they occur?

The list could be extended, but there is no need for more extensive examples. The documents collected here give ample evidence of the birth of a reform movement based on the highest spiritual principles, as well as documentation of the difficulties encountered by the attempt to be true to those principles and to live them out faithfully. The story is one that challenges and chastens us, as it also invites us to engagement and dialogue.

1

Jörg Haugk von Jüchsen

A Christian Order of a True Christian: Giving an Account of the Origin of his Faith (1524)[*]

Introduction

Little is known about Jörg Haugk von Jüchsen. He was obviously literate and, along with Thomas Müntzer and Andreas Karlstadt, influenced by a spirituality that emphasized the importance of an inner, transformational experience of the divine. Like his acquaintance Hans Hut, Haugk was implicated in the Peasants' Uprising of 1525, having been elected preacher by the rebellious peasants in his district. In May 1525 when Hut returned from the defeat at Frankenhausen, Haugk invited him to preach to his congregation at Jüchsen near Meiningen in south Thuringia. It seems likely that Haugk subsequently entrusted the manuscript of his *Christian Order* to Hut and that Hut brought it to Philip Ulhart's press in Augsburg where it was printed in 1526.[1]

Since Haugk's *Christian Order* makes no mention of the Peasants' Uprising or the peasants' defeat, it may be assumed that Haugk had

---

[*]Source: Müller, *Glaubenszeugnisse*, 2-10
Translation: Werner O. Packull with the assistance of Mary Buck

written the *Order* before these events. This scenario is further supported by the lack of any clear references to Anabaptism in his treatise, although the work does suggest the separation of the godly from the ungodly. All the more surprising then seems to be the continuous interest by Anabaptists in Haugk's work. Hans Denck appears to have been responsible for the first reprint of Haugk's *Christian Order* in a volume that included Denck's own writings. This collective volume was printed in Worms by Peter Schöffer Junior during 1527. A third edition came off Heinrich Steiner's press in Augsburg in the 1540s as part of a whole series of Anabaptist prints and reprints. Pilgram Marpeck, then resident in Augsburg, appears to have been the main mover behind these prints and reprints, including Haugk's *Order*. The *Order* has also been preserved in Hutterite codices[2] and reappeared with some of Denck's works in a seventeenth century print, entitled *Geistliches Blumengärtchen*.[3] Thus Haugk's *Christian Order* circulated freely among Anabaptists and their descendants into the seventeenth century, even though it was of pre-Anabaptist vintage.[4] In terms of content, it belongs to the ethos of early South-German Anabaptism as shaped by Hans Denck and Hans Hut.

What was it that interested early Anabaptists in Haugk's semi-mystical tract focusing on the seven stages of divine wisdom? The answer appears to lie in Haugk's connection to Hut and Hut's influence on the emerging Anabaptist movement. What is clear is that Haugk's *Order* was read as a critical alternative to Martin Luther's understanding of justification by faith alone. Like Müntzer, Haugk focused on the issue of how true faith originates and is discerned. He takes issue with the Lutheran notion that faith comes through hearing the spoken Word or by reading the Scriptures. According to Haugk, the Scriptures are a mere outer witness; true faith is an inner work of the Spirit. It is the Spirit's illumination that "lifts" a person out of unbelief and sends the believer on a seven-stage journey that transforms the inner being and thus leads to conformity with Christ. True saving faith is therefore above all transformational.[5]

Haugk's metaphorical, mystical language can be disconcerting at times, but it is revealing, suggesting the influence of the *Theologia Deutsch* combined with Reformation biblicism. Like Hans Hut, Haugk suggests the existence of an elementary revelation in the created order. Indeed, it is tempting to infer that Hut's notion of the "Gospel of all creatures" was in part derived from Haugk's treatise.[6] Haugk also alludes to the "key of David" and the need to consider the "cloven hooves" when interpreting the Scriptures, concepts invoked by Hans Denck and Melchior Hoffman, suggesting a possible borrowing from one another. As noted, Haugk indicated familiarity with mystical vocabulary. He wrote of the *Seelengrund* [ground of the soul] and of *Gelassenheit* [yieldedness].[7] His *Order* contains criticism of the learned, of mere book learning and of the exploitation of the poor, all themes continued in Anabaptist writings; and as already noted, he implicitly argued for the creation of a separated, pure church. In short, the apparent influence and popularity of Haugk's *Christian Order* justifies its inclusion in a volume of Early South German/Austrian Anabaptist sources.

Bibliographical Source:

Werner O. Packull, *Mysticism and the Early South German-Austrian Anabaptist Movement, 1525-1531* (Scottdale, PA: Herald Press, 1977).

A Christian Order of a true Christian: Giving Account of the Origin of his Faith.[8]

Introduction

A Christian life progresses by degrees or steps towards perfection; such progression can be numbered, timed and measured; Wisd. 11[:22]; 2 Esd. 4[:37]. Just as a child increases his understanding daily, so also may a faithful reader increase his understanding of the Scriptures. Such a reader will discover that the number sequence seven is found frequently in the Scriptures, beginning with the seven days in Genesis [Gen. 1-2] and continuing with the seven pillars in the book of Proverbs [Prov. 9:1]; the seven eyes in Zechariah [Zech. 4:10]; the seven candlesticks in Exodus [Exod. 25:31-40]; seven spirits in Isaiah [Isa. 11:2]; seven churches, seven lamps, seven angels, seven trumpets and seven bowls in Revelation [Rev. 1:11, :12, :20, 8:2, 15:7]. The number seven always points to perfection where all is at rest and cannot be more perfect. The human being made one with the Spirit is brought to perfection through the seven gifts of the Spirit. But one reaches this seventh stage of divine blessedness only through great trial and tribulation. At the final stage the Spirit rests on the person and that person is conformed to Christ. All Scriptures witness to this end; they cannot point to anything higher. It follows that the Christian life begins in the fear of God, advancing by degrees from stage to stage until it has been tried and tested to the highest degree through all seven stages and has become conformed to Christ. As will be seen clearly in what follows, this means that such a person has reached the true Sabbath where God's Spirit rests; Isa. 11[:2].

The Spirit of Fear

As David states in Psalm 110[111:10], Solomon in Proverbs 1 and 9 [Prov. 1:7, 9:10], the wise man in Sir. 1, 2[1:15] and Job in chapter 28[:28]: the fear of God is the beginning of wisdom. This is why the prophet in Sir. 1[:20] refers to the holy fear of God as to the root of the tree of wisdom and of life. The trunk, branches and twigs that grow out of the root of this tree, that is out of the fear of God, remain forever. They are divine wisdom, understanding, counsel, strength, knowledge and blessedness [Isa. 11:1-2]. The sacred Scriptures often communicate these seven degrees toward perfection figuratively or through parables; Exod. 25[:31-40]. Thus God shows us his Spirit figuratively through the candelabrum with the seven candlesticks, or in John's Rev. 4[:5] through the seven lamps. Prov. 9[:1] speaks of seven pillars in the house of wisdom; Zech. 4[:10] refers to seven eyes; Isa. 11[:1-2] to seven spirits, to seven degrees or seven gifts of the Spirit. Our spirit must be tested and filtered through seven degrees or stages by the seven gifts of the divine Spirit until the true light, the sun of righteousness, rises in us and illuminates all our darkness. Then we will be encompassed by the clear truth and lifted out of our unbelief; John 8[:12-32]. The fear of God is the beginning of wisdom, that is the root, trunk and the branches of the whole tree of wisdom and of light. From this wisdom sprouts all divine understanding of God in us. It follows that a true Christian life begins in the fear of God and continues in it until the end; Isa. 11[66:5-24]; Luke 1; Ps. 18[19]; Wisd. 10. It is important to note how the fear of God advances wisdom, while fear of humans or of the creatures does the opposite: it hinders the wisdom of God. Note that Christ was put to death because of human fear, as has been the case with all his true followers since the beginning of his ministry; Matt. 23[:30-36]. For when the common people heard the counsel of Caiaphas, that the Romans would come and take their belongings and lives [John 11:47-51] because of Jesus, then their fear of the Romans led them to agree to Christ's crucifixion. Fearing the loss of their material possessions, they picked up a penny and let 100,000 guilders fall to the ground [that is, they forfeited the riches of God in Christ Jesus]. They forsook the innocent anointed one of God, Jesus Christ, for the sake of transient, temporal things, like Esau who gave away his birth right for a bowl of lentil soup [Gen. 25:29-34]. They all lacked spiritual rectitude, selling themselves for material gains as, unfortunately, the whole world now does. Therefore, God's spiritual overtures through which he attempted to draw them back into a proper relationship with him were in vain; for even though the spirit in them desired to do the right things, the bag of maggots, that is the flesh with its love and desire for the creaturely [material], hindered God's work in them; Mark 4[:1-9, :13-20]; Matt. 13[:1-9, :18-23]; for no one can profitably serve two masters; Matt. 6[:24]. A God-fearing person resists the fear of humans and prefers to side with David [2 Sam. 24:14], Daniel, Hananiah, Mishael, Abednego, Susanna and with all of God's blessed ones who committed themselves into the hands of God rather than into human hands, for with God is mercy. Therefore, two fears cannot exist beside each other in the same person, for what the fear of God begins and builds, fear of humans or the creatures destroys. Spirit and flesh cannot triumph at the same time; what profits the flesh diminishes the spirit. Whatever a person loves or fears more than God that is the person's God. Jacob could not fear God as long as he feared humans; therefore he had to overcome his fear of humans by permitting his left hip, in which that fear of humans was located, to be fractured, so that he would fear God only and be assured of God's blessing; Gen. 32[:26-30]. And in as much as he prevailed with God against human fear, the fear of God purged all human fear in him. As the wise man said, the fear of God drives out sin, but the fear of humans is sin [Wisd. 1:21]. The discipline of the Lord cleans the wicks of the seven lamps; for if the wick, that is the flesh, desires to go beyond the spirit, then it dims the light and creates darkness in our temple. It darkens the truth and extinguishes the movement of the Holy Spirit in us. At that point the wick trimmer, that is the discipline and rod of the Father, must cut such hindrance off and throw it out of our temple so that the light can illuminate everything in us again.

All living creatures give witness that the fear of God is the beginning of divine wisdom; for all creatures fulfill their lives in fear, and none trusts the other. We can see that in nature all animals have their enemies, so that through fear they are exercised to become alert and wise and learn to avoid their enemies as the greatest evil. And this is to be an object lesson for humans: indeed, all creation has been ordained and ordered for this purpose. Thus all animals teach us that fear is the way to God's wisdom. No person of right mind knowingly eats or drinks something unfamiliar, no matter how appetizing it looks. This is the result of fearing the unknown; one fears deception and loss of life. Fear in turn leads to questioning and to the examination of all things, whether they are good or evil, beneficial or detrimental. So also does the fear of God give birth to wisdom.

For this reason has God given humans many enemies, as anyone with open eyes can see, unless one is absolutely blind. But because we have locked the fear of God out of our hearts, we must, according to God's righteous judgment, fear other humans and the creatures. Like Adam, we have all forsaken God through our desire for and pleasure in the creatures [Gen. 3:6-13]. And because we have come to love the creaturely in our hearts, God's creation order has been disrupted and we have been in turn cut off from God in height, depth, width and length and become imprisoned to the creaturely, so that we can be returned to God only through much drudgery and misery.

God has shown us the consequences of our unfaithfulness in the warring, quarrelling and deception that goes on in competition for the creatures. Meanwhile all animals cunningly tear, choke, kill and feast on each other, becoming unnecessarily fat and sleek; none are satisfied with the ordained amount of food but live for the sake of the belly. For this reason the fox devours chickens, the wolf sheep, hawks pigeons, etc. Similarly, the tyrants, both temporal and spiritual, devour blood and flesh and sap the strength of all the working poor through usury. These exploiters are animals that live for the belly, born by nature to strangle; 2 Pet. 2[:10-15, :22]; Phil. 3[:18-19]. This is not right. God has not meant it to be that way. He is not the enemy of humankind, nor does he take pleasure in violence. No, God wants to open our eyes; he wants to shake us up and show us our disobedience so that we are ashamed and return to him; as when a son says to his father, "I will never do this again", and the father says, "Well then, I will no longer beat you but break the rod and throw it into the fire." If humankind were obedient to God and feared him, then all creatures would have to serve humans and obey them, but because humans are disobedient to God they are not worthy of the creatures which they use and eat. God created the creatures so that humankind should recognize and understand that they ought to be subject to God just as the creatures are subject to humans.[9]

But fear leads to anxious questioning, to an examination of oneself and of God in all things, persons, places, times, thoughts, words and deeds; yes, in all matters done or undone. Indeed, fear and anxiety lead to a constant examination of the unknown. Fear takes all things into account, examines them carefully and thinks on them until it has understood their true nature. Fear thus distinguishes evil from good, darkness from light, that which is certain from the uncertain, faith from unbelief, truth from lies, righteousness from unrighteousness, God from the devil, the eternal from the temporal, evil from good, appearance from reality, an invented faith from a proven or tested and unfeigned faith. It does not confuse good with evil and evil with good, the sweet with the sour and the sour with the sweet, as now the world does because it lacks proper judgment.

The discernment that comes through the fear of God and the Holy Spirit finds an analogy in the animals with cloven hooves; Lev. 11[:3-8].[10] These animals carefully chew their feed, moving it back and forth as if testing it. Similarly those standing in the fear of God take things to heart, sift them carefully whether they be true. With John they hold steadily to the immovable truth. They are not like the frivolous or foolish who are tossed about by every wind. Standing in the fear of God, they are the pure whom Christ commands to eat [the eucharist] and whom he permits to come into his temple as living sacrifices; for where one God-fearing person joins another, there Christ's body is continually built up, Eph. 4[:14-16], but where the good join the evil ones, there everything deteriorates because what the good build up the evil ones break down; if this one prays, the other blasphemes. Therefore, the good and the evil ones must be separated from each other, so that proper judgment or discernment can reemerge; Matt. 13[:24-30].

The pure fear of God does not fear evil but shuns it; Ps. 18[Ps. 19:10]. It does not embrace the unfamiliar, lest it be deceived. It embraces only the good. Because all wisdom has its beginning in the humble fear of God, the good hearted long to do what is right and to leave the wrong. In contrast, those lacking the fear of God remain like fools without wisdom who proceed thoughtlessly and ruin themselves through the very thing in which they seek pleasure. But a wise person does all things in the fear of God, lest he fail to discern whether a thing be good and proper. Thus the pure fear of God gives birth to proper discernment [*Erkenntnuss*][11] and it follows that the more one fears a thing the more one would like to understand it. Once one discerns it to be in truth wholly good and understands it properly, one loves it all the more; but if one discerns it to be evil, one falls on it with true hatred. For as fear gives birth to discernment and understanding, so understanding gives birth to love. Thus, if a person comes to another seemingly in full friendship and love, no matter how friendly that person acts, the other person will not trust him unless he has known this person previously; I mean truly known this person to be without deceit. All this is the result of fear and not knowing whether that person is honest or deceptive. But if one knows that person, it is easy to love him. For when one recognizes the good in the other, one develops love towards that person and when love flows out of proper discernment and understanding, all fear disappears, for love excludes all fear; 1 John 4[:17-18]. But before one reaches true discernment and understanding, one holds to the middle of the road and examines every thing cautiously, lest one stray from God, either in temporal or in eternal matters.

Now then, when true love has come out of proper discernment and understanding and has driven out fear, then faith or trust is added; for if one loves someone, then one believes that person; thus love gives birth to trust or faith; 1 Cor. 13[:7, :13].

One cannot believe or trust a person totally in earthly matters unless one first knows and loves that person. How then should I trust and hope in the eternal God whom I do not see without first knowing and loving him, trusting and hoping for all the best from him? But when I know him in truth as my highest and only good, then I cannot help but love him in truth with my whole heart as my noblest treasure. For I know with certainty that he is faithful and just and the only singular [*ainfeltig*] good. Such love forces me out of experience to trust him and to expect all the best from him. Thus God's Spirit teaches us through all Scripture that we should recognize his goodness towards us. As a sure witness of his goodness and so that we may properly know him, he has created heaven and earth and everything in it for our good, for our service, and to aid us so that we may use all of it for our needs. Indeed, he so lovingly offers us his mild goodness that if he were human and we were divine, he himself would accept from us what he offers us and demands of us. He wants to be our Father and endows us with the riches of his glory [Eph. 3:15-16], and shares them with us [*gemain machen*], so that we might be his children and heirs eternally [Rom. 8:17].

Abraham feared God from his youth on and oriented his whole life accordingly. As a true servant of God, Abraham raised his son Isaac in the fear of God and gave him Rebecca for a wife so that God-fearing children would be born into the world. It is to the world's greatest detriment that one does not procreate [*erzeucht*] and raise children in the fear of God. The fear of God makes our human fear transparent; it does this in all the chosen. The fear of God is the beginning, middle and end of a true life, and all things must proceed in this fear if one is to fulfil one's life in God's will.

A Short Order [of] How True Faith Grows Properly in a Person

The fear of God gives birth to true understanding [*erkenntnuss*]; Ps. 110[111:10], [Ps. 19:8-10]; and understanding gives birth to true love; 1 John 4[:16]; for we have understood and believed his love. Unfeigned love gives birth to true faith. Love believes all things, etc. and faith works through love [Gal. 5:6]. Love is a fulfillment of the law; he who loves me keeps my commandments.[12] All things serve for the good of those who love God; Rom. 8[:28]. An experienced faith trusts God fully and surrenders completely to him; it wagers everything one has and is capable of; Heb. 11.

The Spirit of Wisdom

Originating in the fear of God, the spirit of wisdom distinguishes between good and evil, true and false. It meditates on and takes to heart the things that are in heaven and in Christ Jesus, who is risen and in whom all the treasures of all wisdom and the fullness of divine knowledge rest and dwell; Col. 2[:3]. Out of his fullness we all receive eternal light; John 1[:9]; according to the measure of our faith; Eph. 4[:7]; Ps. 67[68]. In turn we learn to despise as of little value the wisdom and the things of this world which are corruptible and passing. Yes, divine knowledge provides deep insight into our ignorance and takes cognizance of how far we have turned away from God and through ignorance of divine wisdom have become entangled in matters of this world.

True wisdom points me to heaven and earth and points me to the true head, Christ, who is the eternal truth of the Father; John 1[:17]. But this wisdom is the work of the Holy Spirit, whose loving goodness and power emanates from the Father and the Son, and leads into all truth; John 16[:13]; Rom. 8[:26-30].

Everything that leads me away from God to the creatures is evil. The lies and deception of the creatures had their beginning in the main deceiver, the old serpent, Satan; Gen. 3[:1-5, :13-15]; Isa. 14[:29]; Rev. 12[:9]; [John 8:44].

The Spirit of Discernment[13]

Proper discernment or understanding born out of the fear and wisdom of God holds still and awaits the imprint [*eindruckung*] of the divine will, lest deception enter along with truth and the wisdom of God, for the angel of darkness and of error often disguises himself as an angel of light and intrudes proper discernment and subverts it; 2 Cor. 11:14. These are the wolves or deceivers who disguise their true nature and evil intentions under sheep skins, that is, under a good appearance, in order to destroy mercilessly the sheep fold and sheep stall of Christ. They always come in the name of Christ with the appearance of truth in order to mislead many [Matt. 24:5]. Through the Spirit of God David calls them mid-day devils or devils of light, because they seem to be on the side of plain truth, like the devil himself who addressed Christ politely, citing Scripture: "Are you God's son?" etc. When they wish to deceive, they speak in a high, sweet, flattering voice. They polish their act and scatter their seed like a fowler who throws something out to the unsuspecting little birds [Jer. 5:26]; puts honey into their beaks but means to poison them. When they eat this food, it tastes sweet but is bitter in their belly. At present the whole world eats of it and it tastes very sweet in their mouth, but oh, how very bitter it will become in their bellies! Therefore, it is necessary to examine oneself and to permit Christ the crucified one to open one's discernment within, that is, the Christ who wells up from within. All other discernment is rejected by God and cannot endure, either to the right or the left, because it will not yield to obedience and service of Jesus Christ; indeed, it is incapable of turning away from all that resists the discernment of God in us. For this reason everything anticipated in faith needs to be understood and unlocked by the intellect which through faith in the promise of Jesus Christ justifies and is made manifest through the unconditional righteousness of the divine work in us; Rom. 1[:16-17].

Otherwise the Holy Spirit would be alienated by invented ideas and an invented faith,[14] which hates God's discipline; does not want to suffer the hand of God and does not want to be tested like gold in fire; Wisd. 1[Wisd. 3:4-7]. Therefore proper discernment is a certain assurance in the depth [*abgrundt*] of the soul[15] as to the eternal will of God, so that one knows truly that God has spoken rather than the devil or mere creaturely imagination.[16] Whoever bases himself on his own or on a stranger's discernment builds on sand [Matt. 7:26], remains unsure, creates fantasies and sects and carries contaminated water into the cistern [Jer. 2:13]. But if anyone lacks understanding, let him pray to God and he will be properly instructed; James 1[:5]; Sir. 1[:18-19]; [Prov. 2:3-5].

The Spirit of Counsel

Furthermore, it is highly necessary for the elect to have the spirit of divine counsel so that they exercise proper discernment as to the divine gifts and, as Paul points out, do not despise their neighbour, who may have received a lower or a higher gift from God.

For this reason the judgments [*urteil*] of God must be searched out in a common account of faith in accordance with each person's gift, that is, through the spirit of counsel which leaves nothing undone that pertains to the fear, wisdom and understanding of God.[17] The spirit of counsel helps to recognize the good, so that it will not be misused or removed through thievery and the person deceived. The Spirit's counsel brings one into an unspeakable amazement, because God illuminates the ground of the soul [*grund seiner Seele*] so powerfully and with such wisdom, so lovingly, so kindly, in all things so benevolently and irrefutably, in a way totally unknown to the person who has previously not discerned anything about God's glorious indwelling [*beywonung*].[18]

Such a gift, which is called the spirit of counsel, drives one to leave nothing undone in order to make the acquaintance of such a wonderful God and to come into the proper inheritance of divine fellowship. A person who has experienced the spirit of counsel will be driven by a desire, a longing, a sighing for the Spirit in pursuit of the unknown God, a desire which in turn will give birth to a hunger and thirst for divine understanding, so that all things which are not of God become bitter to such a person[19] and such a person remains inconsolable by things not of God. Such a person can counsel others, tell them about the origin of his faith, what happened to him before he came to such a faith or discernment of God, what he suffered from within and without on account of it and how bitter the struggle was before faith and the inner truth overcame unbelief; indeed, how he had to navigate first through an ocean of contrariness [*widerwertigkeit*]. Through his own experience such a person knows the way and can attest to the dangers that will be encountered in the beginning, the middle and the end. This is what Peter means in 1 Pet. 3[:15] when he writes: "One should be willing to give an account of one's faith."

At this stage one feels like the prodigal son, Luke 15[:11-32], or like the person who fell among the robbers on his way to Jericho; Luke 10[:30-37]. One comes to an inner yieldedness [*Gelassenheit*] regarding all things, including oneself, and with an empty, disconsolate soul one awaits the consolation of God; Matt. 16[:24-28]; Luke 14[:27].

And because from youth on one has consumed and spent one's strength in worldly lusts and in the works of sin as if one pours out water, it is necessary at this stage in accordance with one's own will to reach out to God with all one's strength in order to come to know his loving will. And because one has frivolously and willfully wasted one's strength on all kinds of evil, has become corrupt and is no longer capable of any good and because one has in manifold ways strayed from God, one must in turn be drawn back to God's good will in various ways. One must experience justification and the testing of faith through many trials and much tribulation, yes, in equal measure to the energy or strength formerly expended on the lusts of the flesh; for to become righteous one must be tried and tested like gold in fire; 1 Pet. 1[:6-7]; Sir. 2[:5]; Wisd. 3[:6].

The Spirit of Strength

For the above process of justification one needs to be strengthened by the Spirit of God, who strengthens the person according to that person's yielded strength [*gelassene kraft*], that is, according to the weight and measure of the gift needed [Rom. 12:6]. At this point one becomes courageous and upright [*rechtschaffen*], proclaiming the goodness of God and his marvelous work. Because the riches of grace and the clear, bright knowledge of God have opened wide the understanding [*Vernunft*] of such a person, that person will no longer weaken. Indeed, a person who has trodden the narrow path of dying to all that hinders him from God and has learned the cause of all human failing will be able to distinguish between truth and falsehood, evil and good, sweet and sour, true and false faith. Like Paul, such a person will fear nothing. Nothing will be powerful or influential enough to turn such a person away from Christ and from divine love. Such a person is strong in God, overcomes and subdues himself, accepts patiently everything laid on him as the noblest gift from God and as the necessary work through which God disciplines and prepares him. In this way good overcomes evil [Rom. 12:21]. When such a person experiences trials and tribulations [*Anfechtung*], these become lessons in the life with God for that person. As that person formerly was high in sin, so now he needs in equal measure to be made low: instead of pride humility, instead of riches poverty, instead of gluttony hunger, etc. In whatever manner and measure the person had sinned, in the same manner and measure he is to experience God's discipline; Wisd. 11[:17].[20]

Thus when encountering adversity, one should not rest or remain at peace until one understands what God wishes to teach or why he wishes to test one. For when one realizes that adversity has been sent by God for one's own good, then one is able to remain patient in the midst of suffering; yes, one can have joy and peace. As Christ says in Matt. 5 and 10, God comes not in vain; he encounters us in the paths through which we left him in order to liberate us through the cross of tribulation,[21] for suffering justifies us from the preceding lusts. If we had not strayed from God through lusts, we would not need to suffer.

Without suffering one cannot be freed from that which one has come to love. The more one has come to love the creaturely instead of God, the more painful it will be when God cuts one off from the creaturely and when one has to leave it. If God would not wrench the faithless person from the creaturely through tribulation, that person would remain eternally lost [*ewig auss*] and would never come to God, for it is impossible for a person to leave the creaturely which has become most pleasing to that person. But with God all things are possible. If one does not wish to take account of God in this life, then God cuts one off in the next, as happened to the rich man in Luke [16:19-31]. The creaturely was no longer able to comfort the rich man in the next life. Consequently, a person who does not heed God's voice in this life will have to hear it in the fire of the second death in order to do the right thing.[22] All evil desires must be destroyed; our hearts must be emptied in order to become new vessels into which God's grace can be poured [Matt. 9:17]; [Eph. 4:22-24]. One must put on a new nature.

The Spirit of Knowledge [*Kunst*][23]

In addition, it is necessary to receive the spirit of divine knowledge. To a person experienced in divine knowledge it is clear that all parts originating with and having come from God must be brought back into the whole, that is, into the origin from whence they came; Col. 2[:9-10]; Phil. 3.[24] All things work to the good of those who have this insight; Rom. 8[:28]; and to such persons the yoke is easy; Matt. 11[:30].

Divine knowledge is contrary [*gegentayl*] to what the world cherishes; for it is revealed in the cross and in dying. This knowledge is mastered only by following the crucified Christ.

Divine knowledge is best communicated through opposites: faith versus unbelief; love versus hate; despair versus hope in God; patiently waiting on God versus denial of righteousness; gospel versus fraud; truth versus falsehood; spirit versus flesh; Christ versus Satan; light versus darkness; good versus evil; suffering and the cross versus violence and tyranny; day versus night; summer versus winter; white versus black; sweet versus sour; rest versus labor; joy versus sorrow; life versus death; eternal versus temporal.

When David described a godly person, he did so through opposites, that is, by contrasting the godly with the ungodly. The Scriptures do this consistently and throughout. Yes, one can see it also in the creatures that the good and the evil ones are opposed to each other so that the good may be all the more readily recognized and become all the more attractive by comparison with their evil opposite. Thus one is interpreted through the other and more easily recognized through its opposite. Thus God demonstrates his wisdom wonderfully through opposites or contraries, so that through the visible the invisible and through the temporal the eternal may be perceived, desired and loved, etc.[25]

The Spirit of Divine Blessedness

The spirit of divine blessedness represents the highest degree of faith,[26] that is the believer conformed to Christ has become with Christ God-minded, and his light has been placed on the candlestick to shine for all [Matt. 5:14-16], just as the heavenly father permits the sun to shine on the good and on the evil ones and sends fruitful rain on believers and unbelievers, the grateful and ungrateful alike [Matt. 5:45]. For God wants all people to come to the truth and this will truly take place. The true meaning of this becomes clear to those who reach the highest degree of yieldedness [*gelassenheit*] towards themselves and all creatures and are ignited by the highest zeal for God in all matters so that nothing in the temporal realm satisfies them and they find themselves in constant conflict with the flesh. Yet their spirit finds rest in God, even though God hides himself from them for a while, leaves them without comfort, as if he has no concern for them, etc. Abraham stood in this high degree of yieldedness when he was prepared to sacrifice his son Isaac [Gen. 22:2-18]; similarly Moses, when he zealously interceded on behalf of Israel, wishing himself to be stricken from the book of life rather than for Israel to perish [Exod. 32:32]; so also Paul, when he desired to be cursed in place of his brothers [Rom. 9:3]; David in his flight from Absolom, when Shimei cursed him [2 Sam. 16:5-8]; Christ, when he heard them say, "If he is the king of Israel, then let him climb from the cross, he helped others, now let him help himself, then we will believe" [Matt. 27:40-42]; Job, when his friends mocked him in his suffering [Job 19:3]; Tobias, when his wife said to him, "It is clear as day that your hope in God is useless" [Tob. 2:22]; Isaiah, when during the Babylonian captivity he went into the wilderness of the desert by himself for the sake of the children of Israel [Isa. 42:1-7, 49:1-6, 53:12]; Esther, when she disobeyed the prohibition of King Xerxes in order to redeem her people [Esther 4]; Judith, when she placed herself into great danger for the salvation of God's people [Jdt. 7:12]; Daniel in the lions' den [Dan. 6:17-23; 1 Macc. 2:59]; Shadrach, Meshach and Abednego in the fiery furnace [Dan. 3:14-23; 1 Macc. 2:59]; and so on throughout Scriptures one finds examples of a high degree of yieldedness. But before true faith in God begins and is completely formed, all hindrances to proper understanding must be removed and overcome, whether one likes it or not. One arrives at the degree of blessedness only after falling and rising again and again: indeed, the righteous may fall seven times a day but will rise just as often to praise God. This process grinds one down like a hunted deer that chased by vicious dogs ends up in a well. This is the way one is loosened from one's sinful desires and lusts and begins to call on God for grace; Ps. 41[42:2]. Our soul must thirst for righteousness until it receives it in all fullness; Matt. 5[:6]; Luke 1[:28]; Ps. 41[42:3]; only then does one come to the proper understanding that the righteous lives in faith, Hab. 2[:4]; Rom. 1[:17]. Here the believers and God are joined through faith, like two cherubim that kiss each other. As the power of God manifests itself in the believer, he is one with and in God; Ps. 83[84:6-8].

Faith is a blessed, pleasing and sure understanding through which we assuredly live according to the will of God, and leave all love of the creaturely things behind, knowing full well how to use them properly.

True faith is created and planted in us by the fear of God while we are still in the mother's womb, Sir. 1[:14]. Indeed, the beginnings of faith lie in us like a seed of grain in a field, and this grain of faith grows with us [Matt. 13:1-8, :18-23], for all humans, especially the chosen ones, have God's Spirit in them as a pledge that they will not despise God's goodness for ever; Rom. 8.[27] This is the seal with which we have been sealed unto the day of redemption, Eph. 4[:30]. This is the light through which we will see the eternal light; Ps. 35[36:10]; John 1[:4-9], 8[:12]. Thus we groan inwardly for our adoption and redemption by God; Rom. 8[:23]; John 1. God wants to be recognized, worshipped and honored. We are companions and co-beneficiaries embodying [*einleybig*] the eternal light, 2 Pet. 1[:19]. Through Christ we become one body, one fellowship and participants in the eternal light; John 1[:4], 5:9-13; 1 John 3[:7]. This is the meaning of the parables concerning the mustard seed of faith; Matt. 13[:31-32], 17[:20], the grain of wheat and the treasure in the field; John 12[:24]; Matt. 13[:44-46]. We are made in the image of God through Christ; Gen. 1[:26-27], 2[:7], 5[:3], 9[:6]; Rom. 8:1; 1 Cor. 11[:7-13], 15[:37-49]; Col. 1[:15-23], 3[:9-10]; Heb. 1[:3]. It is the life we have from God, and it is part of God himself, for he is life; John 1[:4], 10[:28]; Deut. 30[:15-16, :19-20]; Rom. 10[:8]; Acts 17[:27-28]. Through Christ we participate in the divine nature and become his kindred, his lineage and offspring; Acts 17[:28-29]. Through him we become heirs of all the treasures of divine wisdom; Col. 2[:2-3]. Through Christ we become capable of receiving the treasures of divine wisdom.[28] That is the heart of the matter[29] from which true life flows and leads to the life God wants us to live; Prov. 4[:4]; Deut. 6; Matt. 22[:37]; Luke 10[:27]. This is the pound which God expects the faithful servant to invest and to increase, etc, Mark 11[4:8, :20]; Luke 8[:8-15]. This is the seed in the field, or in our heart, which brings multiple return; Mark 13[:8, :23]. This is the hundred weight entrusted to the faithful servant to be used, etc. Matt. 11. This is the new creature, the inner person, Gal. 5 and 6; the precious little pearl; the virgin bride who alone is suited to be betrothed to God's son, to be united with him by means of a wedding ring, which is a sign of faith.

God is more than all that has ever been spoken or written about him. The Scriptures warn, admonish, draw, entice and point us to the highest good which must be found in us and without which we will never be satisfied. God, the highest good, accepts nothing and no one except the Son who has proceeded from him. Only through the Son can we be united with the highest good. If God withdraws his Spirit from us, we are incapable of forming proper judgments, for it is the Spirit that leads us into all truth.

But it is the lusts of the flesh that hide the highest good from us, like a hidden, covered stream hides its water. And the lusts of the flesh, like the thorns in the field, seek to choke, smother, stifle and make fruitless the grain of wheat that is God's work in us [Matt. 13:7]. For if the grain of wheat in us is to come alive in our heart, all foreign growth, that is the weeds, must first be weeded out; John 12[:24-26]; Matt. 16[:25]; Luke 14[:33]. Thus Christ states in Matt. 7[:17] and Paul in Rom. 2[:15]; 2 Cor. 3[:3-6] that the law is written into our heart,[30] but that we must make room for it by weeding out the lusts of the flesh and permitting the good seed to grow up and to be recognized. All creatures witness to this truth, for God has commended them as good; Gen. 1[:26], something he would not have done had he not placed goodness in them. Since then all creatures were created for the sake of humankind and were made subject to humankind, something that is true even in terms of mere outer physical subjugation to humans, how much more certain is it then that God has placed good in the human beings created in his own image, for whose purpose all the other creatures exist [Gen. 1:26-27]. Indeed, humans have received a seed to sustain their autonomy and authority [*seines wesens selbstendigkeit*] in relation to the creatures. To this end, all visible creatures serve as examples and object lessons to humankind so that humankind learn its own purpose, rank and role in the divinely order ordained of things. For just as the visible creatures are subject to humankind, so humankind needs to be subject to God. All moisture from below and all sprinkling from above would be fruitless if the seed of grain were not placed in the soil [Matt. 13:1-23]; so also would all prompting, urging, admonition and instruction of the Holy Spirit be in vain if there were not some embodiment [einleybig] of the divine Spirit in the human being. For the earthly cannot receive the heavenly, nor the corruptible receive the incorruptible; 1 Cor. 15[:36-49]; but just as the fruitful rains awaken what they find in the soil, so also the living waters of God's Spirit awaken in the inner human being faith as small as a mustard seed which grows a large tree.[31]

The Scriptures give only an outer witness of a true life, but they cannot create a new being [wesen] in me. For this reason one cannot rely on books or learned persons, because books do not produce Christians, for they tend to lead the reader outward rather than inward. Note that at the time of Christ and the apostles there were few books but many good Christians. Back then, divine knowledge was not stolen from books as is the practice now; back then, it was not a matter of moving from externals to internals, which is like carrying water to the well. Book learning merely puffs up and produces arrogant persons who think highly of themselves and are forever learning[32] but never arriving at an understanding of the truth; 1 Cor. 8[:1-3]; Matt. 23[:2-7, :13-14, :23-33]. But the true Christian life comes from God and begins in the depth of the soul [abgrundt], as is witnessed to by the Scriptures and the creatures.[33]

One should take from books only that which concerns and witnesses of a true life, and one should let the book and the teacher go once they have given witness. One must await the power of God in the heart, for all writing and preaching is in vain if God does not give understanding. This is why David said: "Lord, give me understanding; Lord, teach me your law" [Ps. 119]. The Scriptures have to be opened to us through the key of David[34] as was the case with all who wrote the Scriptures.

I must test the witness of the Scriptures to see if it is true in me. But if I am of a different mind and have a wrong understanding, it will hinder me and hold me back from a true, divine understanding. I must then examine what it is that I love more than God. This is where the struggle between spirit and flesh begins. If the flesh is victorious and the person falls under the sway of the creaturely, the person will be worse off than before; but if the spirit is victorious, then one truth after another will emerge for such a person [Rom. 8:5-14]. When the spiritually illuminated person reads and considers the Scriptures, they witness to him of an unchanging God, while he recognizes himself as the opposite—a changeable human being. The person cannot escape from this realization, indeed, may find himself in a situation as if there were no God. If in his unbelief such a person does not want to become blasphemous but accepts the truth, then that person must hold still in fear between faith and unbelief, await God's revelation and give up his unbelief. Then with truth in the heart, true faith will overcome unbelief. To this end one's own understanding must be opened and the Scriptures must be revealed as they were to all God's chosen patriarchs, prophets, evangelists and apostles; Ps. 61[62]; Job 33[:4-30].

But before this happens, the struggle between faith und unbelief creates great turmoil in the person. During this struggle I must hold still in fear and eagerly desire to do what is right and to abandon evil. That which stirs in me while I am in this state holds and overcomes me and makes itself clear to me, so that I accept it. For if I am to believe, then clear truth must first reveal my unbelief and overcome it; otherwise I am unable to surrender my intellect to the service of God. If unbelief remains victorious in this struggle, one falls away from God to the creaturely; but if faith triumphs, then God reveals himself and to such a person all things serve to the good, [are sweet in God]. Such a person no longer esteems the love of creaturely things, yes, lets go of them.

Some think that one must believe the dead letter of Scriptures without the experience of God's illuminating power, but that would mean nothing less than inventing delusionary truths. Such a person accepts the Scriptures without having the inner experience to which they witness. They accept the witness from those who are contrary to the Scriptures and hence not from God; Ps. 30[31]; John 16; Luke [24:31-32, :44-49].

Nothing on earth is more misleading than if the Scriptures are not experienced and learned in the ground of the soul. Many accept the Scriptures as if they were the essence of divine truth; but they are only a witness to divine truth which must be experienced in the inner being.[35]

If God is to have mercy on me, then I must be illuminated by him and led into an understanding of myself. But if he is to illumine me, he must first frighten me [*entsetzen*] in order to liberate and free me from my darkness and error. If he is to show me my unrighteousness and deliver me from it, then he must first cast me down and afflict me with pain; for it is through his holy cross, through suffering, that he justifies me [*rechtfertigt*] and removes the lusts that have estranged me from God and held up his work.[36] But if he is to help me through his cross, then I must carry it, suffer it and accept it. And if I agree to suffering the cross, then I must be certain that it is for my own good. In this context I must examine my whole life from my youth on and realize how unrighteous I am.

But as one searches and examines one's whole life, one finds nothing but disobedience and turning away from God, and one realizes that one lacks faith and trust in God. Consequently one is overcome by unbelief and placed into the fear of God. This fear gives birth to understanding [*erkendtnuss*], understanding gives birth to love and love gives birth to faith; 1 Cor. 13[:4-7]; 1 John 4[:7-16]; 1 Pet. 1[:7-8]; not all at once, but according to time, number and measure; 2 Esd. 4; Wisd. 11[:20-21].

Some think that the word comes from the outside, through preaching or through the Scriptures. They do not understand what the Scriptures say;[37] Rom. 10[:8]; Deut. 30[:2, :10, :14, :16]; namely that the word has been previously placed and hidden in our heart, and that the Scriptures show us how to find it. If however the word were to be planted from the outside, then God's kingdom would consist of talk [*rede*] and not of power, contrary to what Christ said; [Matt. 15:1-20]; Mark 7[:1-23]. But preaching and Scripture reading are merely a witness to divine truth, a witness that indicates where and how a person may come to this treasure, by what means, in what way, at what time and according to which order [*ordenung*]. A person who does not properly understand this will never be able to use the hidden treasure because the treasure will remain unused, hidden in the field [Matt. 13:44] unless it is revealed to the person and the person learns its significance, its value and how to access it for his/her benefit. This is how it is with the treasure of divine goodness and riches; may we come to know and experience it. To this end help us Jesus Christ, the crucified Son of God. Amen.

A short order of the seven degrees or stages [*staffeln*] through which one is led to perfection by the Holy Spirit:

To fear God with the whole heart gives birth to wisdom; Job 28[:28].

To shun evil brings understanding; Job 28[:28].

Understanding gives birth to love and faith. Blessed are those who act upon it; Ps. 100[111:10].[38]

To remain steadfast is divine counsel [*radt*].

To overcome oneself is strength.

To judge all in God and to accept all as from God is divine learning and wisdom [*kunst*]; 1 Cor. 13[:12].

To become conformed to and like-minded with Christ is divine blessedness; all is at rest; it is the true Sabbath which God requires of us but which the whole world opposes.

2

Hans Hut

Comparing and Interpreting Divine Scripture:[1] A Christian Instruction given in the power of the Holy Spirit together with the three parts of Christian Faith and how they are to be understood.[2] (1527)[*]

Introduction

Born ca.1490, Hans Hut is known for his mystical-apocalyptic thought and as the most important apostle of Anabaptism in south Germany.[3] Hut appears to have been self-taught, but what he lacked in intellectual sophistication, he made up for in native intelligence and ingenuity. His work as a book peddler provided a perfect opportunity for constant travel and contact with a wide variety of people. Hut combined his book peddling with an intense interest in church reform. His missionary zeal was remarkable; in less than two years (May 1526 to December 1527) he had converted hundreds of people to Anabaptism, far more than anyone else in the South German/Austrian region.[4]

Hut was more concerned with the state of the whole Christian social order, as contrasted with Luther's concern for the individual sinner's standing before God. It was because of this focus that Hut joined

---

[*]Source: Müller, *Glaubenszeugnisse*, 28-37.
Translation: Walter Klaassen

Karlstadt and Müntzer in their rejection of Luther's theology. As a travelling book peddler, Hut appears to have met both Karlstadt and Müntzer on several occasions beginning in 1523. Müntzer became the more important influence for Hut. Hut sided with Müntzer particularly in the latter's apocalypticism, which included the belief that the Peasants' War was the last great conflict between the godly and ungodly before the return of Christ.[5]

Hans Hut defended the peasant cause during their revolt in 1525 and was involved in the battle at Frankenhausen, apparently as a noncombatant.[6] A fugitive after that defeat, Hut appears to have sought refuge in Nuremberg, where he could disappear in the crowded town.[7] It was after Frankenhausen that Hut also became acquainted with Jörg Haugk von Jüchsen (ch. 1) who had emerged as a spiritual leader in the area around Hut's hometown of Bibra. As far as is known, Haugk never became an Anabaptist. Hut helped Haugk publish new editions of his *Christian Order*.[8] Hut, like Müntzer, felt that the peasants had failed in their revolt because they had not been the pure, unselfish champions of God's honour for which he had taken them.

In 1526, Hans Hut had his first contact with Anabaptists. He soon found a place for Anabaptism in his apocalyptic understanding: they were the godly Elect that the peasants had not been. Hans Denck baptized Hut on May 26, 1526. Hut's basic insights on suffering discipleship and a separated fellowship are in harmony with Denck's views, but Denck's spiritualist theology did not reduce Hut's apocalyptic enthusiasm; Hut's baptism by Denck did not equal a break from his dependence on Müntzer.[9]

Hut and his baptized followers, including Ambrosius Spitelmaier, Leonard Schiemer and Hans Schlaffer, saw themselves as a persecuted apocalyptic remnant, waiting for the new order that Hut predicted would break out around Easter 1528. Pestilence, famine and invasion of the Turks were the signs of its arrival.[10] The new order was to be based on justice and peace. To the end of his life, Hut believed that religious and social concerns were inextricably interwoven.[11] He saw baptism as a sign or seal of the Elect of the End Times (the sign of TAU, Revelation 7:3) marking those who were to be spared in the approaching judgment. Hut's political ethic was one of suspended vengeance or "sheathed sword." He taught his inner circle that once End Times events began to unfold, they too would participate in the slaying of the ungodly.[12] This point of view did not long survive among Hut's followers past Hut's own death.

Hans Hut's indebtedness to medieval mystical and apocalyptic traditions can be seen in the trinitarian pattern of the following document. As Werner Packull notes, Hut "conceived of the Trinity primarily as a threefold activity present in creation and revealing itself to man in the mystical experience." Hut believed that true knowledge of God can only be achieved through personal experience of the different parts of the Trinity. The scriptural section of Hut's little writing is meant to demonstrate that Scripture cannot be interpreted on literal understanding alone, because of the literal contradictions that exist within it. Understanding can only be achieved through the three-fold creative/redemptive/revelatory activity of the Trinity.[13]

While at the Martyr's Synod in Augsburg in 1527, a warrant was issued for Hut's arrest by the council of Nuremberg; he was arrested a few weeks later.[14] He was tortured, and his connection with Thomas Müntzer came to light, although Hut denied during the interrogation more than casual contact.[15] Before the court could sentence him to death, Hut died in his cell of smoke inhalation in what may have been a failed escape attempt. The Hutterite Chronicle, however, states that after being tortured, Hut was left in his cell like a dead man; a light accidentally set the straw on fire, which killed him. Augsburg officials, apparently frustrated at not being able to execute Hut, tied his body to a chair, officially sentenced Hut to death, and burned his body on December 7, 1527.[16]

Bibliographical Sources:

Chronicle I.
Hans-Jürgen Goertz, ed., *Profiles of Radical Reformers* (Scottdale, PA: Herald Press, 1982).
Werner O. Packull, *Mysticism and the Early South German-Austrian Anabaptist movement: 1525-1531* (Scottdale, PA: Herald Press, 1977).
Werner O. Packull, "Gottfried Seebass on Hans Hut: A Discussion," *MQR* XLIX (1975).
Werner O. Packull, "Hut, Hans," *ME V*, 404-06.
George H. Williams, *The Radical Reformation* 3rd edition (Kirksville, MO: Sixteenth Century Journal Publishers, 1992).

Comparing and Interpreting Divine Scripture: A Christian Instruction given in the power of the Holy Spirit together with the three parts of Christian Faith and how they are to be understood. (1527)

Holy Scripture, a witness of God, written by Moses, the prophets and apostles, was rarely composed in blocks of major topics, but usually in small bits. Only error follows when if we do not understand all the individual sections as parts of the whole. Individually they say on the one hand yes and on the other no on the same topic. The divine art [of interpretation] is done in the truth according to three judgments. Even as we must understand God in three ways, so also with Scripture.

First, God is known through his omnipotence and power in all the creatures.

Second, [God is known] through the perseverance[17] and righteousness of the Son.

Third, [God is known] through the goodness and mercy of the Holy Spirit. Without these three human knowledge of God is impossible. It has to be according to this order, through time, one after the other,[18] until it is understood as a whole. Only then will God's way be known in truth.

God will be known in his omnipotence and power by everyone in the whole world when it is discerned in God's works from the beginning of the creation until now. This understanding of God, however, is not[19] enough even though I know that I am God's creature with all other creatures. I still lack two parts of the proper understanding of God. They are revealed, second, through the perseverance and righteousness of the crucified Son of God. I must suffer him in me so that I might become that for which I was created. For this reason the eternal Son of God set himself as an example for us so that we all become conformed to him. In this conformity is revealed to us, third, the goodness and mercy of God, the Holy Spirit through whom is known the complete fullness of godliness in us. Unless a human being inwardly suffers, is conscious of, and understands these three, he knows no more about God than a Turk or a pagan no matter how much he prattles about it. It is no more than pretence and hypocrisy with which the whole world now tries to cover its nakedness.

To repeat: whoever desires a helpful and fruitful reading of Scripture, must understand it according to the three parts which, however, are rarely found side by side. The three must be kept in mind at each reading in order that there be true understanding of the whole.

First, then, the Holy Scriptures tell us about all divinely created beings, and about the human pleasure in the same. But in doing so they turn away [from God] as you can see. [Through concentrating on this witness alone] their hearts become blinded and confused.

Second, the Scriptures tell us about the suffering, tribulation, and persecution of some people, as you can read, through which a person is led to reject the creatures and the pleasure in them, and turns back to the Creator.

Third, the Scriptures tell us about the perfection which is revealed by the Holy Spirit, when one lives according to the command of God. Where this three-fold order is not observed at every point [of Scripture], it is impossible to interpret Scripture without error or offence. For contradictions are found throughout Scripture which makes it seem that Scripture is opposed to itself. This can be seen in the following:

First

I am not Elijah.	Matt. 11[John 1:21]
He is Elijah.	John 16[Matt. 11:14]
Who knows the mind of the Lord?	Rom. 11[:34]
He has revealed to us the mystery of his will.	Eph. 1[:9]
Without him nothing was made.	John 1[:3]
Pride was not created for human beings.	Sir. 10[:18][20]
For God has not created death.	Wisd. 2[:23?]
Fire, hail, famine and death, all these have been created for vengeance.	Sir. 39[:29]
I can do nothing on my own.	John 5[:30]
No one takes my soul from me, but I give it of my own accord.	John 6[10:18]
Those whom he called he also justified.	Rom. 2[8:30]
Many are called but few are chosen.	Matt. 20[:16]
Who can resist his will?	Rom. 9[:19]
You have always resisted the Holy Spirit.	Acts 7[:51]
You ask and you do not receive.	James 9[4:3]
All who ask will receive.	Matt. 7[:8]

God is no respecter of persons.	Rom. 2[:11]
To whom shall I look, but to the humble and contrite spirit.	Isa. 66[:2]
Preach the gospel of all creatures.	Mark 16[:15]
Do not throw pearls before swine.	Matt. 7[:6]
With one sacrifice he perfected those who are sanctified.	Heb. 10[:14]
In my flesh I am completing what is lacking in Christ for his body.	Col. 1[:24]
I will not be angry for ever.	Jer. 3[:12]
And these will go into eternal punishment.	Matt. 25[:46]
God desires that all should be saved.	Matt. 2[1 Tim. 2:4]
But few are chosen.	Matt. 22[:14]
Whoever comes to me I will not cast out.	John 6[:37]
It is not of him that wills nor of him that runs but of the merciful God.	Rom. 9[:16]
You hate nothing that you have made.	Wisd. 11[:24]
I have hated Esau.	[Rom. 9:13]
I have not come to judge the world but to save it.	John 12[:47]
I came into this world for judgment.	John 3[9:39]
If I testify about myself, my testimony is not true.	John 5[:31]
If I testify on my own behalf, my testimony is valid.	John 8[:14]
God tempts no one.	James 3[1:13]
God tempted Abraham.	Gen. 22[:1]
You are not a God who delights in wickedness.	Ps. 5[:4]
He hardens whomever he will.	Rom. 9[:18]
A bruised reed he will not break.	Isa. 24[42:3]
You will dash them in pieces like a potter's vessel.	Ps. 2[:9]

His mercy is over all his works.	Ps. 24[145:9]
I will have mercy on whom I have mercy.	Rom. 9[:15]
No one has ever seen God.	1 John 4[John 1:18]
I have seen the Lord face to face.	Gen. 32[:30]
Whoever shall drink of the water that I shall give, will never thirst again.	John 4[:14]
Those who drink of me will thirst for more.	Sir. 24[:21]
To the one who conquers I will give a place with me on my throne.	Rev. 3[:21]
To sit at my right hand is not mine to grant; it is for those for whom it has been prepared.	Mark 10[:40]
Judge not that you be not judged.	Matt. 7[:1]
Judge with right judgment.	John 7[:24]
In Christ all will be made alive.	1 Cor. 15[:22]
The Son gives life to whomever he wishes.	1 John 5 [John 5:21]
God has imprisoned all in disobedience, so that he may be merciful to all.	Rom. 12[11:32]
The one who does not believe will be condemned.	Mark 16[:16]
This is my body etc.	Matt. 26[:26]
And when they will say, here is Christ, do not believe it.	Matt. 24[:23]
I will remain with you to the end of the world.	Matt. 28[:20]
You will not always have me with you.	Matt. 26[:11]
He is the atonement for our sins, and not for ours only, but for the sins of the whole world.	John 12[1 John 2:2]
I do not pray for the world.	John 12[17:9]
It is easier for a camel to go through the eye of a needle, than for a rich man to enter the kingdom of God.	Luke 19[18:25]
My yoke is easy and my burden is light.	Matt. 11[:30]

The bars of the earth have closed upon me for ever.	Jon. 2[:6]
He commanded the fish and it spewed him out upon the dry land.	[Jon. 2:10]
There is no law for the righteous.	1 Tim. 1[:9]
You rebuke the proud; all who disobey your commandments are cursed.	Ps. 119[:21]
The law came in so that sin could multiply.	Rom. 5[:20]
God has not commanded anyone to be wicked and has not given anyone permission to sin.	Sir. 15[:20]
There was also an abrogation of an earlier law because it was weak and ineffectual.	Heb. 7[:18]
Do we then overthrow the law by faith? By no means. On the contrary, we uphold the law.	Rom. 3[:31]
The measure you use will be the measure you get.	Matt. 7[:2]
Render to her as she herself has rendered, and repay her double for her deeds.	Rev. 18[:6]
I am the Lord and there is no other. I form light and create darkness, I make peace and create evil.	Isa. 25[45:6-7]
When the devil lies he speaks according to his own nature.	John 8[:44]
Why are you putting God to the test by placing on the neck of the disciples a yoke that neither our ancestors nor we have been able to bear?	Acts 15[:10]
The commandment which I am commanding you today is not too hard for you, nor is it too far away. It is not in heaven, that you should say, who will go up to heaven for us so that we may hear it and observe it.	Deut. 13[30:11-12]
Pharaoh hardened his heart.	Exod. 8[:32]
The Lord said, I will harden Pharaoh's heart.	Exod. 4[:21]

There are many of these and similar statements in the Holy Scriptures that contradict one another.

Therefore one must pay attention and make sure that the right judgment is achieved by which to reconcile the contradictions and understand the whole. If this order is not observed people will inevitably be deceived. The Scripture experts at the time of Christ and also in our time made the same error, for they read Scripture piecemeal. They missed its meaning and the true understanding and deceived themselves and others. They knew the Scripture expertly forwards and backwards, but still their teaching and understanding was wrong. The same is true in our time, no matter that they all teach and preach Scripture. So they preach against each other and no improvement follows from their teaching, nor do they themselves become more godly.

The reason is that they lack the capacity to judge correctly. That capacity can be received only in suffering and poverty of spirit in which one becomes free and detached from the world and incorporated into the body of Christ. There all understanding is revealed. Even the prophets, apostles and all the friends of God could never come to the right understanding before they had become detached and free from the world so that they were the world's and the world their enemy. In that misery and poverty of spirit one learns to use the true judgments of God. Godly David prayed that God should teach him his judgments when he was persecuted by Saul, so that he would neither be a hypocrite nor justify Saul's malice. Yes, even godly David had the Bible and the Scriptures but understood nothing except what he learned under the discipline and punishment of God. Sirach too witnesses to this when he writes that whoever abandons the discipline and punishment of the Lord goes astray and never comes to proper understanding even if he is a master of arts, baccalaureus, or doctor.

Whoever desires to read and judge Scripture with benefit must observe the three parts according to the model of faith in the twelve articles.[21] They are ordered in three parts from which we learn the true Trinity, the one perfect godhead.

As follows:

Father	Son	Holy Spirit
omnipotence	righteousness	goodness
power	severity	mercy

Even as the articles of faith are taught and understood in three parts, the Scripture tells us of many articles which also have to be understood in these three parts, each understood by the others. First, then, we are shown the omnipotence and power of the father when we say: we believe in God the Father, the almighty creator of heaven and earth.

All reasonable persons recognize and experience this first part in nature or creation or creatures in which without argument they see the omnipotence or power of God the Father. We know this from Paul when he writes: For what can be known about God is plain to them, because God has shown it to them. Ever since the creation of the world his eternal power and divine nature, invisible though they are, have been understood and seen through the things he has made. So they are without excuse; for though they knew God, they did not honour him as God or give thanks to him [Rom. 1:19-21]. Paul insists here that although the whole creation and work of God demonstrate that a God exists, what is lacking is the praise which comes with the other two parts, that is, the severe righteousness which the Father practices on Jesus Christ, on the whole body with all its members. Through it is revealed the third part, the most sublime goodness and mercy of the Holy Spirit. Whenever a person does not advance to these two parts and gets stuck in the first, it is not enough. All that remains is vain misunderstanding and darkness. No matter how wise they imagine themselves to be, they are nothing but fools.

Knowledge of the first part alone cannot make one godly, righteous, and a true Christian. That takes place only through the severe righteousness of Jesus Christ which the Father works in all the members of the body. Whoever suffers this righteousness as he has suffered the creation by which he is a creation or power of God, to him is revealed through this justification of Jesus Christ in cross and tribulation the third part, the goodness and mercy of the Holy Spirit. For all creatures[22] are taken in their natural form and made into something better through suffering.[23] An example: many large trees in a forest can be used to build a house. They are all God's creation and work and humankind has dominion over them for good purposes. But no house is made except from those who suffer the work of the carpenter, are cut down, planed and worked into shape according to the pleasure of the master. Only then can they be used for a house.

Likewise many human beings are creatures of almighty God who were unformed through the pleasure and love of the creatures to which they had given their allegiance. Thus they fell away from God and became vain and good-for-nothing. For human beings incline to evil from their youth. It is not that the creatures are evil. The problem is that human beings reject the order in which God has put them which is that they should have dominion over them. Instead people embrace the creatures [as the only reliable reality] and forget their true Lord. Since all have fallen away from God, replace the creator with the creature, and serve the creature and are totally devoted to it, they can never return to that for which they were created, namely to be a house and dwelling for God. That happens only through the righteousness of the cross of Christ through which we are incorporated into the body of Christ of which he is the head. Then only the true knowledge of the Father through the Son comes to life. Then we remain in him and he in us so that we are the one spiritual body of Christ the Crucified. This is the second part of the Creed and the Scripture, condensed to a few words in the Creed: And in Jesus Christ, his only Son, our Lord, who was conceived by the Holy Spirit etc., to judge the living and the dead.

In order to come to the second part (that is the knowledge of the living Son of God) a person must await the work of God through the cross of Christ, which we must carry and follow in the footsteps of Christ. At all points [in this second part] Christ reveals the severity and righteousness of God the Father which he works in Christ. All who wish to grow in the body of Christ, in which the Son of God becomes known, become God's children and co-heirs with Christ, as Paul writes to the Romans, but only if we suffer with him, become one with him, or become the image of the Son of God through the justification of the Father. Whoever does not follow the footsteps and the Way and will not bear the cross of Christ, does not have or know the Son. And whoever does not know and have the Son, does not know and have the Father. Nor can he be illuminated by the goodness of the Holy Spirit who dwells in us.

In this second part only, therefore, are we shown the means, work, truth and righteousness of the crucified Son of God. We must be incorporated in him if we are to participate in the unified Trinity. This is revealed to us when we find ourselves in the most severe suffering which the whole world fears and hates. Each one must personally endure all the articles otherwise one cannot come to the knowledge of the highest good. The Word must be conceived in a pure heart through the Holy Spirit and become flesh in us. This happens with great consternation and trembling as happened to Mary when she heard the will of God from the angel. Then the Word has to be born in us. This cannot happen without pain, poverty of spirit and distress both inwardly and outwardly, etc. When the Word is born and has become flesh in us, and we are able to praise God for this great favour, our hearts rest in peace, and we become Christ's mother, brother and sister. These people, who are at peace with God, become the ridicule and occasion of stumbling for the whole world. With Christ they [come to be called] fanatics and Beelzebub. Everything they say is called a lie. They are regarded as lying spirits because they expose the evil life of the world and will not participate in it. Soon they will have as adversaries the high priests Hannas and Caiaphas and others like them (*und dasselbig geschwüren*) serving their God who is the belly who will be their destruction. They become beggars (*bitteln*) and betrayers of such a person, take him before the magistrates to give testimony against the teaching of Paul. Indeed, if they were not afraid of public shame, God knows, they would themselves beat him with rods.

The same thing is done in our day. They will allow no one to speak or to explain what they believe but scream with their fathers "Crucify him! Crucify him! He will create a disturbance, the people will listen to him and our knavery will be made public." They demand an answer from him in their synagogue and if he will not answer as the expect, then, dear God, Pilate must judge God's Word! Then, as Christ says, he is put in prison or expelled from the city or is silenced, Luke 21[:12-13]. At that point a person enters the test with godly David. He would rather be dead for he receives no comfort at all from the world and all creatures, for he sees that nothing in heaven and on earth can help him. He even thinks frequently that he has been abandoned by the Creator and will perish utterly. Then, for the first time, a person becomes aware of faith. He is dead, dispirited, in hell with Christ, condemned with Jonah to the whale's belly. He looks about for help like a young swallow and finds none. Like Christ when he hung on the cross, he is without comfort and calls out, My God, my God, why have you forsaken me? How can such a person be satisfied with God alone? This kind of thing happens not only once but many times in life. It is the judgment by which his natural life is changed, he is cut to shape and planed, removing all pleasure and love for the world and the creatures, and prepared for the house of God. Such a person in poverty of spirit, who hungers and thirsts for righteousness God cannot forsake. He will nourish him spiritually with his body through which he will be transformed. In this body of Christ is revealed the third part, the goodness and mercy of the Holy Spirit to whom no one can come except through the water of tribulation and the bath of rebirth, by which he is reborn a child of God and brother of Christ. He is comforted, raised from the dead, led out of hell and made alive in Christ. This person does not himself live, but Christ lives in him. And so he is joyful and happy in the Holy Spirit.

These[24] have taken up the cross of Christ through which the Father, the Son and the Holy Spirit are known in truth. They confess that Jesus Christ has come in the flesh and lives in them, for they are governed by the Holy Spirit according to the Word of God. Now appears the third part of the confession of faith which is denied by the whole world.

I believe in the Holy Spirit, the communion of saints, the forgiveness of sins, the resurrection of the body, etc.

Now all the pleasure of the world and the love of the creatures has been taken through cross, suffering and tribulation since the true light Christ has illuminated them. That same light has helped them to comprehend the fullness of God's goodness and mercy. This can never be grasped as long as they are under the domination of the world's pleasure. What is it that they now see in truth through the Holy Spirit? They recognize the Father in the power of his omnipotence who has created them and the Son in whom they are tested, cleansed, justified and circumcized, truly children of God. They now have free access to the Father and have become one with Christ and all his members. These all are his church and one body in Christ. All who oppose sin, love and take pleasure in righteousness, are members of this church. Even though they may sin and fall it is not deliberate. Hence also they are not cast off; the Lord holds them in his hand, the sin is remitted and not reckoned as sin. These are in the kingdom of God and have Christ as Lord. Such persons, whose souls God nourishes, will never suffer death, for all Christians are subject to him and he is lord over them. Then all goodness and mercy, all praise, laud, and honour in the Holy Spirit become visible. Everything is held in common; nothing is private. From the foundation of the world these have been waiting but have never been fulfilled. The prophets foretold that the Lord would pour out his spirit upon all flesh, and that all would eternally be taught by God to live according to God's will and be filled with all goodness. This cannot happen universally until the tribulation of fear and want has humbled the whole world.

Thus all judgments in Scripture, indeed all the words and commandments of the Lord, must be understood and concluded in the Trinity, nor may one part of the three be substituted for another in order to get a proper understanding. The whole Scripture must be divided into three parts and care taken to notice which part is under discussion. Scripture may speak in one place about the creatures and the creation of God in which are shown the power and omnipotence of God. By these, and through lust and surrender to them, human beings are darkened and coarsened in their minds. From it are distinguished the other two parts which must first be grasped, that is, the Scripture in which cross and suffering are proclaimed, and which is the mediator and the righteousness through which we come to the third part which is about how one lives according to the command of God. Thus Scripture must always be properly judged and used in the right order according to the three parts. If Scripture speaks of the means [of salvation][25] one must consider the cause of humanity's suffering and why one is guilty of it, and what purpose it serves. If, on the other hand, Scripture speaks about the truly godly life, one must discover how to achieve it and describe it even if it is not all described at that place. Those who have the Spirit of God judge all things.

The prophets and apostles wrote about the judgments of God in short sketches and for the sake of brevity did not tell the whole story. Scripture is given for the godly; from it they are to learn how God teaches them. Thus a truly learned preacher can easily judge and understand what he should offer and say to the people.

For this reason St. Paul writes his epistles and circular letters to each congregation according to their particular need. To the worldly and creaturely he wrote differently than to the mature and instructed brothers, and differently to the sensual wiseacres than to the weak, etc.

But the Scripture-clever preachers preach to the sensual and worldly people and tell them of the teaching that Peter, Paul, Christ, or the prophets wrote to earlier generations, but omit to mention what is necessary to receive it. Thus they create an indolent and impudent people in whom there is no improvement. They receive [this teaching] as though they had come by it in suffering and severe tribulation. They want to be saved through believing.[26] God has never yet done his work that way. They neglect that through which faith is called into being in the first place. That is why faith is called a work of God. May the eternal merciful God help us to that faith. Amen.

3

Hans Hergot

Concerning the New Transformation of Christian Living (1527)*

Introduction

Hans Hergot (d. 1527) belonged by birth to the group of people referred to as "the common man."[1] He was a printer in Nuremberg and a book peddler, mostly self-taught. Because he was a printer and because he lived in Nuremberg, his contact with Anabaptism was more or less assured.

As regards his writing, he was entwined in a stream of communication in which what was his was mixed with that of others, and was made permanent by the medium of the pamphlet.[2] Hergot was at least acquainted with Hans Hut; in October of 1524, Hut brought Thomas Müntzer's manuscript, the "Special Expose" to Hergot's press in Nuremberg where five hundred copies were printed.

---

*Source: Max Steinmetz, *Leipzig: VEB Fachbuchverlag*, 1977.
Translation: Walter Klaassen

The following document bears the name of Hans Hergot, but his authorship cannot be finally established. It is one of a number of responses to the religious changes of the sixteenth century. It appeared in print in 1527 and was written sometime during the previous two years. Hergot's name is associated with it because he was selling the booklet in the town of Zwickau in Electoral Saxony when he was arrested. The tract clearly reveals the thought world of the common people, and is expressed in a strong polemic style.[3]

The work is divided into two parts. The first is a little utopia, a description of a societal order which God will establish in the Third Age, the age of the Spirit. Its main features are that the two heads of Christendom, Pope and Emperor, will have to yield to a single "shepherd," a priest-king. The envisioned society is hierarchically structured with each leader on the pyramid chosen by leaders one rung lower down. There will be total societal equality, and the system will be self-sustaining. Everything, the author repeats over and over, will be done "for the glory of God and the common good." The author insists that this order will not be the product of revolution by human agency, but will be established by God and confirmed by miracles.

The second part is a bitter attack upon Luther and his fellow-reformers and supporters. Hergot blames them for the bloody suppression of the peasants following the Peasants' Uprising in 1525, and, without naming him the author clearly identifies Luther as the one who promised salvation to those who murdered the peasants. He castigates the Protestant theologians as Scripture wizards who use the Bible and their biblical scholarship as their authority for their own bloody ends. Against them stand the common people to whom God has given his Spirit. Because they have the Spirit they speak the truth and judge justly. But the Scripture wizards have hijacked the Holy Spirit and will not allow him to speak because he will refute their scholarship. This age of the Scripture wizards is part of the Second Age which will be swept away when God comes for judgment. That will happen very soon.

When Anabaptism made its appearance in the Empire early in 1527, its adherents were regarded as part of the continuing threat of the insurrection of the common man. Luther and Zwingli had not interpreted the gospel in the egalitarian terms of popular anticipation, and Hergot's pamphlet clearly expressed the author's dissatisfaction with the existing order, as well as presenting an ancient solution to its basic problem.[4]

Although Hergot refused the use of the sword and revolution because the Age of the Spirit would come by God's own, unassisted action, the authorities of Electoral Saxony saw in Hergot's booklet a new call to revolt and insurrection. Hergot simply said that the present state of affairs after the peasant defeat had long eaten away at him, an ordinary man, until he could no longer contain it.[5]

In spite of his disclaimers, Hergot was seen as a purveyor of seditious ideas, charged with sedition, and executed in Leipzig in Electoral Saxony, by the sword on May 20, 1527.

Bibliographical Sources:

Hans-Jürgen Goertz, ed., *Profiles of Radical Reformers* (Scottdale, PA: Herald Press, 1982).

Walter Klaassen, "The Schleitheim Articles and the New Transformation of Christian Living," *Historical Reflections* 14, no. 1 (1987), 95-111.

Werner O. Packull, *Mysticism and the Early South German-Austrian Anabaptist Movement, 1525-1531* (Scottdale, PA: Herald Press, 1977).

Concerning the New Transformation of Christian Living

Beware, devil!
Hell will be destroyed!
[Hans Hergot]
[1527]

PART ONE[6]

There have been three transformations. The first was the way of God the Father in the Old Testament. The second transformation was the way of God the Son with the world in the New Testament. The third transformation will be that of the Holy Spirit.[7] It will be a transformation from the evil in which they [the world] now find themselves.

I, an ordinary man, make known what is about to take place, for the honour of God and the common good.[8] God will humble all estates, the villages, castles, nunneries and monasteries, and establish a new transformation in which no one will say: "That is mine."

The sects[9] will be humbled. Their houses will be reduced to rubble and their people and activities will disappear. The villages will increase in goods and inhabitants and will be delivered from all oppression. The hereditary nobility will disappear and the common people will possess their houses. The monasteries will lose their four orders[10] and the beggars' staff, and other rich monasteries will also lose their tithes and rents. All sects will disappear and be made into one. All things, wood, water, pasture, etc., will again exist for the use of the whole parish.

Each country will have only one ruler. The spiritual and secular powers in whatever form they have today will pass away. Obedience to spiritual and secular authorities will be dissolved. The servants of rulers and lords will abandon their service. It will be futile for anyone to attempt to maintain his social station.

These articles have grown from the understanding I acquired concerning the Christian sheepfold.[11] I recognized the great affliction of the same and said: "O eternal God! how distressing is the condition of your Christian sheepfold!" Then I understood that God has dismissed the two shepherds,[12] who had been put in charge of the Christian sheepfold, together with all their company. The great efforts they now make to save themselves are in vain.

Then I understood that God has begun anew and that he has appointed one single shepherd over his sheepfold by giving him the whole earth. This took place as follows. God has given every parish its own Common[13] and assigned to it as many people as it will support. Everything that grows on that Common belongs to the parish and to the people who live on it. Everything is designated for common use; they will eat out of one pot, and drink out of one flask. They will be obedient to one man to the degree required by the honour of God and the common good. This man will be called the Provider of the Parish. The people will all work in common at the tasks to which they are suited and are able to perform. All things will be held in common so that no one will be better off than anyone else. The land will be free, for no one will pay either tithe or taxes. Nevertheless, they will be protected by the authorities.[14] The new life of these people will be better than that of all the monastic orders. They will believe in God and prove it by their actions, by prayer, fasting, contemplation on God's suffering and divine mercy, and in other ways.[15]

When these people have children they will bring them to the church at age three or four and dedicate them to God. The Provider will come, receive them, and commit them to the person among them who is most godly. They will be in a house where this man, as a true father, will bring them up to the glory of God and the common good.[16] The girls will be given into the charge of an honourable, godly woman or virgin in that same house. She will teach the children until they are of marriageable age. They will be taught whatever they are most inclined to learn, all to the honour of God and the common good of the people.

From the ranks of these lay people one of every twelve persons will be chosen for the service of God and the common good. These will be in charge of divine worship to teach the people. The monasteries both male and female along with their endowments will no longer have [a special role] in the spiritual care of the people.[17] For all must become part of this new order. The four [mendicant] orders will become part of it, for they will no longer receive alms. The other monasteries and foundations will no longer receive tithes and rents. Even the nobility will be part of the new way. The beggars will come too; they will receive adequate provision along with all others. Thus the human race will be humbled. They will live together in a community of houses in the manner of the Carthusians.[18]

They will always be ready to raise a company of soldiers when it is necessary for the honour of God and the common good. They will have a house in which the aged will be cared for with food and drink and all other physical necessities more adequately than in any hospital.

There will also be a house for those who are ill with leprosy of the body and another for those who have illness in the soul. They will remain in that house until they repent of their sin.

All artisans will be there such as tailors, cobblers, weavers of wool and linen, smiths, millers and bakers, indeed, whatever crafts are required for each Common. All crafts will again be restored to their true usage. The artisans will abandon the striving for their own gain and devote themselves to the common good throughout the whole Common. Then the Lord's Prayer will be fulfilled and they will take to heart the word the Lord uses frequently in that prayer, our, our, our.

Every craftsman will take another and teach him the craft for the sake of the common good and they will prosper. They will call on and worship God, the choice and highest good, and all of God's saints. For God's sake they will forsake their own interests and any mean behaviour.

They will wear one kind of garment which has been produced on the Common in the colours white, grey, black and blue. Their food and drink likewise is what they can produce. Everything on their Common will be theirs such as wood and water; it will all be used for the common good. Whoever produces something on his Common will barter it for other goods. They won't eat meat in Advent and between Ascension Day and Pentecost.[19]

Of the seven sacraments they will observe three; the other four will be regarded as good works.[20] They will be absolutely bound to this and whoever does not adhere will be severely punished. This will be the penalty for anyone from the parish: he will be bound hand and foot and people will walk over him to his great shame whenever he does it. The sacrament of unction will be regarded at that time as prayers to the saints. The sacrament of confirmation will be considered a confession of faith when a person becomes thirty years of age.[21]

The Providers of the parish will choose one head or lord over themselves for the whole country. He will be lord over that same country. They will not be required to pay him tithe or rent.[22] He will travel from one Common to another across the whole land and oversee all the Parish Providers and ensure that the honour of God and the common good be observed in the whole Common. He will eat what they eat and drink and what they can produce on their Common. What ever else he deserves as a recognition of his world he will expect from God.

When the ruler wages war he will be given every third man from every Common insofar as it concerns the honour of God and the common good. They will follow him obediently on foot and mounted. This ruler will mint a coin on which will appear the name JESUS and the inscription will be the name of the Common in which it is minted and the country of that ruler. The coin will be valid in all the Languages[23] of the world. Although he will receive neither tithe nor rent, this ruler will be able to take care of all the needs of the country. Working through the Parish Providers, he will ensure that each one keeps paths and roads in good repair.

The Ruler will engage men who are wise in agriculture and others who are wise in the Scriptures. Those wise in agriculture will know what and how much the fields will yield. The fields will nourish the body and each Common will have its man. The men wise in Scripture will teach the Word of God for the salvation of the soul and thus nourish the soul with Scripture. Again there will be one to each Common. This ruler will rebuild old churches where they will worship God. They will be nourished from the Common.

This ruler will grant each Provider the right to mint coins as needed for the common good. The ruler will live in the centre of that land and everything that is in that land will belong to the people of the Common. Two or three times a year or whenever necessary he will assemble all the Providers and receive reports on any surplus in goods or manpower. He will have special houses built in which to store excess food from the Commons for the benefit of the people of that country or for the help of other countries.

The ruler will support a university in his country where they will instruct men in the honour of God and the common good. All useful books will be found there. He will arange for divine worship in all the Commons which will be oftener and better than anything now done in the monasteries. The soul will be nourished with the Word of God as often as the body is fed. The ruler will be satisfied with one country and will be content with what Common and country will yield. Whatever is in that country will belong to him and the people.

Twelve of these rulers will choose a head or ruler who will travel about and supervise the twelve rulers in order to ensure that they are ruling the twelve countries properly. He will mint a coin which will be worth twelve times that of the coins minted by those under him. It will bear the image of God and the name of the country. He will eat and drink with the Twelve whatever they are able to provide in their houses.

He will be called a Quarter Lord of the Latin Language. The twelve rulers will come to him once or twice a year to report to him the surplusses and shortfalls of their countries. He will confirm the popular election of the Twelve and will be the supervisor of the rulers under him to ensure that none will seek his own good and command them that they also so teach their people in order that none seek his own but the common good. He will be wise in Scripture and agriculture and will mint a coin of bronze and gold with the name of Jesus and the name of the Quarter of the Language in which it is minted. There will be four of these Quarter Lords in the Latin Language. These languages will be given to those lands with which they are identified. Four rulers will exercise authority in them.

Each one of these four rulers will mint a coin of gold and bronze with the same value of all the other coins minted by the subject rulers in his Quarter. Again each one has a university in his Quarter in which the three languages Latin, Greek, and Hebrew will be taught. This is necessary for the ultimate installment of the one shepherd. Every Quarter Lord will have no more than one central retail store large enough for the countries which he governs.

According to the same pattern there will be four Quarter Lords in the Hebrew and Greek Languages. There too each one will mint a coin of gold and bronze which will all be of the same pattern as the others with the name JESUS and the name of the Quarter in which it is minted.

These twelve men of the three Languages will visit the rulers under them, each in his Quarter, to ensure that the rule is just according to the honour of God and the common good. They will decree that they should instruct others under them similarly concerning God's honour and the common good.

These Twelve will also elect a Supreme Ruler who will confirm the Twelve when they are elected in their Quarters. He will travel through the three Languages and ensure that they rule justly according to the honour of God and the common good. If the Supreme Ruler is unable to complete his supervision due to his death, the Twelve will elect someone else to his office who will begin his service where his predecessor left off. This man will be confirmed by God. He, too, will mint a coin of gold and bronze which will have the cumulative value of all the Quarter coins. The image will be the name JESUS and the inscription "One Shepherd and One Flock."

This then, is how the two shepherds of the present will be dismissed, and the one future shepherd established. All their effort and labour will be in vain until the new order comes. Until then there will be no peace.

This gift of the earth and of one shepherd will restore the use of the earth and its fruit for the human needs in body and soul. Because of this gift the little villages will be able to defend their Common against the large cities and lords. Whatever they will find on the Common will be theirs.[24] The cities will surrender their houses and they will be reduced to rubble for they will no longer need them. The monastery buildings on their Common will be adequate and they will occupy them to the honour of God and the common good.[25] It is important to take care that these houses not be damaged in this rebellion of the people. In the gift of this new order no one will remain in the state he now occupies for all will be changed to a unified order.[26]

The aristocracy of virtue[27] will be the boast of this new order, the big cities of the countries will be their artisans' tools, and the master artisan will be God and the common people. Thus all sects will be forged into a single one.

Through this provision the nobility of birth and the present order [will daily yield] to wise and pious men from the common people who will rule in the new order.[28] These men will be chosen from all estates wherever they can be found. By this gift the villages and cities will be delivered from all oppression. And through it there will be one shepherd and one flock on this earth. This shepherd will truly confess "I believe in the Holy Spirit," and will prove it by his actions. All monastic foundations will lose their position, rents, and whatever they have. After their dismissal we will no longer be able to put them to shame with this word of God: "Give Caesar what belongs to him."[29] For they have been dismissed by God and will be dismissed by the world as well. Miracles and wonders will prove the reality of this dismissal, as much as is necessary to ensure belief. Because of them the people will be caught up in the fear and love of God; they will begin to put away selfish striving and act for the common good.[30]

[PART TWO]

This book affects all estates in the whole world, spiritual and secular, noble and common, kings and monarchs, burghers and peasants, and concerns the one as well as the other, cities, principalities, and people. Whatever has been proclaimed by God affects everyone equally. Therefore no one should be wrathful. Whether God's wrath goes forth or relents, it is all the same to him. His punishment will nevertheless take its course. But the world and especially the Scripture wizards[31] at the courts of the princes and in the large cities imagine that their wisdom and understanding is so great that it surpasses God's wisdom. Indeed, all of God's proclamation which he has spoken through all the prophets is worth nothing. All the miracles which he shows us every day in the heavens[32] are as nothing and called mere fables by the Scripture wizards.[33] In this way they seek to overthrow God's power so that nothing is valid except their wisdom.

Can anyone show me one legal judgment from among all those who judge and give justice on earth that is given by the Holy Spirit? All laws are established to be used in truth and justice and not for special favour and advantage. Hence the Holy Spirit has installed twelve men as once God installed the twelve apostles, and for the following reason: even if five of them depart from justice and judge simply in their own spirit,[34] the remaining seven outweigh the five. Justice will be given by the judgment of the seven, and all will be well. He who is Almighty and established the laws on behalf of the poor, will give a proper recompense to all judges and jurists.[35] The time is here and everyone, large and small, is afraid. But no one seeks to improve things as one can see in all the judgments.

Of all who live on earth, from the highest to the lowliest, let someone give us the case where the judgment given was contrary to that of the Scripture wizards! They will acquit whomever they wish whether he is guilty or no. Scripture teaches them and so they always have their way.[36] But the Spirit does not agree with that teaching. He teaches nothing but truth and justice. For this reason he is the enemy of all the Scripture wizards, who, in turn, are the enemies of the Holy Spirit. The Scripture wizards, however, regard all who judge according to the Spirit and the truth to be fools, and with no right to judge.[37] The Spirit's truth is regarded by the Scripture wizards as no more important than a felt hat, but before God it is eternally valid.[38]

There are twelve judges who sit and judge two.[39] But the two are more important than all the rest and therefore they must speak. But God knows their hearts. Do you think that the Holy Spirit will remain a mute forever and allow himself to be buried as though he had no right to speak? No, his voice marches on and resounds like a trumpet in the hearts of all people and exposes all the injustice of the Scripture wizards.[40]

You superpowerful men of authority, whatever your titles are from the most exalted to the lowliest, if you had allowed the old unlearned men to decide and give judgment until now, do you think the world would be in such a bad state as now? I believe that God the Holy Spirit gives more wisdom to an old unlearned man than to a young educated one. Therefore the old man truly says: "If the young man knew what I know he would be undismayed." But nowadays the wisdom of the aged counts for nothing. The Holy Spirit has no place in him. The Scripture wizards have kidnapped the Holy Spirit and won't release him. Whoever boasts of the Lord will have to suffer if he is not a Scripture wizard.

I believe, however, that God won't have anything to do with them [the Scripture wizards]. When he was on earth he did not go much to the Scripture wizards for he feared them. He knew well enough that they would turn his justice and truth into injustice and lies.

Hence he chose only poor simple fishermen and tax collectors who did not think themselves intelligent. God alone is intelligent, and can use only those who boast that they are wise and intelligent through God the Holy Spirit. The Scripture wizards make no appeal to the Spirit; they boast that books and the Scriptures make them wise and clever, indeed, more shrewd than God himself could make them. And so they judge according to the Scriptures and never inquire about God's judgment, as one can clearly see. Moreover, all who have the Holy Spirit are allowed to say only what pleases the wizards.

But now things are happening. He [the common man who has the Spirit] is learning things in a way the Scripture wizards don't like. He is speaking the whole truth and that the Scripture wizards cannot tolerate.

Thus it is that they complain loudly to the princes and kings that the printing presses should be suppressed, and that this vilifying of people and exposing of wickedness ought not to be tolerated. For the devil tells them how their shame will be exposed. As long as one spoke and wrote the truth to princes and kings, knights and counts, noble and commoner, about their injustice, printed it and sent it into the world so that everyone could hear what kind of people these were, the Scripture wizards loved it and agreed that it as right so to expose the injustice of the nobility.

But now that their own injustice also is to be made public they howl "Murder!," and suppress all printing so that it can't happen.[41] Nevertheless, all of God's proclamation must be heard in the whole world, not only once, but often, often even as Noah announced often to the world for one hundred years that God would destroy them.⁴² Now, however, when one announces to the Scripture wizards that God's patience is exhausted, they become furious. They do not consider the great miracles that have taken place in the heavens and on earth.

The nobility and the princes have seen God's power and authority. No house, castle, or city offers security. When God's wrath goes forth none of them can help, and they abandon house and castle and flee. For the fear of God pursued everyone as we have seen. Who is to say? If the Emperor and all the princes had come [with an army] they would not have scared the nobility as much in a year as God did in ten weeks!⁴³ But they don't believe it. They say that the peasants did it, to which I say no. Peasants with threshing flails can't break down a stone wall even if they work a long while. To say that the peasants did it is simply robbing God of his honour. And then they encourage the nobility: "Beat the peasants to death because they are mad and break down your castles!"⁴⁴ This is the wisdom of the Scripture wizards. Thus one blind man teaches another and both fall into the ditch as God himself said. If they would teach the truth according to the Gospel there would not be the disunity and strife on earth which we now have.

The Lord says in the Gospel: "Even the hairs on your head are all counted and none is bent without the will of my Father" (Matt. 12:30; Luke 21:18). If it was God's will, it had to happen. And even if the peasants were no better than anyone else and what they did was not so good, it still had to happen. Had it not been God's doing, I would in truth be glad to say that the Scripture wizards more than the peasants were the cause of it. But the peasants were left with nothing but the hide even though they had to pay twice over for the whole cow. Now she stands in the middle of the market so that everyone can milk her. Hurry up, Scripture wizards, come and suck the cow, and teach the nobility to suck the udder dry so that nothing is left for the children! They've nearly done it now; they have sucked it dry so that neither milk nor blood is left, and mothers and children are near death by starvation. The call to kill and strangle to death whoever can has been amply carried out. If that is just, God will confirm it. But God says: "Be merciful as my Father is" [Luke 6:36]. If that is the mercy of the Scripture wizards, the peasants have tasted it; I want no more of it. If God's mercy were like that of the Scripture wizards, no one would ever enter his kingdom.

No one should think that revolt comes from books or writing; it all comes from the power of God. But the Scripture wizards don't believe it; for their purposes, they consider their wisdom greater than God's. And the mindless world believes them, and so they are able to make the whole world blind so that no one fears God. The only thing they know is to lead the world into blindness. If they knew better, they could teach better, but since they have no understanding they can also not impart any. Whomever they teach wanders into error, unable to find the true path, and suffers grievous loss in time and eternity. God's wisdom has blinded them completely.

I have written this booklet not in anger nor to condemn anyone nor to incite the world to wrath, but to promote peace and concord. Strife creates nothing but strife, but wholesome peace creates wholesome peace. This has been clearly visible in all the recent conflict. Had the Scripture wizards not been so busy teaching strife, there would have been much less of it. The most one can gain from strife is a bit of grease for the shoes; I can do without that meagre gain. Nor do I desire to share with the peasants the loot they gained from their revolt. They have been amply paid for it.

Is it not true that many Scripture wizards and masses of other people on earth acted as unjustly as the peasants? But no one says about them "Stab them to death! Beat them to death!" But God, who summons to battle as the true commander, marches to meet them and will strike them more powerfully than he struck the peasants. But then they have acted with violence a thousand times greater than that of the peasants. God is not much concerned with houses of stone and wood, be they cities or castles. But the houses in which God lives are the poor folk, the peasants and burgers whom God himself has created. He will not suffer that they be destroyed. However, he suffers and allows them to be abused until his time comes.

All things happen according to design. I believe that God will not again arouse the peasants against their masters in a revolt. His work with the peasants was done for the benefit of the nobility and the Scripture wizards. Since in their ingratitude they have not recognized that God did it for them, he is bringing against them, [as payment] for the blood of the peasants they offered him, the Turk and all the infidels. We see the beginning now of the real conflict. And it is not only the Turk. His supreme holiness, our father, the pope and all the high prelates are at strife with each other and each one thirsts for the blood of the other.

God forbid that the conflict also comes to Germany as it has come to Italy, involving all the principalities in antagonism and war. I suspect that it will come to Germany as well. May God have mercy on us, for the rulers and great ones here are as contentious as elsewhere. Anyone pipes a merry tune, and they dance and say First rate, do it again! The Scripture wizards love it; they laugh up their sleeves and approve of growing strife and murder. They interpret the Scriptures in a way that produces feuding and quarreling. Trust that God will hear the prayers of the godly and prevent such discord in Germany. The Scripture wizards believe that the Gospel should be enforced by the sword. It is not true. I believe that if God wills it, a person will believe. Let others believe as they please.

Suppose someone says that this book is no good and teaches error. I say it is good and teaches the truth, but it makes no difference to me. The rain falls from heaven, it gets muddy and I don't like it. It makes no difference to God. What he does is right regardless of whether I like it or not. Similarly, if some wiseacre or Scripture wizard does not like it, it makes no difference. The book is about the wrath of God; we can pray that he relent and treat us more gently. But I am concerned that the punishment and the tribulation will come together. If it does not happen, so much the better. It does no man any harm to be warned. Is it not better for me to be told that I am sinning against God which makes me afraid so that I turn to God and ask for forgiveness, rather than to be told that I am a pious man but am in fact a hypocrite under my skin? How will that help me at God's judgment? What would it be worth if I said: "People regard me as a pious man." It would not change who I am.

That is what it is like if I say It will happen, but in fact does not. My only loss would be to be called a liar. If only the world would be godfearing enough for God to relent in his punishment, I would be glad to be a liar.

My booklet does not cause rebellion. It merely identifies those who sit in wickedness so that they may repent and pray to God for mercy. For God will not be defeated as the peasants were. God himself will fight against you as the booklet clearly states. No innocent person need have any fear. But whoever knows of his own guilt, let him flee to God and beg for mercy without delay, for God intends to pull up the weeds [Matt. 13:25-30]. [Unless that happens soon] they will devour those who believe. They don't know that Moses tells us that if we believe the voice of God we will be blessed in our going out and coming in. We believe God's voice; what he has promised will happen [Deut. 28:1-14].

This matter has long eaten away at my conscience. I am a simple man, but could no longer endure it. I thus make it public in the name of God.

I have seen three tables in the world. The first overflowed with too much food. The second was middling, with enough for every need. The third was very needy. Then those who sat at the overflowing table came and attempted to take the little bread from the third table. That is the source of the trouble. But God will overturn the overflowing and needy tables, and confirm the one in the middle.

4

Ambrosius Spitelmaier

Questions and Answers of Ambrosius Spitelmaier (1527)*

Introduction

Ambrosius Spitelmaier was born in Linz, Austria in 1497. He had enjoyed some university training, and demonstrated a good command of Latin. He was converted and baptized by Hans Hut on July 27, 1527. After this he worked as an Anabaptist apostle around Linz. He soon had to flee. Spitelmaier spent a night in Nuremberg in early September 1527, but the authorities caught him at Erlangen a few days later. He was tortured, tried, sentenced, and then executed by beheading on February 6, 1528. He had been an Anabaptist only two months before he was arrested. He spent five months in jail before being beheaded at Cadolzburg.

Spitelmaier's first trial was on September 9, 1527 in Erlangen. He was first presented with twenty questions of a factual nature. These did not probe into his Anabaptist teaching.[1] He was asked about his

---

*Source: Schornbaum, *Quellen II*, 45-47 and 47-56.
Translation: Friesen/Klaassen

relationship to other Anabaptists, including Hans Hut. Spitelmaier answered that he did not know Hut but later on during the first interrogation, admitted to being baptized by him. It would seem that, although Spitelmaier was a disciple of Hut, his personal relationship with him was a casual one. Indeed, Hut denied knowing Spitelmaier at his own trial.[2]

After being transferred to Ansbach, he was faced with a further thirty-five questions which had been sent from Nuremberg and were also being asked of Hut. The answers to this second set of questions reveals Spitelmaier's understanding of the central place of suffering discipleship and his understanding of water baptism as a covenant with God and the Church. Furthermore, Spitelmaier challenged the right of authorities to control the soul and conscience. He maintained that this was not revolutionary, nor was the idea of Christian sharing. He refused to recant his Anabaptist views in exchange for his freedom, even when tortured.[3]

Spitelmaier's answers (see document B) reflect the theology of his mentor Hans Hut, and are a valuable source for the theology and practice of Hut's followers. They are evidence not only of an individualistic cross mysticism, but also of the view of the church as a disciplined community. Spitelmaier's testimony gives detailed substance to the "seven judgments" that formed the core of Hans Hut's teaching, as well as illustrating how the "gospel of all creatures" functioned as an evangelistic tool.

Spitelmaier put great stress upon the imminence of Christ's second coming (see #23), and also was convinced of the necessity of personal suffering.[4] He attached importance to the year thirty, because it was at thirty years of age that Jesus was baptized by John the Baptist.

Bibliographical Sources:

Claus-Peter Clasen, "Nuernberg in the History of Anabaptism," *MQR* 39 (January 1965), 25-39.

Herbert Klassen, "Ambrosius Spittelmayr: His life and Teaching," *MQR* 32 (October 1958), 251-71.

Werner O. Packull, *Mysticism and the Early South German-Austrian Anabaptist Movement, 1525-1531* (Scottdale, PA: Herald Press, 1977).

George H. Williams, *The Radical Reformation* 3rd edition (Kirksville, MO: Sixteenth Century Journal Publishers, 1992).

A. Questions Prepared by the City of Nuremberg for the Interrogation of [Ambrosius] Spitelmaier. October 23, 1527

Questions which may be used in interrogating the prisoner Albrecht von Linz, as he calls himself.

Firstly, what his real name is, since he is supposed to have a different name depending on his role and clothes?

At which places he recently resided and what his occupation and living were?

Whether he knows Hans Denck, Johann [Ludwig] Hätzer, Hans Hut and doctor Balthasar Friedberger [Hubmaier] who has been living in Moravia, (these being the chief leaders of this new sect)?

Whether he has lived with all these or with some or several of them, or had association with them? Where and how long? Where do these persons now live?—the residence of each to be separately noted.

Whether one or more of them have been in the city of Nuremberg or in some other town or village of our jurisdiction? What are the names of these towns and at what time?

Whether, accompanied by or with these persons or alone by himself he has been in the territories of the council of Nuremberg? At what time and at what places?

What his occupation or business was or that of these persons?

Through whom he or the named persons were secretly or openly harboured each time in the city of Nuremberg or in other places in the jurisdiction of the Council? By whom? Name them specifically.

Which persons besides the above named are also related to this new sect of Anabaptists or are the chief, principal teachers of them?

Who their disciples or apostles are, whom they use at other places or whom they send out and where these customarily stay?

Whether one or more of these principals are now staying in Augsburg and which prominent persons are there connected with this sect?

Further, to investigate particularly what have been the teachings and articles of their union and brotherhood held by himself and the other teachers of this sect?

Also specifically what the seven articles or the seven judgments (as they call them) are, which they have maintained among themselves or taught to others as true? Indicate these separately.

1) He is to be asked whether in this his ignorance he will say, what other sign of their confederation in word or gesture they have besides their ostensible baptism?

2) What they think of Christ? Whether he has sufficiently paid for the sins of all people?

3) What they have taught about the bodily coming of Christ and of the new kingdom which Christ is to set up?

4) Whether they consider it to be true that there should be appointed governments and whether all power and government are of God?

5) What their plots have been to act against the government and whether their use of the "sword of Gideon" does not signify the destruction of the government?

6) What they hold concerning the sacrament of the body and blood of Christ?

7) At what time they have set the coming of the end of the world and with what evidence, since God the almighty has reserved for himself alone the knowledge of the time, which Christ himself indicated in the gospel clearly with plain words?

8) Whether and in what way they have united and bound themselves together with oaths or other duties besides the matter of rebaptism?

9) To what place he or the other principals of this sect had directed their followers or brothers to come, whom they had persuaded to sell goods, and what their plans in this matter had been?

B. The Answers of Ambrosius Spitelmaier to the Points Presented.
October 25, 1527
Recorded on Friday after Ursula, anno 27.

1) Firstly my name is Ambrose, as you have often before heard from me. This name I received at my infant baptism and I still claim it. However, I do not claim my baptism as an infant. We read in Acts 10, that Cornelius, baptized by Philip, did not change his name but kept it as he had received it at his circumcision.

2) Recently I have been living at Linz, where my father and mother are. When I and others at Linz were expelled, I went directly to Augsburg to visit others of my brethren. Other than that I have never lived there. But before I received this baptism, I attended school, since I am a student as my clothes indicate although they are somewhat used and without ornament. Clothes do not make anyone devout nor wicked, but the heart.

3) I know none of them; nor do I know what their Christian walk is.

4) I know about none of them. I have lived with none of them nor heard nor seen any of them. For I am from Linz, and since I was baptized never left until I came here.

5) I know nothing about that.

6) Hans Hut, at the time I was baptized there, was the chief teacher at Linz. Besides him there were three, Lienhart Teutsch, a writer, Christopher his brother [Leonard and Christopher Freisleben (Eleutherobios)] schoolmaster at Wels, 4 miles [20 English miles] from Linz, and Hans Kierschner of Wels. Also I heard from Hans Hut that Caspar Nesler at Augsburg was also of this sect.

7) There is one by the name of Conrad, a binder's apprentice, who was himself ordained by Hans Hut, as Timothy and Titus were by Paul, to instruct the brothers and sisters and to bring others as well to a Christian faith. There is also one by the name of Herons, also Lienhart. Of these two I know nothing more to say than that they were at my place as well as with others in Linz. But where they are now and where they work I do not know.

8) I truly do not know where they are now, for it is about twelve weeks since they were at Linz.

9) Our teaching is nothing else than the eternal pure Word of God. When I or someone else meets someone who is not of our faith, I just ask him whether he is a Christian, what his Christian walk is, how he conducts himself towards his brother, whether he has all things in common with others and they again with him, whether any among them lack food and clothing, whether they have brotherly discipline among themselves, how they conduct themselves towards God in the use of all created things, and how they recognize God and Christ in them, etc. If one or more admit to us that they are ignorant, that they do not know, and if one desires to know, then we show him the will of God clearly through all created things, to each one through his trade according to the trade he has, (John 12; John 15; Matt. 4; Luke 9; Matt. 21). Christ also taught that he should learn his will through his trade as though it were a book that God had given to him. A woman learns this through the flax which she spins or through some other work in the house which she does daily. In sum, our teaching is nothing else than that we clearly make known to all people the will of God through what is created, to help people understand spiritual things through visible things, which is why God has presented them for all to see. This is the way the apostles also learned, for the whole thing is nothing but creature.

The union, however, and fraternity which we maintain with one another, is nothing else but this: wherever we are together we intend to maintain brotherly discipline, wherever one sees or finds the other erring, just as Christ has commanded us. We do not separate from each other in spite of all our differences, nor does one offend the other. One is not to keep anything from the other but hold all things in common whether it be in spiritual or temporal gifts. We wish to harm no one and wish to keep our covenant between God and us as long as body and life last. Such covenanting takes place when we keep the Lord's Supper.

It is certainly not our intent to betray or surrender country and people or to make an insurrection. May that be far from us. The turmoil which will soon come over all people will come from God because of the sin which is daily piled up against God. I say to you awake! Awake! Rise up from your sins and Christ will become your Illuminator. All people carry a dead soul in a living body. They should carry a living soul in a dead body.

10) There are seven judgments in Scripture which completely sum up the will of God, but which in the Scripture are found piecemeal as follows:

The first judgment concerns the covenant of God which he makes with his own when he accepts them as children. This covenant takes place in the Spirit, in baptism and the drinking of the cup which Christ calls the baptism of the blood (Matt. 20, 26; Luke 22; 1 Cor. 11). In one love, Spirit, faith and baptism (Eph. 2) we make a covenant towards God to remain faithful to him. And God, in turn, covenants with us to be our Father, and to assist us in all our tribulations. Scripture is full of this covenant.

The second judgment is about the kingdom of God. God will give it only to those who are poor in spirit (Matt. 5; Luke 6, p[ositi]o 50 [This is an early verse identification]). No one can occupy this kingdom except those who are poor with Christ. A Christian has nothing of his own, indeed, no place where he can lay his head. A real, true Christian is not to have even as much on earth that he could stand on it with his foot. This does not mean that he is to have no shelter or to sleep in the woods, nor not to have fields or meadows or not to work. But he is to count nothing as his own. He cannot say: "This house is mine, that field is mine, this penny is mine; rather, it is all ours." As we say, "Our Father." To sum up, a Christian is to claim nothing as his own, but is to have all things in common with his brother so as not to allow him to suffer need. I am not to work so that my house may be full, that my storeroom is full of meat, but am to look also at what my brother needs. A Christian looks more to his neighbour than to himself (1 Cor. 13). Whoever desires to be rich here, however, so that he lacks nothing as to body or goods, and whoever wants to be looked up to by people and wants all people to fear him and who does not fall down before the feet of the Lord, like Magdalene, the king of Nineveh, and king David, that person will be abased there (Luke 22, 18; 1 Pet. 5). The kingdom of God will be here on earth (Matt. 5), but before that heaven and earth will be renewed by fire (Isa. 66).

The third judgment is about the body of Christ. All who become attached to Christ through his divine word are his members, that is, hands, feet or eyes. Such members are attached to Christ spiritually, not visibly. To such members Christ, true man in the flesh, is the head through whom the members are governed. The relationship of the members to this head is the same as in a visible body. For as in a body there are many members with different functions, yet they still serve one another, for what one member has, the other has also. The members are also humble toward each other and one is obedient to the other (Luke 22; 1 Cor. 12; Rom. 14).

The fourth judgment concerns the end of the world. The time is here when God will purge all things through fire, earthquakes, lightning and thunder. He will overthrow and destroy all buildings, as happened in the great city of Babylon (Hab. 4, 6, 7). Then all defiance and wisdom of the world with its riches must be melted in order that the kingdom of heaven can be established (Ezek. 7; Jer. 30).

The fifth judgment is about the future and about the judgment. After all things are thrown down and all people will have died, Christ will come (Matt. 25; 2 Cor. 5) in his glory in order to judge the living and the dead. Then each will be rewarded according to his works (Matt. 20). As we have sown here, so will we reap there. None of the damned has yet received his damnation and no blessed person has yet received anything.

The sixth judgment is about the resurrection. All people will arise with body and soul: the godly will have a resurrection to life, for they have been dead here (Rom. 6); the godless will arise to death, for they have lived here (Ezek. 18) in the joys and pleasures of this world and have had their heavenly kingdom here (Matt. 19; Luke 12, 16; 1 Tim. 6).

The seventh and last judgment is about the eternal judgment. The godless must receive damnation and go into the eternal fire (Heb. 4; Matt. 25), which is inextinguishable. Then the gnawing worm will begin to gnaw in the hearts of the godless. Then will begin weeping and lamentation and the gnashing of teeth, for here they laughed and had peace all their lives (Matt. 23).

11) I have been baptized again. How many times must I tell you? Do you also want to become my brothers and children of God (John 9)?

12) I was baptized by Hans Hut, a true prophet sent by God (Jer. 1, 23) through the announcing of the creation in which the will of God is proclaimed. When I was baptized, I was 30 years old, like Jesus when he was baptized in the Jordan.

13) In short, I have no regard for my first baptism, for it is not the least use to me. As often as a child is baptized, Christ is slandered, for

a child, although it is conceived and born in original sin, is pure in soul until the time when it understands good and evil.(Ezek. 28; Isa. 7; Matt. 4)

14) We bind ourselves to each other in nothing except what is indicated in article 9.

15) We have no external sign that might be visible, but an invisible sign which was given to us by God, by which God knows us. We greet each other with the greeting which God gave the Jews and with the holy kiss of which Paul speaks so much. So we know each other as Mary and Elizabeth knew each other (Luke 1), and Christ when he says: peace be with you (John 20, 21).

16) We hold and believe that Christ was a true physical man on earth here, as we are, with flesh and blood, a son of Mary according to his humanity. For from her he received flesh and blood, though not in the same manner as we, for he was conceived without a man's seed through the faith which Mary put in the words of the angel. Thus, humanly speaking he was a son of Mary, a son of man as he also calls himself. But according to divinity he was a natural son of God from eternity to eternity, born in the heart of the Father through the Word as John 1 says. Christ true God and man, the head of all his limbs, by himself extinguished the eternal anger of the Father against us with his suffering (Isa. 51) and has made us to be at peace and united with him. He has become our only mediator and with his suffering and dying opened to us the kingdom of heaven from which we had fallen through Adam. If we, his members, would occupy the kingdom of heaven on the day of judgment, we will also have to live accordingly, to suffer and die, as he, as the head, died for us. For whoever does not suffer with him will not inherit with him. We must drink of the cup of which he drank (Matt. 20 concerning the two sons of Zebedee). Whoever does not want to suffer here, however, will have to suffer there in the lake of fire. To speak thus is to say that Christ has not given satisfaction for the sins of the whole world, otherwise no one would be damned. No, no, Christ said at the Supper, "This is my cup of the new testament in my blood, which is poured out for many for the remission of sin." He did not speak of all people. The sins which we do in the body we must also ourselves atone for as Paul says, Rom. 6; Col. 1; Phil. 1. Also Mark 16; Matt. 25. . .

17) Christ will come with a glorified body to judge the living and the dead (John 19; Matt. 25) and afterwards unite the kingdom of God with all his members and be their king.

18) All government which has existed from the time of Adam until now has been instituted by God. But it has not remained in God for it has exceeded its power and still does today. Originally government was instituted by God so that it might judge the words and deeds which had been done against God and man. But the words and deeds which are done against God it does not judge. Therefore it is blind and a leader of the blind. For it seeks only what is its own and not what belongs to God. Therefore its judgment is false. Now, however, the government begins to judge words and deeds which it thinks to be against God, but which are for God. And in this sense it is like Pilate when he condemned Christ. The true, real Christians who are Christians in Spirit and in truth, of whom he says in Matt. 11: "Learn from me, for I am kind and of a humble heart," do not require a government, sword or power, for they willingly do righteousness. Paul says in 1 Tim. 1, "To the righteous no law is given." But those Christians who are Christians only in words, "Lord, Lord," they require their government at all times for their piety, otherwise they would put out each other's eyes. A piety which must be enforced does not please God. God wants a voluntary spirit as he said to the rich young ruler (Matt. 19). If the Jews at the time of Christ had been true Jews and true children of Abraham, they would have required no judges or emperor. It is for this reason that they were severely punished by God 40 years after the resurrection of Christ.

19) We know of no plot which we have made concerning the government nor wish to make in the future, as is indicated above in the 9th article.

20) The body or the blood of Christ are certainly not present in the bread and wine which the priests use in their mass or their Lord's Supper. It is nothing but a sham and a juggling trick by which they deceive the people and murder their souls. May God have pity that the whole world has become and remains so blind. The difference between the Last Supper of Christ and that of the priests is as great as the difference between black and white. They take literally Christ's words in John 6: "Whoever eats my flesh and drinks my blood will have eternal life." But one must not understand these words as they appear outwardly. One must do away with the letter and seek the spirit which is

hidden in the letter. One eats of the flesh of Christ by yielding oneself as a member of Christ's body. In such a one Christ spiritually becomes man, as he became flesh in Mary. In such persons Christ is spiritually conceived, born, circumcised, baptized and preached. A true Christian must do in his spiritual Christ what Christ in the flesh did visibly. That is eating the flesh of Christ (John 1); the word has become flesh and will live in us. Whoever gladly and willingly yields himself through the Spirit of God to the tutelage and the rods of the Father, suffering in all things together with Christ his brother in the flesh and is at all times ready to drink the cup as Christ drank it (Matt. 20, 26), so that the cup is washed and baptized in the blood, that is drinking the blood of Christ. In this way Abel, Abraham, Isaac, Jacob, and all the prophets have eaten and drunk the body and the blood. Whoever will not thus be baptized with Christ in the Spirit in water and blood, will be baptized in the fiery lake.

21) Whenever the name Christ is used in Scripture it identifies a genuine person of flesh and blood, prone to suffering and mortal as we. Thus he is not God, but a man, (that is) a tool through which God's Word has been expressed. Whoever is not able to distinguish the humanity of Christ from his divinity will injure himself severely on this stone [i.e., Christ as the second person of the Trinity]. That Christ was a prophet here according to the flesh can, however, be seen in the following: In Deut. 18, "I will awaken a prophet from among your brethren"; also Luke 7, "If he were a prophet, he would know who the woman is"; also John 4; Matt. 28; Luke 4, "No prophet is accepted in his native land."

22) Mary was only an instrument of the humanity of Christ, for he took from her flesh and blood. Thus Mary was a human being as we, prone to suffering and mortal as we, conceived and born in original sin as we, born through the mixing of the seeds of Anna and Joachim. On the day of judgment God will severely punish that for a long time we have placed her (and still do) beside God and have called her mother of God, mother of mercy, our life and hope, our lady, queen of the heavens and lady of the angels, an advocate for us and more of the like. For he says through the prophet Isaiah, "I will give my honour to no one else." Thus we have also done with all his saints or loved ones, calling them helpers in need. Similarly, in case of the holy cross, we have said that the wood on which Christ hung was better and counted for more than other wood. Thus we have become whores and rogues to God our bridegroom. We have sinned and whored with all the creatures, as God

has often complained, when he says, "My bride has become a whore to me." God is called jealous in Scripture. He wants the whole heart of man.

23) The day and the hour of the coming of Christ is hidden from all people, yes, even from his only begotten Son, but the right conditions for the end of the world are sufficiently present in outward signs. For one kingdom is opposed to another, one nation against another. Now the papacy has been thrown to the ground and a great part of all the vanity of this world has been reduced and is still being reduced until nothing more will remain. The fig tree has blossomed together with other trees. The summer will come soon afterwards and with it the relief of the saints. Let everyone look to himself and present his account books so that he can stand before his Lord. For everyone must give an account for all his words, works and the steps of his feet, for each day and hour he has spent them, for every penny, how he has received, possessed and spent it, how he has related to all creation, and how he has eaten his bread. The powerful of this world, princes and lords, bishops and pastors most of all, must account for how they have ruled their subjects as their sheep from whom they have taken the wool, how they have possessed the kingdom of the earth and how they have used their power. In that day there will be no consideration of persons; being procurator will be of no avail there, nor silver or gold. Therefore we look to paying the ten thousand pounds here. It will go hard with us if we think to do it then. Whoever cannot endure the lash of a foxtail here will have to be beaten with iron rods there.

24) We don't know of any conspiracy made to do anyone any harm. We know only of the union of baptism.

25) We have advised no one to sell anything or to go from house and yard, nor have we directed anyone anywhere to waste such property in sin. Never! However, if anyone leaves wife or child, house or property, he does it because of God and his Word, as also Christ wants us to do. Therefore, also, the Gospel is the power of God. Far be it from us to hatch plots as wolves in sheep's clothing.

26) Those are the exiled of whom all prophets write, who can have no place to stay but must be ever chased and driven from one city into another. For Christ says to all of his disciples, "I have not come to bring peace but the sword." A true Christian can have no rest here. Righteousness can have no peace here in this kingdom. In brief, there must be suffering, whether here or there. We must all be purged in water or fire.

27) This article has been adequately answered in the 17th article and the second judgment.

28) This will happen when the end of the world will have a sudden end. At that time the righteous from all ends of the earth who are still left will assemble in a moment, and strike down all the godless who are still alive. One will strike down a thousand and two ten thousand. This assignment will be given by God to his own (1 Cor. 15; the two epistles to the Thessalonians).

29) God will soon raise up a people whom we call the heathen or enemies of Christ. Those will be the Turks. They will not bring the true cross but one will have little pleasure in it. For all people will be grieved and frightened and the hearts of all people will despair and will run from all their weapons. Then at one time will come pestilence, famine and war and thundering from the firmament. Then the rich of this world will consider their riches, goods and money unclean and throw them on the street. They will put on hair clothes and repent, but it will do no good. This repentance will not please God (Ezek. 7; Dan. 7; Luke 21).

30) I have forgotten why I wrote Müntzer's name in it. If I could see the booklet I will answer for it. But I do not know him and have not seen nor heard him. Nor do I know about his sect nor his actions. Nor do I know where he has been.

31) I have never seen the pastor of Eltersdorf [Wolfgang Vogel]. I have never spoken with him nor communicated with him nor been his disciple.

32) Finally, concerning purgatory. I know of no other purgatory except that a Christian here yields himself to the cross of Christ and allows himself to be cleansed by God and Christ inwardly and outwardly in body, soul and spirit by water and blood. That is the purging and tribulation which the Scriptures call water. David speaks of it when he says: "The waters have gone in unto the soul." All creatures which are to be of use to us must be cleansed by water and fire. Thus the children of God are purged here in water and consuming fire which is God himself (Heb. 4) and the godless there in eternal fire. Beside that I know of no purgatory such as the shepherds and soul-murderers of the people have portrayed until now. God himself charges them through the prophet Jeremiah: "My people have become a lost herd, for their shepherds have deceived them." On the day of judgment God will re-

quire of the shepherds the blood of their sheep (Ezek. 18, 33, 34; Mic. 3; Col. 2; Jer. 27; Matt. 7).

Here the articles presented to me have been most briefly answered according to my heart, spirit and mind given to me by God. If by the decree of God I am placed before a public council I shall sufficiently defend these articles, especially the ones relating to the faith, with divine truth, since I must also give account on the day of judgment before the stern judge who recognizes and knows the hearts of all men.

You servants of God, I see and note that everyone would like to know all things that God intends to do at this time. Now you are being warned by God in a fatherly way to repent and to beware of such cruel punishment. If it were to lead to your amendment it would be well and good. If not, it would have been better you had never known the articles and the secrets. I admonish you, repent before God your Lord with weeping and lamentation. Tear your hearts, not your clothes! Learn from the king of Nineveh, who because of one sermon of the prophet Jonah repented and the whole city with him! If you will repent, then the people of your land will also be moved. See to it that you do not give offence! Make your accounting here. If you save it for yonder, things will go hard with you! Watch what you do and with whom you deal! Whoever has eyes to see, let them see; whoever has ears to hear, let them hear.

Cease to do evil; learn to do good.

5

Leonhard Schiemer

Letter to the Church of God at Rattenberg (1527)*

Introduction

Leonhard Schiemer (d. 1528) grew up in Vöklabruck in Upper Austria. The son of religious parents, he desired to enter the clergy and ended up joining the Franciscan order as a young man. Although the Franciscans were noted for their piety (this seems to be the main reason Schiemer joined), Schiemer recalled that he found nothing but strife and hypocrisy during the six years he spent with the order. He fled the monastery at Judenberg in Styria ca. 1526-27,[1] was given a change of clothes and a guilder from a citizen of the town, and made his way to Nuremberg.

It was in Nuremberg that Schiemer learned the tailor's trade; he may also have met some of the radical reformers. He travelled to Nicholsburg to hear Balthasar Hubmaier, whose ideas he had earlier opposed. After visiting Nicholsburg, Schiemer made his way to Vienna

---

*Source: Müller, *Glaubenszeugnisse*, 58-71.
Translation: Walter Klaassen

to learn more about "true Christianity" from Hans Hut. It was here that he was converted by Hut and baptized by Oswald Glaidt in the spring of 1527.[2]

Schiemer continued to travel after his baptism, going to the economically-vigorous city of Steyr in Upper Austria, known for its radical ideas. He lived in Steyr for a short time, baptizing many to the Anabaptist faith and eventually was made a preacher and sent out to spread the message. He did so, travelling through Bavaria, to Salzburg and the Tyrol, preaching, converting, and baptizing as he went, always with the knowledge that several monasteries in Austria were trying to apprehend him. He was captured in Rattenberg in the Inn valley on November 25, 1527, six months after his conversion.[3]

Although he remained in Rattenberg only a short while, Schiemer's influence on the congregation was tremendous; he considered himself the leader of the congregation after only one day. After his arrest, he spent seven weeks in jail, where the benevolent judge allowed the members of the congregation to visit him and give him ink and paper. Within those seven weeks, Schiemer wrote the most of what is known to us today. His writings were first collected into a pamphlet for the local congregation, but soon found distribution throughout Moravia, Germany and Switzerland.[4]

After a failed escape attempt, the leniency shown to Schiemer was withdrawn. He was subsequently tortured and severely undernourished. He finally was condemned to death by fire under the mandate of King Ferdinand, but this was modified to beheading and the burning of the corpse by the local court. This punishment was carried out on January 14, 1528. Seventy other Anabaptists in Rattenberg were executed soon after, demonstrating his wide influence as a teacher.[5]

Schiemer's writings place a strong emphasis on Christian suffering and faith, which he no doubt in part learned from Hans Hut. Along with Hut, Schiemer maintained that "an untested faith is no faith at all." Furthermore, Schiemer's writings demonstrate a high appreciation for the inner spiritual life. The "outer Word" alone cannot suffice for a true understanding of God's will, rather what is needed is the true light of the Holy Spirit which shines in our hearts.[6] Schiemer's writing on the Three Fold Grace explains this true light of the Holy Spirit and is a description of the spiritual and physical experience of the cross.[7]

Schiemer's writing on "Three Fold Grace" is both a criticism of traditional religious authorities and a lesson for followers of true Christianity. The first grace is an inner light, or the "eternal living Word," which is in all people and which enables everyone to distiguish between good and evil. There are three responses to this first grace but only one response will help one go on to the second grace. The first grace is a help only to those who are shocked into repentance and contrition by the knowledge of their evil nature as sinners. Those who flee from this knowledge remain in darkness.

The second grace Schiemer calls "justification"—one of the few Anabaptist uses of this Lutheran term. But Schiemer invests the word with a non-Lutheran meaning: Justification can never occur apart from "Christ who is our righteousness," he says, but he adds immediately, "that is, when his conception, birth, death and resurrection occurs in us."(74) "Justification" occurs when Christ is born in us, not simply because Christ died for us. The "second grace" of Christ's birth in us will necessarily be a painful process, because Christ is born in the human heart only to the degree that self-will and love of the world have been removed. Schiemer, writing from prison and facing death, encourages his readers not to be tempted by thoughts of having been abandoned by God. The true hindrance to a full reception of the second grace is human weakness and a lack of knowledge of God's true nature.

Schiemer is scathing in his characterization of nominal believers and he enlivens this portion of his letter by describing how the Lord's Prayer is actually prayed by "the heathen," i.e. Catholics, Lutherans and Zwinglians. Schiemer's main point is to underline that a true praying of the Lord's Prayer will be sincerely prayed, matching the words with action, rather than being a merely verbal exercise.

The third grace, which is the comforting joy of the Holy Spirit, cannot be received unless the first two have been received beforehand. The comfort of the Holy Spirit makes even judicial torture and martyrdom an occasion for joy and divine benediction.[8]

Bibliographical Sources:

Chronicle I.
Robert Friedmann, "Leonhard Schiemer and Hans Schlaffer, two Tyrolean Anabaptist martyr-apostles of 1528," *MQR* 33 (January 1959), 31-41.
Robert Friedmann, "Schiemer, Leonhard," *ME IV,* 452-54.
George H. Williams, *The Radical Reformation* 3rd edition (Kirksville, MO: Sixteenth Century Journal Publishers, 1992).

Letter to the Church of God at Rattenberg, Written in 1527.

Found in the Scripture of the Old and New Testament is the three-fold grace (as it is called).

The whole world is chattering about and mouthing back and forth the word grace, especially our Scripture experts. They notice that there is something in Scripture called grace. Since, however, they do not possess it inwardly, they cannot say anything about it except to regard the word grace as the scholastics do when they take from Aristotle the word "chimera" or **ens cognitum**, which means that it exists only in the mind, or whenever one thinks or speaks about it. But when thought and words are completed the essence of a thing is also gone. They call it **entia secunde intentionis**[9] or **secundam intentionem**,[10] or **ens reale**, such as **genus species proprium differentia, accidens propositio categorica** etc., and say it can't be translated into German because the German language is too vulgar. When one thinks about it one can see that they are so rarified that they can never be **realia**, for **res** or **realia** indicates some reality or thing. But this is no thing nor anything and lasts only as long as one thinks about it. Thus in the end we are left with nothing, and those who can chatter most about this "nothing," are called masters and doctors.

This is precisely the case with our Scripture experts. They do not have their skill from God nor are they taught by God. They have all their knowledge from other Christians and have stolen it out of their books. About them Jeremiah says: "I am against the prophets who each steal my word from one another" (Jer. 23[:31]). They have not been sent by the God of heaven but by the god of their belly, and that is why they cannot preach. Christ has not chosen them from the world therefore they do not witness faithfully regarding the world. For their works are evil (John 7[3:19]). And the world lets them be and does not hate them. They are from the world and the world loves them (John 15[:18]). They are just like a person making his living with chopping wood. They do their preaching like any worker who earns his living by his skill. The results prove it. That is why the Lord says that a good tree will not bear bad fruit. God says the same through the prophet: "As the rain and snow water the earth and make it fruitful, so shall my word be that goes out from my mouth. Wherever I send it, it shall not return empty, but accomplish that for which I sent it, what pleases me" (Isa. 55[:10-11]). But they (the belly preachers!) cannot point to anyone who has been improved by their preaching, nor do they know their sheep. The Lord said: "The good shepherd knows his sheep and calls them by name" (John 10[:3]). And these are called masters and some of them doctors of Holy Scripture! They are so called because they have found a word which Scripture often mentions, namely faith. Another is love and yet another community of saints, and others like cancelling of sin, brothers, neighbour, Holy Spirit, God's grace, righteousness, law, Christ, spiritual, preaching, baptizing, the Supper of Christ, hope, remorse, penitence, rising from sin, falling into sin, prayer, justified, word of God (Acts 2). Such words they have stolen from Scripture. If one asks them about the gist of the matter they say one must so believe (John 24 ?). If one asks: what is faith since, as Paul says, [2 Thess. 2:3] not everyone has faith, they say nothing, but are, after all obligated, as Peter says, they give account (1 Pet. 3[:15]). They speak about love and faith, but if they are asked how these are to be had, they don't know. If you ask them whether they know Christ, you learn that they know him only after the flesh. The Lord himself condemned this when he said their ignorance has no limit (John 6[:64?], 8[:12-20?]).

No matter what one asks them, they have words for it. They cannot distinguish the inner word from the outer. If one pushes them to admit that a Christian must be taught by God, they quite brazenly say that they too are taught by God (2 Cor. 5[:12]). However, when they are asked where God conducts his school and what the very first lesson is, they have no answer, and then one can see their deceitfulness. They do the same thing with the little word grace about which I now write. My brothers and sisters, sealed in the Lord; each one of you must share the gift you have received from God and hold it in common (Rom. 4[:1-4], 12[:4-8]; 1 Cor. 12[:4-7]). Likewise in the Acts of the Apostles everything was held in common (Acts 2[:44], 4[:32]). If a brother or sister is pleased [with what I write] it shall not be used privately but copied and shared with those who are favourably disposed toward it.

The three-fold grace, as it is called, is found in the Scriptures of the Old and New Testaments.

The first thing to note is that one must carefully distinguish one grace from the other. John says: We have received grace upon grace (John 1[:16]), and Christ says: To those who have, more will be given and they will have abundance. But from those who have nothing even what they have will be taken away (Matt. 25[:29]). And the worthless slave will be thrown into outer darkness. These three [graces] must remain unconfused, so that one is not mistaken for the other. If Scripture speaks about the first, and it is taken for the second, or the second for the third, the reader is finished and lost in Scripture, and can't find a way out. I will not force the Scripture open for the godless with this booklet; indeed, I can't, for it is sealed with seven seals, and no one can open it except the slaughtered Lamb. It is eternally locked to those who do not have the key of David, which is the cross of Christ.

The First Grace

In the beginning was the Word, and the Word was with God and God was the Word. The same was in the beginning with God. All things were made by it and without it nothing was made that was made. In him was life and that was the light of mortals. And the light shines in the darkness, (etc.)[11] (John 1[:1-5]). John bore witness to this light (etc.) so that they all believed in it, not through John the Baptist, as Luther translated it into German, but through the light.[12] It was the true light that gives light to all who come into the world. Here too Luther has got it wrong when he translates "through his coming into the world."[13] Check all the Latin and Hebrew Bibles! The reason for the errors is that Luther comes **to** Christ, **to** God, **to** the light. He will not have any of them **in** him, but only beside him, under him, near him, as we will soon find in this chapter. There he translates: The Word became flesh and lived among us. But all the scholars know that it should read "lived **in** us, not **among** us.[14] In the same way Luther translates Paul [Col. 1:23] "the gospel **to** all creatures."[15] But that is Luther for you. He hopes for God and believes on Christ. But we hope in God and believe in Christ. We have the Word in us, not among us.

The text continues with the light of grace. It was in the world and the world was made through it and the world did not know it. He came to his own home, and his own did not receive him. But those who did receive him he gave power to become the children of God, (etc.). It continues: from his fullness we have received grace upon grace. For the law was given through Moses; grace and truth through Christ (John 1[:10-12]). Here he identifies the law as the first grace and Christ as the second. When he says that the law was given through Moses externally having said earlier that the light or Word lives in us internally, he means that the external is always a witness to the inner. Moses is an external witness of the first inner grace and Christ the witness to the second internal grace. For he says: John was not the light, but witnessed to the light. In order to understand this better hear what follows: "The eye is the light of the body. If your eye is whole your whole body will be full of light, but if your eye is a rogue your whole body will be dark. If the light that is in you is darkness how great will that darkness be" (Matt. 6[:22-23]). The Lord continues to say that "if your whole body is light with no darkness in it at all it will be total light and will illuminate you as brilliant lightening does" [Luke 11:36].[16]

From all of this I conclude that God enlightens every person that comes into the world. Those who will not receive this light but extinguish it cannot charge God for their condemnation. It is a Lutheran habit to blaspheme and revile God when they say: "I do not have the grace. I would gladly do what is right, but God is to blame because he withdraws his grace and then condemns me afterward etc." Thus they make the whole Scripture into a liar as though God is a respecter of persons, is more concerned about the one than with the other, giving one grace out of special goodwill but not to another.[17] That is contrary to Scripture. Peter says: "I truly understand that God shows no partiality, but in every nation anyone who fears him and does what is right is acceptable to him" (Acts 10[:34-35]). It is also written: "God is not far from each one of us, for in him we live and move and have our being" (Acts 17[:28]). Paul writes: "God's invisible nature, that is his eternal power and divine nature, have been understood and seen through the things he has made ever since the creation of the world. So they are without excuse, for though they knew that God is they did not praise him as God nor give him thanks, but they became futile in their thinking and their ignorant hearts were darkened, although they claimed to be wise," etc. (Rom. 1[:20-22]). Paul says further: "God shows no partiality. All who have sinned apart from the law will perish apart from the law. When the Gentiles who do not possess the law do by nature what the law demands, these, though not having the law are a law to themselves. By this they show that the law is written on their hearts, their consciences also bearing them witness. Their thoughts also, which accuse or excuse them on the day when God will judge the secrets of all through Jesus Christ" (Rom. 2[:11-16]). And Christ says: The whole law and the prophets and all the rest are summed up in these two commandments: "You shall love the Lord your God with your whole heart, with your whole soul, with your whole mind, and with all your strength, and your neighbour as yourself" (Matt. 22[:37-40]; Luke 10[:27]; Mark 12[:30-31]). These two greatest commandments are also written in the old law when the Lord says: "The commandments which I give you today are not too hard for you nor too far away. They are not above you in heaven that you should say `Who will ascend into heaven and bring them down?' Nor are they beyond the sea that you should say 'Who will cross the sea and bring them to us?' No, the word is in your mouth and in your heart for you to do it" (Deut. 14[?], 30[:11-14]). "I call heaven and earth to witness, that I have put before you death and life, good and evil, that you may choose, either death and evil or life and the good so that you may live and come into the land which God has promised you" (Sir. 15[:17]; Jer. 21[:8]). Loving God and the neighbour is the true kingdom of God. John says in his epistle: "God is love, and whoever remains in love, remains in God and God in him" (1 John 4[:16]). That is why the Lord says: "The kingdom of God is in you."

All this makes it certain that there is a light in all people which shows them what is good and evil. Small children, even though the light shines in them, are innocent before they know good and evil, and will come into the promised land (Deut. 1[:39]). That land is not the earthly land of Canaan but the heavenly Jerusalem (Heb. 11[:15-16]). David and Samuel did not receive this promise although they knew they were in the land of Canaan. There is more about this in Ezekiel [28:15-18]: "You were perfect from the day of your creation until iniquity was found in you. In the abundance of your trade you were filled with violence, and you sinned. By the multitude of your iniquities in the unrighteousness of your trade, you profaned your sanctuaries." Christ says: "Let the children come to me for theirs is the kingdom of heaven" (Matt. 19[:14]). This divine light in the soul reveals what is sin and what is not. God in his eternal goodness has not allowed the godless pharisees[18] to conceal it. They have had to speak the truth like Balaam's ass and acknowledge that whoever observes and keeps the Ten Commandments, the Apostles' Creed, the Lord's Prayer and the Two Commandments to love God and the neighbour, will be saved. They said the text of the Gospel standing up, and the lie sitting down that whoever would be faithful in a few things, to him great things would also be entrusted (Luke 16[:10]; Matt. 25[:21]). God will not allow the Lutheran and Zwinglian Scripture experts to conceal God's commandments. I have no direct knowledge of what happens among the Turks and the heathen in all the other countries. Nevertheless, my heart assures me that God is not a respecter of persons, but that he receives everyone who repents. However, no one who has not received it from God himself will believe either Paul or me about this. Although the light is equally there in all persons, peoples' response to the light varies. It happens in three clearly distinguished ways.

The first are those who, when the light shines into their darkness which is their flesh, try to extinguish the light in whatever way they can. This light is not the sun in the firmament of heaven but the eternal living Word. The darkness is our flesh and blood. The light draws us on to all that is good, the flesh to all that is evil. The soul is between the two. Since all of us except Christ have turned with our souls to the flesh, we have all died in our souls. Christ is the physician who brings us all to life through his Word. Thus we have the will through the power of his Word, but not the performance (Rom. 7[:18]). These [carnal] people resist the light of their conscience so vehemently that it is totally ruined. God withdraws his strength and hardens the hearts of those who wantonly strive against the Holy Spirit. Because they have not admitted that they have knowledge of God, God has given them over to a perverted mind to do what is stupid, full of injustice, fornication, deceit, avarice, malice, overcome by hate, murder, feuding, trickery, poisonous gossip, slander, wickedness, pride, arrogance, swindlers, disobeying parents, enemies of God, ignorant, faithless, unfriendly, stubborn, merciless. These are they who know about God's righteousness but not only do not do it themselves, but take pleasure in those who [do not][19] do it. They pay not attention to Peter's rooster who crowed as soon as Peter denied Christ (Matt. 26[:74]). The crowing reminded Peter that he had sinned and then he went out and wept bitterly. These people bind up the beak of the cock when he crows in their hearts. They are frustrated by his crowing and regard him as their enemy. They continue on this course until they no longer hear him crow and they no longer fear to sin. They plunge ahead blindly and no one can get through with a warning about the danger. These people make the best most enthusiastic mercenary soldiers who are unconcerned about danger and who murder, kill, and plunder whatever they can. They are eager to be first over the wall and are effective fighters. They are jolly dancers, leapers, singers, good at cards, excellent hangmen, accomplished Don Juans, suffragan bishops, archbishops, abbots, betrayers, false witnesses. The hearts of these God will harden. Concerning this the Lord says: "If the light that is in you is darkness, how great will the darkness itself be" [Matt. 6:23]. It is forbidden us to speak the Word of God to these hardened people wherever we detect them. They are dogs and swine of whom the Lord says: "Do not give what is holy to the dogs and don't throw your pearls to the pigs," etc., for they will trample them with their feet and dismember those who teach them, and they will kill whoever attempts earnestly to teach them. He will die like a criminal; he wastefully pours perfectly good malmsey wine into the dirt.

The second sort of people are indolent towards the light. They do not exactly bind up the beak of Peter's rooster but also don't really like to leave it free. But when their conscience judges them for sin they are alarmed and fix a hood over the cock's head which means that they generously allow it to crow but pay no attention to it. The Scripture says that such are overcome by a drowsy spirit [Matt. 26:43?]. Elsewhere they are called lukewarm: "If only you were cold or hot, but now that you are lukewarm, I will expel you from my mouth" [Rev. 3:16]. These are the Five Virgins who indeed are very decent like most Christians. They lack only the oil of the Holy Spirit and half-heartedly fear God; they are very self-confident, but fear the opinion of others. Knowledge, understanding, good advice, strength and skill are highly prized by them. They are very inquisitive, ask many questions, and want to experience everything. These people are very beguiling for they often appear as angels of light. Indeed, they are fine Christians until the cross arrives. Then they are shown to be servants who are faithful only when the weather is good or as bad weather loungers[20] who care nothing about the grapes. Their only problem is that they are prepared too late. They walk too slowly and find the door closed. They do not pray fervently. In a time of tribulation they will fall away for they do not truly comprehend their wretchedness. We cannot deny them a place in our congregation because they come with calculating words that they should be allowed to grow until the harvest.[21] However, none of them are steadfast. About them the Lord says: "The servant who knows his lord's will and does not do it will suffer a severe beating, which will be his reward" (Luke 12[:47]). That is why a true leader in our congregation must learn properly to discern the spirits, for if they accept a person who seeks human advice and wants time to consider you will have to let him take the time. As long as he postpones a decision he suffers no pain, but he will be like an extinguished ember.

The third group of people are inwardly shocked at the Word of God as soon as they become aware of the light. They work unsparingly to resist sin, they pray, often listen to sermons, read a lot, and ask many questions with an honest heart. Although sin is their enemy they are not able to resist it in their own strength and are often overcome by the flesh. But they repent immediately, are sorry for it, and submit themselves humbly to God. To these God gives grace and more grace (John 1[:16]). He desires to be gracious and merciful to them (Rom. 9[:15]). The Lord says: "But this is the one to whom I shall look, he who is humble, and who trembles at my word" (Isa. 66[:2]). Likewise David says: "A broken and contrite heart, O God, you will not despise" (Ps. 50[51:17]. Christ says: "Come to me, all you that are weary and are carrying heavy burdens, and I will give you rest" [Matt. 11:28], and elsewhere the following: "The spirit of the Lord is upon me, because the Lord has anointed me; he has sent me to bring good news to the wretched, to bind up the brokenhearted, to proclaim liberty to the captives, release to the prisoners and for the comfort of all who mourn" (Isa. 61[:1-2]; Luke 4[:18]). Surely, these people mourn, have restless and aching hearts, and no Scripture or doctrine can comfort them except God's Word. This fire scorches them and gives them no rest until God gives them light. By this way and means they flee from sin. These know what is means to be in hell. Their inner sorrow creates such remorse that their outer appearance does not express much happiness in their deportment and speech. Since they do not reject this first grace through which they are made aware of their sin, and use it rightly, to them only is promised the second grace, to which we now turn.

The Second Grace

Blessed are those who hunger and thirst after justice, that is, how they might be immediately justified, for they shall be satisfied! Blessed are those who weep and lament for they shall be comforted! This second grace is called justice. To create a person from nothing is a great work of God; it is an equally great work to justify a sinner. This can never happen apart from Christ who is our righteousness, that is, when his conception, birth, death and resurrection occurs in us. Christ says: whoever wants to be my disciple must follow me, and again, without me you can do nothing (Luke 9[?], 14[?]; John 15[:5]). Peter says: "Whoever has suffered in the flesh has finished with sin" [1 Pet. 4:1]. The first light was our taskmaster in preparation for the second light which is Christ, the light of the world. When his Spirit enters me I am no longer under the taskmaster but under grace. It is the end of the law of works, sins, death and the flesh,[22] and the beginning of the law of the Spirit, faith and life or desire. But this Spirit is given only to those who have first surrendered to the cross and discipline of the Lord (Prov. 1[?]; Heb. 12[:6]). One has to trim a particular branch off a tree before another can be grafted in (Luke 14[?]; Matt. 10[?]).[23] Even God in his omnipotence cannot make me blessed without the cross. Blessedness and God itself it is to love nothing except God alone, and to seek joy and comfort, security and life in the one God alone, and to seek none of these in the creatures.[24] If God gives me comfort, pleasure, joy and love in him, and also allows me to enjoy the love, comfort, pleasure and delight of the creatures, he would charge me with marital unfaithfulness because I loved something beside him. But God cannot allow this double love. It is not possible for him to be God and at the same time despise himself. In fact, he is a jealous God who does not give his glory to another. In the same way, the more a husband loves his wife, the less he would force her into unfaithfulness, and she certainly does not desire it from him. If we used to love the creatures and are now to love them no longer, God has no alternative but to trim off the branches, that is to say, to deprive us of the creatures, transfer us naked and exposed into the second birth, give us his Spirit, and teach us to know and love him. This cannot take place without pain, suffering and fear. It is not that God loves our suffering, but he tolerates and puts up with it as a physician puts up with the stench of a sick person when he treats him.

This suffering and pain has its source in our unbelief alone. Our unbelief tortures us before it departs. It is like a man who clings to a woman who is not his wife. She abandons him and he experiences pain. However, no one is torturing him except the unchaste, illegitimate love he has for her. When, therefore, God sends us the loss of wife, children, father, mother, brothers, sisters, property, money, or health in life and limb, what alone tortures us is our refusal to believe firmly that it is for our good and that something better is awaiting us in the future. It is as Christ says: "Everyone who has left houses, brothers, sisters, father, mother, children or fields for my name's sake, will receive a hundredfold and will inherit eternal life" (Matt. 19[:29]).

An even greater form of unbelief that tortures us are the godless thoughts that invade us such as "Yes, but God will forget me. He will not remain faithful and trusting. He is a respecter of persons and won't help me as he helps others." Truly foolish is the unbelief that says: "If I commit myself to God, I will never be secure. I will perish. If I depend on the world I am more safe and won't perish so miserably." Other thoughts: "If I become or remain a Christian, God will perhaps not sustain me. However, if I become or remain a heathen I could easily sustain myself. Or, if I become a Christian my children will die of hunger, but if I don't they will survive." To all of which I respond: clearly you are not yet a Christian but a bad heathen, and you will suffer pain until unbelief is separated from faith. What is needed is a good smelting-house, a strong ordeal, some sharp nitric acid, for an uncrucified Christian is like untested ore or like a house whose boards are still uncut trees.[25] Nothing keeps us from the love of God except that we do not know him. For since he is the greatest good, it would be impossible not to love God alone and above all things, if only one knew him. Indeed, whoever truly knows God begins so to love him that from now on it is no longer possible to love anything else beside even if ordered to do so by threat of eternal damnation. Yes, and if I knew God truly my spirit and soul would be so jubilant that the inward joy would surge into my body so that even my body would be completely insensible, impassible, immortal and glorified. When a person has been purified from love of all creatures and of life itself God will [bring about this change] by means of the sleep of the saints until the resurrection of the dead (1 Pet. 1[:3]).[26] But we cannot know God unless the cover or net which is the creature, and which hides the divine light in us, be first removed (Heb. 11[?]). The more the creature is withdrawn from us for Christ's sake, the more the light and Word of God shines forth. Whoever submits to God under the cross is a child of God (2 Cor. 1[:3-7]). But even that is not enough: there must be separation from all who will not submit to Christ and keeping of love and communion with all who have surrendered themselves to God. These are the neighbours with whom all the gifts of God must be held in common be it teaching, skill, goods, money or whatever. Whatever God has entrusted must be invested for the common good as we have received it in the articles of our faith and everywhere in Scripture, especially in the work of the twelve apostles (Acts 2, 4, 5). Thirdly, one is also committed to brotherly discipline according to the article of faith which speaks of the forgiveness of sins(Matt. 18[:15-20]; Rom. 12[:20-21]). Whoever has not been loosed [from sin] nor admitted by the Christian congregation, that one is also not admitted in heaven (1 Cor. 5[:3-5], 12[?], 16[:1-4]). John says: "Whoever does not love the brother whom he has seen, how can he love God whom he has not seen" [1 John 4:20]?

The Lord says: "By this everyone will know that you are my disciples, if you have love for one another" John 13[:35]. The second grace is the cross. Whoever prays for this grace prays for the cross. Those who pray this prayer, pray it in the name of Christ. However, the heathen, that is, the nominal Christians, write the name Christ on a slip of paper and use it to pray with.[27] They have never yet come to Christ. Christians truthfully say "I believe in Jesus Christ, our Lord." The heathen have another lord. For whenever one speaks to them of the truth they reply that their lords have forbidden it. Asked who their lords are they say the one from Austria or Bavaria. My response to that is: "Why are you lying to God when you say 'I believe in Jesus Christ our Lord?'" Paul rightly says: "No one can submit himself to Christ as Lord except through the Holy Spirit" (1 Cor. 12[:3]). Further he says: "Whoever does not have the Spirit of Christ does not belong to him"(Rom. 8[:9]), that is, he is no Christian. The Lord himself shows us those who truly pray when he says: "God is spirit and those who worship him must worship him in spirit and in truth" [John 4:24]. Therefore, all those who have not yet surrendered life and all that is theirs to the cross of Christ and the communion of the saints, and who have not been loosed from their sins by a Christian congregation are from the devil and the Antichrist (1 John 4[:3]). They blaspheme, reproach, curse, and mock God our creator as often as they open their mouth and imagine that they are praying. But God wants only worshippers in spirit and truth. But they, the heathen or nominal Christians pray without the Spirit and in untruth or the lie. For their father, the devil, is a liar from the beginning and does not stand in the truth [John 8:44].

How the Heathen or Nominal Christians Pray

A brief discussion of their blaspheming prayer will help you to understand better what I mean. It is also a warning to beware of them so that you don't forget yourselves and ask them to pray to God for you for they are unable to pray except in the Spirit. They would blaspheme and mock God for you, and you would become guilty of their wickedness. So take care.

They say: **Our Father** in mocking fashion for they have not even begun to be his children. They do not want to be his children, and have never obeyed him. Like the Jews, they place a crown on Christ's head, put a sceptre in his hand, clothe him in a purple gown and say: Hail, king of the Jews! but certainly do not want him to be king. God is not pleased with such praying. Then they say: **in heaven**, but they are glad to leave heaven to God as long as he allows them their earthly pleasures. They say: **Hallowed be your name**, but spit in his eyes and face, for they are the first to blaspheme his name. It is true; if their prayer were not a mockery they would step out and become angry when they heard God's name being blasphemed and spoken against. Sad to say, no devil's or human name is reviled like the most highly revered name of God. No teaching of monks, priests, nuns and other knaves has after their death been so denounced, dominated, and forbidden as today the teaching of Christ is forbidden. Christ's teaching is called heresy, seduction and rebellion, so that edicts and mandates against it are sent out from the emperor into every nook and cranny. Here run the postmen, there the hangmen, the judge and the jailer arrive, here is the exorcist, there a company of cavalry, and a betrayer is in every house. And even those who don't want to betray, talk about it so openly that the brothers of Christ are scattered and killed. Those who don't want to malign it also say nothing good and excuse themselves: I don't do it gladly, but I need to make sure that I don't earn the displeasure of the king for I am innocent. Yes, just like Pilate! Here comes another, steps up and says: certainly God's Word should not be blasphemed or forbidden, for one must obey God rather than men. But they are afraid that they will be denounced with Christ. Thus when they are called to hallow his name they run and hide so that no one will hear it or suspect them. To this the Lord says: Whoever denies me before others, him I will deny before my father in heaven (Matt. 10[:33]). Paul says that one must confess with the mouth [Rom. 10:9]. But the true Christians and children of God, when they pray, step out with act and word and witness with their blood that one should obey God more than men.

When they pray: **your kingdom come**, Christ answers them: "My kingdom is not from this world [John 18:36]. But they want both kingdoms. They cajole God as an adulteress who wheedles her husband to lie on her left side and allow her lover to lie on the right in the same bed.

Again, they say: **your will be done on earth as in heaven**, but at the same time without interruption they act against God according to the desires of their flesh and blood, their evil heart, their godless neighbours.

They pray: **give us today our daily bread**. But as soon as God gives it to them it is no longer ours, but mine. And today is not enough but they worry about the next day against God's command when he commanded not to be concerned about the next day [Matt. 6:41]. They, however, are worried not only about the next day but about the whole year, and not only about one year but about ten, twenty or thirty years. They are anxious not only for themselves but for their children not only as youth but as adults, how to make a profitable marriage. And when they pray that they may have the bread of the soul, the Word of God, today, and God then gives it to them, it comes too early for them; they will get it at their convenience, and in any case it must always be a new teaching.

Even as they pray with their mouth: **forgive us our offences as we forgive those who offend against us**, they nurture vengeance in their hearts against those who have offended them, although the Lord said: "If someone strikes you on one cheek, offer him the other as well, and if someone quarrels with you about your coat, give him your cloak as well. And if someone compels you to go one mile with him, go with him two" [Matt. 5:39-41]. Paul says: do not complain before the judges but suffer injury patiently [1 Cor. 6:7]. They will have none of it but mock God by saying that he may act in the same way towards them.

Lead us not into temptation. They see that the whole world draws them away from God and tempts them. Nevertheless, they greedily run after it, never have enough, run ever deeper into sin and pray that God will deliver them. **But deliver us from evil.** Whatever keeps us from God is evil, but they desire everything that is against God. **Amen.** With this word Amen they confirm their lies and blasphemy. If perchance they had not sufficiently despised God with their pretty prayers, they complete it with this word Amen. Therefore, dear brothers and sisters in the Lord, we learn clearly that no Christian should ask a heathen: pray to God for me.[28]

The Third Grace

Now I will tell you about the third grace which no one may receive unless the first and second grace have been received first. Many people go astray by starting with the last grace without the first two. The Lord speaks plainly in the parable of the man who went down to Jericho and fell among murderers who left him half dead. A priest came along who had no mercy on the sick man, and likewise an evangelical.[29] But a simple Samaritan came to his aid and poured oil and wine into his wounds, etc. To this point I have spoken about the wine. Now I will speak about the oil of joy. Concerning this oil St. John says: "You have the anointing from him who is holy and you know all things. I did not write you as though you did not know the truth. You know it and you also know that no lie comes from the truth," etc. A little further on he says: "The anointing which you have received from God remains with you, and you have no need for someone to teach you. What the anointing teaches you is the truth and no lie. Remain in what the anointing has taught you" [1 John 2:27]. About this oil the Lord says: "The comforter, the Holy Spirit, whom my Father will send you in my name, the same will teach you all things and remind you of everything I have said to you" [John 14:26]. This oil is the Holy Spirit.

He cannot teach anyone who has not first despaired of all human comfort and wisdom, and has raised the heart to God alone. He comforts and strengthens no one who has not first been terrified [over the soul's condition] and alienated from all human comfort and strength. That is why the Lord says that you should not be called master. But the master Christ receives no one as a learner or disciple who does not reject and hate all that he has and follow him and daily bear his cross. One must hope for the comfort of the Lord and sit still. The Scriptures tell us in many places, especially in the Psalms, the prophets, in Isaiah and the Lamentations of Jeremiah that the whole strength of Christians consists of being still. It is in not giving up in discouragement, but to be patient and thus to await the comfort of the Holy Spirit amid the greatest desolation and misery. This is the true infirmity about which Scripture and especially Paul writes: "When I am infirm, then I am strong" [2 Cor. 12:10]. He also says that even as the suffering of Christ flows over us so does the comfort through Christ. This is the meaning of Christ's words: "A little while and you will see me, and again a little while and you will not see me" [John 16:16]. When the apostles asked him what he meant he answered them: "Very truly, I tell you, you will weep and mourn, but the world will rejoice" [John 16:20]. "Those who kill you will think that by doing so they are serving God" [John 16:2]. [Here follow citations from John 14-16]. "I will not leave you orphaned; I am coming to you" [John 14:18]. The life of the world has a happy beginning and an eternal mournful end. Our life has a mournful beginning, but then the Holy Spirit comes soon and anoints us with the oil of joy unspeakable. It is not a matter of solitary waiting for the comfort of God, but a Christian should and is able to encourage others and give comfort in tribulation. God speaks through Isaiah: "Comfort, comfort my people, says your God. Speak tenderly to Jerusalem and cry to her" [Isa. 40:1]. James also speaks about this oil: "Any who are sick should call for the elders of the church and have them pray over them, anointing them with oil in the name of the Lord. The prayer of faith will save the sick, and the Lord will raise them up; and anyone who has committed sins will be forgiven" [James 5:14-15]. James is not referring to olive oil here. The elect saints who in these days at Salzburg and other places praised God with their holy martyrdom could have bathed in bathtubs full of olive oil and would still not necessarily have remained constant in their faith. But the comfort of the Holy Spirit made their torment bearable. This is the oil of anointing which the apostles used and also we today.

6

Hans Schlaffer

A Brief Instruction for the Beginning of a Truly Christian Life & Confession and Defence (1528)*

Introduction

The Hutterite Chronicle calls Hans Schlaffer a "highly gifted man." He entered the priesthood in 1511 and served in Upper Austria until 1526, when he resigned his office. The influence of Luther brought about his resignation, leading Schlaffer to denounce his priesthood, claiming that it was the estate of false prophets.

The chronology of his life following his departure from the priesthood is not known for certain; he seems to have come into contact with Anabaptists shortly after, most likely with Hans Hut or one of Hut's followers. Whether Hut baptized him is unknown. The Anabaptist congregation at Freistadt relied on him heavily, but he was never their pastoral leader, as Schiemer had been for the congregation at Rattenberg. Schlaffer was at Nicholsburg in 1527 and witnessed the dispute between Balthasar Hubmaier and Hans Hut; he may have been

---

*Source: Müller, *Glaubenszeugnisse*, 85-94.
Translation: Walter Klaassen

converted to Hut's ideas at that point. It is apparent that Schlaffer followed Hut's line of thought for the rest of his short ministry. His main ideas are taken from Hut, often verbatim.[1]

Freistadt soon became unsafe for Schlaffer and so he wandered from one place to another, through Bavaria to Augsburg, where he may have been present at the Martyr's Synod. He then travelled to Nuremberg where he met with Hans Denck and Ludwig Hätzer in September of 1527. From Nuremberg he travelled to Regensburg where he met with two more Anabaptist leaders, Oswald Glaidt and Wolfgang Brandhuber. From Regensburg he travelled to the Tyrol, where he was arrested at an Anabaptist meeting in the mining town of Schwaz on December 5, 1527. Of Schlaffer's nine existing writings, only one, *Vom Geheimnus der Tauff* was written outside prison. All of his other writings were written during his imprisonment between December 6, 1527 and February 3, 1528.

Schlaffer's spiritualistic emphasis is similar to that of Leonard Schiemer, Ambrosius Spitelmaier, Hans Nadler and others connected with Hans Denck and Hans Hut. He believed that "suffering marks the genuine Christian in the world," and his writings are filled with similar thoughts.[2] Schlaffer believed in God reaching the ordinary person, bypassing the university-trained scriptural experts and theologians.

In *A Brief Instruction on the Christian Life*, Schlaffer reveals a gift for praying and communicating with his God.[3] He begins with a prayer and then explains the nature of the three witnesses to a true Christian and God-blessed life, namely, created things, Scripture and Christ. Common to all three is suffering. The first witness, the gospel of all Creatures, is dependent on Hut's *On the Mystery of Baptism* and his teaching on the *Gospel of all creatures*.[4] The second witness, Scripture, testifies to the suffering of the elect, which brings patience and is the mark of the chosen ones.[5] The last witness is Christ, whose example we are to follow again, into the suffering of the cross. It is in this last section that Schlaffer also talks about the three-fold baptism of believers, the baptism of Spirit, water, and fire. Of these three, water is the least important, but necessary because it is what Christ commanded. It is a public confession, to be made in adulthood, or after one's 30th birthday.[6] The covenant between God and the believer has already been made through the baptism of the Spirit, the assurance in the conscience of the grace and mercy of God for the forgiveness of all committed sins. Baptism by fire is the baptism of suffering and martyrdom.

Part B consists of three versions of Schlaffer's confession and defense. The reason for the third (part 3), which is a summary of his defenses (parts 1 and 2) is discussed at its beginning. Schlaffer informed his fellow believers (perhaps the congregation at Schwaz) that the authorities in Innsbruck had falsified his written statement (Part 1), completely changing its meaning. For that reason he wanted to inform his brethren about what he had actually written. Thus we have three different documents in which Schlaffer gives an account of the major ideas of South German Anabaptism as it had evolved at that time.[7]

Of the first two confessions, the second was done under torture, the first without. The defense of his views stated, among other things, that he sought nothing evil but only divine truth; he did not want or consider political rebellion. He also explained his rejection of infant baptism.

Ultimately the death penalty was pronounced and Schlaffer was beheaded on February 4, 1528, probably no more than 6 months after his conversion to Anabaptism. Schlaffer's trial and death received public sympathy, which concerned the authorities.[8] It was perhaps this concern that subsequently led to the execution of 19 others at the same place.

Bibliographical Sources:

Chronicle I.
Robert Friedmann, "Leonhard Schiemer and Hans Schlaffer, two Tyrolean Anabaptist martyr-apostles of 1528," *MQR* 33 (January 1959), 31-41.
Robert Friedmann, "Schlaffer, Hans," *ME IV,* 457-59.
Werner O. Packull, *Mysticism and the Early South German-Austrian Anabaptist Movement, 1525-1531* (Scottdale, PA: Herald Press, 1977).
George H. Williams, *The Radical Reformation* 3rd edition (Kirksville, MO: Sixteenth Century Journal Publishers, 1992).

A. A Brief Instruction for the Beginning of a Truly Christian Life, Written by our Beloved Brother and Witness of Jesus Christ
HANS SCHLAFFER

O Almighty and Merciful God; everyone lives in iniquity, blindness and error and the whole world exists in wickedness (1 John 5[:19]). I pray that you will deliver all good-hearted people out of this blindness and error and draw and bring them to your marvellous light. Jesus Christ alone is this light, your eternal Word and your only Son. O Lord, enlighten with this light all darkened hearts who earnestly and truthfully desire to live and walk in it. For it only is the way, the truth, and the life (John 14[:6]). Beside this light there is no other way, truth and life, but only error, falsehood, and death, no matter how brightly it shines in the world and before all people.

O Heavenly Father, grant us to know this light so that we may abandon what is wrong and take the true way against which the great number of people have striven since the beginning of the world. From among these many a little flock has accepted this way and remained steadfast in it. For it is a very narrow way and few walk on it (Matt. 7[:14]). O Lord, who would not be afraid and tremble (Joel 2[:1]) because of the amazing judgments and deeds (Isa. 58[?]) you have manifested in these last and perilous times (Zeph. 1), anxious to help the world. But alas, the world will not acknowledge it. Therefore, Eternal God, grant us your Holy Spirit who will teach the truth in our hearts that we may worship you in Spirit and in truth (John 4[:23]). Christ our Saviour himself taught us to say: Our Father in heaven. Christ taught us what all pretended Christians also mouth and confess with their hypocritical, external, and invented works but deny with their hearts and the absence of true deeds. Every true-hearted Christian, knowing this prayer, can easily see this. For if God is called Father by the world, how can he have children who love him and live a heavenly life? How can the name of God be hallowed in them, the kingdom of God come to them, and his will be done? Are they hungry for daily bread, that is the Word of God? How do they forgive each other? How are they kept from temptation to sin, and how can they desire to be delivered from evil? (Gloss: The Our Father falsely taught).

From all of this it is easy to conclude who are the true believers and proper Christians and who not. Since not everyone who says Lord, Lord, will enter the kingdom of heaven, but whoever does the will of the heavenly Father, I am certain when I say: if I had all the pretend Christians in the whole world all together, and I asked them to tell me truly if they were Christians, each one would say either I don't know, or I hope so, or I want to become one and the like. And even if someone said yes he would still not be certain of it in his heart since he felt not the least trace of Christian deeds in heart or life. To be brief, that these pretend Christians are worse than Turks or heathen they must themselves acknowledge to each other. For under the sun there is no people who so blasphemes God's name, his suffering, agony and death as these pretend Christians. They are full of terrible public vices such as adultery, fornication, drunkenness, pride, envy, quarrelling and gossip, not to mention the secret sins. Therefore you are not Christians, regardless of how you try to prove it. You are Christians only if you live according to the teaching and commandments of Christ, which are none other than the commandments of God, his Father, and if you continue in his life and follow in his footsteps. Otherwise you are worse than any other unbelieving nation on earth. May God enlighten you. Amen

Whoever desires to be a true Christian must have in himself the witness of the truth and remember that his former life and being was sinful and under condemnation in the light of the commandments of God and the teaching, life, and example of Christ and his disciples. He must remember that he harboured hostility in his heart against Jesus and opposed him in word and deed and still does. He must know that in his own strength it is impossible to act and live as a true believer or Christian should. Moses in the Law and Christ in the Gospel said that every word or truth is valid when supported by two or three witnesses. We also have three witnesses to instruct in and witness to a true Christian and God-blessed life. These are created things, Scripture and Christ.

The First Witness is Created Things

First, therefore, all things that God has created for human necessity and use witness to and teach human beings what a godly and Christian life is. For no creature has been created to live and die for itself alone, but rather to die according to the will and bidding of humans. That is why Christ commands his apostles to preach the "Gospel of all creatures."[9] Christ himself, in his time, taught mainly by means of created things and parables, among them trees, vineyards, fields, seed, dough, bread, fish, weights, oil, lamps, clothing and many others. He did not teach at all without parables.

Without doubt, Jesus' disciples taught the Gospel in the same way as Paul, who had become a servant of the Gospel, said. It has to be done in the same way today. An example: a chicken or a fish or another animal which you plan to eat cannot of its own will be what it must be according to your bidding and will. It cannot kill, remove its feathers and prepare itself for cooking or frying. You have to do it; it must suffer your will. You must turn it into what it must be;[10] the creature can do nothing towards it. It has to surrender and suffer your will and action. It is in its best state for you when it is most contemptible, that is, when you chew it and swallow it. The same thing can be observed and learned from other created things everywhere. Consider what wine and bread have to suffer before you can use or eat them. If we use the created things only to fill our bellies and the nurture this fetid bag of sin, we should be no better than Turks or heathen. Indeed, we would be like the unreasonable animals, as David says. Another parable is a field. If it is covered with grass, thistles, and thorns, it can't be sowed on, as the prophet says (Jer. ?). Notice what work the field must suffer before it is ready for the seed. Again, an ungrafted wild tree will yield only wild fruit. If we expect good fruit from it, it must be slashed, all its branches cut off down to a stump, and a new branch grafted on. Further, no one tills someone else's field, and no one will graft a tree in another's garden without permission, as the prophet says.

Before we come to understanding and are able to distinguish between good and evil we are all by nature and manner a bad tree and can never make ourselves good even as a field cannot till itself nor a tree graft itself; a farmer or a gardener has to do it. Likewise God alone can make us devout, just and useful to his praise, and we have to endure his work and discipline patiently and keep still as the field for the farmer and the tree for the gardener (Prov. 1[:23], 3[:11], 5[:12]). God himself says: Return to me that I may give you my spirit. Learn my words for that is the good seed on the field and the good branch on the tree (Isa. 65[?]; Jer. 7[?]; Hos. 6[?]). Since, however, we are the field of a stranger and growing in someone else's garden, God does not want to sow his seed in us nor graft his branches in us. He will do that only for the one who surrenders all possessions (Matt. 16[:24-26], 19[:21]). Otherwise one cannot be a disciple of Christ (Luke 9[:23-25], 14[:33]). This is what it means to teach and preach the gospel of all creatures as the

Lord commands (Matt. 28[:19-20]). (This is the power and the will of God and his divine work, to save us by grace and mercy through faith in Christ). The created things (Mark 16[:15]) are God's book and living text which everyone can read and understand so that on the day of judgment there can be no excuse before the Lord.

That is why Job says: "Speak to the earth and she will answer you. Ask the animals and they will answer you, the birds of the air and the fish in the sea will show you" (Job 17[12:7-8]). Paul says that "God's invisible nature, that is, his eternal power and divine nature, have been understood and seen through the things he has made from the creation of the world." He goes on to say: "So they are without excuse, for though they knew that God is, they did not honour or praise him, nor give him thanks as God, but they became futile in their thinking and their ignorant hearts were darkened. Claiming to be wise they became fools" (Rom. 1[:20-22]). Elsewhere Paul says that "the invisible things are known by what is visible" (Heb. 11[:3]).

Here we can clearly see how we should understand the creation and all the creatures of God. From those that are visible we see what is invisible, namely God's power and wisdom and work which he, and not we ourselves, performs in us. He justifies, sanctifies and makes us fit for his honour and the glory of his kingdom through his Son Jesus Christ.

Accordingly, all things such as eating, drinking, sleeping, waking, getting dressed and undressed, all that is done and left undone, personally and with others, are clean for the Christian. For in all things the Christian seeks not his own will but God's only, so that at all times there is a willing readiness to be subject to God's will and patiently to submit to it. In the same way all the things that are necessary to life must patiently suffer the Christian's will, although unwillingly because the creation is subject to futility. That is why the creation is afraid and yearns and waits for the liberation of the children of God in hope, as Paul says (Rom. 8[:20-21]). Human flesh is resistant to the Spirit. However, there is no condemnation in those who belong to Christ. For they live not after the flesh but according to the Spirit. That means that the flesh does not govern them but rather the Spirit. The Spirit [in the believer] employs all created things, sees in them the work of God, and is always ready and willing to submit to the Lord. Such a person understands the gospel of all creatures and is called to preach it. There is no need here for intellectual brilliance nor vaulting wisdom; only a simple, obedient, unselfish and humble heart (Ps. 51[:17]). Such a heart God accepts, as the Scriptures witness in many places (Luke 1[:48]).

Much more could be written about the created things. However, I hope that every person of goodwill who desires Christian truth and a godly life will consider the matter diligently and more deeply than I have done here.

The Second Witness is Scripture

Let us now listen to the second witness, the Scriptures.
The whole of Scripture everywhere testifies to the suffering of the elect from Abel down to the apostles (Matt. 23[:35]). That is what is meant when it says that the Lamb was slain from the foundation of the world (Rev. 13[:8]).

Let us consider, therefore, how our fathers Abraham, Isaac, Jacob and others attained salvation (Judg. 8[:18-23]). They struggled to attain faith through much tribulation. We read of the great persecution endured by Elijah, Jeremiah and others from their own fellow believers (that is the Jews), and were even killed by them as Jesus told his listeners in the Gospel (Matt. 23[:29-35]). Especially important here is the 11th chapter of Hebrews where the apostle surveys practically the whole Scripture and describes what the saints suffered and how they overcame through faith.

Paul says that everything that is written is written for our instruction so that through the patience and comfort of the Scriptures we might have hope. Suffering brings patience since all Scripture speaks only about suffering. Patience without suffering is not patience even as fire is not fire without heat and light. Comfort consists in the promise of God to help and rescue his saints from suffering for which there is much Scripture (Ps. 91[:14]). I will be with them, says the Lord, to rescue them from all tribulation and to honour them.

Likewise, God is near to all afflicted hearts, and those of a humble spirit he will save.

Christ says: "Blessed are those who mourn, for they shall be comforted" (Matt. 5[:4]), and "Woe to you who laugh now, for you will howl and weep." Similarly he says, In the world you will have fear, but in me peace. The world will rejoice and you will mourn, but your sorrow will turn into peace, and no one will take that peace from you (John 16[:20-22]). Through much anxiety and sadness we will enter the kingdom of heaven (Acts 14[:23]), for very child which the Father loves he disciplines (Prov. 3[:12]). Whoever is without discipline is a bastard and inherits nothing (Heb. 12[:8]). Search all the epistles of Paul, Peter, and James, and you will read about the sufferings of Christians, and in the book of Revelation of John, which alone speaks of the last times we read: here is the patience of the believers and the saints. Here are those who keep the commandments of God and the faith in Jesus.

By the mercy of God I admonish every sincere Christian (a proper Christian knows it already) to look to Scripture where the Lord himself distinguishes the true from the false Christians (Matt. 24[:31]; Mark 13[:27]; Luke 21[:27]).

Being a true Christian has nothing to do with fur coats, long gowns and hats,[11] good eating and drinking and idleness, honoured sir, highly learned father,[12] beautiful salons, tall houses, warm rooms, gentle brother on your pillow or feather mattress. Poor blind crew! That is not the way it is. I say it without envy as God is my witness; within a very short time you will know it with much greater sorrow and suffering than the pleasure and happiness you have had. I would like to know which way you will look then and where you will find your comfort. Now you are haughty and blind, and pretend to be leaders of the blind. But should not one of your own kind, who knows all about you, who to his own loss himself learned and experienced it, leave you alone and unscathed? Yes indeed, you have already lost part of the game; you understand me well enough, right? The pay-off is on the other, the left side,[13] but not everywhere. Enough, there are already too many words. I repeat, Scripture can never be abolished. It will be fulfilled in whole and in every part, in the members as well as the head, who is Christ.[14]

The Third Witness is Christ,

who has himself said that his life is an example for us according to which we are to live and walk, everyone according to his measure, as Peter said: "Christ has suffered for us and left us a likeness or an example that we should follow in his steps" (1 Pet. 2[:21]). He continues: since Christ has suffered in the flesh for us, arm yourselves with the same mind, for whoever has suffered in the flesh has finished with sin so as to live for the rest of your earthly life no longer by human desires but by the will of God. For it is quite enough that we lived in a heathen way in our past life in licentiousness, passions, drunkenness, revels, carousing, and lawless idolatry. They are surprised that you no longer join with them in the excesses of disorderly living and so they curse you. But they will have to give account to him who is ready to judge the living and the dead.

It should be easy, for God's sake, to tell from these words of Peter who is a Christian and who not. For whoever has been burdened down with the vices of lewdness, gluttony, drunkenness, blasphemers, and idolatry (Paul recalls avarice a service of idolatry, Eph. 5[:5]) in the world for a long time and still is, such a one is not a Christian, says Peter. It is a common saying that the devil has knocked out their bottoms. Paul says likewise that no one should be able to charge you with fornication, uncleanness and greed. That should be obvious for the saints, that is, all Christians. Shameful words, foolish behaviour, and levity that produces no good but rather vexation, and which cannot be reconciled with Christian living, must be avoided. Instead give thanks. For you must know that no fornicator or unclean or greedy person will inherit the kingdom of God.

Those however, are Christians, who have the mind of Christ as Paul writes (Phil. 2[:5]). They prepare themselves to suffer, have nothing to do with the disorder of the world, have no fellowship with the works of darkness but rather with the works of light (Rom. 13[:12]), are not ashamed of their master Christ and of his words (John 13[Mark 8:38]), and [are prepared] to follow him, each in the measure of grace given for it. Therefore also he will not be ashamed of them before God his heavenly Father and all his angels as he himself says (Matt. 16[Luke 9:26]), and then goes on: "Whoever loves his life will lose it, but whoever hates and loses his life in this world for my sake, will save it for eternal life" (Mark 8[:35]; Luke 9[:24], 14[:11?]). Whoever desires to serve me must follow me, and wherever I am, there shall my servant also be. Whoever serves me will be honoured by my Father (John 12[:26]). If anyone wants to be my follower, says the Lord, let him take up his cross daily and follow me (Luke 9[:23]).

To sum up, a follower of Christ is a Christian. Nothing can change that, even though the whole world should shatter and end, which will certainly happen, and, I venture to say, very soon (2 Pet. 3[:10]). For a thousand years are before God as one day, says Peter. For this reason Christians lift up their heads and await their liberation with joy. This will happen when Christ returns to judge the living and the dead (Ezek. 12[:23, :28]).

A goodhearted person is one whom the Father draws. He wants everyone to be saved for he teaches and witnesses to them all. If such a person has been witnessed to in truth by all creatures, the Scriptures of Christ and his teaching, life and example, finds in his heart and is certain that this and no other is the way to salvation, to such a one the gospel of all the creatures has been preached. He is taught and made into a disciple. In the name of Christ repentance and forgives of sins has been proclaimed to him (Luke 24[:47]) provided that he surrenders himself with his whole heart and believes Christ. The Lord says: "Whoever believes" (Mark 16[:15]). This faith is also a work of God in a person. Through this faith God makes a covenant with a person and that person with God. God himself says: Henceforth I will be your God and you my son or daughter, my servant, man or woman together with all my elect sons and daughters who keep my commandments, live and walk according to my will, all of which is written in Moses and the prophets. This is not the old covenant which he made with the Jews who were his people then (Deut. 26). The old covenant, confirmed with the blood of a ram, is only a figure of the new which is a true covenant as Jeremiah says (Jer. 24[:7], 31[:31-34]). Christ himself calls it the new testament in his blood which is shed for the forgiveness of sins (Heb. 8[:8-13]). It is impossible to say too much in words about this new testament. For it only is the work of the Spirit in the human heart and is at the same time the baptism of Spirit and fire with which Christ baptizes. What a holy and blessed covenant it is! It is eternal which no mortal man is able to grant or prevent. Only God through his only Son Christ has that power and orders it through his servants who are not chosen by men but by him. David says: "Gather to me my faithful ones, who look to my covenant rather than to sacrifice" (Ps. 49[:50]).[15] Christ himself confirms it all for his disciples irrespective of the permission of the worldly powers such as emperors, kings, or princes, in the passages mentioned above. This covenant is not against them but rather for them, but their power concerns not the souls but the body and property only. Christ is the only lord in his kingdom and will remain so for ever. Here there is no respect of persons.

For the same reason Christ did not seek permission from the emperor in Rome or his governors in Syria nor the apostles from the kings and lords of the lands in which they preached. If they had tried to gain it, it would not have been given them. They would simply have participated in the same thing with their Lord. The proven and biblical Scriptures do not tell us much about that, since it is as impossible for a rich man to enter the kingdom of heaven as it is for a camel to go through the eye of a needle (Matt. 19[:24]). But what is humanly impossible is possible with God. O that God would grant all rulers [to know] how all true Christians honoured them; they would certainly heartily desire that, if it were possible, all their subjects would be Christians. But I am afraid they do not believe it. Nevertheless, the day of the Lord will reveal all things, for nothing is so hidden or secret that it will not be made known. I could go on here to a discussion of the covenant between God and the believer, but it would be too much. Briefly, I understand this covenant to be nothing other than the baptism of Christ in the Spirit and with fire as described above.

Spirit is the assurance in the conscience of the grace and mercy of God for the forgiveness of all committed sins no matter how great or how many, for Christ has taken them all away and annulled them. The Spirit of God witnesses to our spirits that we are the children of God. By this Spirit we can address God as Abba, dear Father. Whoever does not have the Spirit of Christ is no Christian (Rom. 8[:15-16, 9]).

The fire is the ardour of the love of God and the neighbour in the heart. It enables him to suffer whatever befalls him because of the witness to God's truth, including death. Nothing can turn such a believer from the witness of the truth in the heart. This fiery love of God overflows towards the neighbour, that is, the brothers and sisters, not only with words but with deed and truth. Such goodwill is given also to enemies and evildoers (Matt. 5[:44]), for Christ himself teaches us and says: "By this everyone will know that you are my disciples, if you have love for one another" (John 13[:35]). Paul writes that love does no evil, does not commit adultery or unchastity, does not scold nor give false witness, nor commit any other kind of wrong (Rom. 13[:8-10]). The worldly Christians do such things. Enough has been said about faith, covenant and the inner baptism of Christ.

We go on now to speak about what the Lord says about how to baptize those who believe or have already believed in the past. In Matthew he says baptize them, understand well, those whom you have taught, in the name of the Father, the Son, and the Holy Spirit (Mark 16[:16]; Matt. 28[:18-20]). This is said about water baptism or the external sign. This is for all of us the least important part of baptism but [the part] about which the world is most resentful.

Take note, please, why this water baptism is important for us. In the first place we observe it because Christ instituted and commanded this order, that is, first to preach and teach, secondly to believe, and thirdly to baptize.

Observe first, how strictly God has forbidden not to add or take anything away from his Word and not to pervert it (Deut. 4[:2], 12[:32]). So important are to us the words of Christ, for he is himself the eternal Word of God, and his Word is the very Word of the Father. Heaven and earth will pass away but not his Word (Matt. 24[:35]). That is why we will not alter it or pervert it but accept the commandment and remain in his order. In his grace he has restored our understanding to us regardless of what popes, Fathers, and Councils have ordered and agreed upon. For it is safer and more certain to build on Christ and his teaching than to depend on Fathers and Councils. After all, Christ the Lord (Matt. 25[:31]; 1 Cor. 15[:25]) and not popes, Fathers and Councils will be the judge on the Last Day. Nor is old custom of any avail[16] since Christ and his Word are still older, that is, he is God's Son from eternity and will be in eternity.

Second, we believe that water baptism should be given after the knowledge of and faith in Christ because Christ himself received baptism from John the Baptist for the first time in the thirtieth year of his life (Matt. 3[:13-15]; Mark 1[:9]). After that he was led into the wilderness by the Spirit to be assaulted by the devil whom he also overcame (Luke 3[:21-23]). All this is a great mystery. A Christian life is not child's play. It must be marked by much resolution, truth, courage, and holiness. No external gentility or pleasant pastime as the whole world thinks will count for anything.

Thirdly, water baptism is a sign by which Christians make themselves known to each other by public confession. By this each of them will be prepared to give Christian, brotherly love to each other following the command of Christ. This involves teaching, admonishing, disciplining, excluding, binding, loosing and the like. This is not the least that Christians should do but the most necessary if the church, congregation or gathering of Christ is to remain the virgin and bride of her bridegroom without spot or wrinkle (Matt. 25[:1-13]), and also a holy mother and whatever other names she is called in Scripture. Or else, how has Christ cleansed and sanctified her with his blood if she does not live a spotless and holy life before God with each other and publicly before the world?

Not in any way do we bind salvation to external baptism, for Christ says: Whoever does not believe is condemned. He totally omits baptism. Everyone can read in the book of Acts that Peter, when he preached to the gentiles, witnessing to Christ and proving it with Scripture, all who heard the word and believed it, received the Holy Spirit; only later were they baptized (Acts 10[:44-48]). In this book there is instruction enough concerning external water baptism for anyone who desires it (Acts 8, 10, 19). However, I am afraid that those who are obligated to learn these things have already received their sentence as the Lord and also Isaiah say.

The third baptism, which is the result of water baptism, is the baptism of blood. The Lord speaks about this: "I have a baptism with which to be baptized, and how afraid I am until it is completed" (Luke 12[:50]). He means the baptism of suffering and shedding of his blood. And now he asks his disciples if they desire to be baptized with that same baptism?(Matt. 20[:22]). Here he offers them his suffering. For there are three that give witness on earth by which a person is known,[17] namely Spirit, water, and blood (1 John 5[:8]). These three are one, since there is only one faith, one baptism, one God and Father of us all and of our Lord Jesus Christ (Eph. 4[:5-6]).

To sum up: Since in this last and dangerous time God has raised up again a visible, holy, Christian assembly through his Son Christ, he also expects that this church should become manifest before the world through the external sign of baptism. True to form, the world rages and raves and itself does not know why. It is because God will begin his judgment with his own house. All the writings of the prophets, Christ, and the apostles will be fulfilled and completed first in his own house, and then in the whole world which will not acknowledge the fatherly and faithful visitation of its creator. Therefore she will suffer another judgment and penalty eternally. From which may God protect all those who humble themselves under his mighty hand and suffer patiently the fatherly discipline through Jesus Christ his Son, our Lord. Amen.

May everyone repent and be baptized in the name of Jesus for the forgiveness of sins, and you will receive the gift of the Holy Spirit.

Written in my bondage in Schwaz the 19th day of December, 1527.

Hans Schlaffer.

B. Confession and Defence of Hans Schlaffer Given Twice to the Government and Authority in Innsbruck. How he began to believe and the reason for his baptism.

This First Defence Made in Writing

PART 1

According to Holy Scripture and prophetic preaching Christ Jesus, the Son of the true and living God, came into the world for this reason alone: to be born true man in time from the Virgin Mary, without human seed but through the power of the Holy Spirit; to live on earth, giving us an example for life and teaching which was pleasing to God the Father, so that all who would trust and have faith in him would not be condemned but be saved. For all eternity no way, truth, and life will be found outside this teaching and life of Christ. Our high priest Jesus Christ is the only sufficient sacrifice offered up for the sins of the world. Through him God the Father has established an eternal covenant with his faithful ones.

This Jesus is the true Christ or Saviour and there will be no other, as the Jews continue to hope. He has confirmed this with his own blood and in his suffering and death for our sins. This was in part fulfilled in the writings of the prophets. He is the head of his holy church or body, of which every Christian is a member according to his measure, and all together one body. This body increases daily and must so increase to the end of the world (Matt. 24; Mark 13; Luke 21) when it will develop to its highest and most complete state as at the beginning of Christianity.[18] This healing teaching and life of Christ is called the gospel in Holy Scripture. Christ has chosen or separated disciples or apostles, the evangelists, to teach and preach this gospel as will be shown in what follows.

To begin with Christ says: All authority in heaven and on earth is given to me. Therefore go and teach all nations and baptize those who have been taught in the name of the Father, the Son, and the Holy Spirit, and teach them to observe everything I have commanded you. And remember, I will be with you to the end of the world (Matt. 29[:18-20]).

Second, Christ says: Go into the whole world and preach the gospel of all creatures.[19] Whoever believes and is baptized will be saved. Whoever does not believe will be condemned. The Lord says that it is written that Christ had to suffer and rise from the dead on the third day, and that repentance and the forgiveness of sins should be preached to all nations (Luke 24[:46-47]).

Let me now state it clearly with an oath as Paul did; God is my witness. Since much has been written and spoken concerning the gospel and faith in Christ everywhere in the world, I carefully considered all this for a considerable time in my conscience. I considered my own evil life and of the whole world, and how far we had departed from the true teaching and life of Christ and his holy apostles. But in none of the parties[20] was there any improvement. Rather things only got worse. Little needs to be said about this to those who know, and for impenitent Christians it does no good.

So I was moved and led to consider these matters much more fundamentally. There can be no flaw or incompleteness in the teaching and life of Christ. It is not enough to talk or know or study much about it since, as Paul says, the kingdom of God is not a matter of words but rather of deeds. Christ himself says that whoever does it and teaches it will be great in the kingdom of heaven (Matt. 5[:19]). Consequently, I decided not to be persuaded by the various interpretations,[21] but to take up Holy Scripture myself and to consider the Scriptures mentioned above in which can be found the beginning and basis of Christian living. I continually and fervently called upon God for the sake of the name of Jesus Christ that he would remind me of the truth in my heart through his Spirit. After teaching comes baptism and the keeping of the commandments as Scripture says.[22] He will remain with his own until the end of the world, but remember, through his Spirit, for whoever does not have the Spirit of Christ, says Paul, does not belong to Christ (Rom. 8[:9-10]). It means that he is no Christian. The fruit people bear will reveal whether they have the Spirit of Christ or not. By its fruits one can tell whether a tree is good or bad.

Christ commands in the Gospel of Mark, first chapter, to preach the gospel of all creatures.[23] I am afraid that very few understand what it means to preach the gospel of all the creatures. Paul says that the gospel whose servant he became was preached with or in all creatures under heaven [Col. 1:23]. It would take too long to write about all this but I am ready to speak about it to any who wishes to know.

The second point is that the person who hears believes the preached Gospel; the Lord says whoever believes, that means believes the Gospel about Christ which is preached. Someone may ask: where does faith come from? Paul answers and says that faith comes from hearing and hearing through the Word of God.

Third he says, "and who is baptized . . ." Certainly, we all have been baptized, but no one has known before baptism in truth what Christ's Gospel, his teaching and life is. Christ established the order: first preaching or teaching, then faith, and thirdly baptizing.

Now consider, for God's sake, the perverted order.[24] Baptism is first. I will let everyone judge how the teaching is done and how people believe and become disciples or how they love each other. Christ says: The world will know that you are my disciples if you love one another. John also says that Christ gave his life for us, and that we, too, should give our lives for our sisters and brothers. It is easy to see how what Christ taught and commanded is being observed. To sum up, Christ is Christ, today, yesterday, tomorrow, and in eternity. He is the only redeemer and saviour before ever his truth is taught. Similarly his teaching and salvation is true before there is any baptism. If Christ is not there all other teaching is of no avail, and if there is no true teaching baptism is not true baptism. For baptism before teaching makes baptism more important than teaching and faith. After all, the Lord does say that whoever does not believe the preached gospel is condemned (Matt. 28d[Mark 16:16]).[25] He does not even mention baptism since salvation or the kingdom of God is not bound to external things (Luke 17e[:20]). Many have been saved without water baptism, for example, the children whom Herod slaughtered, the thief on the cross, etc. It follows, therefore, thirdly from the gospel of Luke where the Lord said that Christ had to suffer (Luke 24[:26]) in order that repentance and forgiveness of sin should be preached in his and not another's name. Alas, how many have until now attempted to repent of their sin but not in the name of Christ! Thus they have only fallen deeper into error and have never received remission of sin. Those who have ears let them hear and see what repentance in the name of the Lord is.

John, the forerunner and baptizer of Christ, first preached repentance and, pointing to Christ said, Behold the Lamb of God who cancels and takes away the sin of the world (John 1d[:29]). Meanwhile the whole world is mired in evil and enmity against God since they don't confess Christ as the Lord himself said. Those who desire to repent truly must deny the world, take up the cross and follow Christ. That is the repentance which those who believe must learn from God, as Christ says (John 6[:65?]).

This is how I learned how the true order of Christ's teaching has been perverted as the passages cited above say. Christ says first: All authority is given to me in heaven and on earth. Therefore go, teach all the nations and baptize them, etc (Matt. 28[:18-19]). Since Christ has all authority, why have they dared to pervert his teaching order? For first he commands that all nations ought to be taught, only then to be baptized, and finally to observe all his commandments. These are the teachings which Christ at the beginning of his preaching admonished them to observe.[26] In Luke's gospel he says that if you do not repent, you will all together perish. No one will escape the judgment of God which hangs over the whole world unless they are in Christ and Christ in them.

These and other similar considerations have moved me to submit to and humble myself under the mighty hand of God and the discipline of the eternal Father. For the external witness to this I have accepted the external sign of baptism, which is not re-baptism, for Christ has nowhere commanded children to be baptized. The reason is that the preaching of repentance and of the teaching of the gospel of Christ, who came to call sinners and not the righteous to repentance, is essential. The Lord gave us the example that we should become like children otherwise we could not enter the kingdom of heaven. For of such, he said, is the kingdom of heaven. If it is theirs already, it has not been denied them. That is why I am surprised that the devil is exorcized and expelled from newborn children. But that's what they do nowadays. If they don't remain in all things in the pure teaching of Christ, in which not a jot or tittle, that is the smallest letter, is to be changed, everything will be perverted as is only too evident. Only no one will admit the destruction.

Baptism consists of three things, spirit, water, and blood. John says in his epistle: There are three who witness, the Spirit, water and blood, and those three are one (1 John 5d[:8]). Only Christ confers the baptism of the Spirit as John the Baptist says in Luke: One is coming who is stronger than I. He will baptize with the Holy Spirit and with fire. This baptism takes place with the consent of the heart in obedience to Christ to suffer everything that is laid on us for the sake of Christ and his pure ways. Christ died and rose again so that we should from now on not live for ourselves but for Christ. For all who are baptized are baptized into the death of Christ to walk henceforth in a new life.

The baptism of water is an external sign by which the disciples and followers of Christ and his teaching are known. Wherever such baptism is available it should not be despised since Christ instituted and commanded it and received it himself in his thirtieth year (Luke 3[:21-23]; Matt. 3[:16]). Nothing that Christ has taught us and done himself is so insignificant that we cannot learn something good from it. In the same way, all righteousness from the least to the most important commands must be fulfilled. For whoever is unfaithful and found unrighteous in the least, so also in the great. In the same way, whoever resists water baptism makes known that he has not first been baptized by Christ in the Spirit. But whoever accepts it especially in this time of greatest offense, has already been baptized in the Spirit and fire from Christ. Such a one may also later receive the baptism of blood.

The baptism of blood is the baptism about which Christ spoke: I have to be baptized with a baptism, and how afraid I am until it is accomplished (Luke 12f[:50]). Similarly he said to the two sons of Zebedee: Are you able to be baptized with the baptism with which I am baptized? By this he means the baptism of blood, that is suffering. That is why Scripture everywhere establishes that the true believers in Christ suffer only tribulation and every kind of opposition. Christians must be like Christ the head, whose members they are through suffering. For the disciple is not greater than the master nor the servant than his lord. Peter says: Christ suffered for us and left us an example that we should follow his footsteps. He says further that whoever suffers in the flesh has ceased from sin. If we desire to be God's heirs and joint-heirs with Christ, as Paul says, we must also suffer with Christ. Thus the three baptisms are one even as the three witnesses, Father, Son, and Holy Spirit are one God. There is only one faith, one baptism, one God and Father of us all, and our Lord Jesus Christ.

Thus I have made a short and simple account of my faith for whoever demands it, and have shown the reason for my baptism before God himself who is the knower of hearts and a just judge. Whatever will now be inflicted on me because of it through God's divine will and the powers of the world I will patiently accept in the power of God with a willing and ready heart. And for all who do the work of God with me, as for my own sin, I will pray the Father of all mercy faithfully even to my own death that they too will come to knowledge of the truth, repent, and find grace through Jesus Christ our Lord. Amen.

The above article and defence was subsequently sent to the administration in Innsbruck, following which the magistrate in Schwaz was ordered to bring Hans Schlaffer to the castle of Freundsberg, where he will be questioned under torture about these articles as follows.

PART 2

The Second Defence of Hans Schlaffer in answer to the questions: First, they want a clear understanding of the foundation of the Anabaptist sect.[27]

Reply: as in parts of the above confession.

All authority is given to me in heaven and on earth, says Christ. Therefore go and teach all nations and baptize them in the name of the Father, the Son, and the Holy Spirit (Matt. 28d[:18-19]).

Item:[28] Go into all the world and preach the gospel of all creatures (Mark 16d[:15]). Whoever believes and is baptized, will be saved. It is also written that it was necessary for Christ to suffer and rise again from the dead on the third day, that repentance and remission of sin be preached in his name to all peoples (Luke 24g[:46-47]).

This makes it clear that teaching all people in Matthew and preaching the gospel in Mark is one thing, simply to proclaim in his name Christ's suffering for our sins and rising for our justification for repentance and forgiveness of sins. Whoever wants to know should know that it is necessary to preach repentance to those sinners who understand sin to be simply action against the law of the world or the actions and substance of the alleged Christendom. In my own previous life I regarded the life of godly and upright Christians who lived according to the severe and eternally valid Word of God and unperverted teaching of Christ as godless and wrong for a long time in my restless conscience. Then I learned that no hypocrisy or external appearance, no matter how good and exalted people regard it, proves effectual before God, but is an abomination.[29] Thereupon I prayed to God fervently to deliver me from this evil life which I perceived in my own flesh and in all people, according to his eternal mercy revealed in his Son Christ. This is true, and it is my intention finally to become a true Christian and follower of Christ. This is nothing other than to do the will of God the Father and keep his commandments, and not their commandments.[30]

Not the least among God's commandments is obedience to governmental authority. Christ himself taught and observed it and so did his apostles as is evident from their epistles and accounts. How then could I undertake to foment rebellion as it is rumoured, since I have committed myself to live according to the teaching of Christ by the grace of

God, and which is the fulfilling of God's law? And if insurrection is suspected by the realistic appearance of rebellion or even established not only apparently but in action (which I cannot imagine any Christian doing), I hope that no innocent person would have to pay for it.[31] I also hope that no one on earth will accuse me, a poor sinner, of it. I appeal to the highest authority which I swear now before you, my judge and the jurors, in the face of torture before God in the anguish of my heart, that I know nothing about any rebellion nor old or new uprising in myself or from anyone I know.[32] We are concerned only with putting off our own past evil life and to live in a new life of holiness and uprightness in the truth of God as Paul said. May God help me and all others who hunger and thirst in Jesus Christ. Amen.

Third[33]

This question asks who the actual beginners and principals of this heretical and rebellious sect are, where they are from, what they are called or what each one's name is.

Reply: I know of no beginner or principal of my faith which is called a sect than only the Son of God, Jesus Christ, the crucified, the captain of our salvation (Heb. 12[:2]). For the prophet says: Cursed be anyone who trusts a mortal. That is why I became suspicious of Councils, Fathers, ancient customs or great majorities.[34] They are all oppressed in their consciences as the Jews were to whom Peter said: Repent and let each of you be baptized in the name of Jesus for the forgiveness of sins, and you will receive the gift of the Holy Spirit.

Christ says that he came not to call the righteous but sinners to repentance. He has sent me, he says, to preach the gospel to the poor, to heal the broken-hearted, to proclaim release to the captives, give sight to the blind, and liberate those who are oppressed.

To sum up: First one needs to know what the teaching or Gospel and Christ himself is, and why he was sent by the Father into this world. This truth must be thoroughly known before one is baptized, otherwise baptism is not baptism. For even as one may not add anything to the Word of God, one may not change the order established by Christ. If it is changed everything that follows will be perverted and daily grow worse which, alas, is evident on every side.

Thus Peter says: Save yourselves from this evil and crooked generation. And those who gladly received his words were baptized. Philip, too, demanded faith from the queen's minister before he baptized him, and Peter from Cornelius (Acts 9[:44-48]), [Paul] from the jailor, the worker in purple and others. The twelve men in Ephesus, who had been baptized with the baptism of John had to be baptized later on the orders of Paul in the name of Christ. Christ himself was baptized in his thirtieth year here on earth. Paul writes that we were all baptized into one body. How that is possible with the ordinary baptism of infants I leave for each one to judge. The head is Christ. One should look at Eph. 4 and many other passages.

Second

What plans and plots are hidden under the outward appearance of re-baptism? What new rebellion and insurrection do you plan to foment, as we have learned credibly from the sworn statements of others at several locations in our jurisdiction?[35]

Reply: O Almighty, eternal and merciful God! What shall I say to this since I am not believed despite the horrible pain and torture! I know of no other witness to the truth in my heart than only God my Lord and heavenly Father. My greatest comfort of conscience is that my heart has never entertained any thought of insurrection or rebellion, and that I have not favoured it by others. Indeed, I fled from a house in which people were in conflict. They will support me in this. I know of no plan or plot which is alleged to be hidden under the mantle of re-baptism except only that of the whole.[36] Paul would not allow himself or the other apostles to be called leaders of a group. It is no wonder or odd, nor is it new that they call us a heretical insurrectionist sect. For God's sake, look only at the accusation against Christ before Pilate and of Paul before Felix (Matt. 26[:27]; Acts [24]). If I were to follow other persons I would be ill served, since everyone must himself be convinced of his calling and faith. That is why Christ told Peter not to look at John who was the beloved disciple, but only to follow him. Why should a Christian look to anyone except Christ? The Christian has no greater joy than to know that many follow Christ and live as his followers have lived. (As Paul writes, Be my followers as I am of Christ). To be truthful, I confess that I have seen some in other countries. This past summer I was for a time in Augsburg where there were many. I knew only a few of them, Jacob Wiedeman, Jacob Kautz, Sigmund Hoffer, and Hans Hut who is now in prison there since the Nativity of Mary [8 September] along with some others.[37] In Nuremberg I saw Ludwig Hätzer and Hans Denck, both of whom were striking, godly and learned men. In Regensburg I met Oswald Glaidt and Wolfgang Brandhuber, at one time a pastor in Linz.[38] In all of these I found only a passionate zeal for a godly and Christian life, although there were many strange rumours which were not even human let alone Christian, among the common people [about them]. All of this has to be left to God's time, to that day on which everything will be revealed. Thus I have no knowledge of any heretical or rebellious movement; I know no names or where they come from, since I know no such persons. But God knows the true Christians. As Paul says, God knows his own. May all who call on the name of Christ depart from evil.

The external sign by which Christians are known[39] is given by the Lord himself when he says: The world will know that you are my disciples if you love one another and follow my example. It is no surprise that the world is shocked by the teaching, life, and faith of Christ, and that it is troubled that a new conspiracy is concealed by it. It cannot be otherwise, for the prophets and the words of Christ that God begins his judgment with his own house have to be fulfilled [1 Pet. 4:17].[40] And if the judgment begins with his own house, what will be the end of those who do not believe the gospel? If the just and godly are barely preserved, where will the godless sinner stand?

O, if only God would open the spiritual eyes of all in the world that they could see the terrible and fearful judgments of God predicted long ago by the prophets, Christ, and the apostles, and which, when its signs are observed, (for they are already appearing), cannot be far away. I am afraid that when it happens there will be more who will repent. If I had not already taken all of that to heart, I would now want to be certain that I would not be considered a rebellious, evil person. My plea is to God the righteous judge.

The Fourth

question is, what motivated and brought you, Johann Schlaffer, to abandon your priestly office and estate?

Reply: God and my conscience knows why I accepted the priestly office and estate sixteen years ago. I hope, too, that those with sympathetic understanding will in part know why. But I was urged by the Word of God that one can be called to that office only by God, as Aaron was, and that Christ gave his talent to his chosen servants and commanded them to increase it. I saw that God himself accused the prophets who spoke without being called. This weighed on my heart and, God knows, was to me a heavy burden. Later I was eager to preach the pure Gospel as God gave me strength and people desired it. At that time I was in the country above the Enns,[41] perhaps it is not necessary to say with whom I stayed there. At that time I was forbidden, in writing, to preach any longer, which is, after all, the most important function of a priest.[42] I accepted this as God's will, and then also stopped the daily reading of the Mass. It was against my conscience, but I also found it difficult because I was suffering from headaches. But I spent more time in the daily reading of the Bible, and in the discipline and instruction of the Lord's children which were in my charge. They can confirm what I say without boasting about my life there and where I spent my time. To God alone be the glory.

The Fifth

question: Who decided to send you to this country in order to spread and plant the evil seed under the cover of re-baptism among the ordinary people?

Reply: God knows that no person ordered me to come here or anywhere else. I came of my own decision. While I was ill in Regensburg a man named Ulrich Moser came to me. He told me he was transporting pots from Meissen for Fugger[43] to be smelted down at Matz.[44] I travelled with him to Rattenberg.[45] In Brixlegg I had a friend, a brother of my mother whose name was Leonhart Hauenstein. I had never before seen him nor he me. I stayed with him a few days because of my sickness. Moser himself travelled back to Bavaria. I soon noticed that I was an irritation to my cousin because I had no fixed place to stay. So I left to travel to Schwaz and then on to Hall, intending to find work there to support myself for the winter. I then happened to stop at an inn with people from Münichen called Kripen[46] and stayed there one night. The next day towards evening, which was St. Nicholas' Day,[47] I travelled with Sigmund the accountant, to Schwaz. I asked him to give me a letter of reference to help me get work. On that journey we were arrested by the will of God.

Concerning the evil sect, I know nothing as I already said. It cannot be spoken about to just anyone; only one in a thousand, as the prophet says, will accept it because it is the word of the cross. Not all believe the Gospel. Not everyone can have faith, says Paul. I hope that, contrary to my own will, but not against the will of God, I will write and read and talk about it wherever anyone requests it. May God who is good, the almighty, help me and all needy true believers at the return of Christ when the secrets of every heart will be revealed. Amen. Blessed are the merciful for they will receive mercy.

The foundation and reason for baptism: Rom. 10[:14-15]
Whoever calls on the name of the Lord will be saved.
But how shall they call upon him in whom they do
not believe? How shall they believe in him about whom
they have not heard? And how shall they hear without
a preacher if no one is sent?

The end of two defences given to the authorities.
H: S:

PART 3

A Second Letter From our Beloved Brother Hans Schlaffer in which he sends a written report regarding the two defences he made to the governing authorities in the name of the Lord. AMEN.

First, most beloved brothers and sisters in Christ Jesus our Lord, I want you to know that an order was delivered to me on Saturday before St. Sebastian's[48] from the government in Innsbruck by the sherrif and the jurors here in Schwaz.

This order, read to me by them, was followed by interrogations[49] one with and one without torture. Copies of them are included, written and partly oral[50] concerning rebaptism (as they call it). When I appeared before the court officials, dear brothers and sisters, the court secretary read my written defence (Part 1 of this document) to the governing authorities. Some of what he read was incorrect and some things had been omitted. I objected to this and requested that, to be correctly understood, the record should be my two written defences and confession. The secretary replied that those documents were in possession of the lords in Innsbruck. The officials had prepared short extracts from my written and oral statements according to their judgment, but which did not agree at all points with my words and their meaning.

Because of this, my dear brothers and sisters, I have to explain several things to you. To my opponents it makes no difference, and I am not obligated to them. Certainly you know how much value they place on my confession. They are more fittingly answered by silence than with words according to the example of the just judge, our Lord and Saviour Jesus Christ until his appearance. Amen.

Item. Relating to the last article (Part 1) they said: He warned us judges and jurors to do the same (that is, to be baptized), and if we don't, we will be condemned with the whole world, although salvation is not dependent upon baptism but on faith in Christ alone. I did not say this, and protested it twice. What I did say was: since the whole world lies in wickedness as shown by its actions and is thereby an enemy of God, all must be warned to turn from the world and repent honestly in order to be saved. For Christ says: repent and believe the gospel, and in another place: truly, I tell you, that unless you repent you will all likewise perish. In that first defence (Part 1) I gave them two examples: the account which the Lord gave about the Galileans and the Tower of Siloam [Luke 13:1-5], as well as the uprising of the peasants who also perished shamefully. All these were given as examples and warnings for the amendment of life and for true faith in Christ.

This separation from the world, repentance, and amendment of life and true faith in Jesus Christ is followed by a sign, namely water baptism. This is not a condition for salvation, but rather for a true and complete faith in Christ. If they concluded from these words that I was abandoning baptism or recanting, they did not understand me. It was not my intention and it is not now. I pray to God unceasingly through Christ that he will graciously complete the work he has begun in me, his frail vessel, to the honour and glory of his eternal name. May he do the same for all who fervently desire it. Amen.

To renounce baptism and to regard it as unimportant would be to deny the name in which one is baptized. We are not like infants who do not understand. Rather we are those who have first truthfully confessed and now accepted consciously and with understanding the Father who draws us to Christ and revealed him to us, the Son and his yoke to which we have surrendered, and the Holy Spirit who teaches us and leads us into all truth. May the Almighty protect me from such betrayal. May he not withdraw from me his divine power in my last hour and greatest distress, for it is the teaching and command of Christ. Whoever trespasses against it and does not remain in it has no God. Whoever abides in the teaching of Christ has both the Father and the Son.

Second, I told them how, in the beginning, I stood staunchly against baptism or, as the world calls it, rebaptism, and spoke and wrote against it. At the same time I always prayed to God to teach me to do his will. They falsely point this out to me as a contradiction. It is certain that God who is faithful and true in all his works and words will not abandon to error anyone who trusts in him, nor allow anyone, regardless of who he is, to fall into eternal disgrace. The disgrace and shame which he suffers for the Lord's sake will be transformed by God into the highest honour in his coming kingdom eternally.

Third, I also told them that in Nicholsburg they baptized many, not all of whom amended their lives.[51] I confess that I probably did wrong in this. May God forgive me this and all my sins and misdeeds by his overflowing mercy through Christ. Amen.

I made a special request to renew this article. But here I stand and confess only for myself. I will also be condemned for myself and for no one else.

I did try to distinguish and explain, for where there is only baptism which is not preceded by the truthful witness to the Gospel and the deep planting of faith in the heart, there will be as little amendment as with infant baptism. For in the end even the one who is known to stand firm will pass the test with difficulty as is only too evident.

When they baptized at Nicholsburg they began by first preaching to the assembly, after which they baptized whoever came and desired it. No personal witness or confirmation of faith was required. For this reason our dear brother Hans Hut protested to doctor Balthasar, the result of which was a deep split between him and the brothers there. Hut was imprisoned and miraculously set free again which was known then to many of our brothers. I said this so that they would not consider baptism without faith to be essential for salvation. Therefore, brothers and sisters, I don't want to be criticized for it. Pray that the Lord will forgive me.

Finally, and most important, after they had read my confession to me, the magistrate requested from me confirmation by oath that I would abide by it and to suffer and accept the legal consequences. I said, yes. I was not prepared to do more with the help of God. I begged the magistrate and the jurors to accept my yes, since they too desired to be Christians and had Christian names. For Christ teaches and commands: Your speech must be yes, yes, and no, no; anything beyond that is evil. My no and yes, I said, should have the same validity as an oath. The magistrate ordered me out in order to consult with the jurors. When he called me back and told me that since I despised the common practice and would not swear by oath it needed to be referred to His Royal Majesty for further decision.

Then he ordered me back to prison. I answered: Gladly! I was never there unwillingly, God be praised. I could explain other matters in my statement. However, since I am not in prison and charged by a court as a murderer, thief or evil-doer but as a Christian, I don't need to be ashamed of my imprisonment. God be eternally praised who, although I am afflicted with many weaknesses and failures, has preserved me from an evil life. I will be vindicated not before the world, but before God in his grace. I will gladly suffer injustice, let them write, blaspheme and pass judgment. I am here as a lamb that does not open its mouth when it is slaughtered. For all this Christ, for whose name and teaching I am willing to suffer obediently, will give me strength and his help. I have so little strength that even a rustling leaf would bring me down. But with Christ who gives us strength we can do all things. He will see to everything and turn everything to his glory and praise. He himself is the greatest disgrace and scandal from the beginning of the world until his return and the revelation of his glory. For this we wait with the longing and yearning of our hearts, and pray that he may come soon. Amen.

One more thing, dear brothers. Hear and take note of the inventive trickery of Satan and the deceit of the serpent, how she invents a diversion.[52] Those into whose hands we have been delivered do not ask us about belief but are ready to allow everyone to remain in their heart's conviction. They don't care; believe what you will. But they ask only about water baptism and want to know all about it. So someone tells them that baptism without faith is nothing at all, but only a witness and external sign of the faith in the heart. If evidence is given from Scripture they say: My dear man, we are not here to argue; the hangman will dispute with you. Nevertheless, if they find a passage torn from Scripture which in their view supports their opinion, they belabour you with it. It all has to do with mere water. Is this not worse than when Pilate washed his hands? He at least used water to declare himself innocent of the death of Christ. But these imagine they can be clean and innocent without water. They too sit in bloody judgment and undertake to answer for it at the judgment of the Lord. They have a right to their defence but note what the response will be: I was in prison and you did not comfort me (Matt. 25[:43]). What will he say to those who not only did not comfort, but betrayed like Judas, and who imprisoned, put on trial, condemned and killed?

Please note, dear brothers, how God plays with the world and mocks its wisdom and great violence, that they persecute baptism without faith, that they become so wrathful against a drop of water and use their power against it so violently. Well and good! Let us see how they will fare when the Lord comes with another which, as you know, is put out with water. A single drop of water on that day, for which one would give the whole world! I mean, of course, not mere water, but the power concealed under it, over which the whole world is now so terrified.⁵³ On the last day matters will certainly turn out differently. You understand me, dearest brothers in the Lord.

Now dearest brothers, I have surrendered without condition to the powerful hand of God and the discipline of the Father. May he do with me according to his pleasure to the praise and honour of his holy name, and to witness to Christ his only Son through his witnesses. I will remain quiet and patient until his work in me has been completed to my blessed end. May he help me, in whose name I have been baptized and signed, Father, Son, and Holy Spirit, one God, strong from eternity to eternity.

I admonish you, indeed all at whose heart's door the Lord stands and knocks with longing, to open the door to him and to sup with him. For certainly the Great Supper is near at hand. The householder has long since invited to it, but all have excuses. Now they are coming in from the streets, the squares and the hedgerows until his house is full. So, open the door while he stands and knocks, for he may tire and leave and then, when you open, he is no longer there. Read these parables to the end of the chapter [Matt. 25] for it is all one message. Be aware of how to prepare for the Great Supper. I ask you this because of my Christian obligation. I have done what I could and am finished speaking. For I believe the Lord will not let me live in this mortal hut for much longer, but hope he will call me to his eternal dwelling not made with hands. Amen. Thursday before the Conversion of Paul.⁵⁴

7

Eitelhans Langenmantel

An Anonymous Anabaptist Sermon & An Exposition of the Lord's Prayer (ca. 1527)*

Introduction

Eitelhans Langenmantel (d. 1528) was a patrician, the son of the mayor of Augsburg. As a young man, he had ruined his health (he suffered from gout) and squandered his money travelling through France and Italy.[1]

He became attracted to the ideas of the Reformation. It was probably early in 1527 that Langenmantel became acquainted with Hans Hut. Having been expelled from Nuremberg, Hut had made Augsburg his main base of operations. Hut's goal was to reorganize the Anabaptist community there. In March of 1527, Hans Hut lived with Langenmantel for ten days, after which Langenmantel accepted baptism from him. Jakob Dachser, another leading radical from Augsburg, was also present at the baptism.

---

*Source: *Von der wahren Liebe* (Hans Denck); *Auslegung des Vater unser* (Hans Langenmantel); *Zwei Altevangelische Schriften aus dem Jahre 1527* (Elkhart, IN: Mennonitische Verlagshandlung, 1888), 21-32.

Translation: John C. Wenger; revised by C. Arnold Snyder

Langenmantel came to play a leading role in the Augsburg conventicle, which included Jakob Gross, Sigmund Salminger and Dachser, the latter two of whom had also been baptised by Hut. Langenmantel was the most prolific writer of the leading group.[2] Seven of his tracts survive, written between 1526 and 1527, mostly focusing on the Lord's Supper.

Of the two articles presented here, it is possible that "an Anonymous Anabaptist Sermon" is a work of Dachser (to whom Langenmantel brought his tracts to be published) and not Langenmantel.[3] The tract may have originated in 1527; later it was copied into Hutterite sources together with Langenmantel's "Exposition of the Lord's Prayer."[4] The "Anonymous Anabaptist Sermon" is unique, as there are no other surviving Anabaptist sermons that date from as early as 1527.[5] The Sermon emphasizes leaving sin and the world behind, building instead on the Rock, the living Word that dwells in the heart. The sermon places its strongest emphasis on the inner, spiritual birth which can come only after the heart has been ploughed and prepared—a mystical theme and image repeated often in South German/Austrian Anabaptism. The result of the new birth, however, is obedience and building of a "spiritual house" that will stand for eternity. The preoccupation early in the sermon with blaspheming, slandering and dishonouring God (*Gott gelästern; die Lästerung*) may refer to a concern with "taking God's name in vain" (also seen in the "Exposition of the Lord's Prayer") but seems to have a deeper significance. The misuse of God's good gifts is also described as "blasphemy." The latter part of the sermon, with its condemnation of human judgment, is a plea for freedom of conscience and religious toleration, an increasingly important point for Anabaptists in search of refuge.

The "Exposition of the Lord's Prayer" is a vigorous protest against the carnality of professing Christendom in the early sixteenth century.[6] The "Exposition" continues the central themes of the "sermon" and is written in the same style, giving the impression that both writings were composed by the same author. The "Exposition" continues to be preoccupied with "blaspheming God," but more fundamentally, is concerned with spiritual conversion and a turning from sin and the world. The twin concerns of justice and spiritual renewal are nicely summarized in Langenmantel's gloss on "Give us this day our daily bread." The phrase obligates us, he says, to share our bread with those in need, but also is a prayer to be fed the "bread of the spirit" in the heart.

The South German/Austrian Anabaptists evidently used the Lord's Prayer and the Apostles' Creed as catechetical tools. Readers can compare Langenmantel's exposition with Schiemer's (ch. 5), Schlaffer's brief comments (ch. 6) and Nadler's oral text (ch. 11).

Langenmantel was arrested on September 15, 1527—Hut was arrested on the same day—on the basis of information provided by other Anabaptists seized that day. Because of his standing and influence, he was treated less harshly than were some of the other Anabaptist prisoners. He managed to arrange a disputation with the preacher of the city, which resulted in his temporary withdrawal from the Anabaptists and recognition of infant baptism. He was expelled on October 15 but because of his inability to walk (gout) he was strapped to a chair and carried out of the city.[7] He made his way to Goeggingen, then to Langenneufnach where he bought a house at Leutershofen. He resided there for a few weeks and soon a new conventicle was assembled under his protection.[8] Renouncing his earlier withdrawal from the Anabaptists, he resumed his role as an Anabaptist teacher.

On April 24, 1528 Langenmantel was seized, along with his maid and his servant, by a captain of the Swabian League. He was brought in chains to Weissenhorn where on May 11, he and his servant were beheaded; the young woman was drowned. All were executed without trial.[9]

The translation that follows was done originally by John C. Wenger and was published in *MQR*, January, 1948; it is used with permission. The translation has been substantially revised for this publication.

Bibliographical Sources:

Chronicle I.
Johann Loserth, "Langenmantel, Eitelhans," *ME III*, 289-90.
Werner O. Packull, *Mysticism and the Early South German-Austrian Anabaptist Movement, 1525-1531* (Scottdale, PA: Herald Press, 1977).
John C. Wenger, "Two Early Anabaptist Tracts," *MQR* 21-22 (January 1948), 34-42.
George H. Williams, *The Radical Reformation* 3rd edition (Kirksville, MO: Sixteenth Century Journal Publishers, 1992).

A Sermon on Sin, Repentance, and Salvation
Eitelhans Langenmantel(?)

God says (Jer. 7[:3-4]): Amend your life and your ways, and I will dwell with you in this place; and let none deceive themselves.

Jer. 9: Their evil tongue is a deadly arrow. They speak friendly words to their neighbours, but in their hearts they are planning to lay an ambush.

In the name of the undivided threefold God: May he be with us, and with all those who so desire, to teach and to show us the command of Christ which the Father desires that we fulfill, through Jesus Christ, Amen.

God the Heavenly Father desires that the whole sinful world forsake its sin and from now on sin no more. Then he will not condemn the world, as Christ has shown us. The Father also demands that we recognize Christ's teaching which was sent to us from the Father, given to us in paternal faithfulness. Now those who hear this teaching and these words, and do them, praise God. It is a wise man who builds his house upon the rock; he can therefore be secure in the face of pelting rain and wind, for he builds upon the Word of God. Now there is no other rock before God upon which one may build except this one only (Matt. 9; Ps. 1; Matt. 7; Jer. 17; Ps. 118; Matt. 21; Mark 12).

O dearly-beloved brothers and sisters in the Christian gathering: Let us note well the first plank of this house, as Christ teaches us: "Refrain from sin" (Matt. 3). For sin has no place in this house. If we build with sin we are not building the house of God, but rather the house of darkness. But when we refrain from sin, we will not dishonour the name of God, but praise, extol and honour it, and begin to love him with our whole hearts, for he first loved us. Of this we have abundant external testimony from our Father, as we comprehend and see, which [testimony] is our body, life and all our members (Rom. 1; Heb. 1). Our testimony is heaven and everything which can be known in heaven, the air and everything which moves in the air, the whole earth, the sea and everything which dwells in it. The heavenly Father has created this testimony for us and given it to us as a gift, to those who recognize his name, his glory, his might and his parental love, and who praise him.

O dearest brothers and sisters! Let every one consider with their whole heart whether they have used this testimony, parental faithfulness, and gift, for praise and honour and thanksgiving, to the praise, honour, and glory of the heavenly Father. Oh, it is a great concern that we have wrongly used this testimony and gift which God has granted us, thereby dishonouring God, with our mouths for example, which should have extolled God but have continually blasphemed him. Our eyes should always have been alert to that which opposed our faithful Father. And our ears should always have heard the will of our heavenly Father which he has revealed to us through all his prophets and through Christ, which is a greater gift and testimony and greater parental faithfulness than the testimony of earth, heaven and of all the creatures. But our ears were not able to hear it. Would to God that our ears had not hindered [hearing God's will] and had not paid heed to the esteem of the world; then God would not condemn us.

In this I wish to include all the articles which all persons can consider for themselves if they pay attention to what they hear and to their conduct. Since it is now certain and evident that we have used all the members of our body in this way (of which much could be said but it is not necessary), let everyone pay attention to the Speaker who speaks in all hearts. He will surely teach what is to be done, if one takes good heed. O, dear brothers and sisters! Let all those who hear this immediately begin to praise, extol, honour and thank God with the limbs God gave us. Ever afterwards let them follow what Christ taught us, and never look back to blasphemy. O, dear brothers and sisters! We should no longer look behind us to the dishonouring of God, so we never again slander him, as Christ teaches us truly. Whoever puts hand to the plow and looks back is already disqualified to enter the city to which Christ has shown us the way. O dear brothers and sisters! Give heed to the Speaker who continually speaks in your hearts; thus you shall find in yourselves a true testimony, never to sin against God. O, dear brothers and sisters! All who hear I entreat you for God's sake to pay close attention to this struggle which we continually find in ourselves: the great slandering of God which arises in us. But we also find in us a powerful resistance to help us overcome this slander. Because of the faithful Father's will in heaven, who loved us so dearly, we find the strength to resist through Christ, and we cry to our heavenly Father, as Christ teaches us, that he may answer our prayer and send us the strength to overcome the conflict which arises in us, if we watch well, each over their own house (Matt. 24).

Therefore, dear brothers and sisters, let all be admonished in the Lord to watch, then you will indeed forget all the scribes of the whole earth, of whom we are to beware (Matt. 23; Mark 8; Luke 12). Forget all monasteries, priests, and churches, together with all that is inside them and takes place in them, that we may become a temple of God, since God does not dwell in temples made with hands (1 Cor. 4; Acts 7 and 17) but in temples which come from heaven, the souls and spirits of people who live in faith and do his will. God speaks further: I will dwell in you and walk in you (1 Pet. 2, Exod. 14). If God is to dwell and walk in us, he cannot dwell in this temple until all that is opposed to God is removed. Where we find many pictures and a lot of foreign merchandise, there God cannot dwell. It is a case of the creature having entered into us and having become dearer to us than the Creator. Christ has faithfully warned us about this. That which we prefer to him whom the Father sent to us, makes us unworthy for the Lord to dwell in our house (Matt. 10; Luke 14).

O dear brothers and sisters! Bear in mind that Christ clearly teaches us that God the Father does not sow his Seed (his Word, sent out through Christ who alone teaches us) on the road where the seed cannot grow but is quickly picked up, also not in a thornbush for it would be choked by the thorns, also not on a rock for it would lack earth and could not grow. But where the seed falls in good earth it will yield much fruit (Matt. 13). Now we all know that no one sows seed on a road, in thorns or on a rock. We till first so that we may have a good field into which to sow the seed. And that is what God also does. He comes to our hearts which had become roads, thornbushes and hard stone, to plough and to plant. He roots out all the hedges and thorns with his divine Word, which has been opened to us by Christ and which is truly present in all the world. Would to God that people would listen to that Word, believe in him and follow him. This is what he teaches us to do. Refrain from deceipful wealth and from the overflowing cares of the world (1 Tim. 6) about which God has not commanded us, for they are all thistles and thorns. Whoever does not have these thistles and thorns in their heart may thank God constantly. But let those who have them follow this Tiller who continually comes to our hearts, desiring to clean them out, to plant his field and prepare a good soil so that the Seed of God may be sown there and grow there until the harvest, and may yield much fruit for him who will reap. This Tiller is the living Word of God, which we cannot deny (Matt. 19). It comes to us always, but we do not wish to have it in us, and for this reason we cannot enter into the kingdom of God, as Christ the true Son of God teaches us: unless we are born again we cannot see the kingdom of God (John 3). There is no other birth than hearing God's Word and receiving it into one's heart. Such persons are willing to do everything that the Word teaches them in their hearts, according to the will of God (1 Pet. 4). If they do this, no longer doing the will of the world but the will of God, they are true children of God; they are also truly born again. But those who hear the Word and refuse to do what the Word teaches (which proceeds from God and was opened up by Christ), these can never be born again until they hear the Word in their hearts and obey it, as Christ taught us. This is the law of God which Christ teaches us, which is sealed and which may never be broken, as Christ says: Before one tittle or letter of my law passes away, heaven and earth must rather pass away (Matt. 5).

Therefore, dear brothers and sisters! Let everyone consider well where they stand, whether in the will of the world or in the will of God. When one stands in the will of God, the law and the seal have already been broken (Matt. 11); but when one stands in the will of the world, such a one should know that the seal is too strong and can never be broken. Whoever hears the Word of God, in divine love, with one's whole heart, and does what the Word teaches is wise, as Christ says, for such a one hears and obeys the Word; such a person has heavenly wisdom, can build a house that will never pass away, and it shall be a house of God. But one who hears the Word and does not obey it, as Christ teaches, has an earthly wisdom; such a one will build an earthly house which will fall and pass away along with the whole earth. Let everyone be admonished to be aware of which house we are building. If one builds the house of God, the house of God or Christ, such a one will not be condemned by God. Let all judges be admonished for God's sake, that they consider well which house they are building when they seize the judgment of God, for God taught us through His most beloved Son, whom he commanded us to hear, that we should leave judgment to God. Now if anyone, regardless of who he is, is building a house of this earth, he will always seize the judgment that belongs to God. Yet he should know and be admonished of God that God will judge him at the Last Judgment through his son; and that judgment will be too severe for him, because he acted against God and his omnipotence, whom no one can withstand. Then everyone will repent and see how they have judged [others].

Be admonished accordingly by God, for his sake, to no longer pass judgment against anyone, regardless of who it may be, since the Father has extended such great parental faithfulness to us that no one can deny it, not even the greatest enemy of God who may be found under heaven. But the severest judgment will be against [those who judge others].

AN EXPOSITION OF THE LORD'S PRAYER
[By Eitelhans Langenmantel]

Everyone implores God, crying and saying falsely: *Our Father*, but they do not do what the Father requires. If we want to ask properly, we should be the heavenly children of our heavenly Father; but we act like children born of the devil [yet] who say, *Our Father who art*—but not really believing that it is God [whom we are addressing]. They say also, *who art in heaven*—and seek God not in heaven but rather seek out the father of sin, and then add, *Hallowed be Thy Name*. We are the first to blaspheme God's name and to regard it as profane: All our works give testimony of this. We say, *Thy kingdom come to us*—with great falseness and terrible blasphemy of God. For when the kingdom of God actually comes to us and God wishes to give it to us (as promised us through Jesus Christ, God's most dear Son), we oppose it with all the might of our soul and body, and we regard and treasure the whole world, the kingdom of hell and darkness, as if it were the kingdom of God, just as Christ said: The world knows neither me nor my Father (John 8[:19]).

Therefore we do not say truly, *Thy will be done on earth as it is in heaven*. Here the whole world is reproached by God the heavenly Father, for praying falsely, for when God's will is to be done, it begins in us. The living Word teaches us in our hearts that it is God's will that must always be done in us. Therefore God has no greater enemy opposing his will than we ourselves, since we pray to God as was mentioned and do not trust him [*Ihm nicht glauben geben*] but rather oppose God's words. In the same way God simply slices off our daily bread for us when we pray, *Give us this day our daily bread*. And when God gives me my daily bread as I have asked—and even if God gives me more than I need, and I see my neighbour in need or suffering hunger—if I do not share but rather say, it is mine, then what I prayed for my brothers and sisters is already a lie because I have not shared with them as Christ taught me. Christ says further, you shall not live by natural bread alone but by every Word of God which proceeds from the mouth of God (Matt. 4; Luke 4; Deut. 8). This is the bread of the spirit and the soul that feeds us forever and eternally. And yet when God gives us such bread, as we have asked, we oppose it with all our hearts. Let everyone read this in the book of their mind (*Gemüth*), whether they are following their own mind or the Word of God which is the true Bread. Neither spirit nor soul can ever be fed except by following (*in der Nachfolge*) the living Word of God. Therefore when we pray, let each one see to it that they do not speak against themselves with that prayer.

Forgive us our debts as we forgive our debtors. When the Father comes and wishes to forgive us the debts we have incurred, God says, "sin no more and you shall be forgiven." This is how the Father comes to us. Everyone may [plainly] see the sincerity of our petition. If we never sin again, for the Lord's sake, our debtors are also forgiven, as the Lord has forgiven us. Then we can rightly say, *Lead us not into temptation.* O almighty God! If only we would be satisfied with that, since you lead us and teach us through Jesus Christ, your most dear Son, we would not enter into temptation but into great and endless joy (James 1). But if we allow ourselves to be led of our evil will, and the will of sin which is not from You, we go to damnation, of this we are certain. Therefore let everyone look to what is leading us, whether it is the good will or the evil will. Then everyone will find his place, as God spoke through his dear Son, our Lord [*Herzoge*] Jesus Christ, and will simply pray:

But deliver us from the evil. And even though you, eternal Father, wish to deliver us from evil, [yet] we wish and desire from the whole heart to be bound and taken captive, and led into evil, so that we are continually found to be liars and blasphemers of God. We may be certain that all our sins will testify against us, since they are written before the face of God and will never be forgotten, as long as we do not stop sinning and turn in conversion to God, to whom alone belongs the kingdom, as follows:

Thine is the kingdom. O eternal God! We regard your kingdom as the greatest poverty. O Lord! We give evidence of this with all our works. There is no one who wishes to do your will, even though that is where the everlasting riches of God the eternal Father and of the Lord Jesus Christ are found. We all are ready to fulfill the will of sin, regarding it as the greatest kingdom and as the best. Every person's will testifies to this in their heart, that they love evil more, and act in evil ways. For where the heart's love is, that is where one's treasure and the kingdom are found (Matt. 6; Luke 11). O dear brothers and sisters in all the world! Be admonished of God your Father. Read the book of your heart diligently. Everything is written there, and no learned scribe (against which

Christ warned us), will be able to lead us astray (Matt. 7 and 23). Then we can rightly say:

Thine is the power. O Almighty God! Let all brothers and sisters who crave your power recognize that from this hour forward we may not regard Your power as great weakness. If the greatest sinner on earth commanded us to do something, we regarded it as much more mighty than the heavenly power which God has opened up to us through Christ. We also have sought more strength and comfort from the creature than from the Creator. If we want testimony that is true, we may examine our minds, where we find more desire and joy in obeying and serving the creature than the Creator. Therefore we speak against God [when we pray *thine is the power*].

Thine is the glory from eternity to eternity, Amen. O almighty, eternal God! We are such great blasphemers before your divine face, speaking great and mighty lies which can never be forgotten as long as we seek another glory than yours alone and of our Lord Jesus Christ. We have not sought your glory, although we said it was yours. We have sought glory in many places, regarded them more carefully, and found in them more joy and pleasure than in your glory, which you yourself are. We therefore give testimony of all the desolate abominations we practice in opposition to you. This is evident in the pleasure we take in all our sins, not to mention the accompanying works, all of which is plainly visible. We therefore have caused great offense, which is forbidden us by the Lord Jesus Christ.

Almighty God, the people who read this booklet will say: Who can do such things as are written in this booklet? They say, or will say, It is too difficult (*schwer*). O almighty, eternal God! Grant your strength through Jesus Christ to all those who read or hear this, so that it may become easy (*leicht*) for them in their hearts, because it is your divine teaching and commandment—as Christ the true Son of God teaches—that his commandment is not grievous (*schwer*). O you most beloved brothers and sisters! Do not regard it as burdensome in your hearts; begin with the smallest thing which God teaches and commands through his Son Jesus Christ, and do that with willing hearts for the sake of your Father, from whom you have received great gifts and presents, which no one can deny.

But if you would gladly learn what you ought to receive, ask God for the beginning of the same and he will give it to you. Perhaps you wish to begin by mastering your mouth so that you cease to blaspheme the name of God. When you have started with this item and overcome it you will have made a heavenly beginning. And thereafter when you have begun to extol and praise the name of God, and to become grateful, then you will begin to love God from the whole heart and your neighbour as yourself. This is what Christ has taught us. If we truly believe, we will do this in truth. That which is further to be done the Holy Spirit will teach through Jesus Christ, Amen.

Almighty, eternal God! We ask you to give strength to all who hear your Word, that they may do what your Word teaches them. To those who truly hear, and who repent (*bereuen*) of all their sins, give them the power of the Holy Spirit, that they may resist sin until the end. This we also ask of Christ the Son, that he may intercede with the Father for us, that this may be imparted to us. O almighty, eternal God! That which we have not yet heard from Jesus Christ, and not yet done, grant unto us, and to all who crave it with the whole heart, to hear and to do. God, the heavenly Father, grant this through his Son Jesus Christ our Lord and through the power of the Holy Spirit, and may God be with us from now on, from eternity to eternity, Amen. Amen. May this be true.

8

Anonymous (Simon Schneeweiss?)

Theological Refutation of Anabaptist Teaching (1528)*

Introduction

This is an early refutation, anonymous as it stands. Karl Schornbaum, editor of the volume in which it is printed, suggests it may have been written by Simon Schneeweiss, who was court preacher in the Principality of Ansbach. The refutation reflects contact with the Anabaptism led and shaped by Hans Hut and Hans Denck, both of whom had died the year before.

If the author was Simon Schneeweiss, little is known or written about him. The one certainty is that he was a Lutheran; he signed the Smalcald Articles of 1537, written by Martin Luther. Other notables signing the document were Philip Melancthon, Urbanus Rhegius and Andreas Osiander from Nuremberg. Schneeweiss is listed as being pastor of the Church at Crailsheim, a town near Nuremberg.

Bibliographical Source:

www.iclnet.org/pub/resources/text/wittenberg/concord/web/smc-03p.html May 18, 2001.

---

*Source: Schornbaum, *Quellen V*, 253-60.
Translation: Friesen/Klaassen

Theological Refutation of the Teachings of Anabaptists. (1528)

Answer to the first articles of these new fanatics.

That this self-invented superstitious opinion is a sect both against God's Word and his will, undertaken by themselves or inspired by an evil and not a good spirit, can be shown and proven as follows:

A sect is whatever willfully separates itself from the unity of the Christian church contrary to the divine Holy Word. It is in this sense that Holy Scripture customarily uses the word *heresim*, Titus 3[:10]: A heretic, whom in German we call a *Ketzer* should be avoided after the first and second admonition. You may be sure that such a one is subverted, and sins. He is already condemned.

For the word *heresis* in the Greek language means choose, select, separate. Thus *heresis* is a sect which thinks up and chooses its separate way and form in order to teach, believe and live outside of the unitedly-believing church. And the Scriptures command us strictly to avoid such a rabble or sect. Rom. 16[:17]: I appeal to you, brothers, etc. Also 1 Tim. 6[:3]; 1 Cor. 1. "Now I appeal to you, brothers and sisters, by the name of our Lord Jesus Christ, that you all speak the same thing, and that there be no divisions among you; but that you be perfectly joined together in the same mind and in the same judgment" [1 Cor. 1:10].

In contrast, the true church of God or the Christian Church is gathered in a unified true faith, in which the blessing of the New Testament is offered to the believers through the preaching of the Gospel and through the holy sacraments. Such a congregation or church is one body, and as Paul says, Eph. 4[:5], has one faith, one baptism, one God and Father. Eph. 5[:25]: "Christ also loved the church and gave himself for it, that he might sanctify it, and cleanse it with the washing of water by the Word." We are to cling to this church only, and outside of it there is no salvation. Holy Scripture testifies to this and supremely and fully proves it. In John 15[:4] Christ says: "Abide in me, and I in you. As the branch cannot bear fruit of itself, unless it abides in the vine, no more can you," etc. And as in the time of Noah everything that was outside the ark, which was built through God's Word and command, had to perish in the flood and die, so there is no salvation or life outside this church or congregation which Christ has redeemed through his blood, purified and justified, but only destruction and condemnation. John 10[:27]: "My sheep hear my voice, and I know them and they know me." Luke 11[:23]: "He that is not with me is against me, and he that does not gather with me scatters," etc.

Secondly. Since this new fanaticism or sect does not believe or accept the books of Holy Scripture, neither the Old nor the New Testaments, and since by this means the sword, indeed all power to overthrow the heretical error of their followers is taken from us, it is necessary that they are first of all convinced, and with good reasoning forced to see, that one must believe only such Holy Scripture; that the faith, hope, love, and work of all Christians is to be ruled only according to this guideline, and that from this source all instruction, the nourishing and maintaining of the soul is to be obtained as from a fountain and treasure trove of divine wisdom and divine will.

The truth that Holy Scripture is the sole fruitful pasture of the lambs of Christ and the guideline by which all godly people are duty-bound to guide themselves in faith and life, and not to rely on new inspiration outside of it, can be proven briefly in this way:

If we are not permitted to ground or build an unchanging faith on the Holy Scripture of the Old and the New Testaments, and if we are to believe, to hope and to live according to new inspirations of God, effective at any special time, it must follow that the prophets falsely and unreasonably used the evidence and the authority of the books of Moses, etc. and also that Christ himself with his apostles falsely used the prophets. In addition, where they believe and confess that they are Christians and are baptized in the name of Jesus, they confess at the same time irrefutably that they are the children and heirs of a new covenant. Now the new covenant, that is, the covenant of Christ, is not only a new but an eternal covenant, which is sealed and confirmed with the blood, death, suffering of Christ. All who have been given their name in baptism in Christ are duty bound and obligated to keep its contents and to believe, love, hope, and live in accordance with it until the Son of Man will come to judge the quick and the dead, to liberate the blessed in God and to condemn the godless, to which the words of Christ in the gospels frequently and sufficiently testify.

For if these new fanatics believe in Christ and confess that his is the way, the justice and the truth, then they must also consistently, undeniably and indisputably agree that Christ rightly and reasonably bids the Jews, in John 5[:39], to search the Scriptures, and elsewhere chides them as ignorant of the Scripture [Matt. 22:29]. From this it must follow clearly that only Holy Scripture is the rock and foundation of the faith of all believing Christians, on which they build without doubt, and the only protection on which their comfort, salvation, wisdom and instruction depends. John 20[:30]: "And Jesus did many other signs in the presence of his disciples, which are not written in this book. But these are written so that you may come to believe that Jesus is the Messiah, the Son of God," etc. 2 Tim. 2[3:15]: "And how from childhood you have known the sacred writings that are able to instruct you for salvation through faith in Christ Jesus." Rom. 15[:4]: "For whatever was written in former days was written for our instruction, so that by steadfastness we and by encouragement of the Scriptures we might have hope." 2 Pet. 1[:19]: "So we have the prophetic message fully confirmed. You will do well to be attentive to this," etc., etc.

Further, in Mark 12[:24] Christ scolds the Sadducees by saying: "Is not this the reason you are wrong, that you know not the Scriptures?" etc. In sum, the entire Holy Scripture is everywhere full of these and other irrefutable witnesses that one should obtain knowledge of the truth and divine will, all godly teaching, and the test of good and evil spirits from Holy Scripture alone. John 7[:38]: "Let the one who believes in me drink. As the Scripture has said, out of the believer's heart shall flow rivers of living water." Also, in Luke 16[:29, :31] Abraham says: "They have Moses and the prophets, let them hear them." And soon after: "If they hear not Moses and the prophets, neither will they be persuaded through one rose from the dead."

Thirdly. They reject the outward office of the ministry and count and confess it powerless to forgive sin. This is altogether a terrible error and the great cunning of Satan himself, with which he will attack the evangelical kingdom of Christ unless he is prevented from doing so, and unless his claim is disproved and rejected with good reasons. That this opinion is an altogether pernicious and terrible error, godless and contrary to Holy Scripture can be shown as follows: Firstly, always ever and ever it has been God's usage and custom to impart the treasure of his divine gifts among his own by the use of visible means and outward persons. Scripture shows this in many places, especially, however, in 2 Sam. 12, where God, through his prophet Nathan, forgives David his sins. In the second book of Kings, chapter 18, and Isaiah 38 he does the same for Hezekiah, king of Judah, through the agency of the prophet Isaiah. He has acted similarly in the new covenant and has ordained and commanded that this be done always henceforth to the end of the world. In Matt. 16[:19] Christ commits to Peter the keys, that is, the power to forgive sins and to bind. In chapter 18[:18-19] he says to his disciples, or in the persons of his disciples to all Christians: "Truly I tell you, Whatever you bind on earth," etc. Also John 20[:23]: "Receive the Holy Spirit. If you forgive the sins of any, they are forgiven them." Further, in Acts 2[:38] Peter says to those who had been drawn to Christ through his external office of preaching: "Repent, and be baptized every one of you in the name of Jesus Christ for the remission of sins, and you shall receive the gift of the Holy Spirit." It can further be persuasively shown from Acts 26[:15] that through the outward office of the preacher and the visible dispensing of the holy sacrament forgiveness of sins is given. In that passage Christ appears to Paul, who was still rejecting and persecuting the church, and addresses him thus: "Arise and stand on your feet, for that is why I have appeared to you," etc. See also Acts 10[:6]. Further, in Luke 24[:46] it is written: "Thus it is written, that the Messiah is to suffer and to rise from the dead on the third day, and that repentance and forgiveness of sins is to be proclaimed in his name to all nations." Acts 10[:42] "And he commanded us to preach to the people and to testify that he is the one ordained by God as judge of the living and the dead." 1 Cor. 4[:1]: "Think of us in this way, as servants of Christ, and stewards of God's mysteries." That is the Gospel, through which the treasures of God are offered to us and carried home. In 1 Cor. 3[:9] we read that the apostles or preachers are servants through which you have become believers, etc. Rom. 10[:14-17]: "How are they to call on one in whom they have not believed? And how are they to hear without someone to proclaim him?" And soon after: "How are they to proclaim him unless they are sent? So faith comes from what is heard, and what is heard comes throught the word of Christ." Further, the holy apostle Paul also boasts, that through his office of preaching he has begotten the Corinthians in Christ Jesus, 1 Cor. 4[:15]. Similarly he says to the Galatians, Gal. 4[:19]: "My little children, for whom I am again in the pain of childbirth until Christ is formed in you." Also in John 17[:20] Christ says, "I ask not only on behalf of these, but also on behalf of those who will believe in me through their word".

Fourthly. They accept baptism and approve of it as right, not on the strength or on the assured authority of Holy Scripture, but on their dreams and visions. This is a godless opinion, and contrary to all Holy Scripture, and is also opposed to all reason. Even a person with average intelligence can judge how ridiculous it is to thrust Holy Scripture from its place as unworthy of attention, and to set up and put faith in nothing but visions and dreams. And this after all Christians have for so many centuries adhered to it in unified faith! Such rejection is not only strictly forbidden by God in his Word, but is also contrary to all reason. Holy Scripture commands and warns in many places that no vision or dream is to be credited now that the fullness of time has arrived and the whole will of God has been revealed through Christ. For example, Deut. 13[:3]: "you must not heed the words of those prophets or those who divine by dreams." Also Lev. 19[:31] "Do not turn to mediums or wizards; do not seek them out, to be defiled by them." Also Jer. 27[:9]: "You, therefore, must not listen to your prophets, your diviners, your dreamers." Lev. 20[:27] says that if dreamers are found with you they must be killed [misquoted, ed.]. Not only do their dreams not yield anything godly or good; rather they obviously strive against God's Word and all Christian order ordained by God. Such dreamers and visionaries are not only to be considered liars and spirits of Beelzebub, but are nowhere to be tolerated with their godless interpretations and expositions. Even if the vision or dream exhibits nothing contrary to God's Word, as in the case of this vision by which he confesses and accepts baptism as useful, yet the intent is godless and an insufferable horror. That is, that he approves of baptism not because of Scripture which orders, institutes, and inaugurates it but because of his vision; not because of the divine Word, but because of his baseless dreams.

Fifthly. They do not believe that in our Lord's Supper the actual body and the blood of Christ is present, nor that it may be given to the hungry and the thirsty, that is, the believers by a man. This is no wonder, since they give no credence to the whole Scripture. If, as was indicated in another article, they could through God's grace be brought to the point of accepting Holy Scripture, believing it, and allowing themselves to be shown and convinced, then one could present to them the words of Christ appended to the Supper, which are accepted by all godly people. One could present an earnest and thorough explanation to them and induce and bring them to a right and godly knowledge of the Supper with the majesty of the eternal Word of Christ. Since, however, this has been done in recent times by many in many places against the fanatics in valid and fruitful ways, and since thorough refutation of this error (where it might be necessary) can be obtained from these books, we consider it superfluous to write more about it at present. Nevertheless, the words of Christ at the Supper (This is my body, etc.) are to be presented and carefully explained to them briefly. Use especially the words of Paul in 1 Cor. 10[:16]: "The bread which we break, is it not the communion of the blood of Christ?" etc. From this saying of Paul especially it can be concluded that the body of Christ and his holy blood are present not only with God, as the fanatics dream but also in the Supper in essence, and are distributed according to the order of God.

Some fanatic may confess that he believes the body and the blood of Christ to be present in the Supper, but that since the beginning of his sect he has not wanted to receive it, nor would receive it in future until God commanded him. This kind of personal presumption and dreaming is overthrown and condemned by the clear words of Christ himself. For Christ does not command us that we should deprive ourselves of this spiritual food or to limit our participation until he gives us further faith for the need of our soul without neglect. He says: "Take and eat," etc. "Do this in remembrance of me, hereby declare my death," etc. Thus every Christian must in faith obey the command once given and shall not wait for any other. For the covenant of Christ is an eternally valid covenant in which God has revealed all his divine treasures completely, and presented them to his own. It is such a complete covenant that nothing can be added or removed by anyone. The fullness and sum of all divine promises and will is completely contained in this covenant and is presented as instruction to all those of right faith. We are nowhere commanded to expect any further command outside of this instruction at any time in the future, neither in dream nor in vision. It follows that such intention is nothing but devilish, erring speculation and inspiration. Again, as in the case of infant baptism, the fanatic contradicts himself when he says that the actual body and blood are present in Christ's Supper, and that to receive it is good, but not because of the institution of Christ nor the word of God, but because of his visions and dreams.

Sixthly. They hold in common and contribute their goods each according to his good will, and yet urge no one to deliver or give up all his goods or a certain amount, as the Anabaptists enforce. We do not consider this to be a misdemeanour worthy of any heavy or severe punishment at the present time. Nor can we attack or condemn it especially heavily with Holy Scripture. Yet one is concerned that if such small beginnings were to continue and were to be allowed and tolerated, that they might in time increase and cause larger and wider harm. Therefore we judge that this intent, although small and not in itself sufficiently punishable, should be dealt with and forbidden by suitable, tolerable means, so that out of it in time there might not arise greater harm.

Lastly. Looking at the fanaticisms of this new sect, it seems that they do not believe in Christ, nor think that the suffering of the Son of God was sufficient payment for sin nor eternal reconciliation of believers with God the Father. One of them says: Why Christ suffered he did not know, but God does. With this statement he admits that he has little or no regard for Christ. A Christian who has put on Christ in justifying faith does not doubt. He believes steadfastly, knows, is sure, and confesses that not only God but also he, together with all the elect knows why and for what reason Christ suffered and shed his holy blood. He knows that it was done for the forgiveness of the sin of all believers and for their redemption, purification and sanctification. At all times he stands in good, unshakable hope and trust that he is well off and, together with Christ is a co-heir of all the godly heritage with God the Father because of the mercy of Christ which he has earned and accomplished for us through his holy suffering. He believes that after this sorrowful misery and life he will possess eternal life and the heavenly fatherland full of joy. For thus says Paul, 1 Cor. 2[:12]: "Now we have received, not the spirit of the world, but the spirit which is of God; that we might know the things that are freely given to us by God."

9

Lamprecht Penntz

Recantation Procedures (1528)*

Introduction

Lamprecht Penntz was a baker by trade. He and his wife were both named in a directive from the government of Ferdinand I to the district governor of Hertenberg in June 1528. By this time the case of Lamprecht Penntz had already been discussed once. A report in mid-May had informed the governor of Hertenberg that a fleeing Anabaptist woman had been to see her brother in Telfs and had also met with Lamprecht. Perhaps after this meeting the baker went home and persuaded his wife to join the Anabaptists, too. The sources are not clear on this. We do know, however, that by June both Lamprecht and his wife were in prison in the district of Hertenberg because they were Anabaptists.

---

*Source: Grete Mecenseffy, ed. *Quellen zur Geschichte der Täufer, Österreich II Teil* (Gütersloh: Gerd Mohn, 1972), 173.
Translation: Linda Huebert Hecht

The directive of June 1528 discussed a request for the pardon of all Anabaptist men and women imprisoned in Hertenberg. The government's response was quite explicit. The prisoners could not be excused from the mandate that had been sent out at the end of May. Moreover, two married couples, Hans and Barbara Velcklehner and Lamprecht Penntz and his wife, were singled out and mentioned specifically.

One week later, Lamprecht Penntz and his wife had the possibility of leaving prison. It seems that Hans and Barbara Velcklehner had escaped prison, but the Penntz couple had remained behind. Because of this and the fact that a request had already been submitted on their behalf, orders were given for their release, providing they paid for the expense of their upkeep in prison and performed the proper public acts of penance.

It was not until October of the same year that the government of Innsbruck sent out the exact procedure for the penance and recantation of Lamprecht Penntz and his wife. As was usually the case, it was to take place in the local church on three consecutive Sundays. They were to walk barefoot in procession with the parish priest around the church, kneel in front of the altar during mass, and then read the outlined recantation [*Widerspruch*] publicly to everyone present. Only in this way could they be reinstated into the Roman Catholic church. A translation of Ferdinand's instructions in the Penntz case is presented below.

Since there are no further references in the court records to the baker and his wife, we may assume that they complied and no longer associated with the Anabaptists.

Bibliographical Source:

C. Arnold Snyder and Linda A. Huebert Hecht, eds., *Profiles of Anabaptist Women: Sixteenth-Century Reforming Pioneers* (Waterloo, ON: Wilfrid Laurier University Press, 1996).

RECANTATION PROCEDURES

October 10, 1528, Innsbruck. —The government of Ferdinand I to Lamprecht Haun, Judge of Hertenberg.—Sends a directive to pardon Lamprecht Penntz and his wife. The wording of the recantation is enclosed.[1]

Faithful one! We have read your report regarding Lanndtprechten [Lamprecht] Penntzen and respond with the order that you ensure that they both be present on three consecutive Sundays in front of the high altar in their parish church before the observance of mass, in order to join the usual procession and walk barefoot in front of the priest around the church. Penntz is to bring up the rear and his wife is to carry a cross in her hands.[2] Following that they are to give a public recantation in the church as recorded on the enclosed papers. Then they are to remain in front of the altar on their knees for the duration of the mass and receive absolution from the priest after that. This is the mandate from his majesty, the 10th day of October, 1528.

1. I confess, that through damnable unchristian teaching and instruction, I fell away from the Christian baptism, and no longer adhered to it.

2. In addition, I confess that I did not believe in [*nichts gehaltn*] the holy mass and the most worthy sacrament and did not believe that the bread and the wine truly contained the body and blood of Jesus Christ our Saviour.

3. I confess that I did not place my faith in [*nichts gehalten*] the mediation of Mary, the Mother of God and the saints or in many other articles of the Christian faith. I have erred and did not believe and have gone against the practice of the Christian Church and have instructed others in my erroneous faith.

All this I recant voluntarily and with proper understanding [*mit guetm vorwissen*]. I contradict all of (my previous belief) and praise God the almighty before those assembled in this church, promising to desist from such error, never again to associate with it, and also to believe all that which the united [*gmayn*] Christian church has established and ordained. I also want to attend confession with my priest and partake of the holy sacrament when he deems it appropriate.

10

Ursula Hellrigel

Ausbund, The 36th Song (1529)*

Introduction

Ursula Hellrigel languished in the prisons of Tyrol for five years before finally being allowed to join the Anabaptists in their new home of Moravia. The Tyrolean government had first responded to Ursula's staunch adherence to her Anabaptist belief with severe punishment, then with repeated postponement, and seemingly forgot about her. However, the persistence of family members and others seeking her release finally brought results. Ursula's story is unusual in itself, but the fact that she wrote a hymn makes this young woman all the more significant.[1]

In May of 1538 the seventeen-year-old Ursula Hellrigel, daughter of a peasant farmer, was one of ten Anabaptist prisoners held at the St. Petersberg castle in the upper Inn Valley. Despite various efforts by

---

*Source: *Ausbund, Das ist: Etliche schöne Christliche Lieder, wie sie in dem Gefängnis zu Passau in dem Schloss von den Schweizer Brüdern und von andern rechglaubigen Christen hin und her gedichtet worden* (Elkhart, IN: Mennonitischen Verlagshandlung, 1880).
Translation: Pamela Klassen

local authorities, Ursula stubbornly persisted in her beliefs and refused to recant. Uncertain of what to do, the authorities asked the king for advice on what to do next. The king responded, instructing the authorities in St. Petersberg to do everything in their power to persuade the tenacious Anabaptists to recant in order to save their souls.

Approximately two years later Ursula was still in prison, but was transferred to the castle at Haselburg south of Bozen and then transferred to Sigmundskron, where she was to be kept on a minimal diet and given minimal clothing. Another year passed before further attention was paid to Ursula's case, at which point she was moved to Innsbruck and imprisoned with another group of Anabaptists. Finally, on October 9, 1543, king Ferdinand's government advised local authorities to release Ursula Hellrigel. She had to agree to leave the territory of Tyrol and never return to her homeland on penalty of losing her life. Ursula did agree to leave her home, but refused to swear that she would never return. Surprisingly, the authorities gave in to her objection and agreed to release Ursula merely on the basis of her promise to leave.[2]

The hymn that she wrote, which is translated here, provides some clues as to what sustained her during her five-year imprisonment. It appears that she was not the only member of her family to compose hymns; Zacharias Hellrigel (1580-1630, exact relationship unknown) wrote five hymns. Probably because of her hymn, Ursula's story is one of the few women's stories included in the history later written by the Hutterites in Moravia.

Although there is general agreement that the following hymn was in fact written by Ursula, since it was copied into Hutterite codices under her name, the hymn itself was published and printed only in the *Ausbund*, which attributes the hymn not to Ursula, but to Annelein of Freiburg, about whom very little is known. It is no longer possible to unravel how Ursula's hymn came to be attributed to Annelein in the *Ausbund*, or why it was preserved only in the published Swiss Brethren hymn tradition, and not in the Hutterite hymn tradition. The hymn/prayer is written in the first person throughout, and is a prayerful testament of faith.[3]

Bibliographical Source:

C. Arnold Snyder and Linda A. Huebert Hecht, eds., *Profiles of Anabaptist Women: Sixteenth-Century Reforming Pioneers* (Waterloo, ON: Wilfrid Laurier University Press, 1996).

Ausbund
The 36th Song

Another song of Annelein of Freiburg,
who was drowned and then burned, 1529.

To the tune of "In you I have hoped, Lord."

1. Everlasting Father in heaven,
   I call on you so ardently,
   Do not let me turn from you.
   Keep me in your truth
   Until my final end.

2. O God, guard my heart and mouth,
   Lord watch over me at all times,
   Let nothing separate me from you,
   Be it affliction, anxiety, or need,
   Keep me pure in joy.

3. My everlasting Lord and Father,
   Show and teach me,
   Poor unworthy child that I am,
   So that I heed your path and way.
   In this lies my desire,

4. To walk through your power into death,
   Through sorrow, torture, fear and want.
   Sustain me in this,
   O God, so that I nevermore
   Be separated from your love.

5. Many travel along this road,
   The cup of suffering lies there,
   And also many untrue teachings
   Which try to turn us away
   From Christ our Lord.

6. To you I raise up my soul, Lord,
   I depend on you in misfortune.
   Do not let me come to harm,
   That my enemy not stand over me
   On this earth.

7. They have imprisoned me.
   I wait, O God, with all my heart,
   With very great longing,
   When finally you will awake
   And set your prisoners free.

8. O God, Father, make us like
   The five virgins of your kingdom,
   Who were prudently careful
   To wait for the bridegroom,
   With his chosen flock.

9. Eternal king of heaven,
   Feed us and quench our thirst
   In a spiritual way
   With your food of truth
   Which never perishes

10. If you withhold your food from us
    Everything is lost and useless.
    Without you we bring forth nothing.
    Through grace we trust in you,
    It will not fail us.

11. I do not doubt God's power.
    His judgments all are true.
    He will not abandon anyone
    Who stands firm in the faith,
    And stays on the true paths.

12. Be comforted you Christians and rejoice,
    Through Jesus Christ forevermore,
    Who gives us love and faith.
    God comforts us through his holy Word,
    On that we should rely.

13. I entrust myself to God and his church.
    May he be my protector today,
    For the sake of his name.
    May this come to pass, Father mine,
    Through Jesus Christ, Amen.

11

Hans Nadler

Declaration of the Needle Merchant Hans at Erlangen and the Refutation of the Articles of the Needle Merchant Hans (1529)*

Introduction

Hans Nadler (fl. 1527-1529) became an Anabaptist under the influence of Hans Hut who baptized Nadler and his wife in 1527. Originally from Erlangen near Nuremberg, Nadler was a needle seller by trade and his home became a central meeting place for Hans Hut and Hut's followers. The group was broken up by Nuremberg authorities and Nadler was implicated by Thomas Spiegel, who had been captured. Hut left for Nicholsburg and Nadler, who was not caught at that time, went with him "to explore the new and old faith," leaving his wife and children behind, despite her pleading with him to stay.[1]

Nadler travelled constantly, and wherever he went he preached. This was all the more remarkable because Nadler was uneducated and illiterate. His many business contacts provided opportunities for Anabaptist evangelism, and evidently, the people to whom he preached were also common folk.[2]

---

*Source: Schornbaum, *Quellen II*, 131-41; 143-47.
Translation: Friesen/Klaassen

Nadler may have been present at the disputation between Hubmaier and Hut in Nicholsburg, as was Hans Schlaffer. It could be that Nadler disapproved of the way Hubmaier conducted mass baptisms without requiring individual professions of faith.[3] Sometime after the disputation in Nicholsburg, Nadler had returned to Erlangen where he was arrested on January 17, 1529 and cross-examined.[4] In response to the question of why he had returned he said that God had given him the grace to return to his wife and children.

The first document is Nadler's confession of 1529. The second document is an official refutation of his answers, to which is appended an official consideration of what is to be done with him.

The confession consists of Nadler's answers to specific questions, which were recorded by a court secretary as they were given. The replies are mostly in the third person, but sometimes shift to the first person. The questions asked are no longer extant, and therefore some of the answers are unintelligible.

Nadler's answers shed light on his role as an Anabaptist lay person. He had never baptised others; he had accepted baptism for himself because he did not know anything of his childhood baptism, except what his parents had told him (This was a common reply by arrested Anabaptists). He did admit to providing guidance to those who wished baptism for themselves. He also discussed issues concerning communion, possessions and nonresistance. He did not act contrary to government for it was ordained by God; furthermore, he denied that the Anabaptists were instigating revolt.[5]

Nadler's reflection on the Lord's Prayer reflects an interest in this basic catechetical tool that was often seen in the South German Anabaptist movement. Langenmantel, Schiemer and Hubmaier also wrote expositions of the Lord's Prayer.

On February 13, 1529, Nadler was tried again. This time he was tortured in an attempt to get him to recant; he remained true to his faith but was nevertheless released. Afterwards, he was permitted to sell his property and move to Moravia with his wife and three children. Nothing more is known about him or his life in Moravia.

Nadler's confession provides a a fascinating glimpse into the world of the "common people" of the sixteenth century. These people made up the rank and file membership of the early South German Anabaptist movement. As his testimony demonstrates, Nadler's low social status and lack of education did not signify a lack of religious sophistication or evangelical fervor.[6] To the contrary, his testimony reveals the existence of an elaborate "oral text" that he had committed to memory, and that he utilized when he engaged potential converts. Nadler's "text" included rudimentary instruction in matters of faith, built on the catechetical foundations of the Lord's Prayer and the Apostles' Creed that were common property of the masses, literate and illiterate alike. Preserved for us by a court scribe, Nadler's confession sheds significant light on the functioning of the oral/aural world of common people of the sixteenth century.

Bibliographical Sources:

Christian Neff, "Nadler (Ritter), Hans," *ME III*, 805.

Werner O. Packull, *Mysticism and the Early South German-Austrian Anabaptist Movement, 1525-1531* (Scottdale, PA: Herald Press, 1977).

Russell Snyder-Penner, "Hans Nadler's oral exposition of the Lord's Prayer," *MQR* 65 (October 1991), 393-406.

George H. Williams, *The Radical Reformation* 3rd edition (Kirksville, MO: Sixteenth Century Journal Publishers, 1992).

A. Declaration of the Needle Merchant Hans at Erlangen. January 17, 1529

1. It was God's Word that forced him to this, namely three passages. The first was that many are called but few are chosen. The second is that the way of God is straight and narrow and there are few that find it. The third verse is that not everyone who says, Lord, Lord, will enter the kingdom of God; he who does the will of my Father will enter into the kingdom of God.

2. Hans Hut had helped him to this position and advised him by the power of God which God gave him.

3. It happened in his house about two years ago.

4. He has no knowledge of whether any of his brethren were admitted. He had stayed outside as long as he did because of the weakness of his flesh; he feared torture. In the meantime I heard that in the land of my gracious lord Margrave, who is my lord over body and property, the Gospel and the Word of God were being preached. I prayed to God that it might be his will to give me power and strength so that I might again enter by day without all fear, as I went out by day to my wife and children. The Lord has given me the strength, may He be praised.

5. He traded with needles. With that he earned his living. It was here and there along the Rhine river and other places in the land, with cobblers and tailors.

6. He knew all the others except Ambrosius of Linz and Johan [Ludwig] Hätzer, and he does not know but that they are almost all dead.

7. He was at Nicholsburg below Vienna for fourteen days. There in the church they openly baptized about seventy-two people in one day. The baptism was there, but there was no Christian discipline as is written in the Acts of the Apostles.[7] They were shocked at this and scattered, some here and some there.

8. He hopes that it is still the truth since God's Word clearly indicates so, as is written in Mark 16 when the Lord Christ says: "Go into all the world, proclaim the gospel of all creatures. Whoever believes and is baptized will be saved. Whoever does not believe is damned," says the Lord. By this word I am confident that God's Word is no heresy. As he has spoken and commanded, so I have done and taught. So you also are to do and teach, since Christ himself did this and had himself baptized in his thirtieth year.

9. He may have it here and there in the land, but he has no knowledge of it.

10. He does not know. They have no fixed abode.

11. He knows none of them around here. Half a year ago he was at Berren's place. But he does not know where he is now nor whether he is alive or dead.[8]

12. Yes, if one or more persons came to him or were brought to him, he taught as follows:

I said, "My brother or sister, a Christian must suffer much. Are you prepared, for the sake of truth, to suffer persecution, contempt, scorn, the forsaking of house, yard, wife and child, all for the sake of the Lord? If God gives you the grace so that the Word of God is opened to you, you must abstain from all the joys of the world which the flesh desires, from eating, drinking, whoring, gambling and from blaspheming, from dancing and jumping, which man desires. Do you wish to do this, my brother or sister? If you do not have confidence to do this with the help of God, you may well go your way. For it is written, the Lord desires no enforced service."

If they said, "Yes, my brother, with the help of God," I replied, "Yes, my brother or sister, you must receive the Word of God like a child and must be born anew. For the Lord says to Nicodemus, 'Unless a man is born again, he cannot enter the kingdom of God.' Nicodemus says, 'Can a man, when he is old, return to the body of his mother and be born again?' The Lord says, 'Are you a master in Israel and do not understand that? What is of the flesh is flesh and what is of the spirit is spirit. The wind blows where it wants and you well hear its blowing but do not know where it comes from or where it goes. Unless a man is born again through water and through the Holy Spirit, he cannot enter the kingdom of heaven' [John 3:3-5]. The angel Gabriel, that is the power of God, was sent by the Father. You are to receive the Word of God as Mary received it when she said: 'I am the maidservant of the Lord. Let it happen to me according to your word' [Luke 1:38] Thus you will receive the Word and will now be a child of God and never live according to the pleasure of the world, and will from now on live according to the will of God and be submissive to God, giving your body as a willing sacrifice which is good and holy and pleasing to God. See, my brother or sister, if you submit yourself to God in this way and divest yourself of the world, it will hate you, will be opposed to you, and will say all kinds of evil of you. This you must suffer patiently.

Then the saying will be fulfilled: 'Rejoice if they say all kinds of evil about you if you did not do it.'"

After that I began teaching, starting with the Lord's prayer, and said: "You say, 'Our Father in heaven.' So you must learn, my brother or sister, and consider that you will now be a child of God when you say, 'Father.' You must live according to his divine will and must do as the Word of God and the Holy Gospel teaches, and which you have often heard. That you must do.

Secondly you say: 'May your name be made holy.' Look, my brother or sister, why have you slandered the name of God? You are to make it holy, and you slander it. Look at your prayer. How did you pray? You have chattered a great deal but have not considered in your heart where it goes.

Then you continue: 'May your kingdom come.' How can the kingdom of God come into you while you blaspheme him? My brother, if God comes with his kingdom and wants to come to you, he does not come to his own unless he brings the cross, to each one his own cross. Now whenever God laid something upon you as a punishment, you fled to the devil and cried to one saint here and to another one there. My brother, this you must forsake and must now live like a child of God. Then the kingdom of God can enter you.

'May your will be done.' If God's will is now to happen, we must become completely and wholly yielded and rely upon the Lord, that his will may be done in us on earth as in heaven. In heaven no one is against him. So on earth we are not to be against him either, if we claim to be true Christians.

Now we ask him for daily bread, of body and soul.

'Forgive us our sins.' In the same way we will also forgive and pardon all those who act against us. This you must do," I taught them. "But you ordinarily ask vengeance for yourselves. Now truly the word must become deed.

'And lead us not into temptation,' dear Lord, into which the whole world wants to draw us, so that we are not tempted through our own flesh or through the pleasures of the world. Rather, Lord, deliver us if we have fallen into such evil and from all evil."

That is the way I taught them to pray. Amen.

Concerning faith I have taught as follows:

You are to believe in one God, creator of heaven and the earth. Now since you believe in a God of heaven and of the earth, you are not to have any other god made for yourself, whether it be of stone, wood, silver or gold, nor of bread or cheese.

The next article of the Creed is: I believe in the one Son, our Lord Jesus Christ, who was conceived by Mary the virgin, who suffered under Pontius Pilate, was crucified, died and was buried, descended into hell, rose again on the third day from the dead, descended into hell, rose again on the third day from the dead, ascended into heaven where he sits at the right hand of God the almighty Father, from where he will come to judge the living and the dead.

After that it is written: I believe in the Holy Spirit, a holy Christian church; I believe that there is a communion of the saints and a remission of sin and a resurrection of the flesh and an eternal life after this life.

This I have taught, if a brother or a sister came to me, according to my knowledge.

13. They talked about and discussed the seven judgments. But he had not been able to enter into nor understand them for he is not educated.

14. Yes, he is baptized.

15. Hans Hut baptized him, and the Word of God moved him to it, for Christ says, "Whoever believes and is baptized will be saved" [Mark 16:16]. It was on the strength of this that I did it.

16. No, he did not baptize. I have not been commanded to do it, nor was I ordained to it.

17. He was told that he was baptized. His parents told him. I was present. But I have no knowledge of it for I was a child and had no understanding. Nor did I know of any faith. But the one who was my godfather spoke for me, saying "I believe." It was about forty years ago that this happened. It may be that since all things are becoming perverse these days, the women are beginning to bear children who have faith. That I do not know. But one must first ask the children about it. If they have the faith, they will confess it. If they have faith like a mustard seed and say to that mountain, "Rise, and throw yourself into the sea," it will happen. If they say to this mulberry tree, "Root yourself up and go to a different place," it will happen [Matt. 17:20; Luke 17:6]. We all speak of faith, but we don't much do the works of faith. James says in his epistle that faith without works is dead. He says that the devil also believes and trembles, but will not be saved for the sake of his faith [James 2:17-19]. And now they marshal the Scriptures to maintain infant baptism with it. But there is not a single letter about it that I know of. They want to baptize children and do baptize them

although they are pure already and are a creation of God, good and well made. Who can improve through infant baptism that which God has made good? What kind of woman would it be, who would wash a nice white dress, and would keep on a black one that was soiled? First of all let each one remove himself from sins and cleanse himself and confess before the almighty and learn the faith, and afterwards have himself washed so that he is clean. And the little child which is clean and beautiful, draw it away from sin and teach it the faith when it becomes dirty and falls into sin; if it believes, it may well be baptized according to the command of Christ. This is my understanding.

Whether he really believed, I do no know. My godfather said, I renounce. Did he renounce the devil? I do not know. He said, I want to be a child of God. Was he a child of God? I do not know that either. My godfather will not be saved for me, nor will he be damned for me. I must be saved or damned for myself. I have examined this in my heart, namely that infant baptism has never helped me. I prayed to idols and considered that to be God which is not God. This I have recognized by the help of God my Lord and have given over my body under the hand of God. I now desire to forsake evil and sin as much as God gives me strength and grace. All that I have, body, soul, honour and goods, I have committed to God my Lord and to my brothers and sisters, in order to help where they need it. Therefore I accepted the sign of the water, that by it my brothers and sisters would know that I wanted to be united with them, and to be ready to be rebuked by the Word of God. Where I do wrong, I want to accept such a rebuke. They also will accept a rebuke from me, as Scripture shows when Christ says, "If you see your brother err, rebuke him between yourself and him alone. If he listens to you, you have won his soul. But if he does not listen to you, take one or two more with you so that the witness of two or three may support you. If he does not listen to them either, report him to the congregation, the church of God. If he will not listen to the church of God either, excommunicate him so that he blushes for shame. Consider him to be a heathen until he comes to himself" [Matt. 18:15-17]. That is the Christian order we have among ourselves. If he comes to himself, he is again accepted into the congregation. In the meantime [the congregation] prays to God for him until he comes to himself.

18. They have no other mutual obligation than that indicated in article 17.

19. When one comes to the other, he says, "May the peace of the Lord be with you." He answers, "Amen, with you also, my brother, and with us all."

20. Yes, he bestowed it all on us freely as a present, just as he fared, suffering, persecution, disdain, scorn, and scoffing, and has assigned to each his own cross, to follow him, to die, to be buried, in time to rise and have eternal life. All that he has bestowed on us together. Whoever would have eternal life must also suffer. Whoever will not suffer is a bastard. A bastard does not inherit. One must be a child of God to inherit.

21. He has no knowledge of the new kingdom. He believes that He will come again to judge the living and the dead. He leaves it at that.

22. Yes, one must have government on account of the evil people. They are all ordained by God, whether bad or good.

23. No action is to be taken against the government, for it is not for any Christian to fight or to do battle. There are among us many brethren who want us to lay down completely all swords or defence. I have done this, but it is not a law. One may bear it or leave it according to whether he is strong or weak in the faith.

24. Sacrament is a name indicating a holy thing, an object representing what is holy. But that the body of Christ is in the bread, I do not believe. That were a poor God indeed who allowed himself to be eaten. For the Lord himself spoke it, "That which goes into the mouth goes out again in the natural way" [Matt. 15:17]. For where has there ever been a man as long as the world has stood who has been as lofty, and as great as God the eternal Father who created all that lives and breathes, through the Word? No man has ever reached his eminence and never will reach it whether it be the pope and his party or Luther and his party. Only the eternal Father has made and created his only son Jesus Christ through the Word into the pure body of Mary the Virgin. He was conceived through the Holy Spirit, was incarnated man, and was born. He has shown and prepared the way for us. Him we are to follow. He died on the cross, was buried, descended into hell, rose again on the third day from the dead, and has ascended to heaven and sits at the right hand of God the heavenly Father. He is equal to the Father and to his divine power and glory. No man could accomplish this by the word. Only the eternal Father has been able to do this.

But now they say that when the Lord sat at the table with his twelve disciples, he took bread such as we are accustomed to eat, broke it, and thanking God, his heavenly Father, he said, "Take and eat, this is my body." But he never said that the bread was his body. It is my understanding that he was referring to his members who ate with him. For it is written: "The many are one loaf and one bread." The second evangelist says thus: "This is my body which is offered for you." Here, too, he does not say the bread is my body. If bread were his body, he would have given Judas a piece also and would have said, "Go, give it to the Jews and tell them to torture it." For his body, too, recoiled from suffering. But it could not be the body of Christ, who was with them at the table, and who was to suffer and did suffer. Now the third evangelist says: "This is my body which is broken for you." He also does not say, the bread is my body. It is my understanding that he is speaking of the scourging, of the crowning, of the nailing to the cross, and of the spear. In the breaking of this body no part was spared. If the bread is his body, as they say, and was true flesh and blood as he hung on the cross, I could use those words too[9] I and others, for it has all been translated into German. If that were so I could well make gods for myself so that I could eat my belly full. But it is written that what goes into the mouth goes out again in the natural way. It is my understanding that that would be a great blasphemy. In John 6 it is written: "I am the living bread which has come down from heaven" (not the bread which is baked in the oven), "which gives life to the world. Whoever eats of this bread, will live eternally." Should the living bread then sneak into the perishable bread, as they say, because of the words which they speak over it, since he himself is the Word? They say it is God's Word and one must believe the Word. But is not that also Gods' Word and must they not believe that also? Further John says in chapter 6 in conclusion, "The Bread which I give you is spirit and life."

My understanding is that we are to hear the Word of God from the Holy Gospel and are to live and act according to it. That person lives eternally who lives and acts according to it. That is what it means to receive the body of Christ spiritually. Thus I understand it. But they have said and still say, as I mentioned before, that one must receive him in the form of bread, as he verily hung on the cross. After that they say: one must understand him in spirit. Is flesh and spirit identical? Flesh is tangible, spirit is intangible. Thus the bread is a tangible thing, which one sees and touches. I cannot grasp with my mind that flesh can be spirit. They say, he lives in the bread. Long ago God spoke through the prophet Isaiah [66:1]: "Heaven is my throne, the earth my footstool; what kind of a house or dwelling would you make for me?" I do not want to live in a temple made by human hands. One finds in the

Acts of the Apostles chapters 7 and 17, "I am not served by human hands," and "Which is the place of my rest?" Surely if God lives in the bread, as they say, and surely if bread is made by human hands, then God must surely not be at that spot. It cannot be, since he is that God who is everywhere and has always been. Philip says to the Lord: "Show me the Father." The Lord says to Philip: "Whoever sees me, sees the Father and whoever sees the Father, sees me."

Further they bring out Saint Paul, saying that he too observed the Lord's Supper. I admit it, as long as they had established a Christian order as Paul did, and as is recorded in Acts. That would be a godly people living the Word of God and the command of Christ. Then they could also celebrate the Lord's Supper with one another as those celebrated it, breaking the bread here and there in houses. It was not done also in the temple where the church of God was gathered, not with blasphemers, not with whores, with the avaricious, nor the envious, nor robbers, nor thieves, nor with murderers and the like. Those who live godly lives and show their Christianity in their works as Christ commanded are the church of God, as is written above, and the temple of God in which God desires to live. I would gladly be with such a congregation of God. That is my understanding of the Lord's Supper and the body of Christ. If I err at any points, which I do not now know, I ask God, my Lord, to tear such an error out of my heart. He knows all hearts and I greatly desire to be saved. Amen.

Concerning the sacrament of the blood.

"When they had eaten their supper, he took the cup, blessed it and gave it to the disciples and said: 'Drink, all of you, this is the cup of the new and eternal covenant in my blood.'" He did not say, the blood is in the cup. Since the cup is in his blood as he himself indicated, my understanding is that in this way he indicates his suffering and that this is the earnest and the agreement, that we are to follow him through suffering, as the disciples themselves proved it with their suffering. When the mother of the two sons of Zebedee came and said: "Lord, say that these my two sons may sit one to your right and the other to your left in your kingdom," the Lord said: "Are you able to drink the cup I drink and be baptized with the baptism with which I will be baptized?" "We are," they answered. "You shall drink, but to seat one to the right the other to the left is not in my power. That is prepared by my heavenly Father." The Lord shows us more when he knelt on the Mount of Olives: "Father, if it is possible, take away the cup of this suffering. But let not my will, but yours happen." Thus it is my understanding that the drinking of the cup is his suffering.

25. Christ is the eternal Word and is God in unity with God the Father. He is the prophet who was promised, as is written, "I will raise up a prophet."

26. God has no mother. He is born in eternity. But the Word which went forth from the Father was in the beginning with God, John 1. Mary bore this same eternal Word which went forth from the Father. That is Christ our redeemer become man.

27. Who set the day, the hour, or the year, I do not know. No one but the Father knows the day and the hour. But the time is not far away.

28. With no overt oath nor with any binding promises, only with brotherly love, as is written above.

29. I only know that it was practised in the Christian church. We support one another, especially those who had nothing. This was to avoid becoming a burden to anyone, as Paul says.

30. No one was the disciple of anyone else. I am a poor unprofitable servant of Christ my Lord.

31. Property of one's own is a good thing if one uses it rightly. And if one uses it as Christ has commanded, it serves towards one's salvation.

32. I hold that the government is a servant of God if it executes the command as is written in the books of Moses, I do not know where.

33. Whoever does right, and forsakes unrighteousness, is saved.

34. The devil will not be saved unless he first becomes an angel. Whoever is godless, has no God. If he has no God, in whom will he believe? The Lord said, "Whoever believes will be saved. Whoever does not believe is already condemned." What damnation is or how long it lasts, God knows; I do not know it, for I am a poor creature.

35. It is given to the godless for their instruction, so that they might recognize their God by means of it. God has created all people of whatever faith they are. But to believers it was given for salvation so that they are saved by it if they live according to this word.

36. I do no know whether the spears are ready,[10] whether he will come in 23 hundred or in two hundred or in a thousand years. But the Scripture says: You are all to repent, forsake sin, and turn to God. All that is evil will be destroyed, but the devout and the godly he will take into his kingdom. "Therefore," says Christ, "Struggle to enter by the strait gate" [Matt. 7:13].

37. Whatever is godless has no God and may not rule with God. Whoever is against God is not with God, as Christ says.

38. They themselves do not do what they teach. They do speak of the Word and of faith but do not themselves believe and do not themselves do as they speak. They claim to be teachers of Christ and do not teach according to the command of Christ. Christ spoke and said: "Go out into the whole world, proclaim the gospel of all creatures. Whoever believes and is baptized, will be saved; whoever does not believe is condemned." The Lord said, "Go," and they sit down. He said: "Give freely, for you have freely received." Formerly, it was sufficient to pay thirty or forty guilders to be a priest. Now it costs a hundred or two hundred guilders, perhaps more or perhaps less. Is that giving freely? But it is to be given without cost. It has come to the point that one preaches one or two sermons a week and it costs a farthing a word! If only they believed about faith as they speak of it! The bishop of Mainz, the bishop of Würzburg, the bishop of Bamberg and the bishop of Eichstätt have many good, dear people who also wish to be saved. Of this I have no doubt. As Christ our Lord did, go into the bishoprics and into the churches, wherever you think there is false, unrighteous teaching, and tell them their shortcomings and their misguided faith to their faces. Christ our Lord did this to Jerusalem, when he said, "Woe to you," nine times, as is written in Matt. 23. Christ said that every one of your hairs is numbered and not one falls to the ground without the will of the Father. One buys two sparrows for a farthing, and not one falls to the ground without the will of the Father. If you believe as you talk, nothing will happen to any of you, for the mouth of truth himself has said it. Therefore do not be afraid, for you are worth much more than sparrows.

39. I am not certain that they are united in their practice of the Lord's Supper, for I was not always with them where they are. Nor do I know where they are at any time. But I was with them at a place called Augsburg about a year and a half ago. There at Augsburg we celebrated the Lord's Supper, the Lord's wine and bread. The bread indicates the unity, for many kernels made up one loaf of bread. One must first grind them to a powder; then one makes a loaf of it with water and by the heat of the oven. So must we, the many make up one loaf and one bread as is written. That happens through suffering. As Christ our dear Lord went before us, so we are to follow him. This bread represents unity. Whoever is willing to do this, whoever yields himself willingly thus under the cross with the Lord, may join in the Lord's Supper also. There-

fore each one must examine himself, for it is in this way that he may eat of this bread. It is similar with the wine. Many grapes become one wine and one drink. This happens through the suffering of the wine press. It indicates suffering. It is the same as in the case of the bread. Whoever wishes to be in the brotherly unity may drink from the cup of the Lord, for the cup indicates suffering. This unity we celebrated as described when I was present. But whether they still celebrate it in this way, I do not know.

40. As was indicated before, wherever I travelled in the land, I lived on what people gave me of food and drink for the penny earned with my merchant goods.

41. Wherever I travelled in the land, if I met or found a good-hearted person in inns or on the street, I gave him instruction from the Word of God, as was indicated before.

42. I did not tell each one what my purpose was, for it was not necessary. As it happens with us, wherever one finds one and another elsewhere, one overcomes them all.[11]

Thus I have learned from God and have been instructed by my brethren. Thus I also taught, as is written. I have conducted myself in my activity as I indicated above. That is my faith. If I am in error in any of this, I ask God, my Lord, that he impart grace to me, that I might attain to true, right knowledge. For it is written, "Blessed are those who hunger and thirst after righteousness, for they shall be satisfied" [Matt. 5:6]. For this I trust God, my Lord. Amen.

B. Refutation of the Articles of the Needle Merchant Hans. February 1, 1529

The answer to the first question can be countered by pointing to the 19th chapter of Matthew, where Christ says (as is also written in Genesis, the second chapter), that a man will leave father and mother and cleave to his wife.

It can also be refuted by what Paul said in 1 Cor. 7: "Let the man render to his wife due benevolence and similarly the wife the man. The woman is not ruler over her body, but the man. Similarly the man is not ruler over his body, but the woman." At the same place Saint Paul also says that a believing spouse ought not to separate from the unbelieving one, also that each one remain in his calling.

Further, he says in 1 Tim. 5: "If anyone does not provide for his own, especially those of his household, he has denied the faith and is worse than an infidel."

These sayings of Holy Scripture show clearly, that a married man is to remain with his wife and child, to feed them and provide for them, as nature also teaches. Therefore the needle merchant cannot truthfully say that God's Word and the three passages he cited in his answer urged him to forsake wife and child. For God's Word does not contradict itself nor is it contrary to itself. It is therefore obvious what spirit drives the needle merchant and how his other answers to the questions about the sacraments, etc. are to be evaluated. The Spirit of God is a Spirit of truth, as Christ calls him in John 16, and drives the person in whom he resides or whom he teaches not to act contrary to God's Word and commands (as the lying spirit of the needle merchant has done), but to keep and to obey them.

Refutation of the answer to the eighth question.

In the passage in Mark 16, "Go into all the world," etc., Christ does not command anything about baptism as to when or to whom it is to be administered, but speaks of the office of the preaching of the Gospel, as the words of Christ clearly indicate. Therefore no one can legitimately reject infant baptism with this passage (since Christ nowhere forbids it but leaves it open), nor justify or confirm rebaptism. If, however, one says that in the passage, "Go ye," etc. Christ first says, whoever believes, and after that baptize, and that it is to be understood that one must believe before one is baptized and that the children do not believe, etc., then this is the answer: it is not enough just to say that; one must also prove it, to make it certain and sure that children are not able to believe. Where is the Scripture on which those who say this ground themselves? They probably think it is because children do not speak or have understanding. But such a conceit is obscure and uncertain, indeed manifestly wrong. We have Scripture and example by which it is shown that children well may and can believe even if they have neither speech nor understanding. In Ps. 106 this is written concerning the Jews: "They sacrificed their sons and daughters to devils and shed innocent blood." If it was innocent blood (as the text says) then they were obviously pure and holy children, which they could not have been without the Spirit and faith. The innocent children whom Herod killed were also children but still were holy and blessed. In Matt. 18 Christ says that the kingdom of heaven belongs to the children. Also we read concerning Jeremiah (Jer. 1) that he was sanctified in his mother's womb. Similarly we read in Luke 1 about Saint John the Baptist that he was filled with the Holy Spirit even in his mother's womb. Since the children are capable of and participate in such lofty things as the Word, the Spirit and the kingdom of God, how then can one truthfully say that they are unable to believe and that they are not to be baptized?

In connection with this passage another answer, too, can be given: If the Anabaptists mean to follow their stated opinion, they must not baptize unless they know certainly that the one wanting to be baptized does believe. But in that case they neither may nor will be able to baptize anyone, neither old nor young. For how can they be sure even in the case of an adult person that he believes? See Martin [Luther's] work *Against the Anabaptists*, chapter 1, part 1.[12]

The further evidence of the needle merchant, based on the example or the action of Christ, namely that he did not have himself baptized until his thirtieth year, has no force or effect either. For in that way we might prove or conclude some rather strange and wonderful things, for example: Christ was circumcised in his infancy, he fasted forty days and nights without any natural food in the desert, he walked on the sea, he had no wife, and he had the Last Supper only once, etc.; therefore we ought to do so also. All of this world would follow, if their reasoning were accurate. It is abundantly clear that we don't need to do this and some of it is impossible. Therefore it is not valid if one says: Christ has done or not done this, therefore we must do it or not do it. One must first prove that he also commanded us to do or not do it and only then let his life be our example.

Refutation of the answer to the 17th question:

If one were to reject everything that one has not oneself seen or heard, one would not retain much, neither faith nor love, neither spiritual nor worldly things. Then I might also say: "My dear fellow, how do you know that this man is your father or this woman your mother?" You must not believe people but be sure of your birth yourself. It would follow that all children would henceforth be free, not needing to keep God's commandment which tells them to honour father and mother. I could simply say: I do not know which are my father and mother. See Martin [Luther's] *Against Anabaptists*, chapter 1, page 1.

In his answer to this question the needle merchant further says that the children are not to be baptized for they are already good, etc. By this he means that they are not conceived in that sin which we know as original sin. This may be answered in this way: On this basis one might conclude that one ought not to baptize any adult people either.

For they are also good creations of God, and made whole. But Scripture shows that all people are conceived and born in sin, are children of wrath, and are fit for death and eternal damnation. Gen. 6 and 8; Ps. 51; John 3; Rom. 5, 7, 8 and 11; Gal. 3; Eph. 2, and 1 Cor. 15. Therefore love demands us to baptize children and to help them to the second birth through water and the Spirit.

What he brings up concerning sponsors and godparents in his answer, is easy to reply to, but it is not necessary to do so.

Refutation of the answer to the 24th question.

It is through the order, the institution and the command of Christ that we eat and drink his body and his blood in the Lord's Supper, and not through the consecration or the words of the priest. Therefore see John Pomeramus [Johannes Bugenhagen] in his public confession concerning the sacrament, section d; see also Martin [Luther] in his confession. The needle merchant says that when Christ in the Lord's Supper said, "This is my body," he was referring to his members who ate with him. This you can refute with the words of Christ: "which is given for you." For his disciples were not given into death for us. Therefore they can not be meant here by the word "body." Concerning what he says about John chapter 6, you know that nothing is said here concerning the Lord's Supper. Therefore you can easily answer him. Further, how flesh can be spirit and spirit flesh you will find in the confession of Martin [Luther]. What else is necessary in this question you will already know yourselves.

Refutation of the answer to the 34th question.

That there is an eternal damnation (of which the needle merchant says that he does not know) you can show from Scripture in Matt. 25, Mark 9, and in 2 Thess. 1.

Refutation of the answer to the 38th question:

Christ taught that one ought to hear [and obey] the Pharisees and scribes who sat on the chair of Moses, even though they were evil and did not do what they said, Matt. 23. Christ tolerated Judas. It is true that one should depose those who practise open vices and who will not mend their ways and not gloss over their evil lives. Now the needle merchant requires that preachers are to go from one place to another according to the word of Christ: "Go into the world." You can answer in this way: the proof that the Anabaptists who go about here and there in the land are called and sent by God as the apostles of Christ, is no proof. For they do not prove, or legitimize their calling and commission either by human authority or by miracles, which surely would have to be if things were as they say.

We do not pretend to be apostles but servants of Christ, for an apostle must be sent by God to those places where the Word is unknown. Paul writes to the Ephesians in chapter 5 that in the church God had appointed some to be apostles, some to be prophets, some as evangelists, some as shepherds and teachers. We recognize ourselves as only the lowliest, namely only as shepherds and teachers. Now a shepherd is not to forsake his flock but to remain with them in his calling. What else he says concerning the support of preachers, etc., you can answer from the 10th chapter of Matthew: "A worker is worthy of his food." See also 1 Cor. 9, and Gal. 6. It is not a matter of the large amount if it is not requested and contracted for instead of being freely granted by the government or the congregation. It is a matter of the customary method of support whether it be of preachers, princes, nobles, citizens or peasants. All and everything together depends on this. Let each one now see how he uses his own, whether little or much.

Joh. Rurer to the Representatives and Councillors at Ansbach. 1529.

After careful perusal of the items laid before Johannes, the needle merchant, and of the answers given to them we find that among the chief errors are those concerning the sacraments of the body and blood of Christ, of baptism, of original sin which, it is claimed, children do not have since they are born pure and good, and other such erroneous items. But aside from his we cannot sense nor gather from any of the answers that he and his fellows might perhaps undertake any deed against the government, nor that they were ever, nor are now, minded to cause insurrection. Still, it is a matter of concern that if such factions were to grow and daily gather strength, the devil might easily seduce and deceive them. By means of some misunderstanding of Scripture verses he might seduce them to the extent that disruption of the general peace and a separation from common Christendom, and in the future perhaps insurrection might come about under the pretense of destroying the godless. But since there is no evidence of actual deeds (although secular laws have their own special penalties regarding rebaptism), it is our considered judgment that one or two scholars and men knowledgeable in these matters be sent to the poor prisoner, and that he be turned from his error by the use of divine Scripture. If he would listen to them and would allow himself to be instructed, you, my lords of the Council could show him mercy for leaving the church, and most mercifully allow him to return to his wife and child. If, however, he persisted in his purpose and did not heed instruction nor desisted from teaching other people in the future and from causing other people to err and from poisoning them collectively or singly with his error, we consider common Christendom and other people to be more important than his person. We are, therefore of the opinion that if he and his like were to be exiled from the land, our gracious lord's principality and land might by this means be kept clean of such error and that much mischief thereby be prevented. We submit this for your amendment.

12

Wolfgang Brandhuber

A Letter from our Dear Brother and Servant of Jesus Christ, Wolfgang Brandhuber to the Church of God at Rattenberg on the Inn (1529)*

Introduction

Wolfgang Brandhuber, schoolmaster of Burghausen, Bavaria, has sometimes been confused with his brother Jörg, a tailor by trade, who lived in St. Niclas near Passau.[1] Wolfgang Brandhuber was the son of a bathhouse owner from Obernberg; his wife was Margreth Schernegker from Vilshofen. It is not clear who baptized Wolfgang Brandhuber; Hans Hut seems a likely possibility, since he was in the area around the time when Brandhuber began preaching.[2]

Brandhuber came to Passau because of persecution in Burghausen. In early 1528 he visited Bohemia with like-minded companions; at the same time arrests were being made in Passau. He heard about these arrests and, realising the fate that awaited key members of the Passau congregation, he settled in Linz, therefore escaping certain death in

---

*Source: Müller, *Glaubenszeugnisse*, 137-43.
Translation: Walter Klaassen

Passau. It was in Linz that he set up a model Anabaptist household in which all things were shared.³

Brandhuber's leadership and influence in and around Linz was tremendous, extending all the way to the Tyrol. He preached, comforted and strengthened the congregation as well as providing leadership to other congregations that formed in neighbouring villages. He was acquainted with other Anabaptist leaders of the area, including Hans Schlaffer. Peter Riedemann, Brandhuber's successor in Linz, later became an important bishop and leader of the Hutterian Brethren in Moravia.

Many were attracted to the new doctrine that Brandhuber preached and were served by him and other preachers from Linz.⁴ By 1529 Brandhuber had come under the influence of a group of Anabaptists gathered at Austerlitz, Moravia that was practicing community of goods. He was, therefore, not so much the founding father of the practice of the community of goods (as stated in *ME III*, p. 405) as he was a member and articulator of a form of Anabaptism under a mixed Swiss-Hutian influence.⁵ This influence can be seen in the document that is translated below, where he encourages the practice of community of goods (Hut) but rejects armed vengeance of any sort (Swiss).

In 1529, the authorities in Linz discovered Brandhuber and realised that he was an Anabaptist leader. He was seized with seventy others in December of 1529 and was martyred with fellow preacher Hans Niedermayer that same month.

Brandhuber's letter to the congregation at Rattenberg on the Inn sheds light on his beliefs and doctrines. He put the greatest stress on scriptural faith expressed in a spiritual life rejecting the enticements of the world, lived out in patient endurance of suffering. He rejected worldly splendour, idolatrous images, buying and selling, taking vengeance and military service. He advised followers not to engage in business because of the risk of taking advantage of one's neighbour. He also put forth the idea that governmental authority should be obeyed in everything not opposed to God. As could be expected, he rejected infant baptism and the Roman Catholic mass.⁶

Bibliographical Sources:

Chronicle I.
Christian Hege, "Brandhuber, Wolfgang," *ME I*, 404-05.
Werner O. Packull, *Hutterite Beginnings, Communitarian Experiments during the Reformation* (Baltimore, MD: John Hopkins University Press, 1995).

A Letter from our Dear Brother and Servant of Jesus Christ, Wolfgang Brandhuber to the Church of God at Rattenberg on the Inn (1529)

Wolfgang, an unworthy servant of Christ, called through the grace of God which God has given me, to the church at Rattenberg on the Inn together with all the saints who with us and you have come to share the faith in Christ. Grace be with you and peace in God our Father and our Lord Jesus Christ. Blessed be the God and Father of our Lord Jesus Christ, the Father of all mercy and God of all comfort, who comforts us in our tribulation, that in turn we may comfort those who are in tribulation with the comfort with which we are comforted by God the Father. For even as much suffering for Christ has come upon us, even so much comfort has come through Christ. Amen. So be it.

Much loved brothers and fellow members in the Lord, you know how powerfully and marvellously our merciful God has worked among you at Rattenberg, and how he disciplines and admonished you as his beloved children with so much fatherly discipline for your well-being. For every child which the Father receives he disciplines.

Behold the great love, goodness, and mercy which he has given you after you fell into this sin and the Father has helped you again. Together with all your members I praise and glorify his holy name that he has so often kept you and still does. Be patient in everything which comes your way because of the Word of God, for you know what patience produces. Therefore test yourselves in the Lord so that you may know the spirits of error who invade the people of God. The false prophets, the raging wolves gather to themselves the selfish and the contradictors of the truth. For they see and hear that they are being called to begin to live according to the order and command of the Lord.[7] Not everyone in the church of God is the treasurer, for whatever rich and poor are able to give is distributed by the one chosen to do it. Through frivolous persons disorderly life, offence and provocation has arisen, indeed, in the church itself against the Word of God. They travel about hypocritically and contradict the life of Christ in the Christian church, including the order which the dear apostles taught and observed. They are the ones about whom John said that they went out from us, and Paul, Peter, and Jude make mention of them in their epistles. They say that it is not right that all should be held in common, or for one to tell another in love what he owns. They don't want stewards of physical needs or elders who distribute to the needy. Rather, they want to know what happens to what is theirs, or that all manage their own affairs. I call that wrong. If God permits or makes room for it to be done, all things which contribute to God's praise should be held in common. For if in what is most important we are faithful sharers with Christ in the power of God, why not also in what is lesser, that is, temporal goods? We should not bring together all we have into one place, for such commonness cannot be in all places. But every head of the house and all who are with him and share his faith should work together and have one purse, master, servant, wife, maid or other fellow-believers. Although each labourer is to be given the daily wage according to the words of Christ, since every worker is worthy of his hire, still love should drive each one faithfully to contribute to the common purse. Love must do it.[8]

Faithful oversight should be exercised over all members with admonition and reproof according to godly Scripture until the confession and accounting of faith of each member is well known. Then the Lord's command is to be carried out and men of the Word shall be presented to the congregation, so that the order of the spiritual body of Christ is advanced and the work completed. As the Lord himself says: How blessed are the feet of those who proclaim peace and bring good news. How blessed are the eyes who look to satisfying the need of the neighbour. Blessed is the hand which nourishes itself with its labour and which does honest work, so that she may give to the needy and the whole body be preserved. You know how Paul uses the natural body as an image saying that no member cares for itself alone, but all members for the whole body, and no member may deny the need of others. I'm not writing you something you don't know; you do. But, my brothers and fellow-anointed in the Lord, I admonish you to pay close attention to everything written for us. The Lord has not in vain told us in the power of the Spirit what we are to do and what not. Everything that is pleasing to him he has bid us do in the Scriptures and in the law of our hearts. In love and humility he urges us in many passages to put off the weapons of unrighteousness.

Then he also tells us about the final day of his wrath. If we are not diligently aware and put away what is displeasing to him, he says he will do it himself. On that day he will put away the finery of the anklets, the headbands, the golden crescents, the bodices, the bracelets, the scarfs, the beautiful long tight-fitting dresses, the musk vials, the amulets, the signet rings and head bands, the festal garments, the hats, the cloaks, the veils, the pins, the mirrors, the blouses, the neckcloths, the linen garments, etc. And then instead of perfume there will be stench, instead of a sash a rope, baldness instead of well-set hair, instead of a breast cloth, sackcloth, instead of beauty, blackness.[9] He also proclaims a great Woe! over all merchants, none excepted, small or great, and over all who have traded and committed whoredom with the great Whore of Babylon [Rev. 18:11-17]. The Lord who speaks with might says that innocent blood of the afflicted cries to me without ceasing. Even if I overlooked much else, I will not leave innocent blood unavenged, says the Lord. O my brothers, take heed that in the love of God all these things will be put away and your discipline will appear to be slight. But for the disobedient the punishment will be hard.

Let me also warn you not to make Christ into a Moses as some do who propose to retain the sword from the law of Moses, and who oppose the teaching of Christ and his life. They argue that a Christian may judge and condemn to death, which Christ, the patient Lamb of God, never taught. Dear brothers, please understand that if they overturn all Scripture against you, you must enter into the depths of your hearts and take note of what the Holy Spirit teaches and promises when he says: To him who overcomes as I have overcome, I shall give the heathen as a heritage. He will shepherd them with an iron sceptre and break them in pieces like a potter's vessel. What do those outside concern you, as Paul says? Look to our example, the prince of our faith, our fulfiller, Jesus, who emptied himself of all this even though all judgment and justice were his. He put it all away and called us to follow him. We need to remember that all who judge themselves will not be judged but rather disciplined by the father. The same will also later judge the world and also the angels. Look diligently upon the test that is coming upon us from those who use the sword of Moses. They have already published a booklet about it.[10] They regard the servant to be higher than the Son. I do not, however, reject Moses. He was a faithful servant of God but was still in the shadow.[11] For the curtain [in the temple] had not yet been torn through which the full light could shine. O brothers, we will soon see what the test will be. Whoever survives this crucible, whose faith remains pure, will be loved and accepted by the Lord.

Second, concerning war, you should not transgress and defend your body. That would be disobedience to government and contrary to God. In everything concerning body and goods that is not against God one should be obedient to government. Our attitude to war is not the least of our tests. In this, I believe, will be revealed, as John writes, the name of the Beast. Its marks are already visible in part. They are the two dead elements, namely the foolish sign of the cross on the child's forehead and the dead element, the bread of the Mass. Anyone who thinks this is the truth and seeks to save his life by it denies the will of the Lord publicly before others, and has the sign of the Beast on the hand for eternal damnation.[12]

Infant baptism too is a horror and the name of blasphemy of our God of which only John in the Revelation writes. Whatever else is to be revealed to us the Lord will open to us if only we seek the Lord and remain in his Word and truth to the end. All interpretation is his alone. Beloved in the Lord, I admonish you with great sorrow in godly and brotherly love that with all your hearts you seek the Lord and his righteousness. For the adversary has disguised himself as an angel of light so that everywhere we hear Here is Christ! Or There![13] . . . They imagine that what is Christ is in the externals with those who can speak well and talk a lot about it, who listen respectfully and come together politely, greet one another and offer each other the peace of the Lord. However, our self-satisfied secret adversary hides himself in this pretence and pride. Some think God is pleased with it and think themselves better than others. That is the raising of the golden calf in Israel and all the gold and jewelry of the ears must be used for it. Whoever has wisdom should beware not to worship the work of human hands and that the true goal of faith not be moved from its place. Care should be taken not to build with straw or stubble which will be consumed in fire.

Therefore, dear brothers, do not be turned aside, for the Lord says that the kingdom of God does not come in things that can be seen, nor is it in words, eating and drinking, but in the power and demonstration of the Holy Spirit. God is Spirit and desires to have spiritual servants, for the physical is against the spiritual. That is why we will not look for or find the spiritual word in the dead elements. Since, beloved in God, there is one Spirit, so we, the true worshippers must worship in Spirit and in truth. Worship must be in spirit and truth, not outside, but in the truth. You must also, like David, hear what God speaks in you. The image of God and his likeness in you witnesses against you, that is your flesh. That is why two strive against each other in your soul. If God is your goal you have to enter by the gate through which Adam was expelled. There you will be able to overcome the will, desire and love of the flesh and to follow the law in your heart and also the loud voices of John and Isaiah to prepare the way of the Lord in the desert. Then the weaker will yield to the stronger, the Spirit of Christ. Still, such a person will always experience the struggle and conflict with the flesh. Great distress and fear will grieve his heart to appear thus before the face of the Lord in true humility and lowliness. John points to the true Lamb of God in the depth of the believers' hearts. The Lamb takes upon itself the guilt of every person but especially their own. To them he manifests his salvation and makes his power in them visible. But not in any physical manner for the Lamb has ascended to the Father and will return once only to judge the living and the dead.[14] He works in and remains with his own in power, truth, and spirit to the end of the world. Flesh and spirit struggle constantly even on those who choose the good, which they cannot do in their own power. Since, however, they spare no effort, the anointing of the Holy Spirit takes place and reveals the unspeakable grace of the goodness and mercy of God. Still, they grieve in their hearts that they are not loosed and free from the flesh which continually seeks to prevent the vision of the goodness of God, and gives them much unrest with its opposition. This struggle continues without ceasing. A God-fearing person will therefore constantly keep the eyes on God, living with great cares, but knowing that the victory is God's, and prays without ceasing for deliverance from evil. No one can desire to be delivered from evil until the true good is known. That is the beginning of the Christian life. Then such a person becomes concerned not to misuse any created thing. He distrusts them and curses wealth and extravagance, for they are fatal to his antagonist, the flesh.[15] This person is constantly in the fear of God as Job was, distrusts all his actions, holds himself in low esteem, thinks himself unworthy, and takes the lowest seat at the wedding banquet. He concentrates on the true light, and puts all his thoughts, words, and deeds into that light. The light is Christ in whom the Father has revealed his will. In his true humanity he prepared the way for us so that no one will be able to excuse himself on that day. Our whole outer and inner lives are to be fashioned according to his will, for I and the Father are one, says the Lord. If we are to be one with him we must be one with his will and that happens when we recognize our want and love him. If we love him, we will keep his teaching, for if there is to be love it must be in the heart. Love thinks of nothing but what is loved which she desires without ceasing, as the bride in the Canticle sings and speaks only about her love and gives attention to nothing else. Pretend Christianity does not do this but is satisfied with frivolous talk.

True Christian faith has only love and has no need of law. She fulfils the law of God with overflowing love, expresses it night and day, abandons everything else and casts it into the depths. Why? She strives because she loves. The more she loves the more she desires to love and rejoice in her beloved whom she sees from afar through the lattice resting in the shade of faith. She does not care that others mock her.[16] O brothers, what is it worth to have many words and doctrine, but no love? And what does our cunning adversary do? He also creates and fashions a love of God. But it is orderly with prescriptive words, fixed requirements, and must be visible otherwise no one would know that they are Christians. They have to sound it with a trumpet and what the Spirit works in the faithful and what they have done in love and the bottom of their hearts, must be repeated in their apes' game in order to appear genuine. O brothers, keep the truth of your hearts passionate before God's countenance, for he rejects all pretense. May the gracious Father give to all who are hungry the true bread, that they may judge all Scripture truly without any restriction, for the Spirit of God will not be bound.

Read the epistle with diligence, praying to God for understanding, for he will make learned all who attend his school and accept his discipline. So I commit you all into the powerful hand, protection and shelter of the almighty King. Amen.

All the brothers and sisters in Linz greet you in the Lord. I admonish you to pray for them and us all that the Lord may not allow us to fall into temptation, and we will do the same. Greet each other with the kiss of love. As did Lot's family, leave Sodom and Gomorrah that you be not destroyed with them and partake of their evil works.

I understand that you would gladly have the book about baptism. I can't send it now for it would be too much to copy. If you can't get it, let me know in writing, and I'll make sure you get it. However, the writing in the heart is the true foundation which no one can judge but God alone.

End

[P.S.] This dear brother, servant and witness of Jesus Christ, surrendered and committed his spirit in the fire to his heavenly Father, and became a sacrifice through the hate and ill-will of the ancient serpent in Linz, in the land above the Enns. In the year of Christ, 1529.

13

Jörg Zaunring

A Short Interpretation of the Last Supper of Christ Presented as a Conversation between the World and a Christian to the Honour and Glory of God (ca.1530)*

Introduction

Jörg Zaunring (d. 1531) was born in Rattenberg, where Pilgram Marpeck was born and Leonhard Schiemer was executed. Along with Jacob Hutter, Zaunring became one of the principal leaders of the Anabaptists in southern Tyrol. Little is known about his background, but his writings leave the impression that he was an educated, well-read person. He became an active baptizer throughout the Tyrolean region, proselytizing for Anabaptism as early as 1528. By 1529, he was functioning as the primary treasurer of the Jacob Hutter group, and thus represented a link between the South and North Tyrol.[1] A government search warrant described him as of medium height, no beard and having a little (high-pitched) voice.[2]

Because of excessive persecution in Tyrol, Hutter sent a group of Anabaptists to Austerlitz in Moravia, where a communal group called

---

*Source: Müller, *Glaubenszeugnisse*, 143-48.
Translation: Walter Klaassen

the congregation of God had been established under the leadership of Jakob Wiedemann.[3] Zaunring was sent along as spiritual leader, and despite attempts to apprehend him, the Tyrolean group made it to Austerlitz in early summer of 1530, where they were welcomed by the congregation. The fraternal feelings lasted only a few months, however, and in January 1531 there was a major schism in which Zaunring played a prominent part. In response to what they thought of as "imperfections" at Austerlitz, Zaunring, along with Wilhelm Reublin, left Austerlitz and formed a new community at Auspitz. It was here that Zaunring became servant of the Word in 1531, while Reublin was eventually excluded as a "false Ananias" for withholding money from the community treasury.

Zaunring's leadership was tarnished when it was made public that his wife had had an affair which had been dealt with privately (details of this scandal can be found in the Hutterite Chronicle). The couple was ultimately excommunicated from the church and Zaunring was replaced as leader by Sigmund Schützinger. Zaunring was rehabilitated after he repented of his behaviour and was dispatched soon after as a missionary to Franconia. He was caught by the authorities in the bishopric of Bamberg and was subsequently beheaded ca. 1531.

Zaunring's anticlericalism and rejection of the mass were standard among Anabaptists. The following tract is brief but typical, and takes the form of a dialogue between the Christian and the world. This "Prospectus" reflected the argument of old and new papist alike. Luther, Osiander, and Hesius are named among the latter as "eaters of idols" who misunderstood or deliberately perverted the meaning of the controversial statement, "this is my body." According to Zaunring, the scriptural meaning was to be attained by "interpreting the parts through the whole, [one] saying through other sayings." In keeping with this hermeneutic the New Testament revealed three meanings or definitions of Christ's body: (1) his mortal body; (2) his glorified body, seated at the right hand of God; and (3) his body as the Christian congregation. To postulate the presence of the mortal body in the bread was impossible, for that body was seated at the table when he spoke the words, "this is my body." Furthermore, the Scriptures stated explicitly that "flesh profited nothing" (John 6:63). The clarified body could not be in the bread either because the ascended Christ was seated at the right hand of God as witnessed to by the martyr Stephen (Acts 9). There, in heaven, Christ would continue his work as mediator until his return on Judgment Day. Yet, according to I Corinthians the believers were to eat "until he comes." There remained only one possible correct meaning of the original statement "this is my body," namely "the congregation of God." The ceremony of breaking the bread was, therefore, a remembrance and a sign that the "Christian congregation, as Christ's body on earth, was of the same mind as Christ. The body was prepared to suffer innocently and permit itself to be broken like the bread for the Gospel." Anyone unwilling to make the commitment to suffer with Christ in his body, the congregation, should therefore not participate in the symbolic breaking of the bread; for to do so would be to his or her own condemnation.[4]

Bibliographical Sources:

Chronicle I.
Robert Friedmann, "Zaunring, Georg (Jörg or Juriaen)," *ME IV*, 1018-1019.
Werner O. Packull, *Hutterite Beginnings, Communitarian Experiments during the Reformation* (Baltimore, MD: John Hopkins University Press, 1995).
James Stayer, *The German Peasants' War and Anabaptist Community of Goods* (Montreal, PQ: McGill-Queen's University Press, 1991).
George H. Williams, *The Radical Reformation* 3rd edition (Kirksville, MO: Sixteenth Century Journal Publishers, 1992).

A Short Interpretation of the Last Supper of Christ Presented as a Conversation between the World and a Christian to the Honour and Glory of God.

The world[5] says: you hold the sacrament of the altar of no account and say that Christ is not physically there even though Christ clearly says: This is my body.

Christians: Following the Scriptures we do not admit that there is an idol[6] in the bread. The text clearly says: This is my body (Mark 14[:22], Luke 22[:19]). However, the world takes it out of context and can thus never understand correctly. Using that approach with the words of Jesus: Woman, here is your son, and, Son, here is your mother [John 19:26-27], they would be required to conclude that Mary was John's mother and he her son. These words are as clear as those about the bread.

Anti-Christians: We know full well that John had another mother (Matt. 10[:2], Luke 22[?]) and that Mary was the mother of Christ.

Christians: That is correct. One passage must be interpreted by another, the part through the whole. Scripture speaks of three bodies of Christ. The first is his mortal body which suffered and died for us. The second is his immortal glorified body which ascended into heaven. The third is the Christian church. Which of these three bodies is in the bread?

Anti-Christians: the one who sat at the Last Supper.

Christians: You cannot prove this. Among you, one says it is the one at the Last Supper, another that it is the glorified body after his resurrection, a third that he is there in his deity. You have innumerable opinions about this and don't know ...[7] [We know that you, Lord, sit at the right hand of God][8] where Stephen saw you [Acts 7:56]. Paul heard him say this [Acts 7:58]. Our creed clearly says: Whence you will come to judge the living and the dead and all the godless with the breath of your Spirit at your glorious return. Then the scoffing of these mocking walls will be overthrown and broken down.[9] All the elect fervently await the day when your name will no longer be desecrated and blasphemed but praised and honoured. Amen.

The second body, which God raised up (Matt. 28[:6]), the One who died and is alive, ascended into heaven (Mark 16[:19]) and sits at the right hand of his heavenly Father, is an advocate with the Father and intercedes for us diligently. He will not come down until the Last Day

(Luke 22[:69]). If you confess him in faith he says to you himself: From now on you will see me no longer, for I leave the world and go to the Father (John 26[16:10]). For I came from him (Col. 1[:19?]). Thus the body cannot be in the bread because he will not come down until the Last Day ([1] Thess. 4[:16]). He has no place of his own here on earth so that one could say: See! Here or there is Christ! Don't believe it, for there will be no excuse; he has carefully warned us. All the monks and priests insistently tell us, and especially the new papists[10] urge and compel us to believe that he is in the bread. They show him to us nowhere except in the bread. Christ clearly says that we should not believe it (Rom. 6, 8; Tim. 2; Acts 1; Eph. 4; Col. 3; Luke 21; Matt. 25; John 16; Matt. 24; Mark 13, 17).[11] Paul also agrees with us when he says: As often as you eat this bread and drink this cup you proclaim the death of the Lord until he comes (1 Cor. 11[:26]). If he is still to come, he certainly is not here. What kind of invitation would it be if I said to someone: Sit and eat with me until my lord arrives, and all the time the lord is at the table? You will not say how or with what kind of body Christ is in the bread, nor will you accept any instruction. That is because you are respecters of persons and pay no attention to the Word of God. Whatever Luther, Osiander, or Hesus[12] and the other idol-gluttons, champions, and preachers say, write, teach and preach can be nothing but the truth even if it is a lie. It is the nature of the world to prefer lies to truth.

I will now prove with Scripture that none of the three bodies is in the bread. First, the body which is eaten in the Lord's Supper has died. Jesus himself says about this flesh that it is of no use if it is used and eaten according to the flesh. Whoever eats my flesh and drinks my blood has eternal life even though he has long since died (John 6[:54]). He himself says: the flesh is useless, and then again that it is life. Yes, if we believe in him we too will live, for knowledge of the flesh is of no use (John 9, 14). If we know Christ according to the flesh, how will eating his flesh benefit us, since he himself rejects it? Paul tells us that Christ cannot be in any place in vain for he is the power of God (1 Cor. 1[:2, :24]). His living Word works and bears fruit wherever it is (John 1[:3]). If he is in the bread, he must produce fruit there. However, in reality one sees no fruit, either in the bread or in those who eat it, imagining that they receive it in the bread. The whole world knows that no people are more godless than those who daily receive and eat it in the Mass. Even the heathen live a more godly and honest life than they. They live in all their freedom[13] and lewdness of the flesh, drunkenness, gluttony, drinking, fornication, and blasphemy. This sacrament of the Mass will not tolerate that anyone who desires to depart from evil, be served. For example, if he wishes to abstain from and quit fornication and take an honest wife according to the command of God, he can no longer be a server of this sacrament. On the other hand, if he lives publicly in fornication or adultery, has a whore in the house and many others secretly, he is a good server of this sacrament. He is honoured and held high in this world, awarded a good parish or two, or he is made a canon or provost, or even given a bishopric or two. It is known, after all, in what honour some bishops have possessed, and still do, their dioceses and prebendaries. Such is the fruit which the body of the living Son of God, Christ Jesus our Saviour produces according to their understanding. But it cannot be that he should do such a thing and have pleasure in the service of such knaves, since he is the maker of eternal light. O my Lord Jesus Christ, true Son of God, how long will you suffer this at the hands of this adulterous generation who conceal their roguery and wickedness under your holy name. Although the whole world cannot contain you, they lock you up in a tabernacle or cell and thereby nourish their god, which is their belly, and support their whores. When will you rise up, my Lord and God, and save your temple in which you have said you will abide together with the Father and the Holy Spirit, from this adulterous generation? For they horribly desecrate and destroy this temple. When will you take it again according to your promise that where you are your servant will be also? Let them know and show them where you dwell after your ascension, in the temple of idols, which Peter and Paul refute, or at the right hand of your heavenly Father? It would appear that Paul was wrong when he said: Proclaim the Lord's death until he comes. He says with plain words: He is not there, why do you want him there? He says clearly: Is not the bread we break the sharing in the body of Christ? Paul could have said to confirm your view: The bread we break, is it not the body of Christ? That would be correct in your view. No, Paul was much cleverer than the old and new papists. He is at the right hand of his heavenly Father, that is why he called the bread the sharing in the body of Christ. Those who eat this bread worthily have a share in the body of Christ. They are members of Christ.[14]

The third body of Christ is the one he has here on earth, which is his holy church, the body which even today is tortured, of which he is the head. He may, can, and will be in the bread because it is being tortured, hanged, drowned, burned, beheaded and persecuted. Yes, the church of God is bread here on earth, my dear brother, for we who are many are one bread and body since we all share in one bread. Do you see, now, who is the bread? His church here on earth, which is broken like the bread, and Christ desires to live in this bread. The Christian church is his living temple in which he lives and rests, O brothers, and not in the stone building. Since Christ desires to live in this bread he cannot be in the baked bread. Once you take him out of the baked bread monks, nuns, priests, pope, bishops, cardinals, canonries, masses, pilgrimage, excessive spending and teaching, gowns and tonsures will fall to the ground and disappear. This is the abomination about which Daniel writes in the 9th chapter [:27] and which Christ mentions. O brothers, this idol has made these pilgrims[15] fat and even today brings plenty into the larder. Alas, this generation will not pass away until all has been fulfilled.

I will now tell you, by the grace of God, what Christ means when he says: This is my body. He took bread, gave thanks, broke it, gave it to them and said: Take and eat, for this is my body which is given for you. Do this in memory of me. It is as if he had said: Moses, the prophets and the Psalms have spoken enough about me, that my body would be reviled, mocked and put to death, flogged and tortured so that he would no longer look like a man. He would die the most shameful death, hanged in company of the worst malefactors. All of that will happen so I can redeem you with your father Adam, carry your sins on my back, redeem you from the curse and writ of death and sin, and tear you again out of the mouth of the devil. As certain as you break and eat the bread, so certain is this the body about which the prophets spoke which should crush the head of the serpent and conquer death and hell. I have often told you about this, how he had to suffer, but you considered it to be wrong. However, it had to be if you were to be healed. All the godly have from ancient times looked to him and believed that it had to be so. They were saved because they believed that this body would in future suffer for them and for the whole world.

So you, too, believe that it will happen. That is the Christian church of which I am the head. Now, when you eat you remember that it has already happened, that I offered myself to the Father for you. I have confirmed my love for you with my blood, for by all this you know that I love you beyond measure. Thus I command you that you also love one another as I have loved you. Be ready to give your life for each other. For a sign and memorial of all this you break the bread which is compared to and which represents[16] my body, which is the Christian church. Hence you will also be prepared to suffer with me, and to allow yourselves to be broken, innocently and for the sake of the gospel. Whoever is not minded to suffer with me, but still breaks the bread and drinks from the chalice of suffering, that person eats and drinks judgment, for the heart does not agree with the words and actions. If you desire to eat of the bread and drink from the chalice of suffering, be sure you make me your defence. For I bring suffering to you and all who desire to follow me. The disciple is not greater than his master nor the servant than his lord. Whoever wants to be under my banner will suffer persecution, mocking, fear, disgrace, shame, misery, yes, and the most shameful death in this world, but afterward rule with me in glory for ever and ever. That is why I promise you no abiding city on earth, no peace nor rest but rather disgrace, shame, and viciousness, but in yonder world eternal life and reign. Amen.

This is the true meaning of the Lord's Supper, considered and expressed in few words. Whoever desires to eat the Supper here must keep in mind that it will be bitter for him here, but sweet in the New Jerusalem. May our Father who has called us and the Son whose yoke we have taken and the Holy Spirit whose grace and mercy we have received and will fully receive, help us to that goal. Search the Scriptures, for they bear witness to me.

14

Andreas Althamer and Johann Rurer

Instructions Concerning Anabaptists (1530)*

Introduction

Both Andreas Althamer and Johann Rurer were Lutheran pastors in the town of Ansbach, near Nuremberg and were known for their Anabaptist awareness. Ansbach was where Ambrosius Spitelmaier had the second part of his trial which was conducted by the Nuremberg coucil. Nuremberg had been well-visited by Anabaptist leaders like Hans Denck and Hans Hut.

Johann Rurer was the first Protestant pastor at Ansbach. On Palm Sunday, 1525, he held the first German services at Ansbach, and was soon opposing Margrave Casimir who, for political reasons, thought that Rurer had gone too far in the direction of Lutheran reform. Finding that he could make no impression on Casimir and fearful of arrest, Rurer fled. Before long, however, Rurer was recalled to Ansbach by George, Casimir's successor, who introduced the Reformation to the

*Source: Schornbaum, *Quellen V*, 265-77.
Translation: Friesen/Klaassen

town. Rurer was made preacher at the collegiate church, a position which he retained until his death in 1542. He was active in the struggle against Roman Catholics and Anabaptists and was relgious advisor to Margrave George.[1]

Andreas Althamer was appointed pastor in Ansbach in May of 1528, by Margrave George.[2] His writing entitled "Diallage," was translated by the spiritualist Sebastian Franck.

This "Instruction" translated here reflects the South German Anabaptism which was shaped by the thought and work of Denck and Hut. Both of these men had a view of Scripture that differed markedly from that of Martin Luther, in which they emphasized the supremacy of the inner Word. The writers of this "Instruction" may also have had the "Dreamers" in mind. This was a sect located in the village of Uttenreuth not far from Ansbach. These people specifically based their views on dreams and visions, and had unorthodox views on marriage. They were not Anabaptists, but Althamer and Rurer do not make such fine distinctions, grouping all "sects" together under the same "sectarian" and heretical rubric (see the concluding "Admonition," below). We read in the concluding comments to this "Instruction" an appeal to the civil authorities to enforce Lutheran doctrine and practice, on which (the writers suggest) all social order and harmony rests.

Bibliographical Sources:

Christian Classics Ethereal Library: http://www.ccel.org May 15, 2001.

Irmgard Höss, "Althamer, Andreas," *The Oxford Encyclopedia of the Reformation*, vol. 1 (Oxford: Oxford University Press, 1996), 21.

Werner O. Packull, *Mysticism and the Early South German-Austrian Anabaptist Movement, 1525-1531* (Scottdale, PA: Herald Press, 1977).

George H. Williams, *The Radical Reformation* 3rd edition (Kirksville, MO: Sixteenth Century Journal Publishers, 1992).

Instructions Concerning Anabaptists (1530)

Instructions concerning the new errors and sects that are now arising in many places in the Holy Empire, especially against those who have to do with dreams, visions, and other similar spirits of the devil.

A. Whence heresies, sects or fanaticism arise.

All errors, heresies and factions are a punishment and a plague of God against the thankless children who do not accept the healing Word with joy, delight, fear and thanksgiving. For God wants us to accept and use his grace and gifts with thankfulness. If, however, we do not accept them with thankfulness but despise them, he becomes angry at us and takes away from us again these same gifts and grace of his. As a first example there are the temporal goods, bread, wine and other temporal requirements. These he grants often enough. But if these goods are shamefully misused he takes his blessings away from us again and gives us a curse instead. David, in Psalm 109, shows that instead of plentiful years he sends in its place war and strife. So it also happens with spiritual matters. If we do not desire precious truth and use the Word of God without fear and joy and gratitude, he takes them away again and leaves us lies and untruth in their place. As he himself says, Ps. 81[:12, :13] "But my people would not hearken to my voice; and Israel would have none of me. So I gave them up unto their own hearts' lust: and they walked in their own counsels." Deut. 28[:28]: "The Lord shall smite thee (if you do not obey his Word) with madness, and blindness, and raving of the heart." Isa. 29[:13]: "Wherefore the Lord said, 'Forasmuch as this people drew near me with their mouth, and with their lips do honour me, but have removed their heart far from me, and their fear toward me is taught by the precepts of men: Therefore, behold, I will proceed to do a marvellous work among this people, even a marvellous work and a wonder: for the wisdom of my wise men shall perish, and the understanding of their prudent men shall be hid." 2 Thess. 2[:11, :12]: "They received not the love of the truth, that they might be saved. And for this cause God shall send them strong delusion, that they should believe a lie; that they all might be damned, who believe not the truth, but had pleasure in unrighteousness."

The almighty God in his extraordinary grace has in these last days given us his Holy Word, but with what thankfulness have we accepted it? The Papists oppose it with all their strength, dishonour it and blaspheme most horribly, and kill and persecute many devout, upright people because of it. The common man has now had enough of it, is tired of it, and loathes it as the Jews loathed manna Num. 21[:5]. The powerful are filled and have no more need of it. They now despise both Word and preacher. Briefly, no one pays much attention to it, it is ignored as though only a simple poor person, unworthy of notice, had spoken, and as though it were not God's Word. It is a joke; there is no gratitude, no discipline, no fear, no love nor respect any more. How is God to deal with our frivolity, thanklessness and contempt? Is he now to bake us cookies and shrug off our contempt? Certainly he can punish our thanklessness and reward it with its true reward. He gives us error, heresy, and blindness aplenty and upon these will follow war, dearth, bloodshed, and devastation of land and people. Thus God formerly also punished contempt of his Gospel. God will punish this our thanklessness with spiritual and physical penalties, so that for us too the time will come when we will desire to see the day of the Son of man but shall not see it, Luke 17[:22]. We shall wish that we could hear even one single sermon of the Gospel. How we would praise God, how happy we should be! Now that we have it we sleep and are bored, and in the meantime the enemy, the devil, comes and plants his tares among the good seed, as Christ, Matt. 13[:25] shows in his parable. That is the foremost cause of sects, factions and fanaticisms, although there are other causes besides, such as, that the chosen may be tested 1 Cor. 11[:19]; Deut. 13[:3]. Another is pure arrogance and presumptuousness, so that no one will move from his opinion and listen to anyone else 2 Tim. 4[:3]. There are also other causes, of which we cannot write now.

Since therefore we despise the pure Word of God and will not accept it with thanks God permits Satan to plant weeds, and instigates and awakens one new faction, fanaticism, and sect after another. This sect of dreamers is in our times another new heresy.

B. What a heresy or sect is, and that this error is a sect.

A sect or a heresy, properly called is whatever willfully divides and separates itself from the unity of the Christian church or congregation contrary to the Holy Word of God. Holy Scripture uses the word *haresim* as Saint Paul says in Titus 3[:10]: "Avoid the *haereticum* (called heretic). If he has been admonished once and a second time, one knows that such a one is perverted, and sins as someone who has condemned himself." For *haeresis* in Greek is a self-appointed and schismatic opinion where one does not follow the Christian church but sets out on a separate way to believe, teach and live. The heretics choose their own way and faith, which surely the Holy Scripture strictly forbids and rejects as in Rom. 16[:17]: "I urge you, brothers and sisters, to keep an eye on those who cause dissensions and offences, in opposition to the teachings that you have learned; avoid them"; in 1 Cor. 1[:10]: "I appeal to you brothers and sisters, by the name of our Lord Jesus Christ, that all of you agree and that there be no dissensions among you, but that you be united in the same mind and in the same judgment"; and in 1 Tim. 6[:3]: "Whoever teaches otherwise and does not agree with the sound words of our Lord Jesus Christ and the teaching that is in accordance with godliness, is conceited, understanding nothing, and has a morbid craving for controversy and for disputes about words. From these come envy, dissension, slander, base suppositions, etc. . . ." from such withdraw yourself.

From these quotations we can easily conclude what a heresy or sect is and that we are to flee and avoid such heresies and factions. That this new fanaticism is a heresy and a sect can be recognized in this, that the adherents of this faction reject and condemn Holy Scripture of the Old and the New Testaments, in which our Christian faith is grounded as a useless and dead letter. Secondly, they reject outward oral preaching of the Gospel as useless and vain. Thirdly, they ridicule the holy sacraments and signs of grace such as baptism and the Lord's Supper. Fourthly, they disrupt matrimony, which is contrary to the Holy Word of God and also against the holy Christian church, which we will make known and explain better later on. Whatever is done and undertaken against the Holy Word of God contained in the Scripture and against the unity of the holy Christian church, that is called and is a heresy and sect. We will now show how to recognize the instigators, masters, false prophets, preachers. For we have our rule, line, lodestone, level, protractor and guideline by which we can test and try, estimate and judge every teaching.

C. How the Spirits can be Tested

The Holy Spirit has expressly forbidden us to believe every spirit, but commanded us first to test whether it is of God. For many false prophets shall go out into the world. Christ commands us to be on guard against false prophets, Matt. 7[:15] and to beware that we are not misled and betrayed by them, Matt. 24[:5]. Similarly Saint Paul admonishes us in 1 Thess. 5[:21]: "Prove all things; hold fast to that which is good." Saint John says: "Beloved, believe not every spirit, but try the spirits whether they are of God," 1 John 4[:1]. The touchstone, however, is Holy Scripture and the Word of God, Isa. 8[:20]: "To the law and to the testimony: if they speak not according to his word, it is because there is no light in them." 2 Pet. 1[:19]: "So we have the prophetic message more fully confirmed. You will do well to be attentive to this." Whoever teaches or preaches contrary to Holy Scripture, he is an antichrist, a false prophet and a seducing spirit. All prophecy or prediction must be according to the faith, Rom. 12[:6]. "Whoever speaks must do so as one speaking the very words of God"; 1 Pet. 4[:11]. God's Word, however, is embodied in the Holy Scripture. Therefore, whoever will preach God's Word must have it from Holy Scripture and support it by Holy Scripture. Whoever teaches and preaches against Holy Scripture preaches against God and the faith. By this one can and should know and test the seducing spirits. Let us make this clear with examples: Jesus Christ became man in order to save us poor sinners. That is evidenced by Holy Scripture Matt. 1; Luke 2; 1 Tim. 1[:19]. "Every spirit that does not confess Jesus is not from God," 1 John 4[:3]. Holy Scripture states that Christ the man is very God. Whoever denies that, is not of God, Matt. 16[:17]; John 1[:14] and 6[:40]. Scripture says that baptism has been instituted by Christ for the washing away of sin, Mark 16[:16]; Acts 2[:38]. Any spirit which denies that is of the devil. Scripture says that in the Lord's Supper the body and the blood of Christ was distributed to the communicants, Matt. 26; Luke 22; 1 Cor. 10 and that the just shall live by faith, Heb. 2[:4]; Rom. 1[:17]. But the spirit that teaches that one becomes pious and is saved by one's works, teaches against God and the faith.

Similarly, also, all spirits and dreamers that condemn outward, oral preaching of Holy Scripture are not of God but of the devil, since they shout and teach contrary to God's Word embodied in the Scripture and against faith which comes out of the preaching of the Word of God. Thus they seduce the people. Now since all prophecy, that is proclaiming, teaching and preaching must be according to the faith, Rom. 12[:7] and also since faith comes from the Word of God, Rom. 10[:17], it follows that teaching or prophecy must be God's Word. But how can anyone be sure that his proclamation is God's Word, if he does not have the witness of the Scripture, that is if his teaching is not according to Scripture, but is his own thought, chance or opinion? For the Lord himself speaks through the prophet Isaiah in chapter 55[:8]: "For my thoughts are not your thoughts, neither are your ways my ways, said the Lord. For as the heavens are higher than the earth, so are my ways higher than your ways, and my thoughts than your thoughts." Therefore, dreams here, dreams there, voices here, voices there, prophecy must be according to the faith, that is according to Holy Scripture, and so must the spirits be tested and distinguished.

By this guideline of Holy Scripture and the Word of God, let us now test this named spirit of delusion. Let us prove on the basis of the Word of God that he is a lying, devilish and seducing spirit.

D. Of the Office of Outward Preaching and the Use of Scripture

The office of outward and oral preaching is a command and order of God which was first carried out and practiced by the holy patriarchs, prophets and fathers. Therefore the holy apostle Peter calls the godly Noah a preacher of righteousness, 2 Pet. 2[:5]. The esteemed prophets had a special calling and command for their preaching, as they, the prophets, themselves testify. Thus the Lord Jesus Christ, God's son, also became a preacher, carrying out and instituting the office of oral preaching as the gospel writers testify. Our Saviour Jesus Christ commanded his disciples to preach the Gospel in the whole world, Matt. 28[:19]; Mark 16[:15]; Luke 24[:47]. He confirmed the office of preaching, so that whoever heard them, the apostles, heard the Lord himself, and whoever despised them, despised himself, Matt. 10[:40], Luke 10[:16]. Whoever believed their preaching of the Gospel would be saved, and whoever would not believe it, would be damned, Mark 15[16:16]. Saint Paul confesses that he is not ashamed of the Gospel, for it as a power of God which saves all who believe it, Rom. 1[:6]. So the disciples of Christ went out into the world and preached the Gospel, and the Lord acted with them, affirming the Word through accompanying signs, Mark 16[:20]. What can be stated more plainly than that God instituted the office of preaching in the world and wants it there, and that in this way his kingdom increases and is maintained. As worldly rule is maintained by the sword, good rule and law, so the kingdom of Christ on earth is maintained by the Word.

However, in order that no one preaches his own thoughts, God has prescribed for us what to preach. In the old covenant God gave the law which Moses and the levitical priests and prophets were to preach and explain, and were to teach or preach nothing contrary to it, as it is written in Isa. 8[:20], "According to the law and the testimony." And Jer. 23[:16]: "Do not listen to the words of the prophets who prophesy to you; they are deluding you. They speak visions of their own minds." Thus has he commanded the Gospel to be preached in the new covenant, so that we have a guideline by which we are to guide ourselves. For God wants his Word to be preached and not our dreams or thoughts. His Word is the law and the Gospel, both sufficiently described in the Bible. We are to accept no other teaching, nor hear any other preaching. And even if an angel from heaven should come (says Saint Paul) and preach a different Gospel, it must be cursed, Gal. 1[:9]. Christ the Lord commands most earnestly and faithfully that one is to shun false prophets. Who are the false prophets but those who preach, not God's Word, but their thoughts and dreams, or those who preach contrary to the pure Word of God?

Since God's Word is contained in and described in the Bible, we are to consider and hold all those as seducers of the people who claim to hear heavenly voices, dispute Scripture and reject it. For they are certainly blasphemers and disrupters of the godly order who desire to destroy all consciences. With what do they intend to assure the listeners that their teaching is God's Word? How can they give assurance to men's consciences, since they reject the Holy Scripture? Christ our redeemer himself directs us to Scripture, John 5[:39], and scolds the Sadducees, asserting that they err because they do not know the Scripture, Mark 12[:24]. Similarly Saint Paul admonishes Timothy that he is not to depart from Holy Scriptures, using these words, 2 Tim. 3[:14]: "But as for you, continue in what you have learned and firmly believed, knowing from whom you learned it, and how from childhood you have known the sacred writings that are able to instruct you for salvation through faith in Christ Jesus. All Scripture is inspired by God and is useful for teaching, for reproof, for correction and for training in righteousness, so that everyone who belongs to God may be proficient, equipped for every good work." With these words the holy apostle conclusively shows us in what way Holy Scripture serves us, that it instructs us towards salvation through faith in Jesus Christ. What do all people on earth desire, but to be instructed towards salvation, that they be shown and taught the right and true knowledge of their salvation and that they comprehend true godliness? Such comprehension of godliness does not come from dreams or carnal thoughts, but from Holy Scripture, says Saint Paul, through faith in Christ. For Scripture is useful for teaching, for admonition, for improvement; the Scriptures teach us, admonish us, improve us, comfort us. "For whatever was written in former days was written for our instruction, so that by steadfastness and encouragement of the Scriptures we might have hope," Rom. 15[:4]. The Word of God is contained neatly and orderly in the Holy Scriptures. Whoever therefore rejects Holy Scripture and the oral preaching of the Gospel, rejects God's Word, and is a slanderer of God, for he blasphemes against and despises the order and the command of God, and thereby sins against the Holy Spirit.

This is a warning to all devout and simple people, that they absolutely keep away from these poisonous seducers and dreamers. They are not to greet them or give them shelter, as is commanded by the Holy Spirit in 1 John 1. For the devil does not rest. He is transformed into an angel of light, 2 Cor. 11[:14]; 1 Pet. 5[:8], seeking whom he may devour.

If a seducing spirit says that one must learn directly from God and not from the Scriptures, ask him quickly how he knows that. If he answers, from Scripture, and that such words are written in Isa. 54[:13], then thrust back his own blasphemy under his nose and ask why he invokes this verse from Holy Scripture if he himself has no regard for Scripture? If Scripture is valid for him when it serves him, why should it not much more be valid for us who are constantly served by it and in which and through which we are taught about God? For Holy Scripture and oral preaching are the only means by which God's Word teaches us, gives and preaches, yes through which he awakens faith in us, through which his Spirit witnesses to our spirit, shows us the way, makes known to us his truth, as Paul, the chosen vessel of God, confesses in many places. Particularly significant is Rom. 10[:13]: "Whoever shall call upon the name of the Lord shall be saved. How shall they call on him in whom they have not believed? and how shall they believe in him of whom they have not heard? and how shall they hear without a preacher? And how shall they preach, except they be sent?" As it is written, [Isa. 52[:7]; Nah. 1[:15]], How beautiful are the feet of them that preach the Gospel of peace, and bring glad tidings of good things! But they have not all obeyed the Gospel. For Isaiah said, who has believed what we have heard [53:1]? So then faith comes by hearing, and hearing by the Word of God, [Rom. 10:17]. That is a powerful word against the seducing spirit that destroys the office of external oral preaching and Holy Scripture. In Gal. 3[:2] Paul says: "The only thing I want to learn from you is this: Did you receive the Spirit by doing the works of the law or by believing what you heard?" The

Galatians had certainly not received the Holy Spirit through the works of the law which they did, but through the preaching of the Gospel. So had the gentiles of whom Luke wrote in Acts 10[:44]: "While Peter was still speaking, the Holy Spirit fell on all who heard the Word." Here we have two more witnesses that God pours out his Spirit and faith through the office of preaching and thus imparts it to the hearers. To the Thessalonians he writes thus: "We also constantly give thanks to God for this, that when you received the Word of God that you heard from us, you accepted it not as a human word but as what it really is, God's Word, which is also at work in you believers," 1 Thess. 2[:13]. Does not Paul here declare with clear words that the Thessalonians had come to know God through his preaching, and that they had accepted his oral preaching not as human words but as the Word of God? He writes similarly in 1 Cor. 13 [Rom. 16, 26]. God converted the gentiles to Christian faith through Paul his instrument, as well as through other apostles. Thus the apostle himself confesses to the Corinthians when he writes: "In Christ Jesus I became your father through the Gospel," 1 Cor. 4[:15]. To the Galatians he says, Gal. 4[:19]: "My little children, for whom I am again in the pain of childbirth until Christ is formed in you." God alone is the right master and physician. But he teaches through his accustomed means. He alone is our nourisher who feeds us and gives us drink, Matt. 6[:26]: "Your heavenly Father feedeth them." But he has his customary means by which he feeds the hungry such as bread and meat, etc. He satisfies the thirsty, but with water, wine, or beer, etc. God alone is the helper in need, protector and saviour. But he usually works his salvation through orderly means. Through emperor, king, princes and lords he protects land and people and gives them well-being, peace and prosperity. God alone is the only legitimate Father of all children, who creates and makes all people but again through his common proper means and order. God alone is the Father and master builder of the Christian church, but he builds and maintains it through his customary means, his Word and its preaching. God alone forgives the sins of all people, but customarily through his orderly means, such as the Gospel, the sacraments, and the servants of the Word. He forgave David his adultery through the prophet Nathan, 2 Sam. 12, just as he forgives us our original sin in baptism and imparts to us forgiveness of sin in the Lord's Supper in the bread and wine as his body and blood.

In John 20[:22] we read: "He breathed on his disciples and said to them, Receive the Holy Spirit. If you forgive the sins of any, they are forgiven them; if you retain the sins of any, they are retained." Is that not a clear statement that God forgives sins through his servants and disciples? Did he not himself commit the keys to the kingdom of heaven to them, Matt. 18[:16], that is, give them the power to forgive sins? Does not Saint Paul also say: "For we are labourers together with God," 1 Cor. 3[:9]? Later, in chapter 4[:1] he says: "Let a man so account of us, as of the ministers of Christ, and stewards of the mysteries of God" and as distributors of his sacraments. 2 Cor. 5[:19]: "In Christ God was reconciling the world to himself, not counting their trespasses against them, and entrusting the message of reconciliation to us. So we are ambassadors for Christ, since God is making his appeal through us; we entreat you on behalf of Christ, be reconciled to God." etc.

With these witnesses of Holy divine Scripture we have proven that Holy Scripture and its preachers are appointed instruments of our God, through which he reveals and imparts knowledge of his Word, faith, forgiveness of sin and other treasures and riches. Now since these two have rejected the poor fanatics, one can only consider them to be servants and messengers of the devil, who through them instigates all this misery among the people of God and who turns the people away from the Gospel of Jesus Christ.

E. Their Unchristian Disruption of Matrimony.

In addition these new factions and spirits have another terrible, unheard of error among them, the destruction of marriage, marrying their own espoused wives to others and also taking other wives to themselves. What is your opinion? How does that strike you? How do you like this rabble? They certainly are pious chaps, these apostles, faithfully promoting his kingdom, too, and disrupting both divine and human laws and statutes and order. God has commanded that married people are not to separate, but to live constantly with each other, as Christ our dear saviour indicates, Matt. 5[:32] and 19[:6]: "It was also said, 'whoever divorces his wife, let him give her a certificate of divorce.' But I say to you that anyone who divorces his wife, except on the ground of unchastity, causes her to commit adultery; and whoever marries a divorced woman commits adultery." Similarly the holy apostle in 1 Cor. 7[:3-5]: "The husband should give to his wife her conjugal rights, and likewise the wife to her husband. For the wife does not have authority over her own body, but the husband does; likewise the husband does not have authority over his own body, but the wife does. Do not deprive one another except perhaps by agreement for a set time, to devote yourselves to prayer, and then come together again," etc.

Therefore, according to the judgment of our Lord Christ these spirits are adulterers and adulteresses because they disrupt marriage solely for the sake of their dreams and seductive voices, taking other concubines contrary to the command of God. And since one knows the evil tree by its fruits, Matt. 7[:16] and 12[:35], we can deduce from this one deed that this spirit is of the devil. For God's Spirit teaches no adultery but forbids it. Saint Paul says that no adulterer or fornicator has any part in the kingdom of God, 1 Cor. 5[:6, :9]; Eph. 5[:5]. To the Hebrews, he writes 13[:4]: "Whoremongers and adulterers God will judge." How can people who deal in adultery and fornication, and who defend such vices besides, as though they had acted rightly, be holy and devout? For they say the voice of God so instructed them. Is adultery and marrying one's spouse to another right? Where is it written? What god teaches this except the devil, the god and prince of this shameful world? It is this god's inspiration that these poor people have; he drives, rules and leads them according to his will. It is this unclean spirit who lusts after what is unclean, and who instigates sin, shame and vice. But the Holy Spirit teaches and admonishes towards holiness, chastity and honour. Our God has forbidden adultery and fornication at the cost of the salvation of the soul. He is a steady, truthful, and unchangeable God, as Holy Scripture witnesses, Mal. 3[:6], Ps. 102[:13], James 1[:17]. How can these spirits of the night boast and say that God has bidden it? Does God command something contrary to his Word? He certainly does not do this, nor ever has done.

Just as these spirits of the night act contrary to God's law, so they also act directly contrary to imperial and worldly law and contrary to natural law. For not only God in his Word forbade adultery, but imperial worldly law also forbids it. The pagan histories too testify conclusively that they will not suffer adultery, punishing the perpetrators with severe penalties. Even less will natural law tolerate a strange man sleeping with one's own wife. Each one wants his own for himself and will not have it in common.

Therefore let everyone be warned of these devilish spirits and avoid them, for one may justifiably be concerned that they will not stop with this fanaticism. As soon as their devilish voice drives them they will begin to murder, kill and shed blood. They will undertake to destroy the government, cause all kinds of grief, and say that God's voice told them to do it.

Because of all this the pastors and preachers should admonish the people most earnestly in their preaching to avoid such horrible sects and fanaticisms. For their own good and well-being, they must avoid all this harm, and destruction of soul and body, temporal and eternal.

The admonition of the people, however, can be done in the following manner:

Admonition

Recently there has been generated a new sect and frightful error, doubtless as a special punishment of God in view of our ingratitude and our disdain towards his divine Word. The associates and adherents of this sect reject all Holy, divine Scripture, counting the oral word of preaching neither as useful nor as God's command. But they despise them and base their faith solely on dreams, visions and other similar fantasies which they call the spirit of God. Besides, they recognize no worldly authority and insist on living and acting according to that which they are bidden or instructed to do by these seductive uncertain revelations and dreams of theirs. In addition they presume, on the basis of such devilish inspiration to disrupt marriage, to leave their wives, to marry them to other husbands, to marry other women, as though this were the open command of God and the Holy Spirit. Such devilish marriages they defend as divine and Christian. Added to this they have no regard for the two holy sacraments, baptism and the body and blood of Christ, all of which is burdensome and terrible for Christian ears to hear.

It is the duty of all governments to honour God and his most Holy Word and to watch diligently over their subjects in this matter. This is necessary for the sake of prosperity and well-being and for the furthering and maintenance of the common good and peaceful harmony. These damnable errors are not to be permitted among the people since by them God's public order is despised, oral preaching stopped, and many devout people brought into damnable error. If this sect has its way, all human law, authority, honourable policies and governance, and the common peace and unity would be destroyed.

Our gracious Master N. herewith admonishes us to pray God the Almighty in true confidence that he would graciously turn these and similar horrible errors, attacks and difficulties from his Christian church, to illuminate the erring with the light of his divine truth, to protect those who have recognized truth from all error, and to keep us all in the unity of faith, in brotherly love and true Christian peace.

Finally, our gracious lord most faithfully warns and earnestly commands all in general, that none of his subjects or others in his territory [join the heretics]. This is [in accordance with] his princely grace's mandate, which has been printed, and has now been read and openly posted.

Every one of his princely grace's subjects is, as is fitting, to be obedient and proper in all things.

15

Georg Gross Pfersfelder

Georg Gross, called Pfersfelder, to Hans von Seckendorf. Concerning Persecution of Anabaptists (1531)[*]

Introduction

Georg Gross Pfersfelder was a baron owning property in Weilersburg in the district of Bamberg. He was in the service of the city of Nuremberg but was also an Anabaptist sympathizer. He had close contact with Caspar Schwenckfeld from 1530 on, and had interfered violently in an Anabaptist trial in Brandenberg-Ansbach in 1531, where the Anabaptist in question, Anton Schmied, had been arrested for publicly contradicting Anton Schad, the Protestant pastor in Uttenreuth near Erlangen.

Pfersfelder had Pastor Schad arrested and threatened him before releasing him. The latter then complained to the Ansbach authorities, asking for protection. Pfersfelder, as voluntary council for the

---

[*]Source: Schornbaum, *Quellen II*, 231-234.
Translation: Friesen/Klaassen

Anabaptists, wrote the following letter to Hans von Seckendorf, the bailiff who had arrested Schmied.

The letter shows Pfersfelder to have been a well-trained opponent of Luther and friend of the Anabaptists, as well as a religiously alert layman who knew how to handle words.

It was not possible to allege that Pfersfelder had social revolutionary intentions as was done against Anabaptists, nor was it possible to fasten a charge of disturbing the peace for his arrest of Schad, because of his noble status. It was possible, however, to carry on with the trial against Schmied, and Pfersfelder's actions were ultimately unsuccessful in saving Schmied. After weeks of torture on the rack, Schmied was beheaded on July 10, 1531 on a charge of "setting up a forbidden, illegal, and fundamentally seditious sect and rabble, on account of seductive visionary dreams and ghosts and on account of the dissolving of his marriage."[1]

Pfersfelder, on the other hand, continued to use his position to support radical religious dissenters, writing letters to the Margrave and staying in contact with the "Dreamers" of Baiersdorf. In June of 1531, Andreas Osiander, the leading theologian at Nuremberg, and several other city councillors were commissioned to talk with Pfersfelder concerning his "Anabaptist errors." Pfersfelder did not show up, but submitted a statement of his beliefs. A colloquy between Osiander and Pfersfelder in 1532 was also fruitless. After the bloody suppression of the Anabaptists in Franconia, Pfersfelder transferred to the Schwenckfelders, as did his sister Elisabeth, who had once married the fanatical Anabaptist Claus Frey.

Bibliographical Source:

Eberhard Teufel, "Pfersfelder, Georg," *ME IV,* 159-60.

Georg Gross, called Pfersfelder, to Hans von Seckendorf. Nuremberg Jubilate, April 30, 1531.

I am surprised that you, an old worn-out man, persecute the devout and righteous Christians which are found among the Anabaptists, and that you deal with them wickedly, relying on the teaching of Luther and his following. After all, Luther and his party have done nothing except that they have in part forced the papists out of their avarice and arrogance, and have taken their place. The proof is that they do not submit themselves to the cross, nor do they go out into the world to preach the Gospel to all creatures as Christ taught them. Rather they have allowed themselves to be escorted [before the cross?] in power and glory by mounted soldiers. Briefly put, whoever does not follow Christ, obedient to his Father to the death, is not worthy of him. Those who are not sent by God do not yield fruit, as is clearly seen in the Lutherans.

But God the Father now in these last times, again works mightily among the lowly and ignorant through his Holy Spirit as he did in the beginning when Christ was on earth. He again teaches the unlearned his divine way of salvation. These yield themselves to their Father with body, life and all they do. For a true witness they have the covenant of water baptism just as Christ and his apostles baptized. They do not act contrary to that baptism and that word. By baptism and daily with sighing hearts they ask God that he might work in and through them nothing except that which serves his high praise and divine will. For the sake of divine truth they gladly suffer all kinds of torture and death. The devil and the world do not tolerate this divine truth. The rich are worried that they will have to share their goods with the poor, who hold their goods in common in apostolic fashion, and don't want to do so.

There may at times also be false people among them as among other people. These, if they are evil, ought to be punished. But the concern of your party is much more about property than about salvation. Such, as Christ says, are not worthy of him. Therefore as soon as someone begins to renounce sin and yields completely to God's will, he is despised, ridiculed and persecuted by the world, as also happened to Christ and his disciples at the beginning. But Christ says that whoever does not follow him is not worthy of him. Indeed, if the cross, suffering and total scorn were as easy to bear as eating meat on Friday, going to the sacrament, and marrying, the Lutherans would long ago have yielded themselves to God and would have had themselves baptized in the name of Christ, as Saint Peter on one day baptized about three thousand believers. But I am talking about a covenant of perfection which brings the cross.

Now this Smidt whom you persecute has actually been taught by God. He does not especially emphasize water baptism, for Scripture says that after John baptized with water for repentance, Christ baptized with the Holy Spirit, fire and blood. Indeed, if you were to accept this baptism of suffering and drink the cup, you would not torment Christ, his people and his apostles in this manner. You say that eating a bit of baked bread with a cross on it is the greatest idolatry, and once that has been said you have done with it all. But you will not see how faithfully God warns you against all images. Christ especially says: "Many false prophets will arise, and do miracles and signs. When they say, look here or there is Christ, do not believe it, and note that I have told you this beforehand" [Matt. 24:23-25]. But he has gone up to heaven and will not come except for the last judgment. That, if God wills, will happen soon, after the first persecution. The book of the secret revelation of John is now being opened on earth through his apostles. Your Luther does not know much about it, nor perhaps you either, just as in the times of Noah and Lot few had faith. May God give you and all people grace, that you yield yourselves completely and wholly to the Lord and ask him for his teaching.

All those who would master the Scripture and be wise, miss the narrow gate. Scripture does nothing but give witness about Christ, and is a dead letter. The Lord Christ says: "You must all be taught of God." Whoever cries and prays to him from the heart, will be shown the way of salvation. He will be able to understand Scripture if he follows it. For the Lord says that he does not desire to be in any house made by hands. We are to be the temple of God. If our body is to be his house and his temple, then we have to cleanse it and make it most beautiful. Otherwise he neither can nor desires to live in us with his Word. We know that we are God's creatures even as all animals and birds are our creatures. You can see that if we want to use it as food, we pluck it or skin it, cut it up and clean it most thoroughly. All this our creatures must suffer. In the same way we must also submit ourselves to the Lord and prepare his house for God our Father most carefully, namely desist from all idolatry. That is, we are not to slander our heavenly Father who has made heaven and earth and all that is in them for us, nor to use [his name] idly in our speech. For he says we are not to swear by anything but to abstain from sin. We are to love him above all things and our neighbour as ourselves, although we are unable to be so perfect. But no one can keep from sinning unless as was mentioned above, he yields himself wholeheartedly to his heavenly Father without any concern about how things turn out. He will realize the great faithfulness of the Father. If someone gave you a hundred guilders, you would love him for it. Should the faithful heavenly Father who gives everything, the eternal and the temporal, not be loved enough that we forsake sin as Christ teaches? He calls us to forsake sin and repent, and, if and when he wills, to suffer and die with him. Whoever does not sense this and does not test himself to see that all carnal pride, joy and pleasure has been extinguished in him has not yet really come to know him. He has not yet been born again. Of this Christ said to Nicodemus: "Except a man be born again, he will not see the kingdom of God" [John 3:3]. Paul also says that whoever is born of God, is kept from sinning by that birth. We also have Christ's words in the Gospel that we are not to judge. Woe to one who condemns, judges and persecutes the righteous. I am even more surprised that you want to force those who in knowledge are as far above you as heaven is above the earth to believe in your sacrament as you require.

Above I have pointed out to you three passages. The first, Christ's warning that when they say, look, here or there is Christ, that we are not to believe it. Secondly, that he ascended to heaven bodily and will not return till the last judgment. Thirdly, that he will dwell in no house made with hands. Fourthly, Christ's words, "Take, eat, this is my body which is broken for you" [Luke 22:19]. Now we can never make his words into a falsehood. The body which sat there with them at the table was broken for us and tortured. That same blood was shed on the cross and not in a cup. The Jews did not torture the bread but this same body. Fifthly, the Lord says, "Whatever goes in at the mouth goes out again the natural way" [Matt. 15:17]. That would be poor honour to the high, dear Son of God. Finally and most importantly, Christ, as indicated above, says, "You must all be taught by God" [John 6:45].

I take complete and sufficient comfort in God's teaching, and conclude that Christ became the living bread which came from heaven. For he calls himself bread. And this is the true food and the true drink.

Many have been tested in the fire, who suffer burning at the stake rather than to recant. Through his martyrs God shows that such understanding is true. Even though you say that this happened through the devil, yet I know that Christ's miracles were also ascribed to the devil. For the disciple is not greater than the master. Therefore whoever is born again and who in his heart has [yielded] himself to the Lord to suffer and die and to all that God desires to work in and through him, such a one may with joyous worthiness receive the bread and wine as the Lord's Supper with his brothers as a sign and a seal of his faith and as a memorial of the Lord as he commanded. This, most briefly, I could not in conscience keep from your notice. And even if I begged you strongly to show secular mercy to the poor, yet I know in advance that neither your superior nor you are able to persecute them beyond what God the Lord permits. It will be hard for you to kick against such a prick. May God the Lord instruct you and all people under heaven in his divine truth and show you the way to salvation.

But consider this, that if vengeance were not the Lord's and if I were to give way to the flesh, I would punish you because of your violent, godless actions, so that you would not soon hatch any more chickens even if all the lords of Brandenburg would be even more merciless to me. But I know whose the vengeance is. You will shortly also learn it, at a time when no one will call you or any noble an aristocrat in preference to a peasant.

However that may be, considering your actions in deed, I keep my own need also before me.

16

Katharina Hutter

Testimony of Katharina Hutter, Given before December 3, 1535, at Klausen. (1535)*

Introduction

Katharina Hutter was born most likely near Sterzing, in South Tyrol. Little is known about her parents except that her family name was Purst. In 1532 Katharina was working as a maid in the household of Paul Gall and his wife, Justina. It was during this time that she became acquainted with the Anabaptists. Many Anabaptists found refuge, lodging, and shelter in the household where Katharina worked and the people that she met must have impressed the young maid; she soon was participating in nocturnal Anabaptist meetings. Katharina and Justina Gall often brought food to the Anabaptists hiding in the forests, always in the fear of being caught and made to testify regarding their actions and convictions. In the court proceedings that would take place later, Katharina stated (in the words of the court scribe) that she

---

*Source: Grete Mecenseffy, ed., *Quellen zur Geschichte der Täufer, Österreich III Teil* (Gütersloh: Gerd Mohn, 1983), 300, ll.19 to 301, ll.40.
Translation: Elfriede Lichdi

had been "persuaded and convinced to join the Anabaptist sect" in the Gall household. It was there, following a confession of her faith, that she was baptized by Jacob Hutter, her future husband.[1]

Katharina was arrested by "Anabaptist hunters"—men who were paid a bounty by Ferdinand I to capture Anabaptists—along with all the other members of the Gall household in 1533. After lengthy interrogation and detailed questioning concerning the members, principal leaders, and local leaders of the Anabaptists, Katharina and the Gall couple recanted. Katharina and the Galls were pardoned and set free on the basis that they had seen the error of their ways. The subsequent flight of Justina Gall and Katharina Purst to Moravia demonstrates that their recantation was the result of coercion, and lacked inner conviction. Paul Gall was captured before he could reach Moravia and executed for breaking his oath in Rodeneck, June 25, 1533.

In 1535, Katharina married Jacob Hutter. Soon after, persecution broke out in Moravia, "the promised land" of the Anabaptists, and the Hutters were forced to return to the Tyrol. Unfortunately, Jacob Hutter could no longer travel unrecognized through this country and the Hutters had to be on the move constantly. On November 30, 1535 the couple was arrested in Klausen. Jacob was brought to Innsbruck where he was tortured and burned at the stake in early February 1536. Katharina was taken to the castle at Gufidaun, and her case was given to the judge there. Under threat of punishment and torture, Katharina gave the names of leaders and members of the movement, emphasizing that the key leaders were all in Moravia. Katharina made no secret of her convictions and the fact that she was a *relapsi*, that is, one who had recanted previously and then rejoined the Anabaptist movement. This should have been enough for an automatic death sentence.[2] Why she got another chance is difficult to understand, but orders were given to the religious authorities to try to persuade her to recant. Katharina remained steadfast; she would not deny her faith again. Her stubbornness must have made an impression on the judges, for she was not sent to work in the bishop's residence for fear that she would lead others astray. There were people concerned about her welfare, however, not only among the Anabaptists but also among the officials of the bishop. In fact, she succeeded in escaping the castle of Gufidaun, which could not have happened without outside help. It is possible that pregnancy was the reason for Katharina's leaving prison, but the sources are silent about the end of her imprisonment. They simply state: "Katharina Hutter escaped from the prison at Gufidaun shortly after April 28, 1536."[3]

In 1538, Katharina was arrested for the last time in the village of Schöneck near Bruneck, and since she had rejoined the Anabaptist movement a second time, she was executed immediately. She was approximately thirty years old.

Bibliographical Sources:

Werner O. Packull, *Hutterite Beginnings, Communitarian Experiments during the Reformation* (Baltimore, MD: John Hopkins University Press, 1995).

C. Arnold Snyder and Linda A. Huebert Hecht, eds., *Profiles of Anabaptist Women: Sixteenth-Century Reforming Pioneers* (Waterloo, ON: Wilfrid Laurier University Press, 1996).

Testimony of Katharina Hutter, given before December 3, 1535 at Klausen.

Katharina, legitimate daughter of Lorentzen Pursst testified:

Approximately three years ago she was working in Tryns for Paul Gall. Gall, Paul Rumer and others, some of whom have been executed and some of whom have left for Moravia, persuaded and encouraged her to come to [meetings of] the Anabaptist sect. There Jacob Hutter, a minister and leader, who is now her wedded brother and husband, baptized her. Following that they left for Moravia, and there, around the time of this past Pentecost, she married Jacob Hutter in proper fashion. Hans Tuchmacher, her brother as well as an Anabaptist leader, married them.

And on this past St. Jacob's Day, she and this same man, her wedded brother and husband and another one of her brothers in the faith, a man named Jerome, a schoolmaster, who also was baptized by Jacob Hutter, together came up from Moravia, over the Taurien mountains to Taufers, where they sojourned for a time in the forests. They went to a man named Waldner on the mountainside above Elln. However, he had fallen away from the Anabaptists and had become a destructive person.

From there they went to Hörschwang on another mountain to a man named Ober who was one of their beloved brothers, and also his wife and their daughter, named Dorothea, as well as two male servants, both named Martin, and a young fellow named Wolf, and his wife named Els, all of whom Jakob Hutter converted and baptized. Hutter also baptized the aforementioned Waldner at Elln, but he had become a useless Christian again, and had left the Anabaptists.

After that they visited a man named Prader and one named Braun several times in Lüsen, but Prader is not of their opinion and faith as they are, although his wife and son, named Melchior, are. They stayed often in Prader's house, along with the aforementioned Jerome, who also was with them on these occasions. And Hutter, her husband, baptized many people in the forests of Lüsen.

Approximately fourteen days ago Hutter baptized around seven or eight people in Trens and Sterzing in the cellar of a cartright's house which is named The Shepherd or The Haggler. The man was not home at the time and is not an Anabaptist. She does not know them, and thinks that they may have been miners.

From there, she and Hutter along with Anna, Stainer's daughter, went again to Hörschwang to a man named Ober and stayed with him for a time. After that (when they realized that they were being watched), they went through the forests under cover of darkness and along the streets of Klausen, crossed the bridge at the guard hut and went through the town of Klausen and over the bridge to the Mesner's house, arriving there around midnight. They wanted to leave again right away but did not know where to turn. Her husband and brother, Jacob Hutter, told her that he wanted to go to Villnöss to a man named Niclauer or back to Jörg Müller in Villnöss or wherever God would lead them.

The wife of Niclauer was her dear sister, but not her husband. Like Jörg Müller and his wife in Villnöss, Niclauer had been baptized by Hutter the previous Fall, but Müller had become useless [i.e., had since left the Anabaptists].

Moreover, she could see no use for either the mass or the sacrament of the altar, which monks or priests lift above their heads, nor for the church building, which was nothing but a "pile of stones" [*gemaurten steinerhauffen*], or for the baptism of infants, which was nothing more than a bath in dirty water [*ain sudlwesch*]; and the sacrament was nothing more than an abomination and a stench before God. All this was from the devil.

Niclas Niderhofer from the district of Schonegg and a young woman by the name of Ulian, who worked as a maid at Khyens, and another person whom she did not know, were baptized on St. Jacob's Day by her accused husband, Hutter. They had found protection and lodging several times with these people at Hörschwang.

With whatever means or money available to him, her married brother and husband, Jacob Hutter, provided for the poor widows, poor young children and other poor brothers and sisters who were in need. As far as she knew none of the leaders or her brothers were now in Tyrol, rather they were all in Moravia at this time.

17

Endres Keller

Confession of the prisoner, Anabaptist Endres Keller (Kentlein) in Rothenburg (1536)*

Introduction

The story of Endres Keller is one of the most poignant in Anabaptist literature. He was a member of a prominent family in Rothenburg ob der Tauber. His father had been a member of the City Council. Members of his family occupied various positions in local government in towns around Rothenburg.[1]

A series of letters from members of his family have survived, imploring the magistrates of Rothenburg to relent in their treatment of Keller. Delegations of priests and family members visited Keller in order to get him to recant, but without success. On 30 October, 1536, a letter from the magistrates specifically stated that apart from imprisonment Keller had not been harmed physically. Keller's own statement, however, says that the tortures had ruined his hands and that he had

---

*Source: Schornbaum, *Quellen* V, 193-209.
Translation: Friesen/Klaassen.

been stretched on the rack. That must have happened after 30 October. Even after the application of torture he wrote this confession and was resolved to remain faithful. However, pressure from church and family plus the likely renewal of torture finally convinced him to recant.

He promised to make his recantation in public on the market square and agreed that, in case he should lapse back into Anabaptism, his descendants would be outlaws forever. The recantation is not in Keller's own words because the style is quite different. That means that it was written for him and he merely agreed with it. He had evidently been completely broken.[2]

Bibliographical Source:

Karl Schornbaum, ed., *Quellen zur Geschichte der Wiedertäufer*, V. Bd.(Bayern, II. Abteilung) (Gütersloh, 1951).

Confession of the prisoner, Anabaptist Endres Keller (Kentlein) in Rothenburg.
[between 30 October and 25 November], 1536.

The grace of the Lord be with you all. Amen.

Honourable, prudent, favourable, wise, dear sirs: Since, according to my request, you have permitted me to give an account of my actions, I will do it briefly so that you may not be annoyed with it. I want to indicate to you briefly what I hold concerning the Old and the New Testaments. Concerning the Old Testament I believe as follows. After God had decided to select a person whom he would make into a great nation, he selected the pious Abraham. To him he said: "Truly I will bless you and increase your seed like the stars in the sky and like the sand by the sea, and in your seed I will bless all generations on the earth" (Gen. 12[:2]). There would be much to say about this. Now Abraham believed these words which the Lord promised him and by this faith attained salvation, Gen. 15[:6]. He saw the Lord just as the dear disciples did and all believers do, but in faith, as do all believers. Thus briefly, all Jews are descended from Abraham, who received the law more than four hundred years later. But circumcision was given to Abraham by God, so that he might circumcise them, which he did. He was to circumcise the children on the eighth day. Abraham did as the Lord had commanded him and obeyed his command, neither adding nor subtracting anything. For if he had wanted to follow his own understanding or his thoughts or his wit (of which man is full) he would have had cause to consider. He might, for example, have thought the children were still too weak and too undeveloped, or they might bleed to death and other reasons besides. But Abraham did as the Lord bade or commanded him, no matter how the children would fare. For they (the Jews) did not depart from this one day, neither back nor forward. It was neither the seventh day nor the ninth day, but the eighth day as the Lord had commanded, although circumcision was only an outward sign. And the demonstrative "that" pointed to an inner circumcision of the heart when God said to Abraham: "that" is my covenant which you are to keep, as stated above (Gen. 17[:11]). For Paul says: "Not he is a Jew who is a Jew according to the flesh, but whoever is a Jew according to the spirit, which is the circumcision of the heart,—he is a proper Jew," Rom. 2[:29]. This I hold in conscience also concerning baptism. For look, if God had said they were to circumcise on the first day, they would have done so and not otherwise. Although Moses circumcised no one in the desert, should those children be condemned? No, in no way, even before circumcision was given. It would be a pitiful thing that God should in this way condemn innocent children. And this would have to follow, if salvation were to come through an external sign of baptism or circumcision. How many gentile children were killed by Herod? For many gentiles lived among the Jews at that time Matt. 2[:16]. If it contributes towards salvation of the children to perform such an outward sign, it ought also to contribute towards our salvation. But I do not discount the sign, for I count it important on account of the inner baptism, towards which the outer sign points. From the outward sign I look towards the inner; in baptism, which is now our sign of covenant, as in circumcision which was the Jewish sign of the covenant. For in baptism which Christ commanded, God the Holy Spirit is present through the prayers of the believer or of the servant to whom this has been assigned. He must be one who has the right faith which counts before God and abide in works, as James 2[:26] says: "As the body without the spirit is dead, so faith without works is dead also." Such a prayer God hears, as is written everywhere in Scripture: "Where two or three are gathered together in my name" (Matt. 18[:20]), God will give them whatever they ask for. For the prayer of the righteous is powerful before God (James 5[:16]), but the prayer of the hypocrite is an abomination before God. God does not hear it, but the prayer of the righteous God hears at all times.

When Elijah prayed that it should not rain, it did not rain for three years, and when he prayed again, it rained again. But this did not happen with the others who were sinners. Even though they prayed long, they were not heard. For sinners pray for forgiveness of their sins, if they desist and repent and henceforth live according to the will of God. As he also says: "Whoever loves me will keep my commandments," John 15[:10]. For God wants his commandments to be kept. He says, kept. Not only are we to believe them but we are to keep them. For a true faith which is in God and which comes from God, cannot rest at all. It breaks forth into action like a tree that is good and breaks out with fruit. Now, whoever walks in such faith, loves God from the whole heart and desires to live in all his conduct as God has commanded him. Such a one is not concerned about how his body fares, but whatever God lays on him suits him, whether it be good or ill. He suffers it patiently. Nor does he do any evil to anyone and has hearty love towards all people. This you will learn from me even if I lived thirty years more on earth. But I do not boast with it, for we are human. For if someone stands, let him see that he does not fall. Paul tells the Cornithians bluntly in many places when he says: "If I were to boast, let me boast of my weakness" (2 Cor. 12[:5]). For one who builds on himself will not know when God will let him fall, as happened to Peter. Now then, if I believe with my whole heart everything which our Lord Christ, the saviour, taught us, then one must obey, and neither add nor subtract anything. For all that he has heard from the Father, he told and taught us, as John writes in his Gospel (John 15[:15]). For when we look into the Old Testament where God gave them the command through the mediator Moses that they [the Israelites] were to take the blood of the Easter lamb and apply it to the doorposts so that the angel who killed the firstborn would not strike, they did it. They applied it to the doorposts and not to the windows, as Moses commanded them who at that time was the mediator between God and the Jews, Exod. 12. Further, when he gave them the law and instructed the ark to be made, in which the covenant of the Lord was to lie, they did it and obeyed. Then, when he commanded them to make the priestly garment, they did as he bade them. They did not take what belonged to the pomegranates and made the border out of it, nor did they take that which belonged to the front of the ark and fasten it behind. When he gave a command they executed it in whatever way he told them. If he had said they should each wear a fastening on the front of their garment, they would have done it and not asked why it should be so. Moses did not teach them anything but what God commanded him. And when they transgressed and did not want to or did not obey, God punished them cruelly. As you well know yourselves, it was with fiery snakes, with pestilence and also with the sword, making them slaves to the gentiles, as you can read. For when Moses received the command from God to make the tent of witness God said: "See to it that you make everything according to the plan that you have seen," Exod. 19 or 24[25:40]. I cannot give the chapters accurately, since I have no Bible. Now the Jews were not given anything so small but it had an inner meaning which pointed to God. But among them as with us, very few knew the wonders of the Lord. For the Lord Christ our mediator did no miracle so small, but it had a spiritual explanation. Not, however, that I consider the Lord like Moses. For he far exceeds Moses as you well see by the punishment. For when the children of Israel were commanded something and they thought they knew better and did not obey Moses, God forthwith punished them, no matter with what. For when Urias touched the ark of the covenant when the cattle stepped off the road, he did it with good intentions, for he feared that the ark with the covenant would fall. Yet God punished him so that he died the same hour. That all happened so that the people would see the great dignity of God. How then will we fare who daily walk only in the desires of our hearts in all that serves only the body, thinking that God has paid for everything, that we need do nothing except believe. With this the enemy deceives us badly and leads us to depend on human laws. For the wise man says: you are to add nothing to the Word nor subtract anything from it, so that God does not punish you or that you are not found unrighteous. Also, "Cursed be anyone who is not obedient to the words of this covenant," [Deut. 27:27]; Jer. 11[:3], yes, and who adds or takes away, Deut. 4[:2], 12[:23]. See also in the next book, Josh. 23[:6]; Jer. 26[:2]; Prov., that is, the Wise Man, 30[:6]; Gal. [3:15], and the last chapter of Rev. [22:17-18]. But I do not know this accurately. See for yourselves what is written. I read it there before God granted me grace. Thus I follow him, now that I lie thus in this miserable darkness. Take me for what you will; God knows all and knows the thought of men, Ps. 94[:11], that they are vain. Therefore we cannot think anything good of ourselves apart from the will of God. But the pope and others now ask nothing concerning it, and use the Word of God only for their own benefit, as you know well enough. For when the first indulgence from the pope came to Germany, it cost Augsburg 2000 florins. He never again received so many twelvers.[3] And now your priests say that none of them any longer will offer a prayer for less than a twelver, nor would bury anyone unless he got a fiver.[4] Even if formerly one read twenty-one masses for a guilder, he would not read one again for a twelver.[5] For they did this to me. I could not haggle them down one penny when my mother died. Would God be with people who are thus immersed in greed over their ears and teach nothing but the commandments of men? Thus they drive a hard bargain and ignore what is important, namely the commandments of God, for example, the true faith which counts before God, namely the love of the neighbour. For everything that God has commanded us, John 13, 14, 15, 16, 17, is expressed in the love of the neighbour. For where there is no love, faith is cold, as Paul says: "If I spoke with the tongues of men and of angels and had not love, it would be like a sounding brass or a tinkling cymbal" [1 Cor. 13:1ff]. "And if I had faith that I could move mountains, it would be nothing if I did not have love." For love lasts eternally; one should present that strongly to the people. One should present the law and emphasize it most strongly, so that people almost despair, frightening them thus with damnation. This would go to their hearts and then they should be comforted again with the Gospel. Such preaching yields much fruit. For look at the miserable situation in these times. The small child which cannot yet pray blasphemes God. God certainly will not leave this condition unavenged, and tells us that the end is approaching quickly, as I fear. Daniel prophesied [9:26], concerning the abominating sacrilege which will stand in the holy place. In Matt. 24[:15] Christ himself tells us this and Paul, Peter and John warn us everywhere against the teaching of men, as for instance, Paul to the Col. 2[:8]; Thess. 2 [2 Thess. 2:3]; [1] Tim. 6[:3]; Peter 2 [2 Pet. 2:1]. They describe it so vividly that one should be able to grasp it; but we refuse to take note. You must admit that the popes have created this miserable situation which is obvious and which no one can deny. You must admit that infant baptism was not there during the time of the apostles, and that they did not baptize infants. For if they had done it, it would be written in the Scriptures. But that can be shown by no one, neither Luther nor the pope.

Therefore no one will convince me that I should believe man's commands which are contrary to God. Therefore generous, kind lords, you must not think that I insist on living and at the same time be disobedient to you. You yourselves know well enough and can judge for yourselves whether it is right that we should obey men more than God. This I know, generous and dear sirs, that you will not command me to do it, for I shall not do it even if the executioner puts his sword to my throat, even if the priests have told you so. For I will remain with the truth as long as there is breath in me. For Christ does not agree with Belial nor darkness with light. Whoever does not gather with the Lord, scatters, and whoever is not with the Lord, is against him, Matt. 12[:30]. The Lord himself also says, "If I go, I will send you the Spirit of truth who will teach you everything and remind you of what I have told you"[John 14:26]. He does not say that he will teach them eternal truths that they did not know before, but what they already know from the Lord. He does not say that he would teach you what someone else has said. Christ says: "Everything that I have heard from my Father, I have told you." He says everything, not a part or a piece but everything, everything—which is good German. It simply needs to be believed. Now it would certainly have to follow from this that if the pope's command to baptize infants were right, God would be a liar, or that he had not told us everything. But it cannot be true in all eternity that God lies. You must surely agree that God is true. For surely he remains just and true in eternity. It would also follow that all the infants born after and before the deaths of the apostles would be damned up to the time of pope Eugenius and pope Nikolaus II, who confirmed infant baptism. For whoever has had the eyes of his heart opened by God will confess the truth. Besides, if the apostles had baptized infants, why should the one pope introduce it and the other confirm it? Surely the first pope would have confirmed it but not initiated it? For anything that is initiated has not been before. You can all recognize that, and not one of you can disagree. Take a rough comparison from your building near the Hospital Gate: if the foundation had been already laid as it is now, you would not have had to lay the first stone. But you would have built on the foundation and would not have needed to make a new beginning. For if something already had a beginning, one could not begin it again. Thus it must certainly follow that no apostle ever baptized an infant, even if Luther or all teachers say so. And it would also have to follow that the Holy Spirit was a liar, that he did not teach it to the apostles but had kept silent, and first told it to the pope, whom they call a god upon earth. He allows himself to be worshipped as a god, which is against all Scripture and a great evil. I believe he is the one of whom Paul says to the Thessalonians [2 Thess. 2:4], that he will seat himself in the temple of God and pretend that he is God. This all appears there so clearly that one can grasp it, not only see it. Tell me, which among the popes has not sought to extend his domain? How many popes kept faith with the pious emperors? If you judge correctly here, you will not do me such injustice. For not one pope in a hundred has really kept faith with the emperor, as is written everywhere. For look where the pope comes from. They say: "From Peter." I believe that he never even saw Rome. And if Peter had perpetrated such things he would be to me as Annas and Caiphas and still worse; it would mean that he taught contrary to the Gospel. But it is not credible. For consider the first pope who received power over Rome. I think it was Sylvester; I do not know accurately but guess approximately. But you must not consult the corrupt chronicles, which have been set up by the popes. For that would be as if I were to go to law against someone and let him be judge. But consult a reliable book, and there you will certainly find that the pious emperor Constantine first gave Rome over to the pope Sylvester who lived long after the time of the apostles, I estimate over three hundred years.

But dear sirs, I hope you will not prejudge me, for I truly do not have any ulterior motives, but hope only that you will not violate me in the name of God. What good is it to you that you have mistreated me so pitifully, so that I am now more miserable than miserable, and poor? For I shall never in my life recover. I have been robbed of my trade and my limbs, and am starved so that now I want neither to eat nor to drink. What do you think, five weeks with nothing but water and unboiled bread sops soaked in water? I have lain in darkness on nothing but straw, so that, if God had not granted me his great love, I would have become mentally deranged or insane. For I would have frozen if God had not strengthened me, and you can imagine how a swallow of water could warm one. And I have suffered such great torture, for the torturer twice twisted and maimed my hands, unless the Lord heals them. I have had enough of it to the end of my life. But I know that God will never leave me if I suffer for the sake of his Word. For I well know that the devil accuses me very much before you, which I have learned with much pain. May God forgive you this, and all the dear people who have so falsely accused me before you. For I am now charged with things that happened long ago. But I know that God does these things for my good and shows me his love through them, as David says: "Blessed is he whom you, Lord, punish, for you teach him your law if you give him patience," Ps. 94[:12]. And the wise man says: "Whom the Lord loves, him he punishes and chastises quickly. For he is pleased with him like a father with his child"[Heb. 12:6].

Therefore, dear sirs, you will find nothing in me except patience in words and deeds. Thus I desire to be obedient to you to death and to God also to death and not to depend on this human command, which is against God, as long as I have breath. Nor will I simulate to please anybody or to harm him. I will tell the truth from the heart as David teaches us in Ps. 16[:3] and 24[:2]: "For God takes no pleasure in the hypocrite." There must be no hypocrisy; Job forbids us.

For do you think that the dear prophets and patriarchs have been written for us in vain, and afterwards also the apostles? They are the last messengers sent into the whole world by God. David prophesied this long ago when he says: "Their line is gone out into all the world" [Ps. 19:5] as the Lord commanded them. You say that Paul once baptized a whole household. But infant baptism cannot follow from this, for there are many households here where there is no child.

I am not against baptizing those who have understanding. It does not matter how old they are, if only they understand what they promise in the baptism and hear of the great favour of Christ our faithful mediator. For if the godfather or the witness stands there and simply repeats what he is told you can see well what an error it is. How many peasants and simple laymen stand there and repeat [the words] and do not know what they are repeating. They do not know whether the child will be obedient or disobedient. The simple person stands there as a guarantor and promises that the child believes. But faith comes through hearing as Paul writes in all his epistles. The criminal on the cross heard the words of the Lord, and how he was so patient in all that the Jews did to him, and yet asked his Father for them that he should forgive them. When the criminal heard that, it pricked his heart and penetrated him like a two-edged sword, as Paul indicates. Through this the criminal was saved. If he had not listened or been deaf, he would most likely not have been saved. For what he had done was worthy of punishment, and therefore he had to suffer it. But the infants have done nothing deserving punishment, having done neither good nor ill.

Now if someone says that they have original sin, I agree. But I ask whether the spirit has received original sin or the flesh? You must admit that the spirit is pure and flesh unclean, otherwise God must be a liar and unclean. For the spirit comes from God and the flesh from the earth. It is not that the earth is unclean, of which much could be said, but God remains eternally just, and it is impossible that God lies. For the flesh seduces the spirit, and not the spirit the flesh. For the spirit would gladly again be with God from whence it comes, and the flesh likes to stay on earth from which it comes. Therefore these two are always against each other. Since, now, it follows, that the flesh seduces the spirit, it also follows that it is the flesh that inherits original sin.

I explain such matters concerning infants thus for myself. There may be a better [explanation] and someone who can declare it better. It would take too much writing on my part, so that I think it might annoy you to hear it. The infants must suffer death the same as adults, which death has come upon all flesh from the first man Adam.

So I say that the Lord bore original sin to the wood of the cross. It did not stop bodily death, for we must all die. Yet now bodily death is but a sleep. When Stephen committed his spirit to the Lord, he fell asleep, Acts 7. Therefore I declare the dear children henceforth to have salvation, for they have not sinned. One is not to take anything from or add anything to the Word. For faith comes from preaching, but preaching from the Word of God. It does not come through the teaching of the pope, but through the spoken Word of God.

This is so clearly written. But you say: does not God say that whoever does not believe is damned. And so it must follow that the children are damned since children do not believe nor have faith, since they do not hear and since faith comes from hearing, as the Scriptures report. To this I reply: Certainly not, for little follows from it. For one must observe what has been said before and what he commands, and on what authority he says it. Does he not say in the last chapter of Mark to his disciples, when he explained the Scriptures which were written about him, that what was said about him must be fulfilled? They said that he had suffer thus and arise again afterwards. Then he said: Go! He did not say, Ride! but go, preach the Gospel, that is the good news. He did not say: preach the commands of men. Oh no! Preach the good news to the people, not alone to the Jews, but to all creatures, that is, those who have human form, created in the image of God, Gen. 2[1:27]. He was saying that they were to go and preach to the people that he was the true Messiah for whom they were waiting who had been promised in Deut. 18[:15]. There God said to Moses: "I shall awaken for you a prophet from among your brethren." Him you shall hear for he is as I am in all things; what he says, do. There would be much to say about that: how the children of Israel were obedient to Moses in all things which he commanded. Where they did not, punishment followed surely. That was all written for our instruction as the Scriptures report. Observe carefully. The Jews were to be obedient to Moses who only made more sins for them through his laws and could not keep them himself. Much could be said about that. Now observe the great concern of God in that he gives him to us as a warning. For God is still the same. When, however, they were not obedient to the commands of God, God punished them so that only two of them came into the promised land. This points to the heavenly land. Six hundred thousand came out of Egypt who experienced everything because of their great sin. How will we fare? Therefore my dear sirs, do not favour any person, be they whoever they may be,[6] but on the word and then of the works. A farmer who works the land is to eat from the fruits first, Timothy [2 Tim. 2:6]. People will certainly become Christians if they hear the truth taught and see it done.

The apostles told the people what this one had been like whom they had seen, who was betrayed and killed on the tree of the cross. They confirmed it with the Scriptures and with great miracles. They were shocked at these words when the disciples declared to them old and new things. First they declared the old and then the new, as Christ had taught them by parable. They said, "Dear men, let everyone be baptized in the name of Jesus," not in the name of people but in the name of Jesus. "But as many of them as received the word, they were baptized." It is clearly written: "whoever gladly received the word." Do you not think that they had infants there? The Scripture reports that three thousand believed at one time what they were told by the apostles, Acts 2[:41]. It would have been a marvel if there had been no infants. But the apostles added nothing to the Word of the Lord, nor subtracted from it. For the Holy Spirit in no wise taught them that they were to hold the children guilty of sin. Oh, no! For repentance must come first, which comes from faith. Faith, however, comes from hearing, and hearing from the Word of God, as Paul reports.

Thus John baptized no one at the Jordan who did not hear the preaching of repentance from him, Matt. 3. He told them about Christ, pointing them to the true Messiah. Certainly, if they had believed John, Christ would not have been tortured by them. However, they departed from repentance and did not follow John. When John saw the Lord approaching he recognized him in spirit and said to the people: "Behold the Lamb of God which bears the sins of the world," [John 1:29]. "This is the one about whom I told you, who would come after me, who was before me." If the Jews had [only] paid attention to these words and not simply passed by them, but had paid heed to them! They might have thought: if he came after you and was before you, it must follow that he is more than a man. And since we consider you an excellent prophet, and you say that you are not worthy to untie his shoes, then he must be more than a prophet. If he is more than a prophet, he must be the Messiah, that is, the Anointed One, whom God promised us through Moses. He must surely be he, for the Jews knew it by the times and by the predictions of the prophets, when the three wise men from the east came seeking him of whom David had prophesied long ago. But they had never heard it and lived still in their own lusts of the flesh and in great evil and followed only the flesh in order in satisfy its lusts. They followed the commands of men which they practiced avidly alongside the laws of God. They kept the commands of God only externally, just as the priests, who had been ordained for this, instructed them, Matt. 23[:25]. The Lord had explained it to them so they could grasp it. But it did no good, for they followed their own minds. Therefore God blinded them as David says: "When your people did not walk according to your command, you struck them with darkness and gave them over so that they walked in their own lusts" [Ps. 81:12]. It was still hidden from their eyes that they had eyes but did not see, and had ears but did not hear. That happened to them because they lived in such vice, ignoring the command of God and regarding the commands of men so greatly.

Therefore you should look to this also, and force no one with the commands of men. For the Lord says these words: "Whoever does not believe is condemned." Preach my friendly Gospel [says the Lord] and then, whoever will not believe is condemned. And he closes with these words: even if someone is baptized and had not the faith which God recognized, which exists not only in the mouth with words but is shown in deeds, he is damned. Paul also speaks thus concerning the fruits of faith in all his epistles. Such a faith is recognized by God, for it is a simple faith, which the mind can grasp.

Therefore, as there is renunciation in the baptism with which infants are baptized, so we teach our children to know God. One can daily see that children everywhere learn to curse before they learn to pray. Therefore clement dear sirs, do not violate me wrongfully, for I could at length explain to you the words of the Lord: "Let the children come unto me and forbid them not, for of such is the kingdom of the heavens," Matt. 19[:14]; Mark 10[:14]; Luke 18[:16]. Not one letter of this passage points to infant baptism, even though Martin Luther and his supporters rely heavily on it. Consider me as you will, for it does not concern me. If he would stand before me and not despise me, he would have to let the Word stand, as it is in itself. I should tell him clearly why he discounts the epistles of James and Jude and the Revelation of John so much. The Apocalypse contains great secrets which no one can believe unless he has the grace of God. John speaks truly. Luther admits that his spirit cannot accept the prophecies. He equates it to the third and fourth books of Ezra [Esdras] which are full of great things about our times, that is, the last times after Christ, in which we now find ourselves. Daniel also clearly depicts our times. But we don't believe that either, until Titus and Vespasian come upon the whole world and the elements will melt in heat and vanish with a great noise, 2 Pet. 3[:10]. Things will be much worse than they were in the past. Tell us, who is the beast that rises out of the sea with the seven heads and rises out of the earth with the horns and who are the lamb, the false whore on the beast? Note the woeful crying of the angels in the air who evermore cry: woe, woe, woe. All of that is now in the world, but no one is aware of it. It will be with us as it was with the Jews, who also did not heed their prophecies, nor the fiery sword which they saw for three years before they were scattered down to the present day. Observe the great miracles which God does with the sun and the moon, which we see and know about, and are before our eyes and which were all declared to us by the holy prophets and the apostles. For all prophecies of the Holy Spirit had to be fulfilled. Otherwise the Holy Spirit would be a liar, which eternally can never be. God cannot lie.

For almost all the woes have been poured out, so that I fear that the end is very near. You can observe; one may preach anything, but the people are almost drowned in fleshly pleasures and pay little enough heed to the grace of God. But I wish to leave all that be, for God will judge it. I want to explain only a little. For you tell me that if you let me go I would poison many more people. May it be far, far from me that I should poison anyone, unless you regard good works as poison. I know that you do not say that good is evil. For you must not think I am one who, with the help of God, as you say, does what the Münsterites have done, nor like those who have had women in common, nor like those who were there only because of avarice. The person I told you about warned me threateningly against them. For he said that if any one even hinted at being given anything I ought to have nothing to do with him, no matter what came of it. For he himself would not take one penny from me. I wanted to give him a patched leather [coat], but he did not want it unless I took payment for it. That I did. For he told me not one false word and spoke so gently that in my whole life I never heard a more gentle voice from any person. But it would be far, far from me to build on him. Tell me, would building on a man, however pious he may be, have given me such a firm foundation? Believe me, even if an apostle were to rise from death or an angel were to come from heaven and would tell me what was not in harmony with the New Testament, I should not believe him. And if a poor herdsman, whom I had never seen, were to tell me the truth, I should believe him. For what blinded the Jews the most was that they followed persons because of their fame. It also brought them into fear and anguish. For the secret of God is not in outward appearance of a person, whether he be king or emperor, prince or count, noble or common, burgher or farmer, herdsman or still lower, as you can find written everywhere. For David says in Ps. 25[:14]: "The secret of the Lord is with them who fear him, and he will make his covenant known to them," whether he be rich or poor, king or emperor, prince or count, herdsman or farmer. But whoever fears him does no evil where possible. Thus Job speaks in chapter 28[:12], "Where is wisdom and where is understanding? In all the land of the living one does not find it, nor is it to be bought, neither with gold nor precious stones. Hell says it is not in me and the sea says it is not with me." He does not mean worldly wisdom which is only foolishness before God as Paul writes to the Corinthians [1 Cor. 1:18]. For there he says: "For the word of God concerning the cross is foolishness to those who are lost; to us, however, who believe it, it is a power of God." But Job explains that wisdom to us which God would have of us. He says: "To fear God is wisdom and to avoid evil is understanding" Job, the 28th[18th] chapter. He does not despise worldly wisdom as such. But before God it counts as nothing although it is also a gift of God and not granted to everyone.

Therefore, dear sirs, you will clearly see from my writing that I have turned my heart completely from all that is earthly and want to remain so completely, as much as God gives me grace, and do according to the will of God and as the New Testament teaches me, and depart neither to the right nor to the left. For surely for the Lord's sake one does not add to or subtract from a person's will if it is confirmed by death. How much more ought one to treat the Lord Christ our redeemer likewise. For consider the pitiful torture which I have suffered in all innocence quite willingly and patiently, having been miserably stretched on the rack so that I physically am worth little, for I want neither to eat nor drink. For today is the third day since I could not drink so much as half a measure of wine and I cannot take any meat. But I hope the Lord will take pity on me and take me out of this misery, if it is his will. For I am willing to be obedient to you to death on account of the Lord who was also patient and yet did no sin. For I well know that Satan lies to you about me. For the honourable council well knows my reputation. When I was a gambler and a rowdy, and a wine bibber, Satan did not molest me at all. When I did what was his will [Satan] left me in peace. Now, however, that he sees that I am escaping him, he sets the world on me. I'll say this, if God wants to keep me longer in this vale of tears, you need not be concerned that I will tell anyone much about baptism. One must first take the will out of one's flesh and be able well to resist Satan and to renounce the evil world. For one must not urge it, as your priests do, who baptize away, no matter what. For even if I came out tomorrow, I would not have myself baptized until I had fully subjugated my body to live according to the will of God. For some were pressed into baptism and had not before repented; when the cross came, they soon fell away again. For as soon as the Lord was baptized by John, the Spirit led him into the wilderness,

Matt. 4, where he was tempted by the devil. For there is no miracle so small, but it has a significance for us which certainly God does not reveal to the hypocrite, Ps. 25[:4-5] even if he already knows it in part.

Therefore, dear sirs, I am well aware that you do not do this to me out of ill will. For you mean thereby to turn me from the truth, which you consider, as I myself did before, that it is not the truth, but that it is an [evil] intention. Such an intention is not in me at all. For to whom ten pounds have been given by the Lord, from him they will be required, and five will not be accepted as payment. Also, from the one who has one pound, ten will not be required. It will remain with what and how much one has—that will the Lord require of him. For if we deny that we know what is right, God our Lord will deny us as well; if we confess it, then God our Lord will also confess us. Therefore, if they had not asked me, I would not have gone and told it. If someone had asked me from the heart, so that I noticed that he wanted to desist from sin, I would have told him. Who am I that I should prevent God from giving him his grace? For I have told you more about that than I have told my own wife. But you do not want to believe and only despise it and say that it is from the devil, which is a great wonder. For I know for certain that anyone who hears me carefully could not call what I have done wrong. I have been as much against it as anyone until the Lord himself drew me, though you despise it. But that does not worry me at all, for I well know that God will not remain silent long, but come and judge the world.

Therefore, clement, dear lords, regard my misery and not my family nor relatives. For if they knew it as well as I, they would not be ashamed of me. But what I suffer on account of the Word of God is no scandal to me, if only I suffer it patiently. And I ask you herewith most heartily, dear sirs, release me from this fear, by whatever means pleases you. But beware that you do no violence to the name of God. For even if you kill me off in the dungeon, you will have no glory from it, for we are to be obedient unto death. For what reward should we have if we suffered as evildoers? But we are to suffer as those who do good. Then our reward is great, writes Matthew. And I ask you if it seems time to you that I have suffered enough that you consider my misery and not my relatives. For if you were to command me either to go into a fire or else to depart from the truth, I should go into the fire. You would see that I did not do it out of my own intention. If the love of God were not so powerful to me, one could easily say, considering the miserable pains which I have in my limbs, that there is no God over all. For I have become like a child physically, and do not allow it to carry out its desires. For if a child were to overpower me, I could not defend myself at all. That is the true rebirth which pleases God, John chapter 3, and the turning around to be like children, Mark 10.

> I wish you all happiness and blessing. Amen.
> From a poor, unworthy member of the Lord.
> Dear sirs, if it is not too much trouble to you, give me a copy of this. For I know well, if it should be sent to a Lutheran parson, he would explain it to me as someone who could better instruct me from the Scriptures. Above all, get me a Bible, so that we can speak on that basis. Whoever he is, I am ready to be instructed.
> Peace be with us all. Dear Mr. town secretary, read as considerately as you can. For it is quite improperly written. You must in part read the words according to the sense. For I spell quite wrongly, so that it is not easy to read for one who is not accustomed to it. I am well aware of this, for in eight years I have not written much.

18

Urbanus Rhegius

Justification for the Prosecution of Anabaptists (1536)*

Introduction

Urbanus Rhegius was born in Langenargen on Lake Constance in 1489; he was the son of a priest and his concubine. The ridicule that he suffered as a child because of his father's sinful union may have inspired him to educate himself in order to reform the clergy.[1]

In time, Rhegius attended the Universities of Freiburg, Ingolstadt and Basel, meeting the likes of Balthasar Hubmaier (Freiburg) and Johann Eck (Ingolstadt). He received a Masters degree at Ingolstadt and went on to receive a Doctorate at Basel.[2] In 1520 he was called to Augsburg as a cathedral preacher. A year later he started preaching Protestant themes and was replaced in 1522, after which he retreated to the Tyrol to examine his religious allegiance. In 1523 the Augsburg

---

*Source: Franz, *Quellen IV*, 105-17.
Translation: Friesen/Klaassen

council invited Rhegius to return as a Lutheran preacher and there he stayed until 1530.

Rhegius became the most powerful spokesman of Luther's version of the Reformation in Augsburg, where he persecuted Anabaptists without mercy. It was Rhegius who got Hans Denck, whom he disparagingly called "the abbot of the Anabapists," expelled from the city after a discussion on universal salvation did not convince Denck of his "error."[3] Rhegius also debated with Johann Dachser of Augsburg, a follower of Hans Hut and contemporary of Eitelhans Langenmantel. Rhegius was an active participant in the production of the Augsburg Confession before he was invited by Duke Ernst of Lüneburg, a signer of the confession, to return with him to consolidate the Reformation in the north. Rhegius moved with his family in 1530, where he lived and worked for the new Protestant churches of the north until declining health curtailed his travels. He died in 1541.

It was in 1536 in Lüneberg that he wrote the following document against the Anabaptist movement.

Bibliographical Sources:

Christian Neff, "Rhegius, Urban," *ME IV*, 314.

Scott H. Hendrix, "Rhegius, Urbanus," *The Oxford Encyclopedia of the Reformation*, vol. 3 (Oxford: Oxford University Press, 1996), 429-430.

Werner O. Packull, *Mysticism and the Early South German-Austrian Anabaptist Movement, 1525-1531* (Scottdale, PA: Herald Press, 1977).

George H. Williams, *The Radical Reformation* 3rd edition (Kirksville, MO: Sixteenth Century Journal Publishers, 1992).

Justification for the Prosecution of Anabaptists, 1536.

[1536, June 5] The Consensus of those of Lüneburg concerning the Anabaptists, whether they are to be punished by the sword. Composed by Urbanus Rhegius.

Since, in these last wicked times, the devil is awakening all manner of old heresies by his members, and since therefore not only the consciences of the simple but also all jurisdictions have become disturbed and injured, an urgent question arises:

Should or may a Christian government in official capacity force people who err in the faith back to the right Christian faith, and, if they are disobedient, expel them because of their unbelief and their heresy, punish them in body and in goods, or what the fitting punishment should be.

The answer is given in several articles.

1. Since it is clear from the Scriptures that government is of God, a servant of God for our good, and since without doubt nothing is better for subjects than that they be protected from error in the faith and in healthy teaching and in the true faith, through which they then are made pious and are saved, it follows (Rom. 13; 1 Pet. 2; Titus 3) also that the secular government is bound by God's command, according to the measure of its office, to take responsibility for the Christian religion. First it must prevent, with the sword, the slandering of the most holy name of God through heresy. For as servants and stewards of God, with their sword, they are to execute everything to the honour of God and to the bettering of the kingdom of Christ. Further, they also see to it that the rupture of the common peace does not come about through lying doctrine and through heresy. For it has certainly always happened that heresy, the devil's own work, has brought with it revolt and murder.

2. However, those who err are of many kinds. Some are quickly enticed into error by the seducers because of ignorance or pure simple-mindedness and really would like to know the way of truth. Some, however, are the seducers themselves, who are very hard to help. Some, when they are seduced, become so hardened in error that no teaching or admonition has any effect on them. Here one must act wisely and cautiously. One attacks the error first with the sword of the spirit, which is God's Word, for the sake of the elect. For there is always the hope that not everyone errs deliberately and wantonly. These elect, because they are God's sheep, hear their shepherd's voice and allow themselves

be instructed (John 10); then the poor lost sheep is torn out of the wolf's maw and led again into the sheepfold. This is a very excellent, good work which the holy Augustine in Africa practiced with special earnestness against the evil heretics, the Donatists.

3. However, where teaching, admonition and Christian warning [*bedrauug*, threat] are despised by those who err and where the error is wantonly defended without basis in Scripture or the witness of the ancient church, the government must show its severe aspect and do like the barbers [i.e. surgeons]. If they see that a member of the natural body becomes damaged and cannot be helped by any kind of medicine, and if it is to be feared that the sick member might ruin the whole body, he cuts the bad limb from the body so that the whole body is not harmed by it.

4. Several objections to this exist. First, one can force no one to faith. It is a gift of God and works in us. It is not given to everyone, but to the elect. One must work against heresy only with God's Word. If by punishment one forces the heretics outwardly from their confession, the error nevertheless remains in their hearts and they become "hypocrites, and in place of true Christian they become false Catholics." Second, the one who errs now may eventually improve. Third, the apostles never called upon the worldly sword against heretics and still brought the Gospel fruitfully to the whole world. Fourth, Christ said [Mark 16:15-16]: Preach the Gospel to all creatures, whoever believes, etc. He does not say: force the people to believe. Fifth, belief or disbelief is an invisible thing in the heart which the church cannot judge, and therefore must tolerate many unbelievers within itself. Why would the worldly power want to involve itself with punishment in matters of faith? If the church cannot detect these secrets, how much less the secular power? Let them create order concerning body and goods so that things on earth go peacefully and orderly, and with a firm hand on public affairs, punish the wicked. Sixth, it is for the Supreme Judge to separate the chaff (reprobate) from the good wheat (elect) on the last day [cf. Matt. 3:12]. One cannot judge now; our task is to teach and to admonish, not to force, so that we do not create hypocrites. Augustine was of this opinion at first, but he soon turned to the opposite, namely that one should force the erring ones to the unity of Christ.

5. To the first we answer thus: It is true that one cannot force faith into the heart of the godless with sword, stocks, nor rope, nor drive it out. Otherwise not so many Jews would allow themselves to be killed and in former times there would not have been so many martyrs. God the Father must himself draw the sinner in his heart to Christ, John 6,

give faith and the Holy Ghost through the Gospel, otherwise we would eternally remain without faith. But it is God's order in the conversion of the sinner that he uses the preaching of the Gospel which is a power of God to salvation of all who believe it, Rom. 1[:16]. To his Word he connects his holy seals, the sacraments, so that the faith that makes us pious and also the Holy Ghost come into our hearts through the hearing of the Gospel, Rom. 10; Gal. 3, as the Acts of the Apostles prove. Therefore, although one can force no one to believe this or that, for we cannot illumine another person's heart, and not even our own, that being alone the work of God through the Word (Eph. 2; Phil. 1), yet one can and ought to compel the erring one and the unbeliever to hear the word of faith. It is the responsibility of the government as a duty of its office to induce its subjects to hear the Word of God. For the worldly government has been ordained for us by God for protection, shelter and for the furthering of all that is good as much as father and mother, for which reason it is called fathers with the Father. Now, if it is the father's duty to teach his child and to require it to attend to God's Word and all godliness, if there is need, then the government must also do so and as much as is in them, to require and compel them to this best of all, namely to hear God's Word and to believe. They do not give faith, nor do they force anyone to believe, but they do force you to hear the word of salvation, and it is hoped that God would give his grace and faith so that the listener would be converted and believe in Christ. Who now says that the government has no power to force those who believe wrongly to the right faith in this way, denies God's Word which clearly says that the government is God's servant for good (Rom. 13). Thus you must either deny that it is good to encourage a person to believe, or else you admit that it is good, as you truly must confess.

The truth also thus forces you to confess that the government has the power to force its subjects to listen to the Gospel. You may say: yes, with admonition and with good words, but not by force. Answer: to bring the people to the sermon with good words and admonition is the preachers' obligation. But to force people to attend the sermon and to frighten them from error is the government's duty, for the magistrates are fathers. Now it is the practice of fathers not only to coax their children to the good with friendly words, but where the words are of no avail, to take the switches and to use their authority. That is, "compel them to come in."

6. We also hold that one should first act against heresy with the unconquerable truth of God's Word in the attempt to destroy the error

and save the person. But if the erring person persists in the damnable error and will not yield to the truth, then other means are required. St. Augustine calls it *compelle intrare* [Luke 14:23], namely, that one compels the erring one from error by force, not to teach him and make him confess, but to hear the truth.

7. Someone may now object and say that what the erring one does under force is an abomination and a hypocrisy before God, and therefore one should accomplish it by God's Word alone. Answer: Augustine has dealt with just this same question and case, which we have in our times. He gives good instruction from the words of the Lord in the Gospel according to Luke, ser. 33 concerning the word *Compelle intrare*. He says: The heretics do not want to be forced and say they should be allowed to come by their own good will. But the Lord says, Luke 14[:23]: *Compelle intrare, foris inveniatur necessitas, nascitur intus voluntas*, which means force them to go in; force is applied externally and the will will come internally. In the epistle 48 "To Vincentius against the Donatists," concerning the six ways of correcting the heretics, he says that his city Hippo was at first quite Anabaptist on the side of Donatus. But through the fear of imperial edicts they abandoned their error and left this same heresy so completely that they later cursed the terrible error. He further says that many cities in Africa did this, who at first would like to have remained in error and did not like to be forced. But when the command and edict of imperial majesty came which compelled them to abandon their error under severe torture, God gave his grace that in time they recognized their error, accepted the precious truth and faithfully thanked God that through such fear of imperial authority he had moved them from error to the truth, without which force they would without contrition have perished in error. In the above mentioned epistle Augustine, when he had to deal with an identically similar case at his time, says: Christ forced Saul, later called Paul, also to the truth and also cites this verse from the Gospel: *Compelle intrare*. He also compares Christian severity in punishing heretics with the punishment with which Sara, the true wife of Abraham, punished the refractory maid, Hagar. In the same way the church punishes the ill-behaved, faithless children, namely the hardened heretics through legitimate force.

8. That the worldly government may with God's approval and a good conscience punish with the sword all accursed heretics who hold heretical teaching contrary to our holy faith and who persist in error, is proved by us in the following manner. The worldly government has power to punish with the sword adulterers, thieves, murderers, rebels

and other cases of wrongdoing. It follows that she also has the power to punish with the sword known, open heretics who teach error, who hold it and remain in it. This conclusion cannot be contradicted, for heresy is also counted among the fruits of the flesh, Gal. 5[:19ff], such as rebellion and murder which are punished by the sword. Heresy is worse and more pernicious than stealing, adultery, fornication and murder. For through heresy a person is led from the truth into falsehood and from Christ to the devil so that he perishes eternally in body and soul. Heresy is a cruel blasphemy against the holy Gospel.

Heresy also at all times produces all kinds of revolt, destruction of all good custom, disruption of government. Thus it is with these Anabaptist characters. Through them the devil seeks to destroy all doctrine, discipline and authority, first with hypocrisy under the appearance of God's Word, and then with open mischief. This the horrible example of the miserable city of Münster shows only too clearly. Deuteronomy 13 teaches us that heresy which issues forth deceiving and starting revolt also belongs under the worldly sword. There God commands that the false prophets, who lead the people from the true faith into error, through which factions and splinterings occur in the unity of the church, are to be killed and the evil uprooted from Israel. Similarly, if in a city heresy and error against faith was taught and accepted, that city was to be burned and the erring inhabitants who had accepted false worship and error, contrary to God's Word, were to be killed. See Deut. 17; Dan. 3[:29]: Nebuchadnezzar, the Babylonian emperor, sent out a stern edict to the effect that all nations were to honour the true God of Daniel. Anyone who blasphemed had to die, and have his house destroyed.

(1) Certainly the governments in the New Testament have no less authority than those in the Old.

(2) Scripture teaches that the kings and lords in former times had the power to punish idolaters and blasphemers. Clearly, our heretics are the Anabaptists, who revile the precious Gospel of our God and despise all government which God himself wants honoured, Ps. 82; Rom. 13; 1 Pet. 2.

(3) Thus it follows that our government is to punish and exterminate open heresy and factious heretics with no less zeal than the pious kings in the Old Testament.

Now it may be countered that Moses with his law and its special cases does not bind Christians, but that they guide themselves by imperial or worldly laws of the government under which they live. Therefore Moses has lost his force, and heretics should not be punished by the sword. Answer: Moses had many ceremonial laws which were binding on the Jews for a definite period of time, namely until the rule of the Messiah. His legal system does not bind us. But neither is it forbidden for us. Where Moses and the kings in Israel had some better order or did something which still serves for the maintenance of policies, authorities, mutual peace, and Christian religion, Christian governments may use these things according to the manner, occasion and the requirements of the New Testament. For we are certainly not to think that God had provided his people with a useless, unnecessary legal system. For Moses says in Deut. 4[:8] that there is no people on earth which has such a fine, just order or statutes as the Jews.

9. One must not judge the unrepentant Anabaptists and their like here only by their error in faith but also by their open practice and their actions. For they are not simply heretics. They sin, first, against the holy Christian church from which they wickedly and without any reason or cause separate themselves and are therefore under the ban. Secondly, in addition to their damnable heresy they also do other wicked deeds and wrongdoing, being disobedient to the worldly government ordained by God. They do things in secret and conspire that none of them is to swear the oath of loyalty nor promise obedience, or, if they have promised to obey, not to keep the promise. They consider lawful oaths as wrong, and they destroy the divine order of matrimony. They are all secret enemies of all government which they oppose in action when and where they may. They want to have all goods in common without the consent of others. And the rest of what the evil spirit perpetrates through these blinded people is now evident. God's judgment over those who do wicked things has already been passed, Rom. 12[:2]: Those who oppose the government oppose God's order and will receive judgment on themselves. Therefore a Christian government has no need to fear that it is sinning when it punishes the Anabaptists even with severity, as long as it undertakes the matter in Christian love. This means that it first instructs, admonishes, and warns the erring, so that not the destruction of the person but the suppression of error and the conversion of the person is sought. And if that is of no avail, let the worldly government do its duty according to its office. It does not carry the sword in vain but for the punishment of those who are evil. What is more evil that holding heresy against Christ, persisting in it and wishing to destroy others also in soul, body, honour and goods?

Unbelief and heresy cannot be dispelled nor Christian faith planted with the sword by force alone without the Word of God. But when the government has put forth every effort to demonstrate error and has instructed and sufficiently warned the erring ones, and when all that still bears no fruit with the stiff-necked people, then the government is to resort to the last remedy and prevent such poison from spreading and ruining souls and destroying government and common peace. That is also the teaching of Augustine to Vincentius:

> For if they were only made afraid, and not instructed, this might appear to be a kind of inexcusable tyranny. Again, if they were instructed only, and not made afraid, they would be with more difficulty persuaded to embrace the way of salvation, having become hardened through the inveteracy of custom. ... When, however, wholesome instruction is added to means of inspiring salutary fear, so that not only the light of truth may dispel the darkness of error, but the force of fear may at the same time break the bonds of evil custom, we are made glad, ... by the salvation of many, who with us bless God, and render thanks to Him, because by the fulfilment of His covenant, in which He promised that the kings of the earth should serve Christ, He thus cured the diseased and restored health to the weak.
>
> Not every one who is indulgent is a friend; nor is everyone an enemy who smites. Better are the wounds of a friend than the proffered kisses of an enemy. It is better to love with severity, than to deceive with gentleness. ... He who binds the man who is in a frenzy, and he who stirs up the man who is in a lethargy, are alike vexations to both, and are in both cases alike prompted by love for the patient. Who can love us more than God does? And yet He not only gives us sweet instruction, but also quickens us by salutary fear, and this unceasingly.[4]

10. If heresy remained a secret in the heart, it could be judged by no one else but God. If, however, it breaks out and eats about it like a cancer, so that many simple people are poisoned and misled by it, and if other shameful, carnal vices and rascality begin to spread, as usually happens, then the government must punish the unrepentant heretics not with less but with greater severity than other evildoers, robbers, murderers, thieves, adulterers and such.

11. So the government is to see to it that it does not show untimely mercy where severe wrath and severity must be shown. For what kind

of mercy is it if the government out of mercy allows desperate, unrepentant heretics (of whom I speak) to go free and in the meantime does not take to heart that through such heretical teaching and through such blinded seducers the most holy and fearful name of God is so terribly slandered and that many a precious soul is by this error led into eternal destruction? If at Münster they had not watched Bernhard Rothmann so long, they might have saved the situation. Since, however, they let matters go and spared the seducer, the terrible distress followed which Germany will never forget but which will be a warning to her.

Every power received from a superior lord is to be employed for the use and honour of that overlord from whom the power derives, and not against him. Now all kingdoms, principalities and dominions are of God, Rom. 13[:1]. It follows that they are to use their power for the honour of the divine name and must punish those who despise and insult his Word. But what an abuse of the power received would it be if a lord were to use it to punish thieves, pickpockets and other common criminals and were to overlook and ignore the fact that infamous heretics, enemies of truth, greatly slandered God's name and teaching? Who, as much as might be in them, by means of devilish heresy, murdered souls whom Christ purchased with his precious blood, who despised all civic order and government and who on the other hand acted with unheard-of wanton misdeed, enticing everyone to like wickedness? Indeed, if a government were to fail to punish this frightful wickedness with appropriate severity, it would be unable to account to God for its office, as the holy Augustine teaches in his commentary on John 3: "God raises up the government against the heretics, rabblerousers and splinterers of the Christian church so that Hagar is flogged by Sara." And if the government were not moved against such as these, how would it account to God for its rule? For it is the duty of rulers to see to it that their mother, the Christian church, through which they were spiritually born, has rest in their time. The Donatists murder souls, bringing them eternal death, and they complain that one punishes them with temporal death. Therefore a Christian government is to consider nothing more important than to keep the Christian religion pure with healthy teaching and to remove all which is against the service of God and against Christian faith and teaching. Then God will also give the temporal rule peace and welfare in other matters. If, however, God and the saving religion of Christ is regarded as of no account, there can be no happiness or welfare. Therefore the king of Israel, when he was installed on the throne, was always required to have Deuteronomy, God's law and ordinance copied, to keep it with him and to read in it every day of his life, so that he might learn to fear God, his Lord. Then God would give him and his sons his blessing in their government, Deut. 17.

Examples from Scripture. Thus we read that some Christian kings of Judah held to God's law, seriously tended to religion and destroyed error and heresy. King Asa removed the prostitutes from the earth who were against religion and did away with all abomination of idolatry which his ancestors had practiced. He did not even spare his own mother, Maacah, but deposed her, 3 Reg. 15 [1 Kings 15:13]. Jehu, the tenth king in Israel, killed all the priests of Baal. Therefore God did good to him and promised him the kingdom of Israel into the fourth generation, keeping his promise, 4 Reg. 10 [2 Kings 10:28ff]. Jehoshaphat, the seventh king of Judah, held so strictly to religion that through his princes and Levites he arranged a visitation in which they had to go through the land from one city to another and instruct the people in the Word of God, 2 Chron. 17[:7ff], and God gave him good fortune and well-being and fought for him against his enemies, 2 Chron. 20[:29]. King Josiah acted with equal earnestness, killing all the priests of the hill shrines, burning their bodies on the altar and eradicated all idolatry, root and branch, so that religion was established and maintained through the pure Word of God, 4 Reg. 23 [2 Kings 23:5]. This instruction would become altogether too long if I were to rehearse the zeal and strictness of all Christian emperors and princes in the maintenance of Christian religion. All who know history are aware of what has been done in this by Constantine, Marcian, Valentinus, Gracian, Honorius, Theodosius, Justinian, Charles the Great, Ludovicus and others, for they recognized themselves as being servants of God for the good, according to the teaching of Paul, Rom. 13. They knew that the most necessary and the best thing is to have sound teaching and the right faith and not fall into any heresy. In 1 Tim. 1[:9] Paul says: The law is not made for the righteous but for the unrighteous, the disobedient and the godless, whom he calls the *asebesi*, that is, those who strive and live contrary to right teaching and to Christian religion. Governments should take note of this. The law has been established not only for the obstinate Jews in the Old Testament in order to punish them, but in the New Testament also for all evildoers, fornicators, murderers and perjurers, all vices which Paul recounts. At the end he says that the law is given against all that is contrary to the sound teaching of the Gospel and that is against the glories of the blessed God. He expressly named the godless and the unholy who do not teach and hold correctly concerning religion according to God's Word but blather about divine matters and articles of faith with such disdain and epicurean wickedness as though Scripture and God's Word had been written by any silly old woman. In this way the reprobates of Münster have blasphemed about the humanity of Christ, of holy baptism, of matrimony and of other mysteries of our holy faith until their reward was given them. Now every government is an executor, enforcing the law, for it has the sword from God, in order to punish and remove evil with it according to the law which indicates which are punishable. Thus Paul refers to the godless and blasphemers, names which can be applied to no one more justly than to the unrepentant heretics. It follows that the worldly sword must be applied to them as evildoers, and that by God's command.

12. It is now said that one should not punish any heretic with the sword but await his improvement. That is a protection of evil. For what improvement can one expect from one who has been sufficiently instructed through God's Word, often warned, and who at this time has so often seen into what blindness and desperate barbarism the devil has driven the Anabaptists and who still will not do honour to truth? How can one expect that he will depart from error and confess his wrongful behaviour? If one accepted this argument one would have to conclude that the worldly government could hang no thief, and break no murderer on the wheel, but would rather wait for him to become a pious person. It would have to let everybody live according to his will without all punishment. This is contrary to God's command who has put the government into the world in order to ward off evil with the sword. It is further argued that the apostles requested no help from the worldly government against the heretics and that therefore the government is not to concern itself with teaching or teachers. St. Augustine answers Boniface about the gradual, friendly restraint of the heretics in the 50th letter.[5] Augustine writes that conditions at that time were different from now, for then the heretics and princes were still heathens and themselves opposed the Gospel and the churches. The prophecy of Ps. 2[:1ff, :10ff] was then fulfilled: "Why do the heathen rage and why do the people speak in vain? The kings in the land rebel and the lords take counsel with each other against the Lord and his Christ." The time had not yet come about which we read further in the

same Psalm: "Take instruction, you kings, and be led, you judges on earth, serve the Lord in fear and rejoice with trembling." How can kings serve God their Lord with fear, however, unless it be that with Christian earnestness and severity they forbid and punish whatever is contrary to God's command? A king serves God not only as a person but as a king. As a human being he serves God with a Christian life. But as a king he serves God in a different way also, namely in that with fitting severity he makes good laws by which what is just is commanded, and whatever is against justice is forbidden. *Haec ille.*

Since now in the Roman empire the governments are also Christian, they are to serve God in their assigned office, to establish and protect what is good and to punish what is bad, 1 Pet. 2. And insofar as they are now, in these times, more endowed with God's Word and knowledge of the true service of God than in former times, they should the more earnestly oppose heresy. St. Augustine shows at length of what excellent use the stern edicts of the emperor were in Africa. Through them the Anabaptists and the Circumcellions[6] were prevented by punishment from seducing anyone with their error, and forced to abandon their heresy. He says that through such nurture and the severe imperial command the mother, the holy Christian church, joyfully received into its lap great numbers of the returning Anabaptists who all heard the truth. At Carthage they also heard the dispute held between St. Augustine and the Anabaptist clergymen which was a thorough instruction of the simple who were shown how the Anabaptist separation from the church was a shameful hypocrisy and that all their teaching was pure error. Truth was presented before their eyes so that very many were converted and completely abandoned their heresy. Such lawful means of maintaining the churches in sound doctrine and faith and of keeping civic peace, means that were useful in former times, should still be used according to the wholesome counsel of Augustine: For the experience in many diseases necessarily brings the invention of many remedies. It is known with what cunning and hypocrisy Satan with a thousand tricks misled poor Münster in Westfalia, and if he had shot false teaching in one or two articles into the heart of people, he would have won. He continued so pitifully to seduce and blind people that they became raving animals, and that normal understanding, which even the heathen have, was extinguished in them. Finally no error was too great, no unchastity too shameful, but Satan led them into it, so that, indeed, we could see, yes, actually grasp the same evil spirit in our Anabaptists that drove the senseless Circumcellions into all their wickedness.

13. The fourth objection is that Christ bid us preach but did not bid us force anyone to faith. We well know that spiritual and apostolic authority and worldly force must be totally separated from each other. To the apostles and their successors is committed the office of preaching. They are to teach the truth, and their highest punishment is the ban. But the apostles also preach an article in the Gospel concerning worldly government. It is this, [Rom. 13]: Worldly government has been ordained by God himself. Its order, if it is not contrary to God, the supreme liege Lord, is to be observed, not alone because of punishment but also because of conscience. Whoever acts against it, sins against God's command. The government has authority from God to punish all evildoers. In this article the authority for the punishment of the heretics is found. First one treats them in a friendly way and preaches the saving Gospel to them for their conversion. If they believe it, one leaves them in peace. If they do not believe it but resist and in addition attack the worldly authority and its divine order, then that worldly authority does what it was commanded by God to do, namely to punish the disobedient. It is not, therefore, a matter of forcing them to faith but of cutting the unbelieving, blaspheming evildoers, who under the name and title of Christ would bring Christendom to destruction, from the healthy body as useless and destroyed members.

14. The church does not first judge the unknown, but the known vice of heresy with the ban. Afterwards the government in authority of its office judges open blasphemy and other crimes which flow from such heresy.

15. When the Christian church bans heretics and the worldly government punishes them in body and life, it is not usurping the authority of the supreme Judge in his final judgment when he will separate for ever the blessed and the damned. For he himself commanded us to act thus until the last day, and neither the ban nor the sword are so perfect that all weeds are rooted out. Only the knower of hearts, Christ himself, will gather the pure wheat when he comes in his majesty. Whatever neither church nor government will have been able to recognize and accordingly judge and punish, the righteous judge will find on the great day of his judgment. In the meantime spiritual and worldly authority are not therefore to neglect their work now.

Thus, in answer to the questions laid before us, we have with all possible diligence shown, firstly, that one should make a difference among those who are deceived and that Christian love should first be allowed to deal with them for improvement according to the right way of the new covenant. Perhaps some sheep of Christ may yet be found among them, since love expects the best, 1 Cor. 13. Secondly, a Christian government may properly and justly punish the stubborn unrepentant heretics and the originators and adherents of false doctrine with the sword even as it deals with other crimes. This needs to be done where Christian love, true teaching and admonition do not avail, and where their heresy will not be deterred from despising divine truth but instead leads others away from the way of truth and where it also acts wickedly against the divinely ordered worldly authority. From these actions arise divisions in the church, disruption in worldly sovereignty and danger to body, and goods, social honour and such. All this we have established with divine Scripture of the Old and the New Testaments, with scriptural, well-based arguments and examples from Israelite rule and also with examples from the ancient church in which the teaching was purer and there was more fear of God than now. May your princely grace peruse this with serious diligence, and with timely assistance aid the matter. For what the Anabaptist devil (we do not now want to accuse the poor misled people of desperate wickedness) has in mind with his rebaptism, your princely grace's neighbours, the Westfalians, may well indicate.

> *Sedentes iudicent*
> *Dominus pugnet pro nobis.*
> [Render judgment, you who judge.
> The Lord fights for us].

19

Sebastian Franck

Sebastian Franck on the Anabaptists (1536)*

Introduction

Luther condemned him, saying that one could not learn what a Christian should believe, or even what he himself believed from his writings. Calvin called him "brainless and altogether insane."[1] It is true that Sebastian Franck had few supporters and also little influence in his own time, but he is valued in ours.[2]

Franck was born in Donauwörth in 1499, the son of a weaver. He attended the University of Ingolstadt, where he studied liberal arts. Urbanus Rhegius was his professor for rhetoric and poetry; he wrote Latin, understood Greek, but was ignorant of Hebrew. After he finished at Ingolstadt in 1517, he went to Heidelberg to study theology. There he probably met Martin Luther in 1518 at the famous Heidelberg Disputation. After first entering the priesthood, Franck eventually allied himself with the evangelical movement in 1525, and took up a

---

*Source: Sebastian Franck, *Chronica, Zeitbuch vund Geschichtsbibell von anbegyn bisz in diss gegenwertig...* MDxxxvi iar.... (Ulm, 1536), III, cxciib-ccib.
Translation: Friesen/Klaassen

position near Nuremberg as a pastor. By 1529, however, he had given up this position, and his beliefs had evolved away from those of the magisterial reformers.³ In Nuremberg he had experienced a complete transformation. He became a spiritualist who did not feel at home in any religious organisation, but rather wanted to establish an invisible, spiritual church. It was in Nuremberg that he met Hans Denck and other Anabaptists, but he did not develop a personal friendship with Denck, even though Denck was acquainted with Franck's wife's parents.

It was in 1529 or 1530 that Franck made his way to Strasbourg, a city known for its toleration. Franck became acquainted with Caspar Schwenckfeld and Johann Bünderlin among others. Why Franck moved from Nuremberg to Strasbourg is uncertain, but it may have been that Franck knew of these radicals as well as others, and their acquaintance would have helped in gathering materials for his most famous work, the *Chronica*.⁴ Franck finally published this history in 1531, and the reaction to it was immediate. On December 1531, in response to a complaint by Erasmus (who Franck had cited as a heretic) the city council resolved to put Franck in the tower.⁵ Because of the critical tone of the *Chronica*, Franck created many enemies and few allies, and he was expelled from the city in December of 1531. After a short stay in the nearby town of Kehl, where a petition to be allowed to return to Strasbourg was refused, he moved on to Esslingen where he became a soapmaker. He then moved to Ulm, where he again began publishing. He was banned from that city in January of 1539, again because of his controversial writings. His last move was to Basel, where he made his living as a printer. He continued to write until his death in 1543.

Franck rejected the four contemporary religious groups: Catholics, Lutherans, Zwinglians and Anabaptists. Although he was not an Anabaptist, and was sometimes critical of them, Franck remains important to the history of the movement. He had personal connections with Anabaptist leaders and because of this, his evaluation of the Anabaptists is an important and authentic source of information for their earliest history and doctrine. He was an advocate and defender of the Anabaptists in the face of false accusations directed against them. Franck was also influenced by them, and in particular, by the spiritualist writings of Hans Denck. Franck's own brand of undogmatic spiritualism comes through strongly in his description and evaluation of the Anabaptists.

Bibliographical Sources:

Patrick Hayden-Roy, *The Inner Word and the Outer World, A Biography of Sebastian Franck* (New York, N.Y.: P. Lang, 1994).

Cornelius Krahn and N. van der Zijpp, "Franck, Sebastian," *ME II*, 363-367.

Werner O. Packull, *Mysticism and the Early South German-Austrian Anabaptist Movement, 1525-1531* (Scottdale, PA: Herald Press, 1977).

C. Arnold Snyder, *Anabaptist History and Theology: An Introduction* (Kitchener, ON: Pandora Press, 1995).

George H. Williams, *The Radical Reformation* 3rd edition (Kirksville, MO: Sixteenth Century Journal Publishers, 1992).

Sebastian Franck on the Anabaptists, 1536.

About the year 1526 during and immediately after the peasants' revolt, there arose a new sect and separate church based on a literal reading of Scripture. Some call them Anabaptists, some Baptists. They began to separate themselves from the others by a different baptism and to despise all others as unchristian. Nor would they count anyone who did not belong to their sect or group a Christian or brother. They began to rebaptize those who joined them, or rather, as they claimed, to baptize them according to the command of Christ. For they pronounced infant baptism as well as oral confession to be unscriptural and to be without the command of Christ, adding that these were invented by heretics. They considered it to be a great wickedness if anyone baptized his child or did not allow himself to be baptized.

Their leaders and bishops were first and foremost Doctor Balthasar Hubmaier, Melchior Rinck, Hans Hut, Hans Denck, Ludwig Hätzer. These men moved about so rapidly that their teaching spread quickly and secretly throughout the whole land. They obtained a large following, baptized many thousands and drew to themselves many well-meaning people who were zealous for God. They did this with their appearance of piety and also with the letter of Scripture to which they adhered rigidly. For apparently they taught nothing but love, faith and the cross. They proved themselves patient and humble in much suffering. They broke bread with one another as a sign of unity and love. They conscientiously helped each other faithfully by lending, borrowing, and giving. They taught that all things should be held in common, and called each other brother. But they hardly greeted nor helped anyone who was not of their sect, and kept to themselves.

They increased so suddenly that the world became concerned about a revolt by them, though as I hear they were everywhere found innocent of this. But in many places they were cruelly and violently attacked, especially and firstly among the papists. They were captured, and tortured with burning, sword, fire, water, as well as with all manner of imprisonment, so that in a few years very many were killed in many places. It was claimed that in a number of places over 2000 were killed, in Ensisheim alone over 600. This they bore patiently and steadfastly like martyrs. From the example and witness of their blood many more were moved to join them as the righteous who suffered persecution for the sake of truth. For everyone thought that one could find the proof, mark, and true happiness of the Gospel with them. Therefore many pious and simple people joined them. They were admitted to their congregation by baptism, and because of this many of them steadfastly shed their blood. This tyranny only increased their numbers. Finally, when [the authorities] saw that it not only did not help at all, but that the opposite took place, and that God was mocking them in their use of the sword and of violence, they despaired, and desisted from their tyranny. For everyone thought their own cause and sect right and that they alone were Christians because they suffered so patiently. Because of this their number and church increased still more and grew large, and so the undesirable element, the false brethren, the most carnal of them and the truest chaff, cast out and left over in threshing, raised themselves up above the grain, becoming vain in spirit. They began to judge everyone and became disunited among themselves over many things, to having almost as many teachings as leaders.

But God, who is against all sects, began to confuse them also in their plots, language and counsel, in order to make them desist from their building and to separate themselves in spirit and in truth from sin and from the heathenish churches. He did this so that they might join the spiritual and nonpartisan church of Christ scattered among the heathen, and to all righteousness. Thus they could learn that God is not so concerned about outward things, which he has instituted for our sake and not his, and that one should not separate oneself on their account and tear the bond of love and unity.

I am quite convinced that many devout and simple people have been and still are in this sect, and that many of their leaders have been zealous for God, but in my opinion not according to understanding. But one should not deal with them so tyrannically if in their stubborness they will not be taught, but leave them to God who alone can give faith, eradicate heresy and, as is fitting, give counsel in this matter. Moreover, we should all consider that we too fall short, and that if every error should make us into heretics and separate us from God, where would we all be? True, not only the pope's church and following are nothing but pure error, who at the same time presume to judge others to be heretics, the blind and banned judging and condemning the blind and banned, but also Origen, Cyprian, Augustine, etc., who are all in the same condition. And what about the saints themselves who repent before God and before the world, recanting their error? One ought to go slowly in this, keeping one's hand off, remaining still, and not interfering thus in God's realm and rule, standing with the sword in one's fist instead of on faith, and bursting into spiritual things with an earthly sceptre. For by going too far in this matter, unjustly condemning the misfortune and error of others, we judge ourselves, since we are ouselves similarly full of other and worse errors, and matters are as Paul says, Rom. 2, O man, etc. For these matters do not belong to the judgment of man but to the judgment of God who reserves the judgment to himself alone. Deut. 18; Matt. 5.

Articles and Teachings of the Anabaptists who are all Condemned as Heretics by the Pope and in Part also by Other Sects and Faiths:

Although all sects are divided among themselves, yet the Anabaptists especially are so disunited among themselves and fragmented that I cannot write anything definite or final about them. Some consider their rebaptism or baptism so essential that they count no one else accepted by God; they will not greet them or give them their hand or recognize them as brothers. Some do not consider it as so very essential; hence they like to associate with all devout people, counting them as brothers, but of these there are few.

Some consider infant baptism an abomination and would rather be torn to pieces than have their children baptized. Some consider it a matter of choice for the children, or they permit it to happen as a human commandment or as a matter of indifference, and do not want to make an issue of external things.

Some consider themselves as the sanctified and the pure. These have separated from the others, holding all things in common, no one saying that anything is his, all personal property being a sin with them.

The others have all things in common to the extent that they are not to permit one another to suffer need. Not that one would claim what is another's, but that in case of need everyone's property is to be the other's, that no one is to hide anything from the other but have an open house; that the giver is to be willing and ready but the receiver unwilling, and that he should make as few claims on his brother as possible and not overburden him. But at this point there is much hypocrisy, unfaithfulness, and very much of Ananias as they themselves well know.

In some places, such as for example at Austerlitz and in Moravia, they have leaders in charge of distribution who, out of a common bag of food give to each according to need. But whether it actually happens and whether a correct distribution is made they will need to say. These ban the other brethren as those not on the right road. There is much banning in their congregations so that almost every congregation puts the others who do not subscribe with them in all points under the ban. Apparently there is almost as much freedom of faith among them as among the papists. They believe that whoever in their congregations does not assent to everything, has had his ears closed by God. They begin to plead whiningly for him, and if he does not soon turn back, they excommunicate him.

I have also learned of the special hypocrisy of men who lay claim to great piety, if only it were not for the deviousness of the old Adam. But the transplanted new man never seems to appear. All one sees is the piety of the old Adam and an assumed asceticism by which to control him. In many it is a purely fleshly piety as also among other orders and sects.

The other Anabaptists have little regard for the congregations just described and do not consider community of goods essential. They think it extreme that those consider themselves perfect Christians, despising the others. These work each for himself, helping each other, asking each other's advice, and, as I understand, giving each other the hand hypocritically. However, I do not criticize those who do this with sincerity. But I could wish that they would recognize their hypocrisy and begin to be shamed before the eyes of God and abstain from judging others so readily. For they ought to consider that there are certainly other Christians in other hidden places of the world as well as in their hidden churches.

Some have separated themselves and suffered martyrdom only because, in order to oppose the Antichrist, they did not want to celebrate Sunday when other people celebrated it, since they regarded it as the holy day and law of the Antichrist with whom they would have nothing in common. And thus not the holy days either. On the other hand, others let it be, saying that out of love they want to celebrate Sunday also, and declaring that they do not wish to make an issue of it, and they have their Scriptures for it as well.

Some are scriptural literalists. They say that wife and child, sick or well, and even women with child, should eat without distinction whatever happens to be at hand. They quote the Scripture which says that all things are pure to those who are pure and believe, as if this Scripture refers to the stomach and specifically to the conscience. In the meantime they do harm to themselves, and their wives and children.

Some get to the place where they will have nothing to do with the heathen, not only in fasting, celebrating, living, eating, drinking, etc.

They also establish rules about how simple clothes have to be, how each is to be made, and how many folds the skirt should have. Like the monks, they have rules governing eating, drinking, silence, speaking and clothes. And when one of their wives gives birth to a child, she is not to be modest or to draw a curtain as the heathens do. They quote the Scripture: And be not conformed to this world, etc. Rom. 12, as though faith changed the nature, customs, and laws of the outward man. Or as though Paul meant that we should walk on our head, eat with our feet, speak with our hands and do all the work of nature differently from the world when he says, you are not to be like them, etc. Paul means the vain and wicked ways and practices of the world which we are not to be like, for what is considered great in the world is an abomination before God. Not all practice these fantasies but only a few, the others allowing nature its right at these points.

Some presume to claim the apostolic life and the ways of the first church for themselves. In all things they go by the letter of Scripture, washing each other's feet, moving about from one place to another, preaching, and speaking about their great calling and commission. Some claim to be so certain of their convictions that they take on themselves to be accountable for the whole world at the risk of misleading everyone, if only they would follow them.

Some doubt their calling and regret their unwise zeal for the house of the Lord, and wish that they had not baptized anyone, as for example Hans Denck. Many fall away from them because they see this many-headed division.

Some teach that man should be free to do anything either good or bad, without accepting any responsibility, since nothing he does is sin. Some consider themselves to have risen so high that they cannot sin.

The majority preach the cross, that this is the right and only way to life. This is true enough if only they would not make an idol of suffering, as though they must be saved through suffering and not through Christ, or as though God made a great deal of it because he takes delight in it. They almost ascribe to suffering what the papists do to works and the Christians to grace and to Christ, so that some are zealous for suffering, seeking it and striving towards it.

Some go about preaching repentance to the people, sometimes interrupting the preachers in the pulpit. They boast of a great moving of the Spirit, especially that they have been commissioned by God to speak to them, and suffer martyrdom for it. Others, on the other hand, claim that there is now an end to preaching and that the door is closed; it is time for silence, that the truth which the world has so often rejected is no longer heard.

Some tell of new commands of God revealed daily to evangelize both their brothers as well as strangers. Some go into a trance, distort their faces, and lie prone up to an hour. Some shake, some lie still, some as much as two or three days. Afterwards, when they again come to themselves, they prophesy and tell of wonders as though they had been in a different world. They think they have this in common with Paul, 2 Cor. 11[:12], who was caught up into the third heaven. Many cannot tell the mysteries which they saw in this trance.

To some this trance comes often, to some seldom, to others not at all. Many of them make much of visions and dreams, some nothing. These hold to the letter of the Scriptures.

Some have no regard for either preaching or books and are almost all against the preachers [of the official churches], saying that they are not sent and they do not observe a true order, after the command of Christ.

On the other hand, some go to their preaching and break bread with them, but the other Anabaptists do not think well of them. And if they become aware of them in their congregations, they exclude them with the ban.

Some have regular periods of silence and are much concerned with rules, by which they vex and bind the conscience, and so to speak, put a rope around their necks, by means of preoccupation with clothing, hair, eating, speaking, etc. These are called the silent brethren.

The others allow freedom in all these things. Every person has liberty with respect to them, and they will not make them a matter of conscience for anyone to whom Christ has given freedom.

Some make much of the Scriptures as God's Word. But they rest too much on the letter and carry books wherever they go. On the other hand, the others say that Christ is not necessarily present just because we carry books. These too have little regard for outward preaching and Scripture, saying that we must be taught by God directly, without mediation. They say that the Scripture is not God's Word, and that it is possible to have faith and be saved without it. See Hans Denck's articles, and also Ludwig Hätzer's and Thomas Müntzer's, etc.

Almost all consider children as pure and innocent. Neither young nor old are condemned by original sin. It makes no one unclean except him who makes it his own, bears its fruit and will not leave it. They say that no one will be condemned for someone else's sin. To support this they quote the 18th chapter of Ezekiel.

Therefore the children, because they are pure and not yet accountable are neither capable of receiving baptism nor do they require it. The command of Christ is only for adults who are to be baptized on repentance and enrolled in the church.

Some hold that even if infant baptism were right and proper and godly, everyone ought nevertheless to be rebaptized or, as they put it, rightly baptized, for they consider the formerly-received baptism as no baptism. This is because they were baptized outside of the church by heretics, namely by the pope who cannot baptize, since the only baptism can be performed, not in the divided church, but in the unified church and congregation, just as there is one God, faith, Christ, etc. And this error they have in common with Cyprian who decided this with a whole council in Carthage.

Many do not consider original sin nor evil thoughts and desires as sin, if one does not consent to them and put them into action. Therefore they vigorously compel and force themselves to conquer the flesh, to control all members of the body against the will of the flesh, even if it rebels and objects. They say the kingdom of heaven suffers violence and only the violent (understand, those who deal with themselves violently) will attain it. Christians are knights who must gain the kingdom of heaven by conquest. They point to the quotation from Luke 12[13:24], strive to enter in at the narrow gate, etc. Therefore it is wrong and dangerous to teach that one should not do good works except willingly and if one take pleasure in them. It is enough if the spirit is willing, for the flesh will never take pleasure in them. Whoever waits for that will have to be eternally without good works, and will accomplish nothing good.

Some speak here with conviction, and, it seems to me, not wrongly. That one must be still before God and stand yielded in all things in a free Sabbath, without presumption and self-will. They say that God has his work in us, that he recognizes only that which is his in us and crowns in us nothing but his own work. Thus all have been made alive, etc.

Some hold that those to whom Christ is not preached here are not judged until Christ be preached to them either for life or for death, and if not here, then there. They quote 1 Peter 3 and 4, and say that the children too are not condemned or saved until they reject or accept Christ. For no one is condemned but he who stumbles on Christ, this cornerstone and the rock of offense. Also no one is saved but he who recognizes him and puts him on. To those who do not hear about Christ through the prophets he sent, he will be preached yonder in the darkness for life or death, as Peter says.

Some hold that there are two seeds, the seed of God and the seed of the serpent and that no one can change his kind. Thus the seed of the woman could not or would not become the seed of the serpent. Nor again can a child of God grow from the devil's seed. Neither part can change its birth or kind. So then children of God cannot fall nor the devil's seed choose to come to God. In sum, those cannot be condemned and these not saved. Martin Cellarius in his book *Concerning the Work of God* is also somewhat of this opinion.[6]

Some do almost nothing but pray and want to meet all misfortunes with their regulated prayer, just as though we did God an especially great service in making our mouth and ourselves tired by praying constantly. These also say that one must meet evil only with prayer, and will not permit their people any weapons for any reason. They are to be yielded and surrendered in all things and no vengefulness is to be seen. Some have other opinions and almost everyone a different one, so that hardly two of them are of one mind in all things, except what they pretend to believe as a favour or to oblige each other. Therefore it is impossible to write all their articles, they bring into discussion so many and varied, impertinent and idle questions daily. Yet some are against this, praising a devout simplicity and call these people overweening spirits and scribes who deal in foolish Scotistic questions. These will hear nothing but what speaks of repentance, improvement of life, love and faith, etc.

Some among them think that the matter of being Christian is a kind of holy, simple, blameless, unearthly, perfect thing, so that he, the Christian, no longer lives after the flesh nor seeks that which is on earth. Therefore a Christian no longer lives to the world and worldly things no longer concern him. Dying or living is all the same to him; indeed, to him this life is a burden. In all things he is yielded; if struck, he does not strike back. He even denies that his self exists any longer. He has renounced all that is creaturely, and knows nothing according to the flesh. Dying is counted as gain and riches as dung. He counts the joys of the world, voluptuousness, honour, life, etc. to be sorrow, unhappiness, shame and death. He prides himself on the cross and poverty, and considers temporal fortune as misfortune and sorrows over it. He loves his enemies, blesses those who curse him, always in all things stands before God free, empty and yielded in a free Sabbath. In him God may always have his place and work. He willingly and gladly suffers violence and does not ask back what is taken from him by force. He gives and lends to every man who asks and demands of him not expecting anything in return. He never swears in anything, does not bring a suit before the law, does not go to war, bears no weapons, and needs no worldly government, interest [for money lent], or servants. He goes about as a person no longer alive, without finery. He has nothing of his own, and nothing in common with the world such as parties, banquets, business contracts, craft guilds, companies, estates, weddings, dances, etc. These believe that a Christian may not have any worldly position, such as that of a ruler, nor any connected with the use of force. Nor may he have his own or someone else's servant, may not engage in war nor use his fist, whether on his own behalf or God's or his neighbour's. God is strong enough to avenge himself and so they may not war either for themselves nor for their neighbour in ways other than by prayer, but rather suffer, hope patiently, and wait for the help and vengeance of God. Not only must a Christian not seek worldly pleasure but he must flee it, and take joy only in the cross, misery and poverty, seeking only what is above and nothing on earth. He counts taking as giving, dying as living, privation as possession, poverty as riches, and possessions as though he had none, etc. Yes, he has so far died to the world that he has become insensitive to the flesh. To him all things are equal, in him not one sin, nor passion, nor quarreling, nor concupiscence finds place. Any stirring of the flesh is to be killed and drowned by the spirit, and sin is not permitted to surface. To support all this they cite the saying of Paul about the new man. Also Paul, Rom. 7, did not sin but only accuses himself of the indwelling sin which opposes his spirit and inner man. That is as strict as some are, but only a few. The others are content with the average, and can well get along with the world; but for these the others have little regard.

Many are of the opinion that we can only imagine such people or look for them in heaven or perhaps in the republic of Plato rather than on earth, for they know whether any apostle or any human being aside from Christ has ever attained to this standard. The others think that this is the goal set before us or the prize towards which we are to strive and run, so that if we have not attained it that we might attain it, for nothing imperfect can come into the kingdom of God, Matt. 6. Against this Zwingli, Bullinger and others write in many places. I would that they were as free of and dead to the world and sin within them as they think they are to the outer world. By this I mean love of self, spiritual pride, absolute certainty, thoughtless judgment, their pretense to piety, desire to be admired, and the whole spiritual concern with self and hypocrisy, which, I fear, is not a little present. If they desire to emulate the spiritual inner man, let them do it without banding together and without sectarianism, each by himself, simply watching what he does right, so that the enticing midday devil does not waylay them, and that their perfection does not turn into pure foolishness, hypocrisy and monkery which can so easily happen. But I do not rebuke anyone's piety since I cannot look into the heart to see how he does. A devout person does not boast much of his piety to which also he has died. He is yielded in his yieldedness, having died to all respect of persons and all judging, every man, friend or enemy, being impartially the same to him. For a Christian at the same time loves and hates all people and the whole world. He loves them so that with Christ he would gladly die for them. He hates them so that he does not have anything to do or in common with them, especially with their spirit. But the devil is God's ape; he can imitate everything, adapt himself to everything and pretend extreme piety. But he is unable to love and believe, as Chrysostom says. This is the Christian's mark, and the sure sign by which alone one can know a Christian, as Christ also says, and not by any praying, fasting, giving alms, clothes, food, suffering, pilgrimages, pious foundations, praising God, preaching, Scriptures, tongues, prophesying, performing signs, waking, self-torture, castigations, separating oneself, sects, baptizing, masses, weeping, going to church, reading, hearing sermons, etc.

The devil can also do all of this most beautifully. Matt. 7; 1 Cor. 13; Dan. 7; Acts 13, yes, and all works of mercy as well.

Some of them are ill pleased that many preach Christ as being for us and not in us, that they show him to us as being outside of us, that in his suffering and death he has done for us all that is necessary. They object that Christ did all this for us, and that therefore we need not also do it in him, that is, die and live with him. If he has suffered and died for us so that we need not suffer and die, then he has also gone to heaven for us so that we remain down here. Or has he gone to heaven so that we will also go there in him? If so, then in a similar manner he has fulfilled the law so that we too fulfill it in him and thus might stand the test before God. Therefore one is not to preach Christ outside of or for us, that he alone has done his work for us from a distance. Rather, he is to be preached into our hearts, that we are in him and he in us and that we desire to be what he is and wills.

But the world flees from Christ and will not put him on, and only seeks Christ outside of itself from afar, worshipping him and gladly giving him honour. He has done everything, it is argued, so that it need not do anything but can celebrate on his credit. This world, which has not put Christ on, nor feels him in the heart, is not to be comforted with Christ, for Christ outside or beyond us is of no use, but he must be in us and we in him. It will do the cut off dry branch no good to say according to John 15: "There is the good vine." It must be on and in the vine to live. They speak of it as though one made an idol of Christ if one preaches him outside of us, and honours and knows and worships him alone according to the flesh.

Some have a strange opinion concerning the resurrection, that each would arise again in the precise condition in which he died, that is, that a waiter would pop out with his bottles, a soldier with his armour and halberd. Then the blessed in God will arise peacefully as they fell asleep in Christ and rule with Christ for a thousand years here on earth. Some think that it will be eternally and are of the opinion that the kingdom of Christ will be here on earth literally as the prophets say, and [as] Lactantius understood it, and as the Jews still understand. Some think that there is no saint in heaven nor any damned in hell, but that when we now die, the saved go to Abraham's bosom or into paradise, and the damned also to a prepared place until the judgment. Then each one will be judged and put where he belongs, Matt. 25.

Some think the bodies of both sleep in the earth, but the soul and spirit of the blessed of God, after being released from the body, go to and rest with God, the soul of the godless, however, with the devil.

Some hold to the opinion of Hans Denck and Origen, condemned long ago, that in the end all will be saved, even the lost evil spirits, and that through Christ all things will be returned to the source from which they went forth. For as in Adam all things fell, they must in Christ be restored and brought back. To support this they quote such Scripture, speaking strangely and discrimanently about it. They describe a cruel hell in which the godless with their spirits are tormented eternally, but which they interpret as being a long time.

Contrary to this many agree with the church that there is an eternal damnation no less than on the other hand an eternal salvation.

Some of them, though very few, hold that one must in no case swear if one desires to be a Christian, no matter what the occasion, neither for the sake of God nor for faith nor to please the neighbour. They also believe that a Christian cannot belong to a government that uses the death penalty or judges capital cases or which engages in war, for Christians have only the ban among themselves and not the sword. Also a Christian may not participate in war or kill for any reason. This was the opinion of Michael Sattler, who was burned, and his followers, and a very few others.

Almost all the others believe that one can confirm the truth with an oath if love demands it or if it concerns faith, and appeal to many teachings and examples in both Testaments. Hans Denck was of this opinion. These also admit that government may be Christian, if it acts according to the command of God. They also condone self-defence and war if one does not do it mischievously but is motivated by self-defence or obedience. But all of them teach obedience to the government in all things not contrary to God. This means not only to pay tax and duty, but to give the mantle and the cloak, and anything required. They also say that they are prepared to suffer violence and also to be obedient to tyrants because Paul, when he enjoins obedience in Rom. 13, was speaking of the heathen government such as Caligula, Tiberius and Nero. As many as I spoke to about it, said that they were there in order to suffer with patience for the sake of Christ, and not impatiently to fight. For the Gospel teaches [that it] will not be defended or affirmed with the fist, (as the peasants had in mind) but with suffering and dying. It is not a matter of fighting but of suffering, as one can see in the examples of Christ and the apostles who called on no power to defend their matter with the fist. They criticize all who teach a warlike Christ and who would defend Christianity with the sword, saying that this has no support either in the teaching of Christ and the apostles nor of the first church. Therefore there is no need, according to my thinking, to be concerned about an uprising by them. The devil who likes to see murder and takes delight in bloodbath has deluded many into a foolish zeal. They tyrannize over these poor people as though they did it out of zeal and love towards both God and country to prevent blasphemy and rebellion. God is strong enough to ward off and to punish all heresy, which is directly committed against him, such as heresy, unbelief, etc.

Government has been ordained as avenger in what concerns the neighbour. Now if there is no revolt one should not on suspicion torture anyone so for it. If I were Pope, emperor, or even the Turk, no people would concern me less as fomenters of revolt than these. Only in Hans Hut, at one time their leader, there was a literalistic zeal. Basing himself on Moses and the prophets he was of the opinion that they, as children of God, were to exterminate the godless as Israel did, though not before God commissioned and prepared them to do it. They themselves have written much against him, and so far as I can tell, no one, or at least very few, holds to this opinion now. For they reject this opinion altogether and condemn it in Hut as a failure and an error. They say that all that counts is suffering for Christ and preparing for danger. Whoever wants to be a Christian must endure persecution, suffer, gather up one's hat when it has been knocked off, and not persecute. It is Antichrist's nature to persecute others. It is the nature of the church that it suffers, and overcomes with faith, patience, hope and waiting, Isa. 30; 1 John 5; Luke 8.

They believe unanimously in free will, as far as I have learned. God, they say, comes first, knocks, woos, and lays the first stone. After that we are free and responsible to choose whether we will accept this proffered grace or reject it, whether we give room to the Word and the pleading and courting Spirit in us or not. We choose whether we will admit the knocker. This much is our obligation, for the God of freedom will force no one to accept his gifts and grace.

Also they say that God and his grace never fail. If we desire the good, we can do it through prevenient grace which has urged and drawn us without compulsion to this choice. For God who creates and nurtures in us the will to the good, will do his part, but not without our desire and cooperation. God, who desires and commands the good, denies no one his grace so that we cannot do it; indeed he takes pleasure and joy in preparing the good will. If he had commanded us to do good and did not give us the grace to will it, or that we could accomplish it if we willed it, the fault would be his and he could judge no one. That would be as though he forbade the good and would not give us his grace to do it, but rather worked in us the opposite to harden our hearts and to withdraw the grace to do the good.

Therefore many hold that God is good only and neither wills nor works anything but the good, and that therefore God is not the cause or the creator of any sin. And they deny that God creates both good and evil in man (as many now think) because he hates sin and does not want it. How could he work and create evil in man and then judge this man, condemning his own work in him? Therefore he creates no evil, sin or wickedness but only the good; sin and evil come from the devil only.

They also have a completely different opinion regarding the providence, foreknowledge and predestination of God than any other sects. God, they say, creates and predestines no one to damnation or sin.

Rather, in his eternally present omniscience he foresees who will become an Esau or a Jacob and knows our coming in and going out before we are born. In this foresight and foreknowledge, by which he sees how we will live our whole life, the one whom he knows to be an Esau, even though he is not yet born, is eternally predestined or preordained before the foundation of the world to eternal fire. He hates him in this sense while he is still in his mother's womb. The other, whom he recognizes as a Jacob, he loves to eternal life. It is not that he hardened the heart of the one or that he takes pleasure in his wickedness and would have it so, but that he knew from eternity that he would become an Esau; he could not help him because he would spurn with his foot all proffered grace.

Thus God is not guilty of anyone's ruin but the man himself who will not abandon sin nor admit the grace knocking at his door nor let the gleaming light shine in. Thus God is always and completely guiltless as he has no pleasure in our destruction nor is guilty of it. Our ruin and its cause is our own fault. They do not admit that God hardened Pharaoh's heart as Moses says in Exodus, but he hardened himself as the text also says.

The majority regard Christ very highly. In him they hope, to him they ascribe all grace and salvation and their redemption. But they do not believe in him externally from afar, but put him on and believe in him, following him in all yieldedness [*Gelassenheit*], as they speak of it.

Nevertheless some, though few, almost like Arius, will in no wise accept three persons in the godhead. They say God cannot be a person but only Christ, whom they do not consider as true living God of equal nature and substance, but will allow that he is equal to God in will. Yet they call him their God, a son of God, the world's saviour, the head of the church and more than all prophets and people. They do not regard him as a mere prophet or man, as they complain that they are accused of doing. To sum up, some speak so modestly and imprecisely of Christ that I cannot sufficiently comprehend or understand what they say. I hereby commit them to God to whom, whether they believe rightly or wrongly in this, they will have to give an account.

Some consider separation so necessary that they have no fellowship with those who are of the world and who go to entertainments or inns, and do not recognize them as brethren. Others, however, do not think thus and like to get along with everyone.

The sacrament of the altar they consider to be the bread of the Lord, a meal of remembrance and a sign of brotherly love, and a sign that they are one body and bread in Christ, etc. They do not believe that the body of Christ is bodily and essentially in it. They believe that this sacrament is partaken of by the faithful only in faith, spiritually, so that as the mouth receives the sign, the heart receives the truth of the body of Christ.

They also have a variety of customs in the Supper in different places. In some places they do it very seldom, in some often. Sometimes they make the conditions for participation so extreme in sermons beforehand that hardly two are found who would break bread with one another. There is much quarrelling and sectarianism. Some consider it necessary to break it often; some think it unnecessary, indeed, wrong, and think one ought not to break it except in extremity and even in the fear of death, when one has prepared oneself to die and is ready to stake life and possessions for others.

In some places they ban those who go to the sermons of the scribes [preachers of the established churches] or have anything to do with them, for they are almost all at odds with the preachers whom they contemptuously call scribes and whom, in my opinion, they condemn much too carelessly.

On the other hand, there are some who allow that one should read and hear everything, testing it and keeping what is good. They themselves go to hear the preachers, but in general the manner, commission, order and calling of all preachers does not please them.

Not one image is allowed in their congregations either, which they term idolatry. They call church buildings pagan temples, and some have such a horror about it and such a conscience, that they will hardly look at a picture, and would consider it a sin to walk through the temple of an idol. On the other hand, there are those who are perturbed at nothing, no matter where they are. They could go to a church and even see a mass conducted.

Some urge the cross so much that they virtually persecute or despise those who have no cross, saying that something about them must not be right. For if they truly walked in the way of the Lord, the cross would not be missing. They emphasize this so much that some go looking for the cross. Others, however, are of a different opinion.

Some have taught that a brother or a sister may not live with a heathen spouse, if he does not yield to her in everything she undertakes, such as training the children in her faith, housekeeping, etc. With this foolish teaching they have broken many marriages, so that the wife left the one and the husband the other. But by now this teaching has almost died out and come to shame, so that many of them teach against it themselves.

The consciences of some have been confused by the saying: whoever does not leave everything, wife, children, fields, pastures, father, mother, etc. From this they have concluded that one should give shelter to the brother or have the church meet in his house. Armed with this Scripture they have caused him to leave everything, accept a miserable exile, and become a burden to the people there. He left wife, child, and house, becoming a faithless heathen to his children, by going from them and letting the house fall into ruin. The children are left without discipline. These brothers stormed out, roaming around like spiritual mercenaries, and the one who earlier might have had his own bread, provided for his wife and children, even helping others, now must be a burden to their people. Many of them, however, are against this foolishness, condemning it all as wrong, and will not permit it.

Some elevate the old law almost above the new, introducing into the New Testament all of Moses especially the *judicialia* and the *moralia*, that is, all the laws dealing with morals and justice. They accept not only the sword but also the Mosaic wars and all public policy as though only the ceremonial law were abrogated.

The others are directly against this. Indeed, many of them say that Moses counts for nothing in Christ's covenant. Moses has finished serving, the shadow and the image are gone and only Christ, the Son, is present. They simply will not permit anything that cannot be justified by the New Testament. For Christ only, who is more than Moses and the prophets, was presented to them by the Father to be obeyed. These will not permit swearing, warring or whatever the letter of the New Testament does not permit. Many of them went out daily with new orders to gain converts for their church. The Spirit, they say, told them this, and God disclosed that to them in a vision or a dream. Then the Spirit told them that God would deal thus and so with the world, now that the last day would come, and that the time was fixed. Hut had a good deal to do with this and convinced some, so that they carelessly wasted their property, throwing it away, perhaps thinking they would not need it during the remaining short time, thus not wanting to be friends with their treacherous property, and instead trusting yieldedly [*gelassen*] in God. They did not see that their mischievous Adam was looking to himself and sought and intended his own welfare, namely that he would arise with Christ and avoid the curse and the voice of God, Go ye, etc. He wanted to rule eternally, and thus thought he would not need the goods any more. One can easily see how this prophecy was fulfilled. It is therefore clear they cannot have been sent, because it did not come true, as God, through Moses, taught us to recognize the false prophets Deut. 13, 18. From this it is clear that they had spoken on their own authority without commission and spoke all this without God's command. They were themselves the source of their proclamation. These men whom they had taken to be the best and most spirit-filled lied to them so that they might see how God mocked them, that they should not put their trust in people no matter how they defended their calling.

There has also arisen a sect among them who desired to have all things and also their wives in common. But these were soon silenced and expelled by their brethren. Some accuse Hut and Hätzer as being leaders of this sect. Well, if it is true, they have both received judgment for it.

Some deny the eternal virginity of Mary saying that after Christ whom she conceived, carried and bore as a virgin, she had more children with Joseph, her husband. Others speak against this as a useless question, profiting nothing, and as not an article of faith and as in any way serviceable for edification.

Some say that faith cannot come through studying books, nor from hearing any sermon. Rather, it comes without mediation from the inner true living Word of God when God addresses our hearts and shines the illuminating light into our soul, forming an image, and impressing himself into it like a seal. They call this faith such knowledge and assurance, that the inner man can see and know what he believes more certainly than if the outer man were to see, hear, touch, and perceive it with all five senses, which might all be nonsensical chatter, fantasy and deception. They strongly oppose those who teach that faith comes from the outward Word of God, that faith is uncertainty, and that one must trust without knowing. Which is true enough, they say, if one interprets it as applying to the outer man, but could not be farther from the truth if interpreted as applying to the inner man who does not believe but knows and sees that which he believes. Indeed, he does not believe but grasps and feels; only the outer man believes. In this connection see Paul Heb. 11; and perhaps Luther in many places.

Some leaders with their followers think that faith comes from much reading, hearing, and preaching, and for this reason they go frantically from one place to another. They cite Paul, Rom. 10, that faith comes from preaching. And everything has its Scripture.

Some want to refrain from baptism and other ceremonies eternally till God gives a different command and sends faithful workers into his harvest, for which they honestly desire with great longing, wishing for nothing else.

Some others contradict this and say that the ceremonies were adulterated and ruined immediately after the apostles had departed, and that God no longer regards and wants them. Therefore they will never be reinstated but everything now takes place in spirit and in truth and no longer with outward things. And so, if one has come to the wine, it is not proper to go back to the sign of the tavern, or if one has walked a road to look back again to the mile posts. These will not recognize the Anabaptists as brothers but excommunicate them and fight them verbally and in writing.

There are many more sects and opinions among them which I do not know and cannot describe. Almost no one agrees with anyone else in all matters, by which God shows them that he is just as weary of and as opposed to their sect as to all others. He wants us united not in external baptism but in unity of the spirit and of brotherly love, united to a fellowship more in disposition, spirit and faith than in body, time, place and outward ceremonies. For they should know that God rejects any banding together or sects. For this God will put them to shame as already daily happens so that they will know that the New Testament is no legal requirement; for God wants them to be ground, melted, and knitted into one loaf, union and bread, with spirit, faith, heart and love, and not into an external, worldy alliance of baptism, clothes, food, place, time and ceremonies. They may not claim the glory of the early church and regard the apostles, who shed their blood for the sake of the name of Christ, as predecessors of their bishops. For if they are martyrs of Christ, then God has forgiven them their external error because of their inner justification and their constant zeal and Christian faith, and not imputed it to them. Who will assure us that they have shed their blood for the sake of baptism and for outer ceremonies? Should we not much more believe that these outward things all disappeared in suffering like stubble and wood beside gold in the fire so that the pure, purged and tested faith in God through Jesus Christ, for which they have given their lives, remained constant in their agony? The best among them may have died for the sake of the name of Christ as true martyrs. I cannot condemn them, but I would advise the living that they should not erroneously comfort themselves with or rely on their death, for no one knows how or for what they died or ended their lives.

I recount all of this, especially their articles of faith, besides those of other heretics, in part so that I might present before their eyes their marvelous unity in outward ceremonies and inward faith and spirit. They need to see how, as with other sects, God strikes them all with confusion at this tower of Babel, so that they might realize their foolishness and desist and join the one unified church which is bound together only in spirit and in truth and in no outer ceremonies and elements. I do it so that they might deny the godless ways of the world, no one looking to anyone else, no one believing or holding anything to please or serve another or looking around as Peter looked around at John. Each one must look to himself, to see how certain he is in his convictions and how highly assured, and whether he was taught by God or man. He needs to know where his conscience is at rest, and truly enter the school of Christ of which they speak so much. Then the Lord will put them in remembrance of everything and instruct them how things are in spirit and in truth.

Now I want to warn their enemies and persecutors that they should withdraw their hands and not enter God's domain, that they do not, as often happens, mistake a Christian for a heretic, as though they had the right to lay hold of them. They do not have this right, and if they continue they burden themselves with the blood of Christ and become guilty of his blood with Annas, Caiphas, Pilate and Herod, and thus becoming even worse than these. For there is no sect so wicked that it has not discovered something good. Thus God scatters his favours to the throng and also among the heretics and the heathens so that everyone may tell of having received some of his goodness. Whatever this sect may be, who would be prepared to stake his life on the claim that they teach nothing but heresy and error? And even if they are in error and may be called heretics, I know of no one among their enemies who would let himself be burned to attest to that. For many who do not belong to their sect believe that in many matters we cannot contradict them, no matter how reprehensible they may be in other matters. No one has yet quite fathomed it; but if every word condemns, God help us all. If we were all to see our errors recorded before us, all of us, the Anabaptists and we, would proceed very gingerly in our judgment, and often be ashamed to open our mouth.

Take what is good from each sect and let the rest go to the devil. The worst and most vexing and displeasing aspect of this or any other sect is the partisan separation and the creation of a separate sect. The second is its fragmented, disunified confession, splintered into so many sects, whereby they betray themselves. The third is several unchristian articles of faith. The fourth is the presumptuous, arrogant and insolent judgment which they pass on others more out of love for themselves and self-approval than out of the judgment of the Spirit. Nothing is ever pious enough for this alluring, arrogant, hypocritical devil. Each sect thinks it alone has divined the truth and would, if it could, draw and urge the others to itself by force. The fifth is their legalism, and their ascetic and regulated Christianity. Christian faith cannot be like that. For Christian faith suffers no law nor regulation and cannot be contained in rules; it is liberty of the spirit. In it the Holy Spirit who will not tolerate any law, would be teacher and master. He elevates his own people over every law including God's, making them into freedmen. He inscribes on and pours love into the hearts of his own, so that they do all out of spontaneous love, yes, more than duty calls for, without any forcing, commanding, laws, orders or written rules. The sixth is that their prophesies do not come true and [that] their word goes forth void. This is the test and mark of false prophets, Deut. 18. The seventh is that they always explain and interpret the Scriptures literally and not according to the mind of Christ, by which Scripture, as God intends, is to be understood and explained and not according to the letter. For the letter, as has been demonstrated throughout this Chronicle of heresy, has always made heretics. For since Scripture in its literal rendering is divided and disunited, the letter must make heretics, and thus it can never become the basis of agreement, unless one grasps the sense of the Spirit of Christ in it, and thereby discovers what he meant by each item. This, however, we must be taught in stillness by God. They must also perceive that so many contradictory visions, revelations, dreams and prophesies (which they daily present and which nevertheless do not come true), cannot be of God, since what is spoken by God comes as the Word of God and does not fail to come true. One should not for this reason despise and eradicate all prophecy. Nor ought one simply to accept it but test everything beforehand, and keep what is good. For they should become aware by now how often the devil has lied to them with all their many dreams, visions and prophecies. Even now the last powerful errors are abroad which the devil will confirm not alone with Scripture, but indeed only with Scripture, and most likely also with miracles. Therefore we ought to walk carefully before God, working out our salvation in fear and trembling, holding to God alone, examining the cause of all things, looking to ourselves to see what God says to us concerning all these things. We ought to perceive the witness of our own hearts, and not to understand, do, or accept anything against our conscience. For not everything consists in the bare letter of Scripture, since we see that all heretics have Scripture. The Antichrist of the end and his following have bedded themselves in Scripture. He wants us to be super-scriptural and know all its details. Therefore it all depends on the sense of Scripture and on a spiritual discernment of how God intended it, and why he spoke each individual part. If we thus weigh each matter we find its true meaning in the depth of the spiritual mind and sense of Christ. Otherwise the dead letter makes us all heretics and fools, for everything can be patched, embellished and excused with Scripture. Therefore let no one allow himself to be deafened or bewitched by the letter of the Scripture but let him ponder and test the Scripture beforehand to see how it compares with his heart. If Scripture is contrary to his conscience and the indwelling word, beware; it has not been understood and expounded according to the sense of the Spirit. For the Scriptures are to give witness to our heart and spirit and not to be against them. Just as one is to test the spirits beforehand, so also whether the letter of Scripture is expounded and set forth according to the mind of Christ. For one must not be too sure of the letter and trust everything, because so many heretics come from it, but one must carefully and with fear seek, grasp and receive the sense of the spirit in the letter.

Therefore I beg the Anabaptists to walk in truth, repent, be devout and careful and not sin. If they are so eager for the cross, fearing to miss it if they do not get themselves baptized, let them enter into the power of baptism and its truth; no doubt the cross will find them and not miss them. For the devil is not so much against water baptism as against its power and against the spiritual baptism in truth, which water baptism only symbolizes, namely the godly life dead with Christ to evil. Therefore I ask the Anabaptists that they regard themselves as an example of foolishness, and realize that God mocks them and does not want their sect or any other. For example, a woman of Appenzell in Switzerland, as I am reliably informed, had convinced many that she was Christ, and also obtained twelve disciples, which is too ridiculous for words. Also let them consider how many times they have allowed themselves to be deceived and how often their leaders have deluded them, which they have in part learned, not without harm to themselves. Observe where human stupidity tends to go. If one cocks a snook at it with Scripture and God's name, it is soon convinced and believes that since to God all things are possible and since he is no respecter of persons and since we are all one in Christ, that therefore it may well be that a woman is Christ. Do you see how Scripture proves it? A brother in Switzerland at St. Gall is supposed to have said to his blood brother, Kneel down quickly; I have a command from God to cut off your head. Thereupon the brother patiently and willingly knelt down and was beheaded. The other, captured for it by the magistrate, died for it, claiming and imagining that the Lord had commanded him. This, too, I could easily support with Scripture. But it is nothing but a masquerade of fantasy and nothing but the devil's weapon, this dead letter of Scripture. But the mind of Christ and of the Spirit, is the source of peace, unity and eternal life, for those who are spiritual.

20

Anonymous

Anonymous Hutterite Leaders to Mathes Hasenhan (1538)*

Introduction

Mathes Hasenhan had worked as an Anabaptist leader in Hesse prior to 1532. Sometime after 1533 the Hutterian missionary effort began in Hesse. The letter translated below reveals the concern of the Moravian leaders to get the measure of Mathes, after the Moravian leadership had received a request for help from the Anabaptist group. Peter Riedemann was sent in 1539. When he arrived, Riedemann became involved in settling problems within the local group, where there was dissension and a lack of confidence in their leader, Matthias (Mathes). Mathes was described as "self-willed and obstinate," and when Riedemann suggested that he go to Moravia to learn about communal living and proper leadership, he refused.[1]

The letter here reveals a good deal about the seriousness with which proper church discipline was pursued by the Hutterian Brethren in

---

*Source: Franz, *Quellen IV*, 180-84.
Translation: Friesen/Klaassen

the first years of their common life. The Brethen obviously were uncertain about Mathes, and were anxious to find out more about what he believed and taught.

The apprehension felt by the Hutterites about Mathes seems to have been warranted. Early in 1540 (February) Mathes went to Strasbourg to confer with the lapsed Anabaptist Peter Tasch, who had returned to mainline Protestantism under Martin Bucer's influence.[2] Soon after this visit, Mathes also recanted, as is stated in Bucer's letter of February 7, 1540 to the Strasbourg authorities.[3]

Bibliographical Sources:

The Chronicle of the Hutterian Brethren, vol. I (Rifton, N.Y.: Plough Publishing House, 1987).

Günther Franz, *Urkundliche Quellen zu hessischen Reformationsgeschichte* 4. Bd. Wiedertäuferakten (1951), 269-70.

John J. Friesen, ed., *Peter Riedemann's Hutterite Confession of Faith* (Scottdale, PA: Herald Press, 1999).

Werner O. Packull, "Peter Tasch: from Melchiorite to bankrupt wine merchant," *MQR* 62 (July 1988), 276-95.

Anonymous Hutterite Leaders to Mathes Hasenhan, 1538.

From the elders and ministers of the congregation of God in Moravia and Austria, to be delivered to Mathes [Hasenhan] minister in Hesse. [1538].

We elders and ministers of the church of God, which is gathered through the Holy Spirit and bound together by the bond of love, living in Moravia and Austria are now awaiting tribulation and persecution for the sake of the name of our Lord Jesus Christ. We wish and ask of God, the almighty, merciful heavenly Father, grace, mercy, peace and true knowledge in Christ Jesus, our Lord, to all those who carry and proclaim the message of our Lord Jesus Christ, and who with us preach one kingdom in Christ Jesus. May God, the Lord, give his Word from heaven into their hearts as well as his heavenly grace and his gifts to proclaim his name and the unsearchable riches of his mercy in his Son Christ Jesus. Thus they will be able to fetch his bride, which are all the bruised, zealous and devout hearts who convert themselves to him in truth, and lead her out of this world. May they teach, instruct and lead them in the light of his countenance, so that she might clothe herself in a beautiful white gown, holy, and separate from abominations, uncleanness and sins of the world. They wait, arming themselves with patience, truth and godliness for the time when their King and Bridegroom will come and will appear from heaven together with the angels of his power, and take vengeance with flaming fire on all who are not obedient to his Word. They will be found by him to be holy and blameless in peace, and to have free confidence and expectation that they will enter with him into the eternal joy and glory, where they will rest and will rejoice with all the elect for ever and ever. He who is to come will judge the living and the dead and give their reward to his servants who fear him and are faithful stewards in his house, his church, which he has made holy through his grace, renewed through the Word of divine truth and elected to be kings and priests to God the Father through Christ Jesus, our Saviour. To him be honour and praise for all his saints for ever and ever, amen.

Dear Matthes: We have been informed through Wolf, who is our dear brother in the Lord, that he recognizes you as being zealous for God, and also that God has made you worthy to be a minister to those who bear and confess the Lord Jesus Christ in their hearts wherever they are, in Hesse or elsewhere. These are the ones who are not infected with the error of dreams and works, as they are called. [They are separate from those] who despise Scripture and who also say that there is no devil except our flesh, that even the flesh of Christ was a devil, of which we are horrified to speak, with whom Hans Bott consorted. We hear that you also struggle and fight against them through that grace which has been imparted and given you by God, and are not at ease with the matter. Yes, Wolf also witnesses that he is of the opinion that you are quite of one mind with us in Christ, and he thinks that if you and we might talk and discuss these matters, you would heartily agree with us. Other brethren who know you also have witnessed to us about your piety and fear of God, so that we long from our hearts, if it were God's will, to converse with you concerning the Gospel of God which we announce and proclaim to those who desire it from the heart. Thus, if we recognized the grace which was given to you, and your life and actions in Christ among the heathen, we might from the whole heart be at one with you, rejoicing with you, with fullness of joy. This can or may, however, not be. Yet we have not been able to keep from writing to you and from sending our dear brethren to you, so that you might learn of our concern for you and all who love our Lord Jesus Christ from a pure heart, bearing him in their hearts.

We have been much admonished and urged to do this, especially by our dear brother from the land of Hesse, Jacob Hans Ritter, by his two sons and his whole household, by Lorentz, by Andre Veit and his brother Hänsl, by Hermann, together with his sisters and also by Hans Valtan Schneider. We had long put this off because we did not know to whom to write and because we feared that it would not be accepted by you. For, as far as we know, much evil had been spoken about us by those who have gone out from us and have turned your hearts from us and confused them about us. Nevertheless, we heartily loved you, and at the beginning sent to you dear Jörg Zaunring, who has now completed his course faithfully, confessing and witnessing, with his blood, to his Lord God, his divine truth, as you well know.[4] After that dear brother Christof Gschäll came to you, and disclosed to you our love, life and walk in Christ Jesus, so that many were moved to journey to us. Of these, God have pity, many again left us, being led out by that hireling and faithless servant, Hans Bott. He wanted to mix his falseness and leaven among the people of God. When we tried to prevent this he said that we wanted to stop up the wells of living water. But we acted faithfully in the fear of God with him, expressing our opinion that we could not permit him to speak thus, but that, if he were to keep silent, we would bear him in love. Then he asked again, whether we wanted to refuse him the wells of living water. We said that it was not the wholesome teaching of the Lord Jesus Christ, but leaven. But he persisted, saying that Melchior Rinck took the same position.[5] But we said that even if Melchior Rinck said and taught it, that would not make it right. But we did not believe that he took that position; rather we thought they might not have understood him right. Then they expressed the opinion that we called Rinck a false prophet. They became excited and angry, which is characteristic of Hans Bott. They had influence on those who had recently come to us, stealing their hearts with their views so that they would not hear us. So they left with Hans Bott and Valtan Schuester. They convinced the people to follow them and things became worse and worse for us till in agony we had to commit them to God, and to leave the matter with him who knows us, before whom we stand revealed. [Our understanding is confirmed by] the dear brother Jacob[6] servant of the Lord, who confessed God's Word with great joyfulness. The dear brother Jörg Fasser[7] also gave valiant witness to it with his blood. The same was true of the dear brother Wilhelm, Jeromine, the schoolmaster[8] and many other dear brethren. Now the dear brother Peter of Gmünden[9] of Nuremberg has been released from prison through the gracious will of God, and is living with us in the Lord. He sees and acknowledges our love and mercy in which we stand before God and is heartily satisfied with us.

Our dear brother Christoph[10] is in Styria. God has given a great work into his hand. Indeed, God the Lord is with us richly; to him who is in heaven be praise and thanks. This is the reason why, as long as God keeps us thus, we are zealous for you and for all who in all places call upon our Lord Jesus Christ from a pure heart. If only God would grant us the opportunity to talk with you, my Matthes, and especially with Melchior Rinck, so that each might open his heart to the others. If it cannot be, however, we commend it to God the Lord. However, it is not true that we reviled Melchior Rinck. For how should we slander someone whom we do not know? Let that be far from us. We will not accept this attempt at justifying error by appealing to Rinck. We say that even if an angel from heaven were to do it and teach us differently, we would, with God's help, not obey or move. What Melchior Rinck says and does, he will answer for himself. But we hear that he is honest and steadfast in tribulation so that we rejoice in our hearts. We praise God in heaven for it and say: would to God that we could talk orally with him in the Lord. But we will not accept the mind of Hans Bott. We do not know his voice. He will bear the judgment for having alienated some from us. May the God of all grace and mercy let all those, who seek him and have gone astray, recognize their error and may he have mercy on them through our Lord Jesus Christ.

We formerly also sent brethren out, but they were not accepted since, as we have heard, the worst was said of us. But it is open and known to God that with our life and our walk we are a living, genuine letter of Christ everywhere in the world among this godless, adulterous generation, among whom we are to shine as a light in darkness. This we desire and intend to do with God's help, being a good odour of Christ to the pious for life; to the godless, however, for death. We always hope to appear before the Lord, our God, as faithful and proven, for we know that our teaching and life is not error, delusion, nor dreams, but is the eternal truth in Christ Jesus, which will stand and remain eternally and which is attested to by all prophets and by divine witness. In it we desire, with God's help, to live and walk till death. We also desire always to bear in our body the dying of the Lord Jesus, so that we might also anticipate his resurrection with good confidence. For this we pray and this we implore day and night with supplication to our God in heaven. May he complete this in us to the praise of his great and glorious name and to the comfort of all believers eternally. Amen.

How things stand with us in the Lord and how we daily await tribulation for the sake of the name of Christ, and how we are gathered together in love and unity and in divine peace and how we suffer much for this as well, our dear brethren will witness to you. They will be our living letter and will also make known to you, my Mathes, and to those who want to accept and hear it, our zeal, love and persecution. Now over all who walk by this rule, namely in the footsteps of Christ, be peace, blessing and mercy from God, the Father, through our Lord Jesus Christ. Amen.

P.S. We write this letter out of divine zeal to all those who are zealous for God, and we deliver it to Mathes, your minister, because we think that he ought to receive it first, because we know that the hearts of many have been estranged from us.

May God eternally show mercy to all who seek him from the heart.
Amen.

21

Trieste

Confession of the Brethren, Taken to Trieste as Prisoners (1539)*

Introduction

On December 6, 1539, the congregation at Steinabrunn met with Swiss Brethren led by Philip Plener to discuss the question of a union between the two groups. On that same evening, the group was attacked by the royal provost of King Ferdinand of Austria, who imprisoned 136 men, women, and youth at Falkenstein castle, which belonged to the barons of Fünfkirchen. The main purpose of the attack was to capture the leaders (servants of the Word) in order to get large sums of money and goods from them. But although the people they were after were in the house, they were not found.[1]

The prisoners were separated by gender and were kept in the Falkenstein for eight days, after which the marshall of King Ferdinand appeared with several priests. The intention was to gather information and money and to try to convert the "heretics." Torture was some-

*Source: Müller, *Glaubenszeugnisse*, 190-205.
Translation: Walter Klaassen

times used, but to no avail. After six and a half weeks of imprisonment, the men, totalling 90, were ordered sent to Trieste, where their punishment was to be galley slaves on the war ships of the high admiral Andreas Doria. Although the men warned the king's agents that they would not row to aid war and pillage, it made no difference. In January of 1540, the men were sent off to Trieste, bound in pairs with iron fetters with their hands chained together. The guards were ordered to march the prisoners from one courthouse to the next, through Vienna, Graz, Ljubliana and finally to Trieste. Along the way they endured hunger and hardship but they were able to pray to God every morning and evening without anyone stopping them.[2]

On arrival at Trieste, the brethren were not put on ships right away but imprisoned. After 12 nights, they escaped over the seeward wall of the prison with the help of the rope that had bound them on their journey. Of the ninety that escaped, 12 were seized in the pursuit that followed and were handed over to Doria and taken to the galleys. The others managed to make it all the way back to Moravia, arriving home on the fourth Sunday of Lent, 1540. Their defence and confession of faith follows.

Bibliographical Sources:

The Chronicle of the Hutterian Brethren, vol. I (Rifton, N.Y.: Plough Publishing House, 1987).
The Chronicle of the Hutterian Brethren, vol. II (Ste. Agathe, MB: Friesen Printers, 1998).
Christian Hege, "Steinabrunn," *ME IV*, 624.
Werner O. Packull, *Hutterite Beginnings, Communitarian Experiments during the Reformation* (Baltimore, MD: John Hopkins University Press, 1995).

Defence and Confession of Faith of the Brothers and Friends of God who were Imprisoned in the Falkenstein by the Godless Tyrants and Enemies of Divine Truth. From there they were taken to the Port of Trieste and sold as galley slaves.
[In the 1539th year.]

Prologue. The holy apostle Peter wrote in his first epistle chapter 3[:15-16]: Be always ready to make a defence of the reason for the hope that is in you. Do it with gentleness and reverence with a clear conscience so that those who slander you as evildoers will be put to shame. We are ready and willing to do as you desire and demand from us. We do it as the Lord gives us grace in the pure fear of God and with a good conscience as we commonly do. We do it because we shall have to account for it before the judgment seat of Christ on that day when everything that is hidden and all human injustice will be brought to light and all will receive according to what they have done. We have composed and presented it briefly in writing so that it can be comprehended and understood.

First we believe in the one God who is true, eternal, and almighty, who, according to much Scripture, made the heavens, the earth, the sea and everything that is in and on it (Gen. 1; Exod. 20[:11]; Acts 4[:24]). He is the only God and beside him there is no God, and that is why he desires that he alone should be worshipped, honoured, and praised, and to him alone gratitude is due according to the witness of Scripture: I am the Lord your God who brought you out of Egypt (Exod. 20[:2]). You shall have no other Gods before me (Deut. 5[:6-9]). You shall not make for yourself any graven image nor any other likeness, whether it be of something up in heaven or below on earth or what is in the water or under the earth. Do not honour, worship, or serve them. For I, the Lord your God, am a jealous God who punishes the children for the iniquity of the parents to the third and fourth generation of those who hate me, but show mercy to thousands who love me and keep my commandments.

Again, you shall worship the Lord your God and serve him only (Deut. 6[:4]; Matt. 4[:10]). He is the true God and eternal life. Children, beware of the adoration of images (1 John 5[:21])! Keep watch over your hearts! You saw signs of God on the day when he spoke to you out of the fire (Deut. 4[:12]) so that you should not become perverted and make an image like man or woman or an animal on the earth or bird in the air. There is your witness that God, who is the only God, desires that he alone is to be honoured, worshipped, and served. The whole Scripture is full of this testimony. These texts clearly reject, destroy, and condemn all idolatry, specifically all wooden, stone, golden, waxen, bread idols,[3] frescoes, and carvings of images by all of which God is robbed of his honour. All such things are excluded in this commandment of God.[4]

True worshippers will worship God alone in spirit and in truth. We will now also show how God punished and destroyed those who transgressed against his law and served other gods. First, when the people of Israel prostituted themselves in the desert against the word and will of God and, following other gods, made themselves a calf, the wrath of God came over them and 3000 were killed because of their abomination (Exod. 32). Again, when they forsook the Lord and went whoring after other gods, he gave them into the hands of their enemies whom they were unable to resist. There were many other examples of this sort but it would take too long to relate it all (Judg. 2, 3, 4; 2 Kings 14, 18). Virtually every book of Holy Scripture speaks and witnesses against this abominable idol worship. Of nothing else does God speak so sharply (Jer. 7, 44). Today people think that they will be forgiven for going for an hour or two into the temple of idols and calling upon them, but it is the beginning of all whoredom and apostasy, by which people are led into thoughtlessness and to committing other abominations before God[5] (Wisd. 4[:10-14]). The deceitful Israelites also felt secure in their idolatry, but God punished them horribly. All this God did as a warning that whoever would commit this wrong and become godless in the future would not go unpunished (2 Pet. 2).

2. We also believe in Jesus Christ. We believe in Jesus, that he is the Christ of God, the One who was sent from the bosom of the heavenly Father and took to himself our humanness in the virginal body of Mary to redeem the human race. She conceived him by the Holy Spirit without male seed. She gave birth to him and had him circumcised on the eighth day to fulfil the promise of the Father. Whatever Christ commanded, taught, and promised we confess with word and deed as the eternally valid truth. First, God sent his forerunner John the Baptist. He was a voice calling in the desert and prepared the way of the Lord as it is written (Isa. 40[:3-5]). God commanded him to preach to the house of Israel that they should turn and be converted, for the king-

dom of heaven had drawn near. He baptized them with the baptism of repentance and said: I baptize you with water for repentance. He who comes after me is stronger than I. He will baptize you with the Holy Spirit and with fire (Matt. 3[:11]; Mark 1[:8]; Luke 3[:16]). Jesus himself testified that Moses and all the prophets had prophesied up to the time of John the Baptist. From then on the kingdom of heaven is preached through the Gospel (Matt. 11[:13]). John preached to the people that they should be converted and said that they should bear fruit worthy of repentance. Don't imagine that you can say to yourselves, Abraham is our father. Already the ax is laid to the root of the tree. The tree that does not bear good fruit will be cut down and thrown into the fire.

After this Christ came, accepted this baptism, and said when he was baptized by John that it is proper to fulfill all of God's righteousness (Matt. 3[:13-15]). Later he baptized others through his chosen disciples (John 3[:22], 4[:1-2]). At the end, after he had risen from the dead he commanded his disciples and said: Go out and teach all peoples, baptizing them in the name of the Father, the Son and the Holy Spirit, and teach them to observe all that I have commanded you (Matt. 28[:19-20]).

Again, go into all the world and preach the Gospel to every creature. Whoever believes and is baptized will be saved. Whoever does not believe will be condemned (Mark 16[:15-16]). The disciples obeyed the command of Christ and preached his name after they had received the promise of the Father, the Holy Spirit (John 2[:22]). They witnessed to the people and preached that Jesus was the Christ. When the people said to Peter and the apostles: Men and brothers, what shall we do? Peter said: Repent and be baptized every one of you in the name of Jesus Christ for the forgiveness of sins, and you will receive the gift of the Holy Spirit. Those who received the Word gladly were baptized (Acts 2[:37-38]).

The Ethiopian eunuch came to Philip and said: Here is water. Is there any reason why I should not be baptized? Philip replied: If you believe with your whole heart, it can be done. This clearly shows how the apostles carried out the command of Christ and demanded first the faith that justifies (John 15[:8]; Rom. 8[:30]). If they saw it was there, then only did they baptize. Scripture shows that always they taught Christ first. Those who confessed him and received him as trustworthy, knew their sin and confessed that they had died to it and had risen with Christ, these they baptized. Paul writes: Shall we continue to live in the sin to which we have died? Do you not know that all who are baptized in Jesus Christ are baptized into his death? Thus we are buried with him by baptism into death (Rom. 6[:1-4]). That means that in baptism we have abandoned all sin and unrighteousness and have renounced the devil and the world. Christ says: whoever does not deny all that he has and takes up the cross and follows me cannot be my disciple. Thus we have completely died to sin, so that as Christ was raised from the dead through the glory of the Father, so we too should walk in newness of life. Scripture says further that we have been circumcised without hands with the circumcision of Christ through putting off the sinful body, the flesh. You have been buried with him in baptism and raised up through the faith which God gives. He has made you alive with him when you were still dead in sin (Col. 2[:11-13]).

Those of you who have been baptized have put on Christ (Gal. 3[:27]). He is your forerunner who will sustain you. Baptism is not the removal of the dirt of the flesh but the covenant of a good conscience with God (1 Pet. 3[:18, :21]).

Here one can understand and see how the dear apostles carried out the command of Christ, how they baptized, and who was fit to be baptized, namely those who had heard the Christian preaching of the Gospel, believed it, and confessed their faith. For faith comes from hearing the preaching and the preaching through the Word of God. If one believes with the heart one is justified, and if one confesses with the mouth, one is saved. They baptized those who were bound to God with a good conscience and promised to serve him. With a good conscience they believed what God promised, that he will keep the promise and fulfill it and never put to shame those who trust in him (Ps. 22[:5]; Isa. 28[:16]; Rom. 10[:11]), for the just shall live by their own faith (Hab. 2[:4]).

Thus the papal and anti-Christian baptism of infants is totally excluded by Scripture (Rom. 1[:17?], 3[:24?]). Those who have understanding from God know that it has been invented and instituted against God's command. It is a planting which the heavenly Father has not planted (Heb. 10[Matt. 15:13]), and has therefore to be pulled up by all of God's children, for Christ commands to baptize only those who believe (Matt. 28[:19-20]). So they baptize the young children without faith, for [children] know neither evil nor good (Deut. 1[:39]). They claim that the child has inherited sin (Ezek. 18[:4], 33[:10-17]) and set about to exorcize the devil from it. It is a cruel blasphemy against God to condemn God's good creation. With their godless vanity they think they can make them better than God created them. For it is written that even as through the sin of one, condemnation came over everyone, so through the authentic Word of Christ divine justification includes the children of his faithful ones without the addition of baptism. Christ said: do not hinder the children from coming to me, for theirs is the kingdom of heaven (Matt. 19[:14]; Mark 10[:14]; Luke 18[:16]). At another place, when his disciples asked who was the greatest among them, he called a child to him, placed him among them and said to them: Truly I say to you, unless you return and become as the children, you will not enter the kingdom of heaven (Matt. 18[:1-4]). Now if the child is possessed by a devil Christ has certainly unwisely admonished his own, because it means that he really told them to be like the devil. That is impossible. St. Paul speaks similarly when he says that we should be children in evil but wise in our understanding (Rom. 18[1 Cor. 14:20]).

Thus a great abomination and error has appeared (Matt. 20[24:15?]). Further proof is found where it is written: You were perfect on the day of your creation until transgression was found in you (Ezek. 28[:15]). As long as Adam kept God's commandment he was pure. For God has created humans indestructible after his image (Gen. 3; Wisd. 2[:23]; Sir. 7[?]), and God made them plain and simple. Now since they are obedient again through Christ and placed again at the beginning from which they fell through Adam's disobedience, and since further it is evident that Christ justified the little children by the spirit of his grace without baptism or birth ritual because they know neither good nor evil, the pope's abomination and error is as clear as day. These anti-Christians quote Ps. 5[51:5]: Behold, I was conceived and born in sin. It is easy to believe that all outside of God's grace are totally caught in sin, live in it, were conceived and born in it, and wherever Christ in his grace does not justify, there is no hope. But since he does justify, who will condemn (Rom. 8[:33-34])?

All human flesh has a sinful inclination and desire for what is wrong, but whoever has Christ's Spirit does not perform the works of the flesh. Children also enjoy this grace as Paul says: the unbelieving man is made holy through his believing wife otherwise, the children would be unclean. But now they are holy (1 Cor. 7[:14]). Godly parents raise up, teach, and direct their children to godliness and do not allow them to nourish sin in their flesh. Rather, they bring them up in the fear and admonition of the Lord according to the command of God.

The Antichrist insists on washing the sin away with water, but this does not change them; the inclination is there as before and remains in them as long as they are on earth. But God does not charge those with sin who did not consent to it or do it, for it is written that God judges the thought. The inclination to sin that is not consented to in the heart is no sin before God. It is not living in sin but is sin resisted. The dear Paul in his gospel includes the children in grace and Christian righteousness.

The sum of the matter is that Antichrist has no Scripture, example, or command of God or his holy apostles, not a single letter of Scripture for the baptism and chrism of children and other invented rituals used with small children. He wants to grant them salvation with magic, otherwise they would be unredeemed. It is as though only through him could the children receive grace and be justified. This is to mock the precious suffering of Christ. In many other things as well he usurps God's place (2 Thess. 2[:4]) so that he gets the honour which is due to God alone.

Concerning the new birth

The new birth must take place from water and Spirit (John 3[:5]). In baptism every Christian dies to the old sinful life, and rises with Christ to a new life, and becomes a new person who desires only what is above where Christ is. This new person looks only to the will and command of God and what God desires and expects. The Christian diligently strives to please God and, for recreation, speaks of his law day and night (Ps. 1[:2], 3[?], 7[?]). Christ says: those who hear and keep my command are those who love me (John 14[:15]). This is the way of the love of Christ: it moves through the Holy Spirit which Christ has richly poured out in the hearts of all his faithful, with which they are sealed for the day of redemption (Eph. 4[:30]). They are enemies of all worldly pleasure and desire and listen only to their teacher Christ, who has taught them the will of the Father (Matt. 11[:25-26]). We further find in Scripture, which witnesses to God, that Christ, the Son of God, teaches us also the rest of what all the believers are obligated to do. We will try to describe it, although it is difficult completely to detail everything. Still, we will diligently set it forth and spare no effort so that the grace which God has given us might be felt and known through you, provided that your hearts are inclined to understand.

First, Christ says in Matthew 5 [:33-37]: You have heard that it was said to those of ancient times, You shall not swear falsely, but shall keep your oath made to God. Christ, however, who is the fulfilment of the law says: But I say to you, Do not swear at all.[6] He gives specific instances of swearing, and then concludes: Let your word be yes, yes, and no, no. What is beyond that is from the evil one. Thus we say and confess by the power and command of Christ that it is not proper or incumbent upon any Christian to pledge an oath or to swear. In the Law the false oath was forbidden and only the honest one allowed. Now Christ terminates all of that, establishes divine truth and forbids all swearing to his followers, indeed all commitments and vows, everything that is beyond the yes and no, since no person is able to make a single hair on the head white or black. They are unable to do even this smallest thing, how can they risk and comply with what has been promised by an oath? We will simply hold to this command not to swear or vow but to remain with yes and no insofar as it is God's will. We will not go beyond this.

Second, it is written that it was said to those of ancient times, an eye for an eye, and a tooth for a tooth. But Christ says: I say to you, do not resist that which is evil, but if someone strikes you on the right cheek, turn to him the left one also, and if someone wishes to sue you and take your coat, give your cloak as well. We desire with all our heart to practice this obediently.

All defence and physical resistance, all warring, fighting, insurrection, and resisting evil, and all litigation in worldly courts and quarrelling over temporal goods are excluded. Christ clearly forbids killing or angry resentment (Matt. 5[:38-40]).

To this we add Paul who says: Do not avenge yourselves, my beloved, but give place to God's wrath (Rom. 12[:19]). Going to law with one another is a defeat for you. Why do you not rather suffer injustice (1 Cor. 6[:7])? We and all true Christians accept and obey this. Following the command of Christ, we will not aid any injustice, nor whatever serves warring, murder, rebellion and disunity.

Third, there is the command of Christ concerning those among his believers who sin: If your brother sins against you show him his wrong between you and him alone. If he listens to you you have won your brother. If he will not listen, bring one or two others with you so that every matter is established by two or three witnesses. If he still does not listen, tell it to the congregation. If he will not listen to the congregation, regard him as a heathen and publican (Matt. 1[18:15-17]). Whoever sins against God in the public wickedness of adultery, fornication, idolatry, magic, theft, lying, deceiving, gluttony, drunkenness and the like have broken God's covenant and are admonished and punished differently from the case above. As soon as such offences become public we are commanded by God to expel what is evil. Thus Paul expelled the fornicator in Corinth with the Christian ban as a warning to sin no more, as Christ did with the adulterous woman (1 Cor. 5[:5]; John 8[:11]).

However, we do not accuse or betray anyone in a worldly court and authority. When what is evil has been expelled according to the command of God, we turn that person over to the judgment of God.[7] If they do not repent, God will punish them in his time, for which we have scriptural authority: Leave vengeance to me. I will repay, says the Lord (John 8[:11]; Acts 8[:14-24]; Rom. 12[:19]).

Concerning separation from the world, Christ commanded us to have no fellowship with evil and wickedness and the unfruitful works of darkness, which the devil has planted in the world (Eph. 5[:11]; 2 Cor. 6, 7).[8] St. Peter writes about this: They are surprised that you no longer run with them in the excesses of dissipation and so they slander you (1 Pet. 1[4:4]). St. Paul, likewise, separated the disciples from evildoers and from those who spoke evil of the Lord's name (Acts 19[:9]). Among all creatures there is good and evil, believing and unbelieving, Christ and the world, God's temple and the temple of idols, darkness and light etc., and none may have part in the other since there are only two kingdoms. From all of this we should learn that whatever is not united with our God and Christ is nothing but abomination which we should simply avoid and flee from.

Therefore, following Scripture and the command of God we have separated ourselves from all the unfruitful works of darkness, all popish and worldly wickedness with their idolatry, attending the liturgy, taverns, the singing of songs about sex, citizens' commitments, worldly obligations, and other similar evils. These are considered important in the world but are nevertheless kept contrary to God and his command since those are the places at which God is most egregiously blasphemed (Luke 15[:16]; Sir. 10[?]). We avoid all appearance of evil and hypocrisy. Because the world lies in wickedness, as John writes (1 John 5[:19]), with so much evil living before God, the only thing to be learned from the world is evil. But since by the grace of God we have seen this wickedness, we have gone out from her according to the command of God, that is, we have separated ourselves from all unrighteousness. We cannot serve two masters. Whoever desires to be a friend of the world will be God's enemy. This is our position on separation from all unrighteousness according to God's command.

Four. Concerning the sword we confess to following the command of Christ to his own.[9] The sword is an order of God outside the perfection of Christ which punishes evildoers and protects and shelters those who do good (Isa. 16[:5]; Wisd. 2; Rom. 13[:1-4]). In the Law the worldly sword was given to worldly government. In the perfection of Christ the ban and exclusion are used for admonition, change of heart and conversion of the sinner without killing the body, only with admonition and the command to sin no more.

Many who do not know the will of Christ for us, ask whether a Christian may or must use the sword against evil in order to protect and shelter the good.

Answer: Christ says and commands that we should learn of him, for he is gentle and lowly of heart, and we will find rest for our souls. In the case of the heathen woman caught in the act of adultery, he does not say that she should be stoned according to the law of his Father although he always says that he does what the Father has commanded. No, he acts with mercy, forgiveness, and admonition not to sin again. This is how we use the rule of the ban, for blessed are the peacemakers; they shall be called the children of God (Matt. 5[:9]).

A further question concerning the sword is whether a Christian may be a magistrate if he is chosen. We reply: When they wanted to make Christ a king he fled and again did not follow the ordinance of his Father (John 16[6:15]).[10] We do the same and follow him so that we may not walk in darkness. For the kingdom of Christ is not of this world. He says: Those who will follow me, must deny themselves, take up their cross and follow me (Matt. 15[16:24]). He forbids us the use of the sword when he says: The monarchs of the world rule the peoples and the authorities exercise force. But it shall not be so among you, for whoever wants to be regarded as a power-wielder must be your servant, and whoever wants to be first must be your slave (Matt. 20[:25-27]). Again, those whom God foreknew he decreed that they should conform to the image of his Son (Rom. 8[:29]). Peter also says that Christ suffered. He did not rule, but left us an example that we should follow in his footsteps.

Another question related to the sword is whether a Christian should judge in the worldly disputes and quarrels which unbelievers have with each other. Our witness is: Christ did not wish to and refused to be judge between brothers' strife over an inheritance (Luke 12[:13]). We desire to do likewise. It will be noted that it is our view that it is not proper for a Christian to be a magistrate. Why? Worldly rule is over physical life but Christian authority is over the spirit. Their houses and dwellings are material in this world; the dwelling of Christians is in heaven. Worldly citizenship belongs to this world, but Christian citizenship is in heaven. Their weapons of strife and war are material and used only against physical life. The Christian's weapons are spiritual and used against the fortress of the devil. Worldly people are protected with armour only against the flesh. Christians are equipped with the armour of God, truth, righteousness, peace, faith, salvation, and with the Word of God. Whatever the mind of Christ is must also be the mind of the members of the body of Christ to do and to fulfil. As Christ sought our salvation, so we should seek his praise in all things, so that nothing grows on his body which would violate it. Every kingdom that is divided against itself will fall. The members must be as is written about Christ, so that his body remains totally united for its own improvement and upbuilding.

Five. Concerning the memorial andSupper of the Lord Jesus Christ which he has ordered us to observe, we heartily confess and believe that all who desire to break the Lord's bread as the memorial of Christ's broken body, and all who desire to drink of this cup for the remembrance of the shed blood of Christ, must first be united by baptism to the one body of Christ of which Christ is the head. As Paul points out, we cannot at the same time participate in the Lord's cup and the cup of devils (1 Cor. 10[:21]). This means that all those who have fellowship with the dead works of darkness have no part in the light. Those who follow the devil have no part with those who have been called out of the world by God (2 Cor. 6[:14-16]). All who make their bed with evil have no part in the good. There is no possible alternative. Those who are not united by the call of God into one faith, to one baptism, in one Spirit, for one body with all the children of God, can also not be made one loaf with them. It has to be this way if the bread is broken in truth after the command of Christ (Matt. 26[:26-29]).[11] When he instituted the memorial of his death, the Lord Jesus took bread, thanked his Father, broke it and gave it to his disciples and said: Take, eat; this is my body. He took the cup, gave thanks, gave it to them and said: Drink of it, all of you, this is the cup of the new covenant in my blood, which is shed for many for the forgiveness of sins (Mark 14[:22-24]; Luke 22[:17-20]).

These words of Christ must be understood spiritually, for it is written: My flesh is useless. Rather, the words I speak are spirit and life (John 8[6:63]). From this one can plainly see that the Lord did not mean, as the preachers claim, that the material body of Christ was given to the disciples to eat in the bread. Not at all. Were that the case, he would have had to be broken before them and eaten, when in fact he was broken upon the cross later. Understanding it in the proper spiritual sense, then, he has been of the greatest benefit to us, for he was killed and died for our sin through which all who believe in his name are liberated and redeemed from death. This is what is meant by his words that whoever does not eat the flesh of the Son of Man and drinks his blood, has no life in him. If we believe with our whole heart that he is the true Son of God and the true saviour of all sent from God, who takes away our sin in his death, we truly eat Christ. Through the Holy Spirit we are brought to life, made holy and good, and partakers of Christ. This is the sense in which Christ gives the bread to his disciples and says: this is my body. It does not mean that his body is in the bread. It was only to show that even as he had broken the bread and given it to them he would give his body to be broken on the cross for them all so that through his death we might inherit life. He gives himself to his disciples and says: As often as you do it, do it as a memorial of me. A memorial sign or something by which one may remember is of two sorts. If Christ were always present in his body there would be no need to say that by it they should remember him until he returned. He would not have spoken of coming again if he was always present. He said: you always have the poor with you, but you do not always have me (Mark 14[:7]). He said the same thing about the cup. They did not literally drink his blood. It would have been of no use since what goes into the mouth goes into the stomach and out again in the natural way. It does the soul no good. Rather, he instituted the chalice of the New Testament, which is suffering. As they received it from his hand and all drank of it, they would be required to drink from the cup of the suffering of Christ with him. Were one to take a literal understanding of these words, listen to the words of Paul: This cup is the New Testament in my blood (1 Cor. 11[:25]). Accordingly the wine is in the blood and not, as the preachers say, the blood in the wine. Similarly, Christ spoke to the sons of Zebedee: You will drink the cup that I drink and be baptized with the baptism with which I am baptized. This shows that Christ himself also drank the cup, and he also said: If possible, let this cup pass from me. Yet not my, but thy will be done (Matt. 26[:39]). If, therefore, as the preachers say, Christ's blood is in the cup of wine, Christ would have drunk his own blood, which can't be. Rather, he shed his blood for our salvation on the tree of the cross. It all needs to be understood spiritually as stated above. The members of Christ will remember when they drink, that Christ the Son of God shed his blood for them. He told them: As often as you do it, do it as a remembrance of me. They drink the cup in faith, for they have been washed and cleansed from their sins through the blood of Christ. Thus the faithful drink of his blood. It is against God's own testimony to say that he is eaten physically for we read: He ascended into heaven and took his seat at the right hand of the Father. Further, it is written that the Most High does not dwell in temples made with hands. He is not cared for by human hands since he himself is the one who gives life and breath to all (Isa. 66[:1-2]; Acts 7[:47-50, :24-25]; 1 Kings 6[8:27]). All this shows clearly that he is not in the bread as the preachers say. He is not a God who allows himself to be handled by the godless hands of such shameful, godless, questionable people as monks and parsons who are addicted to immorality, idolatry, gluttony, drunkenness, blasphemy, and every evil. They give this idolatrous bread to the whores and liars, exploiters and deceivers of this world.

Christ observed the memorial of his suffering and death with his disciples and established it for those who are members of his body and of his flesh and bone. These are, as already said, one loaf and one bread in Christ. Therefore they are empowered to truly observe the memorial of his suffering and death and lawfully break the bread for the remembrance of the broken body of Christ in whom they have, by faith, been made into one loaf. All godless, sinful, and unrighteous people are excluded from it, for nothing unclean belongs to the body of Jesus Christ. Whoever lives in sin may not be a member of the body of Christ and cannot observe the memorial of his suffering and death in the right way because he cannot be one loaf with Christ since he is not reconciled, united, and at peace with him nor a member of his body.

The body of Christ must be understood for what it is, writes Paul, for whoever eats this bread and drinks from this cup of the Lord eats and drinks judgment upon himself in the sense that the body of Christ is not understood for what it is, that is, where no distinction is made between the true members of Christ and those who do not live and walk according to the will of Christ (1 Cor. 11[:29]).

To sum up, whatever our Lord Jesus has taught, prescribed and commanded us, namely to love him and to confess him with words and deeds, to testify to his Word with our deeds (John 10[:38]), to keep his commandments and acknowledge him as our example in all things we will do. We also confess and believe that all his faithful ones are obligated to follow him and not to be ashamed of him. After all, he says: Not all who say to me Lord, Lord, will enter the kingdom of heaven, but those who do the will of my heavenly Father (Matt. 7[:21]). The Father's will is that one should believe the Son and listen to him (Matt. 3[17:5]). That Son tells us that those who are not born again will not enter into the kingdom of God, for what is born of the flesh is flesh (John 3[:3, :6]). The lusts of the flesh are, writes Paul, adultery, fornication, uncleanness, idolatry, wrath, quarrelling, gluttony, drunkenness and the like. Those who do such things cannot inherit the kingdom of God (Gal. 5[:19-21]). For all who are of the flesh cannot please God. Christians, however, are not of the flesh but of the Spirit; whoever does not have the Spirit of Christ does not belong to Christ (Rom. 8[:9]). Where the Spirit of Christ is there the body is dead because of sin, but the spirit is alive because of righteousness (Rom. 6).

All who believe Christ and his words (to which Scripture abundantly testifies), are obedient to him and follow him, are, we believe, worthy of the name of Christ. All others, who may also say that they believe in Christ, but do not obey him or do what he taught and commanded, those, we say, are not Christians but anti-Christians.

This is a description of the papal church in which all things begun and done are directly opposed to Christ. They falsely boast of being Christians, for they desire to have Christ as a disguise for their shameful deeds (John 13[?]; Rom. 8[?]). Scripture says that all things must be confirmed by the evidence of two or three witnesses (Matt. 18[:16]).

People everywhere seek to purge their terrible wickedness with the pope's invented baptism of infants and from this same invented baptism take for themselves the beloved name of Christ even though they are fornicators, gluttons, drunkards, thieves, murderers and the like. However, the name Christian does not originate in baptism. To all this we will hold firmly with God's help for we have been buried with Christ in baptism (Col. 2[:12]). We confess our beloved Lord Jesus Christ and testify to him. As soon as, at the command of the Father, he had initiated the true righteousness, namely baptism, he was often persecuted and reviled, betrayed by Judas and horribly tortured under Pontius Pilate, and finally, although Pilate did not like to do it, condemned to death and crucified. With his death and his rose-red blood he achieved salvation for all who believe in him and faithfully follow him. His suffering will testify against all the rest to their condemnation. For whoever does not suffer with Christ, will also not inherit with him. Rom. 8[:17]; 2 Tim. 2[:11-12]; 1 John 5[:10-11]; Matt. 20 and the whole of Scripture teach us that Christ and all the prophets suffered persecution, cross, suffering, tribulation, and self-denial (Isa. 26[:16-18];

Matt. 5[:11]; 1 Pet. 3[:14, :17]). Then, after he had preached his comforting word to the spirits in prison, he rose from the dead in an indestructible and glorified body, and showed himself to his beloved disciples for forty days (Acts 1[:3]). After this he ascended in his body, and even as he ascended, he will come again. He sits now at the right hand of his Father. From there we await him according to Scripture. He will come in the clouds of heaven as the lightening, and many thousands of the holy angels with him (Matt. 24[:27, 25:31]; Mark 13[:26]; Luke 17[:24], 21[:27]; Rev. 19[:11-16]; Acts 7[:56], 17[:29]). The witness of Scripture is that Christ is in heaven, and not in temples made with hands. He will not be handled by human hands and therefore we have nothing to do with the pope's bread idol.

We also believe in the Holy Spirit, the comforter of all grieving and sorrowing hearts. He is sent from the Father through Christ Jesus into the hearts of all the faithful and elect as Christ had promised. Whoever does not have the Holy Spirit is no Christian. Whoever boasts of the Holy Spirit but does the works of the flesh is a liar, as Paul and Christ say at several places (Rom. 8[:9]; Gal. 1[?]; John 4[:23]; 1 John 3[:24], 4[:3]).

We also believe and know that there is a holy Christian church and a godly and Christian communion. This church is the body of Christ, and he, Christ, is the head and governs the whole body. This church is holy and without spot (Eph. 8[5:23, :27]). If an offensive member is found on the body which cannot be corrected in any way, it is expelled from the church and regarded as a heathen (Matt. 18[:17]). No other penalty is used in the Christian church (Mark 9[:43]). It was forbidden by Christ and he did not desire to rule in an earthly kingdom (Matt. 20[:22-23]; Mark 10[:39-40]). My kingdom, he said, is not of this world (John 6[:15], 15[18:36]). But to all authority, emperor, king, or regents we give interest, tithes, rents, discounts, and tax following the teaching of Paul and Peter, as long as it is not used for war (Rom. 13[:6-7]). Peter, the holy apostle, says that we should be subject to all human authority (1 Pet. 2[:13-14]). We also know how he himself did it when the government demanded from him what was contrary to God. He refused to obey like Daniel, Shadrach, Meshech, and Abednego, and many other examples in the Old and New Testament (Dan. 3, 6; 2 Matt. [Macc.] 7).

We also believe firmly with God's help that the Christian church has the key of David to loose from sin and to bind. Christ himself has given her this power (Matt. 16[:19], 18[:18]). Paul also used this power.

It is given to the Christian and not to the papal church (John 20[:22-23]; 1 Cor. 5[:3-5]).

Further, we also believe in this truth that all flesh will be raised up on the great day of the Lord and summoned before the judgment of God. There the Lord will make a judgment, and place the sheep on the right and the rams on the left. Then there will be one sheepfold and one shepherd, and hell will be the place of the rams (Ezek. 33; Dan. 13[12:1-2]; Matt. 25[:32-33]).

We also believe that following this mortal life there will be immortality, eternal life in the kingdom of God, but also eternal life in the lake of fire (Matt. 25[:34, :41]; Rev. 14[:10-11], 21[:8]).

This, then, is a brief confession of the ground of our faith in Christ. May God grant that it will be a good witness to you for eternal life and not for the destruction of your souls. Should anyone not be able to understand sufficiently what we have written, we will gladly give further testimony. If anyone detects something lacking which we have not dealt with here, we will be pleased to explain further to such as ask for the truth with godly earnestness, whatever God reveals and makes known to us. We beg everyone to receive it from us with goodwill and understand it with a humble heart before God. It is a puzzle to the world and can only be understood in the fear of God.

Please, judge, evaluate, and consider what you are doing. Keep God before you, for there is a judge before whom you must appear and give account for all innocent blood, which cannot be hidden (Joel 4[?]; Zech. 2[?]; Isa. 25[?]. We will not ourselves jump into the well, but if someone throws us in we will suffer it patiently and commit it to God. He will, in his own time, give to everyone according to what has been done (Matt. 16[:27]). We desire good for everyone, do not desire and will not do anyone harm whether pope, monks, or priests, emperor or king, or any other creature (1 John 5[:2-3]; Rom. 2[?]; Sir. 9[?]). Our conscience is free, clean, and unencumbered; we have taken no evil deed or vengeance into our hearts. We will gladly, joyfully and with great patience suffer whatever God allows you to do to us. We know that you cannot do to us more than that. Had the godly Joseph surrendered to the villainy of the whore, alas, he would have been her slave. He was godly and so he had to be thrown into prison because of her false witness. But the Lord transformed his bondage and tribulation into great joy (Gen. 39).

In the same way, even if the Babylonian whore accuses us wrongfully with her lies and we are brought into prison, we have the certain hope and do not doubt that God will liberate us out of this misery to joy in his own time as Christ has promised us (John 16[:22]). We have sorrow for you, for we are concerned that you will wrongly lay hands on the pious witnesses of God. The word of the cross is really a mockery to you, but to us it is the power of God. You are zealous for Christ and fervently desire to go with him to heaven, but the zeal to suffer with him and to descend with him into hell is not to your taste (1 Cor. 1[?]). Whoever will not eat the bitter herbs, will not eat the Passover lamb in all eternity (Exod. 12[:8]).[12]

We commit ourselves to God, into the shelter and covering of the Most High who will help us drink the cup of suffering. Amen.

Written at Trieste on the Adriatic.

22

Hans Umlauft

A Letter to Stephan Rauchenecker (1539)*

Introduction

Hans Umlauft (fl.1539-40) was from Raisenberg in Meichsen, Saxony. Little is known about his earlier years; his Anabaptist story is linked with his presence in Regensburg starting around 1537. Sources state that Umlauft was a shoemaker. In fact, he was an exceptional shoemaker, for he also wrote Latin, knew Greek and kept abreast of current reformation literature including that of the Anabaptists. This knowledge leads to the suggestion that before his career as a shoemaker, and his marriage, he had been a priest or a monk. Umlauft became an Anabaptist in 1539. He was baptized by Georg Hueter, a missionary from Austerlitz, Moravia.[1]

Umlauft's story picks up in Regensburg, where he had more than one run-in with the town council. He had been imprisoned in June of 1537 and then two years later in November of 1539, the latter time on charges of Anabaptist behaviour. Umlauft's 1539 arrest is important because it may have made the council aware of an Anabaptist presence in the city, which led to firmer action from the authorities. The Regensburg

---

*Source: Schornbaum, *Quellen V*, 63-71.
Translation: Friesen/Klaassen

council, however, was uncertain as to how to handle the situation. They were afraid of King Ferdinand's possible involvement if he found out that Regensburg was lenient toward Anabaptists. All the same, the council did not want bloodshed either, so it sent a letter to Nuremberg asking for advice on how to treat the prisoners. The case of Umlauft was made more difficult because he had broken his earlier promise to desist from illegal religious activity. In 1537 he had been expelled from the city, but he had since returned and had secretly instructed others.

Ultimately Regensburg followed the advice of the Nuremberg authorities: Umlauft was to be released only upon signing a written recantation. If he refused he was to be placed in the pillory, flogged, and exiled forever from the city. To appease Ferdinand, Regensberg issued an anti-Anabaptist decree so as to leave the impression that the council was taking appropriately severe action.

After eight months in prison, Umlauft finally recanted on July 16, 1540 before a crowd of about two thousand. Once he was released, he moved to Moravia and "relapsed" into Anabaptist errors.[2]

The letter included here was probably written earlier than his 1539 imprisonment and therefore before he became an Anabaptist, because the letter does not mention prison time.[3] The letter provides insight into Umlauft's pre-Anabaptist ideas, which could be described as sacramentist. The letter itself is a response to charges that Umlauft was part of a "heretical, seductive, and insurrectionsist" sect. At issue was his view of the Lord's Supper of which he rejected both old and new papists because they sought Christ in "water and bread" or in the "dead letter, which you call the Word of God, even though it is only a witness of his Word."

Umlauft obviously identified with a reform party that was neither Catholic nor Lutheran but more radical. And if his position on the eucharist qualified him as a sacramentist, his view on the Scriptures would qualify him a spiritualist. He cites Denck's "Recantation" verbatim and although he considered the Scriptures "higher than all human treasures, he did not consider them as high as the Word of God." Umlauft called for a congregational life and discipline not unlike that prescribed in the Swiss and other early Anabaptist orders.[4]

Bibliographical Sources:

Gerhard Hein, "Umlauft, Hans," ML 4, 381.
Werner O. Packull, *Hutterite Beginnings, Communitarian Experiments during the Reformation* (Baltimore, MD: John Hopkins University Press, 1995).

Hans Umlauft to Stephan Rauchenecker, 1539.

Hans Umlauft to Stephan (Rauchenecker?). End of October 1539 or beginning of November (?), Regensburg.

My dear Stephan, I have read the letter which you sent to Balthasar with much anguish on account of the great blasphemy as well as of the reprehensible judging done in this letter, which a Christian ought not to consider, much less do. From it I can sense and judge that you have sharpened your tongue like a sword [Ps. 64:3] and you consider how you can oppress and bring down pious and honest people. For I understand from your letter that they are suspect and an abomination to you with their teaching and their lives, Wisd. 2[:12]; Prov. 13[:8, :5, :9, :19], 29[:7, :10, :27]. This same thing was done by Haman. Because Mordecai would not bend his knee or worship him, he was full of anger and sought to destroy Mordecai's people, Esther 3. Therefore we must seriously cry to God that he might hide us from the assembly of the wicked and from the host of evildoers, Ps. 64[:2]. We pray that he may hide us in secret with him from everyone's pride and cover us in his tabernacle from quarrelsome tongues, Ps. 31[:20], and under the shadow of his wings, give us refuge till the wickedness passes by, Ps. 17[:7], 57[:1]; Rev. 12[:6, :14]. With David we pray: "Oh that we had wings like a dove! For then would we fly away, and be at rest. Lo, then would we wander far off and remain in the wilderness. We would hasten our escape from the windy storm and tempest," Ps. 55[:6-8]. All the while they carefully aim their arrows at us. Such arrows are nothing else than their lies and malicious words, Jer. 9[:2, :7]; Ps. 120[:3-4], with which to destroy the body and soul of the righteous, Ezek. 22[:25ff]. They gnash their teeth against them, string their bow, that is, their tongue, and lay their arrows on the string that they might bring down the distressed and the poor, and butcher those who walk uprightly in the way, Ps. 11[:2]; Acts 5[:28, :40]. They harbour enmity against them Ps. 55[:3], and lie in wait to kill the innocent secretly in their soul through their poisonous teaching or in their body on the charge of insurrection, heresy, and seduction, or whatever they invent as the reason. Sometimes it is because of the evil intention of one or several persons, as it was in the time of the apostles, to bring others into suspicion, to slander and condemn them. For their feet are swift to shed blood, Rom. 3[:15]. They invent false words about the rejected in the land and say, "Look, look, the bleary-eyed ones." Iscariot was a traitor and the Corinthian a fornicator: "Look, look, these are like that also." The pious Davidites must all suffer these things and be silent like the deaf who do not open their mouth, have no reply to make Ps. 39[:2], and may neither read nor write the truth openly. The reason is that through such wickedness, ways and paths are closed to the Davidites; they achieve it with their lies Ezek. 13[:8], in order to support their bellies and their covetousness, 2 Pet. 2[:3]; Rom. 16[:18].

The righteous man, however, rejoices in the Lord. Whoever is in Christ and in whom Christ is and remains, John 15[:4]; Gal. 2[:20], that man is righteous and rejoices in the Lord with good reason, since [the Lord] has thus redeemed and saved him, Ps. 57[:1]. But the papists, whether they be of the old or the new pope, cannot rejoice in the Lord for he is not in them. They seek him outside of themselves in water and bread or through other strange doors, John 10[:1]. If he were in them, they would not need to seek him elsewhere. Yes, they have virtually lost him outside of themselves as well.

Yes, they [the righteous] also all trust in him and all upright in heart boast in it, Ps. 64[:30]. The result of the peace and trust of the righteous is much glory, Prov. 28[:1?], because God shelters and protects them, Ps. 5[:11]. They glory in that they understand God their Saviour and know him, not through the dead letter which you call God's Word, since it is only a witness of His Word, but through the indwelling of Christ, Gal. 2[:20], cessation from sin, 1 Pet. 4[:1ff]; Rom. 6[:6], and lowliness before the world, 1 Cor. 1[:27], 2[:1ff] one is raised up, and becomes righteous before God in one's heart, Luke 2[:79]. Such a person of high degree should rejoice in lowliness, James 1[:9]. Thus one is in Christ and may glory in the Lord, 1 Cor. 1[:31], the crucified, 1 Cor. 2[:2], in that one enters through Him as through a door, John 10[:1]; Matt. 7[:13], that is, through much tribulation, Acts 14[:22], and thus one rejoices in tribulations, Rom. 5[:3], in the cross of Christ, Gal. 6[:14].

But the old and the new pope cannot rejoice thus in the Lord, because [the Lord] is not in them and since they do not seek to enter in this way, but loathe such food. They indeed hope for future glory and joy, Rom. 5[:2], yes, and are even sure and certain that they will inherit with Christ, but suffer with him they will not. Therefore they will also not reign nor inherit with him, Rom. 8[:17]; 2 Thess. 2[:12], nor will they enter with their threat of force, Luke 13[:25ff]; Matt. 16[:24ff]. Yes, it is easy to suffer and witness for Christ by riding high on horses, and with nothing lacking. They put a few beautiful crosses on their horses or something similar, which is really nothing to boast about. The real yoke is too bitter for their stomachs. O, they talk about such boasting, that one should know and recognize the Lord, Jer. 9[:23]. They say the words but, as was said, do not know him themselves, nor where he is. They do not know him spiritually because they deny him with their works and deeds, Titus 1[:16]. Thus all their boasting comes to nothing. They boast that their meetings are Christian, convince the people to believe that it is all true when in fact they have never begun it.

How can it be a Christian congregation when no Christian order or commands are kept such as separation, banning, disciplining, brotherly love and other things, and that one may openly speak after another and present his gifts and revelations clearly before the people for their improvement, 1 Cor. 14[:26]? They do not even know what a Christian brotherhood is, let alone boast that they have it. They have no God because they are transgressors and are not found in the straight teaching and commands of Christ, 2 John 1[:9]. They shout into the wind in vain without any improvement of the heart either last year or this year. They charge that the people have no desire to improve, when in fact it is they as leaders who are guilty of this lack of improvement. They are blind leaders of the blind, seducing the people along with themselves and confirming them in their unrighteousness. Therefore, eternal God, protect all those of a good heart from their destruction, and strengthen, build, lead and keep them in [your] knowledge, love, gentleness, friendliness, long-suffering, patience and other fruits of the Spirit, so that we may grow and increase in a godly, quiet manner without blame in the only saving name of Jesus and in true faith in him. In him and in no one else we do and leave undone, and fulfil our life, cross and death to his praise 1 Pet. 2[:6]. Thus we never come to shame. Such faith is without envy, quarrelling, hatred, wrangling, anger, uncontrolled resentment, scolding, insincerity, bitter passion, evil manners, selfish unlovely fruit or works of the flesh.

To your statement, however, that there is no Word of God except the spoken or written we reply:

If the Scriptures are the Word of God as you say, why did they become a snare and ground for retribution, Matt. 22[:15-22]? Again, all those who did not hear it, and all those who lived the three thousand years before the written Word from Adam to Moses would be damned. It would also follow that the kingdom of God would have to come into us from outside. That would be to deny the living Word, the Spirit and the work of God. In fact, Christ says in Luke 17[:20ff]: "The kingdom of God is not a matter of outward observances but is inside of you." John 5[:39] says: "Search the Scriptures, for in them you think you have eternal life; they testify to me." If, then, they are only a witness of his Word, then they are not themselves God's Word. All the children would also have to be damned who are deprived of hearing the outer word. But Christ called them blessed and presents them to us all as a model and example of innocence, Matt. 18[:3], 19[:14]. Therefore one must ascribe salvation to the inward living Word of God alone, which to the ancients was Christ. It must not be tied in any way to the outer word or the Scriptures, however useful they may be to those whose mind is enlightened by God. The outer word was given as a witness only for the sake of the arguers who deny and do not want to know what they have in themselves, Deut. 30[:14]. Whoever heeds the inner Word in his heart and sees the light that has been set up and lit in him, Matt. 6[:23]; Ps. 5[:11], will leap for joy in his heart, indeed, leap out from inside and give a witness to the external word so that no godless person can withstand him nor excuse himself further, as Paul tells the first Christians, 1 Cor. 11[:1]. Therefore the Scriptures and outer word remain only the witness and light of the living Word of God.

The Holy Scriptures, says Hans Denck, I count above all human treasure, but not as highly as the Word of God, which is alive, powerful and eternal, and which is free and unencumbered from all elements of this world. For as it is God himself, it is Spirit and no letter, written without pen or ink, so that it can never be erased. Therefore, also salvation or the Word of God is not bound to Scriptures. And this is the reason: it is not possible for Scripture to improve an evil heart, even though it is highly educated. A pious heart, however, that is, where there is a real spark or godly zeal, is improved by all things. Thus Holy Scripture is pure to the pure. To believers it acts for good and blessedness, but to the impure and to the unbelievers it is impure and brings damnation. Thus a person who is chosen by God can be saved without preaching or Scripture. Not that on account of this one should not hear any witness taught by God, nor read the Scriptures, but that otherwise no unlearned persons could be saved because they could not read, and that many whole cities and countries [are lost] because they have no preachers sent by God.[5]

All this serves to make us hunger for God and his Word and that we might not beat about with the dead letter of Scripture with such certainty. Rather, we give Scripture the honour due and allow it to be a lantern and a sheath of the Word, knowing that something more belongs to it, namely a sword in the sheath and a light in the lantern, if they are to shine and to cut.

When we say this some say it is a despising of Scripture, and that one cannot honour it too much. It is like the matter of honouring Mary. If Mary is given the honour due only to God, that is making an idol of Mary, as is also the case with Scripture. It is put in the place of God, and given honour and worship. We are expected to be terrified of it as of some relic, to read it with trembling in the fear of God and, as was said, to count it above all human treasures, John 5[:39]; Acts 17[:11]; Matt. 13[:44-46]; 2 Tim. 3[:16]. However, one is not to place it alongside of God and his Word, for he will not give his honour to any created thing. Scripture is all good things to the good as also is the law, to those alone who use it correctly, 1 Tim. 1[:8]. But judging from the way many now self-confidently use it, it would be better if they were sleeping. For it is from the misunderstanding and the misuse of Scripture that all heresies, superstition, and sects flow; so that not only the Jews but also the Turks make use of it, and consider Holy Scripture the basis and foundation of their beliefs.

Further you write that we have no faith, Word nor sacrament and cannot pray to God nor be saved. Even if this were true—from which our gracious Father defend us—you ought not to judge, condemn, nor deny salvation to anyone. Remember that we are humans and just as human as you and your kind, created after the image of God and his handiwork. His law, will and Word is written in our hearts, Rom. 2[:15]. You should grant us the same merciful God you claim for yourself. For God is a God of the heathen also and not a respecter of persons, but whoever among all people fears God and does right is acceptable to him, Acts 10[:35]. At all times and to the end Dan. 11[:16, :30, :36, :41] he has scattered his church. At his coming he will gather the dispersed true Israel from the four winds and corners of the world. Thus also Ruth, a Moabitess and a heathen, was included in the genealogy of Christ, Matt. 1[:5]. From this I conclude that many children of Abraham hewn from stone are among the heathen, Matt. 3[:9], Rom. 9[:8]. Thus the impartial God was pleased with Adam, Abel, Enoch, Noah, Job, and Abraham, who was a heathen before his circumcision. [He also accepted] Naaman the Syrian, Cyrus the Persian king, the king of Babylon Nebuchadnezzar, Nathaniel, the eunuch Moor [Acts 8:26], Acts 2[:9ff], and Cornelius before he had received the external circumcision in baptism. God has not bound his mercy and people so much to external elements and ceremonies. We ought properly to take this to heart and judge no one. We should let God be available to all impartially, since he is no respecter of persons. We should not claim God for ourselves in a partisan spirit as the Jews did. They had to learn the opposite against their will as the Acts of the Apostles shows throughout. [We should stop thinking] that all other people who do not share our views or belong to our group are nothing but pagans. God can make children of Abraham even from stones. We ought well to listen carefully to the saying of Christ that many from the east and from the west (who have been called Turks and heathens) will come and sit at table with Abraham in the kingdom of God [Matt. 11:11]. In contrast the children of the kingdom (that is the ostensible Christians and Jews who want to sit in front and expect God to be their own) will be thrust out. A reversal will take place; the first shall be last, the last the first [Matt. 20:30].

We Gentiles should count ourselves fortunate since we are bastards and strangers in this testament and covenant of grace. We are in our faith a wild olive tree, gentiles grafted onto Christ, Abraham's seed and the true olive tree, Rom. 11[:17].

Augustine in his time considered Donatists and Circumcellions to be heretics. But you and your adherents cannot prove nor establish that heretics of that opinion, which you consider us to be, exist in our times. I might still answer many writings but do not consider it necessary since it would waste much good time and not be to God's praise. Hence I will not do it.

May the Word of God alone be judge of my writing, John 12[:47], and over myself may every Christian government which bears the sword in the place of God be my judge, Rom. 13[:1ff]. With Paul, I ask nothing except examination, judgment and justice, and by it I will let myself be treated well or ill. But where there is nothing but grim force and tyranny through the instigation of some individuals, there I shall make use of the example of Paul at Damascus and not await the conspiracy of the forty [Acts 9:23ff, 23:13], but flee and escape as Christ commands us, Matt. 10[:23], as long as God wills. But I will do it only insofar as it does not tempt him and so that I do not expose others to their anger and rage. Wherever it may be done without violence to God's Word and without harming of the believers I will do it. When, however, the time and hour of my dying is here, no fleeing will help. However, by Jesus Christ and by his last judgment I beg, admonish and warn all those to whom God has given the sword that they do not use it on the instructions of the preachers against the blood of the innocent whether to arrest, expel, torture, hang, drown, or burn. For truly I tell them, the tortured and spilled blood will cry up to heaven to God in accusation together with the innocent blood of pious Abel [Matt. 23:34ff] against these Cains and shedders of blood. He will demand it from their hands and pour out over them and their children his retribution. For whoever sheds human blood (that is, contrary to the order of divine justice), his blood, as God himself says, is to be shed also, Gen. 9[:6]. Whoever takes and uses the sword will also perish by the sword, Matt. 26[:52]. Therefore take heed, O magistrates, what you do. King Jehoshaphat said in the Spirit of God to his judges, 2 Chron. 19[:6ff]: "You have not the office from men but of God and what you judge will come upon you. See to it that you have the fear of God and do everything diligently. There is no evil with God nor respect of persons nor requirement of myrrh and gifts." Take care, take care, oh magistrates, that you do not pollute and wash your hands in the blood of the innocent. You know how things went with the murderer Herod [Matt. 2:16], the fox and whitewashed wall, the priest and bishop Ananias, [Acts 23:2ff], and the criminal judge Pontius Pilate. Remember that you too are subject to a judge in heaven who will judge you with the judgment of Adoni Bezech, Judith [? Josh. 10:26], which you measured out to the others; you cannot escape his sentence. Nor will it help you to say: I had to do it, my lord commanded me. The same is done by our priests and preachers. It is wrong; one must obey God more than man [Acts 5:29]. Pilate also wanted to be a friend of the emperor rather than of the innocent Christ and feared the loss of his position and goods. What good is the emperor to him now? Where is his office? What good do his goods do him? Yes, the emperor for all his power, positions and wealth, could not come to your aid with a drop of cool water [Luke 16:24]. This is what happened to the rich man, Luke 16. Before long God will not receive anything in grace from the unjust magistrates (nor unjust subjects either), even if they sponsored and built [churches] right up to heaven, if they moved mountains and distributed all their goods to the poor. The Spirit of God declares through Isa. 1 and says to the government: "Hear the word of the Lord, you rulers of Sodom; give ear to the law of our God, you people of Gomorrah. What purpose is the multitude of your sacrifices to me? says the Lord: I am full of the burnt offerings of rams, and when you make many prayers, I will not hear: your hands are full of blood. Wash and make yourselves clean; put away the evil of your conspiracies from before my face. Stop burdening me. Learn to do good. Learn to know justice. Relieve the oppressed.

Give justice to the fatherless, assist the widows. Come to me, I beg you. Let us be justified says the Lord. Though your sins be as a scarlet thread, they shall be white as snow" [Isa. 1:10, :15-16].

With this small writing I give you farewell. May the Lord, the almighty God, open his hand and fill you with many divine gifts, spread his wings above you, and keep you under them blameless until the great revelation of the glory of his chosen ones. He will come soon, to liberate his people and you. Amen. Through Christ Jesus our dear Lord and Saviour. Amen.

23

Helena von Freyberg

Helena von Freyberg, Confession (as follows) on Account of her sin. (1535-45)*

The story of Helena von Freyberg is one of the most intriguing in the Austrian territory of Tyrol. That a person from the upper classes would even consider taking the risk of being baptized as an adult was already unusual. Even more unusual were the choices she made to leave her native Tyrol and trade a comfortable life in her castle at Münichau for a life of exile.[1]

Helena was linked to Pilgrim Marpeck, the prominent Anabaptist leader. Her father Gilg and Pilgram's father Heinrich had been friends in Rattenberg and Helena maintained the link to Pilgrim throughout her life.

Helena married a nobleman of Swiss-Bavarian descent by the name of Onophrius von Freyberg. Legend has it that Martin Luther visited Onophrius in his castle at Hohenaschau in 1518. If this event did take place, and if Helena had been present, it would have been her first exposure to Reformation ideas.[2]

---

*Source: *Das Kunstbuch*, No. 28, fol.243r.-246r. From the Mennonite Historical Library, Goshen, IN.
Translation: Linda Huebert Hecht

In 1523, Elizabeth von Frauenberg, Helena's widowed stepmother, relinquished all her rights to the castle at Münichau in order to free herself of a debt of 5000 gulden. Onophrius was the official owner of the property, but Helena occupied the castle and soon made it a centre of Anabaptist activity, despite the fact that her husband chose to remain a Lutheran.

The first mention of Helena in the Tyrolean court records was in a report of March 7, 1528. It states that she and her whole household had been baptized. If this report proved to be correct, local officials had the right to confiscate her property and goods, but it would take almost two years before the proof needed to arrest her was obtained.

The "castle church" that Helena set up at Münichau flourished under her patronage for more than two years, from the fall of 1527 to December of 1529. Here Anabaptists found refuge; Helena herself was head of the congregation.[3] In April of 1529 Helena's husband declared to the government that he was not an Anabaptist while she continued her Anabaptist involvement, providing financial as well as moral support to various members. The government emphasized the work of male Anabaptist leaders, hoping to eliminate the leaders so that the movement would collapse. Since Anabaptism was entrenched in the grass roots, this of course did not happen. But the government miscalculated in another way. While they were obliged to use caution so as not to violate the rights of the nobility, they did not, in these early years, perceive Helena to be a leader among the Anabaptists.[4]

Finally in late 1529, an order for Helena's arrest was issued after testimony of a recanting Anabaptist verified that she was indeed a baptized member. Helena did not react passively. She fled to Bavaria, to her husband's residence. Then, as authorities continued to pursue her, she fled again, ultimately leaving her homeland completely. In July of 1530 Helena was given the opportunity to return if she recanted, but she settled in Constance instead and soon was involved in activities similar to those for which she had been forced to leave Tyrol. Ignoring warnings from city officials, she carried on as she had in Tyrol for the next two years. The city council finally dispossessed Helena of the property she owned in Constance in 1532.

In 1533 Helena decided to recant and return to her husband. But while she was only willing to do so privately, the authorities were determined to have her recant before as many people as possible. It was believed that a public recantation by such an influential Anabaptist would do more damage to the growing Anabaptist movement than any other means that the Protestant authorities of Constance could come up with on their own. Unfortunately for them, Helena ultimately won, recanting in private before the viceroy, a lower-order government official at Innsbruck. Instead of staying in Tyrol, however, Helena moved to Augsburg, where she spent the last eleven years of her life in the company of Anabaptists. Her departure verifies that she had by no means relinquished her Anabaptist faith. Like so many other recanting Anabaptists, she had made a compromise to buy time and her life.[5]

After the defeat of the Anabaptists at Münster in 1535, the governments of Europe became more suspicious of Anabaptists, even in more tolerant cities like Augsburg. Helena was arrested on April 4, 1535 with a group of Anabaptists who had met in a cave near Augsburg. Because Anabaptist meetings were conducted at her home, Helena was required to appear before the city council and give an account of her actions. She ultimately was punished, laid in chains overnight and the next day was expelled from the city. Four years later, after her sons wrote a letter to the Augsburg city council vouching for the Christian character of their mother, Helena was allowed to return to Augsburg where, as far as we know, she remained until her death in 1545.

Helena's confession, which follows, could be called her spiritual autobiography. It is unusual to have something written by an Anabaptist woman, since the majority of the sixteenth-century population could not read and write. At the same time, it is rare to gain insight into the spiritual life and process of development of an Anabaptist, especially a lay leader. The preservation of this confession in the *Kunstbuch*, a book of writings by various members of Marpeck's circle, makes it possible for us to learn more about Helena, the spirituality of the Marpeck circle, and the patient form of fraternal discipline practiced by the followers of Pilgram Marpeck.[6] The specific "sin" of which Helena repents in her confession is not recorded or known. It may have been related to her recantation, or may have had to do more with prideful words and actions.

Bibliographical Source:

C. Arnold Snyder and Linda A. Huebert Hecht, eds., *Profiles of Anabaptist Women: Sixteenth-Century Reforming Pioneers* (Waterloo, ON: Wilfrid Laurier University Press, 1996).

Helena von Freyberg, Confession (as follows) on account of her sin

Beloved in God, I ask you through God's will that you hear my accusation of myself, and the recognition of my guilt, in writing, since I truly cannot speak of it with my mouth, without turning red with shame, for flesh and blood have refused to confront it, sought escape where possible and remained silent when I have tried for a long time in the past (to deal with it).[7] And so flesh and blood must for this (and can no longer avoid it) be disgraced due to its malice (and trickery). The devil has covered me over many times, and distorted the light and made me white while I was black, and perverted the Holy Spirit into a spirit of the flesh. This is what [the devil] does in all spiritual things, he presents himself as if he were white as an angel (and very humble). But God my Lord is even stronger and deprives him of his power and might through Jesus Christ, His beloved Son. To Him be honour and praise. Amen.

First of all: I confess and from the bottom of my heart acknowledge my guilt before God and all his saints in Heaven and on earth, how I have sinned and incurred guilt in the matter which has now been revealed to me by God's grace through the goodness of the Holy Spirit through the mercy and goodness of God my Lord and Father. God does not neglect to discipline his wicked quarrelsome child; unfortunately I have rebelled against God and as a result I have lost the grace of the Holy Spirit.

The fruit of the [Holy Spirit], patience, righteousness, gentleness, humility, kindness, true love, faithfulness, peace, self-discipline, no longer can be seen, which mocks true faith and the Word of God. From the bottom of my heart I am guilty of great impatience before godly discipline and punishment, which has resulted in the bitterness of my heart, in many unfruitful, irresponsible words and behaviour. Also, [I confess] that I have carelessly sworn by the name of God and in disobedience to the Holy Gospel, have not followed its rule, the teachings of Christ my Lord (and Redeemer), where he says, learn of me, I am gentle, patient and humble from the bottom of my heart; He was patient and did not object when injustice was done to him, and yet I do not want to suffer because of my guilt. This is far from the mind of Christ, which a Christian should also have; for children of the Heavenly Father should have his nature. Christ teaches us to leave ourselves and the life of self behind, not to seek ourselves, and to follow him in power, in simplicity and uprightness, like a child without falseness or deceit.

I also confess that my prayer is not righteous, for I do not gladly allow the Lord's will to happen in me, in that I resist what goes against my will or wants to break it.

I am guilty from the bottom of my heart, of not being genuinely god-fearing, of not having God constantly in my sight, therefore I lack the godly wisdom that comes from the fear of God. I exhibit this in my walk; I barely grow or increase in the body of Christ, as an old woman in the faith [should], so that I feel worthless and shameful before God and His own. I am weak, miserable, luke warm and tired in my watching and praying. Wherefore all my trouble has befallen me. In this I have only myself to blame and no one else.

I confess myself to be guilty and to have failed completely in loving God first and my brother, and have broken the command of God, wherein the whole law is contained, that is in forbearance and kindness. For love has no evil passion, and is neither contrary nor complaining, boastful or puffed up, is not undisciplined, bitter or ever angry. Love endures and forbears all things, and trusts that all will go well, has no evil suspicion, does everything for the best according the prompting of the Holy Spirit, and also does not seek its own advantage.

In all this I have failed and broken [faith]. I wanted to teach and discipline my brother, but I was not teachable or amenable to discipline myself. I have sought the twig in him, and not seen the beam in my own eye. Also, I have been troublesome in the way I have acted towards my brother and foremostly in my great impatience, with which I caused anger and great impatience, from which regretfully no good thing followed and happened. Thus the fault is mine alone and falls on me and no one else.

Especially I have sinned and become guilty concerning those in civil authority, (*Hündt*)[8] about which I was spoken to in the beginning; according to my understanding and intention it was not sinful according to the evangelical order. I have resisted at this point with impatience and tactlessness in word and deed. I forcefully wanted to retain the freedom which I thought I had, not wanting to be restricted or compelled, seeking my own good to the detriment of my neighbour, which caused my brother to stumble, resulting in his vexation. In this I did not take into consideration the love of or the good of my brother, and have loved the creature for its own sake. This I confess before God and his own. I have been completely uncooperative and impatient towards those who have resisted me in this. I have often wanted to separate myself from them. In all of this I confess that I have done wrong, above all with those in civil authority [*Hündt*] (having the improper attitude and excessive conduct). Unfortunately, I have not been able to understand it otherwise until now, but God has revealed it to me, through His Holy favourable (charitable) Spirit, to whom be praise eternally. Amen.

Thus, I am guilty from the bottom of my heart of committing a sin and becoming indebted to God and my brothers and neighbours, [both] knowingly and in ignorance as God my Lord knows best for me, inwardly and outwardly. Because of me the name of God has been blasphemed. Consequently, many evil, careless, unfruitful, and blasphemous words have been said before God.

I confess before God, that I well deserve every punishment because of my sin and guilt, yes probably even more than He has given me, and am worthy only of humiliation, disgrace and ridicule. Surely it would not have been a wonder, for all that I have deserved from God, if He had readily allowed me to perish. But God acts as a faithful father to his angry, quarrelsome child, and punishes me until I become aware of [my sin]. Due to the great love from God (through Christ) I have experienced grace and mercy (which will speak for me at the judgment); to God be given thanks eternally.

So I am in the same position as the lost son: I have made a useless mistake, with what my Lord and God the Father (in grace) has given me, yes have used it unfruitfully. I said, I am no longer worthy to be called his child, and I say along with public sinners, God be gracious and merciful, and forgive me (needy as I am) my sin and transgression and provide (for me the poor one) a perfect and appropriate repentance in all yieldedness [*Gelassenheit*], humility and self-denial through the holy blood of Jesus Christ. For I am sorry from the bottom of my heart, God knows what I have done. Therefore I also ask His holy congregation, especially here at Augsburg, whom I have offended greatly, in particular Pilgram [Marpeck] and Valtin [Werner?], to forgive and pardon what I have done against them, for which I am sorry from the bottom of my heart (as previously mentioned) and as God knows. And now however, the consolation and assurance in the shedding of the holy blood of Jesus Christ my God and Lord, promise sanctification and reconciliation. For He says that in the hour in which sinners sigh in their hearts over their sins, they are forgiven. To this I cling in faith, that my sins are forgiven through Jesus Christ, which prepares me for death. This I say in praise, honour and thanks for God's great grace and mercy, to whom be praise, honour and laud from eternity to eternity. Amen.

I ask and plead with God from the depths of my heart through Jesus Christ and through the intercession of the saints and children of God and his holy congregation (whom the Lord knows) whom I ask from the bottom of my heart (and it is also my wish) that they would pray on my behalf (to God) for help and strength, that in future I may withstand all that is opposed to God, end my life following God's will, to the honour and praise of his holy name. Amen.

Thus, I yield myself to the discipline and punishment of God my heavenly father, his holy congregation and Christian church as long and however much, as is pleasing to the Holy Spirit, and may the will of God be done in me according to his grace (along with all those who desire it and who are in need). Amen.

This is at present my will and final decision. May God the Lord require of me whatever he wills. I forgive (forget) and pardon from the bottom of my heart those whom I suppose to have done things against me. I ask God also to forgive and pardon them, yes that God would give them grace to help them recognize their sin (as I have done through God's grace). Amen.

Laus Deo

24

Paul Glock

Letter to his Wife Else
(1563)*

Introduction

Sometimes referred to as "the young" to distinguish him from his father who bore the same name, Paul Glock (c.1530-1585) is an almost legendary figure in Hutterite history. He was born in Rommelshausen, near Waiblingen in the region of Württemberg, and had a rather wild youth until he embraced Hutterite Anabaptism in his late teens.

He was imprisoned for the first time in 1550, along with his father, mother and wife, Else. Little is known about Glock's initial imprisonment except that at some point, he found his way to freedom. In June of 1558 he was arrested again and sent to Stuttgart. He was cross-examined under torture and in autumn of 1558 was transferred to Hohenwittlingen Castle as a recalcitrant Anabaptist. Jailed because

---

*Source: Bossert, *Quellen I*, 1065-78.
Translation: Friesen/Klaassen

he would not recant, Glock spent the next nineteen years of his life at Hohenwittlingen, debating on and off with various Lutheran spokesmen about his faith as compared to theirs.

His time in prison was varied; sometimes his accusers were lenient and sometimes they were not. At first he was tortured in various attempts to win him over, but without success. After a while he was left alone, and after a few years he was allowed the freedom to walk around the courtyard but was not allowed to speak to anyone, lest they be led astray by his "false teaching."[1]

In the various debates in which Glock took part, the concerns centred around four points: infant baptism, the Eucharist, the state and the use of the sword, and the swearing of oaths.[2] It was because of these debates that Glock's confession of faith, as well as his defence, were written for his opponents.

In 1563, the beginning of his thirteenth year in Hohenwittlingen, an exchange of epistles began between Glock and the Hutterites in Moravia. This was made possible because he had gained the sympathy and trust of the warden Klaus von Grafeneck and his wife, who supplied him with paper and ink.[3] Over the next six years he corresponded with his wife, the leaders of the Moravian Hutterites and the community at large.

In 1566, his cell was left unlocked for a full six months, and Glock was sent out as a messenger on the promise that he would come back, which he did without fail. This freedom apparently was part of a larger strategy. His Lutheran opponents had hoped that Glock would concede certain doctrines so that they could report that Glock had yielded and they in turn had graciously granted him this freedom. When Glock refused to yield, he was put into solitary confinement.

The following year he suffered from a severe case of scurvy due to his poor diet; he wavered between life and death for twelve days. Meat and medicine sent from Moravia saved him, as the medicine was a cooked berry juice concentrate full of vitamins. Although the Hutterites knew nothing of vitamins, they knew that this was an efficacious remedy.[4]

In 1569 prison life again improved for Glock. He was moved from his solitary cell to a better, well-heated one where his bread and broth diet was replaced by two daily meals of wine, meat or fish and baked goods. He was also supplied with clothing and blankets which made his life as a prisoner better than life had become outside the prison, due to a general famine in the land.

When fire broke out in the prison in 1576, Glock, along with fellow Anabaptist inmate Matthias Binder, were influential in putting it out. Afterwards they officially requested to be set free as they had never harmed anyone. Before the Lutheran ministers, who were still trying to convert Glock, could react, the prince had commanded their release and had ordered a travelling allowance for them to reach Moravia. On New Years day, 1577, Glock arrived at his Brotherhood home in Moravia. Shortly thereafter he was elected minister and three years later was confirmed in this calling. He died in Schaidowitz on January 30, 1585.

Nine letters written by Glock are included here but they are by no means the only ones in existence. The first is to his wife Else and was the first letter that he wrote after procuring paper and ink from Klaus von Grafeneck. He expressed the hope that God's grace might daily sustain and strengthen her and the whole Brotherhood; he admonished her to be quiet in demeanor as becomes a woman. He then addressed himself to the whole community, exhorting his brethren to open themselves to the mind and spirit of Christ and to exemplify Christ's reputation to both the godly and the ungodly, being a witness to those who were lost, so that the impenitent sinner would have no excuse. He closed this first epistle with a plea for a life of Christian discipleship.[5]

The second document is a lengthy summary of Glock's court hearing of the previous September and was attached to the letter to his wife. Present at the early morning cross-examination were members of the nobility, some citizens, doctors of theology, ministers and the head warden, Klaus von Grafeneck.[6] They said to the two prisoners [Adam Horneck and Paul Glock], that they came with good intent and desired that their imprisonment should end. The prisoners were only to obey and answer well. Glock answered: "We shall speak what God the Lord gives us to speak. Concerning it we will not be silent or hold anything back, with the help of God."

The third document is a letter to Leonard Lanzenstiel (Sailer) who was the *Vorsteher,* or head Brotherhood Leader in Moravia, from 1542 to 1565. When he died, Lanzenstiel was replaced by Peter Walpot and the next five documents are addressed to him. This series includes a letter dealing with Glock's six months of freedom and his subsequent solitary confinement and the 1567 letter Glock wrote while suffering from scurvy and thought that he would soon die.[7]

The last document is a letter to the Church in Moravia, written approximately four years before his release on January 18, 1573. It is Glock's second confession of faith, written when his captors again questioned him about infant baptism, the magistrates, oaths and the Lord's Supper.[8]

Bibliographical Sources:

The Chronicle of the Hutterian Brethren, vol. I (Rifton, N.Y.: Plough Publishing House, 1987).

Leonard Gross, *The Golden Years of the Hutterites,* revised edition (Kitchener, ON: Pandora Press, 1998).

Paul Glock, Letter to his Wife Else, 1563.

Epistle of Paul Glock to his espoused sister [wife] Else in Tajkowitz and to all the devout. Hohenwittlingen. April 14, 1563.

Paul and Adam [Horneck] my fellow prisoner, your loving brethren in the Kingdom, in tribulation and the patience of Christ, to our heartily loved brothers and sisters in the Lord wherever they are in the land of Moravia, and especially to my dear spouse Else. Grace be to all and the inner peace of the heart towards God the Father. We are in prison in the land of Württemberg now into the fifth year for the sake of God's truth. May the longsuffering of Jesus Christ complete your salvation through a great longing for the fatherland and for the daily growth of the inner person. May these increase in you through the operation of the Holy Spirit which proceeds from the Father and the Son. May the Spirit of truth strengthen and fortify you so that you might complete your course to the laud and praise of God and for the salvation of your souls. Amen.

Blessed and highly praised be God the Father whom we rightly ought to praise through Jesus Christ day and night without ceasing. Yes we ought to lift up hands and hearts towards him who lives in heaven. For he is gracious and friendly to all who hold to him firmly as to an anchor of their souls and who do not look back with Lot's wife. For we may well speak with Daniel: "Oh Lord God, have you remembered us? You do not forsake those who love you" [Bel. 1:38]. For when Daniel was in the lions' den forsaken by all, and having no one who gave him food to sustain him, God sent Habakkuk to him, with food which he had cooked for him. Similarly but differently the Lord sent food to us who now sit among the lions so that we might refresh our souls a little. We praise and thank the Lord for this at all times and say with the prophet: "Lord, let us rejoice and be glad in God our salvation. The Lord God is my strength and will make my feet to be like hind's feet and will lead me to a height [Hab. 3:18-19]. That is, he will deliver me out of the hands of my enemies, the victorious conqueror, the strong robber and the swift plunderer who can take the riches of Damascus and the spoil of Samaria and divide them as booty" [Isa. 8:4?]. Let us like King Nebuchadnezzar, write letters to all the lands that the God of Daniel is to be honoured and worshipped. For there is no God more powerful who can save like him from every tribulation. Therefore, our heartily beloved brothers and sisters, especially you Else, my spouse, should not these Scriptures be a comfort to us? Yes, indeed, so that at times we might desire heartily, if it should please God, that they should flog us through the city from one street to the other and then throw us into prison again, as long as the name of Christ be proclaimed. Take note: it was through the tribulations of Daniel that the name of his God was made known in all the lands. If one takes a rose in one's hand and plucks it apart, there is much more aroma from it than if it remains whole.

Why then should we, too, not wish to be a sweet odour of Christ to both the devout and to the godless? For to those who are saved this is a sweet odour to life, and to those who are lost it is a testimony, so that they may have no excuse. For never may the truth be better attested to and sealed than with the blood of the saints. This the Scriptures in many places say so gloriously, that all those who fear God have died to sin are to be hated by those who live in sin. This is clearly stated in the book of Wisdom: "Let us deceive the pious (they say and think), for he is of no use to us and is against our actions; he accuses us of sinning against the law and slanders us as the transgressors of all decency. He pretends to have the wisdom of a son of God. He brings to light our designs and purposes, we do not like to see him; for his life is not like the lives of others and his way is truth" [Wisd. 2:12-15]. Similarly Christ says in the Gospel: "The world cannot hate you. But it hates me for I bear witness that its deeds are evil" [John 7:7]. Peter says: "They slander you that you no longer run with them in the same disorderly excess, in eating, drinking and abominable idolatry" [1 Pet. 4:3-4]. We are now becoming well aware of this prophecy of Peter. For if we refuse to worship the image of the beast and to receive its mark, then we must be cast into the fiery furnace with Shadrach, Meshach and Abed'nego. Still it is better to be cast into the furnace with these three (in which alone we are purged).

Dear Lord, let us not be brought to shame, but deal with us according to your goodness and according to your manifold mercies so that our sacrifice may please you. You forsake no one who puts his trust in you. For we must hear unbearable and terrible things: "If anyone worships the beast and his image and accepts the sign on his forehead or on his hand, he will drink of the wine of God's wrath which is prepared pure in the chalice of his anger. He will be tormented with fire and sulphur before the holy angels and before the Lamb. The smoke of their torment will rise from eternity to eternity and those who have worshipped the beast and its image and who have taken the mark will have no rest day and night. Here is the patience of the saints and of those who have the commands of God and the witness of Jesus Christ" [Rev. 14:9-12].

What do you think of these two rewards? Is it not better to say with Hananiah, Mishael and Azariah [Shadrach, Meshach, and Abed'nego]: "Know, O king, that we shall not serve your gods nor worship the image which you have erected?" [Dan 3:18]. For we say with Christ as it is written: "You are to worship God your Lord and serve him alone" [Matt. 4:10]. He will give his honour to no one else. Therefore let us magnify him in our mortal body, so that he will magnify us with the reward of an immortal body. For it is written: "Whoever honours me, him will I also honour. If anyone is not ashamed of me before men, him will I also confess before my Father in heaven" [Matt. 10:32?] when I shall come to be glorified in my saints and to be made marvellous for the day he will create in all believers who with all their strength have given witness to the Gospel. Notice what reward these warriors will receive: they are to possess all the wealth that is in the city. Ezra says: "A city was situated on a wide field and it is full of all spoil. But there is only one way by which it can be won and it is narrow and strait so that not more than one person can walk on it" [2 Esd. 7:6-8]. That means that everyone must bear his own burden and no one can fight for another. But one can indeed give comfort and strengthen him so that he has joy. For there is great danger on this road and one cannot look around much. On one side is water and on the other side fire, and if we step off the road we die. It is not good to walk this road when there are foggy and dull days and it is dark.

Therefore we advise you, our dear brothers and sisters, and especially you, my dear spouse, Else, that you and we do as is written: "Let your loins be girded and your light be lit and be like those who wait for their Lord, when he will arrive for the wedding, so that when he comes and knocks, the door may be opened. Blessed are those servants whom the Lord finds awake when he comes" [Luke 12:35-37].

First he speaks of girding up our loins. Here we are to understand that this means our walk. In this way the angel of the Lord also girded his loins up, who was to walk with Tobias, for he had gone out to fulfill the work of the Lord. With this girding of the loins we are also to understand that we ought to raise our dispositions and thoughts to heavenly things so that the earthly things do not defile us. We ought to do like the vain people who wear a fresh and pretty garment; they take care to stay clean, taking a belt and gathering it up. How much more ought we to watch our garments that have been washed in such costly blood, and can be cleaned by no soap as the prophet Jeremiah says. We also read that the Lord says to the priest: "Put away the unclean garments for I have taken your sins from you and given you different garments" [Zech. 3:4]. Our burning lights are also highly necessary so that we may not be sent away like the foolish virgins. For the Lord commanded David that in his house a light was to burn perpetually. Christ is that light as John says: "He is that true light who by his coming into this world has illuminated all men" [John 1:9]. This same light David longed for when he speaks in the Psalms: "Your Word is a lantern or a light for my feet, a light on my path. I have decided that I shall maintain the testimonies of your justice. When your Word is proclaimed, it shines and gives knowledge to the humble" [Ps. 119:105-06]. Since this same light now shines and the sun of justice has risen for us through the mercy of God, let us walk in it so that darkness may not take us unaware. Whoever walks in the dark does not know where he is going. Believe in the Light while the merciful Father grants you opportunity so that you may be the children of Light. For Paul calls us children of the day and of light because the morning star has risen in our hearts until day breaks or has broken. God is to be highly praised and to be thanked that he put such light into our hearts, such a bright light through the illumination and the knowledge of the Gospel. For we seldom hear that a thief robs or steals in broad daylight.

If we desire to be free, let us be awake at all times; then the evil one will not attack us. Christ further says, "Whosoever walks in the light will not hurt himself" [John 11:9]. For many stones have been put in our way and many snares, with which they desire to catch us, as David has spoken of in many places. In the book or Regium it is written: "The crushing of death has surrounded me and the streams of Belial have frightened me. The snares of hell had caught me and the nets of death had overtaken me" [Ps. 18:4]. At another place he says: "Save me, my God, from my adversaries and rescue me from my enemies and from the evildoers who are set against me, and deliver me from the bloodthirsty" [Ps. 59:1-2]. In this and other similar passages it is made sufficiently clear that we are to be on guard at all times.

Therefore also David so wisely admonishes us, our dear brothers and sisters, and especially you, Else, my spouse. He says: "With what shall a youth better guard his way, but that he keep to your words or commandments?" [Ps. 119:9]. Moses, who was a prophet more gentle than anyone on earth also says: "These words which I commanded you today you shall take to heart and teach them to your children and think about them and speak of them when you sit in your house or walk on the road, when you lie down or when you rise; you are to bind them as a sign on your hand. They are to be a token of remembrance before your eyes and you are to write them over your doorposts" [Deut. 6:6-9].

This light is God's Word and is the flame of fire which shone for the children of Israel in the desert that they might not go astray in the desert at night. It is also the lamp which the devout woman, of whom Solomon speaks, left burning all night so that she might waken her menservants and her maidservants. It is also the lamp that was to burn day and night in the temple of Solomon. Therefore let everyone see to it that he does not let the light that is in him become dark. For as the day wanes when evening comes, just so the light of righteousness wanes when the obscure darkness which came over the land of Egypt comes to us.

Solomon plainly speaks of this in the book of Wisdom: "Wisdom will not enter into a wicked mind and it does not reside with those who are subject to sins" [Wisd. 1:4]. For the Holy Spirit is repelled by those who only appear to accept training and wisdom and he withdraws from the thoughts of those who are without wisdom; where malice dominates, he draws back. For the spirit of truth is friendly, gentle and good, and has no pleasure in him who speaks evil with his lips. The fear of the Lord hates wickedness, arrogance, pride and the way of evil and one does not find it with those who are double-tongued.

So then also say with Mark: "Watch, for you do not know when the master of the house comes, whether he comes in the evening or at midnight or at cockcrow or in the morning so that he does not come unexpectedly and find you sleeping" [Mark 13:35-36]. For how could we answer for ourselves if we were not prepared for the supper of the Lamb? We would certainly be brought to shame like a thief who is caught with what he robbed. How can he answer? He has to be silent, as is written: "The godless will sigh and their minds will fail. They will be startled when they remember their sin, and their own wickedness will condemn them." Therefore let us watch, so that we do not perish with them. For each will receive recompense from the Lord as he has acted, evil or good. Ezra also says: "Everyone who is preserved and can escape by his works and through the faith which he has will be preserved from the threatened danger and will see prosperity in my land in its borders, for the Lord has sanctified himself before the world. But those who have despised and rejected my ways will live in pain" [2 Esd. 9:7-9].

Since those are especially warned of the Lord who have received his gifts (which are better than gold or jewels) and tasted his friendliness but have not kept them, it is urgent that we be diligent. For that soil which drinks the rain which often comes over it and which bears useful plants for those who work it, receives a blessing from God. That soil, however, which bears thistles and thorns is useless, is cursed more and more, and its end is burning. Let us take these words to heart, for Ezra warns us with these words also: "Those who have received good things in their lives and have not acknowledged me and who have taken displeasure in my law when they were yet at liberty, and who, instead of improving themselves and returning have not understood it but despised it, they will acknowledge it after death in torment" [2 Esd. 9:10-12].

The field is known by its seed, the flower by it colour and the builder by his work. So also a Christian is known by his fruit. For a good tree brings forth good fruit just as the fat land of Canaan brought forth the good bunch of grapes which was shown to the people of Israel by those who spied out the land.

A noble bunch of grapes is shown to us as well. It is the true plant of righteousness, carried by two men. The one goes ahead and is aware of its weight. But he does not fully see the grape. The other walks behind. He also knows the weight but has the advantage in that he sees it. These are the two Testaments, it seems to me, which both bring us Christ, who cools our thirsty mouths with the luscious grapes. He has also let us into a land from where they came, and has planted us in it as a seedling, that we might also all bear such fruit that might be food for the hungry. It is written: "I planted you a noble vine, a true seed, how have you then become a wild vine, wrong and degenerate?" [Jer. 2:21]. Isaiah also says: "Judge now, you citizens of Jerusalem and you men of Judea, between me and my vineyard! What more should I have done to my vineyard that I have not done? Why then did it bear wild grapes when I expected sweet? I will show you what I shall do. I will remove its fence so that it will be trodden down" [Isa. 5:3-5] Christ says that the branches are to be cut off, bound together and thrown into the fire. Therefore in brotherly concern we ask you that you do not become weary or tired on this rough, difficult road which those who are frail have to travel.

For it is a poor life that we lead here. But much good will be given us as reward if we fear God, do right and keep from evil. Notice the friendly answer of the Lord to the servant who earned another five pounds. Grow always in truth, our heartily loved brethren and sisters, and the Lord will not remove his cloud from you. For just as the waters which flow into the garden moisten the tree, the everlasting fountain which at all times flows with grace will never leave you. For it is written that the trees that were watered by the clear streams of water issuing from the throne of God and the Lamb bore their fruit each month and that the leaves served for healing.

Do not say in your hearts: there is a lion in the field. For whoever will not plow because of the cold, will have to go begging in the summer and nothing will be given him. Solomon says: "I went through the field of the lazy man and through the vineyard of the fool and behold, it was nothing but thistles and thorns so that one could not walk though it. The walls had fallen down. When I saw it, I took it to heart and it was a warning to me" [Prov. 24:30-32]. And so it must be a warning to us. For whoever gathers in the summer, is wise, but whoever sleeps during the harvest, will be shamed. Now is the right time and the day of salvation. Let us then prove ourselves as the servants of God so that we may be without offence to the heathen and to the Jews and also the church of God, so that we may have a good conscience which, as Solomon says, is the foundation of a good life. Peter says: "Keep a clear conscience so the those who malign you as evildoers may be brought to shame because they have slandered and reviled your good walk in Christ. For they will speak all kinds of evil against us, but we are to rejoice if they lie in doing it" [1 Pet. 3:16]. Therefore the Lord explained it saying if they lie about you, let your friendliness, which is a fruit of the spirit, be manifest towards all and do not reward evil with evil. For we are God's children born through the Gospel and our heavenly Father lets his sun shine on the devout and on the godless and has never turned his mercy from them. He has at all times shown himself to be fatherly, according to his name, by giving them rain from heaven and fruitful times and has filled their hearts with joy although humanly a person might sometimes think, like John and James: "Lord, shall we ask that fire come down from heaven and devour them?" [Luke 9:54]. But Christ, who had come to save souls and not to destroy, said to them: "You do not know which spirit's children you are." With that he plainly gave us to understand that we are not to avenge ourselves but to learn gentleness and humility from the Master. For he says: "Father forgive them, for they do not know what they are doing" [Luke 23:34]. Indeed, what is more, we should remember that in past times we were also unwise and disobedient enemies of God and served unrighteousness. Therefore we should feel pity for their blinded cold hearts, just as Christ did toward the Jews when they rose up to accuse him. Then he looked about him with anger and was sad because of their hardened hearts.

For he had shown them many good works for the sake of which they meant to stone him. Malchus, who was one of the band who came to arrest him, had the ear which Peter had cut off, healed. He prayed life for those who killed him. In his last extremity he was still concerned about his enemies.

Observe how the Father and the Son are one, friendly and forbearing, who even in his grim anger, says Habakkuk, is mindful of his mercy. Oh, you dearly beloved brethren and sisters, how few people there are who have the mind and spirit of Christ. May the Lord have mercy on us that more and more we may be removed from the unrighteous and defiled Adam into the new and undefiled Adam who is from heaven, the innocent lamb without blemish and without spot. Into his kingdom which he has conquered by much suffering, nothing impure and no abomination may enter, nor those who love or do a lie.

Therefore let us walk in fear and trembling. For Solomon says: "Blessed are those who walk in fear and are circumspect" [Sir. 34:15?]. Paul walked with fear and much trembling among the Corinthians that he might win them. The stars in the sky who are at all times obedient to almighty God serve the Lord with fear and trembling. When they are called they say: "Here we are." How much more and with how much more justice ought sinful man, who drinks mischief like water, serve the great King with fear and great carefulness? We should do it for this reason alone, that our evil and poisoned nature, with which we must at all times be at war, still clings to us. As it is written: "The aim of men and the thought of their hearts are wicked from their youth up." In contrast, we are to note that the Father of light, with whom there is no darkness, is an enemy to sin. For because of the sin of the one man we must all be lost and endure the eternal curse. There was no sacrifice for any holy work in all humanity which might have reconciled God's justice. No one was wise enough to find a means to quiet his anger. But he says to Israel: "For my name's sake I helped you." For it was because of the unsearchable mercy and favouring goodness which he had towards humanity that he went into the treasure of his riches and, according to his wisdom, found a counsel thought out long before, and out of his treasury brought forth a precious gem. This he sent to us on earth so that we people might be cleansed by it. It is as though one were to pour wine into a glass in which there is some poison; if one puts into it a piece of unicorn, the poison does one no harm even though it remains in the glass. So also with us, if the unicorn of which David speaks is put into our hearts, it will take away the power of the poison so that we will not perish.

This is the precious gem for which Zacharias praised and thanked God so fervently when he said: "Blessed be God the Lord of Israel, for he has visited and saved his people, and has raised up the horn of salvation in the house of his servant David, as he spoke before times through the mouths of his holy prophets, that he might save us from our enemies and from the hands of all those who hate us, but showed mercy to our fathers" [Luke 1:68-72].

For just as all the animals in the forest know that they must follow the unicorn and wait on him as on their prince—for through him the water must be purified—even so all the devout are to go to no well except the one to which their unicorn Christ first went and from which he drank himself. Then we will not be punished along with Israel through the prophet Jeremiah who says: "My people have two sins, says the Lord. They have forsaken me, the well of living water and have dug themselves cisterns, yes broken cisterns, that hold no water" [Jer. 2:13]. "Whoever follows me," says Christ, "does not walk in darkness, but will have the light of life" [John 8:11-13]. For he leads his sheep to the right pasture and to the living well which never runs dry. May the Lord give us all a great thirst for this well, like the thirst of a stag for a water brook. Amen.

Further, heartily beloved brothers and sisters, and especially you Else, my espoused wife, it is our request to you that you be quiet. For through the speech of one woman we were all undone. Think of the wonderful admonition of the apostle Peter, that the adornment of women is not to consist of the braiding of hair nor in gold nor putting on of clothes, but in the hidden man of the heart in the incorruptibility of a gentle and quiet spirit which is excellent and great before God. The tongue is a small member and can do much damage. Whoever watches over his mouth, watches over his soul. But whoever is not circumspect and speaks unguardedly will experience misfortune. Therefore weigh your words as the goldsmith weighs out his gold, and at all times consider in your hearts whether your speech is gracious. Do not backbite your fellow members. This is not of God nor is it acting out of love. For Solomon says: "Whoever covers sin, seeks love" [Sir. 2:16?] Do not grieve, dear brother and sisters, that we admonish you so vigorously in this for we admonish you and ourselves also in this. It is better to be warned of danger than unknowingly to fall into it.

Finally, be forbearing in all things and firmly keep the fear of God before your eyes. It is written: "Through mercy and justice evil is reconciled." But through the fear of God one avoids evil. Be strong in the law of the Lord. For out of stones God can raise up children for Abraham. He will give you that courageous and fearless spirit which he gave to the mother of the seven sons. Who ever came to shame that trusted in God? If you do what you are bid by the Lord you will receive praise and honour. It is well known to you what awaits those who have lost patience here. "Woe to you," says Sirach, "who have left the right way and have gone on evil ways; what will you do when the Lord punishes you?" [Sir. 41:8?]. He who is mighty, on the other hand, will keep all believers irreproachable and inoffensive until the day of his appearance. May he strengthen and confirm you to the laud and praise of his holy name. Amen.

The grace of God be with you. Continue in prayer for us and for all saints. Remember Hannah, the mother of Samuel, how she prayed to God in her heart. She made no noise with her voice. Eli said she was drunk. But she spoke with modest words as is fitting for holy women: "No, my lord, I am a sorrowful woman. I have not drunk wine or strong drink, but have poured out my heart before the Lord. Do not count your maid as a daughter of Belial. For I spoke only out of the heaviness of my heart" [1 Sam. 1:15-16]. And she was heard. Consider that we have many more reasons for moving us to pray earnestly and in pain than Hannah had. For now are difficult times, of which Christ speaks. Love has grown cold in many, and it is a wonder that the elect can persevere to the end. Nor can we expect any improvement or freedom for believers. For Ezra says: "The world has lost its youth and times begin to grow old [2 Esd. 14:10]. For as the world and times grow weaker, by so much will sin and wickedness increase in those who live on earth [14:17]. ...The days will come when those who live on earth will be captured in large numbers. The way of truth will be hidden and the land will be without faithfulness. Wickedness will gain the upper hand" [2 Esd. 5:1]. Again we say with Christ: "Watch and pray so that you may not fall into temptation" [Matt. 26:41]. Be firm and immovable for our work is not in vain in the Lord. To him, however, who can keep you in his love and can protect you from all evil, who alone has immortality, who lives in light which no one can approach, whom no one has seen or can see, to this strong God be eternal honour, laud and praise. Amen.

Greet all the saints and fellow citizens of the house of God. Fear not little flock, for it is the Father's will to give you his kingdom. Pilate has no power to kill Christ except what is given him from above. Think of our bonds and never forget those who suffer for Christ's sake. Remember that you are one with them in the body of Christ for the members rejoice and sorrow together. Amen.

Further, our very dear believing brother and sisters, do not bear malice towards anyone, but before God seek the best for them all. In this way encourage yourselves in firm faith and trust in God in obedience to his will with praying, watching, temperance, holiness and purity, in godly wisdom and in the fear of God, in longsuffering, patience, gentleness, humility and in all godliness. Think about every Christian virtue, everything praiseworthy so that you will always be more filled with God's gifts.

Those who the Spirit of God thus drives are the children of God. We know that you spare no effort, and are well aware that you in your part are more comforted than we. We write these things to you in order to refresh ourselves along with you in divine matters and grace. It is not that we are worried that either in small or in large matters you were not diligent without our writing. Oh no, not for that reason, but out of godly love as already said. For we know that you are daily admonished in the Word of God. But as already said, it is that we might enjoy the Lord with you, and in order that the love in your hearts towards us might flourish, grow and become more complete. For we know and have the faith in you, that you will so accept what we have written; that you will accept our simple epistle, and that it can work and accomplish these things in you not as from us but as from the Lord. He will faithfully accomplish it. If something is improperly written, it is not of the Lord. Please attribute it to the fault of our weakness, and so accept our writing in the best way. May the Lord, however, guide your hearts and ours according to the image of Christ, our redeemer, so that we may be formed like him more and more completely. May the life of Christ in us be a mirror to the world, and may we and all the devout eternally take comfort in it. May the true son, Jesus Christ, grant this. Amen.

We commend you, our very dear brothers and sisters, herewith to our strong God and his merciful protection and shelter. Pray faithfully for us that the Lord may at all times open our mouth to confess his truth unto death, as is right. This we will do for you with God's help. Both of us, Paul and Adam, greet you many thousand times in godly love and in the peace of Christ. Greet all the holy congregation of God and be once more commended most faithfully to the Lord. Amen.

25

Paul Glock

First Defense
(1563)*

First defence of Paul Glock, April, 14, 1563.

In September, 1562, the chief overseer, Niklas of Urach [Klaus von Grafeneck] and other nobles, several burghers and also doctors of the Scriptures along with three priests came to Hohenwittlingen. They said to the two prisoners [Adam Horneck and Paul Glock], that they came with good intent and desired that their imprisonment should end. The prisoners were only to obey and answer well. The latter answered[1]

"We shall speak what God the Lord gives us to speak. Concerning it we will not be silent or hold anything back, with the help of God."

So the chief priest began by saying that we were to give him an account of our faith. For Peter says, said he, be ready always to give an answer to every one that asks you a reason of the hope that is in you.

Answer: It is not necessary to give a long account of our faith. For you have now held us in prison into the fourth year, and during this

---

*Source, Bossert, *Quellen I*, 1049-65.
Translation: Friesen/Klaassen

time have sufficiently learned our faith, teaching and life. Therefore that is not now necessary or urgent. But concerning the items for which you have kept us imprisoned now into the fourth year we will talk with you, for instance about the godless baptism of infants which we do not confess as being commanded by God, concerning your teaching, preaching, the Lord's Supper, churches and your godless assembly, that it is not of God. We will also discuss your godless swearing which is neither specified nor commanded by God in Christ, as well as concerning your warring and taking of vengeance, which we confess to be open murder. Further, we will converse concerning the fact that we do not confess that the godless government, which, after all, lives and walks in a heathenish way, is Christian before God, nor that we consider or confess [those in government] to be saved. Those are the items and articles for which you (as said) have kept us imprisoned into the fourth year. Concerning those we wish to talk with you false prophets and seducers.

Then the chief priest spoke, put a New Testament before us, and told us to show him from the Scriptures that infant baptism was not to be practiced or where it was forbidden.

Answer: We can easily attest and prove that the baptism of newly-born infants was not practiced in the New Testament nor introduced, nor commanded in it, Matt. 15[:14]; Rev. 22[:19]. Take note, then, what Paul teaches us. He says: "Faith comes from preaching out of the Word of God," Rom. 10[:10, :17]. He also says: "If you confess with the mouth that Jesus if Lord, and believe in your heart that God has raised him from the dead, you will be saved," Rom. 10[:9]. Since faith comes from preaching, one must first preach and then believe. Not only must one believe, but also confess with the mouth, as mentioned above. Now take a newly born infant, we said to him, and preach to it for a week. And if it believes your false teaching (which surely is no preaching), then you have won, and may baptize it. If, however, it does not confess and you nevertheless baptize it, your baptism is a curse and not a blessing.

Secondly, the apostle Peter proves that your baptism is a curse when he says that baptism is a covenant of a good conscience with God and not the washing off of the filth of the flesh. As said, it is [the covenant] of a good conscience with a certain [sure] witness towards God and also towards all believers. If it is to be the covenant of a good conscience, then a person must surely have a good understanding. For a good conscience towards God is that I recognize that I have a merciful God who has in Christ granted, remitted and forgiven me all my sins.

It means that I recognize that with him all things are possible and that moved by this, I am provoked to enough zeal to give him my allegiance, to subordinate myself to him and to trust him completely as my dearest Father, who will always seek the good, yes the very best for me. On this I raise up my covenant with him, in which I bind myself completely to him, yielding my members to him as instruments of his holy work, Rom. 6[:13]. Henceforth I let him work, effect and do everything in me, while I, as a tool, Acts 9[:15] will suffer his work and allow my master to use me where he will. I will earnestly yield to his gracious will and depart from it neither to the right nor to the left as long as I live. To prove my intention I accept the pure water so that henceforth through his moving I will lead a holy life.

God on the other hand covenants with me that he will be my God and Father, taking care of me as a father cares for his son, giving him everything in Christ. As a surety for this he gives his witness from heaven and imparts to me the grace of his Spirit who will lead me in all truth, 2 Cor. 5[:5]; John 14[:17] complete everything in me, and perform my purpose, so that in this way I begin a new life in his strength. Paul says: "If anyone is in Christ, he is a new creature," 2 Cor. 5[:17]; Gal. 6[:15]. Tell us now, we said to them, whether a child is able to make such a covenant of a good conscience with God. If so, you have won and may baptize it. If, however, it does not occur this way, and you baptize it, nevertheless then, again, your baptism is a curse.

Thirdly, it is very clearly proven by Paul in Acts that your godless baptism is a curse. Here he admonishes the elders in Ephesus and strongly calls them to witness that he is innocent of all blood. It is as though he meant to say that if an evil were to arise hereafter [it would not be his fault] since he had held back nothing from them which he did not proclaim to them, namely, the whole counsel of God. Now he did not mention infant baptism with one word nor report it in any of his epistles. Therefore it cannot be in the counsel of God.

However, he warns them most faithfully and says: "Even if we or an angel from heaven were to preach to you something else than what we have preached, may he be cursed." Be careful, peddler of lies; since infant baptism is no plant planted by the Father in heaven, Gal. 1[:18]; Matt. 15[:13], nor any counsel of God or of the apostles, nor any preaching of Paul, it is a curse before God and all the saints. It follows therefore that infant baptism is forbidden to us as disciples and followers of Christ. We are commanded by God that we subtract nothing from his Word nor add anything to it, Deut. 4[:2]; Prov. 30[:6]; Rev. 22[:19].

Fourthly, Paul clearly proves that your godless baptism is a curse when he says: "How should we live in sin to which we have died? Do you not know that those who have been baptized into Christ Jesus are baptized into his death?" Rom. 6[:3, :4, :6]. "Thus we are buried into his death through baptism so that, just as Christ has been raised from the dead through the glory of the Father, in the same way we are also to live in a new life," 1 Cor. 12[:13]; Gal. 3[:27]; Col. 2[:12]; Eph 4[:17]; 1 Thess. 2[:12]. Since we have been planted into the divine likeness of his death, so we shall also be crucified with him, so that the carnal body may rest. Now Christ shows what sin (in which the whole world lives and walks) is. Evil thoughts, murder, adultery, fornication, theft, false witness, and blasphemy arise constantly from the human heart. These are the things which defile. Matt. 15[:19]; Mark 7[:23]. All these evil things come from the inside and condemn and defile the person. Similarly Paul says especially of those who are full of all injustice, fornication, wickedness, covetousness, malice, envy, murder, quarrelling, deception and evil habits, boasting, maligning, hating God, wicked deeds, pride, invention of wicked things, covenants, and mercilessness, that they are worthy of death. Similarly, he says to the Galatians: "The manifest works of the flesh: lasciviousness, idolatry, witchcraft, enmity, feuding, zeal, wrath, anger, quarrelling, sects, murder, killing, eating, drinking and the like, of which I have formerly told you, that those who do such, will not inherit the kingdom of God," Gal. 5[:21]. Therefore Paul continues: "Do not be deceived; neither the fornicators nor the idolaters not the adulterers nor the effeminate nor the homosexuals nor the thieves nor the avaricious, nor drunkards nor the blasphemers nor the robbers shall inherit the kingdom of God." Christ also warns us, therefore, against such sin, and Paul says, Rom. 6[:2], that the Christians shall have died to them just as Christ, in that he died to sin once. In that he lives, he lives to God. So you, too, consider yourselves to have died to sin but that you now live to God through Jesus Christ our Lord. Observe carefully, we said, how Paul admonishes his brethren or the church (those who are sealed with baptism and the Spirit of Christ), that after baptism we are to be crucified and are to be dead to sin.

Therefore, says Paul, sin is not to rule in our mortal bodies and we are not to obey it in its desires. Do not yield your members, says he, as tools for unrighteousness but yield yourselves to God as those who have risen from death to life, and yield your members as tools of righteousness. Thus, after the baptism of Christ, we are henceforth to lead a pure and holy life and appear holy before God. The devout die daily and decrease in that they do not bear the fruits of sin. You, on the other hand, both groups, Lutherans and popish priests together with your godless congregations, are worse and more godless from day to day following your baptism. Indeed you increase daily in abomination and sin as is recounted above with reference to Matthew, Mark and Paul, so that you are so to speak children of unbelief and wickedness in whom, as Paul says, Eph. 2[:2], the devil has his work. Therefore it is manifest that both of you, Lutherans and papists, are wrong, and not a church of Christ, but a church of the devil. When we said these things to them, they could not truthfully answer us, not even the priest.

But the godless priest attempted to defend his infant baptism with the words said to Nicodemus. Here water is mentioned first, he said, then the new birth. According to that one could also baptize first and after that teach and believe.

Answer: You certainly cannot maintain or protect infant baptism with this verse, because Nicodemus was no child but an old man and a master of Scriptures. Nor does the water come first, but the new birth, which must occur from above through the Spirit from God. It must guide us in all obedience if one walks, lives and remains in the obedience of God. Only then can one legitimately be baptized. Therefore Christ repeats that the new birth comes first and afterwards the water. And because one is to remain in the new birth and walk in it after baptism, he places the water in the middle and the new birth before and after. Now, as was said above, Nicodemus was no child, but a master of the Scriptures, indeed a mentally dull one. When Christ spoke with him he could not even understand earthly things, much less the heavenly.

Had Nicodemus wanted to become a disciple of the Lord and be saved, he would have had to put aside his mental dullness and learn from Christ as his master. It is the same today. If you false prophets want to come to God you will, like Nicodemus, have to lay aside your unrighteousness and mental dullness and learn from Christ and those he sends. Otherwise you cannot be saved nor come to God.

Upon all this the godless priest was forced into silence before us all. The Lord be praised who did not forsake us, his own, as he has promised.

Then another began, not a priest, but a master of Scripture. He asked us whether we believed that all things were possible to God.

Answer: Yes, we believe that all things are possible for God if he wills. As he commands, so it must happen.

Then the master said that therefore he believed that God gave the children faith. Consequently they could also then be baptized.

Answer: It is a small thing to God and easy, to give faith to infants, if only it were his divine will, for all things are possible to him. God the almighty in former times opened the mouth of Balaam's donkey, Num. 22[:28], so that it spoke with a human voice and prevented the foolishness of the prophet. Similarly God did a miracle with the children in the temple at Jerusalem. When Christ entered, Matt. 21[:15, :16], the children cried very loudly in the temple: "Hosanna to the son of David." The priests and scribes said to Christ: "Do you hear what they are saying?" But he said to them: "Why not? Have you not read, 'Out of the mouths of babes and sucklings you have given praise'?" And many other miracles God did. But that does not mean that he wants it to be so now also.

If you believe that everything is possible to God, as you have admitted above, then note what Christ says to the disciples when the children were brought to him that he might lay his hands on them and pray. The disciples had scolded those who brought them, Matt. 19; Mark 10; Luke 18. But Jesus said to them: "Let the children come to me and do not forbid them, for of such is the kingdom of the heavens. I tell you that whoever does not accept the kingdom of heaven as a child will not enter it. And when he had embraced them, he put his hands on them, spoke good things over them and blessed them." Observe how plainly Christ here speaks of the children, promising them the kingdom of God. But he did not baptize them nor command them to be baptized.

Now Christ speaks further about the children: "Truly I say to you, unless you turn and become like children, you will not enter the kingdom of heaven," Matt. 18[:3]; Mark 9[:36-37]; Luke 9[:47-48].

Notice, we said, how Christ here sets the children before us as an example, so that we might turn and become as the children. What does Christ want to teach us through the children? Surely that as the children subordinate themselves to their master, are subject to him and obey him, have not sold themselves to created things, and are innocent of sin and wickedness as well, even so our whole life should be ordered before God. Paul admonishes us: "My brethren, do not become children in understanding, but be children in wickedness. In understanding be perfect," 1 Cor. 14[:20]; Col. 3[:8]. Whoever, then, becomes like children and persists in devotion to the end, he will certainly inherit the kingdom of Christ with the children. It is true, as you have confessed above, that all things are possible to God. Now God has promised and awarded the children his kingdom without your godless baptism. Further he says: "Truly I tell you, until heaven and earth pass away, not one letter or dot will vanish from the law, until it has all happened," Matt. 5[:24]. Christ's words will remain, and Christ has made this promise to the children. If it has been promised them and moreover is given them without baptism, why do you dull people baptize them with your godless baptism?

When we had thus spoken to them, the master of Scripture could say no word against us and had to be silent. Our God be praised! The others also were all silent and no one said anything. So does God capture the wise in their presumption and bring them to shame, Job 5[:13]. To our king, as was said, be the honour eternally!

After this the first priest began to complain against us, again, asking why we did not go to their preaching, teaching, churches and to their assemblies, and why we so despised them.

Answer: Your teaching, preaching church and assembly is a mob and an assembly of fornicators, adulterers, liars, blasphemers, drunkards, proud, usurers, and all unclean spirits in whom the devil has and does his work, Eph. 2[:2]; Acts 18[:2]. There is no true and proper divine service among you, but rather blasphemy and shame before the face of the Almighty. Because of this we are moved to flee and avoid this godless assembly of yours, Jer. 23[:29]. Your teaching and preaching is not done according to the counsel of Christ nor in his Spirit. Therefore, also, it does not bear any good fruit. For Paul says: "The Word of God is alive and active and sharper than any two-edged sword, penetrating soul and spirit, joints and marrow, and sifts the thoughts and purposes of the heart," Heb. 4[:12] Now if the Word of God is alive and is to bear fruit, then the living Word which is God himself in Christ, must live and work in you, and lead and rule you. For the Lord says in the prophet Isa. 55[:10ff], "Just as rain and snow comes down from heaven to the earth, makes it fruitful and green, so that it yields grain and bread to the sower, even so my Word which comes out of my mouth shall not come back to me void, but shall perform my will and accomplish that for which I send it." Here it becomes manifest that, since your teaching and preaching bears no good fruit, it is not from the mouth of Christ nor according to his command, nor is done according to the Spirit of God and Christ.

Then the priest said: "How so is our teaching and preaching not according to the Spirit of Christ? For is it not written that no one can call God Lord except through the Spirit of Christ?"

Answer: It is true that no one can truthfully call God Lord except in the Spirit of Christ. But if one will in truth call God Lord such a person must walk in truth, which truth is God himself, so that God uses all his members according to his own will and pleasure. We, his obedient children, wish to endure and suffer this his work quite willingly with true awareness, and allow him to rule and use all our lives, heart, mouth, eyes, ears, hands, feet and all our members, so that not we but the Lord lives in us and does everything. In this way God is our father and we may in truth call him a father or a lord in the Spirit. If, however, someone is not thus ruled and led by the Spirit of Christ and yet calls God a father and a lord, such a one blasphemes God, which is a lie and an untruth. And when you, false Lutheran and papist priests together with your godless assembly do this, constantly saying: Lord, Lord, yes God is our Lord, then Christ says to you: "Why do you call me Lord and do not do what I have commanded you?" This you false priests do. Besides, the whole world calls God Lord, but in lying and in untruth. The devil also confesses and believes that there is a God, Matt. 8[:29]; Mark 1[:24]; James 2[:19]. But how will such an empty confession help you? Will it save you? Oh no, for Christ says: "Not everyone who says Lord, Lord to me will enter the kingdom of heaven but those who do the will of my Father who is in heaven" Matt. 7[:21].

But that the teaching of you both, Lutheran and papist priests, is not of God or of his Spirit, is shown by your works. Paul admonishes us his brethren or the believers and says: "Are you not the seal in the Lord of my work and of my apostleship? 1 Cor. 9[:2]; 1 Thess. 2[:19]; Phil. 2[:16]. Similarly it is easy to deduce and to recognize by your own people, who are your seal, and which you plant and build or set up with your false teaching and preaching whether you have been appointed by God or by the devil. This is so considering (as stated above) that your assembly is a collection of fornicators, adulterers, and all unclean spirits, who commit all sin and wickedness. Therefore they are children of wickedness in whom (as Paul says) Satan has his work, Eph. 2[:2]. As the people are, so are the apostles and as the apostles are, so are the people: the builder as the building, the seed as the field, the seed as he who has sown. The Lord himself speaks through the prophet when he says: "As is the priest, so are the people and as the master, so is the servant and the woman as her maid, Isa. 24[:2]; Hos. 4[:9]. He wants to say, they are all godless together. They live and walk in that which is against God and none admonishes or speaks to the other about wrong done.

Again, it is demonstrated that you both, false Lutheran and papist priests, are not chosen by God and Christ, because you do not obey the commands of your master Christ (as you boast). Christ himself says: "Just as you, Father have sent me into this world, so do I send them in the world, and I sanctify myself for them so that they, too, may be sanctified in the truth. But I pray not for them alone but also for those who through their word will believe in me, so that they may all be one as you, Father, are one in me and I in you, so that they might also be one in us so that the world might believe that you have sent me," John 17[:20].

Now, my dear man (we said to the priest), where did God command his Son and tell him: "Go, my son Christ, into all the world, for I am putting my word into your mouth and have anointed you. Teach all people, Luke 11[:47] but those who will not believe your teaching and preaching nor accept it, you shall capture and torture. You are to torment them until they believe what I told them and what you preached." Where, my dear sir, did the Father tell and command his Son to do this, or where did Christ approach matters in this way or command his disciples to act in the way you godless Lutherans and papists deal with us and those like us now into the fourth year, which will perhaps end in murder. Tell us, where did Christ do such or tell his disciples to act thus, to force others to faith by means of hangmen and police, with pain and torture and prison as you do? If you can show that they thought and acted thus, you have won and may also act thus and force people to your false teaching and preaching as you prove in our case. If, however, you cannot do it, then you show once more which spirit's children you are. For Christ says: "Truly, truly, I tell you, the servant is not greater than the master nor the messenger greater than the one who sent him. If you now know this, you are blessed if you do it," John 13[:17].

You desire to be greater than Christ your master and Lord, and yet Christ forced no one, nor did the apostles. Peter and Paul say: "We do not rule over your faith but are helpers of your joy," 1 Pet. 5[:3]. They did not want to rule over faith or enforce it with hangmen, bailiffs, torture and imprisonment. But you priests would thus force it on us or force people to it and in this way be lords over the faith. In this way you again show whose servants, messengers or disciples you are, namely the devil's servants and disciples. For the devil forces people into his kingdom using arrests, stocks, dungeons, prison, expulsions and murder. Such things Christ and the apostles never did. Therefore it is manifest that you both, Lutheran and papist priests, are precisely those who fulfill and confirm the work of your father. For the devil is a murderer from the beginning and does not abide in the truth. Therefore Christ says: All those who came before me are thieves and murderers," John 8[:44], 10[:8].

Although in his children, the priests, the devil shows himself to be a murderer, yet he always presents himself as pious. For it is as Paul says, "Their father the devil himself disguises himself as an angel." For such false apostles are deceptive workers who pretend to be apostles of Christ. Nor is this any wonder since, as was just stated, their father himself pretends to be an angel of light. Therefore it is also no wonder when his servants and children also pretend to be servants of righteousness. "Their end will be according to their works," 2 Cor. 1[:15].

Then the godless priest began, and quoted Scripture. But it was with false reasoning. He said: we shall adequately show you that we are permitted to force people to the faith. Consider what Christ says in his parable: A man prepared a great supper and invited many to it. He sent out his servants once and a second time and finally said to them: go out into the highways and to the fences and compel them to come in so that my house may be full. From this you can easily see that one is allowed to force men to the faith. Therefore you Anabaptists (said he) must also be compelled and forced in.

Answer: Here as everywhere else you interpret Scripture falsely and contrary to its nature, and this to your own hurt and to that of all people. That Christ does not want anyone to be forced into his kingdom by means of hangmen, bailiffs, dungeons and prisons has been adequately shown above. But since we have so much divine witness showing that one must not use force in matters of faith, we will look at is more closely and present it, so that your foolishness may be more openly exposed. John says to those who did not fear God: "You nest of vipers, who has taught you to escape future judgment? Bring forth righteous fruit of repentance," Matt. 3[:7ff]; Luke 3[:7ff]. But he did not capture them and force them by means of hangmen and bailiffs.

Christ, when he came into his native country, did not do many miracles there, because of their disbelief. He was himself surprised at their lack of faith. When they took him to the top of the hill in order to throw him down, he passed through their midst with no reference to his forcing them, Luke 4[:29]. What clear evidence we have that Christ forced no one! As we can see, when his disciples said to him, do you know that the Pharisees were annoyed at you when they heard your words, he said to them: "Leave them alone," Matt. 15[:12ff]. They were not to be forced or compelled, but to be left alone, since they were blind leaders of the blind. But if one blind person leads another, both fall into the ditch.

How plainly the apostle speaks of the suffering which he endured for the sake of Christ. It was inflicted by those who did not believe him. He suffered lashes five times, was beaten with rods and was stoned once, 2 Cor. 11[:25]. All that, he says, he suffered. But nowhere is it written that he even once defended himself or that he forced these same rogues and knaves to his faith and to what he preached, neither with hangmen nor with bailiffs. For he says: "Do not avenge yourselves, my dearest ones, but yield place to anger," Rom. 12[:19]. Thus it is manifest that neither Christ nor the apostles used force or violence to force people to their teaching, preaching or their church.

But it was through his word and judgment that Christ compelled people. When he told the Samaritan woman at Jacob's well what she had done and how she had acted, she was compelled to recognize him as the Messiah, and was moved to tell the others this. Then they also came, heard his word, his preaching and his teaching and were compelled by this to believe his teaching in their hearts, John 4. Similarly, when Christ told the Canaanite woman that it was not fitting to take the bread from the children and give it to the dogs, and when he saw that she had faith and when she heard and saw the works and preaching of Christ, she did not relent but was compelled to believe him. Christ himself said: "Your faith is great; it has helped you." How many Christ attracted to him through his word and teaching, as is seen throughout the New Testament!

In this way Christ even today charges and bids us, his servants, by means of the parable you cited to go our into all the streets or into all the lands in order to call them, yes even to the fences. Now what is the fence behind which people hide, flee or conceal themselves? We judge that in part it is your false preaching, teaching, baptism, Lord's Supper, outward ceremonial show and walk, and the result of these, your false hope. All this together is likely the fence behind which you conceal and hide yourselves, and to which you flee. By this means you expect to escape the Lord's judgment and punishment. Even if you enter the Great Supper or wedding of Christ, and are seated at the table with your false hope and unclean robes (for we in part believe that the godless will see the hope and joy of the blessed as the rich man saw Lazarus), Wisd. 5[:2]; Luke 16[:23] how will that help you when Christ the king inspects and looks at the wedding guests, with his Word to see whether they are wearing a wedding garment, which is God's image and divine obedience?

John says that the garments, righteousness, purity and holiness which we are to put on and in which we are to enter and walk, are never to be soiled, Rev. 3[:4]. Nor are we to be found naked, but we are to appear pure before God, Eph. 1[:4]. Now whoever does not enter in and is seated at the table of Christ in this garment, must according to the order and the command of the King of all kings, be cast out again. There will be wailing and the gnashing of teeth. For the hope of the godless will be lost, Prov. 10[:28], and the hope of the ungrateful will vanish as the snow of winter vanishes before the sun. Therefore Christ commands his servants: go forth and call such people out, announce to them that their intention is vain and useless. Therefore with Christ, Matt. 11[:28], we say to such godless people: "Come to me all you who are weary and heavily loaded, I will give you rest. Take upon yourselves my yoke and learn from me." In this way we call people.

Whoever has heard from us the word of preaching and of repentance (the judgment also, on those who will not repent) and allows the preaching of repentance to drive, frighten and force him, such people will begin to recognize their sin, vice, burden of wrong, labour and weariness. They will come to Christ and to his church. They will permit their sins to be removed and prayer for them to be made to God. Those who thus allow themselves to be compelled, urged and driven through God's Word, become God's children and true wedding guests of Christ. Matthew the publican as well as Mary Magdalen did this, Matt. 9[:9]; Luke 7[:36ff]. They all were compelled when they heard the preaching of Christ, to recognize their sins and repent. Therefore, those whom the Spirit of God drives, says Paul, Rom. 8[:14], they are God's children, and are brought and led to the Lord's house, that it might be filled. But whoever will not accept the Word of the Lord from us and will not be compelled by it, will bear his own judgment. Christ says: "Shake the dust from your feet over them as witness," Matt. 10[:14]. For as Christ brought in many hearts with his teaching, preaching, life and walk, so also he shows and teaches us that we are to convince, compel, or win a person. And that is taught by this word of Christ: Let your light shine before men, namely the light of truth which is Christ himself in us. This light is to shine before men, so that they may see our good works and praise our Father who is in heaven. In the same way Paul admonishes us frequently to observe good behaviour among the Gentiles, 1 Pet. 2[:12] or towards those who are outside. His admonitions appear in all his letters, Acts 23[:1]; Rom. 13[:13]; 2 Cor. 1[:12]; 2 Thess. 3[:6]; 1 Tim. 4[:12]. Similarly Peter also says that we are to observe a modest deportment, 1 Pet. 3[:12], especially the women, who are to be subject to their husbands, so that they also who do not believe the Word are won without words by the behaviour of the women when they see their chaste life as well as their fear. That is the compulsion which has been commanded us by Christ and all his apostles that we might compel people in this way and in no other.

Then the priest said to us: Well, I have not been here in the city of Urach long, but just moved here. I do not yet know all of the people nor do they all know me. But when I have been here for a time, he said, I shall raise up a Christian church and congregation here. You will see.

Answer: If you build a Christian church or congregation here by a dead faith and lying preaching, then you will do better than the others who have been here before you. But we do not believe that one can come to life through a dead faith.

So the priest stopped talking with us and in this way did God assist us. To him alone be honour given who cannot forsake his own! They had talked with us close to three hours. Then the chief overseer [Klaus von Grafeneck] said that together we should be given a breakfast. This happened. But all through the time we ate they talked with us. Nothing was said about the Lord's Supper. But the chief overseer said, concerning the government, that he was surprised that God should condemn the government and not pronounce it saved, for God had ordered and instituted it.

Answer: Pay close attention, gentlemen. God has two kinds of servants on earth today, as he did in times past. For you know better than we the story in Scripture concerning Nebuchadnezzar. God himself calls him his servant through the prophet. Yet they were not Jews, much less Christians. For the worldly government exists outside of the kingdom of Christ. The kingdom of Christ and God is his church, his congregation. They are his servants and children whom he had chosen before the beginning of the world. Therefore the world hates us. For his kingdom and church is spiritual. Christ says, John 14[:16], 20[:22]: Receive the Holy Spirit, the Comforter whom the world cannot receive. Thus the government is worldly and not spiritual and is counted as a rod of God in the hand of the Father, which the Father uses on disobedient children. As soon as the rod becomes useless, the Father throws it into the fire. Thus will God do to you, godless magistrates. For just as you are appointed for the condemnation of murderers and evildoers because of their wickedness, so also the judgment and fire of God will come over you magistrates on account of your great vices and wickedness in which you indulge, namely blasphemy, adultery, murder, theft and avarice, full of all unrighteousness, disputing, deception of the heart, evil habits, drinking, and eating. On account of these vices, fire and pain will be your reward, Isa. 9[:17].

Therefore Christ and Paul fittingly say: With the judgment and measure with which you measure and judge, you will yourselves be measured and judged, Matt. 7[:2]; Rom. 2[:1]. Thus it becomes manifest: as the judge, so the culprit, and therefore in the end they both belong in hell and damnation because of their sin. Therefore also, Paul says: "If you bite and devour one another, see that you are not both consumed," Gal. 5[:15]. Since you magistrates and rulers are so surprised that you have been ordained and instituted of God, and yet are to be damned and not saved through your office, notice further what the dear apostle says about Pharaoh the king: "For this very purpose (says God) did I raise you up, that I might show my power on you and so that my name would be made known. He has mercy on whomever he wills, and hardens whomever he will. You say, why does he then blame me? Who can resist his will? Well, my dear man, who are you to want to dispute with God? Does a work perhaps say to the one who made it, why did you make me like this? Does the potter not have power over the clay, so that out of a lump of clay he makes one vessel to honour and one to dishonour? Therefore God, when he intended to be angry and exhibit his power, with great patience brought forth the vessels of wrath which are prepared for damnation, so that he might make known the riches of his glory towards the vessels of mercy which he has prepared to glory which he had ordained, namely us, Rom. 9[:17-24].

Here Paul shows us quite clearly which are the vessels of wrath, fury, and vengeance of God, namely authority and government together with your godless people who thus live together in all unchastity and abomination. Therefore Paul admonishes us further: "In a large house there are not only golden and silver vessels but also wooden and clay vessels, some to honour and some to dishonour," 2 Tim. 2[:20]. The large house is and signifies the whole world, as though Paul said, in this house there will be not only pious children of God, but also many godless who constantly oppose God and his Word and will, as well as the pious who fear God from the heart. That is what you godless magistrates do together with your people, for no righteousness, truth, or faith are to be found among you any more, but only those works which the prophet points out, and which have often been indicated, Hos. 4[:1, :2]. Therefore Paul warns us clearly and says, that whoever purifies himself from such people, will be a vessel sanctified to holiness, useful to the master of the house and prepared for all good works. And so we also say with Paul: whosoever wants to be saved and come to God, must leave the whole world (together with the government) and must turn to God and to his house, yes to his church and to the vessels of honour. Thus he will be saved.

Therefore you magistrates and authorities have been given to the godless people by God in his anger as a punishment and as a rod, though you are yourselves just as evil, Hos. 13[:11]. God has appointed you to this and will sweep you away again in his furious anger. Therefore Paul calls you instruments of vengeance.

You overlords are to punish unrighteous sinners and evildoers, but guard and protect the devout people who fear God. That is why Paul says to us his brethren, Rom. 13[:6], that we are to pay taxes to you for it. But you practice the opposite upon us. You do indeed take the taxes, let the godless sinner go free, but punish the pious, torture, kill, and imprison them, as you openly show in our case. Therefore the punishment you receive from God will be all the greater. Christ calls you magistrates and authorities a power of darkness and the gates of hell, Luke 22[:53]; Matt. 16[:18]. Paul speaks similarly of you, Eph. 5[:8]; Col. 1[:13]; Eph. 6[:12].

That you magistrates are not, and in your office and service cannot be, Christians, Christ shows with these words: "The worldly princes rule over the nations and the overlords lord it over them in might; but you are not to be like that," Matt. 20[:25]. And further Christ says: "My kingdom is not of this world, otherwise my servants would stand there ready to fight for me," John 18[:36]. From this it is manifest that Christ does not want his servants to fight about the kingdom of this world. Since you worldly magistrates fight about the kingdom of this world, you show thereby that you are not servants to salvation but servants to damnation. For the kingdom of this world is the devil's kingdom and domain. He is the father, lord, king, god and prince of the godless world. You magistrates and authorities strive with one another over the kingdom of this world, Matt. 4[:8]; John 8[:44]. Indeed, wherever one can attack the land and realm of another, he does not hesitate, for it is the way of the devil, the father of the world, that he teaches them to murder and do wrong. For the devil himself is a murderer, and therefore he must train his children to this as well. Then they stopped speaking.

Then the priest said to us that he had often intended to come to us and to instruct us and show us the way to God, but he saw now that we would not be instructed.

Answer: You cannot show us the way of God nor faith, for you do not know it yourself. And it is exactly you people who are the thieves and murderers of whom Christ says that they will not come except to steal, murder and do to death, John 10[:10]. Yes it is precisely you priests who are the wolves who would like to tear us, the sheep of Christ, Matt. 7[:15]. Therefore the farther you stay away from us the better we like it. For as often as you godless priests and false prophets come or whenever you have come, you have never yet taught us faith, but only doubt and curse.

So they went on their way and departed. God helped us to win the field and the battle, as he had promised: It will not be you who speak. But the Spirit of my Father will perform in you as he faithfully does. Matt. 10[:20]; Luke 21[:14]. To him be praise!

Written during our imprisonment in Hohenwittlingen, the third day after Easter, Anno 1563.

26

Paul Glock

Letter to Leonhard Lanzenstiel (1563)*

Paul Glock to Leonhard Lanzenstiel, Hohenwittlingen, June 7, 1563.

An epistle written to Leonhard Sailer, servant of the Lord and his congregation. Paul and Adam [Horneck], my fellow prisoner, your loving brethren in the suffering of the cross and the patience of Christ to our dear brother Leonhard Sailer and his helpers in the Word wherever they are in tribulation. We thank our God at all times for you and for the grace of God which has been given to you in Christ Jesus, that you have richly been given all kinds of things in him regarding the Word and knowledge of God. This is confirmed by the witness of Christ in you so that you lack no gift. With us you wait for the revelation of our Lord Jesus Christ who will strengthen us to the end so that we may be blameless in the day of our Lord Jesus Christ. Yes, may God endow

---

*Source: Bossert, *Quellen I*, 1078-81.
Translation: Friesen/Klaassen

and strengthen you still more in this, so that you may pasture the flock of Christ according to the will of God, to the glory of his name, to the comfort of the godly and to your salvation. Amen.

Oh, you dear brethren, how much gratitude and praise we owe our God for the morning meal of Daniel which, to be sure, is much more comforting than Daniel's was.[1] Through your message and letter we were greatly pleased; may God be praised eternally! Your writing and gifts came to us just in time on the day of Pentecost of the year 63. From this we know, dear brethren in Christ, especially you, Leonhard, together with your fellow warriors in the Word and the Gospel, that things still go well with us in the Lord. God preserves us wonderfully among our enemies, as he has promised in many places here and there. He will protect, defend, maintain and keep the devout who have their eye on him. We see this daily with our own eyes, for he leads us with his strong hand. To him be hearty praise! He is still the ancient God and Father who helped Abraham, Isaac, Jacob, Joseph, Moses, Joshua, David and all believers in their distress and tribulation, and will also help us, his believers, to the end as long as we trust him from the heart. Further, dear brethren, we also learned from your writing how willingly and often you write in order to comfort us whenever you can. We know your intentions. You do not spare any diligence, work nor effort daily to help us where it might be possible. But it cannot be and so we are well satisfied with the gift and message from you. Oh our God! We cannot thank him enough for such things. For this message comes to us secretly, contrary to all designs of our enemies.

Further, we have also received word about the writing I sent you. When I did it, I was only throwing pearls and holy things to the dogs and loathsome pigs who do not improve themselves, much less being converted from their sins to God by it. But I am to be quiet about this, and am already calm, dear brethren, although I have already written several articles for them as they required them from me.

For they spoke with us in this year 63 and required of us a statement on every article which they drew up against us. We were to do this in writing. So the lord chief overseer sent us paper and ink for this purpose. We answered them faithfully in the fear of God. What they will do with it, God knows. We have not heard anything about it.

We also hear from you that few become Christian, that concern about it has virtually gone, and that faith has grown cold. We must commit it to God. God has severely attacked the false Lutheranism with punishment and plagues, with death, hunger, and hail and storms, almost like Egypt. There has also been sorcery and fires. There is misery in many places in Württemberg. We have reliable news of this from my blood sister and also from brother Melchior Waal.[2]

We want you to know that we lack for nothing, for they still feed us with bread and water, porridge and soup, a good provision of necessities. Indeed, God has created such a scarcity in the land of Württemberg among the common people that we must say that we still have plenty. For many godless people are dying of starvation. If we lack anything the brethren, Melchior Waal and the others, supply it. For we have good communication with each other, God be fervently praised. The lady and the lord at Urach do much good to us in our bonds without ceasing. May God reward them for it according to his will. The unbelieving people in the castle allow us to come together every day between the cells, so that we may spend the day together. But at night they put each one in his cell. We are cheerful and well satisfied and unified one with the other in faith. God be praised!

We well understand that we are to be faithful to the Lord, to remain devout, and not to allow ourselves to be discouraged. This we intend to do faithfully with God's help and we always comfort ourselves with these words: "The souls of the righteous are in God's hand. No pain of death can touch them. By fools, it is true, they are discounted as though their going out were without honour, and their end a shame. The way of the righteous is counted as destruction. But they are in secure rest and peace and although they suffer some pain from men, yet is their hope on immortal things. They are fed with passing suffering, but will be recompensed with much good. For God tries them so that they are obedient to him. As gold is purified in the smelter, so God has purified and refined and accepted them as a burnt offering. In his time, however, he will look upon them." Christ also says: "Blessed are they which are persecuted for the sake of righteousness, for the kingdom of heaven is prepared for them. If people revile you and persecute you and speak all kinds of wickedness and evil against you falsely for my sake, be happy and rejoice. You will be well rewarded in heaven [Matt. 5:10-12]. They will take you to their council houses and will scourge you in their assemblies. You will be led before kings and princes for my sake as a witness against them and the heathen. When they arrest and try you, do not worry how or what you will speak. For it is not you who speak, but it is the Spirit of your Father who will speak through you" [Matt. 10:18-20].

Certainly this Spirit of God always represents us before our enemies. To God be the praise! Further: "You must be hated by every man for my name's sake. But whoever endures to the end, will be saved" [Matt. 10:22]. Indeed, Christ says: "If the world hates you, know that it hated me before you. If you were of the world, the world would love its own. But since you are not of the world, and I have chosen you out of the world, it hates you. Remember my word when I told you, the servant is not greater than his master. If they have persecuted me, they will also persecute you. But they will do such things to you because they have known neither me nor my Father [John 15:18-21]. I have told you this, however, so that you have peace in me. In the world you have fear, but be comforted, I have overcome the world" [John 16:33]. Paul strongly admonishes us when he says: "We must enter the kingdom of God through much tribulation" [Acts 4:22]. And again he says: "Who will separate us from the love of God, tribulation or anxiety or persecution or hunger or nakedness, danger or sword? As it is written: for your sakes we are killed all day long. We are considered as sheep for the slaughter. But in all that we overcome for the sake of him who loved us. For I am certain that neither death nor life nor angels nor principalities, nor what is in the future nor in the present, nor power nor what is high nor deep nor any other creature can separate us from the love of God which is in Christ Jesus our Lord" [Rom. 8:35-39]. Further he says: "It is given to you not only to believe in Christ but also to suffer for him" [Phil. 1:29]. In another place he also says, "All who would lead godly lives in Christ Jesus must suffer persecution." Be confident of that in us, dear brethren. But ask the Lord together with us and the whole congregation, that he might keep us upright and faithful, to the honour of his holy name, to your comfort, but to our salvation.

With these words we commend you all together with ourselves to the faithful Father in heaven under his merciful protection and safekeeping. May he be your and our champion in all our troubles. We, Paul, and Adam, greet you, especially you, dear Leonhard, together with your helpers in the Word, and also together with the holy congregation of God in the holy and pure love of God. Greet Else especially and encourage her that she commend all things to the Lord. For it pleases him to deal thus with us. It will please us also to do so until it seems time to him to arrange the matter differently. Amen.

Written from the prison Hohen Wittlingen on the 7th day of June of 1563.

27

Paul Glock

Letter to Peter Walpot (1566)[*]

Paul Glock to Peter Walpot, Hohenwittlingen, September 30, 1566.

Paul the younger, your brother and member of the body, cross, suffering, tribulation and the patience of Christ, to Peter Walpot[1] and his coworkers in the Word and the church of God in Moravia, my dear brothers and sisters. The eternal wisdom of God which maintains everything and whose power no one can break, be with you forever. Amen.

Oh, my dear and desired brethren whom I can never forget! Oh my God, how often I think of you and of your love, peace, joy and unity which you have in God our Lord! How much I would like to have seen you once more with a joyful heart before my end. But that will not happen, as I judge.

---

[*]Source: Bossert, *Quellen I*, 1086-92.
Translation: Friesen/Klaassen

First you must know, dear brethren, that I am well comforted in God who enfolds me with his arms so that the defiance of the enemy and of the godless cannot frighten me, and I feel about their threats against me as Joshua and Caleb when they said, "We will eat our enemies as bread" [Num. 14:9]. With many other comforts I strengthen myself in the grace of God.

Now, my dear brethren, the reason that I delayed writing so long is that I had such good news by word of mouth according to the wish of my heart. I thought it unnecessary to write, and also I was in good hopes that God would bring me home soon. But now I no longer have any hope. The Lord, to whom everything is possible, could still arrange it; I leave it with him. Please know, however, that in this 66th year I have experienced much faithfulness from God as the song indicates.[2] In the meantime God has given the unbelieving overseer of the castle such confidence towards me that he trusted my word that no matter where and how far he sent me from the castle, I would return. Thus my going here and there and out and in has continued for fully half a year, so that he never locked me up once, neither day nor night; God be praised!

I have been in the town of Urach many times; I don't know how often. There I have eaten often with the lady and her husband.[3] I planted a pretty vine near the house for them. I have also twice been in their house at Dettling and gotten fruit there. At Wittling I worked a scythe during harvest and earned nine shillings there. I have also been sent three miles [about 15 English miles] from the castle to Blaubeuren and have been over night at the house of the lady's daughter and have washed my hands in the source of the Blau. I also worked in the castle and around it, carting out manure, making fences around the gardens, cutting hay, making and drying it. I also carried many rakes to market for the overseer of the castle. In this way, dear brethren, through God's grace and fear I travelled around among the unbelieving people.

Neither priest nor ruler spoke to me nor to the overseer of the castle, about why he permitted me so much freedom for over half a year. If someone among the people asked me about matters of faith, I told it to them according to the truth, reproving their godless lives and being, admonishing them to repentance and saying that they would not be saved in their false opinions and superstitions. The one liked it, the other despised it as always happens. But the world has become so frivolous because of their false priests that they cannot or do not want to believe the truth. However, all who saw me were very surprised that I was a prisoner, but that I could go out and in and keep my word not to escape. Now the enemy observed this for a while, and as I wrote above, I had hoped to be freed sometime soon.

So the enemy constantly caused the priest knaves and the government to bother me, thinking I would do what they wanted. They wanted to slander me and hypocritically to tell their false church that I had, after all, nicely obeyed them and yielded the matter to them and that therefore they allowed me to go; our prisons are highly to be praised [they said] as well as the laws of injustice which are our strength and by which we have been able to make these rascals do our will. Thus, they had me brought before them; the last time they asked me whether their gracious lord and prince and they as well as his servants were good Christians and would be saved when they died. I answered, "How could that possibly be true, since from the beginning of the world there have never existed such godless men as you abandoned wretches, both Lutheran and papist, who all live and walk in every unchastity, rascality and knavery? The Holy Spirit says that such godless people are cursed whether they die or live. For just as everything that grows out of the earth again returns to the earth, the godless, which you are, come out of the curse and go into destruction or damnation. How do you expect to be saved in your wickedness? With that I put them all out of joint and they all said that I did not deserve to move among the people any more. I was now to remain imprisoned for life, either till I died or until I said they were good Christians.

I answered: "My imprisonment has an end here, but yours, as soon as it begins, has no end eternally." But they derided this and asked whether I believed that God had created everything good and honest. I said, "Yes." "Why then," they said, "do you condemn the government? Has it not also been created good and upright?" I said, "The Holy Spirit says in one place that God has created everything for his own sake, even the wicked for the day of evil. Everything is good, but it will not be good to him who will be struck by pain and torment. At a different place he says that he made it all for the good of the believers, but for the harm of the godless. God has chosen and created the Turk and the devil. Are they saved because of that?" Then they answered, "No." I replied: "You godless magistrates are outside of the kingdom of God and chosen for hell. Always there have been two peoples, a pious and a godless, as it is still. Whoever trusts and believes you priests, and whoever adheres to your false teaching is damned. Whoever comes to us, the church of God, and truly repents from the heart, will be saved.

Then the court preacher of the prince said: "Rabbler, if the rumour went out among the peasants that their lords, servants and priests were not Christian and not saved, they would soon fall upon us, tear our hair and knock us to the ground. Therefore you must be kept prisoner so that what you say does not reach them."

Then they changed the subject and began to speak of the Father, the Son and the Holy Spirit, asking whether I considered them to be three essential persons, as they did. I answered: "I consider the Father essential in his divinity. No one knows about his person or what he looks like. But the Son I consider to be essential in his humanness; he was seen and touched like another person. So there are two names but only one Godhead. The Spirit has no essence in himself, but is the living Word of the Father and the Son and proceeds from them when they will or bid. This Spirit or Word is compared to a wind which passes, you will hear its roaring but do not know whence or whither it blows. This Spirit proceeds from the two and fills our hearts, and makes us intelligent and wise to do God's will. Whoever does not have him, has none; whoever has him has all three. That is my understanding of the matter." They, however, persisted in their harebrained position, that they were three real persons and called me a Turk or a Jew, and so they left, ordering me incarcerated. But I am undismayed in Christ, dear brethren. He knows well how to keep me to the end, and even if I am to lie here my life long, I will comfort myself with his great wonders and goodness.

The goldsmith who was imprisoned with me has been released. But a poor poacher whose home is on the Härtsfeld has been shut up near me in Adam's prison for more than a year. Someone from the outside had sent him a saw and a hatchet, and he has broken out. I heard everything. The man's name is Hans Seng from Eglingen, which is not far from Nördlingen in the Riesz. He has many children and a wife. He spoke much with me concerning faith, because he is a papist. He was surprised that the world cannot be saved. He often said to me that if God were to help him out once more, he would seek the congregation together with his wife and children and become pious. Did he do it and is he with you? I do wish it for him.

Now, however, dear brethren, that he has broken out, they are very diligently building at the castle and at the cells. Where one could formerly see a little to eat—Adam well knows—it is now all closed up and they make it solid from the outside. One can no longer shout or call to another. I am not yet in there, but must wait till they are finished. Since the godless castle overseer has a command to put me in prison and not to allow anyone from Urach to me nor allow any friend or anyone from the lady's house to provide anything for me, he has taken me up into Adam's old prison and has robbed me clean, taking everything I had for writing, and made me quite poor. I was rich in such things, for I bought everything myself. I thought of Sirach when he says: It is easy for God to make a poor man rich and a rich man poor. But praise God! He always gives me more than I know or can think. He has already given me enough that I can write to you once more. But I do not know whether, even if I had enough material for writing, I will be able to see enough in the dark prison. Therefore, dear brothers and sisters, if I can no longer write much, please accept what little I can. But I do not want to forsake my trust in God. Besides the testing he will well give me gracious sufficiency as he has often done before, and will still do to the praise of his name and to our comfort. Amen.

Since I can write again, I will not forget you at any time, if God wills, whom we all serve. Please do the same, do not stop. Write and send it to the old place. You know well where I mean—to the lady of Urach, as I told you before. How things are in the castle, I do not know. I want you to know, however, my Adam, that the servants are gone out of the castle, no one knows where. Albrecht has died. The son has become a smith; the daughter married her old beau from the mill and lives in the village. He keeps house with servants and maids. For a year I was well treated by the maid, for she has made the soups and gruels better for me than for the two of them. How it will go in the future, who will live, God knows well, may that be committed to him, too. My friends have often interceded for me that I might be released. But they have recently not been with me. I think, it does them no good to plead for me because I spoke so strongly against the government.

The brethren have recently been with me and told me that in the congregation things are well. They also know about me. I require nothing, praise God, neither clothes nor food. I am given enough clothes for my need. They still feed me with soups and cooked food, water and bread. The Lord is my helper, praise him! And since my way is so strongly barred, and yours also so that we cannot travel back and forth, do not expect a message from me. I won't expect it either, even if it takes a year or more. But let us thank God for the former frequent times when it happened, and pray that if it be his will that he break the hearts of our enemies and bind their eyes that we might make contact with one another more often than they know. The God of peace, of love and faith be with you all. May he strengthen you, give you increase, and let you grow like the lilies at the water brooks and like the trees whose leaves do not fall off, to the praise of his name. Pray for me at all times that God may save me from the evil and wicked world. For I desire to hold still for the Lord to the end, with his help, whether it costs life or death, whether it be deep or shallow. You may have confidence in me. I commend you to God hereby, to his protection and shelter and the wings of justice. Be united with one another with the inner peace of Christ and be greeted many thousands of times. My whole heart, soul and spirit be with you all, the whole Christian church. Amen, yes, Amen.

Dear Peter, greet all my compatriots, my cousin Hans Egen of Rommelshausen, also Agnes, young Anna Röser, Judith, my neighbour, if she is there, also Bärthel Haugen and his wife, also Jörg and his wife from the Netherlands, my brother-in-law Wolf and his Ottilie, also the daughter of my father's brother, and say to all those who write to me that even if I do not write to all who write to me, they are not to be surprised, because I can no longer manage it as before. Where I can, however, I will be diligent with God's help. Amen.

Written in the prison at Wittlingen on Monday after St. Michael's Day, anno 1566.

28

Paul Glock

Letter to Peter Walpot (1567)[*]

Paul Glock to Peter Walpot, Hohenwittlingen, June 11, 1567.

Paul, your brother and member of the body, of the tribulation and of the pateince of Christ Jesus our Lord, to Peter Walpot, wherever he is in tribulation and to his co-workers, my dear brothers and sisters.

May the true Light, given to us by the Father (who has made all things), increase his divine Word in you more and more through which you may knit the church together so that it might grow still more into the Word of the Lord to the honour of God. Yes, may the Lord, our God, grant this to his praise and for our comfort through Christ Jesus our Lord, redeemer and saviour. Amen.

Oh dear and longed-for brethren and servants of the great God in his church and congregation of Christ Jesus, I cannot refrain from writ-

---

[*]Source: Bossert, *Quellen I*, 1092-95.
Translation: Friesen/Klaassen

ing to you out of love, as is indeed right and just, to let you know how things are with me in all my tribulations which I suffer for the sake of Christ, since God has granted me enough material to write with, to the frustration of all my enemies.

Oh, how much thanks I owe God for this! Therefore I am letting you know how I am. I have been sick this 67th year from Easter [March 30] till now, St. John's day, [May 6] and no improvement is to be expected or hoped for. I shall not be well again in the flesh. May God grant that it will be to your comfort, and to my salvation. Now that I am poor and miserable in body, lame in the knees and in the hips, with aches and a painfully sore mouth, I cannot eat the bread any more and am quite emaciated and run down. I do not have the strength any more to put on or take off my clothes, nor can I make my bed any more. Thus God has attacked me, as Job says: "The arrows of the Almighty have pierced me" [Job 6:4]. But my trust is in him, he will not forsake me. Daily I see and feel his remedies, to him be praise!

Also I have written to the malicious knaves in the chancellory about how poorly I am physically, that I had long been sick, and received only watery soups and bread twice daily which they grudgingly ordered for me. I cannot eat the bread at all. If they do not tend to the matter and help concerning food or other things, they will by this means murder me. I wanted them to know it; then let them do with me as they please. The godless rascals soon replied in a knavish letter and cunningly touched on my sickness. With the letter they sent two crafty rascals or priests who read the letter to me. The meaning and contents were as follows: Since God has thus attacked me with serious illness, I ought really to recognize my sin and convert to their good and godly teaching, obey them, and, if I did so, I could expect every good thing from them, assuming I were to put aside my error. They attempted to catch me as Job's friends did to Job. But Job says: "I mean to hold to my integrity as long as I live and have breath in my nose. You came, but you will not weaken my courage [Job 27:3-5]. You are all together miserable comforters. Will careless words have no end? [Job 16:2-3]. Indeed, you are the people, and wisdom will die with you" [Job 12:2].

Thus these two clerical jacks began to speak with me about faith. Faith saves without works, and accomplishes this by itself. Answer: "Oh no," said I, "Christian faith produces good Christian works. Those works which are done in Christ Jesus or accomplished in him save us, as one can see in Matthew five, Luke ten, fourteen and in many other places." But they opposed this like the company of Korah in the desert who fell alive into hell. Further I said to them: "Show me a Christian group which has grown from your preaching, teaching and faith, and I will go to them. If there is anything in me contrary to God, I want to abandon it and stop it and accept what is better." Then the two knaves said to me that one could not identify the Christian church with hands or fingers. Answer: "Now it is manifest what kind of false prophets you are. Christ identified his church and his disciples when he stretched out his hand over his disciples and said: "These are my brothers, sisters and mothers, which do the will of my Father in heaven" [Matt. 12:49-50]. He also said: "You are to be a light in the world," [Matt. 5:14] and again,"Love one another just as I have loved you, then every man will recognize that you are my disciples" [John 13:34-35]. Peter says: "Have a good walk among the heathen, so that they are compelled to believe in God without words. Observe, you false serpents, how God identifies his church and sets it into the light for the godless world to see. Therefore you cursed knaves are children of darkness together with the perverted world. The true light of Christ in us shines into your false faces so that you can neither see, hear nor tolerate us." Thus the two knaves were put to shame before all who were there. And the fact that they could not show me a single Christian man was a still greater shame to them.

Then I said to them: "You godless scum, am I to trust or give myself to you so that you can make a Christian out of me while you have not yet made a single Christian in your churches? You, precisely are the knaves, the four hundred prophets of Ahab. God has put a false spirit into your cheating mouths in order to seduce the whole world. Indeed you are the thieves and murderers of whom Christ says that they come only to steal and to kill, who do not serve the Lord Christ but their belly which is god, in whom you will come to shame. You malicious recreants," I said to them, "lie in all your dealings." Thus they were discomfitted together. But the Lord made me joyous in the presence of my enemies so that they were amazed that in my weak sickness I was able to answer them this way. Praise God who gave me the words!

They also talked much about baptism and Christ's supper. I could write much about their folly in these matters, as you know from my previous reports. When I showed them the truth about this, they were once again frustrated in their intent, and the two priests angrily asked me whether I presumed to know the secret of Christ, for that was theirs to do. "Yes, indeed," I said. "I hear well enough that I and the elect of God are not supposed to know or preceive his secret, but are to entrust ourselves to you so that you might lead us as well as the whole world into hell with your cunning knavery. No, we praise God in Christ who has given us his Spirit through which we can recognize your trickery and may separate ourselves from you as from unclean spirits whom God condemns. For you conduct your preaching without the Spirit of Christ. Therefore it yields neither fruit nor life or the saving of the soul. For where has the Holy Spirit preached infant baptism or used it as you abominable scum say and do?" And I said to them: "This is the last straw; your preaching baptism and Lord's Supper purifies your people and churches for the kingdom of God like the ugly mud of autumn cleans. Just so is your congregation of whoredom clean." Oh, brethren, that cut deeply into their dishonest hearts and at this point they and the others left. Thus did the Lord stand by me, he who does not forsake his own; to him be praise!

And thus do the malicious knaves let me lie in the throes of my illness, quite lame. The food has not improved nor have they had the barbers[1] nor doctors in to help me, so that I think, dear brethren, they will in this way murder and kill me. But I am well comforted in Christ our Lord and am not afraid of what flesh can do to me. I have committed it all to my God to do with me according to his good will. To him I will be true and firm to the end, for I see and feel his means, help and strength and his miracles to me, a simple and poor man. To him be praise! He has taken all struggling from me, although at times it does stir within me. Faith in Christ is our victory which overcomes the world, death, devil, hell and its servants, as well as our flesh.

But if this letter reaches you while I am still alive, do faithfully pray to God for me, that he arrange my affairs for the best and to his honour, to your comfort, and to my salvation, and to the increasing sentence and condemnation of the malicious tricksters. They have exhausted all their cunning tricks and knavery so that they do not know what more they can do to me, for their bag of lies has been almost emptied and they have been put to shame. In all their folly they know nothing, the dirty liars. But since they are so repelled by the communion of Christ, you must continue in preaching, teaching and admonition all the more, since that has been assigned to us by Christ. Let us walk, live and exist in that certainty, even though the world were to burst because of it.

Otherwise, dear brethren, do not worry now about me on account of food. I have enough, may God be given praise and thanks for it. It appears that I will live a while longer, for I buy much for myself. Otherwise I think I would have died before this. If I cannot come to you any more nor am able to write, make do with this letter. For I write in great illness. Continue in prayer, in community, and in the love of God and also in true obedience, to which we have been called in Christ. May the Lord infuse and grant this in you through his Holy Spirit. Amen.

With this I take leave of you in the peace of Christ, in the love and unity of Jesus Christ. My greetings to all many times in divine love as was mentioned before. I need not teach you for you are already well taught. Remain firm to the end. Amen.

Given at Wittlingen, from prison, on the 11th of June, ao. 1567.

29

Paul Glock

Letter to Peter Walpot (1569)[*]

Paul Glock to Peter Walpot, 1569 during Easter week, Hohenwittlingen.

To Peter Walpot and his co-workers in the service of the Word, my dear brothers and sisters. May the Lord, the almighty God, who at all times extends his care over his church and children, increasingly strengthen you, as those who are looked upon and are chosen to be pillars in the house of God, to build his church. May he send his Spirit down upon you, the Spirit of wisdom and understanding, the Spirit of counsel and of strength, the Spirit of the knowledge and the fear of God. Through him may you pasture his sheep for him with sound teaching in which God might take sweet pleasure at all times. I wish from the depth of my heart that God who can do everything, will in Christ Jesus, his Son, give it. Amen.

---

[*]Source: Bossert, *Quellen I*, 1096-99.
Translation: Friesen/Klaassen

My fathers and fathers of the church of God especially, beloved brethren, I want you to know how I am faring in my bonds, which I bear for the sake of Christ among an ill-behaved and wicked generation whose face is estranged and who consider it an offence to have to hear the truth of God. I am quite well in the Lord Christ. Praise be to him! I am well and comforted in everything the Lord has put upon me in whatever manner to suffer for his sake. For a great reward awaits us which no one can tell. But in spirit and in faith we grasp it. Therefore we wait with patience until the Lord relieves us. I am of good cheer and have no complaints, may God be praised eternally! Although the devil tries, he cannot accomplish anything. I am determined to hold still for the Lord, whatever he does with me whether the price is death or prison. My hope is firm that he will keep me to the end to the honour of his name, to your comfort, and to my salvation. Please don't doubt me, for I know that God strengthens me through your prayers which he hears daily.

How have things gone with me this winter? They have gone well, the Lord be praised! Each day they heated a warm room for me so that I was never cold. They also give me good food and drink, meat twice each day or fish or baked goods instead. There are two dishes at one time and I eat twice daily and each time receive a quarter of wine. Nor do they allow me to lack clothes or blankets. Also they don't bother me with talk about their faith. When they come here, they talk only with the priest who is imprisoned next to me, for he also quarrels with them about faith. But he errs in several things and will not agree with our confession. Therefore I am not yet satisfied with him. However, I still hope that the Lord will grant him further grace that he will allow himself to be shown right. They allow us to be together only a little. But I think they may allow us together more.

I received a letter from Christoph Achznit from which I received much comfort and joy. God be thanked, who still allows messages to come to me despite my enemies, no matter how they fume. I have heard, therefore, that things go well with you all, and the whole congregation, in both body and soul, and how God still adds daily those who belong to him. The Most High be praised! May he bring in more who learn to praise and acknowledge his name. Also, the brethren who have come out,[1] such as Leonhart and those belonging to him, have written me that things are going well with you. I can also believe that zeal is at a low ebb. For Satan has quite turned schoolmaster in the world and insists strongly that no one become godly. May the Lord, however, seek those who belong to him!

The messages reached me approximately ten days from the end of March in the 69th year. Other than that I have had no message since the autumn of the 68th year. I wrote that to you once and sent the message. But I have not heard whether you received it or not. I should like very much to know, dear brethren, for otherwise I don't know whether the messengers are reliable or not. Dear brother Peter, tell Jobst Lackhorn and his old wife that I received their present before the autumn of the 68th year, but that there was no letter with it. How that happened, I do not know, but the Lord be praised! May he be their recompense in eternity. I have received the laxative as well as the note accompanying the gift.

In the 68th year both of my princes died, the young duke Eberhart, and his father Christoph, duke of Wurttemberg. For a time there was a strong rumour that all the prisoners would be released and that I would be included. But the rumour has died out. In any event, my life does not depend upon that. Rather, God knows my time. I will await it with patience. The length of time that pleases him shall please me also. The young prince, duke Ludwig, still lives. What God will allow him to do with me, he well knows; may God keep me true to the end to his honour. Amen.

With this letter I am also sending you a song which I composed two years ago. I sent it to you before too, but have not heard whether you received it. The song relates how things went.[2] Since then they leave me in peace. When the priests do come they are very compatible and give me good information. But they no longer debate with me, so I don't say anything either. For what I am not asked I do not answer. The reason, however, that they are so quiet is that they are themselves confused and are building the tower of Babel. For God has confused them through their blindness.

Whatever is clumsy in the song, please remove, for at that time I could do no better because they had a very godless intention with me, as you know. I simply was very ill. They came to comfort me just like the three friends of Job. But God was my support as always. To him be the honour!

At present I sing, I read, I write, I braid cords for the citizens of Urach, and each time earn a groat. Whatever I lack the brethren outside supply faithfully. May the Lord be praised! Every day I have backaches, though the Lord helps me to bear it. Messages will reach me better than during the last two years. To God be the honour eternally.

Dear Peter, if possible, do not forget the faithful people who for such a long time have done good to me and still do. Send them another two pairs of knives as before. For the lord of the castle told me himself that the brother Ludwig [Dorker?] had been with him for the night and told him good things about the congregation, which I was very glad to hear; to God be the praise! Such great things the Lord does for me. In my simplicity I cannot thank him enough. I can't think of anything more to write to you, except that you hear of my well-being in Christ. Other than that, dear brethren, take care of the flock of Christ. Watch the lazy and the indolent; and whoever will not submit to the obedience of Christ. Sweep it out, and allow no splintering among you, contrary to those who claim that there must be divisions in the church of Christ. I say no! Such frivolous people are not to be tolerated in the Christian congregation. In the church there is to be one faith, one love, one obedience, one Lord, one baptism and one God. I well know that you spare no diligence in this, but I say it for the sake of even more diligence. May the God of peace sanctify you through and through. Your spirit, soul and body must be kept blameless for the future of our Lord Jesus Christ. Faithful is he who will do it. Dear brethren, pray for me at all times, that he may keep me faithful to the end, as I know that you and the whole congregation do at all times for me and all who sorrow. Yet I admonish you to still more diligence. I do this for you and mean to do it at all times. And even if it is not God's will that you see me face to face or I you, yet we see each other in spirit daily. May God also keep me to himself to the end. Herewith I greet you with a peaceful heart many thousand times in Christ, especially you elders in the Word, together with the entire holy church of God. Greet Christof Achznit for me and my brother-in-law Wolf Ruemer at Gostall, as well as my cousin and brother Hans Egen, the cobbler, and his old wife.

Given at Wittlingen from the room of the bailiff during Easter week in the year of Christ 1569.

30

Paul Glock

Letter to Peter Walpot
(1569)*

Paul Glock to Peter Walpot, Hohenwittlingen, August 24, 1569

To Peter Walpot and to his fellow warriors, my dear brethren in Christ be grace and mercy from God, our Father, from our Lord Jesus Christ. This is my hearty wish for you. May he bear you at all times on eagles' wings and himself watch you, the sheep of his dear flock. May he provide you with faithful shepherds who divide the Word of truth rightly with sound teaching so that the church of Christ may nowhere suffer loss. This I wish you all together again from him who bears up all things, who is God, a Light to which no one can come unless he is pure in heart. Amen.

Oh my longed-for brethren and fathers, all you elders of the Word and of temporal care; know that your dear message reached me just

---

*Source: Bossert, *Quellen I*, 1099-1102.
Translation: Friesen/Klaassen

three days before Bartholomew [August 24] in the 69th year. I was overjoyed and comforted when I heard that you are all really well and that you grow and increase abundantly in Christ and live and walk in peace, love and unity as is fitting for the children of God. The Lord of heaven be greatly praised for this, who blesses you so richly, lets you flourish and blesses you despite all the bloodhounds and enemies of truth who constantly seek our lives, to eradicate us for the sake of his righteousness which they will neither tolerate nor accept and in which they will much less live and walk. For they consider it a disgrace, while to us it is an introduction and a way to the kingdom of Christ and to eternal life. May the Lord grant it to us and let us walk in it more and more until we arrive.

I want you to know, dear brethren, how I am faring in my bonds for the sake of the name of Christ. I desire to remain with him, by his help, to the end of my life. I know of nothing more to write to you except that I am well in Christ in soul and body. The one exception is that my back is not well. But I thank God for the discipline of his love because he has shown me his manifold grace, love and his benign hand. I cannot sufficiently express myself for what he has manifested in me, a poor, simple man. To him be praise eternally! I am well comforted in my heart and have no special concerns. To him be the praise! I sing, I read. At times I work braid and in this way pass the time as long as God grants it to me. And I am not bothered by those false knaves, the apostate priests, nor by the government. For they leave me in peace even though they sometimes come up here and have to do and talk with other prisoners. They only take me out so I can eat with them, but concerning faith they are silent towards me. For I have stated to them orally and in writing that if they can show me a better way to salvation than I show them in my written or oral confession, I shall follow them. If not, I shall certainly remain by that which is most certain. They say that even if I or we were in the right, they could still not tolerate it.

I answered: "Thus you do just as your fathers did also who always persecuted the truth, and you will receive the same reward, too. Therefore I warn you about your treatment of us." Thus there is no improvement in their attitude and they will not release me either. But I am in the Lord's hand, and he knows the right time and hour to deal with me. May he keep me true and devout in the truth. Amen.

I want you to know that I have copied our account of our faith[1] and given it to the deputy overseer of Urach, who is well-known to me as well as the chief overseer. They are both agreed with me. I have especially asked the deputy to have it bound for me. He is without a doubt a learned man in Latin and German. He will read it carefully, but how it will please him I do not know yet. The Lord will do what is best.

I have given our *Account* to the priest who is imprisoned near me, of whom I wrote you earlier, and of whom I hoped, that he might turn to us. He actually criticizes many articles in it and slanders us, although he agrees with us at some points. But he wants to go his own way and if it were possible he would like to turn me away from you so that I would adhere to him or to others. But whoever does not adhere to the teaching which we have learned from Christ, him I will not take home or to heart. He does not believe that we have inherited original sin from Adam. He also confesses that a magistrate may be a Christian but only so long as his duty does not conflict with or fight against his conscience. However, a Christian cannot be in government. He says that a Christian may give all kinds of war tax or blood money but that he himself may not fight, but only pay taxes towards it, and other such fantasies. He will not allow himself in any way to be instructed. Therefore I must separate myself from him and not have much to do with him. May the Lord grant him better grace and knowledge, if that is his will.

You will be glad to hear that they have now put me into a room that is airy, panelled and comfortable, and has a large window so that one can see people in the valley, and can look into the vineyards and highways. There is no physical hardship except that I am imprisoned, and must be deprived of your words and the Lord's. It is a struggle for me that I am not able to see your face nor hear the voice of God. But the Lord is my comfort as also are your letters and prayers for me. Therefore, dear brother Peter and the whole congregation, be diligent in prayer for me and all the afflicted, because the times are so dangerous.

May God keep you to his honour, to your comfort, and to my salvation. I know well that you constantly do this, but I write it to increase your zeal. May the Lord, pour out his good blessing over all, and may he increase you like the sand at the sea and the stars in the sky. May he guard you and me from all evil for ever. Amen.

I suppose the brethren tell you how things are outside. Bread and wine are fairly cheap, but the whole land is polluted with whoredom and defiled with all manner of unchastity like Sodom. May the Lord grant them to know this. Besides this they still treat me quite well as to food, with meat, wine and bread, and also as to clothes. Besides, the brethren still come here often and send to ask me about what I require.

May the Lord be your reward for your concern about me. Thus I have no lack in anything. God be praised!

So far this year I have made 2000 ells of braid. For each I earn about one kreutzer so that I can buy something. I do not lack money, to the Lord be the praise! Right now I do not know anything special to write, either. The brethren have written me that there is little interest in the Gospel outside; thus they will soon return to Moravia again. "To him, however, who is able to do superabundantly all that we ask and understand according to the power which works in us, to him be honour in the church which is in Christ Jesus at all times from eternity to eternity. Amen."

I greet you with a peaceful heart many times in the love of God, you fathers first together with the holy Christian church. Please greet Jobst Lackhorn and his whole house, as well as my compatriots from my homeland. Greet my cousin Hans Egen, the cobbler, also Bartl Haugen, and Jorg and their wives with them in the holy love of God.

Given at Wittlingen, the 24th day of August anno 1569.

31

Paul Glock

Letter to Peter Walpot (1571)[*]

Paul Glock to Peter Walpot, Hohenwittlingen, March 14, 1571

Paul, the Younger, your brother and member of the body of Christ (which you are), imprisoned thirteen years at Wittlingen for the faith and for the sake of God's truth, to be delivered to Peter Walpot and his assistants in the Word, my beloved brothers and sisters in the spirit.

The eternal and true God whose counsel and wisdom exists only through himself, is the protector of his people Israel, tends them like lambs and sheep and provides them with faithful servants and herdsmen as he did in former times, still does, and will do to the day of his appearance. He will provide us with all things, especially with servants whom he will give and present to his people, as God himself said to Joshua, saying: "Moses my servant is dead; now therefore arise, go over this Jordan, thou, and all this people. There shall not any man be

---

[*]Source: Bossert, *Quellen I*, 338-43.
Translation: Friesen/Klaassen

able to stand before thee all the days of thy life: as I was with Moses, so I will be with thee: I will not fail thee, nor forsake thee..." [Josh. 1:2-5] Now Christ is our Moses (with the law of the Gospel), and after his death chose his Joshua, praying over him. These are all the true servants in the church of Christ and his congregation. God the Father himself chose them with his Spirit of truth, so that through them the church of Christ has been led. With this strong power of his Spirit of strength and wisdom may the Almighty train you, firstly yourself, my Peter, and then all your assistants in the Word and in temporal care so that you have no failure of supply and may lead the people of Israel through the wilderness of this desert and godless world. Through Christ our redeemer I wish you this abundance of the foretaste of the peace of God eternally. Amen.

Oh, you my especially beloved brethren, servants in the Word, and especially you, Peter, who together with the others and the whole congregation are written as a living epistle into my heart with the Spirit of Christ, which I daily read and know! I have received the writing and gift from you, Peter, and the others, the knives, the cloth and the scarf, and also the spoon on St. Michael's day in the year 70, as the messenger no doubt has told you. This has heartily pleased me and comforted me in the Lord, although God always gives me comfort. But I am now still more fully and overabundantly pleased, since I see how God cares for us, who does not bar our way to communicate with one another by which we are gladdened and God is honoured. Praise be to him eternally.

I have heard that God blesses and protects you in all things and especially in the famine which again pleases my heart. For this I praise the Lord at all times. I thank you for reminding me of the firmness of the old heroes, and to stay faithful in the Lord's work to the end of my years, life and imprisonment. I intend to do this as you have reminded me steadfastly and faithfully, with God's help. May he deal with me as is his will, if it is to God's praise and to your comfort, and towards my salvation. That is my prayer to him always. I also pray that my writing may cheer you as yours has me.

You have heard of the abundance of the Lord's assistance and help to me. This is how. There is a great scarcity here now in the year 71 (as it has been with you), and many people are hungry. One gallon of grain costs a guilder or fifteen shillings and half a loaf of bread twenty pennies in the city of Urach. A bushel of corn is eight guilders. But no matter how great the dearth is, it has not yet reached me. But they have raised and improved the allowance for me to the castle overseer, so that the allotted food remains the same for me, such as wine, meat, bread and other good food. Also I have clothes enough, and they let me lack nothing. This I really did not expect. In addition the beadle let me out every day in the winter. And I heated my own room as much as I wanted, with plenty of wood. Many people badly lack wood, but I have an abundance. The Lord, our God, at these times treats my enemies outside much harder, more roughly and to more fear than me in my bonds. The castle overseer also allows me to walk about the castle where I please, but in secret from the priests, and also upon my promise that I will not escape without his permission. So (as formerly also) I promised it to him for a time, and my condition is as though I were not imprisoned. I live like a town burgher, but in fear of the Lord.

What more do I want from our God in my affliction? Are these not mighty wonders? I can also earn money for upkeep by working. How should I then become faithless to God? And although it does not always go this well, yet I want to let God's Word and grace be sufficient for me, trusting in him, for he will not let me or you be tested beyond our strength. Trust him, all of you, from the heart, for he has promised and will keep it, as long as we keep faith with him and confess him honestly in all kinds of tribulation. Also I perceive that you cannot express your love to me with ink or pen as also I cannot express mine to you. May God, however, who himself is love in us, keep us in this, that we do not forget one another, neither here nor there. Now since God makes me struggle so in all my tribulation and suffering, let such grace and kindness be sufficient for you, even if God were to delay my matter for some time more and you be deprived of me altogether. Our hearts constantly long that we might see each other face to face, yet we will commit it to God, letting him do it. He knows the right time. To him be praise eternally!

I have also heard about the blood tax [taxes for war] or levy, and that the godless [ruler] threatens to drive you out if you do not pay it. Because it is a sinful gift and a tax against the Turks, it is my opinion and feeling that you should not give it, but that you conduct yourselves according to the order of [Peter Riedemann's] *Account* which indicates how far you are bound to give the government its dues. Beyond that we have reason to give them nothing for the war. Therefore, dear brethren, we allow ourselves much rather to be wronged, than that we should accede to them and give. If they were to take it themselves, suffer this as well. The reason is that the sins of the Canaanites had to be filled before Israel could enter in. But Israel, who was to occupy and receive the good, fertile land worthily, had to be refined in the desert. Similarly now God has struck with the scythe of judgment, so that he raises the godless up above us, that they practice violence, thus becoming ripe for punishment. Thus also God the better establishes your faith, so that we might become ripe for the kingdom of God. It has been given to us not only to believe in Christ, but also to suffer for him. Admonish all the people, dear brother Peter, and the others with you that they remain firm and trust in our God. For he will work something special through you if you trust him fully. I have experienced it, even as you have often seen, that at times he allows us to experience hard times. He does not intend to exterminate us or test us beyond our strength. But he tests us whether we are willing to suffer for him, as we promised in baptism, although he already knows our hearts. Yet at times he allows a testing to come over us, so that we become known and acquainted with one another the better. For true friends and Christians become known, dear, valued and pleasant to each other in need. Therefore suffer it willingly. The time which we have to live in this age is short. Even if it is nothing but sorrow, yet it is not worth the glory which will be revealed to us.

The angel says to Esdras, [2 Esd. 6-7 was a favourite passage dealing with the endtime] that there will be an affliction of the pious. They will be robbed, torn, ejected out of their houses and their goods taken. Then will it become evident who his elect are. But be of good cheer, dear brethren, when all this is evident our redemption is very near! Praise God! Dear brethren, you know all this through God's grace, that you might comfort the people. Nor do I write to you as though I know more than you; not at all, but I admonish myself along with you in the Lord. To him be the glory! Further, it is my humble opinion that if the rulers were to seek and exact the tenth penny or whatever they want whenever you buy anything, since you must buy much grain for the whole community, it seems to me that wherever possible when the brethren work for the lords or the burghers they take only grain as payment. If one of them does not himself have grain, request that he buy it and pay you your wages that way. This should be for any kind of worker, carpenters, masons, and hewers, wherever one works for the heathens. Thus I believe that you won't need to give a tenth or, as they call it, Turk money. This is my humble opinion.

I also understand concerning Adam [Horneck's] wife, that she is well. I wrote to her briefly. I should like to report more detail if I only could. My simplicity is at fault. You must be content.

You have also written me that I report in my writing what gifts I received. Except for the scarf I had nothing to report. Please know that the scarf did not come with the first message, but only about St. Michael's day by Paul Prele of Esslingen. I still have it all with me, and if I may I shall carry the one pair of knives with me for your sake, Peter. The reason why I have the scarf is this: The lady of the castle, [wife of the castle overseer at Grafeneck] fled from the epidemic to the city of Ulm. She went there before winter and has not yet returned. I have no certain knowledge concerning her. I expect she may soon come home. I shall see what I can do about it, God willing. Actually, I did not write for any wrap or scarf. Perhaps you did not understand my writing, or perhaps you sent it out of love yourself. I do not know. In any case, the Lord be praised! Tell Claus [Braidl] the cobbler that I received his letter and gift. May the Lord be his reward and may he recompense you all richly.

I also understand that three brethren have been captured and that (as far as you know) they are still in the faith. God be praised! Know further, also, that in the 70th year I earned a good wage with making cloth. For four shillings I bought yarn and made nine hundred ells to send to you. My request to you, my brother Peter, is to deliver one bolt of the woolen cloth, if feasible, to our two cotton rooms at Nembtschitz and at Gostal. Ursula Wurm of Kaufbeuren, if she is still alive, is also to share the cloth, even if she gets only one ell. It is as a greeting. And the other bolt you are to give to your wife Maria and to all the wives of servants of the Word and temporal care, also as a greeting. I can send them nothing else. Please assign the other seven bolts where the community requires it. Here also you may perceive God's miracle, in that the Lord gives me the grace among my and your enemies to complete this. Honour be to our God!

Herewith I commend you all to God's strong protection. May he care and watch over you at all times as of old, and be a bronze wall about you. I, Paul, greet you many thousand times in the holy and unadulterated love of God, you my dear brother Peter together with the elders of the Word and of temporal care, and after you also the whole congregation of God in the love of God. Tell them I am in all respects well according to God's will. Pray for me at all times that he keep me faithful and true. I shall do likewise for you, as long as I live, and not depart from the truth in which God has set and established us, in which also we are saved with the strength and help of God and of your intercession to God for me. For I know that God hears us together for each other. To him be the praise. Now you know everything, how things are with me to the present. May God grant that all things at all times contribute to our comfort and blessedness and to God's honour. Amen.

If possible, you might send me two pairs of knives. The one I want to present to the castle overseer. Perhaps he will allow the brethren in to me the sooner. They can still come to me, but secretly. Felix the clothmaker is to come to you, as I think. He will tell you of the knives. He is at Urach and has friends at Brunn and in the city of Vienna. He is to stop with you and tell you what I am doing. I have also written him a note to several brethren. I am sending the secretary Haupprecht [Zapf] a braided bolt as a greeting. He has admonished me frequently and comfortingly. To the Lord be the honour. Amen.

Given at Wittlingen, the 14th day of March, anno 1571.

32

Paul Glock

Letter to the Church in Moravia (1573)[*]

Epistle of Paul Glock to the Congregations in Moravia. Hohenwittlingen, after January 18, 1573.

In this 72nd year, the councillors, lords of the chancery and the prince have fled here from Stuttgart to Urach on account of the plague and remained here the winter. The lords of the chancery came up here to the castle for the third time just for a visit and each time spoke with me concerning the faith. The Lord gave me wisdom to speak, praise to him.

But now in the 1573rd year they fetched me to Urach and had me led into their chancery. There were present the two court preachers, the city preacher, and four lords of the chancery besides; also the senior steward, the one just below the prince in authority. Then the court preacher brought forth four items, i.e., infant baptism, the Lord's Supper, government and whether magistrates are Christians, and the oath. I am to show why they are not of God.

---

[*]Source: Bossert, *Quellen I*, 350-58.
Translation: Friesen/Klaassen

I replied: Infant baptism is the first thing we will discuss. Now since you think that forcing people to accept your views is truly godly and Christian, you must attest and maintain them with Christian Scripture. Otherwise it is not valid before God. Thereupon they said that they would gladly do it, and this was their attestation of infant baptism: Firstly, they said, that the children have faith, adding that without faith it is impossible to please God; therefore the children had to have faith, which is why they ordered them to be brought to baptism. Secondly, they referred to the household of Stephanas where all were baptized. Thirdly they referred to the house of Philip, where also all were baptized. Here you have divine evidence that one must baptize infants. They added besides that I would find nowhere where it was written that children should not be baptized. Then they bid me answer.

Then with God's grace and help I answered: In Hebrews the apostle does not speak about or with children but with adults, as the whole chapter shows. He clearly says: "Whoever would come to God, must believe that he, God, is, and that he will be a rewarder of those who seek him" [Heb. 11:6]. Therefore place a child here, and if it can make that confession and has that faith, then baptize it and you have won. Then they said, "The child needs no confession." I answered: "Then it does not require any baptism either." Then they were silent.

Now about the household of Stephanas. The last chapter of this same epistle mentions the house of Stephanas again and shows clearly that no child was baptized here. It says: "You know the house of Stephanas, that it is the firstfruits of Achaia, that they have committed themselves to the ministry of the saints." Now the children could not serve even themselves, let alone the others. So there were no children included in this.

Thirdly, concerning the house of Philip: he rejoiced with his whole house that they had come to a belief in God. Again, bring an infant before us. If it understands the work of God and rejoices at it, then baptize it and be right and win. If not, then you are wrong and cannot prove or maintain that one should have infants baptized from these three passages. I will not be convinced by uncertain evidence. Then they were silent.

Then I spoke further to them. Although it is not written that one must not baptize children, yet one can judge from the words of Christ and of the apostles. Firstly, John baptized, but whom? Those who confessed their sins. Infants have done no actual sins, and so they require no repentance or confession. Secondly, Christ promises them the kingdom of God without faith, without preaching, without the sign in the church, without baptism. Therefore we are happily satisfied with the words of Christ, since he does not bid them be baptized. For if they had to be baptized, he surely would have commanded it. Thirdly, Jesus says: "Every plant which my Father has not planted, shall be rooted up" [Matt. 5:13]. Infant baptism is no plant of God, otherwise Christ would have mentioned it. Fourthly, Christ says: "Teach all nations and baptize them" [Matt. 28:19]. Observe: the nations are first to be taught, otherwise you baptize the untaught. Fifthly, faith comes from the hearing of divine preaching. Thus you baptize without faith, for Christ clearly says: "Whoever believes and is baptized will be saved" [Mark 16:16]. Sixthly, nowhere in the Acts of the Apostles do we find anyone baptized without faith as you do. The apostle said that he wanted to be free from all responsibility for any destruction that would arise after his departure for, he said, "I have declared to you the whole counsel of God and kept back nothing" [Acts 20:27]. He ought to have told them, "See to it, that you baptize your infants," since for them too he was responsible. But he never had that in mind, and therefore it must not have been a counsel of God. In addition he earnestly warned them when he said, "If an angel from heaven preached a different Gospel than the one we preached to you, let him be cursed" [Gal. 1:8] Then I said to the priest, "You are not even angels from heaven and preach other than the Gospel. Therefore I do not believe it."

Thereupon they said I was quite perverted and that I would not allow myself to be corrected and taught. "I will not be taught by false words," said I, "as Christ warns me." Further I said to them, "Since you so proudly consider yourselves to be apostles, prove it with the good works of Christ, for the disciples of Christ evidenced their office of apostleship with good works. Then I would follow you. For Christ says, "As my Father sent me into the world, so send I you" [John 20:21]. Then I asked them where the Father had commanded the Son, or Christ his disciples that they were to force people to faith or infant baptism and put them into prison, as you now do. Then the rascals had to be silent. "Well, since I see you acting other than Christ your master or the apostles your predecessors, I will follow you less than him. For the messenger is not to be greater than he who sent him, nor should the servant be over his lord, nor the disciple over his master. Where that is not the case they will be cast out like Satan."

Government

Then they began to speak of the government. Surely magistrates were Christians, since Paul calls them the servants of God. I said: "Paul calls them servants of vengeance. Vengeance does not belong in the house of Christ but in hell." Then they said that vengeance belongs to the house of God. I replied: "Show me one worldly government in the house or the congregation of Christ. For the apostle established all offices in the house of God. Tell me, where did he order bailiffs, princes or worldly kings with their offices to be there?" Then the priests responded and said that there were in fact worldly governments in the house of Christ, mentioning Cornelius. He was a centurion among the soldiers and became a Christian. They said I could not prove that the apostle had bid him abandon his office. They also referred to Sergius Paulus, saying he was a deputy of the country. Answer: "Do you believe that the apostle preached the Gospel to them, through which they had to become believers, and was the apostle Paul a true follower and teacher of Christ?" They said yes. "Did Paul have worldly government or carry a sword?" They said, no but that he used a spiritual sword and judgment. "If you confess that," said I, "then the apostle also preached that Gospel to Cornelius and Sergius Paulus, where John writes that when people wanted to make Christ a king, he fled. 'The worldly princes rule the nations and the overlords use violence,' but to the disciples he says, 'It is not so with you' [Luke 22:25]. Further, Christ says, 'Those of old have been told, an eye for an eye, a tooth for a tooth, a foot for a foot, a blow for a blow. But I say to you that you are not at all to resist evil or fight' [Matt. 5:38-39]. Look," I said, "from all this these two and all Christians were able to learn that they could no longer be worldly princes, lords or bailiffs if they wanted to be and become followers of Christ. Beyond that Paul says to his whole church and brotherhood, 'Be followers of me just as I am of Christ.' From this also they could learn that they could no longer use worldly weapons, but instead, faith, love, peace, friendliness, patience, gentleness. Now I have proved that no worldly government may or can be in the kingdom or church of Christ." Then they had to be silent. But I continued to them: "If your teaching were of God or Christ, it would also bring corresponding fruits so that you could show it to me. For the apostle Paul boasts and says to the brotherhood: 'You are the seal of my apostleship, my joy, my crown' [1 Cor. 9:2]. If I am asked, I respond similarly. Now if you were to show me your seal (that is, the congregation truly living in Christ), or at least show me the fourth seed, which bears fruit for Christ—as Christ himself says, 'The fourth seed bringing fruit, some hundredfold, some sixtyfold, some thirtyfold' [Matt. 13:23]—I would certainly join that congregation. If their life were better, more devout, more honest and more Christian, I should learn it also. Since, however, I see that my life and that of my brotherhood is more faithful or Christian than yours, and since you can show me no pious people in your churches, I shall stay with mine until I see a more devout life among you. For until now I see that only a godless life follows from your teaching, such as blasphemy, fornication, arrogance, drinking, and eating." Then the priests said that I always came up with this or with similar arguments, expecting that they should show me pious people. "Certainly, why not?" said I, "After all, Christ and the apostles told their congregations that they were to be lights in the world, so that they could be like mirrors to the godless so that they would serve God also." That stuck in their throats not a little, for they could show me no one. On the contrary, they had to admit that they were wicked and godless. It was a joy to me to hear that we (praise God) were more pious than they.

Evildoers

It also happened that the priests spoke of evildoers. God, they said, forgave all people or sinners, no matter how great a sinner one was. I said, "Yes, I believe that too, if one has real contrition and repentance." Then I asked them whether they also forgave and pardoned such a one as their dear member and brother. They said, yes. Then I said, "Why do you hang your evildoers, such as thieves, murderers and the like on gallows and on the wheel if, as you say, you have forgiven them?" Then all of them laughed and said that that was what the government was ordered to do, to punish evil. I then asked whether repenting was also a sin. They said, no, but that it was a good deed. Then I said, "Where in the Old or New Testament does the government have the power to kill the repentant or pious (since, as you say, he has partaken of your Lord's Supper and is a Christian)?" They said that he was nevertheless forgiven although the body had to suffer as a warning to others. I asked whether they believed that they made a good man of an evildoer by imprisonment? Or whether, if he accepted their preaching about infant baptism and their Lord's Supper, they would consider him a Christian? Yes, said they. Then, I said, "Since he has become a believer, as you say, then, according to the words of Paul, he has also been sealed with the Spirit of God." They said, yes. So I said, "Then his body must be a temple of God, since the Holy Spirit dwells in him. It is written: 'If any man defiles or desecrates the temple of God, God will defile and spoil him also' [1 Cor. 3:16-17] Look," said I, "what you are doing. You hang the temple of God on the gallows, defiling it. It is written, as you know, that whoever is hanged on the wood is condemned." They said, yes. Then I said to them: "Look, you and your government are such fine Christians, but you shed innocent blood, you slaughter the repentant, and defile the temple of God. Where did Christ command or tell his church to do that? For Christ forgave the woman caught in adultery everything, saying: 'I do not condemn you either, go and sin no more' [John 8:11]. Such was his pardon, and he taught us, his disciples, also to forgive. He did this when he said, 'As you forgive people their trespasses, so the Father in heaven will forgive you your sins or trespasses' [Matt. 6:14]. We see it done thus in the churches of Paul, and sinners are forgiven who also were nothing but rascals and rogues. He himself says: 'Do not be deceived, neither fornicators, nor idolators, nor adulterers, nor effeminate, nor homosexuals, nor thieves, nor covetous, nor drunkards, nor revilers, nor extortioners, shall inherit the kingdom of God. And such were some of you: but you are washed, you are sanctified, you are justified in the name of the Lord Jesus, and by the Spirit of our God' [1 Cor. 6:9-11]. See how the apostle here forgives the evildoers out of love and not envy, while you hang them on gallows, defiling the temple of God. Paul also speaks of Philemon's servant who, after all, was also a thief, and who would also have been worthy of the hangman. But Paul did not hang him nor have him hanged, but out of the love of God forgave him as their member, because he had been converted now, had improved himself, and repented. Elsewhere Paul writes: 'Whoever has stolen or overcharged, let him no longer steal or overcharge, but work something honourable with his hands, so that he might have something to give to the poor' [Eph. 4:28]. Again therefore, observe the order the true Christian church has been given by Christ and the apostles. Where things are done differently, however, there is no church of Christ, but a worldly, pagan and godless intention and essence, as of those who cannot receive the Holy Spirit of Christ, through which sin is forgiven. It is the worldly government which has the charge to kill the evildoers who do not desire the good, nor improvement, nor repentance. To these the church has nothing to say. Nor does God forgive them, for they are cursed here and condemned there." Their response to my words was to look at each other as if to say, "In that case we were all wrong everywhere in our rule and Christianity." They could not truthfully contradict me.

Lord's Supper

Then they began to ask me what I thought about the Lord's Supper. I answered: "I believe it is very important if it is kept the way Christ ordered it. But I reject the way you observe it. Christ showed us a true Christian community through bread and wine. We, the many, are to be one body with him and members of one another. We are to help where one requires the other, the rich is to have no more than the poor and the poor no less than the rich. This is repugnant to you, and it is therefore in vain to talk much with you about this." They were silent. I added, "Why should we talk much with each other, since you have no Christian order at all?" So they were silent about the remaining items.

The gentlemen from the chancery had been silent through all this, listening diligently to what I spoke with the priests, and writing it down. Finally the senior steward began to speak with the court preacher in Latin, and when he had finished, the priest asked me whether I would be prepared to move out of the country again and not back in again. Upon this condition my lord would release me to liberty. I replied: "If you will give me a letter and seal that wherever I go, I would be allowed to live, then I would leave your land." They answered that they could not do that; I said: "Then I cannot leave, either. But I want to get out, and if I come back and do something to merit the sword, then use it. More I cannot promise." They did not like that. The former again spoke in Latin with the priest, and then said to me that even if I would remain pious by myself and continue in my opinion but mislead no one any more, they would let me out again. Then I said: "If I am wrong, use the sword, since you are ordained to use it. If I am right, it is also right for him who hears or learns something good from me, and on that I will stake my life." Then the priest said that I had misled many, that they did not want to force me in my faith, but only to keep me imprisoned so that I should not seduce more people.

We talked about many other things which I am not recording. I wrote only what was most necessary. Thus we conversed about three hours, on the 18th day of January, the 73rd year. So they ordered me brought to the castle again.

And now I lie here, firmly trusting in the Lord Christ, may he be praised. In his grace I await what God ordains or permits them concerning me.

May God protect me and us all, who call to him and trust in him, from their false and erring designs. For God's saying is fulfilled in them, which says: "I will harden their hearts and stop their ears and blind their eyes so that they shall not know nor understand anything godly" [Ezek. 6:9?]. It is also written: "I will make the wisdom of this world to be foolishness" [1 Cor. 3:19].

May the Lord Christ give us his grace and strength. So that we persevere in the good to the end of our lives. No matter what the cost, death or imprisonment, to the praise of God and to the comfort of the pious. Amen.

Paul Glock
Now imprisoned fifteen years at Wittlingen.

33

Walpurga von Pappenheim

Ausbund, Song 75
(ca. 1571)*

Introduction

Walpurga von Pappenheim was the daughter of the aristocrat Joachim von Pappenheim who, along with Walpurga's aunt Magdalena, came into contact with the Marpeck circle in the early 1530's. After Joachim's death in 1536, the two women continued to associate with the circle.[1]

Walpurga was in possession of an early copy of the *Verantwortung*, which was a lengthy response by Marpeck to Caspar Schwenckfeld's *Judicium*.[2] Walpurga's copy of the *Verantwortung* still survives, and the comments that she made when she corrected and revised it, (which she did "for the sake of God's glory") give us virtually all the information that is known about this noble woman turned Anabaptist.

---

*Source: *Ausbund, Das ist: Etliche schöne Christliche Lieder, wie sie in dem Gefängnis zu Passau in dem Schloss von den Schweizer Brüdern und von andern rechglaubigen Christen hin und her gedichtet worden*, Song 75 (Elkhart, IN: Mennonitischen Verlagshandlung, 1880).
Translation: Pamela Klassen

She obviously had a close personal identification with the Marpeck circle, as well as a commitment to the Anabaptist community of believers. She saw the hand of God at work through the persecution of the Anabaptists, and her correction and annotation of the *Verantwortung* testifies to its importance to her.[3]

As well as being an editor of Marpeck's work, she was also known as a song writer, an example of which follows here. Song 75 of the *Ausbund*, the Swiss Brethren Hymnal, is attributed to her, and is the only song in the collection explicitly credited to a female composer.[4] There is some question, however, as to whether Walpurga actually composed the song. The song was first published in 1531 in the "Songbook of the Bohemian Brethren," and the compiler of that book, Michael Weisse, did not credit Walpurga with authorship. But Weisse is known to have used songs composed by others while not giving credit to them. Therefore, it remains possible that Walpurga wrote Song 75. If this is true, Walpurga would have been a very young woman (as the *Ausbund* introduction notes) when she composed the song, probably no more than twenty years old.

As was common practice in the sixteenth century, the text was written to be sung to the tune of a popular song, in this case to the tune of the popular Lutheran hymn, "Out of Deep Distress" (*Aus tieffer Not*).[5]

Bibliographical Sources:

C. Arnold Snyder, *Anabaptist History and Theology: An Introduction* (Kitchener, ON: Pandora Press, 1995).

C. Arnold Snyder and Linda A. Huebert Hecht, eds., *Profiles of Anabaptist Women: Sixteenth-Century Reforming Pioneers* (Waterloo, ON: Wilfrid Laurier University Press, 1996).

Ausbund, Song 75 (ca. 1571)

Another beautiful sacred song written by a young noblewoman, Walpurga of Pappenheim.

To the tune of: "Out of Deep Distress"

1. Oh pious heart, so glorify,
   And give praises to your Lord,
   Be mindful he is your father
   Whom you should honour always,
   Without him there is not one hour
   With all the worry in your mind
   That your life can be nourished.

2. He is the one who loves you from his heart,
   His blessing he shares with you,
   Forgiving you your misdeeds,
   And healing you of your wounds,
   Arming you for the spiritual war,
   So Satan not overcome you,
   And disperse all of your treasures.

3. He is merciful and so good
   To the poor and destitute,
   Who turn from all their arrogance,
   And convert to his truth.
   He accepts them like a father,
   Seeing that they reach the end
   Of the true path to salvation.

4. How like a true father he bends,
   Doing good to his children,
   God has opened himself to us
   Blessing us poor sinners.
   He has loved us and has graced us,
   Forgiving us our trespasses,
   Making us victorious.

5. And he gives us his good spirit,
   Which renews all of our hearts,
   Through this we fulfill his commands,
   Although with the pain of love.
   He helps our need with grace and healing,
   Promising us a glorious share,
   Of the eternal treasures.

6. According to unrighteousness,
   He has not recompensed us,
   Instead he showed us compassion,
   When we should have been doomed.
   His mercy and his goodness
   Is readied for every one of us
   Who love him from the heart.

7. What he has begun out of love,
   He also wants to finish.
   We offer ourselves to God's grace
   With loins that have been girded,
   With all we have, even our flesh,
   Hoping that, to his praise,
   He will change our every way.

8. Oh Father! Be gracious to us,
   While we are in wretchedness,
   May our actions be upright,
   And come to a blessed end.
   Light us all with your shining Word,
   So that we can, in this dark place
   Be not beguiled by false light.

9. Lord God! Accept our praise and thanks,
   That we are humbly singing,
   Let your Word sound in us freely,
   Let it penetrate our hearts.
   Help us that we, with your power,
   Through true spiritual knighthood
   May achieve the crown of life.

   Amen.

34

Hans Schmidt

Experiences of a Hutterite Missionary in Württemberg (1590)[*]

Introduction

Hans Schmidt (d. 1602) was from Rommelshausen in Württemberg and converted to Anabaptism in 1581; who converted him is unknown. After his conversion he left Württemberg for Moravia, where he joined the Hutterites and married. In 1590 he was chosen to be a missioner in his homeland of Württemberg to spread the Gospel. He did this readily and with success, preaching for several months before being apprehended by the local authorities.

Schmidt was treated badly by the authorities: tortured, interrogated repeatedly, and sent from prison to prison where at times he was placed in dank, dark dungeons infested with vermin. His family, who still lived in the area and attended the state church there, tried to persuade him to change his mind in order to free himself, but he was steadfast in his faith. He was finally released upon the intercession of his father and

---

[*]Source: Bossert, *Quellen I*, 652-65.
Translation: Friesen/Klaassen

was expelled from the country. He had been in prison for approximately five months, between August and December 4, 1590.

After his release, he wrote the following report on his experiences for the Moravian brotherhood. He goes into great detail about being racked and tempted by all means. The story was excerpted from the original by Gustav Bossert. Extensive sections of it are abridged. The original was in the first person; the editorial summaries in the third. For better reading the translators have put it all in the first person.

One of the more interesting passages regards Schmid's response to the bailiff's question on his opinion of the "sword." It is almost a word for word repetition of Michael Sattler's statement at his trial of 1527, where he was ultimately martyred. Schmidt was obviously familiar with Sattler's case and had more than likely read one of the booklets in circulation that contained the Schleitheim Articles as well as accounts of Sattler's trial and martyrdom. Copies of these booklets also made their way into Hutterite manuscripts.[1] The report also gives rare insight into the life, thoughts and the practices of Hutterite missioners at the end of the sixteenth century, a time when many were of the mistaken opinion that Anabaptism would soon be nonexistant.[2]

Schmidt eventually made his way back to Moravia, where he was chosen as preacher in 1591. He was confirmed to the office in 1596 and served as "servant of the Word" until his death at the Stignitz Bruderhof near Moravian Kromau in 1602.

Bibliographical Sources:

The Chronicle of the Hutterian Brethren, vol. I (Rifton, N.Y.: Plough Publishing House, 1987).

Robert Friedmann, "Schmidt, Hans von Rommelshausen," *ME IV*, 466.

Robert Friedmann, "Schmidt, Hans," *ML* 4, 79.

C. Arnold Snyder, "The Influence on the Anabaptist Movement: An Historical Evaluation," *MQR* 63 (October 1989), 323-44.

Wilhelm Wiswedel, *Bilder und Führergestalten aus dem Täufertum*, III Bd. (Kassel, 1952), 36-39.

Hans Schmidt's experiences in Württemberg, after December 4, 1590.

Hans Schmidt's experiences in Württemberg

God has disclosed his counsel and will to the church and the churches, namely, that it should do the work of God. The greatest and most important work is to visit the people who do not know, to present to them God's counsel and will, to be a light in the world, to strengthen the cords of the tabernacle, and to proclaim repentance to sinners . . . so that the number of saints be fulfilled, and the will of the Father be made known to the children of men, in order that they might not, at the end, have any excuse.

In the year 1590, through the counsel of the Lord I, together with others, was assigned by the congregation to the visitation of Württemberg. I went gladly and willingly, as my conscience bears witness. I also hoped to be blessed by God in this.

The summer was almost past and my companions and I were already thinking of going home. But I still had some urgent business to take care of in Rienharz, not far from Welzheim. An evil man lived there (an enemy of the pious), who saw me from a distance and not distinctly. But he urged the constable to pursue me and the latter, when he had caught up with me, told me to halt. With false words he told me that someone was following me who knew me well. With a show of eagerness he told me of a different village where he lived. Even if I had noticed the deception I would not have been able to escape because of physical weakness. Soon the mayor came who, with scorn and hard words took me home into his house as a prisoner. They soon began to eat and drink greedily. The mayor reviled us that we misled the people, sneaked into their homes at night, separated the husband from his wife, the children from the parents and also [reviled] the manner or our life in the congregation. I told him that we directed the people only to what is good and to piety. The mayor and his wife demanded knives from me, but I told them I was no knife monger. The mayor said that I had a large sack and that he wanted to search it to see if there were any knives in it. I replied that in all my travels I had never been robbed; if that were to happen in this house, I could not prevent it. Then the mayor desisted from his purpose, had his horse saddled, and with four armed men led me to the monastery of Lorch.

There I was questioned the first day by the superintendent, who asked about my name and home. When I answered, the superintendent showed me a letter from the Stuttgart chancery, according to which they were to watch for Anabaptists, and especially for Hans Schmidt from Rommelshausen, who annually came into the country and who had his residence near Schorndorff, Beitelsbach and Aichenberg. I agreed that I was Hans Schmidt. The superintendent wanted to know where the Anabaptists had their residence and whom I had intended to seduce. I did not want to betray my benefactors. The superintendent threatened: You will be taught to confess. He told me to go into a room where the abbot and the armed escort waited. He addressed me rudely: "You hedge preachers, inciters and seducers. You seduce the people, separating the man from his wife, the wife from the man and the children from the parents." He asked me what business I had in the territory of his gracious prince and lord. He would not let me answer, but was quite wrathful, calling me a fool who did not know his own teacher. He ordered me to tell him who sent me into this land and where they lived. I told him I would not say that, since it was no article of faith. I would gladly have told him of how I became a Christian, the reason of my commission, and about the sacraments. But the abbot interrupted me again and again, trying to confuse me with false, poisonous words, such as I have seldom experienced. But I noted that the abbot did not want to be bested before those present. Therefore he said violently that I did not want to answer but was silent because his position was unassailable; I said that since they thought they were the best, they ought not to fear but let me speak also. Then everyone could judge. The abbot asked what criticisms I had of their teaching and preaching, to persuade us to leave the church. But I was told to speak only of the teaching, not of the life and the conduct of the Württemberg clergy. From this I noticed that he was anxious about their knavery being broadcast and their avarice and pride being exposed. But I wanted to speak first about their priests' lives, since they presumed the office of preachers and presumed to be the teachers.

For the third time the abbot repulsed me. I said: "My dear man, tell me whether when a householder wants to hire a servant or a worker, whether it be a vintner or another worker, he would not first want to know whether he were honest and also whether he were able to perform the work. Otherwise he would not hire him. Consequently we want to speak first of the servant or worker, whether he is honest or devout. We want to talk about your life and walk, and why I cannot recognize your teaching as good." But the abbot would not agree to this. Then I said: "If you were the honest, sincere people or teachers you claim to be, you would not need to be ashamed of speaking of your life and walk." Since the abbot was silent, I recounted before them their wicked, offensive lives. "You preach that one is not to be avaricious, arrogant, proud, envious with too much eating and drinking and with other vices. But you are the foremost in this, together with your wives and children. You and they persist in sin while you forgive them their sin. Firstly you consider yourselves Christian through your fabricated infant baptism. Then, through the sacrament, you take away and wash all their sins away for them. You give them peace but there is no peace. All this you do only in order to maintain your custom and your selfishness.

For where you know of a large benefice, you go after it, no matter what the sheep are like. And all that is against the Word of God. For the apostle says: 'If you have enough to eat and to drink, you are to let that suffice.' Christ says: 'You have received freely, you are to give freely.' But you did not receive it freely from God, but have bought it for money in the university at Tübingen or elsewhere, where God's wisdom is not taught, but instead all sorts of unchastity and mischief, and human trickery to deceive one another. This is what those who come from there to us report, and how you get what you have for money. The abbot became angry, and with his false leaven he often misapplied Scripture. The apostles, he argued, had all been sinners, especially Paul. I reminded him of the travels, the persecutions and deaths of the apostles. "But you," I said, "have the power in the whole land. Whoever opposes you and is pious, must present his back and has soon lost everything. You have placed your houses near to the churches, so that you will not have to walk far. The apostles did not have things that easy, nor did they sit around in fox-trimmed coats like you." Thereupon the abbot again became very excited and the spirit of evil was on his forehead.

Finally the abbot threatened me with torture and with death, and had the prison prepared. But I said that the apostles did not prepare the prison for others, but suffered it themselves. Certainly there had never been a sheep that had harmed a wolf, but it was the wolf who killed the sheep. That is what we experienced from them. Then the abbot tried kindness, and promised to bring a Testament to me in prison. I was to think it over this night. I was still young, he said, and had been misled, and I was to pray to God. Tomorrow he would speak with me again. But things happened differently, for I was put in irons with both feet. This was Wednesday, August 26.

The next day I was led by the guards to Schorndorf. The following Saturday, the 29th, I was interviewed in the presence of my father and my brother who pleaded for me. The overseer told my father that it was good that they had me, for they had been looking for me for a long time. He could not oblige him. The overseer asked me whether I was single, who had misled me, how long I had been in Moravia, who had gone with me, who had baptized me and who had been baptized with me. I answered that I was not single and that I had gone into Moravia about nine years earlier. But I would not say any more, for I did not want to betray anyone. The overseer described my secret departure as a breaking of the regulations of the country and the misleading of others as rebellion and transgressions of the fourth commandment. "You have forsaken your father and are a cause of grief to him in his old age." He named places and people with whom I had been in contact. "For a long time," he said, "no one has come into the land of my gracious prince and lord, who has done more damage than you." I answered, "I have not been misled. God made his will known to me and I knelt down before him and prayed for understanding and for the right way. I did not leave secretly but openly by day while I was still single. I did not mislead anyone but only pointed others from evil to good, on account of which I am now charged. Thirdly, I am not a disgrace to my father, before God. I could not be pious in the world and so I had to move away. My father cannot help me on the Last Day. If he were to go with me, I would help him as far as I am able. One must leave everything for the sake of God. Thus neither I nor my brothers and sisters are sorry that I took them with me. God disclosed it to me."

Then the special priest said, "The living devil disclosed that to you and if you do not forsake it, you are the devil's body and soul." I answered with Scripture verses, referring to the mote and the beam, to the fruit and the tree. God would not give anything evil to one asking him. The special priest should, I said, be conscious of his responsibility with respect to the Last Day.

The overseer asked about the right of the government to use the sword. I pointed to Rom. 12, saying that vengeance belongs to God. The government closed its eyes to crime and punished the good. The overseer said, "If a murderer came to you in the field and killed you while you could defend yourself and did not, you would be your own murderer. If the Turk were to come into the land, would you not defend yourselves either?" I said, "No. We will defend ourselves with prayer and will refrain from fighting. God fights for us." I also said,

"The Turk professes to be a Turk and is a Turk. The alleged Christians, however, profess to be Christians after the flesh, but nevertheless persecute the true Christians, and drive them out of house and home. They are Turks in spirit."[3]

Then the dean asked about baptism, the Lord's Supper, original sin and whether it harmed the children, about the Trinity and the origin of Christ, and whence he received his flesh and his blood.

The interrogation in four sessions lasted three and a half hours. The priest became bored. He often stood up and said he had to go. But the overseer remained seated. I again spoke of their lives of vice, pride and greed.

On the 30th day of September I was taken by four men to Sindelfingen into an evil, dark, small prison, so that I was robbed of the light of day. At night I had little rest because of the vermin which scurried around my head. They seemed to me to be hunting for food. Because it was crowded with much refuse and straw, I could find no rest at night, whether I lay with my head this way or that. Such was my condition. Afterwards, when I was freed again, I learned from some people that there were snakes there. But I do not know, for I did not see them.

Every pious person may well consider that at such times it is good that one is pious and that one has achieved some self-control, for temptation will not long be absent. What a glorious thing is the lovely light and glow of day. No one realizes it except someone who has experienced its lack.

After seventeen days five men took me to Stuttgart. There, after three more days, on Wednesday before [probably after] St. Gall's day, (October 16), I was interrogated by the overseer and by the city secretary. Asked what I was doing, I answered that I was bringing my friends messages from their friends. We also wished to tell those who desired to join us in Moravia the basis of the truth and the cross and the tribulation which awaited them, so that they would not make the long trek from house and home in vain. The city secretary called me a detestable toady. He said that I misled the people with loose, mischievous talk, and that I should be dealt with according to the law as all others. He asked me of which faith I was: a Schwertler, (An Anabaptist who allowed Christians to bear sword) a Gabrielite, or an Austerlitzer? In the chancery the chancellor shook hands with me in a friendly way, called me by name and told me of the request of my father. He knew my family well, and I was not to do this harm to my father. The old priest was present, as were several others.

Then I was asked whether I was a leader, and a teacher, whether I had studied to prepare for it, whom I had planned to take with me, how long I had been in the country, who had misled me, who my companions were, whether there was a teacher among them, how often I had already been in the country, who had sheltered me, when I had misled my brother and sister, where my wife was from and whether she was also of my persuasion. I answered without betraying anyone. The prior said they only wanted to correct those whom I had misled. Their questions were sharp and cunning. They also asked about the inns at which we had stopped outside of the land. Since I refused to answer, they scolded me, saying that no one as proud as I had ever come into their hands. To be sure, they had no jurisdiction outside of the country, but the Anabaptists were cunning, sly people. They threatened me with the hangman.

They asked why a minister of the Word had not travelled this way and why I had taken up this work myself. Another remarked that the ministers did not come where there was danger. I answered that I had also been sent into Turkey. To the question about my work I replied that I studied with the hoe and the flail. One said that I did not look like that. They required of me that I report my companions and adherents, and said I was a fool to suffer for others. Another was of the opinion that such holy and pious people ought to confess freely, even if it were a matter of their own or other people's lives. I replied that Christ also did not answer all the questions of Pilate. They further asked whether I thought that only the likes of me would be saved and whether my father and my brother were damned. I was also asked about Paul Glock, Mathes Binder, Petter Scherer [Walpot?] and Simon Kresz. Anabaptists were slandered as traitors to the country.

They told me that an Anabaptist had said that Samson's hair would likely grow again. By this they meant Simon Kresz. No subject was discussed to completion. I noted that the men had the record of the Schorndorf interrogation lying before them. They also told me that I was imprisoned not for the reason of faith, but for my disobedience to the government and because of my pride. Five times I was admonished to save myself, for they would question me with the hangman. I answered, "May it happen as God wills, for all my life I have prepared myself to suffer." In vain they reminded me of my wife and asked whether I had children. I said that my brothers would take care of my wife and child. I also knew, I said, that they are pious people. Among us they are not infected with vice as they would be if they were with you. I said they were not as dear to me as my own soul. They replied that there was a great difference between an Anabaptist who came into the land at random and one who came in with the intention of misleading people.

On the next day I was taken from the prison and lowered into a deep and dirty dungeon. Above this was a common prison into which people were put daily. There was only iron grating over the hole. I heard many rats and mice scurrying in the straw, climbing up the wall and falling down. I was afraid the vermin would attack my body. The next day I received a little clean straw and did not know how to thank the Lord enough for this. For I could boldly kneel and sit on it, and it was a good gift for me.

On the third day I was again pulled up and taken into the house of the overseer, where the hangman was also present. The overseer began to annoy and slander me, putting the old questions to me and pointing at the hangman. I did not allow him to confuse me, even when the overseer called for a stick with which to beat me to make me confess. Instead I told the overseer about the beginning of my faith, told him what kind of people we were who had forsaken everything for the sake of salvation. The overseer said, "You lead a virtous life at that." I answered: "I could hope that God would help you understand it." Then the overseer said, "I should not like to know it, for then you would mislead me also."

After eighteen days, on November fourth about midnight, I was set on a horse, blindfolded, my hands tied behind my back, my body tied to the saddle with ropes, my feet tied together under the horse, and I was taken out of the city. When I asked about our destination I was given no clear answer. I was afraid I would be executed secretly and prayed that God would let me be executed publicly. We went over hedges and fences, and over such stony and rough roads, that I was concerned that the horse might stumble and fall on top of me. I was sorry for the horse. Sometimes they led the horse back or in a circle. Then they trotted ahead again. They called and whistled to each other and complained they had lost each other in the woods and were lost in the night. They asked me about the inns as well as other questions, but I gave evasive answers.

When day dawned they said, in the Black Forest there are many overseers and nice pine branches, whether I also wanted one. I gradually noticed that one of them went ahead and warned those we met not to tell me where I was. I said that I would not be surprised if the horse began to speak, and thanked God that I was suffering innocently for the sake of Christ. About 9 or 10 o'clock, we came to a castle just as the people were coming out of the church, it being a Sunday. They got me off the horse and dragged me up the steps, sat me down again, and again asked me about those whom I had misled saying that I was still young, and that my beard would grow white before I got back to Moravia. Then they led me up some high steps into a prison, took off my blindfold and untied my hands. They searched me, taking what they wanted. When food was brought to me, they would not tell me the name of the castle. But I nevertheless learned that it was the Reichenberg, where a forest ranger was stationed.

After six days the overseer from Stuttgart came to the prison, together with the forest ranger and a secretary. They put the questions to me again and threatened me vehemently. The overseer complained and said I was a rogue and caused him much trouble and that I ought to regard my young life and obey. They were now getting serious, they said, and that they would put me on the rack. I was to think about it seriously this night. When I answered but briefly, the overseer said that in his whole life he had not come upon such a stiff-necked and proud person. I replied that I was not proud nor impertinent but that I feared God. God knows it all. They left indignantly.

However, I did not confer with flesh and blood, but with my God, who is still my helper. I will not fear what men can do to me. Early in the morning they asked me again and I said, "I shall yield my limbs to be stretched." In the evening they put me into an evil dungeon with a dissolute person, a leader of mercenaries. He was from Lorraine and, with a troop of his countrymen, had destroyed Montbeliard which belonged to Count Frederick. He had done much damage besides, and had been caught freebooting. He had been racked without confessing anything. After that he had been led out about 30 miles and put into this prison. Only there did he betray his master and whatever he knew of his captain. Because he had not behaved well in prison, especially with the maid, and had made a hole in the prison and had spoken shamelessly against the government, he was forced to be in this dungeon. When he heard that they wanted to put another man in with him, he shouted loudly that if they put a thief in with him he would kill him immediately. I also heard that in this prison a man had become insane, as also happened to Simon Kresz. So I thought that the mercenary had also become insane. But he did me no harm, nor did he understand German too well. His speech, thought and aim were wicked, carnal, shameful, unchaste. He cursed. In his rage he often said that he would kill himself. I chastised him, but for a long time it did no good. Gladly would I have been alone, for our two aims did not agree. That was my greatest grief and complaint. If someone came and asked what Hans was doing, the mercenary answered, "Hans prays and I curse; thus we are even."

In this dungeon there were no vermin. They could not survive there, for it smelled like a lime kiln. The maid who brought the food went away again quickly from the hole because of the rising vapour. The odour weakened all my limbs and made my head quite dizzy so that I lost the desire to speak. When I lay down I thought I should never get up again. They told me that it was still worse in summer.

But the Lord, who gives the fire its strength and takes it again, who stops the water so that it does not flow, who stops the mouth of the lion, is stronger. To him I cling.

The lady of the castle sent word to me urging me to yield, to think of my wife and child and of my father, and that I ought to obey. But I sent word to her that my suffering had to do with my salvation, and that she ought to be concerned not with me, but with her own soul. I also had the mercenary and the maid against me. After fourteen days the lady sent a message urging me to reconsider, for the overseer from Stuttgart was coming again. She said she was warning me as a sister warns her brother. I should not be so obstinate. Another before me had been imprisoned there and he had listened to her. I sent her the message that each one would have to account for himself before God.

In the morning they pulled me up and arraigned me. The overseer said, "Now things are serious." He had, he said, told me for a long time but that I had not believed it. He was willing to give ten guilders of his own money if I were fifty miles away. If I would now obey, things would go well with me. Otherwise they would rack me so that the sun would shine through me.

I answered, "God put my limbs together, so I shall maintain them till he takes them again. With his help I shall await what he has decided about me. The position I took at the beginning I still hold and I do not intend to become a liar. But know this; God will visit this upon you and yours, that you thus torment a pious and innocent man. Since the time when I was able to distinguish good from evil I have never desired to do anyone wrong. But the Lord will reward me also." The overseer said that it was his duty, and had the hangman open his tools, telling him to take over. I took off my coat and stepped under the rope. The hangman said, "You know what to do, I believe you have been at this before." They all reminded me of my wife and child, but I said, "At our parting my wife said that I should remain devout and true if I were caught. That I will do with God's help. No one is as dear to me as my salvation. In the Holy Scripture Christians were promised tribulation and suffering, and also death. This happened to Christ our master and to many other pious people who were perhaps better than I. Therefore I am not too good for it."

My hands quickly became black from the tight bonds, for the hangman had no pity on me but was angry at me like the others. He hoisted me up (A form of torture by which a person was hoisted up by a rope by the wrists with heavy weights attached to the feet), all of them standing around. If one stopped the other began gnawing at me. Then the overseer said, "Let him hang there; we will go for lunch. When we come back, he will obey." Another said, "He will get very hot hanging like that. Let's let him down again and let him lie for an hour. Then we can pull him up again, and then we will succeed." The overseer read the items to me, and because I could not speak well, he let me down, but I would not give in even if it cost body and life.

They said, "The devil has taught you. He is closing your mouth; you belong to him." The hangman again applied tension. Then they tried something else. They let me down and fastened a screw to the floor. They tied my feet to it with a rope and said: "Now then; either you yield or else your body breaks." In spite of mild and rough admonitions concerning my life and of my father's grief, I did not yield. The overseer would have been satisfied with an answer about the stopping places of our people, but I would rather have died than to betray anyone. So they left; only the hangman and a secretary stayed with me. The hangman said, "Do you think that only you people will be saved?" I said, "I cannot prevent anyone from receiving salvation, but there must be improvement of life." The overseer and the others had gone to the prison and asked the mercenary, "My dear man, they are torturing Hans severely and racking him. What does he say when he is with you?" He said, "Why do you torment the poor devil? I can see nothing wrong in him except that he prays day and night. He says he has the right religion and will not depart from it. Bring him back to me, I will convert him."

They came back. The overseer had the hangman release me and said, "Thomann says he will convert him. Anyway we must have breakfast. After that we shall again come to you; meanwhile you can think about it." And so I was never really racked at the screw. Since I could not put my coat on alone, the overseer told the hangman to help me.

Then I was again lowered into the dungeon. After eating, the secretary called down whether I would now obey. But I had him tell the overseer that even if they racked me every day, I would not depart from the truth.

The lady of the castle twice came to the prison, full of pity, brought me wine, and in a friendly way urged me to comply, for the government would not give in. Did I want to rot in the dungeon? My father and my mother had been there, she said, but they had to let them go again, they were such fine people. I answered that everyone would have to give an account to God for himself. During the week she had the maid tell me several times that I should obey or else I would have to suffer hunger. She had been ordered to tell me. But she let me have some food nevertheless. During the last two days I did not lack for anything. When I had been imprisoned in Reichenberg for four weeks, the overseer from Stuttgart came again and had me brought in. But I stood as before. I wanted to stand by the recognized truth whether the price was fire or water, death or life.

The overseer disclosed to me that my father had pleaded for me, and because it was established at the questioning that my father was a devout man, who had nothing to do with the Anabaptists, but that he regularly went to church, for the sake of my old father, they would be prepared to let me out if I swore to leave the country and never to return, the penalty being the loss of body and life. This would be done in spite of the fact that never had such a seducer as I, misleading so many hundreds of people, and doing the Duke so much damage, come into the country, and although no one had ever been shown such mercy. Thomann would also be released upon an oath that he would fight against the Turks. Thus I would have a companion on my way back to Moravia. But I refused the oath or the promise with a handshake because God had forbidden to swear oaths. The overseer said my father would swear for me, but I could not be bound by this, because my father could not answer before God for me. Moreover I had forbidden my father to be guarantor or to swear for me. Upon this the mercenary was sworn in my presence and the overseer wanted to let that oath count for me also, but I objected. This made them angry.

They led me bound to Backnang. On the way those riding with me, the overseer and his son, the forest ranger and the secretary, spoke to me, but I was too weak to talk or walk. At the city hall the council and my father and my brother were assembled.

The overseer first spoke sternly to me in a little room, and said he had the power to have me beheaded. He struck at my mouth with the hilt of his sword, but missed. My father objected, but the overseer said that if I did not cooperate now, I would be taken again to the old prison. I told him that they need not have brought me to Backnang at all, for I would keep to my opinion. The overseer said that he had a pigtrough into which he would have me put so that I would not be able to turn. I told him that God's will would be done.

My father and my brother begged me to yield a little so that I could leave. But I did not yield. Since they did not ask anything about my faith but kept me imprisoned because of my recalcitrant manner and because I resisted the government, I was not obligated to answer questions. I also refused the promise with the handshake because Solomon says that he is a fool who promises with his hand. I also would not promise to stay out of the land, for in the Psalms David says that the earth belongs to the Lord and all that is in it. The overseer suggested that in this exigency my brethren would have nothing against a promise. Moreover it was not an eternal obligation. In the case of an emergency I could again come through the land or return, if God converted me into leaving this sect. Then the overseer, from Backnang, said to the overseer from Stuttgart that he should not attack the Anabaptists with such hard, evil words and with cursing. That did no good. One would gain more with friendly words.

The latter said that he had now tried everything, even the worst prisons in the land. Now only lifelong imprisonment was left. Now I had to express my mind before the whole council in the presence of my relatives: "What God has revealed to me and what separates me from the world this I will keep with God's help as I have said before." To the insults against my brethren or the elders I said: "Our elders are pious and faithful, stand in the breach and ward off evil."

Then the overseer disclosed to me that on the plea of my father I would be released and banished from the land. "If, however, you are caught again, your sentence has already been passed." My father had pleaded that his son be given over to him, so that he could get him out of the country. That was now to happen. My father had to stand surety for me on the strength of his own life and goods. Should I return, he and his goods would be taken. Also, spies were already ordered to watch me so that I should mislead no one else. That was my release on December 4, 1590.

I remember the difficulty with the other prisoners with whom I had to be together. In Schorndorf with a poacher, with a forestry assistant and with a fornicator; in Stuttgart with drunkards, quarrelsome men, debtors and other dissolute people, in Reichenberg with the mercenary. A pious person might judge for himself how the time passed for a believer with such people and what mischievous talk they had against the believer. A pious person likes to be alone when he prays. There was also the trouble when they had to divide the food.

I thank God that he kept me faithful and led me again to the children of God, for the pleasant living together of the devout or the children of God is the most precious jewel. Whoever has to do without it in this time will yet see them again if he overcomes and receives the crown together with the sign of victory.

How good it is to be devout, to have the Lord's Word, the comfort of souls. The zealous can find instruction, the troubled can find good counsel, the sick can find a physician, the weak a place of rest and shelter, the righteous justice, and to the unrighteous his unrighteousness can be told. The hungry find bread, the thirsty find drink. How good it is if one can have the bright light of day and not be shut up in darkness!

Let each one consider this and invest these riches usefully. This is my desire for everyone. Amen.

(On the Sunday, Oculi 1591, Schmidt was inducted into the service of the Gospel and served the church at Stiglitz, until he finished his course and fell asleep in the Lord July 1, 1602.)

Notes

Introduction

[1] See James Stayer, Werner Packull and Klaus Deppermann, "From Monogenesis to Polygenesis: The Historical Discussion of Anabaptist Origins," *MQR* 49 (April 1975).

[2] C. Arnold Snyder, *Anabaptist History and Theology: An Introduction* (Kitchener, ON: Pandora Press, 1995).

[3] Werner O. Packull has done the most comprehensive and foundational work on this branch of the Anabaptist movement. The indispensable introduction to the beginnings of South German/Austrian Anabaptism is Packull's *Hutterite Beginnings: Communitarian Experiments during the Reformation* (Baltimore, MD: Johns Hopkins University Press, 1995). Also crucial to understanding the origins of Anabaptism in these regions is his earlier monograph, *Mysticism and the Early South German-Austrian Anabaptist Movement, 1525-1531* (Scottdale, PA: Herald Press, 1977).

[4] John H. Yoder, trans. and ed., *The Legacy of Michael Sattler* (Scottdale, PA: Herald Press, 1973), Leland Harder, ed., *The Sources of Swiss Anabaptism* (Scottdale, PA: Herald Press, 1985), and H. Wayne Pipkin and John H. Yoder, trans. and eds., *Balthasar Hubmaier* (Scottdale, PA: Herald Press, 1989). Some selected Swiss Anabaptist sources also were published from time to time in *MQR*.

[5] For a preliminary report on later Swiss Brethren writings, see C. Arnold Snyder, "The (not-so) 'Simple Confession' of the later Swiss Brethren. Part I: Manuscripts and Marpeckites in an Age of Print," *MQR* (October 1999); "The (not-so) 'Simple Confession' of the later Swiss Brethren. Part II: The Evolution of Separatist Anabaptism," *MQR* (January 2000). See also Hanspeter Jecker, *Ketzer-Rebellen-Heilige. Das Basler Täufertum von 1580-1700* (Liestal: Verlag des Kantons Basel-Landschaft, 1998).

[6] *Biblical Concordance of the Swiss Brethren, 1540*, trans. by Gilbert Fast and Galen A. Peters (Kitchener, ON: Pandora Press, 2001).

[7] A complete collection of Hoffman's writings was gathered by Klaus Deppermann in preparation for a critical edition of Hoffman's German writings. Following Deppermann's untimely death in 1990, this collection was moved to the Library of the University of Amsterdam, where it resides at present. The project of preparing a critical edition of Hoffman's German writings has come to a stop. Those interested in reading Hoffman's works must locate and consult the original prints.

⁸ Robert Stupperich, ed. *Die Schriften Bernhard Rothmanns*, I (Münster: Aschendorff, 1970).

⁹ Leonard Verduin, trans., *The Complete Writings of Menno Simons* (Scottdale, PA: Herald Press, 1956), C. J. Dyck, William Keeney, and Alvin Beachy, eds. and trans., *The Writings of Dirk Philips* (Scottdale, PA: Herald Press, 1992), Thieleman J. van Braght, *The Bloody Theater or Martyrs' Mirror*, trans. by Joseph F. Sohm (Scottdale, PA: Herald Press, 1972); for a sample of early confessions, see Howard John Loewen, *One Lord, One Church, One Hope, and One God: Mennonite Confessions of Faith* (Elkhart, IN: Institute of Mennonite Studies, 1985).

¹⁰ Gary K. Waite, trans. and ed., *The Anabaptist Writings of David Joris, 1535-1543* (Scottdale, PA: Herald Press, 1993).

¹¹ Jacob Hutter, *Brotherly Faithfulness: Epistles from a Time of Persecution*, trans. by the Hutterian Society of Brothers (Rifton, N.Y.: Plough Publishing House, 1979); John Hostetler, Leonard Gross, and Elizabeth Bender, eds. and trans., *Selected Hutterian Documents in Translation, 1542-1654* (Philadelphia, PA: Communal Studies Center, Temple University, 1975); *The Chronicle of the Hutterian Brethren*, vol. I (Rifton, N.Y.: Plough Publishing House, 1987); *The Chronicle of the Hutterian Brethren*, vol. II (Ste. Agathe, MB: Crystal Springs Colony, 1998); John J. Friesen, trans. and ed., *Peter Riedemann's Hutterite Confession of Faith* (Scottdale, PA: Herald Press, 1999).

¹² William Klassen and Walter Klaassen, trans. and eds., *The Writings of Pilgram Marpeck* (Scottdale, PA: Herald Press, 1978); Walter Klaassen, Werner Packull, and John Rempel, trans. and eds., *Later Writings by Pilgram Marpeck and his Circle*, vol. 1 (Kitchener, ON: Pandora Press, 1999). Still to be completed are the writings of the Marpeck-circle preserved in the *Kunstbuch* and the large biblical concordance composed by Marpeck and members of his circle, the *Testamentserläuterung*. Work on both of these projects is underway at Pandora Press.

¹³ A good translation and introduction is *The Theologia Germanica of Martin Luther*, trans. by Bengt Hoffman (New York, N.Y.: Paulist Press, 1980), although the introduction contains some misinformation about the Anabaptist movement as such.

¹⁴ See the useful collection in Edward J. Furcha, ed. and trans., *The Essential Carlstadt* (Scottdale, PA: Herald Press, 1995), vol. 8 of the Classics of the Radical Reformation series.

¹⁵ Peter Matheson, ed. and trans., *The Collected Works of Thomas Müntzer* (Edinburgh: T & T Clark, 1988); Abraham Friesen, *Thomas*

Muentzer, a Destroyer of the Godless (Berkeley: University of California Press, 1990) minutely examines Müntzer's reading of Tauler.

[16] Clarence Bauman, trans. and ed., *The Spiritual Legacy of Hans Denck* (Leiden: E. J. Brill, 1991), includes all of Denck's writings in English. Denck's mystical "Propositions" are found on 263-67.

[17] "The *Theologia Deutsch* is more than just congenial to Franck. It is a source for his own ideas and vocabulary—a statement about the action of God in the small regenerate portion of the human soul." Patrick Hayden-Roy, *The Inner Word and the Outer World. A Biography of Sebastian Franck* (New York, N.Y.: Peter Lang, 1994), 113. Hayden-Roy notes Franck's indebtedness to the writings of Hans Denck, *ibid.*, 31-35.

[18] Hoffman, *Theologia Germanica*, 26-29.

[19] See for example, Karlstadt's tracts on *Gelassenheit*, especially his second tract written in 1523 which explicitly names the *Theologia Deutsch* as a background, in Furcha, *Essential Carlstadt*, 27-39, 133-68. Thomas Müntzer's writings all reveal the influence of mystical thought, but his "On Counterfeit Faith" (1523) is particularly revealing for the way it bridges the mystical and Reformation worlds, and provides an new "evangelical" reading of the former. Matheson, *Collected Works*, 210-25.

[20] Bauman, *Spiritual Legacy*.

[21] Michael Baylor, *The Radical Reformation* (Cambridge: Cambridge University Press, 1991), 152-71.

[22] Hans Denck had published a similar series of scriptural contradictions a year earlier, called "He Who Truly Loves the Truth," in Bauman, *Spiritual Legacy*, 163-77. Sebastian Franck later did the same thing in his *Paradoxa* of 1534. See Hayden-Roy, *Inner Word*, 109. The point of these collections of "contradictions" was essentially the same, namely to demonstrate the inadequacy of a "literal" reading of Scripture, and to point to the need for a spiritual understanding.

[23] See the *Biblical Concordance of the Swiss Brethren, 1540*, for an example of one of the earliest collections of biblical citations, topically organized.

[24] Packull, *Hutterite Beginnings*, 263.

[25] See his "Sermon to the Princes" (July 1524), titled "Interpretation of the Second Chapter of Daniel," in Matheson, *Collected Writings*, 230-52.

[26] Adding to Müntzer's general anticlericalism and distrust of the established clergy, both Catholic and Protestant, was added the personal animosity between Müntzer and Luther. See Müntzer's "Vindi-

cation and Refutation," in Matheson, *Collected Writings*, 327-50, for a striking example of sixteenth century invective.

[27] There was a tight circle involving people writing, producing, and promoting radical printed texts. Hans Hut had brought Müntzer's *Exposé* to Hans Hergot's press in Nuremberg to be published, and Hut probably was responsible for getting seeing to the printing of Haugk's *Christian Order* in Augsburg. See Packull, *Hutterite Beginnings*, 56, 338, n. 18.

[28] Hergot was a radical printer and supporter of Anabaptists, although not baptized himself. He was executed May 20, 1527.

[29] On the Peasants' War and Anabaptism, see James Stayer, *German Peasants' War and Anabaptist Community of Goods* (Montreal, PQ: McGill-Queen's University Press, 1991); on the Peasants' War in the Tyrol, see Packull, *Hutterite Beginnings*, 169-75; Walter Klaassen, *Michael Gaismair: Revolutionary and Reformer* (Leiden: Brill, 1978).

[30] The case of Hans Römer, although not a widespread phenomenon, demonstrates the staying-power of a visionary, apocalyptic, and revolutionary Anabaptism. See Stayer, *Sword*, 189ff.

[31] See Walter Klaassen, *Living at the End of the Ages: Apocalyptic Expectation in the Radical Reformation* (Lanham, MD: University Press of America, 1992).

[32] One of the earliest (September/October, 1524) was by the soon-to-be Anabaptist, Balthasar Hubmaier, "On Heretics and Those Who Burn Them," in Pipkin and Yoder, *Hubmaier*, 58-66. See also the selection from Sebastian Franck, #17 in this collection. Jacob Otter, Protestant preacher at Neckarsteinach, was one of a few Protestant clerics to plead for toleration of Anabaptists, while at the same time warning parishoners against secret preachers and divisions. Packull, *Hutterite Beginnings*, 82-83.

[33] See Packull, *Hutterite Beginnings*, ch. 11, 258-82.

[34] Now available in a new translation, vol. 9 of the *Classics of Radical Reformation* series, Friesen, *Peter Riedemann's Hutterite Confession*.

[35] The above summarizes Packull, *Hutterite Beginnings*, 70-73. For the years of prosperity in Moravia, see Leonard Gross, *The Golden Years of the Hutterites*, revised edition (Kitchener, ON: Pandora Press, 1998). Anabaptist presence in Moravia came to an end only when Ferdinand II defeated the nobility at the Battle of White Mountain, 1620. Packull, *ibid.*, 73.

[36] For example, Heinrich Bullinger, *Der Widertöufferen Ursprung, Fürgang, Secten, Wäsen, fürnemme und gemeine irer leer Artickel, auch ire*

Gründ, und warumm sy sich absünderind, etc. (Zürich: Froschauer, 1561; photo reprint, Leipzig, 1975).

[37] Packull, *Hutterite Beginnings*, 62-63; see all of ch. 3, 55-61.

[38] Werner Packull has established the centrality of communal sharing of goods among the first Anabaptist communities in Zollikon, Switzerland. Even though conditions in Zollikon soon made communal living impossible, the "congregational order" that emerged from the Zollikon community provided the template for congregational order not only for later Hutterite communities, but also for Pilgram Marpeck's groups. See *Hutterite Beginnings*, 33-53 and Appendix A, 303-15.

[39] See Packull, *Hutterite Beginnings*, ch. 5, 99-132.

[40] *Ibid.*, ch. 4, 77-98.

[41] *Ibid.*, ch. 6, 133-58, esp. 135ff.

[42] Gabriel Ascherham seems to have been connected with Brandhuber at Linz before moving on to Moravia to found his community at Rossitz. See *ibid.*, 121.

[43] Based on the testimony of several of his followers, Hut held to a provisional pacifism, with the sword held in check until the divine signal came to use it. This is how Sebastian Franck also characterized Hut's position, #19 below.

[44] See Yoder, *Legacy*, 34-43 for the text of Schleitheim, especially Article 6 on the sword, 39-41.

[45] James Stayer, *Anabaptists and the Sword*, (Lawrence, KS: Coronado Press, 1972), provides the foundational study of this issue for Anabaptism as a whole, with reliable studies of the South German/Austrian movement. Packull, *Hutterite Beginnings*, 174-75, notes the slow and late emergence of a "resolute pacifism" among the Tyrolean Anabaptists.

[46] The sorry tale with all relevant details is told in Packull, *Hutterite Beginnings*, ch. 9, 214-35.

[47] Well documented in Gross, *The Golden Years of the Hutterites*.

[48] See Klassen and Klaassen, *Writings*.

[49] Packull, *Hutterite Beginnings*, 293-301.

1 Jörg Haugk von Jüchsen

[1] The German title reads: *Ain Christlich ordenung/ aines warhafftigen Christen/ zu verantwurtten die ankufft seynes glaubens/*. The *Order* appeared first in 1526 from the press of Philip Ulhart Senior in Augsburg.

[2] Müller, *Glaubenszeugnisse*, 3-10 is incomplete.

³ *Flugschriften vom Bauernkrieg zum Täuferreich (1526-1535)*, ed. by Adolf Laube with assistance of Annerose Schneider and Ulman Weiss, vols. I and II (Berlin, 1992), esp. I, 667-86.

⁴ Cf. Packull, *Mysticism*, 77ff.

⁵ It is noteworthy that Peter Riedemann's allegorical first *Confession* identified the seven gifts of the Spirit with seven pillars on which to build the house of God. "Ein Rechenschaft und Bekanntnus des Glaubens vom Peter Ridemann" in *Glaubenszeugnisse oderdeutscher Taufgesinnter*: vol. II: *Quellen zur Geschichte der Täufer*, ed. by Robert Friedmann (1967), 4ff; translated as *Love is Like Fire. The Confession of an Anabaptist Prisoner*, ed. and transl. by Hutterian Brethren (Rifton, N.Y.: Plough Publishing House, 1993).

⁶ The notion that the created order contains a witness of the creator is not new. What is new is that the suffering of the creatures contains the Gospel witness, an idea articulated in variations by Hut, Leonard Schiemer and Peter Riedemann.

⁷ *Gelassenheit*, here applied in its original mystical theological meaning as yieldedness to the cathartic work of God in the person, was reinterpreted by the Anabaptist-Hutterites to designate a yielded attitude toward private property.

⁸ Marginal scriptural references are omitted; biblical references are given according to NRSV format.

⁹ This was the thrust of Hans Hut's Gospel of all creatures. Cf. Packull, *Mysticism*, 97-98.

¹⁰ The notion of the "cloven hooves" as a metaphor for the proper discernment in reading the Scriptures is also found in the writings of Melchior Hoffman.

¹¹ *Erkentnuss* is translated here as discernment. It could also be translated as understanding.

¹² The original *helt meine rede* could also mean "keep my word." It is noteworthy that Erasmus had preferred "speech" to "word" in his translation of the New Testament.

¹³ The original is *Verstandt* which could also be translated as understanding.

¹⁴ This distinction clearly echoes a key concern of Thomas Müntzer.

¹⁵ The reference to the ground of being is the typical language of mystical theology.

¹⁶ This language–*oder von abcontrofehung der natur einzogen sey*–is difficult to translate. The main point is that an outer witness is not sufficient; it must be the true inner witness. But to hear that witness,

one must focus on the true ultimate spiritual reality. The underlying assumption is a medieval realism.

[17] Searching out the will of God together implies a fellowship of sorts, functioning as the hermeneutic community.

[18] *Beywonung* designates mystical spousal or bridal language of consummating a spiritual union.

[19] Thomas Müntzer described it as a bitter experience.

[20] Like the medieval penitential system.

[21] For Luther this concept could mean temptation or tribulation.

[22] Here Haugk seems to be giving an allegorical account of an inner process rather than suggesting a second chance in purgatory.

[23] *Kunst* in this context could also be interpreted as divine learning.

[24] A neo-Platonic notion also found in Hans Denck.

[25] The theology of contraries, especially in neo-Platonic thought, contrasts the physical or material with the spiritual.

[26] The margin has *Pietatis* apparently as the equivalent to the highest degree of faith or divine blessedness [*gotseligkeit*].

[27] The notion that the chosen have a special promise of the spirit plays a role in some Anabaptist thinking regarding children.

[28] The passage reads *In dem sein wir fehig des eindrucks aller schetze götlicher weysshait*.

[29] *hertz korn darauss unser leben fleusst* does not seem to fit because it changes metaphors. The original must have been "born."

[30] A literal rendering would read "written in the flesh" but that seems to confuse the main point.

[31] The analogy between field and heart was a medieval favorite.

[32] The word is actually *leren* or always teach, but the meaning intended is forever learn.

[33] Sometimes creature could also be interpreted to mean the creation order or nature.

[34] The "key of David" appears in the writings of Müntzer, Hut, Denck and Jeronimus Käls.

[35] A warning is intended against bibliolatry.

[36] Justification is understood as God's cleansing work in the believer. The cleansing process is a painful dying to the old life, rising to a new life, hence transformational.

[37] This seems an obvious criticism of Lutherans.

[38] The emphasis is on faith in action.

2 Hans Hut

[1] This document shows a dependence on Hans Denck's pamphlet: *Unterricht, wie das Gesetz Gottes aufgehebt und doch erfuellt muss werden* ("He who truly loves the truth"). See Müller, 11, n. 3.

[2] While churchly instruction was available for those who wanted it both in the old church as well as in the emerging Protestant movement, Hut appears to suggest here that "Christian" instruction was lacking, especially proper understanding of the interpretation of Scripture.

[3] Werner O. Packull, *"Hut, Hans," ME V*, 404.

[4] Packull, *Mysticism*, 62.

[5] Hans-Jürgen Goertz, ed., *Profiles of Radical Reformers* (Scottdale, PA: Herald Press, 1982), 55.

[6] Packull, *Mysticism*, 63.

[7] Goertz, 55.

[8] Packull, *Mysticism*, 63.

[9] *Ibid.*, 64.

[10] Packull, *ME V*, 405.

[11] Packull, *Mysticism*, 64.

[12] Packull, *ME V*, 405.

[13] Packull, *Mysticism*, 66-67.

[14] Goertz, 54.

[15] Packull, *Mysticism*, 62.

[16] George H. Williams, *The Radical Reformation* 3rd edition (Kirksville, MO: Sixteenth Century Journal Publishers, 1992), 285.

[17] The text here has *ernst*. This can be variously translated as seriousness, determination, resolution. Perseverance seems to fit best with what Hut appears to have in mind here.

[18] This is an echo of Joachim of Fiore's three ages of Father, Son and Holy Spirit, a scheme which for Joachim was indispensable for understanding the Scriptures. See Bernard McGinn, "*Intellectus Spiritualis*: Joachim's Understanding of Scripture," ch. 4 of *The Calabrian Abbott: Joachim of Fiore in the History of Western Thought* (New York, N.Y.: Macmillan, 1985), 123-44.

[19] Müller has *mit*, but the context demands *nit*=not.

[20] Hut's references to the Hebrew Scriptures are to one of the late medieval translations, since Luther's were not yet available.

[21] The Apostles' Creed.

[22] The word creatures here does not mean simply animals as in modern usage. It means all particular created things, created by God and human hands, that belong to human existence. These objective creatures stand in contrast to non-objective spiritual realities.

[23] The original is somewhat convoluted and reads: *Dan alle creatur und geschoepf werden grob durch den einzug und das annemen der creatur gebraucht oder zu einem bessern wesen gefueert werden, dan durch leiden.* Since this translation is made from Müller's transcription, including her punctuation and occasional explanation in square brackets, one cannot always be certain of the nuances of the original. The translation of this sentence was arrived at in part through the context, especially the example given by Hut which follows immediately.

[24] Hut uses the second and third person singular and third plural of the personal pronoun randomly to refer to the believer. The translator has chosen to use the third person plural, which in no sense changes the meaning of what Hut is describing. It has the added advantage of avoiding the third person masculine singular which Hut frequently uses.

[25] The word here is *mittel*.

[26] This is a charge Hut makes against Luther's teaching that salvation is gained by external consent to Christian teaching, rather than through the mystic purgation and struggle to true faith.

3 Hans Hergot

[1] Walter Klaassen, "The Schleitheim Articles and the New Transfromation of Christian Living," *Historical Reflections* 14, no.1 (1987), 96.

[2] Goertz, *Profiles*, 97.

[3] *Ibid.*, 97.

[4] Klaassen, *Historical Reflections*, 106.

[5] *Ibid.*

[6] This translation is based on a facsimile of the original print of 1527 and a transcription of it under the title *Hans Hergot und die Flugschrift 'Von der Newen Wandlung Eynes Christlichen Lebens.' Faksimilewiedergabe mit Umschrift.* Introduction by Max Steinmetz, (Leipzig: VEB Fachbuchhandlung, 1977). The small volume also has a complete bibliography of all the printed literature on this tract.

[7] Hergot likely borrowed this trinitarian scheme from Joachim of Fiore whose prophecies were popular in the early sixteenth century.

[8] "The honour of God and the common good" was a popular peasant slogan in the 1520s.

⁹ Often, in the sixteenth century, a reference to the various monastic orders.

¹⁰ Meant, presumably, are the mendicant orders because they begged for their support. Which four Hergot means is not clear but they would certainly have included the Franciscans, Dominicans, and Augustinians. Carmelites, Servites, and others also had mendicant privileges.

¹¹ See John 10:1ff.

¹² Pope and emperor, who had for many centuries been regarded as the two heads of Christendom.

¹³ Hergot's *Flur* means meadow, pasture, open area. It also meant the common land. The designation "Common" with upper case has been chosen to translate *Flur*. The reasons for this choice will become obvious to the reader.

¹⁴ This was unheard of because refusal to pay tithe and tax was usually the first sign of revolt.

¹⁵ That there are still considerable elements of Catholic piety here is not surprising. There are several reasons for this. First, Reformation teachings had hardly penetrated into the consciousness of the peasantry by 1527. Second, the lower classes abandoned the traditional practices of piety much less readily than intellectuals, and third, Hergot's whole vision is the restoration of an old dream and not the proposal of a new one.

¹⁶ The communal raising of children was a common feature of utopian schemes. It is found first in Plato's *Republic*, and in most of the societal programmes drawn up in the sixteenth century. The Hutterites, a branch of the Anabaptist movement, actually instituted this feature in their communities in Moravia in the 1530s.

¹⁷ The original, which is somewhat confusing, reads as follows: *Der selbigen menschen wirdt also kommen/ das man alle mal den zwelfften menschen wird auskisen zu dem dienst Gottes und gemeynem nutz/ das sie stets auf Gots dienst warten/ die do geschickt wollen werden/diesen Gottes dienst zubestellen ist nicht gnug alle Cloester menlich vnd frawlich/nach auch stifftung dartzu.*

¹⁸ The Carthusians were noted for their silent ascetic and contemplative life. More important, it was an order that had never required reform. Apparently Hergot regarded them as the epitome of what it meant to live in a manner pleasing to God, and is another indication of how traditional his vision was.

[19] In a clear departure from traditional practice, periods of fasting will now be the times of rejoicing.

[20] This provision reflects the new evangelical practice of Luther and his followers. There was, however, a continuing tradition in the church which elevated the three, baptism, eucharist and confession as primary, and relegated the others to a lower order of importance.

[21] Thirty years was considered to be Jesus' age at his baptism.

[22] The repeated reference to the abolition of tithes and rents indicates how burdensome people found the feudal exactions of lay and spiritual lords.

[23] "Language" is anticipated here and refers to the three main geographical areas into which the world will be divided, Latin, Greek, and Hebrew, the three sacred languages. Thus space is "trinitarian" even as time is.

[24] It will no longer go to the support of the nobility and the urban rich.

[25] In Michael Gaismair's draft for a new agrarian society he also provides for the destruction of the cities because they are concentrations of wealth and privilege. He too provided for the public use of vacated monastic buildings. See Walter Klaassen, *Michael Gaismair: Revolutionary and Reformer*, (Leiden: Brill, 1978), Appendix I, no. 4.

[26] This is a direct repudiation of the principle of everyone remaining in the estate to which he was born held in traditional society and supported strongly by Martin Luther.

[27] This reflects the common idea among the non-nobility of these centuries that virtue was not inherited but a function of one's moral behaviour. A common peasant could possess the nobility of virtue. An example of this view is Pilgram Marpeck's letter to Magdalena von Pappenheim which was copied under the title "Men in Judgment and the Peasant Aristocracy." This text can be found in *The Writings of Pilgram Marpeck*, trans. and ed. Klassen and Klaassen, 464-483.

[28] The original text, not quite clear here, reads: *Durch dise vorleyhung wird der adel der gepurt vnd auch der verstand der yetzo ist, dem man wird teglich anhengen weyse vnd frome menner von dem gemeynen volcke, die den verstand regieren werden.*

[29] Monasteries and clergy enjoyed extensive exemption from civil taxes.

[30] Hergot was evidently convinced that even ordinary people could not be so virtuous without miracles. Thomas Müntzer and others said after the defeat of the peasants in May 1525, that they had been de-

feated because they had not acted according to the honour of God and the common good.

[31] The term *Schriftgelehrte*, literally, those learned in Scripture, was used often in the sixteenth century as a term of reproach. It was aimed by peasants and artisans especially at the Lutheran leaders who made so much of the Bible. The point of the reproach was that, in popular perception, they could always find ways of making the clear counsels and precepts of Jesus ineffective by means of their scholarly ingenuity. The term was borrowed from the Gospels where it is frequently used pejoratively, sometimes synonymous with hypocrisy.

[32] Planetary conjunctions, eclipses, and comets were widely regarded in the sixteenth century as omens of disaster. This was based partly on popular astrology as well as on a variety of Bible passages.

[33] Actually many of the Scripture scholars also believed these things. It is true that Martin Luther himself poured scorn on such things when they were put forward by ordinary people. Nevertheless, in 1527 he wrote an extensive introduction to a work of astrology. See Klaassen, *Living at the End of the Ages*, 31-32.

[34] "*vnnd liessen sich den blossen geyst regieren ...*"

[35] This reflects the peasant hostility toward all lawyers and especially toward the centralization of the judiciary in the sixteenth century on the basis of Roman law which made the dispensing of justice alien and impenetrable to the peasant accustomed to regional common law.

[36] Hergot constantly opposes Scripture and Spirit as had been done by Thomas Müntzer and Hans Hut, both of whom he had known personally. This does not reflect hostility to Scripture, but to the manipulation of Scripture with the syllogistic devices of the scholars. The Spirit could not be so controlled and perverted.

[37] This appears to be a reference to Luther who had violently attacked the appeal to the authority of the Spirit in his polemic *Against the Heavenly Prophets* of 1524.

[38] The appeal to the Spirit by assorted dissenters of the 1520s reflected the inability of many people to read, who therefore had no immediate access to the Bible, and were always at the mercy of those who could read. The appeal to the Spirit represented what has been called "the democratization of revelation." The Spirit could not be controlled and many believed that the Spirit spoke directly especially to the poor who could not read. Hence they had access to the wisdom of God as well as those who appealed to Scripture.

[39] The Twelve referred to are evidently the spirit-possessors from among the common people, while the two are representatives of the Scripture wizards. Twelve is a symbolic number here reminiscent of Twelve Tribes and Twelve Apostles.

[40] The Holy Spirit as a trumpet was an image Thomas Müntzer used in his Prague Manifesto in 1521.

[41] Luther had suppressed the published writings of one of his early opponents, Andreas Karlstadt whenever he could. See Calvin A. Pater, *Karlstadt as the Father of the Baptist Movements: The Emergence of Lay Protestantism* (Toronto, ON: University of Toronto Press, 1984), 5, 39, 157.

[42] Gen. 6:3-13.

[43] A reference to the peasant movement during the ten weeks from beginning March to mid-May, 1525.

[44] See Luther's pamphlet *Against the Murdering Robbing Hordes of Peasants*, 1525, for Luther's words to that effect.

4 Ambrosius Spitelmaier

[1] Herbert Klassen, "Ambrosius Spittelmayr: His Life and Teaching," *MQR* 32 (October 1958), 253.

[2] Packull, *Mysticism*, 119.

[3] Klassen, *MQR*, 253.

[4] Williams, *The Radical Reformation*, 272.

5 Leonhard Schiemer

[1] Williams, *The Radical Reformation*, 271.

[2] See Robert Friedmann, "Leonhard Schiemer and Hans Schlaffer, two Tyrolean Anabaptist martyr-apostles of 1528," *MQR* 33 (January 1959), 31; Williams, *The Radical Reformation* states first that Hut baptised Schiemer (271), but later Williams writes that Schiemer was converted by Hut and baptised by Oswald Glaidt (273).

[3] Friedmann, *MQR*, 32.

[4] *Ibid.*

[5] *Chronicle I*, 55.

[6] Friedmann, *MQR*, 32.

[7] Williams, *The Radical Reformation*, 273.

[8] *Ibid.*, 276.

[9] Schiemer's text says *nitentois*.

[10] Schiemer's text has *nitentionem*.

¹¹ The (usw.), used several times in this text, appears to indicate that parts of Scripture quotations have been omitted. They are almost certainly the work of Lydia Müller to reduce the length of the text. Were they by the original author, etc. would have been used.

¹² Luther translated the Greek text correctly at this point. The Greek *di'autou* can read through him, that is through John, or through the Word, since in John 1:2-4 the pronoun referring to the Word is masculine.

¹³ Schiemer got this wrong: *durch sein zuekunft in die welt* is Zwingli's translation in the Froschauer Bible.

¹⁴ The Latin Vulgate as well as the Greek text literally read *in nobis* and *en hemin* respectively. In that respect Schiemer has a point. However, the translations of John 1:14 without exception translate "among us" not "in us." Schiemer is here constrained by his mystical theology.

¹⁵ Again, the Vulgate and Greek texts read, literally *in universa creatura* and *en pase ktisei* respectively, whereas the translations all read **to** every creature. The reason for this is that with the locative case *en* can mean in in the usual sense, but also among. The context of the two passages John 1:14 and Col. 1:23 clearly shows that Luther translated accurately and that, literally, Schiemer is wrong. His mystical theology determines his reading.

¹⁶ This rendering of Luke 11:36 shows that even though Schiemer sharply criticizes Luther's translation at some points, he is in fact using Luther's translation.

¹⁷ Schiemer had evidently become acquainted with Lutheran teaching during his stay in Vienna and especially in Steyr where he worked for a few months in 1527. No doubt he had become aware how attractive some elements of Lutheran teaching were to his own converts in Steyr. See Grete Mecenseffy, *Geschichte des Protestantismus in Östrreich*, (Graz-Köln: Hermann Boehlaus Nachf., 1956), 10, 13.

¹⁸ This is a reference to the "pharisees" contemporary with Schiemer, by which he means the Protestant divines.

¹⁹ The sense here requires the negative which is absent in the text.

²⁰ The word here is *wintertrollen*.

²¹ This appears to reflect conflict between Lutheran and Anabaptist views in the congregation in Steyr.

²² The word here is *glider*.

²³ When Schiemer was imprisoned in Rattenberg he was, at his request, given paper and ink. Local Anabaptists visited him without hindrance at the beginning of his imprisonment. One wonders,

however, if he had a Bible when he wrote, since he is often not sure of his references.

²⁴ The term creatures means all created things physical and spiritual. It was a term commonly used by the western mystics from Meister Eckhart onwards.

²⁵ This is a favourite image in Anabaptist mystical writing of the pain and reordering of life necessary for the advent of faith. The tree has to be cut down and sawed into building lumber before a house can be built.

²⁶ This is perhaps as strong and eloquent a statement as can be found in Anabaptist writings reflecting the patristic conviction of the divinization of the believer, a change brought about by God with the consent of the believer. See for example J. Pelikan, *The Emergence of the Catholic Tradition (100-600)* (Chicago, IL: University of Chicago Press, 1971), 155, 206, 216, 344-45.

²⁷ This is clearly a reference to the Breviary, the book of Psalms, Scripture readings and prayers used in the Catholic church at that time.

²⁸ This seems to be a warning that believers should not be tempted to go to the parish priests to whom they have been accustomed to go and ask them to pray for them.

²⁹ This is a reference to Lutherans and Zwinglians.

6 Hans Schlaffer

¹ Friedmann, *MQR* 33, 40.
² *Ibid.*
³ *Ibid.*, 38.
⁴ Müller, *Glaubenszeugnisse*, 85, n. 1.
⁵ Williams, *The Radical Reformation*, 277.
⁶ *Ibid.*, 278.
⁷ Friedmann, *MQR* 33, 39.
⁸ Packull, *Mysticism*, 213, n. 154.
⁹ This view was based on an older mystical theology and justified by a faulty reading of Mark 16:15 where the German reads *predigt das Evangelium aller Kreatur*. The adjective *aller* has the same form in the genitive and the dative. Schlaffer chose the genitive reading.
¹⁰ Schlaffer here uses the word *rechtfertigung*, to justify.
¹¹ The formal attire worn by civic and academic officials.

¹² The text says *geistloser vater*, which is not parallel with what precedes. It should probably be *geistvoller vater*, meaning highly learned father.

¹³ This sentence is somewhat obscure. *Es haft nur noch an der andern seiten, das ist auf der linken, aber doch nit allenthalben.* Haft means the kernel of something. The reference to the left side is perhaps an allusion to being put on the left at the Great Judgment, Matt. 25.

¹⁴ At this point Müller has omitted part of the text.

¹⁵ Luther's translation of 1524 has the opposite of modern renderings. The NRSV reads: "Gather to me my faithful ones, who made a covenant with me by sacrifice."

¹⁶ This is Schlaffer's response to the argument that ancient church custom legitimized the baptism of infants.

¹⁷ Schlaffer evidently means here that a true Christian has to participate in all three baptisms.

¹⁸ These are simply general references to the discourse of Jesus about the end of all things.

¹⁹ See note 9, p. 395.

²⁰ By this he means Lutherans, Zwinglians, and Catholics.

²¹ The Lutheran, Zwinglian, and Catholic versions of what constitutes true teaching.

²² The text is corrupt at this point and therefore the translation is a conjecture. The text reads: "...*dieweil alle Christen oder recht warhaftige nach tauft und gepot haltet* ..."

²³ He evidently means last chapter, Mark 16:15. See note 9, p. 395.

²⁴ This is the order in use by all other Christians of the time.

²⁵ The letter added to the chapter indicates the relative position of the reference in the chapter.

²⁶ The text is obscure here. The translation is a conjectural reading of: "*Wen man nun also leert, deren auch Christus selbs im anfang seiner predig ermanet hat.*"

²⁷ These questions were asked by the interrogators and Schlaffer's answers were recorded by a secretary.

²⁸ This word is used to indicate similarity, meaning "in the same way," or "also."

²⁹ This section, beginning with "Whoever wants . . ." is very difficult syntactically and grammatically. Schlaffer seems to be contrasting the understanding of sin as institutional cultic infractions with sin as ethical according to God's law in Scripture.

³⁰ This is a reference back to obeying cultic rules earlier in this paragraph.

³¹ This is probably an allusion to the talk of the overthrow of all existing authority in the confessions of Hans Hut of late 1527, whose links with Thomas Müntzer had been established. Schlaffer was influenced by Hut's theology, especially in his adoption of Hut's "Gospel of all the creatures."

³² The first decree of King Ferdinand against the Anabaptists of August, 1527, had stated that Anabaptism was a new form of the old peasant revolt of 1524-1526.

³³ For some reason the order of the questions was changed by the interrogators.

³⁴ By majorities Schlaffer alludes to the argument Anabaptists often faced, namely that, for example, infant baptism had been the practice of the whole church for many centuries. How did they dare to set themselves against this majority?

³⁵ This is likely a reference to the confessions of Hans Hut of late 1527 as well as of several of Hut's converts. See Packull, *Mysticism*, 88-117.

³⁶ The sentence ends here. It is not clear whether he meant to say something specific or if by "the whole" he is referring to the plot of the whole world against him and those of his faith.

³⁷ Evidently the news of Hut's death in November, 1527 had not reached Schlaffer, since he himself had been arrested and imprisoned on December 6, 1527.

³⁸ Evidently, under torture, Schlaffer decided to mention the names of prominent Anabaptists who lived outside Habsburg jurisdiction so as not to endanger them.

³⁹ The text has Christ*um*, but the context suggests that it should be Christ*en*, i.e. Christians.

⁴⁰ From this point onwards virtually no Scripture references are included. Evidently, although Schlaffer quotes Scripture copiously, the stress of the interrogation under torture made it difficult to add these details.

⁴¹ The area north of the Enns River.

⁴² This was obviously an official order from his bishop because his preaching departed from what was required.

⁴³ The Fuggers were one of the most prominent banking houses of the Empire.

⁴⁴ A castle near Brixlegg in the Inn Valley.

[45] The text says Rottenburg. I take it to mean Rattenberg on the Inn, which often appears in the records as Rottenburg. Rattenberg lay on the Inn River a few kilometres east of Brixlegg.

[46] Münichen was perhaps the small hamlet Münichau near Kitzbühel. The inn was presumably somewhere along his route between Brixlegg and Schwaz.

[47] December 6.

[48] St. Sebastian's day was January 20.

[49] Müller notes that the text, which is difficult to read here, reads *gerichtstag*. What follows makes clear that this is a reference to two interrogations that followed the submission of the first confession (Part 1).

[50] Presumably Schlaffer's own memory.

[51] In 1526-1527 Balthasar Hubmaier carried out an Anabaptist reform with the co-operation of the Lord Leonhard von Liechtenstein. Many were baptized. Hans Hut and others protested against what they considered to be a careless administration of baptism. See Snyder, *Anabaptist History and Theology: An Introduction*, 118-21.

[52] Diversion is a pure conjecture. The word is *schrauflucken* which is unintelligible. The conjectural rendering is based on the context.

[53] This is not to be interpreted as hyperbole or the prideful ranting of a sectarian. The introduction of the baptism of adult believers threatened to undermine the role of the clergy as the sole authorities on Christian belief and life. Moreover, the interwovenness of church and civil society gave the baptism of infants a civil as well as a religious character. The proposal of Anabaptists to baptize only believing adults was therefore perceived as a threat which could undermine Christendom.

[54] The Conversion of Paul is January 25.

7 Eitelhans Langenmantel

[1] Johann Loserth, "Langenmantel, Eitelhans," *ME III*, 289.

[2] Packull, *Mysticism*, 208, n. 44.

[3] *Ibid.*, 208-09, n. 48.

[4] *Ibid.*

[5] John C. Wenger, "Two Early Anabaptist Tracts," *MQR* 21-22 (January 1948), 35-36.

[6] *Ibid.*, 36.

[7] *Chronicle I*, 61.

[8] Loserth, *ME III*, 289.

[9] *Ibid.*

9 Lamprecht Penntz

[1] This is the editor's summary. What follows is a translation of the original document as printed in Grete Mecenseffy, ed. *Quellen zur Geschichte der Täufer, Österreich II Teil* (Gütersloh: Gerd Mohn, 1972), 173, ll. 11-38.

[2] The penance procedures sent out in November 1527 to administrators [*Pfleger*] by the Archbishop of Salzburg stipulated that penitent men and women were to wear plain clothing onto which a cross was sewn. *Ibid.*, 18, #18B, #1.

10 Ursula Hellrigel

[1] C. Arnold Snyder and Linda A. Huebert Hecht, eds., *Profiles of Anabaptist Women: Sixteenth-Century Reforming Pioneers* (Waterloo, ON: Wilfrid Laurier University Press, 1996), 195.

[2] *Ibid.*, 197.

[3] *Ibid.*, 199.

11 Hans Nadler

[1] Packull, *Mysticism*, 92.

[2] Russell Snyder-Penner, "Hans Nadler's oral exposition on the Lord's Prayer," *MQR* 65 (October 1991), 395.

[3] Packull, *Mysticism*, 113.

[4] Christian Neff, "Nadler (Ritter), Hans," *ME III*, 805.

[5] *Ibid.*

[6] Snyder-Penner, *MQR* 65, 395.

[7] This was Balthasar Hubmaier's Anabaptist church.

[8] Answers 9-11 are responses to questions that are virtually impossible to reconstruct.

[9] The words "This is my body" which, when said by the priest, were believed to change the bread into the very body of Christ.

[10] Perhaps the arms for God's avenging forces.

[11] This statement is not clear because we do not know the question.

[12] This is a reference to Luther's booklet *Von der Wiedertaufe an zwei Pfarrherrn*, 1528, found in vol. 26 of the Weimar Edition of Luther's works. Schornbaum, *Quellen II*, pp. 144-45 provides the relevant page references.

12 Wolfgang Brandhuber

[1] Both *Chronicle I* and Packull's work, *Mysticism*, say that Brandhuber was a tailor. This error has been corrected in Packull's latest work, *Hutterite Beginnings*, 60.

[2] Packull, *Hutterite Beginnings*, 60.

[3] *Ibid.*, 121.

[4] Christian Hege, "Brandhuber, Wolfgang," *ME I*, 404-05.

⁵ Packull, *Hutterite Beginnings*, 60-61.
⁶ *Chronicle I*, 61-62.
⁷ There appears to have been some trouble in the church relating to the place of private property. That is likely the sin to which Brandhuber has already alluded.
⁸ In other words, no one must be coerced in any way to contribute to the common purse; it must be voluntary and motivated from within.
⁹ This list of female finery, somewhat contemporized by Brandhuber, comes from Isa. 3:18-24. It should, however, not be understood as sexist, but simply as a scriptural list of worldly indulgence applicable to male and female alike.
¹⁰ This could be a reference to Martin Luther's *Ob Kreigsleute auch in seligem Stande sein koennen (Whether Soldiers, too, Can be Saved)* published in 1526. In it Luther argues that the sword has been divinely instituted to punish evil and that the military profession legitimately bears that sword.
¹¹ The use of shadow in contrast to light may be an echo of Joachim of Fiore (ca. 1132-1202) who used this image to denote the forward movement of God's purpose from darkness, through shadow, to full light.
¹² Three years later Pilgram Marpeck would similarly identify the Whore of Babylon with the Protestant attempt to justify the use of the sword to protect the gospel. See "Exposé of the Babylonian Whore" transl., Klaassen, *Later Writings of Pilgram Marpeck*, 21-48.
¹³ The last part of this sentence is incomprehensible: *"vermaindlen und beschidens und ist doch nichts anders,"* and is left untranslated.
¹⁴ This is an allusion to the Mass in which Christ was physically present according to church doctrine. Christ, says our author, does not return every time the Mass is celebrated but only once at the End.
¹⁵ This passage seems contradictory, for Brandhuber's whole argument is that created things are a threat to the spirit, not the flesh. The passage reads: "...*darumb flucht er reichtumb und pracht, dan sie dem widersacher, dem fleisch, toedlich sein* . . ."
¹⁶ These images are all drawn from the Song of Solomon or canticle.

13 Jörg Zaunring

¹ Packull, *Hutterite Beginnings*, 200-01.
² *Ibid.*, 63.
³ *Ibid.*, 215.
⁴ *Ibid.*, 201-02.

⁵ For Zaunring and for most Anabaptists world meant primarily those in the papal and Lutheran churches. In making that judgment Zaunring was simply being a man of his time, for Anabaptists, in turn, were identified as opponents of God and the Gospel by the other confessions. However, Zaunring was also speaking as an Anabaptist who rejected the assumption that European society was Christian despite its claim to be Christendom. World, or worldly behaviour was anything that did not express the life of Christ and the apostles. A tree, they said, is known by its fruit. Doing evil and at the same time claiming the Christian name was incompatible for Anabaptists. Faith in Christ had to be expressed in a Christ-like life, not merely in theological or confessional words.

⁶ This term, drawn from Old Testament models (see Isa. 46:6-7) is used in this manner because of the veneration accorded the consecrated bread in particular on the Feast of Corpus Christi when the Host was taken in procession through the community.

⁷ There is a gap in the text here.

⁸ The words in brackets are Müller's conjecture and appear to be justified by the context.

⁹ Zaunring's word *Spottmauer* probably refers to the strength of the old church, using the word Mauer, wall, as Luther used it in his 1520 work *Appeal to the Ruling Class of the German Nation*.

¹⁰ Martin Luther and his followers.

¹¹ Zaunring's references in this section are extremely general. It is usually impossible to assign a specific verse.

¹² Eobanus Hessus (1488-1540), humanist scholar and firm supporter of Luther.

¹³ One remembers here Luther's insistence on the freedom of the Christian.

¹⁴ By this time the reader may conclude that we are dealing here with a cramped biblicism in Zaunring's argument about the presence of Christ's body at the right hand of God instead of in the bread. He was, however, using arguments used also by the Swiss reformers. A number of Zaunring's arguments are made by Oecolampadius and Zwingli at the Marburg Colloquy with Luther in 1529. See Donald J. Ziegler, ed., *Great Debates of the Reformation* (New York, N.Y.: Random House, 1969), 75, 83, 88, 90-91, and 101. In fact that whole colloquy dealt with the true location of the body of Christ.

¹⁵ Zaunring's word is *Walitten*. It is probably linked to *Wallfahren* which means to go on pilgrimage. A Waller is a pilgrim.

[16] Zaunring's word is *asimuliert*, which is derived from the Latin verb simulo-are, to represent.

14 Rurer/Althamer

[1] Christian Classics Ethereal Library website: http://www.ccel.org May 15, 2001.
[2] Irmgard Höss, "Althamer, Andreas," *The Oxford Encyclopedia of the Reformation* vol. 1 (Oxford: Oxford University Press, 1996), 21.

15 Georg Pfersfelder

[1] Eberhard Teufel, "Pfersfelder, Georg," *ME IV*, 159.

16 Katharina Hutter

[1] Snyder and Hecht, *Profiles*, 179.
[2] *Ibid.*, 182.
[3] *Ibid.*, 183.

17 Endres Keller

[1] Schornbaum, *Quellen V*, 20.
[2] *Ibid.*, 218-222.
[3] A twelver was a 20th of a florin, about half a day's pay for a carpenter.
[4] A fiver was a 12th of a florin.
[5] A guilder and a florin were equivalent.
[6] The translation here is a conjecture, following the context and train of thought. The original reads *sie sein wie lailg vmer wol*?

18 Urbanus Rhegius

[1] Scott H. Hendrix, "Rhegius, Urbanus," *The Oxford Encyclopedia of the Reformation*, vol. 3, 429.
[2] Williams, *The Radical Reformation*, 283.
[3] Packull, *Mysticism*, 41.
[4] This translation of selections from Augustine's letter to Vicentius is by J. A. Cunningham in *Letters of St. Augustine, Nicene and Post-Nicene Fathers*, vol. I (Grand Rapids, MI: Eerdmans, 1956), 383.
[5] "A Treatise Concerning the Correction of the Donatists" in *The Nicene and Post-Nicene Fathers*, vol. IV, 633-51.
[6] Fanatical ascetics in North Africa at the time of the Donatists and of Augustine.

19 Sebastian Franck

¹ Hans J. Hillerbrand, *A Fellowship of Discontent* (New York, N.Y.: Harper and Row, 1967), 32.
² Cornelius Krahn and N. van der Zijpp, "Franck, Sebastian," *ME II*, 363-67.
³ Patrick Hayden-Roy, "Franck, Sebastian," *The Oxford Encyclopedia of the Reformation*, vol. 2, 134.
⁴ Hayden-Roy, *Inner Word*, 42.
⁵ *Ibid.*, 96.
⁶ Martin Cellarius (Borrhaus), born 1499, was educated at Tübingen and Ingolstadt in the humanist disciplines. Once a friend of Melanchthon and supporter of Martin Luther, he moved towards the radical side of reform. He opposed infant baptism, but never became an Anabaptist himself—although he was often accused of it. In Strasbourg in 1526 he opposed Hans Denck for teaching freedom of the will. Cellarius supported a predestinarian view in public disputation and also in the book cited by Franck, which was published in 1527. He taught in Basel, first as a professor of rhetoric and then of theology, from 1536 to the time of his death in 1565 (*ME I*, 538-39).

20 Mathes Hasenhan

¹ Friesen, *Peter Riedemann's Hutterite Confession of Faith*, 39-42.
² Werner O. Packull, "Peter Tasch: from Melchiorite to bankrupt wine merchant," *MQR* 62 (July 1988), 283, n. 42.
³ Franz, *Quellen IV*, 269-70.
⁴ Jörg Zaunring was executed at Bamberg in 1532.
⁵ Melchior Rinck was not an advocate of a legislated community of goods.
⁶ Jacob Hutter, the leader of the Moravian Brethren, was burned at the stake in 1536.
⁷ Jörg Fasser was executed in Lower Austria in 1537.
⁸ Hieroniums Käls of Kopfstein, community schoolmaster, was burned at the stake in Vienna in 1536.
⁹ Peter Riedemann of Hirshberg was imprisoned in Gmunden from 1529 to 1532, and imprisoned in Nuremberg from 1533 to 1537.
¹⁰ Christoph Gschäl was sent to Styria and Carinthia in 1537.

21 Trieste

[1] *Chronicle I*, 188.

[2] *Ibid.*, 194.

[3] This is the term Anabaptists often used of the bread of the eucharist, because it was adored as the very body of Christ.

[4] This repetitive tirade against all religious representation of which the late medieval churches were full shows how seductive it all was. It should be understood that this is not a tirade against what we today call medieval art. It was drawing attention to and warning against the invisible line between the function of the image as a form of religious instruction for the illiterate and the adoration of the image itself since it was visible and God, to whom ideally it pointed, was not. The bread idol is, of course, the consecrated wafer of the Mass, which, housed in a jewelled case, was everywhere taken in solemn procession through the streets on the feast of Corpus Christi for the adoration of the faithful. The attention was on the sacred wafer which represented the actual presence of Christ's body.

[5] Conforming outwardly to required religious observance by attending the Catholic Mass or the Protestant communion was a continuing temptation for Anabaptists everywhere because it helped avoid confrontation with the authorities over religious differences. Faced with the prospect of prison, exile, or even execution, attending Mass, which involved a minimum of participation, seemed to many like a small thing for which God would forgive them.

[6] Parts of the article on the non-swearing of oaths parallel Schleitheim, Article 7 very closely. Cf. Yoder, *Legacy*, 41-42.

[7] I accept here the conjecture of Müller to clarify a damaged text. It reads: *Wann wir das boes haben hinausgetan nach dem bevelch [Gottes, uebergeben] wir si Gott nachmals in seim gericht.*

[8] The section on separation from the world closely copies and paraphrases Schleitheim, Article 4. Cf. Yoder, *Legacy*, 37-38.

[9] The section following contains verbatim copies of large parts of Schleitheim, Article 6. Cf. Yoder, *Legacy*, 39-41. It would appear that the writers had a copy of the Schleitheim Articles in hand.

[10] This sentence gave Yoder some difficulty. See Yoder, *Legacy*, 53, n. 80. In this confession there is no such difficulty since a reference has been made in the previous paragraph to the Father's law in the Old Testament that Christ disregarded in his judgment about the woman

taken in adultery. Here Jesus withdrew from being made king which was also an "ordinance of His Father."

[11] Beginning with the section on separation from the world on 268 and ending at this point, the authors have drawn on the Swiss Schleitheim Articles. They used all of Article 3, most of Article 4, and all of Article 6, although not in that order. Most of what they use is a verbal rendering, with some omissions and some additions. Cf. the critical text of the Articles in *Quellen zur Geschichte der Täufer in der Schweiz. 2. Bd. Ostschweiz*, ed. by Heinold Fast, (Zürich: Theologischer Verlag, 1973), 22-30. See also the English translation in Yoder, *Legacy*, 34-43. This dependence on the Schleitheim Articles appears to suggest that this document was not only well-known among the Hutterians, but also used with approval. Perhaps there were among the prisoners Anabaptists from Switzerland who had joined the Hutterians.

[12] As Müller points out in a note on 205, the reference to the absolute necessity of the believer's descent into the hell of tribulation before the ascent into the heaven of the vision of God is likely an allusion to the 11th chapter of the "German Theology." Anabaptists who shared in the legacy of late medieval mysticism, especially Hans Hut and Hans Denck, knew and used this work. See *The Theologica Germanica of Martin Luther*, trans. by Bengt Hoffman (New York, N.Y.: Paulist Press, 1980).

22 Hans Umlauft

[1] Packull, *Hutterite Beginnings*, 147.
[2] *Ibid.*, 148.
[3] *Ibid.*, 149.
[4] *Ibid.*, 151.
[5] This paragraph is virtually a literal citation of the first article of Hans Denck's so-called *Recantation* which can be found in Bauman, *The Spiritual Legacy of Hans Denck*, 245-59.

23 Helena von Freyberg

[1] Snyder and Hecht, *Profiles*, 124.
[2] *Ibid.*, 125.
[3] *Ibid.*, 126.
[4] *Ibid.*
[5] *Ibid.*, 128.
[6] *Ibid.*, 131.

[7] Round brackets are words in the original text; square brackets are inserted words.

[8] In her confession she uses the word *Hündt* which is a reference to a person in civil authority at the local level. See Hans Fink in *Tiroler Wortschatz an Eisack, Rienz und Etsch* (Innsbruck: Universitätsverlag Wagner, 1972), 134. Perhaps Helena was referring to the *Statthalter* before whom she had recanted at Innsbruck in 1534.

24 Paul Glock: Letter to his wife Else

[1] Gross, *Golden Years of the Hutterites*, 101-02.
[2] *Chronicle I*, 450.
[3] Klaus von Grafeneck was present at the trial and execution of Michael Sattler in 1527, and wrote an account of the events. See Yoder, *Legacy*, 67-76, 81, n. 4.
[4] Gross, *Golden Years of the Hutterites*, 107.
[5] *Ibid.*, 102.
[6] *Ibid.*, 103.
[7] *Ibid.*, 105.
[8] *Ibid.*, 112.

25 Paul Glock: 1st defence

[1] Up to this point, this report has been a summary by the editor Gustav Bossert. It now shifts to verbatim testitomony.

26 Paul Glock: Letter to Leonhard Lanzenstiel

[1] This is a legend about Daniel found in the apocryphal book Bel and the Dragon. The prophet Habakkuk brought a meal to Daniel in the lion's den.
[2] A cobbler, until 1559 servant of the word with the Swiss Brethren, after 1561 with the Hutterian Brethren.

27 Paul Glock: First Letter to Peter Walpot

[1] Peter Walpot was the leader of the Hutterian Brethren 1565-1578.
[2] See *Die Lieder der Hutterischen Brüder*, (Cayley, AB: Hutteritschen Brüder, 1962), 734. This is a song Glock himself composed.
[3] Margaret von Grafeneck, a follower of Schwenckfeld, and her husband, the chief overseer of Urach, Klaus von Grafeneck.

28 Paul Glock: Second Letter to Peter Walpot

[1] In the sixteenth century, barbers also functioned as surgeons.

29 Paul Glock: Third Letter to Peter Walpot

[1] Hutterite missionaries went out to Europe every spring on their evangelizing journeys.
[2] *Die Lieder der Hutterischen Brüder*, 709.

30 Paul Glock: Fourth Letter to Peter Walpot

[1] See Friesen, *Peter Riedemann's Hutterite Confession of Faith*.

33 Walpurga von Pappenheim

[1] Snyder and Hecht, *Profiles*, 111.
[2] Selections from the *Verantwortung* can be found in Klaassen, Packull and Rempel, *Later Writings by Pilgram Marpeck and his Circle* (Kitchener, ON: Pandora Press, 1999), 67-144.
[3] *Ibid.*, 119.
[4] Snyder, *Anabaptist History and Theology: An Introduction*, 262.
[5] Snyder and Hecht, *Profiles*, 119.

34 Hans Schmidt

[1] C. Arnold Snyder, "The Influence of the Schleitheim Articles on the Anabaptist Movement: An Historical Evaluation," *MQR* 63 (October 1989), 323-44.
[2] Robert Friedmann, "Schmidt, Hans," *ML* 4, 79.
[3] Michael Sattler had used these words at his trial. Cf. Yoder, *Legacy*, 72-73.

Index of Names and Places

Althamer, Andreas, 171-72, 402n
Allstedt, xix
Amon, Hans, xxxviii
Anabaptists, 1-3, 22, 50, 51, 52, 65, 81, 100, 110, 111, 112, 127, 129, 130, 132, 133, 136, 137, 151, 152, 156, 163, 164, 172, 185, 186, 187, 191-93, 194, 195, 214, 215, 219, 220, 224, 225, 229, 231, 233-34, 248, 249, 251, 277, 288, 289, 318, 363, 369, 373, 378, 379, 381n, 384n, 385n, 390n, 394n, 397n, 398n, 399n, 401n, 404n, 405n
Ascherham, Gabriel (See Gabrielites)
Augsburg, xiv, xxxvi, xxxviii, 1, 2, 23, 52, 54, 82, 102, 110-111, 148, 201, 213, 214, 289, 292, 384n, 385n
Augustine, xl, 216, 218, 221, 222, 224, 225, 232, 284, 402n
Ausbund, xlix
Auspitz, xliii, 164
Austerlitz (Brethren), xxxvii, xliii-xliv, xlvii-xlix, 156, 163, 164, 233, 277, 372
Austria, xxxviii, li, 50, 64, 65, 77, 81, 255, 259, 403n
Bamberg, 148, 164, 185, 403n
Basel, 213, 229, 403n
Bavaria, 65, 77, 82, 104, 155, 288
Belial, 202, 301, 307

Bibra, 22
Blesdijk, Nicholas van, xvii
Bohemia, xxxviii
Brandhuber, Wolfgang, xxiv, xxxii, xliv-xlvii, xlix, 82, 102, 155-57, 385n, 399n, 400n
Brixlegg, 104, 397n, 398n
Bruneck, 193
Bünderlin, Hans (Johann), xli, li, 229
Bullinger, Heinrich, xli
Burghausen, 155
Catholics, 66, 130, 156, 172, 216, 229, 278, 383n, 390n, 395n, 396n, 404n
Cellarius, Martin, 403n
Charles V, xxxviii
Denck (Denk), Hans, xx-xxii, xxv, xxxi, xxxiii, xli, l, 1, 2, 3, 22, 52, 82, 102, 121, 171, 172, 214, 229, 231, 235, 236, 241, 242, 278, 282, 383n, 387n, 403n, 405n
Donatists, xl
Eck, Johann, 213
Eckhart, Meister, 395n
Entfelder, Christian, li
Falkenstein, 259, 261
Fasser, Jörg, xxxvii, 257, 403n
Ferdinand I, xxxvii, xxxviii, xlvii, 65, 129, 131, 192, 259, 278, 397n
France, 110

Franck, Sebastian, xx, xli-xlii, 172, 228-31, 383n, 384n, 385n, 403n
Frankenhausen, xxx, 1, 22
Frederick (Count), 375
Frey, Claus, 186
Freyberg, Helena von, xxvii, xlix, 287-93
Froschauer, 394n
Gabriel(ites), (Gabriel Ascherham) xxxvii, xliii-xliv, xlviii, li, 372
Gaismair, Michael, xxxi, xxxvi, 384n, 391n
German(y), 2, 21, 47, 48, 65, 67, 69, 83, 111, 112, 122, 137, 145, 171, 172, 201, 202, 222, 346, 375, 381n, 385n, 395n, 405n
Glaidt, Oswald, 65, 82, 102, 393n
Glock, Paul, xxiv, xxviii, xxxv, xxxix, xl-xli, xlix, 294-98, 308, 324, 329, 335, 340, 344, 348, 354, 361, 373, 406n
Grafeneck, Klaus von, xli, 295, 296, 309, 321, 406n
Grafeneck, Margaret von, xli, 352, 406n
Graz, 260
Griesinger, Onophrius, xxxvii
Gross, Georg (see Pfersfelder)
Hätzer, Ludwig, 82, 102, 139, 231, 236, 247
Hapsburgs, xxxviii
Hasenhan, Mathes (Matthias), 253, 255
Haugk, Jörg (von Jüchsen), xxii, xxv, xxix-xxx, xxxiii, 1-3, 22, 384n, 387n
Hellrigel, Ursula, xxxv, 132-33
Hergot, Hans, xxv-xxvi, xxx, xxxii, 35-37, 384n, 389n, 390n, 391n, 392n

Hesse, 253, 255, 256
Hoffman, Melchior, xiii, xvii, 3, 381n, 386n
Horneck, Adam, 296, 298, 309, 325, 352
Hubmaier, Balthasar, xlii-xliii, 52, 64, 81, 137, 213, 231, 384n, 398n, 399n
Hut, Hans, xxi-xxii, xxiv-xxxiii, xlii-xlvi, 1, 2, 21-23, 35, 50-51, 52, 54, 57, 65, 81, 82, 102, 107, 110, 111, 112, 121, 136, 137, 139, 142, 155, 156, 171, 172, 214, 231, 242, 246, 247, 384n, 385n, 386n, 387n, 388n, 389n, 392n, 393n, 397n, 398n, 407n
Hutter, Jacob, xxxii, xxxvii, xlvii-xlix, 163, 192, 382n, 403n
Hutter, Katharina, xxxv, xxxvii, xlviii-xlix, 191-93
Hutterian Brethren (Hutterites), xvi, xviii, xxii, xxv, xxix, xxxii, xxxvii-xxxviii, xliv, xlviii, l-li, 2, 23, 81, 111, 133, 156, 164, 253, 254, 294, 295, 366, 367, 382n, 385n, 386n, 390n, 405n, 406n, 407n
Inn Valley/River, 65, 156, 157, 132, 397n
Jews, 58, 59, 77, 88, 91, 95, 101, 123, 145, 150, 174, 189, 198, 199, 200, 205, 206, 207, 208, 209, 216, 220, 223, 241, 283, 284, 304, 321
Joris, David, xviii
Käls, Jeronimous, xxxvii
Karlstadt, Andreas, xix-xxii, xxv, xxxiii, 1, 22, 383n, 393n
Keller, Endres, xxviii, xxxv, xli, xlvi, 196-197, 198,
Klausen (Tyrol), xlix, 192, 194, 195
Langenmantel, Eitelhans, xxiv-xxv, 110-112, 113, 117, 137, 214, 398n
Lanzenstiel (Sailer), Leonhard, 296, 325

Linz, xliv, 50, 52, 54, 102, 139, 155, 156, 162, 385n

Ljubliana, 260

Lochmaier, Leonhard, xxxvii

Luther, Martin, xix-xxii, xxv, xxix, xxxii, xxxiv, xl, 36, 69, 81, 121, 144, 152, 164, 167, 172, 186, 187, 188, 202, 203, 208, 228, 247, 287, 382n, 383n, 387n, 391n, 392n, 393n, 394n, 400n, 401n, 403n

Marburg Colloquy, 401n

Marpeck, Pilgrim, xviii, xxii, xxvii, xliv-xlv, xlix, li, 2, 163, 287, 289, 292, 362, 363, 381n, 382n, 385n, 391n, 400n

Melancthon, Philip, 121, 403n

Mennonites, xiii, xvii

Moravia, xiv, xxxvi-xxxviii, xlii-xliv, xlvii-l, 52, 65, 137, 156, 163, 194, 195, 233, 253, 254, 255, 260, 277, 278, 295, 297, 298, 329, 347, 354, 366, 367, 371, 372, 375, 378,

Müller, Jörg, 195

Müller, Lydia, 388n, 389n, 394n, 396n, 398n, 401n, 404n, 405n

Münichau, 287, 288, 398n

Münster(ites), xvii, xxxvii, xl-xli, 209, 219, 222, 224, 225, 289

Müntzer, Thomas, xix-xxii, xxv, xxx-xxxii, xxxvi, xl, 1, 2, 22, 23, 35, 62, 236, 382n, 383n, 384n, 386n, 387n

Nadler, Hans, xxiv, xxvii-xxviii, xxxi-xxxii, xxxv, xxxix, xlv, 82, 112, 136-138, 399n

Nicholsburg, xlii-xliv, 64, 81, 107, 136, 137, 139

Nuremberg, xiv, xxxvi, xxxviii, 22, 23, 35, 50, 51, 52, 64, 82, 102, 110, 121, 136, 171, 185, 186, 187, 229, 257, 278, 384n, 403n

Osiander, Andreas, 121, 164, 167, 186

Orlamünde, xix

Packull, Werner, 23, 381n, 382n, 385n, 399n

Pastor, Adam, xvii

Palatinate, (the), xlii-xliii

Pappenheim, Walpurga von, xlix, 362-63, 364

Passau, xlix, 155-56

Peasants' War (Uprising), 1, 22, 36, 165, 384n

Penntz, Lamprecht, 129-30, 131

Pfersfelder, Georg (Gross), xli, 185-86, 187, 402n

Philip, 54, 101, 146, 263, 355

Philip(ites), (Philip Plenner), xxxvii, xliii, xlviii-xlix, 259

Philips, Dirk, xvii

Plener, Philip (See Philipites)

Rattenberg, 65, 81, 104, 156, 157, 163, 287, 394n, 398n

Regensburg, 82, 102, 104, 277

Reublin, Wilhelm, 164

Rhegius, Urbanus, xxxvi, xl-xli, 121, 213-14, 215, 228, 402n

Rhineland, xiv, xxxvii, xliii

Riedemann, Peter, xxxviii, xlix, 156, 253, 350, 386n, 403n

Rinck, Melchior, 231, 257, 403n

Ritter, Jacob Hans, 256

Rossitz, xliii

Rothmann, Bernhard, xvii, xli, 222

Rurer, Johann, xxxix, 153, 171-72

Salzburg, 65, 80, 399n

Sattler, Michael, xlv, 242, 367, 406n, 407n

Schiemer, Leonhard, xxiv, xxvi, xxxii, xxxv, 22, 64-66, 81, 82, 83, 112, 137, 163, 386n, 393n, 394n

Schlaffer, Hans, xxiv, xxvii, xxxi-xxxii, xxxv, 22, 66, 81-83, 84, 94, 95, 99, 103, 105, 112, 137, 156, 393n, 395n, 396n, 397n, 398n

Schleitheim Articles, xlv

Schmidt, Hans, xxxv, xxxix, xlv, xlix, 366-67, 368, 369, 380, 407

Schneeweiss, Simon, 121

Schwenckfeld, Caspar, xli, 185, 186, 229, 362, 406n

Schwaz, 82, 83, 94, 99, 104, 105, 398n

Silesia, xiv, xxxvii, xlii-xliii, xlviii

Simons, Menno, xvii

Spitelmaier, xxiv, xxvi-xxvii, xxxi-xxxii, xxxv, 22, 50-51, 52, 54, 82, 171, 393n

Steinabrunn, 259

Steyr, 65, 394n

Strasbourg, xxxviii, xli, li, 229, 254, 403n

Swabian League, 112

Swiss Brethren, xvi, xvii, xxxvii, xliii-xlvi, xlviii-xlix

Switzerland, xlii-xliii, 65, 251, 252, 385n, 405n

Tasch, Peter, 254

Tauler, Johannes, xx

Thuringia, xiv

Trieste, xxxv, xlv-xlvi, 260, 261, 276

Turk(s), xxxi, xxxvii-xxxviii, 22, 24, 47, 62, 71, 85, 86, 242, 283, 284, 331, 332, 350, 351, 371, 378

Tyrol(ean), xiv, xxvii, xxxi, xxxvi-xxxviii, xlii, xliv, xlvii-xlviii, 65, 82, 132, 133, 156, 163, 164, 191, 192, 195, 214, 287, 288, 289, 384n, 385n

Ulhart, Philip, 1, 385n

Umlauft, Hans, xl, 277-78, 279

Vienna, 64, 139, 260, 353, 394n, 403n

Villnöss, 195

Vogel, Wolfgang, 62

Walpot, Peter, 296, 329, 335, 340, 344, 348, 373, 406n

Waldshut, xlii

Wartburg, xix

Wiedemann, Jakob, xliii, 102, 164

Wittenberg, xix

Württemberg, xxxvii-xxxviii, xlii-xliii, 294, 298, 327, 366, 368, 369

Zaunring Jörg, xxiv, xlvi, 163-65, 256, 401n, 402n, 403n

Zollikon, xliii

Zürich, xiii, xli, xliii

Zwingli, Ulrich (Zwinglians), 36, 66, 71, 229, 239, 394n, 395n, 396n, 401n

Scripture Index

*sixteenth century bibles did not have verse numbers. Scripture references in the text that appear in square brackets have been added by the editor.

OLD TESTAMENT

Genesis
Gen. 1 p. 261 Trieste
Gen. 1-2 p. 4 Jüchsen
Gen. 1:26-27 p. 16, 17 Jüchsen
Gen. 1:26 p. 17 Jüchsen
Gen. 2 p. 149 Nadler
Gen. 2:7 p. 16 Jüchsen
Gen. 2[1:27] p. 206 Keller
Gen. 3 p. 265 Trieste
Gen. 3:1-5, :13-15 p. 10 Jüchsen
Gen. 3:6-13 p. 6 Jüchsen
Gen. 5:3 p. 16 Jüchsen
Gen. 6 p. 152 Nadler
Gen. 6:3-13 p. 393 endnotes
Gen. 8 p. 152 Nadler
Gen. 9:6 p. 16 Jüchsen
    p. 285 Umlauft
Gen. 12:2 p. 198 Keller
Gen. 15:6 p. 198 Keller
Gen. 17:11 p. 198 Keller
Gen. 22:1 p. 26 Hut
Gen. 22:2-18 p. 15 Jüchsen
Gen. 25:29-34 p. 5 Jüchsen
Gen. 32:26-30 p. 6 Jüchsen
Gen. 32:30 p. 27 Hut
Gen. 39 p. 275 Trieste

Exodus
Exod. 4:21 p. 28 Hut
Exod. 8:32 p. 28 Hut
Exod. 12 p. 200 Keller
Exod. 12:8 p. 276 Trieste
Exod. 14 p. 115 Langenmantel
Exod. 19 p. 200 Keller
Exod. 20:2 p. 261 Trieste
Exod. 20:11 p. 261 Trieste
Exod. 24[25:40] p. .200 Keller
Exod. 25:31-40 p. 4 Jüchsen
Exod. 32 p. 262 Trieste
Exod. 32:32 p. 15 Jüchsen

Leviticus
Lev. 11:3-8 p. 7 Jüchsen
Lev. 19:31 p. 126 Schneeweiss?
Lev. 20:27 p. 126 Schneeweiss?

Numbers
Num. 14:9 p. 330 Glock (ch. 27)
Num. 21:5 p. 174 Althamer/Rurer
Num. 22:28 p. 314 Glock (ch. 25)

Deuteronomy
Deut. 1:39 p. 71 Schiemer
    p. 264 Trieste
Deut. 4:2 p. 92 Schlaffer
    p. 201 Keller
    p. 311 Glock (ch. 25)
Deut. 4:8 p. 220 Rhegius
Deut. 4:12 p. 262 Trieste
Deut. 5:6-9 p. 261 Trieste

Deut. 6 p. 16 Jüchsen
Deut. 6:4 p. 261 Trieste
Deut. 6:6-9 p. 302 Glock 9 (ch. 24)
Deut. 8 p. 117 Langenmantel
Deut. 12:23 p. 92 Schlaffer
  p. 201 Keller
Deut. 13 p. 219 Rhegius
  p. 247 Franck
Deut. 13:3 p. 174 Althamer/Rurer
  p. 126 Schneeweiss?
Deut. 13[30:11-12] p. 28 Hut
Deut. 14[?] p. 71 Schiemer
Deut. 17 p. 219, 223 Rhegius
Deut. 18 p. 60 Spitelmaier
  p. 233, 247, 250, Franck
Deut. 18:15 p. 206 Keller
Deut. 26 p. 91 Schlaffer
Deut. 27:27 p. 201 Keller
Deut. 28:1-14 p. 48 Hergot
Deut. 28:28 p. 173 Althamer/Rurer
Deut. 30:2, :10, :14, :16 p. 20 Jüchsen
Deut. 30:11-14 p. 71 Schiemer
Deut. 30:14 p. 282 Umlauft
Deut. 30:15-16, :19-20 p. 16 Jüchsen

Joshua
Josh. 1:2-5 p. 349 Glock (ch. 31)
[?]Josh. 10:26 p. 285 Umlauft
Josh. 23:6 p. 201 Keller

Judges
Judg. 2, 3, 4 p. 262 Trieste
Judg. 8:18-23 p. 88 Schlaffer

1 Samuel
1 Sam. 1:15-16 p. 307 Glock (ch. 24)

2 Samuel
2 Sam. 12 p. 124 Schneeweiss?
  p. 180 Althamer/Rurer
2 Sam. 16:5-8 p. 15 Jüchsen
2 Sam. 24:14 p. 5 Jüchsen

1 Kings
1 Kings 6[8:27] p. 272 Trieste
1 Kings 15:13 p. 223 Rhegius

2 Kings
2 Kings 10:28ff p. 223 Rhegius
2 Kings 14 p. 262 Trieste
2 Kings 18 p. 124 Schneeweiss?
  p. 262 Trieste
2 Kings 23:5 p. 223 Rhegius

2 Chronicles
2 Chron. 17:7ff p. 223 Rhegius
2 Chron. 19:6ff p. 285 Umlauft
2 Chron. 20:29 p. 223 Rhegius

Esther
Esther 3 p. 279 Umlauft
Esther 4 p. 15 Jüchsen

Job
Job 5:13 p. 315 Glock (ch. 25)
Job 6:4 p. 336 Glock (ch. 28)
Job 12:2 p. 336 Glock (ch. 28)
Job 16:2-3 p. 336 Glock (ch. 28)
Job 17[12:7-8] p. 87 Schlaffer
Job 19:3 p. 15 Jüchsen
Job 27:3-5 p. 336 Glock (ch. 28)
Job 28[18] p. 210 Keller
Job 28:12 p. 209 Keller
Job 28:28 p. 4, 20 Jüchsen
Job 33:4-30 p. 19 Jüchsen

Psalms
Ps. 1 p. 113 Langenmantel
Ps. 1:2 p. 266 Trieste
Ps. 2:1ff, :10ff p. 224 Rhegius
Ps. 2:9 p. 26 Hut
Ps. 3[?] p. 266 Trieste
Ps. 5:4 p. 26 Hut
Ps. 5:11 p. 280, 282 Umlauft
Ps. 5[51:5] p. 265 Trieste
Ps.7[?] p. 266 Trieste

Ps. 11:2   p. 279 Umlauft
Ps. 16:3   p. 204 Keller
Ps. 17:7   p. 279 Umlauft
Ps. 18:4   p. 301 Glock (ch. 24)
Ps. 18[19]   p. 5 Jüchsen
Ps. 18[19:10]   p. 8 Jüchsen
Ps. 19:5   p. 204 Keller
Ps. 19:8-10   p. 9 Jüchsen
Ps. 22:5   p. 264 Trieste
Ps. 24:2   p. 204 Keller
Ps. 24[145:9]   p. 27 Hut
Ps. 25:4-5   p. 211 Keller
Ps. 25:14   p. 209 Keller
Ps. 30[31]   p. 19 Jüchsen
Ps. 31:20   p. 279 Umlauft
Ps. 35[36:10]   p. 16 Jüchsen
Ps. 39:2   p. 280 Umlauft
Ps. 41[42:2]   p. 16 Jüchsen
Ps. 41[42:3]   p. 16 Jüchsen
Ps. 49:50   p. 91 Schlaffer
Ps. 50[51:17]   p. 74 Schiemer
Ps. 51:17   p. 88 Schlaffer
Ps. 51   p. 152 Nadler
Ps. 55:3   p. 279 Umlauft
Ps. 55:6-8   p. 279 Umlauft
Ps. 57[:1]   p. 279, 280 Umlauft
Ps. 59:1-2   p. 301 Glock (ch. 24)
Ps. 61[62]   p. 19 Jüchsen
Ps. 64:2   p. 279 Umlauft
Ps. 64:3   p. 279 Umlauft
Ps. 64:30   p. 280 Umlauft
Ps. 67[68]   p. 10 Jüchsen
Ps. 81:12, :13   p. 173 Althamer/Rurer
Ps. 81:12   p. 207 Keller
Ps. 82   p. 219 Rhegius
Ps. 83[84:6-8]   p. 16 Jüchsen
Ps. 91:14   p. 88 Schlaffer
Ps. 94:11   p. 201 Keller
Ps. 94:12   p. 204 Keller

Ps. 100[111:10]   p. 20 Jüchsen
Ps. 102:13   p. 182 Althamer/Rurer
Ps. 106   p. 150 Nadler
Ps. 109   p. 173 Althamer/Rurer
Ps. 110[111:10]   p. 4, 9 Jüchsen
Ps. 118   p. 113 Langenmantel
Ps. 119   p. 18 Jüchsen
Ps. 119:9   p. 301 Glock (ch. 24)
Ps. 119:21   p. 28 Hut
Ps. 119:105-06   p. 301 Glock (ch. 24)
Ps. 120:3-4   p. 279 Umlauft

Proverbs
Prov. 1[?]   p. 74 Schiemer
Prov. 1:7   p. 4 Jüchsen
Prov. 1:23   p. 86 Schlaffer
Prov. 2:3-5   p. 11 Jüchsen
Prov. 3:11   p. 86 Schlaffer
Prov. 3:12   p. 88 Schlaffer
Prov. 4:4   p. 16 Jüchsen
Prov. 5:12   p. 86 Schlaffer
Prov. 9:1   p. 4, 5 Jüchsen
Prov. 9:10   p. 4 Jüchsen
Prov. 10:28   p. 320 Glock (ch. 25)
Prov. 13:8, :5, :9, :19   p. 279 Umlauft
Prov. 24:30-32   p. 304 Glock (ch. 24)
Prov. 28:1[?]   p. 280 Umlauft
Prov. 29:7, :10, :27   p. 279 Umlauft
Prov. 30:6   p. 201 Keller
         p. 311 Glock (ch. 25)

Isaiah
Isa. 1   p. 285 Umlauft
Isa. 1:10, :15-16   p. 286 Umlauft
Isa. 3:18-24   p. 400 endnotes
Isa. 5:3-5   p. 303 Glock (ch. 24)
Isa. 7   p. 58 Spitelmaier
Isa. 8:4[?]   p. 298 Glock (ch. 24)
Isa. 8:20   p. 176, 178 Althamer/Rurer
Isa. 9:17   p. 322 Glock (ch. 25)
Isa. 11:2   p. 4 Jüchsen

Isa. 11:1-2 p. 4, 5 Jüchsen
Isa. 11[66:5-24] p. 5 Jüchsen
Isa. 14:29 p. 10 Jüchsen
Isa. 16:5 p. 269 Trieste
Isa. 24:2 p. 316 Glock (ch. 25)
Isa. 24[42:3] p. 26 Hut
Isa. 25[?] p. 275 Trieste
Isa. 25[45:6-7] p. 28 Hut
Isa. 26:16-18 p. 273 Trieste
Isa. 28:16 p. 264 Trieste
Isa. 29:13 p. 173 Althamer/Rurer
Isa. 30 p. 243 Franck
Isa. 38 p. 124 Schneeweiss?
Isa. 40:1 p. 80 Schiemer
Isa. 40:3-5 p. 262 Trieste
Isa. 42:1-7 p. 15 Jüchsen
Isa. 46:6-7 p. 401 endnotes
Isa. 49:1-6 p. 15 Jüchsen
Isa. 51 p. 58 Spitelmaier
Isa. 52:7 p. 179 Althamer/Rurer
Isa. 53:1 p. 179 Althamer/Rurer
Isa. 53:12 p. 15 Jüchsen
Isa. 54:13 p. 179 Althamer/Rurer
Isa. 55:8 p. 177 Althamer/Rurer
Isa. 55:10ff p. 315 Glock (ch. 25)
Isa. 55:10-11 p. 68 Schiemer
Isa. 58[?] p. 84 Schlaffer
Isa. 61:1-2 p. 74 Schiemer
Isa. 65[?] p. 86 Schlaffer
Isa. 66 p. 56 Spitelmaier
Isa. 66:1 p. 145 Nadler
Isa. 66:1-2 p. 272 Trieste
Isa. 66:2 p. 26 Hut
          p. 74 Schiemer

Jeremiah
Jer. [?] p. 86 Schlaffer
Jer. 1 p. 57 Spitelmaier
       p. 150 Nadler
Jer. 2:13 p. 11 Jüchsen
          p. 306 Glock (ch.24)
Jer. 2:21 p. 303 Glock (ch. 24)
Jer. 3:12 p. 26 Hut
Jer. 5:26 p. 10 Jüchsen
Jer. 7[?] p. 86 Schlaffer
Jer. 7 p. 262 Trieste
Jer. 7:3-4 p. 113 Langenmantel
Jer. 9 p. 113 Langenmantel
Jer. 9:2, :7 p. 279 Umlauft
Jer. 9:23 p. 281 Umlauft
Jer. 11:3 p. 201 Keller
Jer. 17 p. 113 Langenmantel
Jer. 21:8 p. 71 Schiemer
Jer. 23 p. 57 Spitelmaier
Jer. 23:16 p. 178 Althamer/Rurer
Jer. 23:29 p. 315 Glock (ch. 25)
Jer. 23:31 p. 67 Schiemer
Jer. 24:7 p. 91 Schlaffer
Jer. 26:2 p. 201 Keller
Jer. 27 p. 63 Spitelmaier
Jer. 27:9 p. 126 Schneeweiss?
Jer. 30 p. 57 Spitelmaier
Jer. 31:31-34 p. 91 Schlaffer
Jer. 44 p. 262 Trieste

Ezekiel
Ezek. 6:9 p. 361 Glock (ch. 32)
Ezek. 7 p. 57, 62 Spitelmaier
Ezek. 12:23, :28 p. 90 Schlaffer
Ezek. 13:8 p. 280 Umlauft
Ezek. 18 p. 57, 63 Spitelmaier
         p. 236 Franck
Ezek. 18:4 p. 264 Trieste
Ezek. 22:25ff p. 279 Umlauft
Ezek. 28 p. 58 Spitelmaier
Ezek. 28:15 p. 265 Trieste
Ezek. 28:15-18 p. 71 Schiemer
Ezek. 33 p. 63 Spitelmaier
Ezek. 33 p. 275 Trieste
Ezek. 33:10-17 p. 264 Trieste
Ezek. 34 p. 63 Spitelmaier

Daniel
Dan. 3 p. 274 Trieste
Dan. 3:14-23 p. 15 Jüchsen
Dan. 3:29 p. 219 Rhegius
Dan. 6 p. 274 Trieste
Dan. 6:17-23 p. 15 Jüchsen
Dan. 7 p. 62 Spitelmaier
    p. 240 Franck
Dan. 9:27 p. 169 Zaunring
Dan. 9:26 p. 202 Keller
Dan. 11:16, :30, :36, :41 p. 283 Umlauft
Dan. 13[12:1-2] p. 275 Trieste

Hosea
Hos. 4:1, :2 p. 323 Glock (ch. 25).
Hos. 4:9 p. 316 Glock (ch. 25)
Hos. 6[?] p. 86 Schlaffer
Hos. 13:11 p. 323 Glock (ch. 25)

Joel
Joel 2:1 p. 84 Schlaffer
Joel 4[?] p. 275 Trieste

Jonah
Jon. 2:6 p. 28 Hut
Jon. 2:10 p. 28 Hut

Micah
Mic. 3 p. 63 Spitelmaier

Nahum
Nah. 1:15 p. 179 Althamer/Rurer

Habakkuk
Hab. 2:4 p. 16 Jüchsen
    p. 264 Trieste
Hab. 3:18-19 p. 298 Glock (ch. 24)
Hab. 4 p. 57 Spitelmaier
Hab. 6 p. 57 Spitelmaier
Hab. 7 p. 57 Spitelmaier

Zephaniah
Zeph. 1 p. 84 Schlaffer

Zechariah
Zech. 2[?] p. 275 Trieste
Zech. 3:4 p. 301 Glock (ch. 24)
Zech. 4:10 p. 4, 5 Jüchsen

Malachi
Mal. 3:6 p. 182 Althamer/Rurer

APOCRYPHA

2 Esdras
2 Esd. 4 p. 20 Jüchsen
2 Esd. 4:37 p. 4 Jüchsen
2 Esd. 5:1 p. 307 Glock (ch. 24)
2 Esd. 6-7 p. 351 Glock (ch. 31)
2 Esd. 7:6-8 p. 300 Glock (ch. 24)
2 Esd. 9:7-9 p. 302 Glock (ch. 24)
2 Esd. 9:10-12 p. 303 Glock (ch. 24)
2 Esd. 14:10 p. 307 Glock (ch. 24)
2 Esd. 14:17 p. 307 Glock (ch. 24)

Tobit
Tob. 2:22 p. 15 Jüchsen

Judith
Jdt. 7:12 p. 15 Jüchsen

Wisdom
Wisd. 1:4 p. 302 Glock (ch. 24)
Wisd. 1:21 p. 6 Jüchsen
Wisd. 1[3:4-7] p. 11 Jüchsen
Wisd. 2 p. 269 Trieste
Wisd. 2:12-15 p. 299 Glock (ch. 24)
Wisd. 2:12 p. 279 Umlauft
Wisd. 2:23[?] p. 25 Hut
Wisd. 2:23 p. 265 Trieste
Wisd. 3:6 p. 12 Jüchsen
Wisd. 4:10-14 p. 262 Trieste
Wisd. 5:2 p. 319 Glock (ch. 25)
Wisd. 10 p. 5 Jüchsen
Wisd. 11:17 p. 13 Jüchsen
Wisd. 11:20-21 p. 20 Jüchsen
Wisd. 11:22 p. 4 Jüchsen
Wisd. 11:24 p. 26 Hut

Sirach (Ecclesiasticus)
Sir. 1, 2[1:15] p. 4 Jüchsen
Sir. 1:14 p. 16 Jüchsen

Sir. 1:18-19 p. 11 Jüchsen
Sir. 1:20 p. 4 Jüchsen
Sir. 2:5 p. 12 Jüchsen
Sir. 2:16[?] p. 306 Glock (ch. 24)
Sir. 7[?] p. 265 Trieste
Sir. 9[?] p. 275 Trieste
Sir. 10[?] p. 268 Trieste
Sir. 10:18 p. 25 Hut
Sir. 15:17 p. 71 Schiemer
Sir. 15:20 p. 28 Hut
Sir. 24:21 p. 27 Hut
Sir. 34:15[?] p. 305 Glock (ch. 24)
Sir. 39:29 p. 25 Hut
Sir. 41:8[?] p. 307 Glock (ch. 24)

Bel and the Dragon
Bel.1:38 p. 298 Glock (ch. 24)

1 Maccabees
1 Macc. 2:59 p. 15 Jüchsen

2 Maccabees
2 Macc. 7 p. 274 Trieste

NEW TESTAMENT
Matthew
Matt. 1 p. 176 Althamer/Rurer
Matt. 1:5 p. 283 Umlauft
Matt. 1[18:15-17] p. 267 Trieste
Matt. 2 p. 26 Hut
Matt. 2:16 p. 199 Keller
p. 285 Umlauft
Matt. 3 p. 113 Langenmantel
p. 207 Keller
Matt. 3:1 p. 263 Trieste
Matt. 3:7ff p. 318 Glock (ch. 25)
Matt. 3:9 p. 283 Umlauft
Matt. 3:12 p. 216 Rhegius
Matt. 3:13-15 p. 93 Schlaffer
p. 263 Trieste
Matt. 3:16 p. 99 Schlaffer
Matt. 3[17:5] p. 273 Trieste
Matt. 4 p. 55, 58 Spitelmaier
p. 117 Langenmantel
p. 211 Keller

Matt. 4:8 p. 323 Glock (ch. 25)
Matt. 4:10 p. 261 Trieste
p. 300 Glock (ch. 24)
Matt. 5 p. 13 Jüchsen
p. 56 Spitelmaier
p. 116 Langenmantel
p. 233 Franck
Matt. 5:4 p. 88 Schlaffer
Matt. 5:6 p. 16 Jüchsen
p. 149 Nadler
Matt. 5:9 p. 269 Trieste
Matt. 5:10-12 p. 327 Glock (ch. 26)
Matt. 5:11 p. 274 Trieste
Matt. 5:13 p. 356 Glock (ch. 32)
Matt. 5:14 p. 337 Glock (ch. 28)
Matt. 5:14-16 p. 15 Jüchsen
Matt. 5:19 p. 96 Schlaffer
Matt. 5:24 p. 315 Glock (ch. 25)
Matt. 5:32 p. 181 Althamer/Rurer
Matt. 5:33-37 p. 266 Trieste
Matt. 5:38-39 p. 357 Glock (ch. 32)
Matt. 5:38-40 p. 267 Trieste
Matt. 5:39-41 p. 79 Schiemer
Matt. 5:44 p. 92 Schlaffer
Matt. 5:45 p. 15 Jüchsen
Matt. 6 p. 118 Langenmantel
p. 239 Franck
Matt. 6:14 p. 359 Glock (ch. 32)
Matt. 6:22-23 p. 70 Schiemer
Matt. 6:23 p. 72 Schiemer
p. 282 Umlauft
Matt. 6:24 p. 5 Jüchsen
Matt. 6:26 p. 180 Althamer/Rurer
Matt. 6:41 p. 78 Schiemer
Matt. 7 p. 63 Spitelmaier
p. 113, 119 Langenmantel
p. 240 Franck
Matt. 7:1 p. 27 Hut
Matt. 7:2 p. 28 Hut
p. 322 Glock (ch. 25)
Matt. 7:6 p. 26 Hut
Matt. 7:8 p. 25 Hut
Matt. 7:13 p. 147 Nadler
p. 280 Umlauft
Matt. 7:14 p. 84 Schlaffer

Matt. 7:15 p. 176 Althamer/Rurer
          p. 324 Glock (ch. 25)
Matt. 7:16 p. 182 Althamer/Rurer
Matt. 7:17 p. 17 Jüchsen
Matt. 7:21 p. 273 Trieste
          p. 316 Glock (ch. 25)
Matt. 7:26 p. 11 Jüchsen
Matt. 8:29 p. 316 Glock (ch. 25)
Matt. 9 p. 113 Langenmantel
Matt. 9:9 p. 320 Glock (ch. 25)
Matt. 9:17 p. 14 Jüchsen
Matt. 10 p. 13 Jüchsen
          p. 115 Langenmantel
          p. 153 Nadler
Matt. 10[?] p. 74 Schiemer
Matt. 10:2 p. 166 Zaunring
Matt. 10:14 p. 320 Glock (ch. 25)
Matt. 10:18-20 p. 327 Glock (ch. 26)
Matt. 10:20 p. 324 Glock (ch. 25)
Matt. 10:22 p. 328 Glock (ch. 26)
Matt. 10:23 p. 284 Umlauft
Matt. 10:32[?] p. 300 Glock (ch. 24)
Matt. 10:33 p. 78 Schiemer
Matt. 10:40 p. 177 Althamer/Rurer
Matt. 11 p. 17 Jüchsen
        p. 25 Hut
        p. 59 Spitelmaier
        p. 116 Langenmantel
Matt. 11:11 p. 284 Umlauft
Matt. 11:13 p. 263 Trieste
Matt. 11:14 p. 25 Hut
Matt. 11:25-26 p. 266 Trieste
Matt. 11:28 p. 74 Schiemer
          p. 320 Glock (ch. 25)
Matt. 11:30 p. 14 Jüchsen
          p. 27 Hut
Matt. 12:30 p. 46 Hergot
          p. 202 Keller
Matt. 12:35 p. 182 Althamer/Rurer
Matt. 12:49-50 p. 337 Glock (ch. 28)
Matt. 13 p. 115 Langenmantel
Matt. 13:1-23 p. 17 Jüchsen
Matt. 13:1-8, :18-23 p. 16 Jüchsen
Matt. 13:1-9, :18-23 p. 5 Jüchsen
Matt. 13:7 p. 17 Jüchsen

Matt. 13:23 p. 258 Glock (ch. 32)
Matt. 13:24-30 p. 8 Jüchsen
Matt. 13:25 p. 174 Althamer/Rurer
Matt. 13:25-30 p. 48 Hergot
Matt. 13:31-32 p. 16 Jüchsen
Matt. 13:44 p. 20 Jüchsen
Matt. 13:44-46 p. 16 Jüchsen
          p. 283 Umlauft
Matt. 15:1-20 p. 20 Jüchsen
Matt. 15:12ff p. 318 Glock (ch. 25)
Matt. 15:13 p. 264 Trieste
          p. 311 Glock (ch. 25)
Matt. 15:14 p. 310 Glock (ch. 25)
Matt. 15:17 p. 144 Nadler
          p. 189 Pfersfelder
Matt. 15:19 p. 312 Glock (ch. 25)
Matt. 15[16:24] p. 269 Trieste
Matt. 16 p. 90 Schlaffer
Matt. 16:6 p. 181 Althamer/Rurer
Matt. 16:17 p. 176 Althamer/Rurer
Matt. 16:18 p. 323 Glock (ch. 25)
Matt. 16:19 p. 124 Schneeweiss?
          p. 274 Trieste
Matt. 16:24ff p. 280 Umlauft
Matt. 16:24-26 p. 86 Schlaffer
Matt. 16:24-28 p. 12 Jüchsen
Matt. 16:25 p. 17 Jüchsen
Matt. 16:27 p. 275 Trieste
Matt. 17:20 p. 16 Jüchsen
          p. 142 Nadler
Matt. 18 p. 150 Nadler
Matt. 18:1-4 p. 265 Trieste
Matt. 18:3 p. 282 Umlauft
          p. 314 Glock (ch. 25)
Matt. 18:15-17 p. 143 Nadler
Matt. 18:15-20 p. 76 Schiemer
Matt. 18:16 p. 181 Althamer/Rurer
          p. 273 Trieste
Matt. 18:17 p. 274 Trieste
Matt. 18:18 p. 274 Trieste
Matt. 18:18-19 p. 124 Schneeweiss?
Matt. 18:20 p. 199 Keller
Matt. 19 p. 57, 59 Spitelmaier

Matt. 19 p. 115 Langenmantel
    p. 149 Nadler
    p. 314 Glock (ch. 25)
Matt. 19:14 p. 71 Schiemer
    p. 208 Keller
    p. 265 Trieste
    p. 282 Umlauft
Matt. 19:21 p. 86 Schlaffer
Matt. 19:24 p. 91 Schlaffer
Matt. 19:29 p. 75 Schiemer
Matt. 20 p. 56, 57, 58, 60 Spitelmaier
    p. 273 Trieste
Matt. 20:16 p. 25 Hut
Matt. 20:22 p. 94 Schlaffer
Matt. 20:22-23 p. 274 Trieste
Matt. 20:25 p. 323 Glock (ch. 25)
Matt. 20:25-27 p. 269 Trieste
Matt. 20:30 p. 284 Umlauft
Matt. 20[24:15?] p. 265 Trieste
Matt. 21 p. 55 Spitelmaier
    p. 113 Langenmantel
Matt. 21:15, :16 p. 314 Glock (ch. 25)
Matt. 22:14 p. 26 Hut
Matt. 22:15-22 p. 281 Umlauft
Matt. 22:29 p. 123 Schneeweiss?
Matt. 22:37 p. 16 Jüchsen
Matt. 22:37-40 p. 70 Schiemer
Matt. 23 p. 57, Spitelmaier
    p. 115, 119 Langenmantel
    p. 148, 152 Nadler
Matt. 23:2-7, :13-14, :23-33 p. 18 Jüchsen
Matt. 23:25 p. 207 Keller
Matt. 23:29-35 p. 88 Schlaffer
Matt. 23:30-36 p. 5 Jüchsen
Matt. 23:34ff p. 285 Umlauft
Matt. 23:35 p. 88 Schlaffer
Matt. 24 p. 95 Schlaffer
    p. 114 Langenmantel
    p. 167 Zaunring
Matt. 24:5 p. 10 Jüchsen
    p. 176 Althamer/Rurer
Matt. 24:15 p. 202 Keller
Matt. 24:23 p. 27 Hut

Scripture Index / 419

Matt. 24:23-25 p. 188 Pfersfelder
Matt. 24:27 p. 274 Trieste
Matt. 24:31 p. 89 Schlaffer
Matt. 24:35 p. 93 Schlaffer
Matt. 25 p. 57, 58, 59 Spitelmaier
    p. 109 Schlaffer
    p. 152 Nadler
    p. 167 Zaunring
    p. 241 Franck
    p. 396 endnotes
Matt. 25:1-13 p. 93 Schlaffer
Matt. 25:21 p. 71 Schiemer
Matt. 25:29 p. 68 Schiemer
Matt. 25:31 p. 93 Schlaffer
    p. 274 Trieste
Matt. 25:32-33 p. 275 Trieste
Matt. 25:34, :41 p. 275 Trieste
Matt. 25:43 p. 108 Schlaffer
Matt. 25:46 p. 26 Hut
Matt. 26 p. 56, 60 Spitelmaier
    p. 176 Althamer/Rurer
Matt. 26:11 p. 27 Hut
Matt. 26:26-29 p. 270 Trieste
Matt. 26:27 p. 102 Schlaffer
Matt. 26:39 p. 271 Trieste
Matt. 26:41 p. 307 Glock (ch. 24)
Matt. 26:43[?] p. 73 Schiemer
Matt. 26:52 p. 285 Umlauft
Matt. 26:74 p. 72 Schiemer
Matt. 27:40-42 p. 15 Jüchsen
Matt. 28 p. 60 Spitelmaier
    p. 97 Schlaffer
Matt. 28:6 p. 166 Zaunring
Matt. 28:18-19 p. 98, 100 Schlaffer
Matt. 28:19-20 p. 87, 92 Schlaffer
    p. 263, 264 Trieste
Matt. 28:19 p. 177 Althamer/Rurer
    p. 356 Glock (ch. 32)
Matt. 28:20 p. 27 Hut
Matt. 29:18-20 p. 95 Schlaffer

Mark
Mark 1:8 p. 263 Trieste
Mark 1:9 p. 93 Schlaffer
Mark 1:24 p. 316 Glock (ch. 25)

Mark 4:1-9, :13-20 p. 5 Jüchsen
Mark 7:1-23 p. 20 Jüchsen
Mark 7:23 p. 312 Glock (ch. 25)
Mark 8 p. 115 Langenmantel
Mark 8:35 p. 90 Schlaffer
Mark 8:38 p. 90 Schlaffer
Mark 9 p. 152 Nadler
Mark 9:36-37 p. 314 Glock (ch. 25)
Mark 9:43 p. 274 Trieste
Mark 10 p. 212 Keller
       p. 314 Glock (ch. 25)
Mark 10:14 p. 208 Keller
       p. 265 Trieste
Mark 10:39-40 p. 274 Trieste
Mark 10:40 p. 27 Hut
Mark 11[4:8, :20] p. 16 Jüchsen
Mark 12 p. 113 Langenmantel
Mark 12:24 p. 124 Schneeweiss?
       p. 178 Althamer/Rurer
Mark 12:30-31 p. 70 Schiemer
Mark 13 p. 95 Schlaffer
       p. 167 Zaunring
Mark 13:8, :23 p. 17 Jüchsen
Mark 13:26 p. 274 Trieste
Mark 13:27 p. 89 Schlaffer
Mark 13:35-36 p. 302 Glock (ch. 24)
Mark 14:7 p. 271 Trieste
Mark 14:22 p. 166 Zaunring
Mark 14:22-24 p. 270 Trieste
Mark 15[16:16] p. 177 Althamer/Rurer
Mark 16 p. 58 Spitelmaier
       p. 139, 150 Nadler
Mark 16:15 p. 176 Althamer/Rurer
       p. 396 endnotes,
Mark 16:15-16 p. 26 Hut
       p. 87, 91, 100 Schlaffer
       p. 216 Rhegius
       p. 263 Trieste
Mark 16:16 p. 27 Hut
       p. 92, 97 Schlaffer
       p. 142 Nadler
       p. 176 Althamer/Rurer
       p. 356 Glock (ch. 32)

Mark 16:19 p. 166 Zaunring
Mark 16:20 p. 177 Althamer/Rurer
Mark 17 p. 167 Zaunring
Mark 26:26 p. 27 Hut

Luke
Luke 1 p. 5 Jüchsen
       p. 58 Spitelmaier
       p. 150 Nadler
Luke 1:28 p. 16 Jüchsen
Luke 1:38 p. 140 Nadler
Luke 1:48 p. 88 Schlaffer
Luke 1:68-72 p. 306 Glock (ch. 24)
Luke 2 p. 176 Althamer/Rurer
Luke 2:79 p. 280 Umlauft
Luke 3:7ff p. 318 Glock (ch. 25)
Luke 3:16 p. 263 Trieste
Luke 3:21-23 p. 93, 99 Schlaffer
Luke 4 p. 60 Spitelmaier
       p. 117 Langenmantel
Luke 4:18 p. 74 Schiemer
Luke 4:29 p. 318 Glock (ch. 25)
Luke 6 p. 56 Spitelmaier
Luke 6:36 p. 46 Hergot
Luke 7 p. 60 Spitelmaier
Luke 7:36ff p. 320 Glock (ch. 25)
Luke 8 p. 243 Franck
Luke 8:8-15 p. 16 Jüchsen
Luke 9 p. 55 Spitelmaier
Luke 9[?] p. 74 Schiemer
Luke 9:23 p. 90 Schlaffer
Luke 9:23-25 p. 86 Schlaffer
Luke 9:24 p. 90 Schlaffer
Luke 9:26 p. 90 Schlaffer
Luke 9:47-48 p. 314 Glock (ch. 25)
Luke 9:54 p. 304 Glock (ch. 24)
Luke 10:16 p. 177 Althamer/Rurer
Luke 10:27 p. 16 Jüchsen
       p. 70 Schiemer
Luke 10:30-37 p. 12 Jüchsen
Luke 11 p. 118 Langenmantel
Luke 11:23 p. 123 Schneeweiss?
Luke 11:36 p. 70 Schiemer
       p. 394 endnotes

Luke 11:47 p. 317 Glock (ch. 25)
Luke 12 p. 57 Spitelmaier
   p. 115 Langenmantel
Luke 12:13 p. 269 Trieste
Luke 12[13:24] p. 237 Franck
Luke 12:35-37 p. 300 Glock (ch. 24)
Luke 12:47 p. 73 Schiemer
Luke 12:50 p. 99 Schlaffer
Luke 13:1-5 p. 106 Schlaffer
Luke 13:25ff p. 280 Umlauft
Luke 14 p. 115 Langenmantel
Luke 14[?] p. 74 Schiemer
Luke 14:11[?] p. 90 Schlaffer
Luke 14:23 p. 218 Rhegius
Luke 14:27 p. 12 Jüchsen
Luke 14:33 p. 17 Jüchsen
   p. 86 Schlaffer
Luke 15:11-32 p. 12 Jüchsen
Luke 15:16 p. 268 Trieste
Luke 16 p. 57 Spitelmaier
   p. 285 Umlauft
Luke 16:10 p. 71 Schiemer
Luke 16:19-31 p. 14 Jüchsen
Luke 16:23 p. 319 Glock (ch. 25)
Luke 16:24 p. 285 Umlauft
Luke 16:29, :31 p. 124 Schneeweiss?
Luke 17:6 p. 142 Nadler
Luke 17:20 p. 97 Schlaffer
Luke 17:20ff p. 281 Umlauft
Luke 17:22 p. 174 Althamer/Rurer
Luke 17:24 p. 274 Trieste
Luke 18 p. 56 Spitelmaier
   p. 314 Glock (ch. 25)
Luke 18:16 p. 208 Keller
   p. 265 Trieste
Luke 19[18:25] p. 27 Hut
Luke 21 p. 62 Spitelmaier
   p. 95 Schlaffer
   p. 167 Zaunring
Luke 21:12-13 p. 32 Hut
Luke 21:14 p. 324 Glock (ch. 25)
Luke 21:18 p. 46 Hergot
Luke 21:27 p. 89 Schlaffer
   p. 274 Trieste

Luke 22 p. 56, 57 Spitelmaier
   p. 176 Althamer/Rurer
Luke 22:17-20 p. 270 Trieste
Luke 22:19 p. 166 Zaunring
   p. 189 Pfersfelder
Luke 22[?] p. 166 Zaunring
Luke 22:25 p. 357 Glock (ch. 32)
Luke 22:53 p. 323 Glock (ch. 25)
Luke 22:69 p. 167 Zaunring
Luke 23:34 p. 304 Glock (ch. 24)
Luke 24:26 p. 97 Schlaffer
Luke 24:31-32, :44-49 p. 19 Jüchsen
Luke 24:46 p. 125 Schneeweiss?
Luke 24:46-47 p. 96, 100 Schlaffer
Luke 24:47 p. 91 Schlaffer
   p. 177 Althamer/Rurer

John
John 1 p. 16 Jüchsen
   p. 60 Spitelmaier
   p. 147 Nadler
John 1:1-5 p. 69 Schiemer
John 1:2-4 p. 394 endnotes
John 1:3 p. 25 Hut; 167 Zaunring
John 1:4 p. 16 Jüchsen
John 1:4-9 p. 16 Jüchsen
John 1:9 p. 10 Jüchsen
   p. 301 Glock (ch. 24)
John 1:10-12 p. 69 Schiemer
John 1:14 p. 176 Althamer/Rurer
   p. 394 endnotes
John 1:16 p. 68, 74 Schiemer
John 1:17 p. 10 Jüchsen
John 1:18 p. 27 Hut
John 1:21 p. 25 Hut
John 1:29 p. 97 Schlaffer
   p. 207 Keller
John 2:22 p. 263 Trieste
John 3 p. 115 Langenmantel
   p. 152 Nadler
   p. 212 Keller
   p. 222 Rhegius
John 3:3 p. 189 Pfersfelder
John 3:3, :6 p. 273 Trieste
John 3:3-5 p. 140 Nadler
John 3:5 p. 266 Trieste

John 3:22 p. 263 Trieste
John 3[9:39] p. 26 Hut
John 4 p. 60 Spitelmaier
  p. 319 Glock (ch.25)
John 4:1-2 p. 263 Trieste
John 4:14 p. 27 Hut
John 4:23 p. 84 Schlaffer
  p. 274 Trieste
John 4:24 p. 77 Schiemer
John 5:9-13 p. 16 Jüchsen
John 5:21 p. 27 Hut
John 5:30 p. 25 Hut
John 5:31 p. 26 Hut
John 5:39 p. 123 Schneeweiss?
  p. 178 Althamer/Rurer
  p. 282, 283 Umlauft
John 6 p. 59 Spitelmaier
  p. 145, 152 Nadler
  p. 216 Rhegius
John 6:15 p. 274 Trieste
John 6:37 p. 26 Hut
John 6:40 p. 176 Althamer/Rurer
John 6:45 p. 189 Pfersfelder
John 6:54 p. 167 Zaunring
John 6:64[?] p. 68 Schiemer
John 6:65[?] p. 97 Schlaffer
John 6[10:18] p. 25 Hut
John 7:7 p. 299 Glock (ch. 24)
John 7:24 p. 27 Hut
John 7:38 p. 124 Schneeweiss?
John 7[3:19] p. 67 Schiemer
John 8:11 p. 268 Trieste
  p. 359 Glock (ch. 32)
John 8:11-13 p. 306 Glock (ch. 24)
John 8:12 p. 16 Jüchsen
John 8:12-20[?] p. 68 Schiemer
John 8:12-32 p. 5 Jüchsen
John 8:14 p. 26 Hut
John 8:19 p. 117 Langenmantel
John 8:44 p. 10 Jüchsen
  p. 28 Hut
  p. 77 Schiemer
  p. 318, 323 Glock (ch. 25)
John 8[6:63] p. 270 Trieste

John 9 p. 57 Spitelmaier
  p. 167 Zaunring
John 10 p. 216 Rhegius
John 10:1 p. 280 Umlauft
John 10:1ff p. 390 endnotes
John 10:3 p. 68 Schiemer
John 10:8 p. 318 Glock (ch. 25)
John 10:10 p. 324 Glock (ch. 25)
John 10:27 p. 123 Schneeweiss?
John 10:28 p. 16 Jüchsen
John 10:38 p. 272 Trieste
John 11:9 p. 301 Glock (ch. 24)
John 11:47-51 p. 5 Jüchsen
John 12 p. 27 Hut
  p. 55 Spitelmaier
John 12:24 p. 16 Jüchsen
John 12:24-26 p. 17 Jüchsen
John 12:26 p. 90 Schlaffer
John 12:47 p. 26 Hut
  p. 284 Umlauft
John 12[17:9] p. 27 Hut
John 13[?] p. 273 Trieste
John 13:17 p. 317 Glock (ch. 25)
John 13:34-35 p. 337 Glock (ch. 28)
John 13:35 p. 76 Schiemer
  p. 92 Schlaffer
John 13 p. 90 Schlaffer
  p. 201 Keller
John 14 p. 167 Zaunring
  p. 201 Keller
John 14:6 p. 84 Schlaffer
John 14:7 p. 311 Glock (ch. 25)
John 14:15 p. 266 Trieste
John 14:16 p. 321 Glock (ch. 25)
John 14:18 p. 80 Schiemer
John 14:26 p. 79 Schiemer
  p. 202 Keller
John 15 p. 55 Spitelmaier
  p. 201 Keller
  p. 241 Franck
John 15:4 p. 122 Schneeweiss?
  p. 280 Umlauft
John 15:5 p. 74 Schiemer
John 15:8 p. 263 Trieste
John 15:10 p. 199 Keller

John 15:15 p. 200 Keller
John 15:18 p. 67 Schiemer
John 15:18-21 p. 328 Glock (ch. 26)
John 15[18:36] p. 274 Trieste
John 16 p. 19 Jüchsen
         p. 25 Hut
         p. 150 Nadler
         p. 167 Zaunring
         p. 201 Keller
John 16:2 p. 80 Schiemer
John 16:13 p. 10 Jüchsen
John 16:16 p. 80 Schiemer
John 16:20 p. 80 Schiemer
John 16:20-22 p. 88 Schlaffer
John 16:22 p. 276 Trieste
John 16:33 p. 328 Glock (ch. 26)
John 16[6:15] p. 269 Trieste
John 17 p. 201 Keller
John 17:20 p. 125 Schneeweiss?
         p. 317 Glock (ch. 25)
John 18:36 p. 78 Schiemer
         p. 323 Glock (ch. 25)
John 19 p. 59 Spitelmaier
John 19:26-27 p. 166 Zaunring
John 20 p. 58 Spitelmaier
John 20:21 p. 356 Glock (ch. 32)
John 20:22 p. 180 Althamer/Rurer
         p. 321 Glock (ch. 25)
John 20:22-23 p. 275 Trieste
John 20:23 p. 125 Schneeweiss?
John 20:30 p. 124 Schneeweiss?
John 21 p. 58 Spitelmaier
John 24[?] p. 68 Schiemer
John 26[16:10] p. 167 Zaunring

Acts

Acts 1 p. 167 Zaunring
Acts 1:3 p. 274 Trieste
Acts 2 p. 69, 76 Schiemer
Acts 2:9ff p. 283 Umlauft
Acts 2:37-38 p. 263 Trieste
Acts 2:38 p. 125 Schneeweiss?
         p. 176 Althamer/Rurer
Acts 2:41 p. 207 Keller

Acts 2:44 p. 68 Schiemer
Acts 4 p. 76 Schiemer
Acts 4:22 p. 328 Glock (ch. 26)
Acts 4:24 p. 261 Trieste
Acts 4:32 p. 68 Schiemer
Acts 5 p. 76 Schiemer
Acts 5:28, :40 p. 279 Umlauft
Acts 5:29 p. 285 Umlauft
Acts 7 p. 115 Langenmantel
         p. 146 Nadler
         p. 205 Keller
Acts 7:47-50, :24-25 p. 272 Trieste
Acts 7:51 p. 25 Hut
Acts 7:56 p. 166 Zaunring
         p. 274 Trieste
Acts 7:58 p. 166 Zaunring
Acts 8 p. 93 Schlaffer
Acts 8:14-24 p. 268 Trieste
Acts 8:26 p. 283 Umlauft
Acts 9:15 p. 311 Glock (ch. 25)
Acts 9:23ff p. 284 Umlauft
Acts 9:44-48 p. 101 Schlaffer
Acts 10 p. 93 Schlaffer
Acts 10:6 p. 125 Schneeweiss?
Acts 10:34-35 p. 70 Schiemer
Acts 10:35 p. 283 Umlauft
Acts 10:42 p. 125 Schneeweiss?
Acts 10:44 p. 180 Althamer/Rurer
Acts 10:44-48 p. 93 Schlaffer
Acts 13 p. 240 Franck
Acts 14:22 p. 280 Umlauft
Acts 14:23 p. 88 Schlaffer
Acts 15:10 p. 28 Hut
Acts 17 p. 115 Langenmantel
         p. 146 Nadler
Acts 17:11 p. 283 Umlauft
Acts 17:27-28 p. 16 Jüchsen
Acts 17:28-29 p. 16 Jüchsen
Acts 17:28 p. 70 Schiemer
Acts 17:29 p. 274 Trieste
Acts 18:2 p. 315 Glock (ch. 25)
Acts 19 p. 93 Schlaffer
Acts 19:9 p. 268 Trieste

Acts 20:27 p. 356 Glock (ch. 32)
Acts 23:1 p. 321 Glock (ch. 25)
Acts 23:2ff p. 285 Umlauft
Acts 23:13 p. 284 Umlauft
Acts 24 p. 102 Schlaffer
Acts 26:15 p. 125 Schneeweiss?

Romans
Rom. 1 p. 113 Langenmantel
Rom. 1:6 p. 177 Althamer/Rurer
Rom. 1:16 p. 217 Rhegius
Rom. 1:16-17 p. 11 Jüchsen
Rom. 1:17 p. 16 Jüchsen
   p. 176 Althamer/Rurer
Rom. 1:17[?] p. 264 Trieste
Rom. 1:19-21 p. 30 Hut
Rom. 1:20-22 p. 70 Schiemer
   p. 87 Schlaffer
Rom. 2 p. 233 Franck
Rom. 2[?] p. 275 Trieste
Rom. 2:1 p. 322 Glock (ch. 25)
Rom. 2:11 p. 26 Hut
Rom. 2:11-16 p. 70 Schiemer
Rom. 2:15 p. 17 Jüchsen
   p. 283 Umlauft
Rom. 2:29 p. 198 Keller
Rom. 2[8:30] p. 25 Hut
Rom. 3:15 p. 279 Umlauft
Rom. 3:24[?] p. 264 Trieste
Rom. 3:31 p. 28 Hut
Rom. 4:1-4 p. 68 Schiemer
Rom. 5 p. 152 Nadler
Rom. 5:2 p. 280 Umlauft
Rom. 5:3 p. 280 Umlauft
Rom. 5:20 p. 28 Hut
Rom. 6 p. 57, 58 Spitelmaier
   p. 167 Zaunring
   p. 273 Trieste
Rom. 6:1-4 p. 264 Trieste
Rom. 6:2 p. 312 Glock (ch. 25)
Rom. 6:3, :4, :6 p. 312 Glock (ch. 25)
Rom. 6:6 p. 280 Umlauft
Rom. 6:13 p. 311 Glock (ch. 25)
Rom. 7 p. 152 Nadler
   p. 239 Franck

Rom. 7:18 p. 72 Schiemer
Rom. 8 p. 16 Jüchsen
   p. 152 Nadler
   p. 167 Zaunring
Rom. 8[?] p. 273 Trieste
Rom. 8:1 p. 16 Jüchsen
Rom. 8:5-14 p. 18 Jüchsen
Rom. 8:9 p. 77 Schiemer
   p. 273, 274 Trieste
Rom. 8:9-10 p. 96 Schlaffer
Rom. 8:14 p. 320 Glock (ch. 25)
Rom. 8:15-16 p. 92 Schlaffer
Rom. 8:17 p. 9 Jüchsen
   p. 273 Trieste
   p. 280 Umlauft
Rom. 8:20-21 p. 87 Schlaffer
Rom. 8:23 p. 16 Jüchsen
Rom. 8:26-30 p. 10 Jüchsen
Rom. 8:28 p. 9 Jüchsen
   p. 14 Jüchsen
Rom. 8:29 p. 269 Trieste
Rom. 8:30 p. 263 Trieste
Rom. 8:33-34 p. 265 Trieste
Rom. 8:35-39 p. 328 Glock (ch. 26)
Rom. 9 p. 92 Schlaffer
Rom. 9:3 p. 15 Jüchsen
Rom. 9:8 p. 283 Umlauft
Rom. 9:13 p. 26 Hut
Rom. 9:15 p. 27 Hut
   p. 74 Schiemer
Rom. 9:16 p. 26 Hut
Rom. 9:17-24 p. 322 Glock (ch. 25)
Rom. 9:18 p. 26 Hut
Rom. 9:19 p. 25 Hut
Rom. 10 p. 217 Rhegius
   p. 247 Franck
Rom. 10:8 p. 16, 20 Jüchsen
Rom. 10:9 p. 78 Schiemer
   p. 310 Glock (ch. 25)
Rom. 10:10, :17 p. 310 Glock (ch. 25)
Rom. 10:11 p. 264 Trieste
Rom. 10:13 p. 179 Althamer/Rurer
Rom. 10:14-15 p. 105 Schlaffer
Rom. 10:14-17 p. 125 Schneeweiss?
Rom. 10:17 p. 176, 179 Althamer/
   Rurer

Rom. 11 p. 152 Nadler
Rom. 11:17 p. 284 Umlauft
Rom. 11:34 p. 25 Hut
Rom. 12 p. 235 Franck
    p. 371 Schmidt
Rom. 12:2 p. 220 Rhegius
Rom. 12:4-8 p. 68 Schiemer
Rom. 12:6 p. 13 Jüchsen
    p. 176 Althamer/Rurer
Rom. 12:7 p. 176 Althamer/Rurer
Rom. 12:19 p. 267, 268 Trieste
    p. 319 Glock (ch. 25)
Rom. 12:20-21 p. 76 Schiemer
Rom. 12:21 p. 13 Jüchsen
Rom. 12[11:32] p. 27 Hut
Rom. 13 p. 215, 217, 219, 223, 226 Rhegius
    p. 242 Franck
Rom. 13:1 p. 222 Rhegius
Rom. 13:1ff p. 284 Umlauft
Rom. 13:1-4 p. 269 Trieste
Rom. 13:6 p. 323 Glock (ch. 25)
Rom. 13:6-7 p. 274 Trieste
Rom. 13:8-10 p. 92 Schlaffer
Rom. 13:12 p. 90 Schlaffer
Rom. 13:13 p. 321 Glock (ch. 25)
Rom. 14 p. 57 Spitelmaier
Rom. 15:4 p. 124 Schneeweiss?
    p. 179 Althamer/Rurer
Rom. 16 p. 180 Althamer/Rurer
Rom. 16:17 p. 122 Schneeweiss?
    p. 175 Althamer/Rurer
Rom. 16:18 p. 280 Umlauft
Rom. 18 p. 265 Trieste
Rom. 26 p. 180 Althamer/Rurer

1 Corinthians
1 Cor. 1[?] p. 276 Trieste
1 Cor. 1:2, :24 p. 167 Zaunring
1 Cor. 1:10 p. 122 Schneeweiss?
    p. 175 Althamer/Rurer
1 Cor. 1:18 p. 210 Keller
1 Cor. 1:27 p. 280 Umlauft
1 Cor. 1:31 p. 280 Umlauft
1 Cor. 2:1ff p. 280 Umlauft

1 Cor. 2:2 p. 280 Umlauft
1 Cor. 2:12 p. 128 Schneeweiss?
1 Cor. 3:9 p. 125 Schneeweiss?
    p. 181 Althamer/Rurer
1 Cor. 3:16-17 p. 359 Glock (ch. 32)
1 Cor. 3:19 p. 361 Glock (ch. 32)
1 Cor. 4 p. 115 Langenmantel
1 Cor. 4:1 p. 125 Schneeweiss?
    p. 181 Althamer/Rurer
1 Cor. 4:15 p. 125 Schneeweiss?
    p. 180 Althamer/Rurer
1 Cor. 5:3-5 p. 76 Schiemer
    p. 275 Trieste
1 Cor. 5:5 p. 268 Trieste
1 Cor. 5:6, :9 p. 182 Althamer/Rurer
1 Cor. 6:7 p. 79 Schiemer
    p. 267 Trieste
1 Cor. 6:9-11 p. 359 Glock (ch. 32)
1 Cor. 7 p. 149 Nadler
1 Cor. 7:3-5 p. 181 Althamer/Rurer
1 Cor. 7:14 p. 265 Trieste
1 Cor. 8:1-3 p. 18 Jüchsen
1 Cor. 9 p. 153 Nadler
1 Cor. 9:2 p. 316 Glock (ch. 25)
    p. 357 Glock (ch. 32)
1 Cor. 10 p. 176 Althamer/Rurer
1 Cor. 10:16 p. 126 Schneeweiss?
1 Cor. 10:21 p. 270 Trieste
1 Cor. 11 p. 56 Spitelmaier
1 Cor. 11:1 p. 282 Umlauft
1 Cor. 11:7-13 p. 16 Jüchsen
1 Cor. 11:19 p. 174 Althamer/Rurer
1 Cor. 11:25 p. 271 Trieste
1 Cor. 11:26 p. 167 Zaunring
1 Cor. 11:29 p. 272 Trieste
1 Cor. 12 p. 57 Spitelmaier
1 Cor. 12[?] p. 76 Schiemer
1 Cor. 12:3 p. 77 Schiemer
1 Cor. 12:4-7 p. 68 Schiemer
1 Cor. 12:13 p. 312 Glock (ch. 25)
1 Cor. 13 p. 56 Spitelmaier
    p. 180 Althamer/Rurer
    p. 227 Rhegius

1 Cor. 13 p. 240 Franck
1 Cor. 13:1ff p. 201 Keller
1 Cor. 13:4-7 p. 20 Jüchsen
1 Cor. 13:7, :13 p. 8 Jüchsen
1 Cor. 13:12 p. 20 Jüchsen
1 Cor. 14:20 p. 265 Trieste
 p. 314 Glock (ch. 25)
1 Cor. 14:26 p. 281 Umlauft
1 Cor. 15 p. 62 Spitelmaier
 p. 152 Nadler
1 Cor. 15:22 p. 27 Hut
1 Cor. 15:25 p. 93 Schlaffer
1 Cor. 15:36-49 p. 18 Jüchsen
1 Cor. 15:37-49 p. 16 Jüchsen
1 Cor. 16:1-4 p. 76 Schiemer

2 Corinthians
2 Cor. 1:3-7 p. 76 Schiemer
2 Cor. 1:12 p. 321 Glock (ch. 25)
2 Cor. 1:15 p. 318 Glock (ch. 25)
2 Cor. 3:3-6 p. 17 Jüchsen
2 Cor. 5 p. 57 Spitelmaier
2 Cor. 5:5 p. 311 Glock (ch. 25)
2 Cor. 5:12 p. 68 Schiemer
2 Cor. 5:17 p. 311 Glock (ch. 25)
2 Cor. 5:19 p. 181 Althamer/Rurer
2 Cor. 6 p. 268 Trieste
2 Cor. 6:14-16 p. 270 Trieste
2 Cor. 7 p. 268 Trieste
2 Cor. 11:12 p. 236 Franck
2 Cor. 11:14 p. 10 Jüchsen
 p. 179 Althamer/Rurer
2 Cor. 11:25 p. 319 Glock (ch. 25)
2 Cor. 12:5 p. 200 Keller
2 Cor. 12:10 p. 80 Schiemer

Galatians
Gal. 1[?] p. 274 Trieste
Gal. 1:8 p. 356 Glock (ch. 32)
Gal. 1:9 p. 178 Althamer/Rurer
Gal. 1:18 p. 311 Glock (ch. 25)
Gal. 2[:20] p. 280 Umlauft
Gal. 3 p. 152 Nadler
 p. 217 Rhegius

Gal. 3:2 p. 179 Althamer/Rurer
Gal. 3:15 p. 201 Keller
Gal. 3:27 p. 264 Trieste
 p. 312 Glock (ch. 25)
Gal. 4:19 p. 125 Schneeweiss?
 p. 180 Althamer/Rurer
Gal. 5 p. 17 Jüchsen
Gal. 5:6 p. 9 Jüchsen
Gal. 5:15 p. 322 Glock (ch. 25)
Gal. 5:19ff p. 219 Rhegius
Gal. 5:19-21 p. 273 Trieste
Gal. 5:21 p. 312 Glock (ch. 25)
Gal. 6 p. 17 Jüchsen
 p. 153 Nadler
Gal. 6:14 p. 280 Umlauft
Gal. 6:15 p. 311 Glock (ch. 25)

Ephesians
Eph. 1:4 p. 320 Glock (ch. 25)
Eph. 1:9 p. 25 Hut
Eph. 2 p. 56 Spitelmaier
 p. 152 Nadler
 p. 217 Rhegius
Eph. 2:2 p. 313, 315, 316 Glock (ch. 25)
Eph. 3:15-16 p. 9 Jüchsen
Eph. 4 p. 102 Schlaffer
 p. 167 Zaunring
Eph. 4:5 p. 122 Schneeweiss?
Eph. 4:5-6 p. 94 Schlaffer
Eph. 4:7 p. 10 Jüchsen
Eph. 4:14-16 p. 8 Jüchsen
Eph. 4:17 p. 312 Glock (ch. 25)
Eph. 4:22-24 p. 14 Jüchsen
Eph. 4:28 p. 359 Glock (ch. 32)
Eph. 4:30 p. 16 Jüchsen
 p. 266 Trieste
Eph. 5 p. 153 Nadler
Eph. 5:5 p. 90 Schlaffer
 p. 182 Althamer/Rurer
Eph. 5:8 p. 323 Glock (ch. 25)
Eph. 5:11 p. 268 Trieste
Eph. 5:25 p. 122 Schneeweiss?
Eph. 6:12 p. 323 Glock (ch. 25)
Eph. 8[5:23, :27] p. 274 Trieste

Scripture Index / 427

Philippians
Phil. 1 p. 58 Spitelmaier
   p. 217 Rhegius
Phil. 1:29 p. 328 Glock (ch. 26)
Phil. 2:5 p. 90 Schlaffer
Phil. 2:16 p. 316 Glock (ch. 25)
Phil. 3 p. 14 Jüchsen
Phil. 3:18-19 p. 7 Jüchsen

Colossians
Col. 1 p. 58 Spitelmaier
Col. 1:13 p. 323 Glock (ch. 25)
Col. 1:15-23 p. 16 Jüchsen
Col. 1:19[?] p. 167 Zaunring
Col. 1:23 p. 69 Schiemer
   p. 96 Schlaffer
   p. 394 endnotes
Col. 1:24 p. 26 Hut
Col. 2 p. 63 Spitelmaier
Col. 2:2-3 p. 16 Jüchsen
Col. 2:3 p. 10 Jüchsen
Col. 2:8 p. 202 Keller
Col. 2:9-10 p. 14 Jüchsen
Col. 2:11-13 p. 264 Trieste
Col. 2:12 p. 273 Trieste
   p. 312 Glock (ch. 25)
Col. 3 p. 167 Zaunring
Col. 3[:8] p. 314 Glock (ch. 25)
Col. 3[:9-10] p. 16 Jüchsen

1 Thessalonians
1 Thess. 2:12 p. 312 Glock (ch. 25)
1 Thess. 2:13 p. 180 Althamer/Rurer
1 Thess. 2:19 p. 316 Glock (ch. 25)
1 Thess. 4:16 p. 167 Zaunring
1 Thess. 5:21 p. 176 Althamer/Rurer

2 Thessalonians
2 Thess. 1 p. 152 Nadler
2 Thess. 2:3 p. 68 Schiemer
   p. 202 Keller
2 Thess. 2:4 p. 203 Keller
   p. 266 Trieste
2 Thess. 2:11,:12 p. 173 Althamer/Rurer
2 Thess. 2:12 p. 280 Umlauft

2 Thess. 3:6 p. 321 Glock (ch. 25)

1 Timothy
1 Tim. 1 p. 59 Spitelmaier
1 Tim. 1:8 p. 283 Umlauft
1 Tim. 1:9 p. 28 Hut
   p. 223 Rhegius
1 Tim. 1:19 p. 176 Althamer/Rurer
1 Tim. 2:4 p. 26 Hut
1 Tim. 4:12 p. 321 Glock (ch. 25)
1 Tim. 5 p. 149 Nadler
1 Tim. 6 p. 57 Spitelmaier
   p. 115 Langenmantel
1 Tim. 6:3 p. 122 Schneeweiss?
   p. 175 Althamer/Rurer
   p. 202 Keller
[?]Tim. 2 p. 167 Zaunring

2 Timothy
2 Tim. 2:6 p. 206 Keller
2 Tim. 2:11-12 p. 273 Trieste
2 Tim. 2:20 p. 322 Glock (ch. 25)
2 Tim. 2[3:15] p. 124 Schneeweiss?
2 Tim. 3:14 p. 178 Althamer/Rurer
2 Tim. 3:16 p. 283 Umlauft
2 Tim. 4:3 p. 174 Althamer/Rurer

Titus
Titus 1:16 p. 281 Umlauft
Titus 3 p. 215 Rhegius
Titus 3:10 p. 122 Schneeweiss?
   p. 174 Althamer/Rurer

Hebrews
Heb. 1 p. 113 Langenmantel
Heb. 1:3 p. 16 Jüchsen
Heb. 2:4 p. 176 Althamer/Rurer
Heb. 4 p. 57, 62 Spitelmaier
Heb. 4:12 p. 315 Glock (ch. 25)
Heb. 7:18 p. 28 Hut
Heb. 8:8-13 p. 91 Schlaffer
Heb. 10 p. 264 Trieste
Heb. 10:14 p. 26 Hut
Heb. 11 p. 9 Jüchsen
   p. 247 Franck

Heb. 11[?] p. 76 Schiemer
Heb. 11:3 p. 87 Schlaffer
Heb. 11:6 p. 355 Glock (ch. 32)
Heb. 11:15-16 p. 71 Schiemer
Heb. 12:2 p. 101 Schlaffer
Heb. 12:6 p. 74 Schiemer
           p. 204 Keller
Heb. 12:8 p. 89 Schlaffer
Heb. 13:4 p. 182 Althamer/Rurer

James
James 1 p. 118 Langenmantel
James 1:5 p. 11 Jüchsen
James 1:9 p. 280 Umlauft
James 1:17 p. 182 Althamer/Rurer
James 2:19 p. 316 Glock (ch. 25)
James 2:26 p. 199 Keller
James 3[1:13] p. 26 Hut
James 5:14-15 p. 80 Schiemer
James 5:16 p. 199 Keller
James 9[4:3] p. 25 Hut

1 Peter
1 Pet. 1:3 p. 76 Schiemer
1 Pet. 1:6-7 p. 12 Jüchsen
1 Pet. 1:7-8 p. 20 Jüchsen
1 Pet. 1[4:4] p. 268 Trieste
1 Pet. 2 p. 115 Langenmantel
        p. 215, 219, 225 Rhegius
1 Pet. 2:6 p. 281 Umlauft
1 Pet. 2:12 p. 320 Glock (ch. 25)
1 Pet. 2:13-14 p. 274 Trieste
1 Pet. 2:21 p. 89 Schlaffer
1 Pet. 3 p. 237 Franck
1 Pet. 3:12 p. 321 Glock (ch. 25)
1 Pet. 3:14, :17 p. 274 Trieste
1 Pet. 3:15 p. 12 Jüchsen
           p. 68 Schiemer
1 Pet. 3:15-16 p. 261 Trieste
1 Pet. 3:16 p. 304 Glock (ch. 24)
1 Pet. 3:18, :21 p. 264 Trieste
1 Pet. 4 p. 116 Langenmantel
        p. 237 Franck
1 Pet. 4:1 p. 74 Schiemer
1 Pet. 4:1ff p. 280 Umlauft

1 Pet. 4:3-4 p. 299 Glock (ch. 24)
1 Pet. 4:11 p. 176 Althamer/Rurer
1 Pet. 4:17 p. 103 Schlaffer
1 Pet. 5 p. 56 Spitelmaier
1 Pet. 5:3 p. 317 Glock (ch. 25)
1 Pet. 5:8 p. 179 Althamer/Rurer

2 Peter
2 Pet. 1:19 p. 16 Jüchsen
           p. 124 Schneeweiss?
           p. 176 Althamer/Rurer
2 Pet. 2 p. 262 Trieste
2 Pet. 2:1 p. 202 Keller
2 Pet. 2:3 p. 280 Umlauft
2 Pet. 2:5 p. 177 Althamer/Rurer
2 Pet. 2:10-15, :22 p. 7 Jüchsen
2 Pet. 3:10 p. 90 Schlaffer
           p. 208 Keller

1 John
1 John 1 p. 179 Althamer/Rurer
1 John 2:2 p. 27 Hut
1 John 2:27 p. 79 Schiemer
1 John 3:7 p. 16 Jüchsen
1 John 3:24 p. 274 Trieste
1 John 4 p. 27 Hut
1 John 4:1 p. 176 Althamer/Rurer
1 John 4:3 p. 77 Schiemer
          p. 176 Althamer/Rurer
          p. 274 Trieste
1 John 4:7-16 p. 20 Jüchsen
1 John 4:16 p. 9 Jüchsen
           p. 71 Schiemer
1 John 4:17-18 p. 8 Jüchsen
1 John 4:20 p. 76 Schiemer
1 John 5 p. 27 Hut
        p. 243 Franck
1 John 5:2-3 p. 275 Trieste
1 John 5:8 p. 94, 98 Schlaffer
1 John 5:10-11 p. 273 Trieste
1 John 5:19 p. 84 Schlaffer
           p. 268 Trieste
1 John 5:21 p. 261 Trieste

2 John
2 John 1:9 p. 281 Umlauft

Revelation
Rev. 1:11, :12, :20 p. 4 Jüchsen
Rev. 3:4 p. 320 Glock (ch. 25)
Rev. 3:16 p. 73 Schiemer
Rev. 3:21 p. 27 Hut
Rev. 4:5 p. 5 Jüchsen
Rev. 8:2 p. 4 Jüchsen
Rev. 12:6, :14 p. 279 Umlauft
Rev. 12:9 p. 10 Jüchsen
Rev. 13:8 p. 88 Schlaffer
Rev. 14:9-12 p. 300 Glock (ch. 24)
Rev. 14:10-11 p. 275 Trieste
Rev. 15:7 p. 4 Jüchsen
Rev. 18:6 p. 28 Hut
Rev. 18:11-17 p. 159 Nadler
Rev. 19:11-16 p. 274 Trieste
Rev. 21:8 p. 275 Trieste
Rev. 22:17-18 p. 201 Keller
Rev. 22:19 p. 310, 311 Glock (ch. 25)

About Pandora Press

Pandora Press is a small, independently owned press dedicated to making available modestly priced books that deal with Anabaptist, Mennonite, and Believers Church topics, both historical and theological. We welcome comments from our readers.
Visit our full-service online Bookstore:
www.pandorapress.com

Pedro A. Sandín Fremaint y Pablo A. Jimémez, *Palabras Duras: Homilías* (Kitchener: Pandora Press, 2001).
 Softcover, 121 pp., ISBN 1-984710-17-7
 $12.00 US/$16.00 Canadian. Postage $5.00 US/$7.00Canadian
[Spanish. Reflections on the "hard words" of Jesus in the Gospels.]

James C. Juhnke and Carol M. Hunter, *The Missing Peace: The Search for Nonviolent Alternatives in United States History* (Kitchener: Pandora Press, 2001; co-published with Herald Press.)
 Softcover, 321 pp., includes index. ISBN 1-894710-13-4
 $26.50 US/$37.50 Canadian. Postage $5.00 US/$7.00 Canadian
[The myth of redemptive violence, re-examined historically.]

Ruth Elizabeth Mooney, *Manual Para Crear Materiales de Educación Cristiana* (Kitchener: Pandora Press, 2001).
 Softcover, 206 pp., ISBN 1-984710-12-6
 $15.00 US/$20.00 Canadian. Postage $5.00 US/$7.00 Canadian
[Spanish. Manual for creation of Christian education programs.]

Esther and Malcolm Wenger, poetry by Ann Wenger, *Healing the Wounds* (Kitchener: Pandora Press, 2001; co-published with Herald Press).
 Softcover, 210 pp. ISBN 1-894710-09-6.
 $18.50 US/$21.00 Canadian. Postage $5.00 US/$7.00 Canadian
[Experiences of Mennonite missionaries with the Cheyenne people]

Pedro A. Sandín Fremaint, *Cuentos y Encuentros: Hacia una Educación Transformadora* (Kitchener: Pandora Press, 2001).
 Softcover 163 pp ISBN 1-894710-08-8.
 $12.00 US/ $16.00 Canadian. Postage $5.00 US/$7.00 Canadian.
[Spanish. Stories and discussion questions for Christian education]

A. James Reimer, *Mennonites and Classical Theology: Dogmatic Foundations for Christian Ethics* (Kitchener: Pandora Press, 2001; co-published with Herald Press)
 Softcover, 650pp. ISBN 0-9685543-7-7
 $52.00 U.S./$65.00 Canadian. Postage: $5.00 U.S./$7.00 Can.
[A theological interpretation of Mennonite experience in 20th C.]

Walter Klaassen, *Anabaptism: Neither Catholic nor Protestant*, 3rd ed. (Kitchener: Pandora Press, 2001; co-pub. Herald Press)
 Softcover, 122pp. ISBN 1-894710-01-0
 $12.00 U.S./$15.00 Can. Postage: $3.00 U.S./$4.00 Can.
[A classic interpretation and study guide, now available again]

Dale Schrag & James Juhnke, eds., *Anabaptist Visions for the new Millennium: A search for identity* (Kitchener: Pandora Press, 2000; co-published with Herald Press)
 Softcover, 242 pp. ISBN 1-894710-00-2
 $20.00 U.S./$26.00 Canadian. Postage $4.00 U.S./$5.00 Can.
[Twenty-eight essays presented at Bethel College, June, 2000]

Harry Loewen, ed., *Road to Freedom: Mennonites Escape the Land of Suffering* (Kitchener: Pandora Press, 2000; co-published with Herald Press)
 Hardcover, large format, 302pp. ISBN 0-9685543-5-0
 $35.00 U.S./$39.50 Canadian. Postage: $7.00 U.S./$8.00 Can.
[Life experiences documented with personal stories and photos]

Alan Kreider and Stuart Murray, eds., *Coming Home: Stories of Anabaptists in Britain and Ireland* (Kitchener: Pandora Press, 2000; co-published with Herald Press)
 Softcover, 220pp. ISBN 0-9685543-6-9
 $23.00 U.S./$26.00 Canadian. Postage: $4.00 U.S./$5.00 Can.
[Anabaptist encounters in the U.K.; personal stories/articles]

Edna Schroeder Thiessen and Angela Showalter, *A Life Displaced: A Mennonite Woman's Flight from War-Torn Poland* (Kitchener: Pandora Press, 2000; co-published with Herald Press)
 Softcover, xii, 218pp. ISBN 0-9685543-2-6
 $22.50 U.S./$25.00 Canadian. Postage: $4.00 U.S./$5.00 Can.
[A true story: moving, richly-detailed, told with candor and courage]

Stuart Murray, *Biblical Interpretation in the Anabaptist Tradition*
(Kitchener: Pandora Press, 2000; co-published with Herald Press)
    Softcover, 310pp. ISBN 0-9685543-3-4
    $30.00 U.S./$33.00 Canadian. Postage: $4.00 U.S./$5.00 Can.
[How Anabaptists read the Bible; considerations for today's church]

Apocalypticism and Millennialism, ed. by Loren L. Johns
(Kitchener: Pandora Press, 2000; co-published with Herald Press)
    Softcover, 419pp; Scripture and name indeces
    ISBN 0-9683462-9-4
    $39.50 U.S./$45.00 Canadian. Postage: $5.00 U.S./$6.00 Can.
[A clear, careful, and balanced collection: pastoral and scholarly]

Later Writings by Pilgram Marpeck and his Circle. Volume 1: The Exposé, A Dialogue and Marpeck's Response to Caspar Schwenckfeld
Translated by Walter Klaassen, Werner Packull, and John Rempel
(Kitchener: Pandora Press, 1999; co-published with Herald Press)
    Softcover, 157pp. ISBN 0-9683462-6-X
    $22.00 U.S./$25.00 Canadian. Postage: $4.00 U.S./$5.00 Can.
[Previously untranslated writings by Marpeck and his Circle]

John Driver, *Radical Faith. An Alternative History of the Christian Church*, edited by Carrie Snyder.
(Kitchener: Pandora Press, 1999; co-published with Herald Press)
    Softcover, 334pp. ISBN 0-9683462-8-6
    $33.00 U.S./$36.00 Canadian. Postage: $5.00 U.S./$6.00 Can.
[A history of the church as it is seldom told – from the margins]

C. Arnold Snyder, *From Anabaptist Seed. The Historical Core of Anabaptist-Related Identity*
(Kitchener: Pandora Press, 1999; co-published with Herald Press)
    Softcover, 53pp.; discussion questions. ISBN 0-9685543-0-X
    $5.00 U.S./$6.25 Canadian. Postage: $2.00 U.S./$2.50 Can.
[Ideal for group study, commissioned by Mennonite World Conf.]
    Also available in Spanish translation: *De Semilla Anabautista*, from Pandora Press only.

John D. Thiesen, *Mennonite and Nazi? Attitudes Among Mennonite Colonists in Latin America, 1933-1945.*
(Kitchener: Pandora Press, 1999; co-published with Herald Press)
Softcover, 330pp., 2 maps, 24 b/w illustrations, bibliography, index. ISBN 0-9683462-5-1
$27.00 U.S./$30.00 Canadian. Postage: $4.00 U.S./$5.00 Can.
[Careful and objective study of an explosive topic]

Lifting the Veil, a translation of *Aus meinem Leben: Erinnerungen von J.H. Janzen*. Ed. by Leonard Friesen; trans. by Walter Klaassen
(Kitchener: Pandora Press, 1998; co-pub. with Herald Press).
Softcover, 128pp.; 4pp. of illustrations. ISBN 0-9683462-1-9
$14.50 U.S./$16.00 Canadian. Postage: $4.00 U.S. and Can.
[Memoir, confession, critical observation of Mennonite life in Russia]

Leonard Gross, *The Golden Years of the Hutterites*, rev. ed.
(Kitchener: Pandora Press, 1998; co-pub. with Herald Press).
Softcover, 280pp., index. ISBN 0-9683462-3-5
$24.00 U.S./$27.00 Canadian. Postage: $4.00 U.S./$5.00 Can.
[Classic study of early Hutterite movement, now available again]

The Believers Church: A Voluntary Church, ed. by William H. Brackney
(Kitchener: Pandora Press, 1998; co-published with Herald Press).
Softcover, viii, 237pp., index. ISBN 0-9683462-0-0
$27.00 U.S./$29.50 Canadian. Postage: $4.00 U.S./$5.00 Can.
[Papers from the 12th Believers Church Conference, Hamilton, ON]

An Annotated Hutterite Bibliography, compiled by Maria H. Krisztinkovich, ed. by Peter C. Erb (Kitchener, Ont.: Pandora Press, 1998).
(Ca. 2,700 entries) 312pp., cerlox bound, electronic, or both.
ISBN (paper) 0-9698762-8-9/(disk) 0-9698762-9-7
$18.00 each, U.S. and Canadian. Postage: $6.00 U.S. and Can.
[The most extensive bibliography on Hutterite literature available]

Jacobus ten Doornkaat Koolman, *Dirk Philips. Friend and Colleague of Menno Simons*, trans. W. E. Keeney, ed. C. A. Snyder (Kitchener: Pandora Press, 1998; co-pub. with Herald Press).
  Softcover, xviii, 236pp., index. ISBN: 0-9698762-3-8
  $24.50 U.S./$29.50 Canadian. Postage: $4.00 U.S./$5.00 Can.
[The definitive biography of Dirk Philips, now available in English]

Sarah Dyck, ed./tr., *The Silence Echoes: Memoirs of Trauma & Tears* (Kitchener: Pandora Press, 1997; co-published with Herald Press).
  Softcover, xii, 236pp., 2 maps. ISBN: 0-9698762-7-0
  $19.00 U.S./$21.00 Canadian. Postage: $4.00 U.S./$5.00 Can.
[First person accounts of life in the Soviet Union, trans. from German]

Wes Harrison, *Andreas Ehrenpreis and Hutterite Faith and Practice* (Kitchener: Pandora Press, 1997; co-published with Herald Press).
  Softcover, xxiv, 274pp., 2 maps, index. ISBN 0-9698762-6-2
  $29.00 U.S./$34.00 Canadian. Postage: $4.00 U.S./$5.00 Can.
[First biography of this important seventeenth century Hutterite leader]

C. Arnold Snyder, *Anabaptist History and Theology: Revised Student Edition* (Kitchener: Pandora Press, 1997; co-pub. Herald Press).
  Softcover, xiv, 466pp., 7 maps, 28 illustrations, index, bibliography. ISBN 0-9698762-5-4
  $38.50 U.S./$40.00 Canadian. Postage: $5.00 U.S./$6.00 Can.
[Abridged, rewritten edition for undergraduates and the non-specialist]

Nancey Murphy, *Reconciling Theology and Science: A Radical Reformation Perspective* (Kitchener, Ont.: Pandora Press, 1997; co-pub. Herald Press).
  Softcover, x, 103pp., index. ISBN 0-9698762-4-6
  $16.00 U.S./$18.50 Canadian. Postage: $3.50 U.S./$4.00 Can.
[Exploration of the supposed conflict between Christianity and Science]

C. Arnold Snyder and Linda A. Huebert Hecht, eds, *Profiles of Anabaptist Women: Sixteenth Century Reforming Pioneers* (Waterloo, Ont.: Wilfrid Laurier University Press, 1996).
 Softcover, xxii, 442pp. ISBN: 0-88920-277-X
 $28.95 U.S. or Canadian. Postage: $5.00 U.S./$6.00 Can.
[Biographical sketches of more than 50 Anabaptist women; a first]

The Limits of Perfection: A Conversation with J. Lawrence Burkholder 2nd ed., with a new epilogue by J. Lawrence Burkholder, Rodney Sawatsky and Scott Holland, eds.
(Kitchener: Pandora Press, 1996).
 Softcover, x, 154pp. ISBN 0-9698762-2-X
 $12.50 U.S./$15.50 Canadian. Postage: $2.00 U.S./$3.00 Can.
[J.L. Burkholder on his life experiences; eight Mennonites respond]

C. Arnold Snyder, *Anabaptist History and Theology: An Introduction* (Kitchener: Pandora Press, 1995). ISBN 0-9698762-0-3
 Softcover, x, 434pp., 6 maps, 29 illustrations, index, bibliography.
 $38.50 U.S./$40.00 Canadian. Postage: $5.00 U.S./$6.00 Can.
[Comprehensive survey; unabridged version, fully documented]

Pandora Press
33 Kent Avenue
Kitchener, Ontario
Canada N2G 3R2
Tel./Fax: (519) 578-2381
E-mail:
info@pandorapress.com
Web site:
www.pandorapress.com

Herald Press
616 Walnut Avenue
Scottdale, PA
U.S.A. 15683
Orders: (800) 245-7894
E-mail:
hp@mph.org
Web site:
www.mph.org

www.ingramcontent.com/pod-product-compliance
Lightning Source LLC
Chambersburg PA
CBHW070305230426
43664CB00015B/2644